Women in American History

Series Editors

Mari Jo Buhle
Nancy A. Hewitt
Anne Firor Scott

A list of books in the series appears
at the end of this book.

U.S. Women in Struggle

U.S. Women in Struggle

A *Feminist Studies* Anthology

EDITED BY

Claire Goldberg Moses and
Heidi Hartmann

UNIVERSITY OF ILLINOIS PRESS   Urbana and Chicago

©1995 by the Board of Trustees of the University of Illinois
Manufactured in the United States of America
1 2 3 4 5 C P 5 4 3 2 1

This book is printed on acid-free paper.

Library of Congress Cataloging-in-Publication Data

U.S. women in struggle: a feminist studies anthology/edited by
    Claire Goldberg Moses and Heidi Hartmann.
        p.   cm.—(Women in American history)
        Includes index.
        ISBN 0-252-02166-5.—ISBN 0-252-06462-3 (paper)
        1. Feminism—United States—History. 2. Women—United States—
History. I. Moses, Claire Goldberg, 1941–   . II. Hartmann,
Heidi I. III. Series.
HQ1426.U17 1995
305.42'0973—dc20
                                                        94-38319
                                                            CIP

Contents

Acknowledgments

☐ This book is an example of women's collective political struggles. We wish to acknowledge that the work of many people have made this book possible. First are the authors: although most have now achieved positions of high rank in the academy, they struggled against great odds for many years to establish the legitimacy of scholarship that focuses on women. Most also worked to establish women's studies, now well-respected programs or departments in colleges and universities and the tangible results of the collective struggles of feminist scholars and students.

We would also like to acknowledge the contributions of the board of editors of *Feminist Studies,* both to this volume and to the collective effort, over the past two decades, of developing feminist scholarship. Originally founded in 1969 by Ann Calderwood, the journal has, since 1977, been edited by a collective which has included Kathryn Pine Parsons Addleson, Lynn Bolles, Barbara Christian, Rachel Blau DuPlessis, Judith Kegan Gardiner, Ruth Milkman, Marilyn Mobley, Judith Newton, Rosalind Petchesky, Rayna Rapp, Deborah Rosenfelt, Ellen Ross, Mary Ryan, Judith Stacey, Christine Stansell, Rosalind Terborg-Penn, Marian Urquilla, Martha Vicinus, Judith Walkowitz, and Rhonda Williams, as well as, of course, we editors of this particular book. All the *Feminist Studies* editors share the credit for this book—for soliciting these articles and for nurturing them through the original revising and editing process. Here we want to acknowledge also the contributions of the many others whose work has appeared in *Feminist Studies* and whose scholarship has helped to build our understanding of women's collective struggles. Unfortunately, the wealth of articles we have published on this theme over the past twenty years could not be included in its entirety in one volume.

And, finally, we wish to thank two individuals without whose help this anthology would not have come into being: Carole Appel of the University of Illinois Press, who initially encouraged this anthology, and

Alden Waitt, who, since 1978, has done the copy editing for *Feminist Studies,* and who, once again, carefully and patiently reviewed the edited and shortened versions of the articles presented here.

Heidi Hartmann and Claire Goldberg Moses

Introduction

☐ The question of women's political activism is particularly timely at this historical moment. To most observers, the 1980s appeared to be a period of quiescence, but we can now look back and locate the reemergence of organizing, especially among students on U.S. campuses, already in the final years of the Reagan-Bush era. The struggle against apartheid in South Africa and other antiracism campaigns were particularly noteworthy. Feminists—young and old—took to the streets, this time in defense of reproductive rights, victories once thought secure but once again clearly endangered. Peace activists responded to the resurgence of a militaristic policy by demonstrating against the war in the Persian Gulf.

At the same time, women looking to academe for intellectual support for their activism were expressing concern that women's studies scholarship had become preoccupied with a kind of theorizing that seemed divorced from the concrete realities of political struggle. Women's studies scholars responded by organizing conferences[1] that attempted to move questions of activism back into the center of our inquiry. This book is offered in the desire to sustain this renewed activism.

We have brought together a collection of essays that focus on women's collective political struggles in the United States. All were originally published in *Feminist Studies,* a journal which from its inception has sought to link scholarship to activism. To quote from the journal's statement of purpose: "The feminist movement has demonstrated that the study of women is more than a compensatory project. Instead, feminism has the potential fundamentally to reshape the way we view the world. We wish not just to interpret women's experiences but to change women's condition." Pioneering, then, in the publication of politically engaged scholarship, *Feminist Studies* has provided a home for an extraordinary wealth of material on "women in struggle."

The essays presented here make visible the remarkable diversity of these struggles. Women's struggles have not, for example, all been self-consciously feminist. Indeed, women have participated in just about every type of political activity men have participated in, including movements to strengthen patriarchy and white supremacy. In this volume, however, we have focused on activities in which women organize as women, whether feminist or not, and we place greater emphasis on those activities in which women sought to better their lives and the lives of their families and communities.

U.S. Women in Struggle covers the chronology of women's activity in the United States, beginning with the early 1800s. For this volume, the original essays have been newly edited, somewhat updated, and, in many cases, shortened to permit us to publish as many as possible. The essays we have selected not only describe significant areas of women's collective struggles but also shed light on important theoretical and practical questions related to collective activity.

For example, many of these essays reflect on the conditions that have discouraged or encouraged women's organizing. In the nineteenth and early twentieth centuries, women's exclusion from those state or religious activities deemed "public" precluded certain kinds of organizing but did not inhibit women from coming together in neighborhood settings or creating associational structures that were neither absolutely "public" nor "private." Such groups usually addressed issues traditionally considered appropriate for women's attention, such as the price of food or sexual behavior and morality. Some women were encouraged to enter arenas not generally considered "womanly" by male co-workers, friends, or spouses. And if their activism was often confined to "auxiliary" work in male-led movements like antislavery or labor, they were also sometimes inspired by emancipatory ideologies to challenge their own oppression, usually in opposition to the wishes of their male allies. Many women were inspired to daring activism by other women—teachers, mothers, sisters, friends.

Around which issues have women organized? Not surprisingly, sex and sexuality have played a central role from the female moral reform societies of the 1830s to the lesbian and reproductive rights movement of our time. The family has also played a central role, with some women organizing in defense of what they viewed as traditional and therefore best; other women labored to reform the family; and still others worked to destroy it. The politics of race and class have been significant in women's organizing as well, reminding us that women's interests have been shaped by multiple positionalities, not just sex/gender ones.

Women have also organized around improving conditions of daily life, for example, providing food and shelter for their families or changing the conditions of both their own and their husbands' work lives. But women's concerns have not only been local. They have organized as well to transform relations between nations, and if not wholly successful, they have at least prodded the government to take some limited steps, such as a nuclear test ban treaty. Nor have women's activities been only emancipatory, for women have also organized to defend hierarchical, male-dominant families and the "purity" and supremacy of white, Protestant families.

The essays also reflect on the *ways* women have organized and consider how these have differed from men's ways of organizing. For example, nonhierarchical, structureless groupings of peace activists could frustrate McCarthyite witch-hunters who had destroyed male groups simply by obtaining their membership lists. Women have used their kin and neighborhood ties to create self-help groups and organizing networks that, in their dependability, made up for what they may have lacked in national organization. And, finally, women have often organized most effectively when they have organized separately from men, as community activists, voters, professionals, unionists, and feminists.

But if sisterhood has often been powerful, it has also been elusive. Sometimes this has been intended, as was the racially divisive stance of Klanswomen. But sometimes this has been an unexpected consequence of poorly thought-through positions, as was the case, for example, with the moral reformers in the nineteenth century whose antiprostitution politics slipped into a woman-hating, victim-blaming discourse, or the abortion rights movement of more recent times which has often seemed class- and race-biased, because of its failure to rigorously challenge sterilization abuse and Medicaid funding cutoffs or to fight strenuously for improved access to maternity and child health care.

These essays also address the problematic status of women's power and women's oppression. Each strives to identify not only the oppression against which women struggled but also their possibilities for effective resistance. Sometimes women's possibilities for resistance were enhanced by their class or race position. Women, by virtue of their gender, are members of an oppressed group, but—as the chapters that explicitly focus on questions of race or class make clear—they are also members of oppressor groups. Oppression is structured along axes that include race, class, ethnicity, religion, age, and sexual orientation, as well as gender.

In *U.S. Women in Struggle* the chapters are arranged chronologically, according to the time period in which the activities occurred. We have selected three main areas of women's activity in collective struggles: women's participation in traditional women's associations; women's participation in progressive (or reactionary) movements not focused solely on women, for example, the labor, peace, and civil rights movements or the Ku Klux Klan; and women's participation in self-consciously feminist movements.

Our first selection, Mary P. Ryan's case study of female moral reform societies in New York State in the 1830s and 1840s, illustrates one way that women, activating networks from within their traditional sphere and organizing around an area of concern considered legitimately female, were able to assert power in the society at large. In the homogeneous, white, Protestant culture of Oneida County, at a moment when rapid urbanization had weakened traditional paternal and religious authority, women stepped into a power vacuum and succeeded in setting social standards, controlling sexual behavior, altering moral values, and even reshaping class ideology.

Many historians trace the origins of feminist consciousness to these Protestant, mostly evangelical, moral reformers; but Nancy A. Hewitt, in "Feminist Friends: Agrarian Quakers and the Emergence of Woman's Rights in America," discovers an alternative path from religious to feminist activism. Examining the antebellum women's rights movement in Rochester, New York, she identifies the extraordinary presence of Quaker women, many of whom had been raised in relatively egalitarian farm villages. Although their move to the city introduced them to the concept of separate spheres of activity, in their economically, residentially, and culturally distinct Quaker community, they continued to work alongside men in radical causes like the Indian rights and abolition movements. Twenty-five percent of the signers of the Seneca Fall Resolutions were these Quaker women.

The radical Quaker women of Rochester would seem to confirm Ellen Carol DuBois's thesis, in "The Radicalism of the Woman Suffrage Movement: Notes toward the Reconstruction of Nineteenth-Century Feminism," that suffragists confronted the public/private dichotomy in ways quite unlike that of moral reformers. In claiming the vote, suffragists asserted their desire to break out of the confines of women's sphere and enter the public sphere on equal terms with men, as citizens, not as social housekeepers. Their newly won public power would then be extended back into the private sphere. DuBois reminds us that this was an intentionally radical strategy. Suffragists were not only demanding women's admission to the public sphere but also undermining the familial basis of citizenship in which male heads represented the household, a vestigial remnant of pre-Enlightenment ideology, and thus completing the liberal revolution. It was also an eminently reasonable strategy, given that nineteenth-century politics were much more responsive to electoral pressure than politics today.

In Ellen Carol DuBois and Linda Gordon's "Seeking Ecstasy on the Battlefield: Danger and Pleasure in Nineteenth-Century Feminist Sexual Thought," we hear multiple feminist discourses that recall both the early moral reformers and more radical feminists. DuBois and Gordon focus first on the ambiguities of a type of collective action that seeks to extend the values of women's traditional sphere into the social arena, challenging some aspects of sexual inequality, especially the double standard of nonconsensual sex in marriage, but leaving unexamined the consequences of their sexual repressiveness to women. They also identify a counterdiscourse in nineteenth-century gender politics among the advocates of sexual liberation but note the ambiguities of this stance as well. Although advancing a seemingly liberatory position, these advocates failed to offer a critique of the male construction of the sexual experience available to most women. Nor did either camp—the social purity group or the sexual liberationists—ever give public expression to the pleasures of the homoeroticism that many women had explored in private.

Estelle Freedman, in "Separatism as Strategy: Female Institution Building and American Feminism, 1870–1930," revisits many of these same issues; but by re-visioning the relationship of sex-segregated social spheres and women's power, she challenges us to reconsider our notion of the radical. It was in women's separatist organizations and institutions, she points out, that women became politicized and a feminist politics was nurtured. Here we have an example of women's sphere not only empowering women but also presenting a radical challenge to the inequality of the sexes.

Kathleen M. Blee's study of Ku Klux Klan women comes then as a sobering reminder that women's activism may take a deliberately anti-progressive route. In "Women in the 1920s' Ku Klux Klan Movement," Blee documents the widespread participation of rather mainstream midwestern women, some of whom had been active in the campaign for women's suffrage, in the Women's Ku Klux Klan, which sprang up as part of a national resurgence of nativism during the 1920s. This account illustrates a particularly vicious outcome of women's leadership and consciousness built both on women's increased participation in the public sphere and on their special role within the family. The safeguarding of race "purity" was justified as a proper activity for women because it could be regarded as an extension of the safeguarding of purity in the home. Like the moral reformers of the 1830s and 1840s about whom Ryan writes, Klanswomen attempted to impose an order that was deeply repressive. More disturbing yet, Blee finds in the Klanswomen's rhetoric and political activity the fruition of the nativism characteristic of a portion of the woman suffrage movement. Klanswomen advanced racist and anti-Semitic ideas while simultaneously arguing for increased equity between white Protestant women and men.

Readers will likely feel more comfortable reflecting on women's organizing as workers. But even if this volume—and *Feminist Studies* over the past two decades—is especially attentive to this history, the belief that women workers have not organized on the job to improve their working conditions is still widespread. Alice Kessler-Harris and several other authors in this book (Beverly W. Jones, Sharon Hartman Strom, Dorothy Sue Cobble, and Molly Ladd-Taylor), however, all reclaim this crucial aspect of working women's history, examining the conditions that have enabled or inhibited women's organizing.

In the first of these chapters, Kessler-Harris points out that women have organized in disproportion to their number and with great militancy when they worked in an industry where unionism was common. She relates the wide fluctuations in women's union activity to the attitudes and behavior of male unionists and the hegemony of the ideology of home and motherhood rather than to women's disinterest or incapacity to make collective demands on their own behalf.

Although Kessler-Harris's study focuses primarily on white and immigrant women of the Northeast, Beverly Jones's research on Black female tobacco workers in the South between 1920 and 1940 illustrates how race, as much as gender and class, influences the development and political expression of women's consciousness. As was often typical of women's organizing efforts on the job, Black women tobacco workers organized a local that turned out to be short lived, largely because it received no support from male union locals, either Black or white. In this instance, and in many others, Black women turned elsewhere to establish solidarity and build their strength—to their families and communities.

According to Sharon Hartman Strom, in "Challenging 'Woman's Place': Feminism, the Left, and Industrial Unionism in the 1930s," women clerical workers, in the 1930s, looked to the newly formed Congress of Industrial Organizations (CIO) and the Communist Party (CP) for strength and solidarity. Through legislation, policies, and practices, governments and employers excluded married women from many of the better jobs yet did not keep married women—many of whom had to increase their waged work time during the Depression—from working. The decline of feminist politics, combined with official policies and male attitudes unfavorable to women, all contributed to making it difficult for women workers to organize. Yet many women clerical workers did so in CP-dominated clerical worker unions, which were later expelled from the CIO because of postwar anticommunism. But even though the CP encouraged clerical organizing, members too viewed the women workers in these jobs as temporary workers, not fit for serious roles in union governance.

Dorothy Sue Cobble's inspiring tale of strong unionism among waitresses points to a different strategy. By organizing separate women's locals in the craft-based Hotel Employees and Restaurant Employees International Union, women workers were able to get effective voice and leadership roles even beyond their locals. Cobble shows, too, how the nature and organization of waitresses' work and the family backgrounds of many waitresses contributed to their ability to organize. Engaging in verbal repartee with customers, learning how to size them up, and working with male cooks and bartenders all taught waitresses how to hold their own in the mixed-sex regional and national conventions. Waitresses' work also offered considerable "down time" on the job, between split shifts and during meals, when they could engage in female bonding. And, finally, waitresses were more often single, divorced, or widowed than married, perhaps affording them more freedom to engage in union activity. When the success of the separate female locals is compared with the alternative of "women's committees" in mixed unions, it becomes clear that the female locals allowed women to combine their unionism with their women's concerns. As union locals they carried out all the union functions, incorporating their needs as women. If their union brothers did not respect their feminism they had at least to acknowledge their unionism. Women's committees in mixed unions, in contrast, had no union functions to conduct and were left only with identifying and speaking for women's special needs, often finding a hostile male audience.

Reading Strom and Cobble together, one realizes that the radical wave of industrial unionism that swept the United States in the 1930s and led to the considerable expansion of the union movement did not, despite its ideal of a more inclusive unionism than the craft-based American Federation of Labor could offer, do much to incorporate women as equal members of the working class. In Strom's view the absence of feminism as a strong mass movement during this period allowed male unionists to get away with their dual strategy of excluding and subordinating women and precluded working women from developing strong cross-class alliances with other women that would have strengthened their hand both in leftist political parties and labor unions. Yet, as Cobble shows, echoing Freedman's theme and Tronto's observations (discussed below), it is precisely in a time when mass feminist activity has declined that separatist women's organizations can keep women's voices and viewpoints alive and in contention. Thus, the waitress locals were able to raise issues and speak for all working women.

Annelise Orleck challenges us to rethink not only the separatist strategy, but also the view that dichotomizes working women and housewives. The women who organized as housewives during the Great Depression did not challenge the sexual division of labor; yet they knew that feeding, clothing, and sheltering their families were their "jobs" and that, like their husbands in unions or in the Socialist or Communist parties, they were organizing as workers when resisting evictions and protesting the high cost of food and clothing. In cities throughout the country—New York, Detroit, Seattle, Chicago, Philadelphia, Richmond —women organized self-help groups and food exchanges with farmers. They organized neighborhood councils to boycott high-cost food or clothing. They lobbied in state capitals and in Washington, D.C., to regulate prices and establish publicly owned farmer-consumer cooperatives. They discovered their power as a voting bloc and ran their own candidates for public office.

Politicized housewives also effectively used the separatist strategy in organizing as peace activists in the 1950s and early 1960s. According to Amy Swerdlow, Women Strike for Peace used quintessentially female networks—personal telephone calls, contacts in Parent Teacher Associations, Christmas card lists—to build a movement that, by 1962, was strong enough to attract the attention of the House Committee on Un-American Activities. "Ladies' Day at the Capitol: Women Strike for Peace versus HUAC" describes the face-off between thirteen women (and their many supporters) and the committee members. These were women who had, for the most part, internalized the "feminine mystique." Although generally well educated and politically sophisticated, few were employed outside the home. But they imaginatively used traditional sex-role ideology to enhance women's political power. Their defense was grounded in a "mom and apple pie" rhetoric. They even brought their babies into the sanctum of male power, the congressional hearing room, which they transformed from an inquisition room where lives and careers were broken into a laughter-filled, flower-bedecked setting. Moreover, according to Swerdlow, they did in fact prepare the way for the reemergence of feminism later in the 1960s by (1) pointing out men's failure to fulfill their part of the bargain in a sex-segregated world by keeping the world safe for women and children; (2) expanding the sphere of women's activism into the political sphere and, indeed, into the until-then exclusively masculine sphere of international politics; and (3) raising women's sense of political empowerment and self-esteem.

Might not the taking on of starkly stereotypical butch and fem roles by lesbians during the intensely homophobic 1940s and 1950s be viewed similarly? According to Madeline Davis and Elizabeth Lapovsky Kennedy, lesbians also made imaginative use of sex-role ideology in developing an independent lesbian culture. For them, separatism was a survival strategy and sex roles an imaginative means of creating an authentic lesbian sexuality. Although Second Wave feminists were sharply critical of the earlier lesbians' prescriptive roles and role-playing behavior, Davis and Kennedy contend that role-playing was crucial to nurturing the more confrontational political stance of the later period.

Perhaps, then, the distance from role-playing lesbians or role-following housewives of the McCarthy period to Second Wave 1970s' feminist—even radically feminist—groups is not so great as we once thought. This is certainly the view of Judith Sealander and Dorothy Smith, in their case study of three large women's organizations in Dayton, Ohio. Their overview of the range of activities and types of organizing characteristic of this moment in feminist history affords us an opportunity to reflect on the effectiveness of this kind of organizing for the long term. Focusing on Dayton Women's Liberation, the Dayton Women's Center, and Dayton Women Working, Sealander and Smith show how these groups grew out of the nearly spontaneous formation of many small consciousness-raising groups, indicating broad mobilization. Yet they all self-destructed within less than a decade, at the end of the 1970s. The organization of Dayton Women's Liberation and the Dayton Women's Center was built along egalitarian and participatory lines, often making it difficult to set priorities and resolve personal and political conflicts. Dayton Working Women, on the other hand, had a strong socialist feminist leader who was able to lead the organization in significant activity that garnered media attention and led the federal government to investigate Dayton's banks for sex discrimination, but it did not sow deep grass roots. All three organizations depended largely on government funds. When these funds began to dry up, all the organizations failed to sustain themselves, because they either lacked broad participation or were unable to harness and organize the participation they had. Thus, the kind of organizing that Swerdlow found worked so well for Women Strike for Peace proved to be a problem for developing any kind of sustained activity. As Sealander and Smith point out, all three groups also failed to involve many working-class women or women of color, thus limiting their membership and effectiveness.

Bonnie Thorton Dill, in "Race, Class, and Gender: Prospects for an All-inclusive Sisterhood," further explicates the origins and consequences of class and race differences among women. She argues that, as a basis for political and economic actions, the feminist concept of sisterhood, premised on the shared needs and experiences of women, is necessarily limited by the differences in women's race and class backgrounds. A quite different concept of sisterhood—one that is less removed from its original familial sense—is the sisterhood that many Black women have found in churches, associations, and extended families. But this concept, too, Dill contends, has proved of limited political utility, for Black women have used this sisterhood in antiracist politics and community building but not "to forge [their own] political identities." Dill calls for increased awareness of the differences among women and especially for a recognition that these differences may lead to conflict. She is optimistic, however, that cross-race and cross-class alliances can be formed around particular issues, such as school deseg-regation campaigns that would focus on both race and gender equity in education.

Bernice Johnson Reagon's prose poem follows Dill's analysis in identi-fying how Black women's consciousness has emerged from race con-sciousness. But unlike Dill—more like Swerdlow and Orleck—she insists on the *politically* radical nature of women's daily family work. "Black women as mothers have been the heart" of the "nationalist" battle: "I am in fact doing the same thing that my mother did and that my sisters did. The sands have shifted, but the motion I carry is from them." African-American women's participation in civil rights struggles is born of their need to preserve their race, their families, and themselves. Reagon reminds us that the civil rights movement included more women than men and that the majority of the people who went to jail, who marched, and who attended the mass meetings were women. And these women are not different from, but *are* her mother, sisters, teachers, and the women she sat with in church.

Kristin Booth Glen returns us to the troubling issue of racism within the women's movement. In reading "Abortion in the Courts: A Laywoman's Historical Guide," which tracks feminists' use of legal strategies to obtain abortions, we discover that some feminists at least were challenging this racism already in the 1970s. Working closely with Hispanic women in their efforts to end sterilization abuse, feminists were led to examine the quite different historical experiences of women of color and white women around issues of birth control, population control, and eugenics. Writing in 1978, when feminist strategies had been successful in secur-ing legal rights to abortion but had failed to secure economic access, Glen warns that assaults on poor women's access to abortion and health care would one day undermine the abortion rights of all women. She calls for a coalition movement that links abortion rights to access and links both to a reproductive rights politics that places a high priority on ending sterilization abuse and improving the health of women and children. It is chilling to contemplate how prescient she was in identifying the agenda of the antichoice movement. And it is saddening to recognize, as Joan Tronto (discussed below) does, that the abortion rights movement has not for the most part refocused its politics in the directions Glen suggested and that racism still pervades much feminist abortion rights rhetoric and action.

Lise Vogel also considers legal strategy as a form of women's collective action. Reading "Debating Difference: Feminism, Pregnancy, and the Workplace," however, leaves us more optimistic about its potential for progressive change. Vogel explicates opposing feminist legal strategies regarding the most appropriate way to treat women's pregnancy in employment. Policymakers show signs of a willingness to address these issues now that they seem to have learned that women's labor force participation is not a fleeting phenomenon. How they address these issues, whether they adopt an "equal treatment" or "special treatment" philosophy, could make substantial difference in the economic progress women achieve. Both local and national advocacy groups are involved in developing these legal strategies and in lobbying for appropriate legislation.

The next two essays included in this volume, by Judy Aulette and Trudy Mills and by Molly Ladd-Taylor, return us to grass-roots labor union struggles. Aulette and Mills focus on a women's auxiliary reactivated to support Mexican-American unionists during the 1983–86 copper strike in Arizona. Racial factors figured in the strike—most of the striking workers were Mexican American, and the imported "scabs" were mostly Anglos—but because of training in union solidarity, the workers sought not to escalate these ethnic differences. More significant among the strikers and their supporters were gender differences. The work of the women's auxiliary was much like the work of most auxiliaries throughout the twentieth century, including both "domestic" work (typically female activities such as making food for the strikers) and "political" work (establishing picket lines, organizing speaking tours and media coverage, and raising funds). But the gender conflicts that arose between this auxiliary and the union seem new. Mills and Aulette speculate that the discouragements of a long, drawn-out, and ultimately unsuccessful strike, coming at a moment of declining union strength nationally, may explain these internal conflicts. The fact that the union leaders were more tied to their international, while the women were more tied to their communities, may also have played a role. But, most significant, it seems, was the existence in the 1980s of a feminist discourse and politics that shaped the women's perceptions of their actual and potential roles and led them to make demands upon the male unionists, demands that were met with stiff resistance.

Recent feminism also played a role in the strike of the predominantly female clerical workers at Yale University who are the subjects of Molly Ladd-Taylor's "Women Workers and the Yale Strike." This strike, however, was successful. From Ladd-Taylor's account, we learn how political consciousness can be developed through a self-consciously grass-roots effort that takes as its primary goal the building of a strong organization. Developing a sisterly community was the first step in ensuring that the union's direction would not be determined by outsiders. Further, a Black caucus was set up to encourage the emergence of Black leaders. This contrasts with the strategy of Dayton Women Working, one of the organizations described by Sealander and Smith, which failed to sow deep grass roots, and therefore disappeared within a decade. In contrast, the Yale women workers prevailed, relying not only on their own efforts but also marshaling the support as well of the New Haven community, Yale faculty and students, the blue-collar Yale union, and its national union. The women's success, then, seems to have come from a successful wedding of strategies dependent first and foremost on themselves (not unlike the separatist strategies that proved successful in Freedman's and Cobble's histories) and also on the support of people of influence. This was the kind of support that, according to Kessler-Harris and Strom, has too often been denied to women but when offered has served women well.

We conclude this volume with Tronto's review of the varying political strategies pursued by the women's movement, particularly since World War I. Her essay chronicles a movement that has shrunk and expanded over time but has never disappeared. This has important implications for the future. We may pine for the exciting mass activity characteristic of "movement" times, but it is well to remember that there is much that has been accomplished by narrowly focused, small, but solid, groups in periods when mass activity has declined. In Tronto's view, for example, the U.S. women's movement was kept alive during the period from 1945 to 1960 by small groups like the National Woman's Party or the network created by women who worked in the federal government. The activity of these women—Tronto calls them the "elite sustained movement"— during that period led to the adoption of the Equal Pay Act in 1963 and the inclusion of sex as a protected category in the 1964 Civil Rights Act. She considers as well the organizing activities of working-class women and argues from their example that "politics" must be conceptualized more broadly than simply governmental action. Noting that many of the problems (e.g., work-family conflicts, the division of labor within families, and economic rewards) confronting women are considered private matters by the ideology of liberalism and therefore placed beyond the reach of governmental action, she urges us to extend "the notion of politics to include questions of power, domination, and 'respect' at work, at home, and in the community." This volume is inspired by that goal.

Note

1. "Feminist Theory and Women's Activism," a "Polyseminar" and Lecture Series, sponsored by the Women's Studies Program, University of Maryland, Fall 1990; "Bridging the Gap: Between Theory and Practice," sponsored by the Collective on Women of Color and the Law and the *Yale Journal of Law and Feminism,* Yale University, 9–10 Feb. 1991; and "Women, the Environment, and Grassroots Movements," the Eighteenth Annual Scholar and the Feminist Conference, sponsored by the Barnard Center for Research on Women, Barnard College, 13 Apr. 1991.

1 Mary P. Ryan

The Power of Women's Networks:
A Case Study of Female Moral Reform
in Antebellum America

☐ One of the first impulses of the feminist historians in the early 1970s
who set about discovering women's past was simply to chart the course
of sexual inequality and the oppression of women. The advances in
women's scholarship since then have raised more complicated historical issues. Women's historians are now looking to the past for evidence
of women's power and autonomy rather than their simple subordination.
Within segregated female spheres and women's networks they have
discerned evidence of the ability of women to maximize their freedom
and exert considerable social influence. This trend in women's history
has given new currency to Mary Beard's notion, first enunciated in the
1940s, that contrary to being oppressed and victimized, women have
acted throughout the American past to shape events and to make
history. This scholarly perspective has given us a richer, multidimen-
sional picture of women's history. There are, at the same time, some
hazards inherent in this emphasis on women's culture and women's
power. The first possible risk is that by exonerating the women of the
past from the charge of being eternal victims and passive objects of
history, we will also lose sight of the societal inequality which has
consistently marked womanhood and been a central component of
nearly every sex/gender system. Second, we are in some danger of
oversimplifying the historical process. If women are a force in history, if
they make their own history, then we must also face the possibility that
females have participated in creating and reproducing the less-sanguine
aspects of the gender system. We are now in a position to recognize
women as full agents in history, who for all their power and freedom

Reprinted, with changes, from *Feminist Studies* 5, no. 1 (Spring 1979): 66–85. ©1979 by
Feminist Studies, Inc.

have not circumvented the constraints, ironies, and contradictions that confront human beings in the past and into the future.[1]

This essay explores one manifestation of this more complex historical relationship drawn from the annals of antebellum American reform movements. The American Female Moral Reform Society seems to represent women entering history in a powerful, militant some have said, feminist posture. More than four hundred chapters of the national moral reform association grew up throughout New England and the Middle Atlantic states in the 1830s and 1840s. Their goal was to reform standards of sexual morality and regulate sexual behavior in their communities. They assailed the double standard, forcefully pursued and exposed licentious men, and extended their protection to seduced women and reformed prostitutes. In female moral reform, Carroll Smith-Rosenberg has found expressions of women's discontent with their assigned sphere, contempt for tyrannical males, and militant defense of members of their own sex. More recently, Barbara J. Berg has relied heavily on the records of the American Female Moral Reform Society to argue that the origins of U.S. feminism lay not in the abolitionist movement but in the women's benevolent organizations that flourished in the nineteenth-century city and often dated from an earlier period.[2] At the same time, any casual reader of the society's periodical, the *Advocate of Moral Reform,* will also notice a contrary tendency. The *Advocate* reveled in portraying the innate purity, domestic virtue, and maternal priorities of the female sex. In fact they were among the earliest and most enthusiastic exponents of these features of the nineteenth-century stereotype of "true womanhood." Female moral reform, in other words, presents two apparently contradictory uses of woman's power—to attack the double standard, on the one hand, and to celebrate a domestic feminine stereotype, on the other. Thus, the case of female moral reform offers an excellent opportunity to examine the relationship between women's power and the history of the sex/gender system. It may illuminate the nature, sources, and ambiguous historical impact of women's efforts to exert influence on society at large.

This historical objective is best achieved by minute analysis at the level of local reform organization. This narrow but sensitive compass can locate the specific origins of the female moral reformers' power. The focus of this inquiry is a chapter of the American Female Moral Reform Society founded in Utica, New York, in 1837. The Utica Society was also served by rural tributaries, including chapters in such satellite farming and factory villages as Whitesboro, Clinton, New York Mills, and Westmoreland. In the 1830s and 1840s, Utica and the surrounding towns of Oneida County were alive with moral reform and, consequently, prolific in documents for historians of women.

Female moral reform grew up in the interstices of the expanding agricultural market economy which centered in the village of Utica. As late as 1800, Utica was merely a river crossing and trading post situated in the midst of a few pioneer homesteads. The commercial preeminence of the town was established in the 1820s when it became a port along the Erie Canal, bustling with trade and exploding with a population of eight thousand. By the mid-1830s, the canal boom had subsided and the population stabilized at around twelve thousand people. The majority of the employed males of the newly incorporated city made their livelihoods as small merchants or manufacturers—shopkeepers and artisans who served the nearby commercial farmers. Utica also boasted a number of banks and insurance companies; many stockholders in the nearby railroads and textile factories; and a bevy of ambitious entrepreneurs, large and small, who proudly announced themselves as capitalists. Just on the outskirts of the town stood the industrial village of New York Mills, one of the nation's largest textile producers outside of New England. Yet neither large-scale manufacturing nor wage labor dominated local economic activity. Rather, the small independent producer, whether a farmer or artisan, characterized the regional economy and made Utica a bustling, open marketplace.[3]

At this precise historical moment—while still a small, youthful, preindustrial, but flourishing, market economy—Utica earned its place of moderate renown in social history. The plethora of religious revivals and reform activity which Whitney Cross portrayed in his classic study, *The Burned-Over District: The Social and Intellectual History of Enthusiastic Religion in Western New York,* originated in and around Oneida County. The region had been overrun with evangelism since the first settlers arrived from New England in the late eighteenth century. The first benevolent association, a missionary society, was founded in Utica in 1806, and the long, lively, revival cycle ensued soon thereafter—beginning in 1814, peaking in 1826, and dissipating late in the 1830s. It was in the 1830s and 1840s that the "Burned-Over District" spawned the species of reform organization to which female moral reform properly belongs. The city directory for 1832 listed no fewer than forty-one voluntary associations. These groups performed a multitude of community functions: care of the poor, instruction of children, self-improvement of young men, and simple conviviality for their members.[4]

The first associations, founded at the turn of the century, generally united women or men of elite status in order to perform community services, such as providing relief for the poor in a condescending fashion. The voluntary associations of the 1830s were set up for a different purpose—to reform individuals and institutions—and exhibited a new mode of organizing. Most were congregations of peers—members of similar age groups, occupations, and ethnic backgrounds. Most rejected a rigid governing hierarchy and condescending manners. The Washingtonian Temperance Union was the most extreme expression of this leveling tendency, enthusiastically welcoming even acknowledged inebriates into its fraternal embrace. All these associations occupied a distinctive space in the social order of the community, somewhere along a muted boundary between private and public life. The "association," or "society" as it was alternately called, was clearly not an enclosed private space. Yet it was not exactly public, at least not in the way Utica's New England founders used the term to designate the formal institutions of town and church where male heads of households met to exercise official authority. Rather, the association relied on informal but expansive social ties, a voluntary network of like-minded individuals, as its organizational machinery and political leverage. Combined, these associations actually functioned as a major structure of social organization for Utica in the 1830s and 1840s. Whatever the community need—be it police or fire protection, a new industry, poor relief, education, an orphanage—some association rose to meet it.

Social organizations of this nature were particularly receptive to female participation. Sex, first of all, was a legitimate common characteristic around which to form an association of peers. Furthermore, the blurred distinction between private and public space which characterized the association effectively removed a barricade which so often consigned females to domestic confinement. Finally, the social organization of the 1830s and 1840s worked through informal personal associations, the sustained, everyday contacts between neighbors and kin, social networks which were especially familiar and comfortable to women. Thus, it is not surprising that one in three of Utica's associations was a congregation of females. Women's associations were formed, beginning in the first decade of the nineteenth century, for a variety of purposes—to support the frontier ministry, to educate poor children, to circulate religious tracts. Soon women began to organize in a more democratic manner and in a spirit of mutuality rather than noblesse oblige. Groups such as the Maternal Association, the Daughters of Temperance, and the Female Moral Reform Society were all dedicated to serving the reciprocal needs of the members themselves, especially in rearing their children and ridding their homes of vice. All these groups assumed a basic commonality between their members and those they might serve. The victims of alcohol or lechery were all perceived as errant children of the same Protestant, native-born, industrious, and respectable culture. In sum, women were among the most active participants in the rich social life that transpired within the voluntary associations, that American mode of antebellum social organization that so fascinated de Tocqueville. It could also be argued, in the case of Utica at least, that women played a formative role in creating the associational system. The region's first voluntary benevolent organization was the Female Charitable Society. The prototype of the more democratic associations was the Maternal Association which predated its male analogue, the Washingtonian Temperance Union, by over a decade. At any rate, the social order of antebellum Utica and environs was replete with women's organizations, of which the Female Moral Reform Society was only one special case.

The immediate antecedent of female moral reform appeared in Oneida County early in the 1830s when John McDowall of New York City alerted the local population to the need to control seduction, prostitution, and obscenity. The very first issue of *McDowall's Journal*, appearing in 1833, recorded a ground swell of support in the city of Utica. The *Journal* reported individual donations from city residents as well as contributions from associated women, such as the "Female Benevolent Society of Utica." Moral as well as financial support soon followed. Abigail Whitellsey, the editor of the *Mother's Magazine*, another offshoot of the women's organizations of Utica, also sent her appreciation and endorsement. Tokens of support also came from anonymous women, such as "a Lady from Utica" who poignantly offered up "two rings and a breast pin" to help finance the cause. The small towns outside Utica were the first to mobilize behind moral reform. Whitesboro had a chapter of the American Female Moral Reform Society as of 1835 which enrolled approximately 40 members. By 1837 when the Utica Society was formally established, the chapters in Clinton and Westmoreland had acquired a membership of 84 and 181, respectively. The 100-member Utica association pledged to wage a pious women's crusade: "We do feel dear sisters" announced the first annual report of the Utica Female Moral Reform Society, "that we have enlisted in the warfare for life and that we are not at liberty to lay down the armor till called upon by death to other services."[5]

The names of only a handful of the Utica reformers have been recorded on an occasional circular or newspaper account. These few identifiable members, however, represented a relatively wide range of women from the middling and upper classes. Wives of artisans joined those of merchants and prominent attorneys. Two seamstresses brought the interests of wage-earning women into the society. Although veterans of evangelical reform based in the Utica First Presbyterian Church formed the core of the Female Moral Reform Society, women of Baptist affiliations also joined the ranks. The single and the widowed, furthermore, joined with middle-aged wives and mothers in the moral crusade.[6] Significantly, the rural areas of Oneida County, including both farming communities and industrial villages, displayed equal, if not greater, enthusiasm for female moral reform than did the city proper.

What then stimulated women from such a broad spectrum of the population to take an interest in moral reform? It might be expected that these women were simply reacting to a sudden upsurge in the incidence of "adultery and seduction," the species of vice that they were most determined to eradicate. Yet a survey conducted by the Utica Society in 1843 uncovered a paltry record of sexual offenses—nine cases of illegitimacy and two arrests for prostitution. Although no more refined estimate of the frequency of sexual relations outside of marriage is available for Oneida County, there are some indications that the rate of sexual license was actually on the decline in the northeastern United States. Analysis of vital statistics and church records suggest that the proportion of births conceived before marriage had peaked in the late eighteenth century and actually reached its nadir in the era of moral reform.[7] These statistics, however, hint at more complex changes in sexual behavior than a simple decrease in premarital sexual relations. These cases of premarital sex were exposed by examining genealogical records, proceeding, couple by couple, to simply subtract the number of months between the date of marriage and the date of first birth. Premarital sex which did not culminate in a marriage record, then, is not recorded by these statistics. Hence, it may be that the young women and men of Oneida County and the northeastern United States were engaging in sex outside of marriage at the same or even a higher rate than in previous decades but were now evading marriage to their sex partners. If this were true then the decline in "early births" may indicate not a lower incidence of premarital sex, but, rather, the breakdown of those methods of social control which formerly insured that illicit intercourse and conception usually culminated in matrimony.

This second interpretation of changing sexual behavior in antebellum America is substantiated by evidence from Oneida County. Although the actual level of premarital sex cannot be accurately determined, it is quite clear that the community's ability to monitor and regulate such behavior had eroded substantially. After 1830, neither the church nor the family retained its former control over private sexual activity. Before then, the local churches, Baptist, Methodist, and Presbyterian alike, regularly called their members to account for committing fornication and adultery. Seducers and adulterers were brought before the elders of the church to confess their sins, vow to change their ways, or be excommunicated. Early in the 1830s, after heated ecclesiastical debates too complicated to recount here, the local churches discontinued this method of enforcing sexual morality.[8] At the same time, the rapid increase in the population of Utica and its increasing religious diversity prevented a single church (including the once-ruling Presbyterians) from overseeing the sexual behavior of the entire town.

At the same time, parents' ability to restrict the sexual activity of their daughters and sons was being undermined by the extreme geographical mobility of the commercial era. The population of Utica quadrupled between 1820 and 1840, due in large part to the influx of young women and men unaccompanied by their parents. One-quarter of the city's population was between the ages of fifteen and thirty; as much as 30 percent of all those listed in the city directory called themselves boarders, most of whom were young men living apart from their kin. Many of these young urban dwellers were migrants from rural Oneida County, where after the exhaustion of unimproved agricultural land in the 1820s, parents could no longer provide a livelihood for all their progeny on nearby farms. Thus, Utica was inundated with young unsupervised women and men seeking jobs as seamstresses, clerks, canal boys, and servants. The industrial village of New York Mills, meanwhile, was filling up with unchaperoned factory girls of similar origins. Parents and the deacons of the church were not available then to control or protect these young migrants.

It was the Female Moral Reform Society that came to the aid of this peripatetic generation. Although the espoused goal of the society was to rout out seduction and adultery, the Utica chapter was most concerned about the former sexual transgression, the peculiar pitfall of the young and unmarried. The appearance of at least two seamstresses on the rolls of the Utica chapter represented a population of women who seldom enlisted in local reform groups. These working girls were especially vulnerable to seduction and the fateful consequences of becoming unwed mothers and may well have joined the society for their own sexual self-protection. The bulk of the members of the Utica chapter, however, were married women who seemed to act more out of concern for their children than their own immediate self-defense. The brothels of the city, according to the reformers, were the "known cause of ruin to multitudes of the rising generation" and were responsible for "rending the hearts of fathers and mothers." One mother from Clinton wrote the *Advocate of Moral Reform* describing the demographics of her interest in sexual control: "A daughter and a son have returned to their widowed mother from visiting distant cities and pined away victims of this sin [of sexual indulgence]." The secretary of the New York Mills chapter explained the sources of maternal concern in this region as follows: "The state of society in this place is peculiar to manufacturing villages. Multitudes of youth are here collected who need light and instruction on this subject." The records of the female moral reform societies of Oneida County were most of all a repository of the anxieties of mothers. "Even our children are infested with [obscenity]," wrote the alarmed matrons. "Who amongst us have not had our hearts pained by the obscenity of little children? Who among us does not trouble at least if some who are dear to us should be led away by the thousand snares of the destroyer?" They feared for their sons as well as their daughters, whom they envisioned leaving home only to be enticed into brothels and descend therewith to the almshouse, prison, or the gallows. The female moral reformers, in sum, anticipated the dangers of unbridled sexuality in the fluid circumstances of commercial and early industrial capitalism, and they constituted themselves as a force to regulate and control such threatening behavior.[9]

Female moral reform, then, constituted a concrete, specific attempt to exert woman's power. Led and initiated by women, it was a direct, collective, organized effort, which aimed to control behavior and change values in the community at large. Because female moral reform entailed explicit social action it is possible to examine its origins, impact, and limitations as an exercise of woman's power. Several manifestations of this power will be identified. First of all, the case of moral reform suggests how women could use their social position in a specific time and place as leverage with which to influence others, including males. Second, within the Female Moral Reform Society, women can be seen giving direction to the future of their sex. Specifically, it will be argued that the members of the Female Moral Reform Society helped to lay the groundwork for the Victorian sexual code which placed particular stock in the purity of females. Finally, the case of female moral reform will illustrate the proposition that associated women were a force in history at large. In this instance, women played a vital role in working out the ideology of sexual control which characterized the middle classes of the nineteenth-century city. Female moral reformers, it will be seen, clearly made history and reshaped aspects of the American sex/gender system. Yet their impact on the status of women was rife with ambiguities. In the end they used their social power to create a moral code which exacted particularly stringent sexual repression from their own sex.

How then did the women of the Female Moral Reform Society grasp the power to enact their program of purification? They began simply enough by activating the machinery of reform which had been operating in Oneida County for nearly a generation. One of the first endorsements of female moral reform was sent to *McDowall's Journal* by a matron calling herself "A Friend of my Species," who had arrived in Utica forty years before. For the benefit of readers, McDowall described the correspondent as "a lady moving in the very first circle of society, a mother, a philanthropist, a Christian."[10] This writer, while anonymous to historians, was undoubtedly widely known among her Utica contemporaries. She might have been Sophia Clarke, founder of the city's Female Missionary Society and the Maternal Association, active abolitionist, and prominent Presbyterian. Or she may have been Mrs. Clarke's colleague, Sophia Bagg, the mistress of Bagg's Hotel who sat at the center of local society and founded the city's most august charitable institution, the Utica Orphan Asylum. Perhaps the identity of the "friend of my species" was the same as the unnamed woman who nearly rent apart the First Presbyterian Church a few years previous when she censored a leading parishioner "on his political opinions." Regardless of individual identity, this matron, described as a "lady moving in the very first circle" was representative of a whole web of associations between women that had been growing and reinforcing itself since the first decade of the nineteenth century.

The oldest and strongest stand in this network linked together the members of the Presbyterian Church. The female parishioners were assembled at the First Presbyterian Church of Utica in 1834 when Samuel C. Aiken, pastor and veteran revivalist, announced from the pulpit that "a whole tribe of libertines" was about to invade the city of Utica. Aiken then turned to the females of the congregation, saying, "Daughters of America! Why not marshall yourselves in bands and become a terror to evil doers."[11] It was not until three years later that the women of Utica put this plan into operation, forming their own chapter of the American Female Moral Reform Society. Two parishioners, Fanny Skinner and Paulina Wright, played the major leadership roles in the Utica chapter. Mrs. Skinner's ties to the local network of female associations went back to 1806 and the founding of the Female Charitable Society of Whitestown. The 1830s found her embroiled in abolitionism as well as moral reform and exploiting her personal contacts in order to convince Angelina Grimké Weld to speak in Utica. Paulina Wright was a relative newcomer to Utica reform, yet she quickly found her way into the women's network as she peddled tracts and petitions for the Martha Washington Temperance Union as well as the Female Moral Reform Society. Her personal network of women's reform would also take her to the border of feminism; for example, she circulated petitions for the reform of married women's property rights in the company of Elizabeth Cady Stanton.[12] Again the trail of women's associations followed deeply rutted paths through local neighborhoods, churches, and reform circles.

Female moral reformers discovered a portal to public responsibility and power through the same social circle. Mrs. Whitellsey's letter to John McDowall in 1833 described a practice of moral reform which predated any formal association. Whenever she came in contact with defenseless young women, Mrs. Whitellsey resorted to this strategy: "I have either written a note or sent with them a messenger to such of my friends as might be able either to employ them themselves or direct them to others. Whether this course or some other equivalent is oftener pursued, many of the unfortunate victims of vice and wretchedness . . . would be greatly diminished." Mrs. Whitellsey was proposing that women could use the bonds of friendship which linked local households, that is, the existing female social network, as the mechanism of moral reform. The same device could be used to secure financial support for reform activity, as was inadvertently revealed by the editor of a local evangelical periodical. Charles Hastings wrote to the *Advocate of Moral Reform* (the periodical of the national organization) apologizing for his own inability to devote time to the worthy cause. He happily announced, however, that "a female in my family says she will go around among the families and see if she can't get something for your support." This door-to-door, woman-to-woman approach was also the means of expanding the ranks of reformers and influencing public opinion. The circulation of tracts and petitions was a routine of female organization in charities, temperance, and Bible societies. In other words, female moral reform simply sent a new message, a new set of demands, through a familiar and personal network of communication.[13]

Faced with what they saw as an epidemic of vice, female moral reformers soon entertained the notion that more heroic measures were necessary, and they began to tread outside of their familiar social circles. They formed a visiting committee in 1841 which ventured into the more unseemly haunts of the town. Entering into some of the hovels of the poor, they met a sympathetic response among Utica's mothers and wives. Poor widows tearfully accepted their tracts and offered in return personal reports about sexual offenses and domestic crimes against women. The stories grew more lurid than a dime novel as these pious women of Utica encountered real-life cases of seduction and betrayal, of drunken and tyrannical husbands, and abused and battered wives. One of the visiting committee's informants told the sordid tale of her invalid neighbor. Night after night, the sick woman's husband took her nurse to his bed. This report like many others was accompanied by a remark which identified the offending man to his neighbors. "This man has the charge of a paper, the object of which is to uphold public morals," wrote the female reformer: "May we not ask how long shall men like this occupy responsible stations and be tolerated among Christian people?" Through the agency of the Female Moral Reform Society such stories transformed gossip into a public instrument of protest.[14]

The reports of the visiting committee also offered examples of militant assaults upon the forces of vice. One Utica matron became a heroine of moral reform after her unilateral attack on a local brothel. She told the following story. Her son had been keeping late hours night after night while she paced, prayed, and wept for his soul. Finally, she could endure such passivity no longer. She marched straight to the nearby brothel, bounded up the stairs, pounded on the door of the chamber which harbored her son, and shouted that a constable was on his way. This enraged mother was hurled down the stairs by the brothel's owner, but she returned home to find a repentant son. It was stories like these that the officers of the Female Moral Reform Society had in mind when they reported that the monthly meeting had been "rendered highly useful and interesting from the reports of the visiting committee which have been replete with heart-stirring facts and appeals."[15]

Buoyed by encounters such as these, the reformers became even more energetic and audacious. A committee of eight women secured between two and three thousand signatures on a petition to outlaw prostitution in 1841. Another woman visited twenty-two families in a one-month period. Ultimately, the membership of Utica's Female Moral Reform Society began to encroach upon the male centers of authority. One cadre of the movement marched to city hall and demanded statistics on sex offenders. Others accosted men of dubious character on the city streets and entered taverns to interrogate bartenders. The Female Moral Reform Society even took their cause into the courts. When a young servant woman came to the society with a report of sexual exploitation by her employer, the members acted swiftly and decisively in her defense. They brought the culprit to trial and provided the victim with legal counsel, personal support, and a new job in a respectable home. In this instance, the Utica Female Moral Reform Society acted as a special police force and public prosecutor, whose jurisdiction was sexual assaults on women. They had mobilized not only to perform a community function once assigned to male ministers and elders of the church, but they had also carried their moral mission outside their own congregations and into the streets and thoroughfares of Utica.[16]

In the process, the new female custodians of sexual morality also

altered the standards of propriety. Church trials were primarily concerned with cases of adultery, that is, the infidelity of married men and
especially women. The members of the Female Moral Reform Society,
however, were most concerned about the sexual behavior of the young
and unmarried and demanded stricter purity from both their sons and
daughters. Moral reformers repeatedly lamented the lax standards of
the recent past. For example, one reformer noted that until recently a
"young boy who was not afraid to trifle with the most forward girls was
esteemed above his years and almost a man." Female moral reformers
would not tolerate such permissive attitudes and attempted to purge
local culture of all suggestions of casual, lenient sexuality. The goal of
moral reform, as the minister of a largely female congregation put it,
was to eradicate all "unchaste feelings and licentious habits," not just to
condemn and punish sexual intercourse outside of marriage. Toward
this end, the Female Moral Reform Society instructed women to
"encourage both by precept and example, simplicity with regard to
dress and at their children's tables, that unseen snares are not laid
which shall lead to the vice we are striving to exterminate."[17] They were,
in other words, making connections between a child's dress and diet
and his or her disposition to sexual indulgence in later life. The Female
Moral Reform Society, as well as the overlapping membership of the
local maternal associations, propounded methods of childcare which
were designed to instill sexual control in the very personalities of the
rising generation. They turned from external control of sexual behavior
to an internalized repression of physical drives.

The women of the Female Moral Reform Society of Utica had
traveled a considerable ideological and social territory within a few
short years. They began simply by taking advantage of a vacuum of
moral authority in the commercial city and proceeded to adapt traditional and previously male-directed methods of moral surveillance to a
new environment and their own interests (primarily as mothers). By the
early 1840s, they had revised the code of sexual morality and created
novel and forceful methods of circulating these revised standards.
Coincidentally, they had opened a new social space through which
their sex could maneuver for power in the community.

The nature of their power is indicated by a major community
conflict instigated by the female moral reformers of Utica in 1836 and
1837. The incident was one skirmish in a prolonged battle between the
Female Moral Reform Society and the city's clerks. The moral reformers
charged these youthful employees of stores and countinghouses with
major responsibility for seduction in the city. When, for example, some
members of the society spotted the alleged perpetrators of some unnamed

nocturnal infamy on a city thoroughfare, they jumped from their carriage and presented the offending clerks with a tract appropriately entitled "Run Speak to That Young Man." In 1836 the Utica Society commissioned a Reverend Dodge to deliver a public lecture indicating the same class of young men on charges of licentiousness. The members of the society were so pleased with Dodge's discourse that they published an endorsement of his remarks in the local newspaper. Suddenly they found themselves at the center of a raging local controversy. First a delegation of clerks held a public meeting and placed a newspaper advertisement to defend their good name. Then another group of citizens who also purported to represent the city's clerks rose to concur with Dodge's opinion.[18]

These two broadsides displayed a growing cleavage in antebellum sexual ideology. The supporters of female moral reform proposed an old-fashioned solution to the problem of sexual license in the commercial sector of the local economy. They recommended that employers assume the responsibility for overseeing the private behavior of their clerks; and they proposed that this obligation be written into a formal contract between the merchant and his young workers, just as in the ancient practices of indenture and apprenticeship, and on that same principle of paternal surveillance which once prevailed in stable farm households. In other words, these supporters of female moral reform seemed to hark back to more traditional methods of controlling sexual behavior. They had been compelled to announce their position, however, by the actions of a novel social organization, a band of reforming females who were considerably more sophisticated in their thinking about sexual questions. The clerk faction, on the other hand, rejected both paternal control of sexual behavior and the zealotry of the female reformers. As they saw it, "one of the first lessons to be learned by young men is to carry their lives and the regulator of their conduct in their own bosoms" independently of the commands of their superiors or the moral pressure of evangelizing women. Theirs was a highly individualistic and liberal position, which proclaimed the rights of private conscience.

Analysis of the signatories of these two lists reveals that these differences in sexual attitudes reflected the divergent social status of the two factions. The clerks who were appalled by Dodge's sermon garnered support from their employers and hence some of the city's largest and most influential merchants. The bulk of the signatories of the second resolution, that in support of female moral reform, turned out to be neither clerks nor the employers of clerks. In fact the largest single occupational group represented on this second document was that of artisans. The proponents and opponents of female moral reform also differed markedly in their family status. The opponents were not only clerks, but also boarders, and very often residents of the largest and most impersonal lodging houses and hotels of Utica. The allies of the Female Moral Reform Society, on the other hand, tended to reside with their biological families. Even among the minority who called themselves boarders, a significant proportion still shared a household with either their parents or their employers. In sum, the Utica Female Moral Reform Society had raised issues which divided the population by occupation as well as pattern of residence. It pitted artisans who favored a more traditional household structure against merchants and clerks who had chosen the residential pattern germane to a thriving commercial town, namely boarding.[19]

Still the fact remains that both factions and a substantial portion of the community's leadership were forced to respond to issues that had been introduced into public debate by an organized group of women. The clerks in fact felt obliged to endorse many of the values expounded by the Female Moral Reform Society. They advertised their own chastity and proclaimed it a young man's "highest interest" and "most valuable capital." The financial establishment of Utica soon issued similar demands for sexual self-control. During the 1840s, the Mercantile Agency (forerunner of Dun & Bradstreet) sentenced many a young man to business failure by denying credit on the basis of a "bad reputation" or "running after the women."[20] In the risky enterprises of the aggressively capitalistic town of Utica, self-control was one predictor of financial prudence and soon became a measure of middle-class respectability. It would become even more important as the city industrialized after 1845 and as more and more young women and men were permanently exiled from the farms and artisan workshops where fathers once enacted direct sanctions against the sexual irregularities of their children. The progeny of native-born artisans and farmers would increasingly find themselves in the more solitary and insecure circumstances represented by the city clerks of the 1830s. The ideology of individual internalized sexual control first formulated and most aggressively publicized by female moral reformers eased young women and men through this transition from farm to city, from the family economy to individualized occupations. In the end then, the history of the Utica Female Moral Reform Society suggests that women could play a central and initiating role in the transformation of class and ideology. They devised and implemented sexual standards and practices which would distinguish the urban middle class from their artisan and farming parents.

In sum, the events of 1837 provide a public illustration of how a few active, organized, well-situated women could exert power in history.

They had a direct effect on the opinions of men and had found leverage that extended beyond their households, outside the women's networks, and across the social and economic divisions within the city. In achieving their goals, the female moral reformers demonstrated a distinctive variety of women's power. This power did not take the covert and privatized form which nineteenth-century writers venerated as "women's influence." Rather the women of the Female Moral Reform Society set social standards, commanded public attention, and caused a major commotion right in the center of the local social system.

Their power is attributable not merely to the energy and ingenuity of the women involved but also to the hospitable environment of a small commercial city in the antebellum period. These women were still located in relatively close proximity to the centers of public power. Fanny Skinner was particularly well situated in relation to the male leadership of the youthful city. The instigator of the male defense of Utica Female Moral Reform in 1837 was Cyrus Hawley, a clerk who happened to reside in the boardinghouse full of young lawyers which Skinner had managed for over a decade. But women's influence was not limited to such domestic associations. Most importantly, it extended to a rich social network based on the long-term, habitual cooperation of women in church and reform activities. The collective power of these groups, finally, was situated in easy reach of the arenas in which the male leaders of the city jostled for authority. In the 1830s and early 1840s, the polity of Utica was still composed largely of innumerable associations of men.

Informal networks not so different from the Utica Female Moral Reform Society made decisions on everything from political candidates to the founding of factories. Accordingly, a well-organized women's network, operating parallel to these male associations, had at least a fighting chance of affecting the policies and opinions of the community at large. These historical conditions, as well as the social form of the voluntary association, confused the boundaries between public and private life, thus allowing women to form circles of influence outside their homes and put ideological and moral pressure on the male authorities of the public sphere. In Oneida County in the 1830s and 1840s, as in similar cases described by anthropologists, this muting of the barrier between private and public life seems to have enhanced the power of women within their communities.[21]

Neither these conditions nor the American Female Moral Reform Society would survive for very long. The last notice of an active local chapter of the Utica Society appeared in 1845, at about the same time that the city's first steam-powered cotton factory was put into operation, and just as the town was inundated with unskilled workers hailing from Ireland, Germany, and the British Isles. By mid-century, Utica had become a city of more than twenty thousand inhabitants with a major industrial sector and increasingly segregated pattern of residence. Once the old commercial community had become hopelessly fractured by ethnic and class differences, a band of Protestant women could no longer presume to make moral pronouncements for the city at large. Concomitantly, as Utica and Oneida County became more closely integrated into the national economic and political system, vital decisions were transferred from the neighborhood to a formidable city hall and then on to Washington and Wall Street, that is, to a remote, more formalized public sphere. The local conditions which allowed female moral reform to obtain this position of social power did not survive into a second generation.

This is not to say that the movement ended with a quiet failure in the backwaters of social history. Such a thesis can be rebutted by several arguments. First of all, the members of the female moral reform societies of Oneida County were willing participants in the destruction of their own organization. In fact, the disappearance of the society can be interpreted as a measure of successful sex reform. The Utica association disbanded in the midst of a quarrel over whether to hold a convention in nearby Clinton. Some of the members deemed it improper to conduct a public discussion of sexual matters in a town full of young seminary and college students.[22] It would seem that the Female Moral Reform Society had become caught up in its own propaganda, converted by its own increasingly exacting standard of propriety, which in the end prescribed almost complete reticence about sexual questions. Furthermore, the sexual reform movement did not end even with the demise of the society. The banners of purity which its members once hurled in the streets now paraded through popular culture. Wherever the young women and men of the 1850s might travel their path would be strewn with admonitions and expectations of sexual continence. The *Advocate of Moral Reform* itself survived the collapse of local chapters of the American Female Moral Reform Society and continued to propagate the ideology of sexual control.

That ideology had become increasingly detached from organized women's networks. The *Advocate of Moral Reform* soon presumed an alternative social mechanism through which women could control sexual behavior, that is, through the private relationships of wives and especially mothers. The *Advocate of Moral Reform* was happy to announce that moral reform now took place "where it should begin, in the right instruction of children." The journal's editors embraced the same doctrine of women's domestic influence celebrated in the ladies' magazines of the era: "A mother's love will accomplish more than anything else except omnipotence."[23] From the first, female moral reformers had placed special emphasis on maternity. In fact, they were among the first and most forceful exponents of women's glorified role as the socializers of children. With the dissipation of local associations after 1845, women were left stranded in this isolated private sphere which the reformers themselves had done so much to cultivate. In the last analysis, Victorian women were guided into domestic confinement by members of their own sex. Such is the convoluted and ironic history of this example of the power of women's networks.

This history can be instructive for contemporary feminists. It suggests, first of all, that women can find sources of organizational strength at the local level. The formal and national organizational structures which eluded the female moral reformers and which still have a fragile existence in today's women's movement can be strengthened and reinforced by connections with the everyday associations and informal social networks of local and neighborhood women. In fact, such a bridge between local networks and national organization still exercises substantial social power. It is, however, the Right which has proven particularly successful in utilizing such power, but for antifeminist purposes. Through neighborhood organization and affiliation with local and national churches, these right-wing women conducted yet another campaign to control sexual mores—attacking homosexuality, fighting abortion and the ERA, and venerating the heterosexual nuclear family. Furthermore, like the moral reformers of the 1830s and 1840s, the women of the Right have come to public prominence at a time of major social and sexual change, when, for example, the rising divorce rate threatens to sever the ties between wives and husbands nearly as frequently as children were separated from parents by the frenetic geographical mobility of the nineteenth century. Now, as then, some women are reacting to this crisis by defending the domestic institutions which seem to offer them security along with inequality. The rise of the New Right, like the power of female moral reform, may presage yet another readjustment of the sex/gender system with dubious consequences for women. In fact, it prompts some skepticism as to whether women's culture and female networks, which continue to be rooted largely in the relations of housewives and mothers, can generate much more than reflexive and defensive, rather than critical, responses to social and familial change.[24]

It should be clear, at any rate, that not every incident and every species of women's social and historical power merits our applause. It is the use of that power which concerns feminists. In the case of female moral reform, the laudable ability to maneuver for social influence fell short of the feminist goal of subverting the restrictions and inequality delegated to women by the American sex/gender system. The power of women's networks, be it manifest in female moral reform or the New Right, deserves more than either congratulations or condemnation. It requires serious, critical attention to both its historical permutations and diverted feminist possibilities.

Notes

I would like to thank Bert Hansen and the editors of *Feminist Studies* for their help in revising this article.

1. These ideas were raised and debated at the session, "The Legacy of Mary Ritter Beard," chaired by Ann J. Lane, at the Fourth Berkshire Conference on the History of Women, Mount Holyoke, Massachusetts, August 1978.

2. Carroll Smith-Rosenberg, "Beauty and the Beast and the Militant Woman: A Case Study in Sex Roles and Social Stress in Jacksonian America," *American Quarterly* 23 (October 1971): 562–84; Barbara Berg, *The Remembered Gate: Origins of American Feminism* (New York: Oxford University Press, 1978).

3. The exact population figures for Utica are as follows: 1820 = 2,972; 1830 = 8,323; 1840 = 12,782; 1850 = 17,565; 1860 = 22,529. The changing occupational structure of the city is represented in the following table:

	Merchants Manufacturers	Professionals	Shopkeepers	White Collar	Artisans	Unskilled Factory
1828	11.1%	4.8%	12.5%	4.8%	46.1%	14.1%
1845	2.7%	10.2%	11.9%	10.2%	45.4%	20.2%
1855	2.9%	8.6%	6.6%	8.6%	40.9%	24.1%

4. Whitney Cross, *The Burned-Over District: The Social and Intellectual History of Enthusiastic Religion in Western New York* (Ithaca: Cornell University Press, 1950); Mary P. Ryan, "A Woman's Awakening: Evangelical Religion and the Families of Utica, N.Y., 1800–1840," *American Quarterly* 30 (Winter 1978): 602–23.

5. See *McDowall's Journal*, January, March, May, July, and November 1833, for correspondence from Utica.

6. Only thirty-four female moral reformers were identified by name, and only nineteen of these could be traced to the city directories. Of this latter group, six were married to merchants or shopkeepers, five to professionals, two to artisans; two were seamstresses and four had neither occupations nor employed husbands. Seven single women, as well as wives and widows, were found in the

same group. This range of class and marital status is the widest of any of the reform groups studied.

7. Daniel Scott Smith and Michael S. Hindus, "Premarital Pregnancy in America, 1640–1971: An Overview and Interpretation," *Journal of Interdisciplinary History* 5 (Spring 1975): 537–70.

8. "The Session Records of the First Presbyterian Church," First Presbyterian Church Utica, New York, vol. 3, 3 Dec. and 17 Dec. 1834; 2 Jan. and 2 July 1835.

9. *Advocate of Moral Reform*, 15 June 1843; 1 Feb. 1838; 15 Sept. 1837.

10. *McDowall's Journal*, November 1833.

11. Samuel C. Aiken, *Moral Reform* (Utica: R. R. Shepard, 1834), 8–9.

12. Information about Fanny Skinner is drawn from scattered references in local histories, church records, and reform society publications; for a biographical sketch of Paulina Wright, see Alice Felt Tyler, "Paulina Wright Davis," *Notable American Women 1607–1950: A Biographical Dictionary*, 3 vols. (Cambridge: Harvard University Press, 1974), 1:444–45.

13. *McDowall's Journal*, June 1834; *Advocate of Moral Reform*, 7 Feb. and 22 Feb. 1836.

14. *Advocate of Moral Reform*, 15 Sept. 1842.

15. Ibid., 1 July 1842.

16. Ibid., 15 Dec. 1841; 1 Apr. 1844.

17. *McDowall's Journal*, June 1834; *Advocate of Moral Reform*, 15 Feb. and 30 July 1840.

18. *Oneida Whig*, 27 Dec. 1836; 27 Jan. and 14 Feb. 1837.

19. The occupations and residences of the parties to the moral reform controversy of 1836 and 1837 are summarized in the following table:

	Supporters of Female Moral Reform	Opponents of Female Moral Reform
Total Number Identified	118	50
Occupations		
Merchants/Manufacturers	22.9%	2.0%
Shopkeepers/Farmers	13.6%	4.0%
Professionals	17.8%	12.0%
Clerks	9.3%	72.0%
Artisans	36.4%	10.0%
Residence		
Home of Own	78.3%	11.8%
Boards with Relatives or Employers	3.3%	9.8%
Boards Alone	18.6%	78.4%

20. Early handwritten credit reporting ledgers of the Mercantile Agency (Utica), R. G. Dun & Company Ledgers, vol. 476, Baker Library, Harvard Business School, Cambridge, Massachusetts.

21. Rayna R[app] Reiter, "Men and Women in the South of France: Public and Private Domains," in *Toward an Anthropology of Women,* ed. Rayna R[app] Reiter (New York: Monthly Review Press, 1975), 252–82; Michelle Zimbalist Rosaldo, "Woman, Culture, and Society: A Theoretical Overview," (Stanford: Stanford University Press, 1974), 17–42.

22. *Advocate of Moral Reform,* 15 Sept. 1845.

23. Ibid., August 1838; August 1835.

24. The parallels between female moral reform and the New Right were brought to my attention during the discussion of this paper at the Women and Power Conference, University of Maryland, College Park, November 1977.

Feminist Friends: Agrarian Quakers and the Emergence of Woman's Rights in America

☐ Historian Nancy Cott captured the paradox of women's status in early-nineteenth-century America by identifying "two seemingly contradictory visions of women's relation to society: the ideology of domesticity, which gave women a sex-specific role to play, primarily in the home; and feminism, which attempted to remove sex-specific limits on women's opportunities and capacities." Cott argues that historically the emergence of feminism "depended on" the slightly earlier "subtle changes in women's view of the domestic role."[1] What was essential about that new domestic experience was the sex-consciousness it fostered, a sex-consciousness most forcefully depicted by Carroll Smith-Rosenberg. The "female world of love and ritual" that she discovered in the private interstices of middle-class life revealed the domestic circle as a seedbed not only of sex-consciousness but also of sex solidarity.[2] Suddenly, women's separation from productive labor and relegation to the private sphere appeared less restrictive and isolating; rather, it provided the necessary resources for women's reemergence as public arbiters of moral and social order.

Numerous other historians have sought the roots of feminism first in extensions of women's domestic roles through missionary and charitable societies and then in elaborations of evangelical theology. Female neighbors, kin, and coworshipers served as agents of evangelical revivals and had their own sisterly bonds strengthened through the conversion experience. It was these tightly knit circles of women who joined forces to eradicate prostitution, intemperance, and enslavement. In these latter campaigns, women met barriers to their public efforts based

Reprinted, with changes, from *Feminist Studies* 12, no. 1 (Spring 1986): 27–49. © 1986 by Feminist Studies, Inc.

solely on sex, leading some to claim rights for themselves as a precondition for aiding others.[3]

It is this last step in the scenario, from moral crusades to feminism, that proved the most difficult, for both the women who took it and the historians who attempted to explain it. Conventional evangelical Protestantism, which initially liberated women from the domestic circle, nonetheless proved a barrier to overt feminism. Blanche Glassman Hersh, for example, notes that "emancipation from religious orthodoxy was a crucial element in the development of a feminist leadership." Of the fifty-one feminist abolitionist leaders Hersh studied, twenty-one grew up in Quaker, Unitarian, or Universalist families. Of the twenty-seven who were raised in orthodox or evangelical faiths, nine rejected these youthful affiliations to become Unitarians, Universalists, or Quakers; and nine others "deconverted" to join radical religious sects or to join no sect at all. Nonetheless, Hersh claims that the ideology her feminist abolitionists bequeathed to later generations was rooted in the doctrine of sexual spheres and in the belief in female moral and spiritual superiority, that is, in the social and cultural mores of middle-class evangelicals.[4] Thus, the existing historical literature suggests that the birth of feminism was a two-step process—from domesticity to humanitarian reform via evangelical religion, and from evangelical crusades to feminism via a second conversion to unconventional Protestantism.[5]

This article puts this scenario to the test by examining the origins of the woman's rights movement in early-nineteenth-century Rochester, New York. In Rochester, boom-town growth, the development of a market economy, the building of the Erie Canal, and the appearance of evangelical ministers nurtured a large number of charitable and reform associations in the 1820s and 1830s, several of which were founded and directed by women. Many Rochester women, then, did take the first step from domesticity to reform. They were aided, moreover, by the preachings of Charles Grandison Finney and his local evangelical counterparts, who convinced the wives of lawyers, land speculators, artisans, and merchants to shift their emphasis from amelioration to the wholesale eradication of society's vices. As I have demonstrated elsewhere, however, neither boom-town benevolence nor evangelically inspired perfectionism proved adequate to transform these female activists into feminist advocates. When national and local clergymen and editors began to balk at women's expanding role in the public domain, Rochester's evangelical women listened to their paternal censors and retreated.[6] Most either discontinued their activist careers during the 1840s or redirected their energies to church and charitable efforts. The reasons for this self-imposed detour from the feminist path were complex, but they included the internalization of the tenets of "true womanhood"—piety, purity, domesticity, and submissiveness—combined with the ritual humiliation before God demanded in the conversion experience and with upward economic and social mobility.[7]

Those few Rochester women who did accept Elizabeth Cady Stanton's call to attend the first woman's rights convention in Seneca Falls, New York, in July 1848, and who organized an even more radical gathering in Rochester that August took an alternate path to the public platform. They were among the large contingent of Quakers who gathered for the convention from Waterloo and Auburn, New York, and Philadelphia as well as from Rochester. At least one-fourth of the one hundred signers of the Declaration of Sentiments drafted at the 1848 meeting were members of the Society of Friends. Frederick Douglass, the lone Black participant, was the only non-Quaker among five Rochester signers. These feminist Friends did not perhaps answer Stanton's call at all. Rather, they answered the call of American Quakerism's leading spokeswoman, Lucretia Mott, and of her three coreligionists—Mary Ann McClintock, Jane Hunt, and Martha Wright—who helped Stanton organize the historic event in Seneca Falls.[8]

The Quaker women who attended the 1848 meetings had bypassed, for most of their lives, the basic elements of the new urban bourgeois gender system—the separation of spheres, the sex-consciousness of domesticity, and the ideology of female moral and spiritual superiority. Instead, they worked alongside husbands in downstate and central New York farming communities; imbibed a group consciousness rooted in religious persecution; proclaimed woman's equality before God and in the religious "meeting"; and viewed change, both personal and social, as a gradual unfolding of the Divine presence. These agrarian Quakers were active before 1848 as advocates of Indian rights, communitarianism, temperance, and abolition but not alongside urban evangelicals. Within Quaker meetings and within "popular" associations dominated by Quakers, women and men shared public labors. Accused of being extremists, this group of agrarian Quakers lived up to its detractors' fears and extended its critiques to the land monopoly, capital punishment, and gender roles.

Radical Quakers' uniqueness within the nineteenth-century reform community is best exemplified by their justification for women's entrance into the public realm. Rejecting claims for separate spheres or female superiority, they argued for women's natural right to equality. Thomas Paine, Charles Fourier, and Mary Wollstonecraft, along with a pantheon of Quaker pietists, were their theoretical guides. This ideological divergence from dominant definitions of woman's place was directly related to the group's agrarian Quaker heritage. The social relations of production and politics in native villages, combined with a supportive brand of sectarian theology, allowed some female Friends to resist the attractions of true womanhood and to view equality as a sounder basis for progress than moral superiority.[9]

The path to Rochester and to woman's rights originated for feminist Friends in Jericho, Westbury, Milton, Farmington, Scipio, and similar villages in New York, New Jersey, Pennsylvania, and western Massachusetts. Within these communities, work, worship, and social welfare were defined by a greater diffusion of power and equality of status than were to be found in commercial New England towns. Following "quietistic ideals" developed in the eighteenth century, the residents of Quaker villages dwelt "upon withdrawal from contact with the world," isolating themselves from the cultural and social as well as the economic and political developments that shaped the lives of other female activists.[10]

The demand for labor on family farms assured that women's work would be visible and that, at least during planting and harvesting, women and men would work side by side. At the same time, religious precepts promoting social duties and condemning finery and display limited the elaboration of domesticity within Quaker households. Even in urban Philadelphia, Lucretia Mott ordered her domestic life so that no "excess duties," including "unnecessary stitching" or "ornamental work" on clothes would take time away from reading, meditation, and community work.[11] Quaker farm women, further removed from the accoutrements of the new domesticity, would have had less time or use for the fancy dress, abundant furnishings, or lavish social entertainments that characterized affluent urbanites and those who sought to emulate them. Plainness, according to Quaker doctrine, was "the surest way to avoid 'those gaieties which tend to divert and alienate the mind from the simplicity and gravity of the Truth' and as a garrison against 'fashion-mongers.'" Regular "family visits" by those appointed by the meeting increased conformity to these general principles.[12]

In the 1820s, when Rochester's future feminists made their marital choices, they applauded each other on finding "kind, affectionate husbands, ready to share with us whatever may attend us through life."[13] Thus, as romantic love entered the fantasies of urban, middle-class daughters, Quaker farm girls continued to follow the model of their parents' generation, combining mutual respect and affection with hard work. Courtship was to unfold gradually within circles of families and friends, and women were to play a specific role in the courtship process.[14] Marriage proposals were laid before the women's and men's meetings by the couple, accompanied by both sets of parents and by two female and two male friends. Committees from both meetings were then appointed to "consider the proposal" and to report on the "life and conversation" of the concerned couple. When approved, the marriage would be solemnized a month later at a regular midweek meeting during which the bride and groom rose, exchanged identical promises, and received a certificate of marriage from an elderly Friend.

Newlyweds were admonished to "take care of one another" so as to become an "invaluable companion" and "friend."[15] Young brides simultaneously urged each other to maintain social contacts and community activities. Thus, Elizabeth Mott wrote to her sister, Amy Kirby, that she "fear[ed] that the domestic concerns of life will become all" and sought "more substance for the mental power to act upon" so that "they will be occupied with something of a higher nature than patching [one] thing and making another."[16] Many married Quaker women found such substance by serving as ministers, caring for orphans, visiting prisoners or Indians, and attending to religious and social duties. Even in their domestic labors, they were rarely as isolated as their urban, middle-class counterparts. A constant flow of relatives, as visitors and boarders, joined in household and farm labor, and the major burdens—spring housecleaning, farm chores, and painting and repairs—were shared by household members of all ages and both sexes.[17] This is not to suggest that there were no distinctions of tasks by gender in agrarian Quaker families but, rather, that those distinctions were less rigid and more frequently abandoned than in the households of the new urban middle class.

Indeed, for Quaker farm daughters, young men's desire to attain middle-class status by heading to the rich farmlands or urban centers to the west necessitated a renewed concern with self-sufficiency that limited the appeal of true womanhood ideals. In 1823, Amy Willis wrote to her friend Amy Kirby that their native village of Jericho would "be quite stripped of beaus" within a year.[18] One friend, rather than fearing spinsterhood, feared that her lot would be "cast in a distant land" with a pioneering husband, and another noted that she would feel "lonely and dejected . . . without one female to whom I could unbosom my feelings."[19] A few who had earlier achieved the status of frontier wives were already returning home as widows, "severed" as one proclaimed "from the friend to whom her heart was most dear."[20]

Amy Kirby, who was born in Jericho, New York, in 1802 and moved to Rochester in 1836, became that city's leading feminist activist in the 1840s. In the early 1820s, her older sister, Hannah, moved to central New York upon her marriage to Isaac Post. Hannah soon wrote Amy, begging that she visit in order to alleviate her isolation and to assist in farm and household chores. Having spent several months with Hannah in 1823 and 1824, Amy planned to move permanently to central New York upon her marriage to a Quaker youth in a neighboring town. Her plans were abruptly foreclosed, however, when the young man died just months before the wedding. While mourning his loss, Amy heard that a close friend, newly married and living on an isolated homestead, was languishing with a terminal illness; she died the same year. The husband of another childhood friend was jailed for drunkenness and wife abuse. A year and a half later Hannah died, and Amy left her childhood home for good to care for the grieving Isaac and his two young children. Finally, in 1829, at age twenty-seven, Amy agreed to give up her role as nursemaid to her niece and nephew in order to become their stepmother. She thus entered the wifely role, having already labored side by side with Isaac and knowing, as one friend reminded the new couple, that "connubial happiness" and "domestic felicity" could be short-lived.[21]

The experiences of Amy Kirby Post were not unlike those of many of her Quaker sisters who surrounded her on Long Island, in central New York, and later in Rochester. Of the two dozen Quaker women who led woman's rights efforts in Rochester, one-half were single or widowed during the early years of their activism. Four others married widowers with children prior to joining public campaigns. Several wrote of female relatives or friends who suffered abuse or abandonment at the hands of husbands. At least fourteen of the twenty-four feminist Friends helped support their families, either by providing labor on family farms or by pursuing jobs as teachers, seamstresses, nurses, or lecturers. A far smaller proportion of Rochester's nonfeminist female activists experienced spinsterhood, widowhood, or wage labor; and those who did did not have the tradition of female self-sufficiency that gave independent women and women's work status in agrarian Quaker communities.[22]

Agrarian Quakers were a mobile lot in the nineteenth century, but only when they moved to urban centers like Rochester did geographical change mean significant experiential change. The entry of the Posts, DeGarmos, Fishes, Burtises, Anthonys, and other agrarian Quaker families into the heterogeneous, dynamic, and non-Quaker environs of Rochester forced them to confront new economic, political, and cultural options. The power of communal norms was diminished at the same time that extended kinship networks were disrupted. Opportunities in shopkeeping and manufacturing drew Quaker men toward urban life-styles and Yankee ethics of individualism while the cult of true womanhood encouraged Quaker farm wives to retreat to domesticity.

Isaac Post, for instance, opened a butcher shop upon his arrival in the city, then within a few years shifted to the cleaner and more respectable occupation of pharmacist. Each of these moves took his work farther from home and Amy's involvement. Some of his coreligionists entered the commercial arena by cultivating cherry or apple orchards and developing nurseries. Others turned to selling drygoods or establishing woolen manufactories. A few entered artisanal ranks as stonecutters, jewelers, or tailors as well as butchers, defying the general trend among that class of workers by enjoying some financial success. As these ex-farmers looked around them, they saw Rochester's earliest Quaker settlers, who had arrived two decades before, leading prosperous lives as merchants, manufacturers, and professionals.

The wives of Rochester's pioneer Quaker families had already accepted the accoutrements of domesticity. As urban economic and political institutions diminished women's access to power in the community, pioneer Quaker women accepted the double-edged sword of glorification in the private and subordination in the public domain. The availability of manufactured goods, such as clothing, shoes, and medicine, added weight to the argument that women should trade productive for consumptive roles, public labors for privatized domesticity. Those Quaker women who wished to maintain some influence in civic affairs could do so by joining one of the existing female benevolent or reform organizations. Societies to aid the sick, poor, orphans, homeless women, and slaves—all single sex, all asserting female moral superiority, and all justifying their efforts on religious grounds—offered female Friends an acceptable mode of public activism, one based on female separation and subordination. In addition, the Quaker meeting still offered women an opportunity to assert their influence within their own religious community.

The female migrants of the 1830s and 1840s were encouraged to follow the paths of their Quaker forerunners. Their husbands sought upward mobility, often in occupations that required less labor from wives outside the domestic circle. The women were invited to support local benevolent efforts, and some, like Amy Post and Sarah Fish, briefly joined the Female Charitable Society, contributed to the orphanage fund, and affixed their signatures to petitions circulated by the evangelically inspired Female Anti-Slavery Society. Even relatives who remained in Quaker farm villages on Long Island or in central New York may have unwittingly pushed their newly urbanized sisters to adopt domesticity. As Mary Post complained to her sister-in-law, Amy, she expected more letters and visits from her since "retirement from farm life must give you more leisure time."[23]

Yet several dozen of the newly arrived Friends ultimately rejected the options offered them and instead forged a new style of public activism and a new set of associations through which to pursue their goals while retaining their "woman's right" within the family, the meeting, and the community.[24] Some of these women would join male kin and coworshipers in efforts to revitalize the Society of Friends, some would move on to worldly activism in campaigns to abolish slavery, and a smaller number would press forward with demands for economic and racial equality and woman's rights.

The women who forged this new path had gained the bottom rungs of Rochester's emerging bourgeoisie, but they retained some distance from their more fully urbanized neighbors both geographically and ideologically. A few of these families, such as the Anthonys, continued to survive by agriculture; others, like the Posts, returned to that pursuit during hard times. All of them retained strong ties to agrarian Quakers in their native communities as well as to those who migrated further west. Most of the women also continued to assume some productive roles, whether married or single. Their male kin, moreover, did not enter existing political parties but remained, like their wives and daughters, self-conscious nonparticipants in the electoral system.

This circle of Quaker families attempted to maintain or re-create strong kinship networks and extended community ties by living in close proximity and by hosting newly arrived kin, newly married or widowed children, and itinerant Quaker preachers and reformers. By the early 1840s, for instance, Amy and Isaac Post; their daughter, Mary; and her husband, William Hallowell; Amy's sister, Sarah; and her husband, Jeffries Hallowell; Isaac's nephew, Edmund Willis; and at least five other Post relatives lived within a ten-block area of the city's First Ward. Another cluster of Fish relatives, numbering at least ten persons, lived in a single large house in the Second Ward, while the Anthonys, their cousins the Burtises, and the DeGarmos inhabited neighboring farms in the northwest corner of the city. A number of these families temporarily moved to Sodus Bay together in the mid-1840s to join a Fourierist phalanx and then returned to one of the existing Quaker enclaves by the late 1840s. These families visited regularly, held religious and reform meetings in their homes, traveled together to other parts of the state, sent their children to live in each other's houses, and joined forces to reform society.

One final factor that divided these new Rochester Quakers from the pioneer Friends and from some of their fellow migrants was religion itself. The structure of the Society of Friends and its role in reforming the world as well as the role of women in the Society became sources of bitter dispute in the 1820s and again in the 1840s. By the late eighteenth century, some broad guidelines, officially written into the *Rules of Discipline* and accepted by all Quaker meetings, defined women's role in the Society and Society's role in the world. In general, women and men sat in separate meetings, each having responsibility for the care and discipline of its own sex. The women's meeting often had greater responsibility for the "oversight of marriages"; but they had to gain the concurrence of men to discipline, disown, admit, or reinstate women members and to approve women ministers. The men's meeting did not necessarily have to seek such concurrence from the women. Still, as traveling ministers or speakers within their home meeting, women held absolutely equal rights with men and were similarly acclaimed or criticized for the theological soundness and clarity of their presentations.[25] In politics, the religious proscription against the "deceitful spirit of party" equalized women's and men's participation in the electoral process.[26] Views on political issues were expressed but generally through religious testimonies which necessitated the consent of both the women's and men's meetings. Itinerant ministers also articulated such testimonies, including such notable women as Rachel Hicks, Priscilla Cadwallader, and Lucretia Mott.

As the numbers of Quakers expanded and as the concerns of the meeting became more complicated, most Quaker groups came to depend on a core of leaders known as the ministers and elders. They initiated testimonies and sanctioned ministers as well as administered the affairs of the monthly, quarterly, and yearly meetings. By the 1810s and 1820s, the ministers and elders were implementing most major policies and programs of the Society of Friends. Women had the right to serve in this select group, but, as with other hierarchical institutions, men tended to dominate in the upper echelons of the administrative structure. Despite this, even some men were disturbed at the increasingly "churchly" structure of their Society.

In 1828, protracted debates within the Society over increasing bureaucratization, the role of the Society in worldly reform, and the proper interpretation of early Quaker texts led to the group's division into Orthodox and Hicksite branches. The latter attracted most of the agrarian and reform-minded members. They followed the teachings of Elias Hicks, who emphasized the revelatory power of "Inner Light" over any laws or principles provided in "external aids," including the Bible. Women and men were equally endowed with this Light. In addition, Hicksites rejected Original Sin, asserting that women and men could use their rational powers to "rise above that innocent state" in which they were "created, to the exalted state of virtue and glory."[27] They also rejected churchly structures and sought to return to the simplified and democratic forms of worship advocated by the Society's founders.

It was at the time of the Hicksite separation that the Society of Friends began its most rapid expansion into western New York, an expansion in which Hicksites predominated.[28] By 1834, a sufficient number of Hicksites resided in central and western New York to form a Yearly Meeting, the boundaries of which extended north to Ontario, Canada, and westward into Michigan. Future feminists were prominent in the early deliberations of this Genesee Yearly Meeting, and they often invited Lucretia Mott to their annual gatherings to address the membership on any of the reform issues of the day. In 1836, several of Rochester's most reform-minded women and men were appointed to consider changes in the Society's *Rules of Discipline*. The issues they raised—women's full equality in the Society, the role of Quakers in the antislavery cause, and the reemergence of ministers and elders—initiated a decade-long series of debates that ultimately led to the division of the Hicksites.[29]

Although the Yearly Meeting did not act quickly on the reform proposals, many of those who advocated changes in the *Rules of Discipline* did begin to act. In 1837, Phebe Post Willis of Long Island had written Amy and Isaac Post, asking, "How is it that you tell us nothing about abolition movements in Rochester? I should scarcely suppose you were members of that society by your silence on the subject."[30] That silence diminished as the Yearly Meeting proved intractable in furthering the antislavery cause. First dissenting Hicksites began holding "numerous little abolition meetings" in their homes. Soon the Posts began wondering why they should "exclude all who do not happen to be included within the pale of our religious faith" from such associations and, with a Long Island Friend, concluded that "our light (if we have any) would be more likely to shine where it would do good by uniting with all without distinction of Sect or creed."[31] Then in 1842, when ex-Quaker antislavery lecturer Abby Kelley appeared at Rochester's Washington Street Presbyterian Church, a large body of disaffected Hicksites were in attendance. At least twenty were among the first thirty-four officers of the Western New York Anti-Slavery Society (WNYASS) founded there. The WNYASS, which extended membership equally to both women and men, attracted no evangelical women to its roster and only a few of their male relatives. One of the latter, Samuel D. Porter, served as the first WNYASS president, but he feared being lumped unjustly with "agrarians, disorganizers, infidels, & fanatics" and withdrew from the society in 1844. After that year, the WNYASS consisted solely of self-styled "fanatics."[32]

Throughout this period, disowned and disaffected Hicksites asserted ever more radical positions on woman's rights. In some cases this meant putting into practice existing principles of equality. It also meant that women themselves labored against a heritage of quietist ideals in order to claim the rights they sought. Women called their own "free meetings" to discuss "subjects of Social and Pecuniary interest" and trained themselves as speakers, pamphleteers, healers, and ministers.[33] Their actions began to take effect and as early as 1845, Boston abolitionist Jeremiah Burke Sanderson wrote to Amy Post: "Woman is rising, becoming free. The progress manifest at present of the idea of Woman's Rights in the public mind" demonstrates "what a few years comparatively may effect."[34] By 1846, Amy Post and her female coworkers were selling copies of Samuel J. Mays's "Sermon on the Rights of Women" at their WNYASS fair and complaining openly when the "Lords of Creation" in their own midst refused to recognize women as equals.[35]

Even the most radical Hicksite women still performed some gender-specific tasks within antislavery organizations, but unlike other female activists, they claimed the right to equality with men in the decision-making bodies of such associations.[36] WNYASS women were not yet the equals of men in officeholding, policy-making, or public speaking, but they advanced their position considerably during the 1840s. By this time, the causes they advocated and women's place in them aroused the kind of vociferous opposition once visited upon evangelical women, but Hicksite women refused to retreat. Rather, they extended and intensified their efforts. "Cold looks, unyielding purse strings, and repelling voices and actions" could not "dishearten" the antislavery sisters, but instead "inspir[ed] them with courage for fresh victories."[37] Indeed, condemnation was viewed as a badge of honor, a sign that one had been "more faithful in the cause of the downtrodden." "Blessed are they who are persecuted for righteousness's sake," wrote one Hicksite, "for theirs is the kingdom of Heaven."[38]

In 1843, the Genesee Yearly Meeting began aiding radicals seeking the kingdom of heaven, such as Isaac and Amy Post, Mary Hallowell, and Lewis Burtis, by releasing them from membership. Within a few years, the efforts of local meetings in Rochester and Michigan to increase women's role and diminish the power of the ministers and elders shattered the fragile consensus that had been built on years of postponing action. On June 6, 1848, the Genesee Yearly Meeting disowned a large group of dissidents for their disregard of the "injunctions of the discipline and the authority of the church."[39] They were followed out of the meetinghouse by those like-minded Friends who had escaped formal censure. Still wishing to create a religious association based on the principles of equality and free thought, these rebel Quakers called a meeting at Waterloo, New York, for June 14 and 15 to form a new society, the Yearly Meeting of Congregational Friends. Lucretia Mott, who observed the proceedings at the Genesee gathering, was invited to participate as were all who sought a Society in which there would be no ministers and elders, no rules of admission or disownment, no limits on worldly activity, and no tolerance for racial or sexual discrimination.[40] Satisfied after two days' labor that they had created the basis for a new and better form of religious association, the Congregational Friends adjourned with a call for a second and larger gathering in October.

Lucretia Mott remained in upstate New York after the dramatic events of June to visit her sister, Martha Wright. It was when the two sisters returned to Waterloo in July to visit Congregational Friends Thomas and Mary Ann McClintock that Mott was reunited with Elizabeth Cady Stanton, and the two put into effect the plan for a woman's rights convention they had devised at the World Anti-Slavery Convention in 1840. For the recently formed Congregationalists this was the perfect opportunity to extend the attack on religious tyranny and sexual oppression. Thus, the call went out for the Seneca Falls Woman's Rights Convention.[41] The event attracted a wide range of participants, one hundred of whom, including Rochesterian Amy Post and four neighbors, signed the final Declaration of Sentiments that declared "woman is man's equal." At the end of the meeting, believing that "there were still many new points for discussion, and that the gift of tongues had been vouchsafed to them," the audience "adjourned, to meet in Rochester in two weeks." Amy Post, Mary Hallowell, Sarah Fish, and Sarah C. Owen were appointed the local arrangements committee for this second gathering.[42]

The Rochester Woman's Rights Convention, held August 2, 1848, was dominated by Congregational Friends. Among the officers, however, were two women who were not Quakers and yet illustrate the tenuous relationship between evangelical Protestantism and feminism. Abigail Bush was raised in the orthodox First Presbyterian Church and joined her mother in charitable works at a young age. In 1831, she experienced conversion and became a "Brick church perfectionist" in the midst of Finney's revival fervor.[43] A few years later, she married abolitionist Henry Bush and spent the next decade bearing and rearing five children. She reemerged in the public domain in 1843 as a member of the WNYASS but only after withdrawing from the Brick Presbyterian Church. Another Brick church member turned feminist was Sarah C. Owen. She moved to Rochester in the mid-1830s and was soon active in the Female Moral Reform Society. However, in 1840, as evangelical women retreated from their critiques of the sexual double standard and their advocacy of abolition, Owen, like Bush, joined forces with Quaker dissidents. In doing so, Owen brought upon herself the condemnation of her congregation and was excommunicated in 1845.

These ex-evangelicals were never able to convert others among their former coworshipers to feminism, and they remained active themselves only a few years. Both Owen and Bush moved west in the 1850s, losing their circle of Congregational coworkers and finding it impossible to forge a new network. They did not lose their interest in radical causes. Yet without the support of those Quaker women whose experience and ideology provided the preconditions for feminism, these evangelical women were left alone with their unorthodox views and their memories of earlier campaigns.[44]

The highpoint of Owen's and Bush's activist careers was the Rochester Woman's Rights Convention. The meeting was a direct outgrowth of the Seneca Falls gathering, yet it differed from it in two crucial ways. First, the earlier convention was called to discuss the "social, civil, and religious condition and rights of women"; the Rochester meeting was called to consider the "Rights of women, Politically, Socially, Religiously, and Industrially." The greater emphasis on rights, and on economic rights in particular, showed the influence of women well practiced in public pursuits and productive labor. Unlike at Seneca Falls, a woman, Abigail Bush, served as president of the Rochester meeting, for these seasoned activists had come to realize that woman could only be redeemed from her "degraded position" by "the most strenuous and unremitting effort" to "claim an equal right to act."[45] At the opening session, Elizabeth Cady Stanton and Lucretia Mott proclaimed it "a most hazardous experiment to have a woman President and stoutly opposed it. . . . They were on the verge of leaving the Convention in disgust" when Amy Post "assured them that by the same power by which they had resolved, declared, and debated, they could also preside at a public meeting."[46] The audience, filled with Amy's kin and coworkers, approved the proposed slate. Here the grassroots experiences of local Friends put them in advance of their more prominent national leaders.

The presentation of the agenda by the female officers revealed a bold and broad conception of woman's rights. The elective franchise, the ninth of eleven proposals at Seneca Falls and the one that received the most opposition, topped the Rochester agenda. Yet political rights were only a small portion of the demands of the Rochester organizers. Their own experience in relatively egalitarian families, joint-sex religious meetings, paid labor, and public service made them sensitive to women's relative deprivation in many domains of modern urban life. The leaders of the convention urged "women no longer to promise obedience in the marriage covenant" and to allow "the strongest *will* or the superior intellect" to "govern the household." They beseeched women to claim equal authority "on all subjects that interest the human family," one of the most important of which was women's economic status. Many women were plying "the needle by day and by night, to procure a scanty pittance for [their] dependent famil[ies]." The husband's "legal right to hire out his wife for service" and "collect her wages" was labeled "a hideous custom" that reduced woman "almost to the condition of a slave."[47]

The committee of arrangements appointed women to investigate the wrongs of the laboring classes and "to invite the oppressed portion of the community to attend the meetings of the convention and take part in its deliberations."[48] At the convention, Owen read an address on "woman's place and pay in the world of work" which was elaborated upon by Mrs. Roberts, who reported on the "average price of labor for sempstresses." Mrs. Galloy "corroborated the statement, having herself experienced some of the oppression of this portion of our citizens." For participants who were in more secure economic circumstances, the conveners noted that "those who believe the laboring classes of women are oppressed" should do "all in their power to raise their wages."[49]

Moreover, Rochester's feminists predicated woman's political, familial, and economic rights on historical proofs of her capacity for equality. "From Semiramis to Victoria," declared one speaker, "we have found the Women of History equal to the emergency before them!" Recognizing that most women failed to match the achievements of such historical role models, feminists reminded their audience that "only by faithful perseverance in the practical exercise of those talents so long 'wrapped in a napkin and buried under the earth'" would woman "regain her long-lost equality with man." This mythohistorical perspective on women's oppression and the possibilities of its overthrow was combined with a sensitivity to socialization. The speakers granted that "woman's intellect is feeble" but claimed it was so "because she has been so long crushed.... Let her arise and demand her rights and in a few years we shall see a different mental development." Here, they compared women with slaves of the South and saw foreshadowed woman's rise in the "progress [made] within the past few years" by escaped slaves resettled in the free environs of the North.[50]

By arguing that history and education, custom and deprivation, were the key forces in the oppression of women, Rochester's feminists rejected the argument of separate spheres and separate natures that dominated the discussion of women's role in nineteenth-century America. Lucretia Mott voiced the sentiments of her Congregational sisters when she objected to the very "language of flattering compliment" that portrayed women as more devoted, spiritual, and altruistic than men. These mid-nineteenth-century feminists did not seek a matriarchate that would replace the domination of men by that of women, nor did they make special pleadings based on woman's nature. Rather, they proclaimed it the "duty of woman, whatever her complexion, to assume, as soon as possible, her true position of equality in the social circle, the Church, and the State."[51]

Immediately after the Rochester Woman's Rights Convention and for the next six decades, Congregational Friends worked to achieve equality in their own lives and in the lives of all women. Amy Post and Sarah Owen helped organize a Working Woman's Protective Union in August 1848, declaring that women were entitled "equally with men to the products of their labor or its equivalent."[52] They and their coworkers assisted their working-class sisters by providing jobs, temporary housing, and childcare to Black women escaping from the South and to white women escaping from intemperate or abusive husbands.[53] In 1853, Sarah Burtis opened new job opportunities for local women by becoming the first female store clerk in Rochester, though she was married and had several children.[54] Within their own families, these same women sought to provide models of egalitarian relations. Owen went so far as to declare that if a man sought to dominate her, "I would let him know that I *could* live without him."[55] Already-married women sought to share decision making; to provide equal educations to daughters and sons and to assert their right to travel, speak, and act independently of even the most beloved spouses.[56]

This concern with model behavior derived in part from feminists' belief that the personal was political and in part from their economic circumstances. Hicksite abolitionists had resolved in 1843 that they should apply "their principles in all their social, political, and religious relations"; in the following years they frequently provoked public condemnation by so doing. Women in particular faced verbal and physical harassment for traveling and socializing in racially mixed company, for speaking before mixed-sex audiences, for wearing turkish trousers instead of long skirts, and for casting ballots in the 1872 presidential election, almost a half-century before women gained the "right" to vote.[57] These and similar badges of radicalism were the most accessible forms of social commentary for those with limited resources. The choice then was both pragmatic and ideological. Political statements that were expressed through the events of everyday life required no hierarchy of administration, allowed for independent and decentralized action, and were equally available to all.

The blueprint for social change lived out by feminist Friends was most often debated at the annual meetings of the Congregational Friends, where the campaign for woman's rights was placed in the larger context of a "thorough re-organization of Society."[58] Meeting just two months after the Rochester convention, the Congregational Friends proclaimed: "When we speak of the Rights of Woman, we speak of Human Rights." They rejected innate sexual differences and declared instead for "common natures, common rights, and a common destiny" for women and men.[59] They may have been unique among their contemporaries, including other activists and other Quakers, in extending this belief in human equality across the color line: "Every member of the human family," they asserted, "without regard to color or sex, possess potentially the same faculties and powers, capable of like cultivation and development and consequently has the same rights, interests, and destiny."[60]

Most feminist Friends sustained their arguments into the post–Civil War period despite the pressure of changing circumstances. When William Lloyd Garrison and other abolitionist leaders concluded that their goals had been achieved, members of the WYNASS were among the dissenters who formed the Equal Rights Association. Its first annual meeting was held in Rochester in 1866, but when president Wendell Phillips proclaimed it was the "Negro's hour," several local feminists disagreed, believing that it was possible to obtain votes for women and Blacks simultaneously. They maintained this position after joining the National Woman Suffrage Association whose leaders gave female suffrage primacy.[61] Rochester's feminist Friends also gave a feminist presence to other progressive organizations, such as the National Liberal League, which mounted campaigns for the reorganization of government along social scientific lines and against Victorian sexual standards. In the league's proposed "Liberal compact for government," Amy Post discovered a critical omission—"that omission was the word *woman.*" She cautioned her "thoughtful and conscientious" colleagues not to "forget that we—Women—are the long downtroden [*sic*] class of National Citizens."[62] Finally, as a wider range of women entered women's rights campaigns, reshaping the goals and strategies of the movement, feminist Friends remained adamant in rejecting any basis for woman's rights except their natural equality of condition.

A few feminist Friends continued to fight for their goals into the twentieth century, although they could not maintain control of the movement. Instead, the goals were narrowed, almost exclusively to suffrage, to gain a mass following, and arguments were adopted that were rooted in the cults of domesticity and true womanhood. Although this mass movement rejected the ideology of its radical foremothers, it was nonetheless born from their agitations. Only after several decades of public advocacy of absolute equality between the sexes was it possible for large numbers of women and men to accept women's equal access to the ballot as a reasonable, even moderate, proposal. Thus, feminist Friends provided the preconditions for the later suffrage victories even as the suffragists themselves rejected their fundamental beliefs.

In the same way, the evangelical environment of Rochester that radical Quakers rejected provided the preconditions for a feminist rebellion. For only when women raised in the relatively egalitarian enclave of Quaker farm villages moved into a heterogeneous urban arena, where women's and men's roles were increasingly distinct and unequal, were they provoked to reconsider the very nature of sex roles. Because the first feminists remained economically, residentially, and culturally marginal to the emerging bourgeoisie, they were able to elaborate a wholly different concept of gender roles. Believing that "corrupt customs," a "perverted application of the Scriptures," exclusion from education and occupations, and women's own self-effacement had limited their development, the feminist sought to "move in the enlarged sphere which her great Creator" had "assigned her," opening up new avenues for women at large and thereby "freeing the entire human family from thraldom both physical and moral."[63] Feminists did not achieve this final goal, but they did illuminate the path along which later generations of women could seek their own emancipation.

Notes

The author wishes to thank Mary Huth, Marcus Rediker, Steven F. Lawson, and Judith Wellman for their many and various contributions to this article.

1. Nancy F. Cott, *The Bonds of Womanhood: "Woman's Sphere" in New England, 1780–1835* (New Haven: Yale University Press, 1977), 5; also 197–206 generally.

2. Carroll Smith-Rosenberg, "The Female World of Love and Ritual: Relations between Women in Nineteenth-Century America," *Signs* 1 (Autumn 1975): 1–29.

3. The earliest versions of this interpretation appeared in Eleanor Flexner, *Century of Struggle: The Women's Rights Movement in the United States* (Cambridge: Harvard University Press, 1959); Andrew Sinclair, *The Emancipation of the American Woman* (New York: Harper & Row, 1965); and Alice Rossi, ed., *The Feminist Papers: From Adams to de Beauvoir* (New York: Columbia University Press, 1973).

4. Blanche Glassman Hersh, *The Slavery of Sex: Feminist-Abolitionists in America* (Urbana: University of Illinois Press, 1978), ix, 136–39, 204–9.

5. In addition to Hersh, see Cott, 204; Carroll Smith-Rosenberg, "The Cross and the Pedestal: Anti-Ritualism, Liminality, and the Emergence of the American Bourgeoisie," in *The Rising Tide of Evangelical Religion,* ed. Leonard I. Sweet (Mercer, Ga.: Mercer University Press, 1984): 199–231; and Ellen DuBois, *Feminism and Suffrage: The Emergence of an Independent Women's Movement in America, 1848–1869* (Ithaca, N.Y.: Cornell University Press, 1978). This interpretation has been reinforced by historians' reliance on Elizabeth Cady Stanton's account of her own transition to feminism in *Eighty Years and More: Reminiscences, 1815–1897* (1898; reprint, New York: Schocken Books, 1971), esp. 127–48.

6. See Nancy A. Hewitt, *Women's Activism and Social Change: Rochester, New York, 1822–1872* (Ithaca, N.Y.: Cornell University Press, 1984), chaps. 4 and 5; and "Yankee Evangelicals and Agrarian Quakers: Gender, Religion, and Class in the Formation of a Feminist Consciousness in Nineteenth-Century Rochester, New York," *Radical History Review,* nos. 28–29–30 (1984): 327–42.

7. Barbara Welter, "The Cult of True Womanhood, 1820–1860," *American Quarterly* 18 (Summer 1966): 151–64, 171–74; Smith-Rosenberg, "The Cross and the Pedestal"; and Hewitt, *Women's Activism,* 59–60, 123–24.

8. Seneca Falls residents who attended the first convention included Wesleyan Methodists, Baptists, Episcopalians, and at least one Catholic. Unlike the Quaker participants, the more diverse group from Seneca Falls did not remain active in feminist causes beyond this first meeting. Judith Wellman has generously shared with me both her statistics and her insights from her study of the Seneca Falls convention.

9. Mary Kirby and Sarah Hallowell to Amy Post, 20 Feb. 1838; and Amy Post to Frederick Douglass, 13 Feb. 1860, Isaac and Amy Post Family Papers (hereafter cited as IAPFP), University of Rochester, Rochester, New York; the *Phalanx,* 4 Nov. 1843, and 5 Jan., 4 May, 15 June, and 9 Dec. 1844; "Address to Reformers," from the Yearly Meeting of Congregational Friends, in *Liberator* 19 (6 July 1849); Isaac Post, *Voices of the Spirit World* (Rochester, N.Y.: Charles H. McDonnell, 1852); and Anna Davis Hallowell, ed., *James and Lucretia Mott, Life and Letters* (Boston: Houghton Mifflin, 1884), 186–87. Although a high percentage of early feminists were Quakers, only a small percentage of Quakers were feminists. Those Quakers most likely to become feminists moved from rural to urban areas, were economically marginal to the new bourgeoisie, maintained strong ties with agrarian Quakers, sought reforms within the Society of Friends, advocated the abolition of slavery, and experienced many of the uncertainties of women's lot in their youth.

10. Rufus M. Jones, *Later Periods of Quakerism,* 2 vols. (1921; reprint, Westport, Conn.: Greenwood Press, 1970), 1:101.

11. Hallowell, 251.

12. Jones, 1:175.

13. Maria Willetts to Hannah Kirby Post, 18 Apr. 1823, IAPFP.

14. See in IAPFP, Mary W. Willis to Amy Kirby, 182–; Mary W. Willis to Hannah Kirby Post, 1 July 182–; Amy Willis to Amy Kirby, 8 Dec. 1822; and Abbey Gifford to Amy Kirby, 16 May 1823.

15. Mary Kirby to Hannah Kirby Post, 2 June 182–; and Amy Willis to Amy Kirby, 30 Aug. 1823, IAPFP.

16. Elizabeth Mott to Amy Post, 17 June 183–, IAPFP.

17. Amy Kirby to Mother, 24 May 1823; Phebe Kirby to Amy Kirby, 26 May 1823; Sarah Hallowell to Amy Post, 5 May 1841; and Susanna Hallowell to Sarah Hallowell, 8 June 1847, IAPFP.

18. Amy Willis to Amy Kirby, 30 Aug. 1823, IAPFP.

19. Hannah Kirby Post to Amy Kirby, 182–; and Amy Willis to Amy Kirby, 30 Aug. 1823, IAPFP.

20. Amy Willis to Amy Kirby, 30 Aug. 1823, IAPFP.

21. John Ketcham to Isaac and Amy Post, 20 Jan. 1829, IAPFP.

22. In contrast, very few of the sorts of problems noted among Quaker feminists in the IAPFP are discussed in the correspondence of evangelical women activists. Either their circumstances were sufficiently more secure to minimize such difficulties, or they did not feel such problems should be discussed, even in private correspondence.

23. Mary W. Post to Amy Post, 183–, IAPFP.

24. Isaac Post to Amy Post, n.d., IAPFP.

25. Jones, 1:186–87; *Rules of Discipline of the Yearly Meeting of Friends Held in Philadelphia* (Philadelphia: J. Mortimer, 1828), 114–17. Also, Mary Robbins Post to Amy Post, Nov. 183–; Jane Johnson to Priscilla Cadwallader, 4 Jan. 1833; Noah Haines to Isaac Post, 10 Feb. 1834; and Phebe Post Willis to Isaac and Amy Post, 4 May 1837, IAPFP.

26. *Rules of Discipline,* 109.

27. Jones, 1:453.

28. See A. Day Bradley, "Progressive Friends in Michigan and New York," *Quaker History* 52 (1963): 95–103; and Carlisle G. Davidson, "A Profile of Hicksite Quakerism in Michigan, 1830–1860," *Quaker History* 59 (Autumn 1970): 106–12.

29. Genesee Yearly Meeting of Women Friends (hereafter GYMWF), Minutes, June 1835, June 1836, June 1837, June 1838, June 1839, and June 1840, Haviland Records Room, New York City.

30. Phebe Post Willis to Isaac and Amy Post, 5 Apr. 1837, IAPFP.

31. John Ketcham to Isaac and Amy Post, 11 Mar. 1841, IAPFP. See also, Ida Husted Harper, *The Life and Work of Susan B. Anthony,* 3 vols. (Indianapolis: Bowen-Merrill Co., 1899), 1:48.

32. Samuel D. Porter to Abby Kelley, 16 Sept. 1842, Abby Kelley Foster Papers, American Antiquarian Society, Worcester, Massachusetts; "American Anti-Slavery Society" report on Rochester meeting, *Liberator* 13 (6 Jan. 1843);

"First Annual Meeting of the Western New York Anti-Slavery Society," *Liberator* 14 (5 Jan. 1844); "Second Annual Meeting of the Western New York Anti-Slavery Society," *National Anti-Slavery Standard* 5 (6 Mar. 1845).

33. Notice of a Free Meeting, n.d., IAPFP.

34. Jeremiah Burke Sanderson to Amy Post, 8 May 1845, IAPFP.

35. Samuel J. May to Isaac Post, 20 Dec. 1846. On controversies with men in the WNYASS, see William C. Nell to Amy Post, 11 Aug. 1849, IAPFP.

36. For a comparison of evangelical and Hicksite forms of activism, see Nancy A. Hewitt, "Yankee Evangelicals and Agrarian Quakers"; and "The Social Origins of Women's Antislavery Politics in Western New York," in *Crusaders and Compromisers: Essays on the Relationship of the Antislavery Struggle to the Antebellum Party System,* ed. Alan M. Kraut (Westport, Conn.: Greenwood Press, 1983): 205–33.

37. "Anti-Slavery Bazaar," *Rochester North Star* 11 (7 Jan. 1848).

38. Nathaniel Potter to Isaac Post, 18 Sept. 1845, IAPFP.

39. GYMWF, June 1847 and June 1848. These Minutes indicate no dissension over the issues discussed. For a more conflict-filled version, see Yearly Meeting of Congregational Friends (hereafter YMCF), *Proceedings of the Yearly Meeting of Congregational Friends, Held at Waterloo, N.Y., from the Fourth to the Sixth of the Sixth Month, Inclusive, 1849* (Auburn, N.Y.: Oliphant's Press, 1849), 32–35. Those who withdrew voluntarily included feminist activists Sarah A. Burtis, Rhoda DeGarmo, and Sarah Fish.

40. "Basis of Religious Association," in YMCF, *1849 Proceedings,* appendix.

41. Existing studies of the convention rely heavily on Stanton's *Eighty Years and More,* and on Stanton, Susan B. Anthony, and Matilda Joslyn Gage, *A History of Woman Suffrage,* 4 vols. (New York: Fowler and Wells, 1881). These works do not note the importance of the Hicksite-Congregational Friends as a group. Judith Wellman's work does contain significant information on this circle of activists.

42. Rochester Woman's Rights Convention (hereafter RWRC), "Proceedings," in *The Concise History of Woman Suffrage,* ed. Mari Jo Buhle and Paul Buhle (Chicago: University of Illinois Press, 1978), 99.

43. William Channing Gannett thus identified Abigail Bush in his speech for the Fiftieth Anniversary of the RWRC, 1898, Unitarian Society of Rochester Records, University of Rochester.

44. See Abigail Bush to Amy Post, 185–; and Sarah C. Owen to Amy Post, 12 Feb. 1850 and 24 Sept. 185–, IAPFP.

45. *Report of the Woman's Rights Convention, Held at Seneca Falls, N.Y., July Nineteenth and Twentieth, 1848* (Rochester: John Dick, 1848), 3; RWRC, Minutes, 2 Aug. 1848, Phebe Post Willis Papers, University of Rochester. Because the Seneca Falls Convention had already provoked considerable criticism, the choice of more radical language seems particularly noteworthy.

46. RWRC, "Proceedings," 99. For the disappointed response of one agrarian Quaker to Lucretia Mott's role in the RWRC, see Mary Robbins Post to Amy Post, 2 Sept. 1848, IAPFP.

47. RWRC, Minutes; and RWRC, "Proceedings," 102.

48. *Rochester Daily Advertiser*, 3 Aug. 1848.

49. RWRC, "Proceedings," 102.

50. RWRC, Minutes.

51. Ibid.

52. "Women's Protective Union," *Rochester North Star* 1 (15 Sept. 1848).

53. For example, see Linda Brent, *Incidents in the Life of a Slave Girl* (Boston, 1861), written by Harriet Brent Jacobs, an escaped slave who lived with the Posts from about 1849 to 1851. Also Nancy Hassey to ————, n.d.; E. Bowen to Amy Post, 19 Nov. 1857; and Jenny Dods to Amy Post, n.d., IAPFP; and Lucy N. Colman, *Reminiscences* (Buffalo: H.L. Green, 1891), 85.

54. Blake McKelvey, *Rochester: The Water-Power City, 1812–1854* (Cambridge: Harvard University Press, 1945), 349.

55. Sarah C. Owen to Amy Post, 185–, IAPFP. At the same time, Owen praised the Post's marriage, based as it was on the "principles of equal rights" (Sarah C. Owen to Amy Post, 31 July 185–, IAPFP).

56. Sarah E. Thayer to Amy Post, 9 Mar. 1853 and 1 Aug. 1857; Jacob Post to Amy Post, 4 May 1858; Sarah Hallowell Willis to Amy Post, 6 Mar. 1852, IAPFP; and Colman, 3, 20–41.

57. *Liberator* 13 (6 Jan. 1843). See also Mary Robbins Post to Isaac and Amy Post, 184–; Rebecca M.C. Capron to Amy Post, 1 Apr. 1850; and Sarah Thayer to Amy Post, 1 Aug. 1857, IAPFP; WNYASS, Fair Report, n.d. IAPFP; and Harper, 1:423–39; and *Rochester Democrat and Chronicle*, 1 Nov. 1872.

58. YMCF, *1849 Proceedings*, 6.

59. YMCF, *Proceedings of the Yearly Meeting of Congregational Friends, Held at Waterloo, N.Y., from the Third to the Fifth of the Sixth Month, Inclusive, 1850* (Auburn, N.Y.: Henry Oliphant, 1850), 14, 15.

60. YMCF, *Proceedings of the Yearly Meeting of Congregational Friends, Held at Waterloo, N.Y., on the Fifth, Sixth, and Seventh of the Sixth Month, 1853* (Auburn, N.Y.: Knapp & Peck, 1853), 6.

61. DuBois, 56–64. On Rochesterians specifically, see Amy Post to Aaron M. Powell, 186–, IAPFP.

62. Amy Post to A.L. Rawson, 9 Sept. 1879, IAPFP. See also William Leach, *True Love and Perfect Union: The Feminist Reform of Sex and Society* (New York: Basic Books, 1982), 137–38, 293.

63. *Seneca Falls Report*, 5; and YMCF, *1850 Proceedings*, 6.

3   Ellen Carol DuBois

The Radicalism of the Woman Suffrage Movement: Notes toward the Reconstruction of Nineteenth-Century Feminism

☐ In this essay, I would like to suggest an interpretation of nineteenth-century suffragism that reconciles the perceived radicalism of the woman suffrage movement with the historical centrality of the family to women's condition. My hypothesis is that the significance of the woman suffrage movement rested precisely on the fact that it bypassed women's oppression within the family, or private sphere, and demanded instead her admission to citizenship, and through it admission to the public arena. By focusing on the public sphere, and particularly on citizenship, suffragists demanded for women a kind of power and a connection with the social order not based on the institution of the family and their subordination within it.

Recent scholarship has suggested that the sharp distinction between public and private activities is a relatively modern historical phenomenon. In his work on the evolution of the idea of childhood in Western Europe, Phillipe Ariès demonstrates that there was considerable overlap between family life and community life in the premodern period. He traces a gradual separation of public and private life from the sixteenth century to the nineteenth century, when "family" and "society" came finally to be viewed as distinct, even hostile, institutions.[1] This development seems to have been clear and compact in U.S. history. In seventeenth-century New England, all community functions—production, socialization, civil government, religious life—presumed the family as the basic unit of social organization.[2] The whole range of social roles drew on familial roles. The adult male's position as producer, as citizen,

Reprinted, with changes, from *Feminist Studies* 3, nos. 1/2 (Fall 1975): 63–71. ©1975 by Feminist Studies, Inc.

as member of the church, all flowed from his position as head of the family. Similarly, women's exclusion from church and civil government and their secondary but necessary role in production coincided with their subordinate position within the family.[3] A few women enjoyed unusual economic or social privileges by virtue of their family connections, but, as Gerda Lerner has pointed out, this further demonstrated women's dependence on their domestic positions for the definition of their roles in community life.[4]

By the nineteenth century, this relationship between family and society had undergone considerable change. Although the family continued to perform many important social functions, it was no longer the sole unit around which the community was organized. The concept of the "individual" had emerged to rival it. In the nineteenth century, we can distinguish two forms of social organization—one based on this new creature, the individual, the other based on the family. These overlapping but distinct structures became identified, respectively, as the public sphere and the private sphere. The emergence of a form of social organization not based on the family meant the emergence of social roles not defined by familial roles. This was equally true for women and men. But because women and men had different positions *within* the family, the existence of nonfamilial roles had different implications for the sexes. For women, the emergence of a public sphere held out the revolutionary possibility of a new way to relate to society not defined by their subordinate position within the family.

However, only men emerged from their familial roles to enjoy participation in the public sphere. Women on the whole did not. Women were of course among the first industrial workers, but these were overwhelmingly unmarried women, for whom factory work was a brief episode before marriage. Adult women remained almost entirely within the private sphere, defined politically, economically, and socially by their familial roles. Thus, the public sphere became man's arena; the private, woman's. This gave the public/private distinction a clearly sexual character. This phenomenon, canonized as the nineteenth-century doctrine of sexual spheres, is somewhat difficult for us to grasp. We are fond of pointing out the historical durability of sexual roles into our own time and miss the enormous difference between the twentieth-century notion of sexual roles and the nineteenth-century idea of sexual spheres. The difference is a measure of the achievements of nineteenth-century feminism.

The contradiction between the alternative to familial roles that activity in the public sphere offered and the exclusion of women from such activity was particularly sharp with respect to civil government. In seventeenth-century New England, citizenship was justified on the basis of familial position; the freeholder was at once the head of the household and a citizen. By contrast, nineteenth-century citizenship was posed as a direct relationship between the individual and her or his government. In other words, patriarchy was no longer the *official* basis of civil government in modern industrial democracy. However, in reality, only men were permitted to become citizens. The exclusion of women from participation in political life in the early nineteenth century was so absolute and unchallenged that it did not require explicit proscription. It was simply assumed that political "persons" were male. The U.S. Constitution did not specify the sex of citizens until the Fourteenth Amendment was ratified in 1869, after women had begun actively to demand the vote. Prior to that, the equation between "male" and "person," the term used in the Constitution, was implicit. The same, by the way, was true of the founding charter of the American Anti-Slavery Society. Written in 1833, it defined the society's membership as "persons," but for six years admitted only men into that category.

The doctrine of separate sexual spheres was supreme in the nineteenth century and even suffragists were unable to challenge certain basic aspects of it. Most notably, they accepted the particular suitability of women to domestic activities, and therefore their special responsibility for the private sphere, and did not project a reorganization of the division of labor within the home. Antoinette Brown Blackwell, pioneer suffragist and minister, asserted that "the paramount social duties of women are household duties, avocations arising from their relations as wives and mothers. . . . The work nearest and clearest before the eyes of average womanhood is work within family boundaries—work within a sphere which men cannot enter."[5] No suffragist of whom I am aware, including the otherwise iconoclastic Elizabeth Cady Stanton, seriously suggested that men take equal responsibilities with women for domestic activities. "Sharing housework" may be a more specifically twentieth-century feminist demand than "smashing monogamy." To nineteenth-century feminists, domestic activities seemed as "naturally" female as childbearing and as little subject to social manipulation.

Although suffragists accepted the peculiarly feminine character of the private sphere, their demand for the vote challenged the male monopoly of the public arena. This is what gave suffragism much of its feminist meaning. Suffragists accepted women's "special responsibility" for domestic activity but refused to concede that it prohibited them from participation in the public sphere. Moreover, unlike the demand that women be admitted to trades, professions, and education, the demand for citizenship applied to all women and it applied to them all of the time—to the housewife as much as to the single, self-supporting woman. By demanding a permanent, public role for all women, suffragists began to demolish the absolute, sexually defined barrier marking the public world of men off from the private world of women. Even though they did not develop a critical analysis of domestic life, the dialectical relationship between public and private spheres transformed their demand for admission to the public sphere into a basic challenge to the entire sexual structure. Thus, although she never criticized women's role in the family, Stanton was still able to write: "One may as well talk of separate spheres for the two ends of the magnet as for man and woman; they may have separate duties in the same sphere, but their true place is together everywhere."[6]

Suffragists' demand for a permanent, public role for all women allowed them to project a vision of female experience and action that went beyond the family and the subordination of women which the family upheld. Citizenship represented a relationship to the larger society that was entirely and explicitly outside the boundaries of women's familial relations. As citizens and voters, women would participate directly in society as individuals, not indirectly through their subordinate positions as wives and mothers. Mary Putnam Jacobi identified this as the revolutionary core of suffragism. The American state, she explained, is based on "individual cells," not households. She went on: "Confessedly, in embracing in this conception women, we do introduce a change which, though in itself purely ideal, underlies all the practical issues now in dispute. In this essentially modern conception, women also are brought into direct relations with the State, independent of their 'mate' or 'brood.'"[7] Without directly attacking women's position within the private sphere, suffragists touched the nerve of women's subordinate status by contending that women might be something other than wives and mothers. "Womanhood is the great fact in her life," Stanton was fond of saying; "wifehood and motherhood are but incidental relations."[8]

On one level, the logic behind the demand for woman suffrage in a country professing republican principles is obvious, and suffragists made liberal use of the tradition and rhetoric of the American Revolution. Yet this is not sufficient to explain why suffrage became the core of a *feminist* program, why enfranchisement was perceived as the key to female liberation. I hypothesize that because enfranchisement involved a way for women to relate to society independent of their familial relations, it was the key demand of nineteenth-century feminists. It was the cornerstone of a social movement that did not simply catalog and protest women's wrongs in the existing sexual order but also revealed the possibility of an alternate sexual order. Unlike the tradition of female protest, from the moral reformers of the 1830s to the temperance women of the 1880s, which was based in the private sphere and sought to reinterpret women's place within it, suffragism focused squarely on the public sphere.

In part, the feminist, liberating promise of enfranchisement rested on the concrete power that suffragists expected to obtain with the vote. Suffragists expected women to use the ballot to protect themselves and to impose their viewpoint on political issues. They anticipated that by strategic use of their political power women would break open new occupations, raise the level of their wage scales to that of men, win strikes, and force reforms in marriage and family law in order to protect themselves from sexual abuse, the loss of their children, and the unchecked tyranny of their husbands. The demand for suffrage drew together protest against all these abuses in a single demand for the right to shape the social order by way of the public sphere. No longer content either with maternal influence over the future voter's character or with an endless series of petitions from women to lawmakers, suffragists proposed that women participate directly in the political decisions that affected their lives. "Like all disfranchised classes, they began by asking to have certain wrongs redressed," Stanton wrote. But suffragism went beyond what she called "special grievances" to give women's protest "a larger scope."[9]

In evaluating suffragists' expectations of the power that the vote would bring women, it is important to keep in mind the structure of political power in the nineteenth century. Political decisions were less centralized in the federal government and more significant at the local level than they are now. Herbert Gutman's analysis of the assistance which local politicians gave labor activists in nineteenth-century Paterson, New Jersey, suggests that Susan B. Anthony's prediction that woman suffrage would win women's strikes had some basis in reality.[10]

Even granted the greater power of the individual voter over political decisions that would affect her or his life, suffragists did not understand the ballot as merely a weapon with which to protect their interests in the political process. They also expected enfranchisement to transform woman's consciousness, to reanchor her self-image, not in the subordination of her familial role but in the individuality and self-determination that they saw in citizenship. This was a particularly important aspect of the political thought of Elizabeth Cady Stanton, the chief ideologue of nineteenth-century suffragism. It is developed most fully in "Solitude of Self," the speech she thought her best. She wrote there: "Nothing strengthens the judgment and quickens the conscience like individual responsibility. Nothing adds such dignity to character as the recognition of one's self-sovereignty."[11] Elsewhere, she wrote that from the "higher stand-point" of enfranchisement, woman would become sensitive to the daily indignities which, without due appreciation for her own individuality, she ignored and accepted.[12] She developed the theme of the impact of enfranchisement on women's self-concept most fully in a speech simply titled "Self-Government the Best Means of Self-Development."[13]

Given the impact on consciousness that suffragists expected from the vote, they generally refused to redirect their efforts toward such partial enfranchisements as municipal or school suffrage. Although these limited suffrages would give women certain political powers, they were suffrages designed especially for women and justified on the basis of women's maternal responsibilities. Their achievement would not necessarily prove women's right to full and equal participation in the public sphere. Suffragists did not simply want political power; they wanted to be citizens, to stand in the same relation to civil government as men did. As a result, it was primarily clubwomen who worked for school and municipal suffrage, while those who identified themselves as suffragists continued to concentrate on the admission of women to full citizenship.[14]

An important index to the nature and degree of suffragism's challenge to the nineteenth-century sexual order was the kind and amount of opposition that it inspired, especially from men. Male opponents focused on the family, its position vis-à-vis the state, and the revolutionary impact of female citizenship on that relation. In response to suffragists' demand that modern democracy include women, opponents tried to reinstate a patriarchal theory of society and the state.[15] The family, they contended, was the virtual, if not the official unit of civil government, and men represented and protected the women of their families in political affairs. Male opponents regularly charged that the enfranchisement of women would revolutionize the relations of the sexes and, in turn, the character and structure of the home and women's role within it. The 1867 New York Constitutional Convention expressed this fear for the future of the family when it rejected suffrage because it was an innovation "so revolutionary and sweeping, so openly at war with a distribution of duties and functions between the sexes as venerable and pervading as government itself, and involving transformations so radical in social and domestic life."[16]

Most suffragists were much more modest about the implications of enfranchisement for women's position within the family. They expected reform of family law, particularly of the marriage contract, and the abolition of such inequities as the husband's legal right to his wife's sexual services. They also anticipated that the transformation in woman's consciousness which enfranchisement would bring would improve the quality of family relations, particularly between wife and husband. Stanton argued that once women were enfranchised they would demand that democracy be the law of the family, as well as of the state.[17] Her comment suggests that by introducing women into a form of social organization not based on patriarchal structures, she expected enfranchisement to permit women a much more critical perspective on the family itself. However, suffragists regularly denied the antisuffragists' charge that woman suffrage meant a revolution in the family. Most would have agreed with Jacobi that if antisuffragists wanted to argue that familial bonds were mere "political contrivances," requiring the disfranchisement of women to sustain them, suffragists had considerably more faith in the family as a "natural institution," able to survive women's entry into the public sphere.[18]

Suffragists worked hard to attract large numbers of women to the demand for the vote. They went beyond the methods of agitational propaganda which they had learned as abolitionists, and beyond the skills of lobbying which they had developed during Radical Reconstruction, to become organizers. As suffragists' efforts at outreach intensified, the family-bound realities of most women's lives forced more and more domestic imagery into their rhetoric and their arguments. Yet suffrage remained a distinctly minority movement in the nineteenth century. The very thing that made suffragism the most radical aspect of nineteenth-century feminism—its focus on the public sphere and on a nonfamilial role for women—was the cause of its failure to establish a mass base. It was not that nineteenth-century women were content, or had no grievances, but that they understood their grievances in the context of the private sphere. The lives of most nineteenth-century women were overwhelmingly limited to the private realities of wifehood and motherhood, and they experienced their discontent in the context of those relations. The enormous success of the Woman's Christian Temperance Union (WCTU), particularly as contrasted with the nineteenth-century suffrage movement, indicates the capacity for protest and activism among nineteenth-century women and the fact that this mass feminism was based in the private sphere. The WCTU commanded an army in the nineteenth century, while woman suffrage remained a guerrilla force.

Unlike the woman suffrage movement, the WCTU took as its starting point woman's position within the home; it cataloged the abuses she suffered there and it proposed reforms necessary to ameliorate her domestic situation. As the WCTU developed, its concerns went beyond the family to include the quality of community life, but its standard for nonfamilial relations remained the family and the moral values women had developed within it. The WCTU spoke to women in the language of their domestic realities, and they joined in the 1870s and 1880s in enormous numbers. Anchored in the private realm, the WCTU became the mass movement that nineteenth-century suffragism could not.

The WCTU's program reflected the same social reality that lay beyond suffragism—that the family was losing its central place in social organization to nondomestic institutions, from the saloon to the school to the legislature, and that woman's social power was accordingly weakened. Yet the WCTU, Luddite-like, defended the family and women's traditional but fast-fading authority within it. Its mottoes reflected this defensive goal: "For God and Home and Native Land"; "Home Protection." In 1883, the WCTU formally endorsed the demand for female enfranchisement but justified its action as necessary to protect the home and women within it, thus retaining its family-based analysis and its defensive character. The first resolutions introduced by Frances Willard in support of suffrage asked for the vote for women in their roles as wives and mothers, to enable them to protect their homes from the influence of the saloon.[19] This was the woman suffrage movement's approach to female oppression and the problem of spheres stood on its head—women entering the public arena to protect the primacy of the private sphere and women's position within it. Yet, the very fact that the WCTU had to come to terms with suffrage and eventually supported it indicates that the woman suffrage movement had succeeded in becoming the defining focus of nineteenth-century feminism, with respect to which all organized female protest had to orient itself. Even though the WCTU organized and commanded the forces, the woman suffrage movement had defined the territory.

Suffrage became a mass movement in the twentieth century under quite different conditions, when women's position vis-à-vis the public and private spheres had shifted considerably. Despite, or perhaps because of, the home-based ideology with which they operated, the WCTU, women's clubs, and other branches of nineteenth-century feminism had introduced significant numbers of women to extradomestic concerns.[20] Charlotte Perkins Gilman noted the change among women in 1903: "The socialising of this hitherto subsocial, wholly domestic class, is a marked and marvellous event, now taking place with astonishing rapidity."[21] Similarly, Susan B. Anthony commented at the 1888 International Council of Women: "Forty years ago women had no place anywhere except in their homes, no pecuniary independence, no purpose in life save that which came through marriage. . . . In later years the way has been opened to every avenue of industry—to every profession. . . .

What is true in the world of work is true in education, is true everywhere."[22] At the point that it could attract a mass base, suffragism no longer opened up such revolutionary vistas for women; they were already operating in the public world of work and politics. The scope and meaning of twentieth-century suffragism requires its own analysis, but the achievement of nineteenth-century suffragists was that they identified, however haltingly, a fundamental transformation of the family and the new possibilities for women's emancipation that this revealed.

Notes

I wish to thank Amy Bridges, Mari Jo Buhle, Ann D. Gordon, Linda Gordon, Carolyn Korsemeyer, and Rochelle Ruthchild for their comments and suggestions on earlier versions of this article.

1. Phillipe Ariès, *Centuries of Childhood: A Social History of Family Life* (New York: Vintage Books, 1962), esp. 365–407.

2. Edmund Morgan, *The Puritan Family: Religion and Domestic Relations in Seventeenth-Century New England* (New York: Harper & Row, 1966), esp. chap. 6; John Demos, *A Little Commonwealth: Family Life in Plymouth Colony* (New York: Oxford University Press, 1970), 2–11.

3. Morgan, chap. 2. Demos, 82–84.

4. Gerda Lerner, "The Lady and the Mill Girl: Changes in the Status of Women in the Age of Jackson," *Midcontinent American Studies Journal* 10 (1969): 6.

5. Antoinette Brown Blackwell, "Relation of Woman's Work in the Household to the Work Outside," reprinted in Aileen S. Kraditor, *Up from the Pedestal: Selected Writings in the History of American Feminism* (Chicago: Quadrangle Books, 1968), 151.

6. Elizabeth Cady Stanton, "Speech to the 1885 National Suffrage Convention," in *History of Woman Suffrage*, ed. Elizabeth Cady Stanton, Susan B. Anthony, and Matilda Joslyn Gage (Rochester, N.Y.: Susan B. Anthony, 1889), 4:58.

7. Mary Putnam Jacobi, *"Common Sense" Applied to Woman Suffrage* (New York: Putnam, 1894), 138.

8. Stanton, Introduction, *History of Woman Suffrage,* 1:22.

9. Ibid., 15.

10. Herbert Gutman, "Class, Status, and Community Power in Nineteenth-Century American Industrial Cities—Paterson, New Jersey: A Case Study," in *The Age of Industrialism in America,* ed. Frederic C. Jaher (New York: Free Press, 1968), 263–87. For Anthony's prediction on the impact of woman suffrage on women's strikes, see "Woman Wants Bread, not the Ballot," reprinted in *The Life*

and Work of Susan B. Anthony, ed. Ida Husted Harper (Indianapolis and Kansas City: Bower-Merrill, 1898), 2:996–1003.

11. Elizabeth Cady Stanton, "Solitude of Self," reprinted in *History of Woman Suffrage,* 4:189–91.

12. Stanton, Introduction, *History of Woman Suffrage,* 1:18.

13. Stanton, "Self-Government the Best Means of Self-Development," reprinted in *History of Woman Suffrage,* 4:40–42.

14. See Lois B. Merk, "Boston's Historical Public School Crisis," *New England Quarterly* 31 (1958): 196–202.

15. See, for instance, Orestes A. Brownson, "The Woman Question," reprinted in *Up from the Pedestal,* 192–94.

16. "Report on the Committee on Suffrage," reprinted in *History of Woman Suffrage,* 2:285.

17. Elizabeth Cady Stanton, "The Family, the State, and the Church," unpublished manuscript speech, Elizabeth Cady Stanton Papers, Manuscript Division, Library of Congress, Washington, D.C.

18. Jacobi, 108.

19. Mary Earhart, *Frances Willard: From Prayers to Politics* (Chicago: University of Chicago Press, 1944), chap. 10.

20. This process is described in Anne Firor Scott, *The Southern Lady: From Pedestal to Politics, 1830–1930* (Chicago: University of Chicago Press, 1970), chap. 6.

21. Charlotte Perkins Gilman, *The Home: Its Work and Influence* (New York: McClure, Phillips, & Co., 1903), 325.

22. Susan B. Anthony, "Introductory Remarks," *Report of the International Council of Women* assembled by the National Woman Suffrage Association (Washington, D.C.: Rufus H. Darby, 1888), 31.

Seeking Ecstasy on the Battlefield: Danger and Pleasure in Nineteenth-Century Feminist Sexual Thought

□ It is often alleged that female sexuality is a more complex matter than men's, and, if so, a major reason is that sex spells potential danger as well as pleasure for women. A feminist politics about sex, therefore, if it is to be credible as well as hopeful, must seek both to protect women from sexual danger and to encourage their pursuit of sexual pleasure.

This complex understanding of female sexuality has not always characterized the feminist movement. In general, feminists inherit two conflicting traditions in their approach to sex. The strongest tradition, virtually unchallenged in the mainstream women's rights movement of the nineteenth century, addressed primarily the dangers and few of the possibilities of sex. Another perspective, much less developed despite some eloquent spokeswomen by the early twentieth century, encouraged women to leap, adventurous and carefree, into sexual liaisons, but it failed to offer a critique of the male construction of the sexual experience available to most women. It is no use to label one side feminist and the other antifeminist, to argue by name-calling. We cannot move ahead unless we grasp that both traditions are part of our feminism.

Neither feminist tradition is adequate to our needs today. Both were thoroughly heterosexist in their assumptions of what sex is. Even the nineteenth-century women who experienced intense emotional and physical relationships with each other did not incorporate these into their definition of what was sexual. Certainly women had relationships with other women that included powerful sexual components, but the feminists who are the subject of this paper did not theorize these

Reprinted, with changes, from *Feminist Studies* 9, no. 1 (Spring 1983): 7–25. ©1983 by Feminist Studies, Inc.

relationships as sexual.[1] Furthermore, both feminist lines of thought—that emphasizing danger and that emphasizing pleasure—were often moralistic. They condemned those whose sexual behavior deviated from their standards, not only sexually exploitive men but also women who did not conform.

Still, without an appreciation of these legacies and the processes of thought and experience that produced them, we cannot have much historical insight into our own concerns. Without a history, political movements like ours swing back and forth endlessly, reacting to earlier mistakes and overreacting in compensation, unable to incorporate previous insights and transcend previous limitations. Today we observe some of that pendulumlike motion. In reaction to the profound disappointments in what has passed for "sexual liberation," some feminists are replicating an earlier tradition, focusing exclusively on danger and advocating what we believe to be a conservative sexual politics.

We use a label like "conservative" cautiously. Such terms, like "Left" and "Right," come to us from class politics. When applied to sex and gender, they fit less comfortably. The oppressions of women, the repressions of sex, are so many and so complex, by virtue of their location in the most intimate corners of life, coexisting even with love, that it is not always obvious in which direction a better world lies. We use the term "conservatism" to characterize strategies that accept existing power relations. We are suggesting that even feminist reform programs can be conservative in some respects if they accept male dominance while trying to elevate women's "status" within it. In this case, we believe that the nineteenth-century feminist mainstream accepted women's sexual powerlessness with men as inevitable, even as it sought to protect women from its worst consequences. Its appraisal of women's sexual victimization was not, on balance, offset by recognition of women's potential for sexual activity and enjoyment. We think our judgment will be justified by the historical description which follows. Through that description we hope to show, too, that despite the stubborn continuities of women's sexual oppression, there have also been momentous changes in the last one hundred fifty years, changes that require different strategies today.

The feminist movement has played an important role in organizing and even creating women's sense of sexual danger in the last one hundred fifty years. In that movement, two themes more than others have encapsulated and symbolized women's fears—prostitution and rape. There is a certain parallel construction between the nineteenth-century focus on prostitution and the modern emphasis on rape as the quintessential sexual terror. It is remarkable, in fact, how little emphasis nineteenth-century feminists placed on rape per se. It is as if the norms of legal sexual intercourse were in themselves so objectionable that rape did not seem that much worse. Instead, feminists used prostitution as the leading symbol of male sexual coercion. Although rape is an episode, prostitution suggests a condition that takes hold of a woman for a long time—possibly for life—and is difficult to escape. The symbolic emphasis in prostitution is on ownership, possession, purchase by men but in rape it is on pure violence. Rape can happen to any woman; prostitution involves the separation of women into the good and the bad, a division with class implications, as we shall see, even when the division is blamed on men.

Lest it seem trivializing to the real sufferings of women as prostitutes or rape victims to treat experiences as symbols or metaphors, let us emphasize again our subject. We are looking at how feminists conceptualized different sexual dangers, as a means of organizing *resistance* to sexual oppression. We want to look at how these feminist strategies changed, so that we can examine historically how we conduct feminist campaigns around sexual issues today.

In different periods, feminists emphasized different aspects of prostitution. In the 1860s and 1870s, for example, they focused on the economic pressures forcing women into sexual commerce; but in the Progressive Era their primary theme was "white slavery," the physical coercion of women into the trade. Despite these shifts, however, aspects of their approach to prostitution were consistent. First, they exaggerated its magnitude.[2] They did so because their definition of prostitute included virtually all women who engaged in casual sex, whether or not they were paid. Second, feminists consistently exaggerated the coerciveness of prostitution. In their eagerness to identify the social structural forces encouraging prostitution, they denied the prostitute any role other than that of passive victim. They insisted that the women involved were sexual innocents, helpless young women who "fell" into illicit sex. They assumed that prostitution was so degrading that no woman could freely choose it, not even with the relative degree of freedom with which she could choose to be a wife or a wage earner. Thus, the "fallen woman" was always viewed as a direct victim, not only of male dominance in general, but of kidnapping, sexual imprisonment, starvation, and/or seduction in particular.[3] These attitudes toward prostitution were not exclusive to feminists, but they were also part of the ideological outlook of many male reformers, including some antifeminists. Our point here, however, is that feminists not only failed to challenge this oversimplified and condescending explanation of prostitution but also made it central to their understanding of women's oppression.

The feminists' exclusive emphasis on the victimization of the prostitute ultimately prevented their transcending a sexual morality dividing women into the good and the bad.[4] They wanted to rescue women from prostitution and to admit prostitution's victims into the salvation of good womanhood; but they clung fast to the idea that some kinds of sex were inherently criminal and were confounded by the existence of unrepentant whores. Furthermore, their equation of prostitution with any illicit sex indicates that a crucial element of their fear was loss of respectability. The power of prostitution rested on the common understanding that once a woman had sex outside of marriage she was "ruined" and would become a prostitute sooner or later. This potential loss of respectability was not imaginary but a real, material process with sanctions that varied by culture and class. For middle-class and many white working-class women, the loss of purity—we would call it getting a bad reputation—damaged prospects for marriage. It led to a total loss of control over one's own sexuality; once "used" by a man, a woman became free game for that entire sex.

Maintaining respectability was an especially severe problem for Black women, fighting to free their entire race from a slave heritage that tended to place them at the disposal of white men's sexual demands. Thus, the Black women's movement conducted a particularly militant campaign for respectability, often making Black feminists spokespeople for prudery in their communities.[5] White feminists assimilated the horror of Black slavery to their fears of prostitution. They understood the sexual tyranny of slavery as central and as a form of prostitution. Among their most powerful antislavery writings were images of beautiful, pure Black womanhood defiled, and white feminist abolitionists found it difficult to accept the possibility of willing sex between Black women and white men.[6]

The fear of prostitution represented also a fear of direct physical violence but in a displaced manner. In the nineteenth century, as today, women encountered sexual and nonsexual violence most often at home. Rape in marriage was no crime, not even generally disapproved; wifebeating was only marginally criminal. Incest was common enough to require skepticism about the idea that it was taboo. Although feminists occasionally organized against domestic violence, they did not make it the object of a sustained campaign, largely because they were unable to challenge the family politically.[7] The focus on prostitution was a focus on extrafamilial violence. Nineteenth-century feminists came closer to intrafamily matters in the temperance campaign. Their criticisms of drinking were laced through with imagery of the bestial, violent quality of male sexuality, but blaming alcohol also allowed a displacement of focus, an avoidance of criticizing men and marriage directly.[8]

Certain dangers in marriage had to be faced. One was venereal disease, and this too was assimilated to the central imagery of prostitution, for men who patronized prostitutes could then transmit diseases to their wives. In keeping with the division of women between good and bad, feminists implicitly considered prostitution as the source of venereal disease. The communicability and incurability of these diseases proved to them that absolute monogamy was women's only source of safety amid the sexual dangers.[9] (One is reminded of the conservatives' response to sexually transmitted diseases today.) Feminists also opposed the sexual demands of self-centered husbands on their wives, which law and convention obligated women to meet. But instead of protesting "marital rape," as we do, they criticized what they called "legalized prostitution" in marriage.[10]

Sex posed another serious danger in marriage—unwanted conception. Given the equation of sex with intercourse and the lack of access to reliable contraception, desire to control conceptions often resulted in the antisexual attitudes of women.[11] Despite a great reverence for motherhood, an unexpected pregnancy was often threatening. For poor women, for virtually all Black women, having children meant introducing them into social and economic circumstances where their safety and well-being could not be guaranteed. Even for prosperous women, mothers' economic dependence on men was extreme. Single motherhood was an extremely difficult situation in the absence of any regular welfare or child-care provisions. Mothers were frequently forced to remain with abusive men for fear of losing their children. Indeed, prostitution was sometimes seen as an option for a single mother, for at least she could do it while she remained at home with her children.[12] A bitter irony surrounds the place of motherhood in the sexual system of nineteenth-century feminism. Clearly, it was some women's greatest joy and source of dignity; for many women it was what made sexual intercourse acceptable. But at the same time motherhood was the last straw in enforcing women's subordination to men, the factor that finally prevented many from seeking independence. What was conceived of as women's greatest virtue, their passionate and self-sacrificing commitment to their children, their capacity for love itself, was a leading factor in their victimization.

Of the many factors constructing the feminist fear of prostitution perhaps none is so hard for contemporary feminists to understand as religion. But we would miss the dilemma that these women faced in dealing with sex if we did not thoroughly appreciate their religious culture. Those actively rebelling against established religion were as influenced by it as the dutiful church members or Christian reform activists. All had been raised on the concept of sin, especially sexual sin. They all shared the view that there could be high and low pleasures, and the guilt they felt about indulging in the low was not just psychological self-doubt. It was a sense of self-violation, of violation of the source of their dignity.[13]

We are arguing here that the feminist understanding of sexual danger, expressed so poignantly in the fear of prostitution, must be seen as part of a sexual system in which they were participants, sometimes willing and sometimes unwilling, sometimes conscious and sometimes unaware.[14] Their very resistance often drew them into accommodation with aspects of this oppressive system. What is surprising is the extent of resistance that actually challenged this sexual system. Some women labeled "loose," who might or might not have been prostitutes, rejected the notion that their disreputable sexual behavior was something to be ashamed of or something that had been forced upon them.[15] There were young sexual "delinquents" who took pleasure and pride in their rebellion.[16] There were women who passed as men in order to seize male sexual (and other) prerogatives and to take other women as wives.[17] Even respectable, middle-class married women had orgasms more than they were supposed to. One survey had 40 percent of women reporting orgasms occasionally, 20 percent frequently, and 40 percent never, proportions which may not be so different than those among women today.[18] About the present, it is angering that so many women do not experience orgasm; about the past, it is impressive—and analytically important—that so many women did. In other words, our nineteenth-century legacy is one of resistance to sexual repression as well as victimization by it.

☐ Despite resistance, the weight of the nineteenth-century feminist concern was with protection from danger. This approach, usually known as "social purity," reflected an experienced reality and was overwhelmingly protectionist in its emphasis.

The major target of the feminist social purity advocates was the double standard. Their attack on it had, in turn, two aspects: seeking greater safety for women and more penalties for men. Their object was to achieve a set of controls over sexuality, structured through the family, enforced through law and/or social morality, which would render sex, if not safe, at least a decent, calculable risk for women. Social purity feminists railed against male sexual privileges, against the vileness of male drunkenness and lust, and they sought with every means at their disposal to increase the costs attached to such indulgences.[19]

The most positive achievements of social purity feminism were in the homes and communities of the middle-class women most likely to be its advocates. Here, efforts to make marriage laws more egalitarian, upgrade women's property rights, and improve women's educational and professional opportunities altered the balance of power between wife and husband. Social purity thought emphasized the importance of consensual sex for women and insisted that even married women should not be coerced into any sexual activities they did not choose freely; inasmuch as they believed that sexual drive and initiative were primarily male, they understood this as women's right to say no. Through organizations like the Woman's Christian Temperance Union, feminists propagandized for these standards, with tirades against the threat to civilization caused by immorality, and with energetic moral and sex education programs.[20] And they succeeded in changing culture and consciousness. Without knowing precisely how much peoples' lives conformed to this standard, we can say that the ideal of marital mutuality and a woman's right to say no were absorbed into middle-class culture by the turn of the century. There is mounting evidence that, for reasons not yet clear, immigrant and poor women did not establish the same standards of marital mutuality but fought for power within their families differently, by accepting certain patriarchal prerogatives while asserting their power as mothers and housewives.[21]

The negative consequences of social purity's single-minded focus on sexual danger come into focus when we look at their vigorous campaign against prostitution. Over time the repressive tendencies of this campaign overwhelmed its liberatory aspects and threw a pall over feminism's whole approach to sexuality. The beginning of women's reform work on prostitution in the early nineteenth century was a big step forward in the development of feminism. That "respectable" women took the risk of reaching out, across a veritable gulf of sexual sin, to women stigmatized as whores, was a declaration of female collectivity that transcended class and moralistic divisions. The reformers visited and talked with prostitutes, conducted public discussions of the issue, and established homes into which prostitutes could "escape." In doing so they were opening a crack in the wall of sexual "innocence" that would eventually widen into an escape route for women of their class as well. The attitudes that we today perceive as a patronizing desire to "help" were initially a challenge to the punitive and woman-hating morality that made sexual "ruin" a permanent and irredeemable condition for women.[22]

In the 1860s and 1870s feminists reactivated themselves into a militant and successful campaign to halt government regulation of prostitution.

The system of regulation, already in existence in France and parts of England, forced women alleged to be prostitutes to submit to vaginal examinations and licensing; its purpose was to allow men to have sex with prostitutes without the risk of venereal disease. Feminist opposition drew not only from their anger at men who bought female flesh but also reaffirmed their identification with prostitutes' victimization. Feminists asserted that all women, even prostitutes, had a right to the integrity of their own bodies.[23]

But after a relatively easy victory over government regulation, social purity feminists began to press for the abolition of prostitution itself. They sponsored legislation to increase the criminal penalties for men clients, while continuing to express sympathy with the "victimized" women. The catch was that the prostitutes had to agree that they were victims. The "white slavery" interpretation of prostitution—that prostitutes had been forced into the business—allowed feminists to see themselves as rescuers of slaves.[24] But if the prostitutes were not contrite, or denied the immorality of their actions, they lost their claim to the aid and sympathy of the reformers. "The big sisters of the world [want the] chance to protect the little and weaker sisters, by surrounding them with the right laws for them to obey for their own good," one feminist explained, unwittingly capturing the repressive character of this "sisterhood."[25] The class nature of American society encouraged these middle-class feminists to conduct their challenge to the double standard through other women's lives and to focus their anger on men other than their own husbands and fathers.

Another attack on prostitution which sometimes turned into an attack on women was the campaign to raise the age of sexual consent.[26] In many states in the nineteenth century this had been as low as nine or ten years for girls. The feminist goals were to deny the white slavers their younger victims, to extend sexual protection to girls, and to provide punishments for male assailants. Like most of these feminist sexual causes this one had in it a radical moment: it communicated an accurate critique of the limitations of "consent" by women in a male-dominated society. Yet by late in the century, when urban life and the presence of millions of young working girls changed the shape of family and generational relations, age-of-consent legislation explicitly denied women the right to heterosexual activity until they were adults or—and note that this qualification applied at any age—married. In fostering this hostility to girls' sexual activity, the feminists colluded in the labeling of a new class of female offenders—teenage sex delinquents. Sex delinquency was soon the largest category within which young women were sent to reformatories.[27] These moralistic reformers, some of them feminists, allowed the criminal justice system to take over the task of disciplining teenage girls to conform to respectable morality.

This inability to see anything in prostitution but male tyranny and/or economic oppression affected not only "bad" women but the "good" ones as well. Feminists' refusal to engage in a concrete examination of the actuality of prostitution was of a piece with their inability to look without panic at any form of sexual nonconformity. We do not suggest that prostitutes were necessarily freer than other women sexually. Our point is that feminists remained committed to the containment of female sexuality within heterosexual marriage, despite the relative sexual repressiveness that marriage meant for women at that time.[28] "Are our girls to be [as] free to please themselves by indulging in the loveless gratification of every instinct... and passion as our boys?" the social purity feminist Frances Willard asked her audience in 1891; and we can imagine that they answered with a resounding "No!"[29]

Feminist politics about sex became more conservative in the period up to World War I because women's aspirations and possibilities outstripped the feminist orthodoxy. Growing feminist organizational strength and the ability to influence legislation, combined with the class and racial elitism of the world in which the feminists moved, further strengthened their conservative political tendencies. Social purity feminists not only accepted a confining sexual morality for women, but they also excluded from their sisterhood women who did not or could not go along. The prostitute remained, for all their sympathy for her, the leading symbol of the woman excluded, not only from male-bestowed privilege but also from the women's community.[30]

Yet, just as there was behavioral resistance to the sexually repressive culture of the nineteenth century, so too there was political resistance within the women's movement. Although a decidedly minority viewpoint, a thin but continuous stream of feminists insisted that increased sexual activity was not incompatible with women's dignity and might even be in women's interests. We refer to this as the "prosex" tendency within the feminist tradition. It began with the free love and utopian movements of the 1820s through the 1840s. These radicals challenged the identification of sexual desire as masculine; and even though they remained for the most part advocates of the strictest monogamy, they challenged the coercive family and legal marriage as the channels for sexuality.[31] In the 1870s the free lover Victoria Woodhull appeared as a spokesperson from within the women's movement, idealizing as "true love" sex that involved mutual desire and orgasms for both parties.[32] At the same time Elizabeth Cady Stanton, a revered if maverick heroine, also asserted women's sexual desires.[33] In the 1880s and 1890s a few extremely visionary free love feminists began to formulate the outlines of a sexuality not organized around the male orgasm. Alice Stockham, a physician and suffragist, condemned the "ordinary, hasty and spasmodic mode of cohabitation . . . in which the wife is a passive party" and envisioned instead a union in which "the desires and pleasure of the wife calls forth the desire and pleasure of the husband."[34] Still, on the whole, these nineteenth-century feminists were only relatively "prosex," and most of them shared with social purity advocates a belief in the need to control, contain, and harness physiological sex expression to "higher" ends. Furthermore, even this limited sex-radical tradition was so marginal to American feminism that when the twentieth-century feminist Margaret Sanger searched for a more positive attitude to sex, she had to go to Europe to find it.

The only issue within mainstream nineteenth-century feminism where "prosex" ideas had a significant impact was divorce. Led by Cady Stanton, some feminists argued that the right to divorce and *then to remarry*—for that was the crucial element, the right to another sexual relationship after leaving a first—was a freedom important enough to women to risk granting it to men as well. Still, most feminists took a strict social purity line and opposed divorce for fear it would weaken marriage and expose women to even greater sexual danger.[35]

Ironically, one sexual reform strongly supported by social purity advocates became the vehicle by which a new generation of feminists began to break with the social purity tradition. This was birth control.[36] Nineteenth-century feminists had argued this as "voluntary motherhood," the right of women to refuse intercourse with their husbands if they did not want to conceive. Voluntary motherhood was a brilliant tactic because it insinuated a rejection of men's sexual domination into a politics of defending and improving motherhood. Consistent with its social purity orientation, voluntary motherhood advocates rejected contraception as a form of birth control for fear it would allow men to force even more sex upon their wives and to indulge in extramarital sex with even greater impunity. In the early twentieth century, by contrast, an insurgent feminist support for contraception arose, insisting that sexual abstinence was an unnecessary price for women to pay for reproductive self-determination and that sexual indulgence in the pursuit of pleasure was good for women.

That this new generation of feminists could break with social purity was possible in part because they were no longer controlled by their fear of becoming, or being labeled, prostitutes. They no longer saw the prostitute as only a victim; they began to break the association between sexual desire and prostitution. Indeed, they embraced and romanticized sexual daring of all sorts.[37] The specter of the white slaver no longer haunted them, and they were willing to take risks. They ventured unchaperoned into theaters and bars, lived without families in big cities, and moved about the city to discover the lives of those across class and race boundaries where their mothers would not have gone. Some of their names you recognize—Emma Goldman, Margaret Sanger, Crystal Eastman, Elizabeth Gurley Flynn, even Louise Bryant—but there were many, many more. Above all, they asserted a woman's right to be sexual. They slept with men without marrying. They took multiple lovers. They became single mothers. Some of them had explicitly sexual relationships with other women, although a subsequent repression of evidence, along with their own silences about homosexuality, make it hard for us to uncover this aspect of their sexual lives.[38]

In many ways these women were beginning to explore a sexual world which we are determined to occupy. But as pioneers they could explore only part of it and they did not imagine changing its overall boundaries. Even when it contradicted their own experience, they continued to accept a male and heterosexual definition of the "sex act." They were, so to speak, upwardly mobile, and they wanted integration into the sexual world as defined by men. The man's orgasm remained the central event, although now it was preferable if a woman had one at the same time; stimulation other than intercourse was considered foreplay; masturbation was unhealthy. And sex, all the more desirable now because of the transcendent possibilities they attributed to it, remained bound up with the structure of gender—it could only happen between a woman and a man.[39] These feminists criticized male dominance in the labor force and in the public arena, but they did not seem to notice how it shaped sex. They fought for women's freedom, but they rarely criticized men.

Once the organized women's rights movement began to fade, women who advocated this "prosex" politics were more and more alienated from a larger community of women; they seemed to feel that to enter the world of sex, they had to travel alone and leave other women behind. This rejection of women occurred both because the dominant tradition of feminism was so antisexual and because their own understanding of sex was so heterosexual. They were part of a generation that branded intense female friendships as adolescent.[40] The tragedy was that in rejecting a community of women which they experienced as constricting and repressive, they left behind their feminist heritage.

At the same time these pioneering sex radicals offer us a positive legacy in their willingness to take risks. It would be easier if we could progress toward sexual liberation without sufferings, if we could resolve the tension between seeking pleasure and avoiding danger by some simple policy; but we cannot. We must conduct our sexual politics in the real world. For women this is like advancing across a mined field. Looking only to your feet to avoid the mines means missing the horizon and the vision of why the advance is worthwhile, but if you only see the future possibilities you may blow yourself up.

If this is warlike imagery, it is not bravado. The dangers are substantial; women are assaulted and killed. But each act of violence against women would be multiplied in its effect if it prevented us from seeing where we have won victories and if it induced us to resign ourselves to restriction of our sexual lives and constriction of our public activities.

Seen in this light, the contemporary focus on rape and other sexual violence against women represents an advance over the earlier campaign against prostitution. Through this new conceptualization of the problem of sexual danger, feminists have rejected the victim blaming that was inherent in the notion of the "fallen woman"; we know that any of us can be raped. Our critique of sexual violence is an institutional analysis of the whole system of male supremacy which attempts to show the commonalities of women, as potential agents as well as victims. Thus, the campaign against rape comes out of our strength as well as our victimization. Whether the actual incidence of rape has increased or decreased, the feminist offensive against it represents an escalation of our demands for freedom. We have redefined rape to include many sexual encounters that nineteenth-century feminists would have considered mere seduction and for which they might have held the woman responsible; we have included in our definition of rape what was once normal marital intercourse. We have denied impunity to any men: we will bring charges against boyfriends, fathers, and teachers; we will label as sexual harassment what was once the ordinary banter of males asserting their dominance. We declare our right—still contested, viciously—to safety not only in our homes but in the streets. We *all* intend to be streetwalkers.

It is vital to strategy building to know when we are winning and when losing, and where. Failing to claim and take pride in our victories leads to the false conclusion that nothing has changed. When the campaign against rape is fought as if we were the eternal, unchanged victims of male sexuality, we run the risk of reentering the kind of social purity worldview that so limited the nineteenth-century feminist vision.[41] It is important to offer our comprehensive critique of misogyny, violence, and male dominance without ceding the arena of sexuality itself to the men, as the nineteenth-century feminists did.

We have tried to show that social purity politics, although an understandable reaction to women's nineteenth-century experience, was a limited and limiting vision for women. Thus we called it conservative. Today, there seems to be a revival of social purity politics within feminism, and it is concern about this tendency that motivates us in recalling its history. As in the nineteenth century, there is a feminist attack on pornography and sexual "perversion" in our time, which fails to distinguish its politics from a conservative and antifeminist version of social purity, the Moral Majority and "family protection movement." The increasing tendency to focus almost exclusively on sex as the primary arena of women's exploitation and to attribute women's sexual victimization to some violent essence labeled "male sexuality" is even more conservative today, because our situation as women has changed so radically. Modern social purists point to one set of changes. The rise of sexual consumerism and the growing power of the mass media to enforce conformity to sexual norms are debilitating for women's sexual freedom. As feminists, we are learning to be suspicious of a sexual politics that simply calls for "doing your own thing" and to ask whether women's desires are represented in these visions of sexual "freedom." We must not make the same mistake as the early twentieth-century sexual libertarians who believed that ending sexual inhibition in itself could save women. Instead, we have to continue to analyze how male supremacy and other forms of domination shape what we think of as "free" sexuality.

But there have been liberating developments as well that we can ill afford to ignore. Women have possibilities for sexual subjectivity and self-creation today that did not exist in the past. We have a vision of sexuality that is not exclusively heterosexual nor tied to reproduction. We have a much better physiological understanding of sexual feeling and a vision of ungendered parenting. We have several strong intellectual traditions for understanding the psychological and social formation of sexuality. Perhaps most important, we have today at least a chance at economic independence, the necessary material condition for women's sexual liberation. Finally, we have something women have never enjoyed before—a feminist past, a history of one hundred fifty years of feminist theory and praxis in the area of sexuality. This is a resource too precious to squander by not learning it, in all its complexity.

Notes

Because this paper grew out of material we have been thinking about for years, our intellectual debts are literally innumerable. For specific critical comments on this paper we want to thank Ann Ferguson, Vivian Gornick, Amber Hollibaugh,

Jill Lewis, Cora Kaplan, Esther Newton, Ann Snitow, Carol Vance, and Marilyn B. Young. About this paper we need to add, more than ever, that we alone are responsible for our conclusions. This paper was originally written for the Ninth Barnard Conference on the Scholar and the Feminist, New York City, April 1982.

1. These "homosocial" relationships are documented and analyzed in Lillian S. Faderman, *Surpassing the Love of Men: Romantic Friendship and Love between Women from the Renaissance to the Present* (New York: William Morrow & Co., 1981); Carroll Smith-Rosenberg, "The Female World of Love and Ritual: Relations between Women in Nineteenth-Century America," *Signs* 1 (Autumn 1975): 1–29; Blanche Wiesen Cook, "Female Support Networks and Political Activism: Lillian Wald, Crystal Eastman, Emma Goldman," *Chrysalis*, no. 3 (Autumn 1977): 43–61.

We distinguish here between behavior recognized as sexual by its actors and behavior not so recognized, aware that some historians will not agree. Furthermore, we are also emphasizing the importance of conscious sexual thought, theorizing, and politicizing for the feminist effort to transform women's sexual experience. We do so aware that, in the past decade, in an exciting renaissance of feminist historical scholarship, women's history scholars have chosen to focus more on behavior and culture than on political ideology. In the history of American feminism, for reasons that are undoubtedly important to explore, the initial focus for explicitly sexual politics was on the relations between women and men. The history and chronology of feminist conceptualization of what we today call lesbianism is different and we do not address it here, but Carroll Smith-Rosenberg and Esther Newton do so in their paper, "The Mythic Lesbian and the New Woman: Power, Sexuality, and Legitimacy," delivered at the Fifth Berkshire Conference on the History of Women, Poughkeepsie, New York, June 1981.

2. For instance, in 1913, a suffrage newspaper estimated that there were 15,000 to 20,000 prostitutes in New York City, who serviced 150,000 to 225,000 male customers daily; this would work out to roughly 1 out of every 100 females in all five boroughs and 1 out of every 10 males. See *Women's Political World*, 2 June 1913, 7. Using a more precise definition of prostitution, for example, women who supported themselves solely by commercial sex, a member of New York City's Vice Commission estimated less than one-half that number (Frederick Whitten to Mary Sumner Boyd, 17 Mar. 1916, National American Woman Suffrage Association Collection, New York Public Library), New York.

3. The historical literature on nineteenth-century and early-twentieth-century reformers' views of prostitution is extensive. The best recent study is Judith R. Walkowitz, *Prostitution and Victorian Society: Women, Class, and the State*

(Cambridge: Cambridge University Press, 1980); much less aware of issues concerning gender, see Mark Connelly, *Response to Prostitution in the Progressive Era* (Chapel Hill: University of North Carolina Press, 1980).

4. Marian S. Goldman, *Gold Diggers and Silver Miners: Prostitution and Social Life on the Comstock Lode* (Ann Arbor: University of Michigan Press, 1981), chap. 7. Also see Elizabeth Jameson, "Imperfect Unions: Class and Gender in Cripple Creek, 1894–1904," in *Class, Sex, and the Woman Worker*, ed. Milton Cantor and Bruce Laurie (Westport, Conn.: Greenwood, 1977).

5. *Black Women in White America: A Documentary History*, ed. Gerda Lerner (New York: Pantheon, 1972), 150–72; Cynthia Neverdon-Morton, "The Black Woman's Struggle for Equality in the South, 1895–1925," in *The Afro-American Woman: Struggle and Images*, ed. Sharon Harley and Rosalyn Terborg-Penn (Port Washington, N.Y.: Kennikat, 1978), 55–56.

After attending the 1914 convention of the National Association of Colored Women, white feminist Zona Gale wrote of Black women's effort to work "against the traffic in women (which I hope I shall never again call the 'white slave' traffic)." See "National Association of Colored Women's Biennial" *Life and Labor* 4 (September 1914): 264.

6. For examples of feminist abolitionists' focus on sexual abuse in their attacks on slavery, see Lydia Maria Child, "Appeal in Favor of That Class of Americans Called Africans," in *America through Women's Eyes*, ed. Mary R. Beard (New York: Macmillan, 1933), 164; and Elizabeth Cady Stanton, "Speech to the [1860] Anniversary of the American Anti-Slavery Society," in *Elizabeth Cady Stanton–Susan B. Anthony: Correspondence, Writings, Speeches*, ed. Ellen C. DuBois (New York: Schocken, 1981), 84.

The reluctance of white feminist abolitionists to acknowledge the possibility of affection and/or voluntary sex between Black women and white men can be seen in the initial response of Angelina and Sarah Grimké to the discovery that their brother had fathered a child by a slave woman. They assumed that Thomas Grimké had raped the woman; but their nephew, Archibald, who had been raised as a slave, objected that this was untrue and cast his parents and the circumstances of his birth in a sordid light.

7. Linda Gordon, *Woman's Body, Woman's Right: A Social History of Birth Control in America* (New York: Viking, 1976), chaps. 5 and 6; William L. O'Neill, *Everyone Was Brave: A History of Feminism in America* (Chicago: Quadrangle, 1971).

8. Barbara Leslie Epstein, *The Politics of Domesticity: Women, Evangelism, and Temperance in Nineteenth-Century America* (Middletown, Conn.: Wesleyan University Press, 1981), 100–14; Ruth Bordin, *Woman and Temperance: The Quest for Power and Liberty, 1873–1900* (Philadelphia: Temple University Press, 1981), 7, 26.

9. Walkowitz, chap. 3; Gordon, *Woman's Body, Woman's Right*, 106; E.M.

Sigsworth and T.J. Wyke, "A Study in Victorian Prostitution and Venereal Disease," in *Suffer and Be Still: Women in the Victorian Age*, ed. Martha Vicinus (Bloomington: Indiana University Press, 1972); Connelly, chap. 4.

10. For example, see Elizabeth Cady Stanton, "Speech to the McFarland-Richardson Protest Meeting," 1869, in *Elizabeth Cady Stanton–Susan B. Anthony*, 129; Clara Cleghorne Hoffman, "Social Purity," and Lucinda B. Chandler, "Marriage Reform," in *Report of the International Council of Women* (Washington, D.C.: R.H. Darby, 1888), 283, 285.

11. See Gordon, *Woman's Body, Woman's Right*, chap. 5, "Voluntary Motherhood."

12. Evidence of these problems abounds in case records of social service agencies used by Linda Gordon in her research on family violence, and in her paper, "Child-Saving and the Single Mother: A View from the Perspective of the Massachusetts Society for the Prevention of Cruelty to Children, 1880–1920."

13. For an exceptionally good account of the religious culture of nineteenth-century women and the conflicts it generated, see Kathryn Kish Sklar, *Catherine Beecher: A Study in American Domesticity* (New Haven: Yale University Press, 1973). The major nineteenth-century feminist opponent of women's religious traditions was Elizabeth Cady Stanton; see *Elizabeth Cady Stanton–Susan B. Anthony*, pt. 3.

14. In taking this approach, we are drawing on two recent schools of historical interpretation: feminist historians, for instance, Nancy Cott, Gerda Lerner, and Ann Douglas, who emphasize the role of women as active agents of cultural change but who have concentrated on domesticity rather than sexuality; and male theorists of sexuality, notably Michel Foucault, who regard sexuality as a socially constructed historically specific cultural system but leave women out of their accounts.

15. Ruth Rosen and Sue Davison, eds., *The Maimie Papers* (Old Westbury, N.Y.: The Feminist Press, 1977).

16. Estelle B. Freedman, *Their Sisters' Keepers: Women's Prison Reform in America, 1830–1930* (Ann Arbor: University of Michigan Press, 1981); Rosalind Rosenberg, *Beyond Separate Spheres: Intellectual Roots of Modern Feminism* (New Haven: Yale University Press, 1982), chap. 5 and p. 228. Sheldon Glueck and Eleanor T. Glueck, *Five Hundred Delinquent Women* (New York: Alfred A. Knopf, 1934), chap. 5; Mabel Ruth Fernald et al., *A Study of Women Delinquents in New York State* (New York: Century, 1920), chap. 12.

17. Jonathan Katz, *Gay American History: Lesbians and Gay Men in American History* (New York: Crowell, 1976), pt. 3; Erna O. Hellerstein et al., eds., *Victorian Women: A Documentary Account of Women's Lives in Nineteenth-Century England, France, and the United States* (Stanford: Stanford University Press, 1981), 185–89.

18. Carl Degler, *At Odds: Women and the Family in America from the Revolution to the Present* (New York: Oxford, 1980), 262–63. Beatrice Campbell, "Feminist

Sexual Politics: Now You See It, Now You Don't," *Feminist Review,* no. 5 (1981): 1–18. For a contemporary assessment of women's orgasms, see Shere Hite, *The Hite Report: A Nationwide Study on Female Sexuality* (New York: Macmillan, 1976). Despite conceptual problems, Hite's study points to women's continuing problems with having orgasms, at least in partnered sex.

19. David J. Pivar, *Purity Crusade: Sexual Morality and Social Control, 1868–1900* (Westport, Conn.: Greenwood, 1973); Degler, chap. 12; Walkowitz, chap. 12; Gordon, *Woman's Body, Woman's Right,* chap. 6; "Social Purity Session," *Report of the International Council of Women,* 251–84.

20. Epstein, 125–37; Bordin, chap. 6.

21. For a good summary of Black and immigrant family life, in contrast to middle-class families, see Degler, chap. 4 and passim. For specific evidence of poor women's weaker marital position vis-à-vis their husbands' sexual demands, see Eli S. Zaretsky, "Female Sexuality and the Catholic Confessional," Special Issue on Women—Sex and Sexuality, *Signs* 6 (Autumn 1980): 176–84; and Ruth Hall, ed., *Dear Dr. Stopes: Sex in the 1920s* (New York: Penguin, 1978), chaps. 1 ("The Lower Classes") and 2 ("The Upper Classes"). Note that we deliberately avoid expressing this difference as a contrast between middle- and working-class families. We suspect that greater male sexual dominance is not so much a matter of proletarian experience as it is of peasant authoritarian background and women's extreme economic dependence.

22. Carroll Smith-Rosenberg, "Beauty, the Beast, and the Militant Woman: A Case Study in Sex Roles and Social Stress in Jacksonian America," *American Quarterly* 23 (October 1971): 562–84; Mary P. Ryan, "The Power of Women's Networks: A Case Study of Female Moral Reform in Antebellum America," *Feminist Studies* 5 (Spring 1979): 66–85; Barbara J. Berg, *The Remembered Gate: Origins of American Feminism* (New York: Oxford, 1978).

23. Walkowitz, pt. 2; Pivar, chap. 2; Degler, 284–88; John Burnham, "Medical Inspection of Prostitutes in America in the Nineteenth Century: St. Louis Experiment and Its Sequel," *Bulletin of the History of Medicine* 45 (May–June 1971): 203–18.

24. Connelly, chap. 6; Pivar, 135–39; Walkowitz, Epilogue; Deborah Gorham, " 'The Maiden Tribute of Modern Babylon' Re-Examined: Child Prostitution and the Idea of Childhood in Late Victorian England," *Victorian Studies* 21 (Spring 1978): 353–79; Mari Jo Buhle, *Women and American Socialism, 1870–1920* (Urbana: University of Illinois Press, 1981), 253–56.

25. Jeanette Young Norton, "Women Builders of Civilization," *Women's Political World,* 1 Sept. 1913, 5.

26. On efforts to raise the age of consent, see Pivar, 139–46; Degler, 288–89; Gorham; Michael Pearson, *The Age of Consent: Victorian Prostitution and Its Enemies* (London: Newton Abbot, David & Charles, 1972).

27. Steven Schlossman and Stephanie Wallach, "The Crime of Precocious

Sexuality: Female Juvenile Delinquency in the Progressive Era," *Harvard Educational Review* 48 (February 1978): 65–94; Steven Schlossman, *Love and the American Delinquent* (Chicago: University of Chicago Press, 1977); William I. Thomas, *The Unadjusted Girl, with Cases and Standpoint for Behavior Analysis* (Boston: Little, Brown, 1923).

28. Leslie Fishbein, "Harlot or Heroine? Changing Views of Prostitution, 1870–1920," *Historian* 43 (December 1980): 23–35.

29. Willard, quoted in Pivar, 157.

30. This is one of the themes in *The Maimie Papers*. Wrote sometime prostitute Maimie Pinzer, "I would like to have women friends—but I can't have . . . I dreaded [they] would find out, perhaps inadvertently, something about me, and perhaps cut me, and I couldn't stand that" (p. 10).

31. On the free love movement in general, see Taylor Stoehr, *Free Love in America: A Documentary History* (New York: AMS Press, 1979); Hal D. Sears, *The Sex Radicals: Free Love in High Victorian America* (Lawrence: Regents Press of Kansas, 1977); Gordon, *Woman's Body, Woman's Right*, chaps. 5 and 6; Mary S. Marsh, *Anarchist Women, 1870–1920* (Philadelphia: Temple University Press, 1981), chap. 4; William Leach, *True Love and Perfect Union: Feminist Reform of Sex and Society* (New York: Basic Books, 1981), 82–83 and passim. We use the term "prosex" provisionally, in lieu of a more precise term which is yet to emerge.

32. Victoria C. Woodhull, *Tried as by Fire, or, the True and the False Socially: An Oration* (New York: Woodhull & Claflin, 1874).

33. *Elizabeth Cady Stanton–Susan B. Anthony*, 94–98, 185–87.

34. Alice Stockham, *Karezza: Ethics of Marriage* (Chicago: Alice B. Stockham, 1897), 22.

35. William L. O'Neill, *Divorce in the Progressive Era* (New York: Franklin Watts, 1973); *Elizabeth Cady Stanton–Susan B. Anthony*, passim; Leach, passim.

36. Gordon, *Woman's Body, Woman's Right*, chap. 5; James Reed, *From Private Vice to Public Virtue: The Birth Control Movement and American Society since 1830* (New York: Basic Books, 1978).

37. Caroline Ware, *Greenwich Village, 1920–1930* (Boston: Houghton Mifflin, 1935); Floyd Dell, *Love in Greenwich Village* (New York: George H. Doran, 1926); Rheta Childe Dorr, *A Woman of Fifty* (New York: Funk & Wagnalls, 1924); Judith Schwarz, *Radical Feminists of Heterodoxy, Greenwich Village, 1912–1940* (Lebanon, N.H.: New Victoria Publishers, 1982); Buhle, 257–68; Gordon, *Woman's Body, Woman's Right*, 189–99.

38. For lesbianism among the Greenwich Village feminists, see Schwarz, 30–31, 67–72. Also see Marion K. Sanders, *Dorothy Thompson: A Legend in Her Time* (Boston: Houghton Mifflin, 1973). Emma Goldman's relationship with Almeda Sperry is discussed in Katz, 523–29. Elizabeth Gurley Flynn's long relationship with the pioneering lesbian, Marie Equi, is traced in Rosalyn F. Baxandall's Introduction, "Selected Writings of Elizabeth Gurley Flynn,"

unpublished manuscript; there is also some suggestion that Flynn gave lesbian-ism a positive treatment in her original draft of *The Alderson Story: My Life as a Political Prisoner* (New York: International Publishers, 1972) but that Commu-nist party officials insisted that she rewrite the material and make her portrait more judgmental and negative (Baxandall, private communication to authors, 1982). The larger issue of repression of evidence of lesbianism is considered in Blanche Wiesen Cook, "The Historical Denial of Lesbianism," *Radical History Review* 5 (Spring/Summer 1979): 55–60.

39. Gordon, *Woman's Body, Woman's Right,* 359–80; note the *new* insistence on the importance of the vagina, replacing an older recognition of the role of the clitoris in women's experience of orgasm.

40. Faderman, pts. 2 and 3; Christina Simmons, "Compassionate Marriage and the Lesbian Threat," Special Issue on Lesbian History, *Frontiers* 4 (Fall 1979): 54–59; Nancy Sahli, "Smashing: Women's Friendships Before the Fall," *Chrysalis,* no. 8 (Summer 1979): 17–27.

41. For a major modern feminist study of rape, extremely important to our movement but marred by its ahistorical assumptions, see Susan Brownmiller, *Against Our Will: Men, Women, and Rape* (New York: Simon & Schuster, 1975).

5 Estelle Freedman

Separatism as Strategy: Female Institution Building and American Feminism, 1870–1930

Scholarship and Strategies

☐ The feminist scholarship of the past decade has often been concerned, either explicitly or implicitly, with two central political questions—the search for the origins of women's oppression and the formulation of effective strategies for combating patriarchy. Analysis of the former question helps us to answer the latter; or as anthropologist Gayle Rubin has wryly explained:

> If innate male aggression and dominance are at the root of female oppression, then the feminist program would logically require either the extermination of the offending sex, or else a eugenics project to modify its character. If sexism is a by-product of capitalism's relentless appetite for profit, then sexism would wither away in the advent of a successful socialist revolution. If the world historical defeat of women occurred at the hands of an armed patriarchal revolt, then it is time for Amazon guerrillas to start training in the Adirondacks.[1]

Another anthropologist, Michelle Zimbalist Rosaldo, provided an influential exploration of the origins-strategy questions in her 1974 theoretical overview of women's status.[2] Rosaldo argued that "universal sexual asymmetry" (the lower value placed on women's tasks and roles in all cultures) has been determined largely by the sexually defined split between domestic and public spheres. To oversimplify her thesis: the greater the social distance between women in the home and men in the public sphere, the greater the devaluation of women. The implications for feminist strategy become clear at the end of Rosaldo's

Reprinted, with changes, from *Feminist Studies* 5, no. 3 (Fall 1979): 513–29. © 1979 by Feminist Studies, Inc.

essay in which she says that greater overlap between domestic and public spheres means higher status for women. Thus to achieve an egalitarian future, with less separation of female and male, we should strive not only for the entrance of women into the male-dominated public sphere but also for men's entry into the female-dominated domestic world.

Rosaldo also discusses an alternative strategy for overcoming sexual asymmetry, namely, the creation of a separate women's public sphere; but she dismisses this model in favor of integrating domestic and public spheres. Nonetheless, the alternative strategy of "women's societies and African queens" deserves further attention.[3] Where female political leaders have power over their own jurisdiction (women), they also gain leverage in tribal policy. Such a separate sexual political hierarchy would presumably offer women more status and power than the extreme male-public/female-domestic split, but it would not require the entrance of each sex into the sphere dominated by the other sex. At certain historical periods, the creation of a public female sphere might be the only viable political strategy for women.

I would like to argue through historical analysis for the alternative strategy of creating a strong, public female sphere. A number of feminist historians have recently explored the value of the separate, although not necessarily public, female sphere for enriching women's historical experience. Carroll Smith-Rosenberg's research[4] has shown how close personal relationships enhanced the private lives of women in the nineteenth century. At the same time, private "sisterhoods," Nancy F. Cott has suggested, may have been a precondition for the emergence of feminist consciousness.[5] In the late nineteenth and early twentieth centuries, intimate friendships provided support systems for politically active women, as demonstrated by the work of both Blanche Wiesen Cook and Nancy Sahli.[6] However, the women's culture of the past—personal networks, rituals, and relationships—did not automatically constitute a political strategy. As loving and supportive as women's networks may have been, they could keep women content with a status that was inferior to that of men.

I do not accept the argument that female networks and feminist politics were incompatible. Rather, in the following synthesis of recent scholarship in American women's history, I want to show how the women's movement in the late nineteenth and early twentieth centuries provides an example of the "women's societies and African queens" strategy that Rosaldo mentioned. The creation of a separate, public female sphere helped mobilize women and gained political leverage in the larger society. A separatist political strategy, which I refer to as "female institution building," emerged from the middle-class women's culture of the nineteenth century. Its history suggests that in our own time, as well, women's culture can be integral to feminist politics.[7]

What Happened to Feminism?

□ My desire to restore historical consciousness about female separatism has both a personal and an intellectual motivation. As a feminist working within male-dominated academic institutions, I have realized that I could not survive without access to the feminist culture and politics that flourish outside of mixed institutions. How, I have wondered, could women in the past work for change within a men's world without having this alternative culture? This thought led me to the more academic questions. Perhaps they could not survive when those supports were not available; and perhaps this insight can help explain one of the most intriguing questions in American women's history: What happened to feminism after the suffrage victory in 1920?

Most explanations of the decline of women's political strength focus on either inherent weaknesses in suffragist ideology or on external pressures from a pervasively sexist society.[8] But when I survey the women's movement before suffrage passed, I am struck by the hypothesis that a major strength of U.S. feminism prior to 1920 was the separate female community that helped sustain women's participation in both social reform and political activism. Although the women's movement of the late nineteenth century contributed to the transformation of women's social roles, it did not reject a separate, unique female identity. Most feminists did not adopt the radical demands for equal status with men that originated at the Seneca Falls Convention of 1848. Rather, they preferred to retain membership in a separate female sphere, one which they did not believe to be inferior to men's sphere and one in which women could be free to create their own forms of personal, social, and political relationships. The achievements of feminism at the turn of the century came less through gaining access to the male domains of politics and the professions than in the tangible form of building separate female institutions.

The self-consciously female community began to disintegrate in the 1920s just as "new women" were attempting to assimilate into male-dominated institutions. At work, in social life, and in politics, I will argue, middle-class women hoped to become equals by adopting men's values and integrating into their institutions. A younger generation of women learned to smoke, drink, and value heterosexual relationships over female friendships in their personal lives. At the same time, women's political activity epitomized the process of rejecting women's culture in favor of men's promises of equality. The gradual decline of female separatism in social and political life precluded the emergence of a strong women's political bloc which might have protected and expanded the gains made by the earlier women's movement. Thus the erosion of women's culture may help account for the decline of public feminism in the decades after 1920. Without a constituency a movement cannot survive. The old feminist leaders lost their following when a new generation opted for assimilation in the naive hope of becoming men's equals overnight. To explore this hypothesis, I shall illustrate episodes of cultural and political separatism within American feminism in three periods: its historical roots prior to 1870, the institution building of the late nineteenth century, and the aftermath of suffrage in the 1920s.

Historical Roots of Separatism

☐ In nineteenth-century America, commercial and industrial growth intensified the sexual division of labor, encouraging the separation of women's and men's spheres. Although white males entered the public world of wage labor, business, the professions and politics, most white middle-class women remained at home where they provided the domestic, maternal, and spiritual care for their families and the nation. These women underwent intensive socialization into their roles as "true women." Combined with the restrictions on women which denied them access to the public sphere, this training gave American women an identity quite separate from men's. Women shared unique life experiences as daughters, wives, childbearers, childrearers, and moral guardians. They passed on their values and traditions to their female kin. They created what Smith-Rosenberg has called "The Female World of Love and Ritual," a world of homosocial networks that helped these women transcend the alienation of domestic life.[9]

The ideology of "true womanhood" was so deeply ingrained and so useful for preserving social stability in a time of flux that those few women who explicitly rejected its inequalities could find little support for their views. The feminists of the early women's rights movement were certainly justified in their grievances and demands for equal opportunity with men. The Seneca Falls Declaration of Sentiments and Resolutions of 1848, which called for access to education, property ownership, and political rights, has inspired many feminists since then, and the ridicule and denial of these demands have inspired our rage. But the equal rights arguments of the 1850s were apparently too radical for their own times.[10] Men would not accept women's entry into the public sphere, but more importantly, most women were not interested in rejecting their deeply rooted female identities. Both women and men feared the demise of the female sphere and the valuable functions it performed. The feminists, however, still hoped to reduce the limitations on women within their own sphere, as well as to gain the right of choice—of autonomy —for those women who opted for public rather than private roles.

Radical feminists such as Elizabeth Cady Stanton and Susan B. Anthony recognized the importance of maintaining the virtues of the female world while eliminating discrimination against women in public. As their political analysis developed at mid-century, they drew upon the concepts of female moral superiority and sisterhood, and they affirmed the separate nature of woman. At the same time, their disillusionment with even the more enlightened men of the times reinforced the belief that women had to create their own movement to achieve independence. The bitterness that resulted when most male abolitionists refused to support women's rights in the 1860s, and when they failed to include woman suffrage in the Fifteenth Amendment (as well as the inclusion of the term "male citizen" in the Fourteenth Amendment), alienated many women reformers. When Frederick Douglass proclaimed in defense that "this is the Negro's Hour," the more radical women's rights advocates followed Stanton and Anthony in withdrawing from the reform coalition and creating a separatist organization. Their National Woman Suffrage Association had women members and officers; supported a broad range of reforms, including changes in marriage and divorce laws; and published the short-lived journal, the *Revolution*. The radical path proved difficult, however, and the National Woman Suffrage Association merged in 1890 with the more moderate American Woman Suffrage Association. Looking back on their disappointment after the Civil War, Stanton and Anthony wrote prophetically in 1881:

> Our liberal men counselled us to silence during the war, and we were silent on our own wrongs; they counselled us to silence in Kansas and New York [in the suffrage referenda], lest we should defeat "Negro Suffrage," and threatened if we were not, we might fight the battle alone. We chose the latter, and were defeated. But standing alone we learned our power: we repudiated man's counsels forevermore; and solemnly vowed that there should never be another season of silence until woman had the same rights everywhere on this green earth, as man. . . .
>
> We would warn the young women of the coming generation against man's advice as to their best interests. . . . Woman must lead the way to her own enfranchisement. . . . She must not put her trust in man in this transition period, since while regarded as his subject, his inferior, his slave, their interests must be antagonistic.[11]

Female Institution Building

☐ The "transition period" that Stanton and Anthony invoked lasted from the 1870s to the 1920s. It was an era of separate female organization and institution building, the result, on the one hand, of the negative push of discrimination in the public, male sphere, and, on the other hand, of the positive attraction of the female world of close, personal relationships and domestic institutional structures. These dual origins characterized, for instance, one of the largest manifestations of "social feminism" in the late nineteenth century—the women's club movement.

The club movement illustrated the politicization of women's institutions as well as the limitations of their politics. The exclusion of women reporters from the New York Press Club in 1868 inspired the founding of the first women's club, Sorosis. The movement then blossomed in dozens and later hundreds of localities, until a General Federation of Women's Clubs formed in 1890. By 1910, it claimed over one million members. Although club social and literary activities at first appealed to traditional women who simply wanted to gather with friends and neighbors, by the turn of the century women's clubs had launched civic reform programs. Their activities served to politicize traditional women by forcing them to define themselves as citizens, not simply as wives and mothers. The clubs reflected the societal racism of the time, however, and the Black women who founded the National Association of Colored Women in 1896 turned their attention to the social and legal problems that confronted both Black women and men.[12]

The Woman's Christian Temperance Union (WCTU) had roots in the social feminist tradition of separate institution building. As Ellen Carol DuBois has argued, the WCTU appealed to late-nineteenth-century women because it was grounded in the private sphere—the home—and attempted to correct the private abuses against women, namely, intemperance and the sexual double standard.[13] Significantly, though, the WCTU, under Frances Willard's leadership, became a strong prosuffrage organization, committed to righting all wrongs against women, through any means, including the vote.

The women's colleges that opened in these same decades further attest to the importance of separate female institutions during this "transition period." Originally conceived as training grounds of piety, purity, and domesticity, the antebellum women's seminaries, such as Mary Lyon's Mt. Holyoke and Emma Willard's Troy Female Academy, laid the groundwork for the new collegiate institutions of the postwar era. When elite male institutions refused to educate women, the sister colleges of the East, like their counterparts elsewhere, took on the task themselves. In the process they encouraged intimate friendships and professional networks among educated women.[14] At the same time, liberal arts and science training provided tools for women's further development, and by their examples, female teachers inspired students to use their skills creatively. As Barbara Welter noted when she first described the "Cult of True Womanhood,"[15] submissiveness was always its weakest link. Like other women's institutions, the colleges could help subvert that element of the cult by encouraging independence in their students.

The most famous example of the impact of women's colleges may be Jane Addams's description of her experience at Rockford Seminary where she and other students were imbued with the mission of bringing their female values to bear on the entire society. Although Addams later questioned the usefulness of her intellectual training in meeting the challenges of the real world, other women did build upon academic foundations when increasingly, as reformers, teachers, physicians, social workers, and in other capacities, they left the home to enter public or quasi-public work. Between 1890 and 1920, the number of professional degrees granted to women increased 226 percent, at three times the rate of increase for men. Some of these professionals had attended separate female institutions such as the women's medical colleges in Philadelphia, New York, and Boston. The new female professionals often served women and children clients, in part because of the discrimination against their encroachment on men's domains, but also because they sincerely wanted to work with the traditional objects of their concern. As their skills and roles expanded, these women would demand the right to choose for themselves where and with whom they could work. This first generation of educated professional women became supporters of the suffrage movement in the early twentieth century, calling for full citizenship for women.

The process of redefining womanhood by the extension, rather than by the rejection, of the female sphere may be best illustrated by the settlement house movement. Although both women and men resided in and supported these quasi-public institutions, the high proportion of female participants and leaders (approximately three-fifths of the total), as well as the domestic structure and emphasis on service to women and children, qualify the settlements as female institutions. Mary P. Ryan has captured the link which these ventures provided between "true womanhood" and "new womanhood" in a particularly fitting metaphor: "Within the settlement houses, maternal sentiments were further sifted and leavened until they became an entirely new variety of social reform."[16] Thus did Jane Addams learn the techniques of the political world through her efforts to keep the neighborhood clean. So too did Florence Kelley of Hull House welcome appointment as chief factory inspector of Illinois, to protect women and children workers; and Julia Lathrop, another Hull House resident, entered the public sphere as director of the United States Children's Bureau; and one-time settlement resident Katherine Bement Davis moved from the superintendency of the Bedford Hills reformatory for women to become in 1914 the first female commissioner of corrections in New York City. Each of these women, and other settlement workers who moved on to professional and public office, eventually joined and often led branches of the National American Woman Suffrage Association.[17] They drew upon the networks of personal friends and professional allies that grew within separate female institutions when they waged their campaigns for social reform and for suffrage.

Separate female organizations were not limited to middle-class women. Recent histories have shown that groups hoping to bridge class lines between women existed within working-class or radical movements. In both the Women's Trade Union League and the National Consumers League, middle-class reformers strived for cooperation, rather than condescension, in their relationships with working women. Although in neither organization were they entirely successful, the Women's Trade Union League did provide valuable services in organizing women workers, many of whom were significant in its leadership. The efforts of the Consumers League, led by Florence Kelley, to improve working conditions through the use of middle-class women's buying power was probably less effective, but efforts to enact protective legislation for women workers did succeed. Members of both organizations turned to suffrage as one solution to the problems workers faced. Meanwhile, both in leftist organizations and in unions, women formed separate female organizations. Feminists within the Socialist party met in women's groups in the early twentieth century, while within the clothing trades, women workers formed separate local unions which survived until the mid-1920s.[18]

As a final example of female institution building, I want to compare two actual buildings—the Woman's Pavillion at the 1876 Centennial Exposition in Philadelphia, analyzed recently by Judith Paine, and the Woman's Building at the 1893 World Columbian Exposition in Chicago. I think that the origins and functions of each illustrate some of the changes that occurred in the women's movement in the time interval between those two celebrations.

Originally, the managers of the 1876 Centennial had promised "a sphere for woman's action and space for her work" within the main display areas. In return women raised more than $100,000 for the fair, at which point the management informed the Women's Centennial Executive Committee that there would not be any space for them in the main building. The women's response surprised the men: they raised money for a separate building, and although they hoped to find a woman architect to design it, there was no such professional at the time. From May through October 1876, the Woman's Pavillion displayed achievements in journalism, medicine, science, art, literature, invention, teaching, business, and social work. It included a library of books by women; an office that published a newspaper for women; and an innovative kindergarten annex, the first such day school in the country. Some radical feminists, however, boycotted the building. Elizabeth Cady Stanton claimed that the pavillion "was no true exhibit of woman's art" because it did not represent the product of industrial labor or protest the inequalities of "political slavery."[19]

By 1893, there was less hesitation about the need for a woman's building and somewhat less conflict about its functions. Congress authorized the creation of a Board of Lady Managers for the Columbian Commission, and the women quickly decided on a separate Woman's Building, to be designed by a woman architect chosen by nationwide competition. Contests were held to locate the best women sculptors, painters, and other artists to complete the designs of the building. The Lady Managers also planned and provided a Children's Building that offered nursery care for ten thousand young visitors to the fair. At this exposition, not only were women's artistic and professional achievements heralded but industrial organizations were "especially invited to make themselves known," and women's industrial work, as well as the conditions and wages for which they worked, were displayed. Feminists found this exhibit more agreeable; Antoinette Brown Blackwell, Julia Ward Howe, and Susan B. Anthony all attended, and Anthony read a paper written by Elizabeth Cady Stanton at one of the women's symposia. The Board of Lady Managers fought hard to combine their separate enterprise with participation in the rest of the fair. They demanded equal representation of women judges for the exhibitions and equal consideration of women's enterprises in all contests.[20] Although they had to compromise on some goals, their efforts are noteworthy as an indication of a dual commitment to separate female institutions—but only if they had equal status within the society at large.

The Political Legacy

□ The separate institution building of the late nineteenth century rested on a belief in women's unique identity which had roots in the private female sphere of the early nineteenth century. Increasingly, however, as its participants entered a public female world, they adopted the more radical stance of feminists such as Stanton and Anthony who had long called for an end to political discrimination against women.

The generation that achieved suffrage, then, stood on the border of two worlds, each of which contributed to its ideology and politics. Suffragists argued that women needed the vote to perform their traditional tasks—to protect themselves as mothers and to exert their moral force on society. Yet they also argued for full citizenship and waged a successful female-controlled political campaign to achieve it.

The suffrage movement succeeded by appealing to a broad constituency —mothers, workers, professionals, reformers—with the vision of the common concerns of womanhood. The movement failed, however, by not extending fully the political strengths of woman bonding. For one thing, the leadership allowed some members to exploit popular racist and nativist sentiments in their prosuffrage arguments, thus excluding most Black and immigrant women from a potential feminist coalition. They also failed to recognize that the bonds that held the constituency together were not "natural" but social and political. The belief that women would automatically use the vote to the advantage of their sex overlooked both the class and racial lines that separated women. It underestimated the need for continued political organization so that their interests might be united and realized.

Unfortunatley, the rhetoric of equality that became popular among women and men (with the exception of the National Woman's Party) just after the passage of the Suffrage Amendment in 1920 subverted the women's movement by denying the need for continued feminist organization. Of course, external factors significantly affected the movement's future, including the new Freudian views of women, the growth of a consumer economy that increasingly exploited women's sexuality, and the repression of radicalism and reform in general after World War I.[21] But, at the same time, many women, seemingly oblivious that these pressures necessitated further separate organizing, insisted on striving for integration into a male world—sexually, professionally, and politically.

Examples of this integrationist approach can be found in the universities, the workplace, and politics. In contrast to an earlier generation, the women who participated in the New York World's Fair of 1937 had no separate building. Woman, the Fair Bulletin explained, "will not sit upon a pedestal, not be segregated, isolated; she will fit into the life of the Exposition as she does into life itself—never apart, always a part." The part in this world's fair, however, consisted primarily of fashion, food, and vanity fair.[22] In the universities, the success of the first generation of female academics did not survive past the 1920s, not only because of men's resistance, but, as Rosalind Rosenberg has explained, "Success isolated women from their culture of origin and placed them in an alien and often hostile community." Many academics who cut off their ties to other women "lost their old feminine supports but had no other supports to replace them."[23]

The lessons of women's politics in the 1920s are illustrated by the life of one woman, Emily Newell Blair, who learned firsthand the pitfalls of rejecting a separatist basis for feminism.[24] Blair's life exemplified the transformation of women's roles at the turn of the century. Educated at a woman's college, Goucher, this Missouri-born, middle-class woman returned to her hometown to help support her family until she married and created her own home. Between 1900 and 1910 she bore two children, supported her husband's career, and joined in local women's club activities. In her spare time, Blair began writing short stories for ladies' magazines. Because she found the work, and particularly the income, satisfying, she became a free-lance writer. At this point, the suffrage movement revived in Missouri, and Blair took over state publicity, editing the magazine, *Missouri Woman,* and doing public relations. Then, in World War I, she expanded her professional activities further by serving on the Women's Council of the U.S. Council of National Defense. These years of training in writing, feminist organizing, and public speaking served Blair well when suffrage passed and she entered politics.

In 1920, women faced three major political choices. They could become a separate feminist political force through the National Woman's Party, which few did; they could follow the moderates of the NAWSA into the newly formed, nonpartisan League of Women Voters, concentrating on citizen education and good government; or they could join the mainstream political parties. Emily Newell Blair chose the last and rose through the Democratic party organization to become national vice-chair of the party in the 1920s.

Blair built her political life and her following on the belief that the vote had made women the political equals of men. Thus, the surest path to furthering women's goals was through participation in the party structure. Having helped to found the League of Women Voters, Blair then rejected nonpartisanship and urged women not to vote as women but as citizens. In a 1922 lecture on "What Women May Do with the Ballot," Blair argued that "reactions to political issues are not decided by sex but by intellect and emotion...." Although she believed that lack of political experience and social training made women differ from men temporarily, she expected those differences to be eliminated after a few years of political activity. To hasten women's integration into the mainstream of party politics, Blair set up thirty "schools of democracy" to train the new voters during the early twenties, as well as more than one thousand women's clubs. Her philosophy, she claimed, was one of "boring from within." Blair rejected the sex-conscious feminists of the National Woman's Party and those who wanted "woman cohesiveness." Although she favored the election of women, she wanted them to be chosen not as women but as politicians. "Give women time," she often repeated, and they would become the equals of men in politics.

By the late 1920s, however, women had not gained acceptance as men's political equals, and Blair's views changed significantly. Once she had claimed that the parties did not discriminate against women, as shown by her own powerful position. After she retired from party office in 1928, however, Blair acknowledged that the treatment of women by the parties had deteriorated since the years immediately after suffrage passed. As soon as male politicians realized that there was no strong female voting bloc or political organization, they refused to appoint or elect powerful women, and a "strong masculine prejudice against women in politics" surfaced. Now they chose women for party office who seemed easiest to manage or who were the wives of male officeholders.

By 1931, Blair's former optimism had turned to disillusionment. She felt herself "ineffective in politics as a feminist," a term that she began to use positively. Blair realized that women could not command political power and the respect of their male colleagues unless, like the suffrage leaders, they had a visible, vocal following. "Unfortunately for feminism," she confessed, "it was agreed to drop the sex line in politics. And it was dropped by the women." In the pages of the *Woman's Journal*, Blair called for a revival of feminism in the form of a new politics that would seek to put more women into office. Reversing her former stance, she claimed that *women* voters should back *women* candidates, and use a *women's* organization to do so. They could remain in the parties but should form "a new organization of feminists devoted to the task of getting women into politics."

The development of Emily Newell Blair's feminist consciousness may have been unique for her time, but it is a familiar process among educated and professional women today. Having gained access to formerly male institutions, but still committed to furthering women's struggles, today's "new women" are faced with political choices not dissimilar to the generation that achieved suffrage. The bitterness of Stanton and Anthony in their advice to the younger generation in 1881, and the strategy that Emily Newell Blair presented in 1931, may serve as lessons for the present.

The Lessons of Separatism

□ The strength of female institutions in the late nineteenth century and the weaknesses of women's politics after the passage of the Suffrage Amendment suggest to me that the decline of feminism in the 1920s can be attributed in part to the devaluation of women's culture in general and of separate female institutions in particular. When women tried to assimilate into male-dominated institutions, without securing feminist social, economic, or political bases, they lost the momentum and the networks which had made the suffrage movement possible. Women gave up many of the strengths of the female sphere without gaining equally from the man's world they entered.

This historical record has important implications for the women's movement today. It becomes clearer, I think, why the separate, small women's group, organized either for consciousness raising or political study and action, has been effective in building a grass-roots movement over the past ten years. The groups helped to reestablish common bonds long veiled by the retreat from women's institutions into privatized families or sexually integrated, but male-dominated, institutions. The groups encouraged the reemergence of female networks and a new women's culture which in turn have given rise to female institution building—women's centers, health collectives, political unions, even new women's buildings, like the ones in Los Angeles and San Francisco.

The history of separatism also helps explain why the politics of lesbian feminism has been so important in the revival of the women's movement. Lesbian feminism, by affirming the primacy of women's relationships with each other and by providing an alternative feminist culture, forced many nonlesbians to reevaluate their relationships with men, male institutions, and male values. In the process, feminists have put to rest the myth of female dependence on men and rediscovered the significance of woman bonding. I find it personally gratifying that the lesbian feminist concept of the woman-identified woman[25] has historical roots in the female friendships, networks, and institutions of the nineteenth century. The historical sisterhood, it seems to me, can teach us a great deal about putting women first, whether as friends, lovers, or political allies.

I find two kinds of political lessons in the history of the separatist trend. In the past, one of the limitations of separate female institutions was that they were often the only places for women to pursue professional or political activities, while men's institutions retained the power over most of the society. Today it is crucial to press for feminist presence both outside and within the bastions of male dominance, such as politics, the universities, the professions, the unions. But it is equally important for the women within mixed institutions to create female interest groups and support systems. Otherwise, token women may be co-opted into either traditionally deferential roles, or they will assimilate through identification with the powers that be. In the process, these women will lose touch with their feminist values and constituencies, as well as suffer the personal costs of tokenism. Thus, in universities we need both to strengthen our women's centers and women's studies programs and to form women's groups among faculty as well as students. In all of our workplaces we need women's caucuses to secure and enlarge our gains. And unlike much of the movement in the past, we need to undertake the enormous task of building coalitions of women's groups from all classes, races, and cultures.

I argue for a continuation of separatism not because the values, culture, and politics of the two sexes are biologically, irreversibly distinct but because the historical and contemporary experiences that have created a unique female culture remain both salient for and compatible with the goal of sexual equality. Our common identities and heritage as women can provide enormous personal and political strength as long as we claim the power to define what women can be and what female institutions can achieve. I argue for renewed female institution building at this point in the contemporary women's movement because I fear that many feminists—faced with the isolation of personal success or dismayed by political backlash—may turn away from the separate women's politics that have achieved most of our gains in the past decade. And I argue as well for both greater respect for women's culture among political feminists and greater political engagement on the part of cultural feminists because we now face both external resistance and internal contradictions that threaten to divide our movement.

The contradictions faced by contemporary feminists are those experienced by an oppressed group—in this case, women—which needs both to affirm the value of its own culture and to reject the past oppression from which that culture in part originated.[26] To survive as a movement we must avoid two kinds of pitfalls. In this essay, I have concentrated on the dangers of rejecting our culture through individualist integration of the kind that undermined feminism after the first wave of political and educational progress. The other pitfall is that of embracing our culture too uncritically, to the point of identifying with the sources of our own oppression. Rayna Rapp has warned that "as we excavate and legitimize women's history, social organization, and cultural forms, we must not allow our own need for models of strong female collectivities to blind us to the dialectic of tradition"[27] in which women are both supported and constrained. Although we must be self-critical of women's culture and strive to use female institutions to combat inequality, not to entrench it, at the same time, we must not be self-hating of that which is female as we enter a world dominated by men. Even as women retrain in the skills that men once monopolized—in trades, professions, politics—we should not forsake, but rather we should cherish, both the values and institutions that were once women's only resources. Even if the Equal Rights Amendment someday legally mandates equality, in the meantime, and for some time thereafter, the female world and separatist politics will still serve the interests of women.

Notes

I would like to thank Irene Diamond for inspiring me to write about history and strategy; Mary Felstiner for the perceptive comments she and members of the graduate seminar in women's studies at San Francisco State University offered; the members of the women's faculty group at Stanford University and the members of the history of sexuality study group for forcing me to refine my thinking; and both Yolaida Durán and John D'Emilio for support and criticism as I rewrote this essay.

1. Gayle Rubin, "The Traffic in Women: Notes on the 'Political Economy' of Sex," in *Toward an Anthropology of Women*, ed. Rayna R. [app] Reiter (New York and London: Monthly Review Press, 1975), 157–58.

2. Michelle Zimbalist Rosaldo, "Woman, Culture, and Society: A Theoretical Overview," in *Woman, Culture, and Society*, ed. Michelle Zimbalist Rosaldo and Louise Lamphere (Stanford: Stanford University Press, 1974), 36: "Women's status will be lowest in those societies where there is a firm differentiation between domestic and public spheres of activity and where women are isolated from one another and placed under a single man's authority in the home." For a reconsideration of her views, see M. Z. Rosaldo, "The Use and Abuse of Anthropology: Reflections on Feminism and Cross-Cultural Understanding" *Signs* 5 (Spring 1980): 389–417.

3. Rosaldo, "Theoretical Overview," 37–38. Rosaldo lists women's trading societies, church clubs, "or even political organizations" and cites both the Iroquois and West African societies in which "women have created fully

articulated social hierarchies of their own." This strategy differs significantly from the argument that women's domestic sphere activities are a source of power. On the recent anthropological literature on domestic and public, see Rayna Rapp, "Review Essay: Anthropology," *Signs* 4 (Spring 1979): 505, 508–13.

4. Carroll Smith-Rosenberg, "The Female World of Love and Ritual: Relations between Women in Nineteenth-Century America," *Signs* 1 (Autumn 1975): 1–29.

5. Nancy F. Cott, *The Bonds of Womanhood: "Women's Sphere" in New England, 1780–1835* (New Haven: Yale University Press, 1977).

6. Blanche Wiesen Cook, "Female Support Networks and Political Activism: Lillian Wald, Crystal Eastman, Emma Goldman," *Chrysalis*, no. 3 (Autumn 1977): 43–61; and Nancy Sahli, "Smashing: Women's Relationships before the Fall," *Chrysalis*, no. 8 (Summer 1979): 17–27.

7. Feminist historians need clear definitions of women's culture and women's politics to avoid such divisions between the personal and political. Women's culture can exist at both private and public levels. Women's politics, too, can be personal (intrafamilial, through friendship and love, for example) as well as public (the traditional definition of politics). The question of when women's culture and politics are *feminist* has yet to be fully explored. At this time, I would suggest that any female-dominated activity that places a positive value on women's social contributions, provides personal support, and is not controlled by antifeminist leadership has feminist political potential. This is as true for the sewing circle, voluntary civic association, and women's bar as for the consciousness-raising group, coffeehouse, or women's center. Whether that potential is realized depends in part on historical circumstances, such as the overall political climate, the state of feminist ideology and leadership, and the strength of antifeminist forces. Women's culture can remain "prefeminist," as in the case of some nineteenth-century female reform associations that valued women's identity as moral guardians but did not criticize the status quo. When the group experience leads to insights about male domination, however, the reformers often become politicized as feminists. Women's culture can also become reactionary, for instance, when women join together under the control of antifeminist leadership, as in the case of Nazi women's groups in prewar Germany or right-wing movements in America today. The more autonomous the group, the more likely it is to foster feminist political consciousness. Cott raises some of these questions for the early nineteenth century in her conclusion to *The Bonds of Womanhood*. On moral reformers, see Carroll Smith-Rosenberg, "Beauty, the Beast, and the Militant Woman: A Case Study in Sex Roles and Social Stress in Jacksonian America," *American Quarterly* 23 (October 1971): 562–84; and Mary P. Ryan, "The Power of Women's Networks: A Case Study of Female Moral Reform in Antebellum America," *Feminist Studies* 5 (Spring 1979): 66–85. Jo Freeman's discussion of the communications network

as a precondition for the rebirth of feminism in the twentieth century is also relevant. See Freeman, *The Politics of Women's Liberation* (New York and London: Longman, 1975).

8. These theories are surveyed in Estelle B. Freedman, "The New Woman: Changing Views of Women in the 1920s," *Journal of American History* 61 (September 1974): 372–93.

9. Smith-Rosenberg, "The Female World of Love and Ritual." On changing ideologies of womanhood, see Mary Ryan, *Womanhood in America: From Colonial Times to the Present* (New York: Franklin Watts, 1979); and Gerda Lerner, "The Lady and the Mill Girl: Changes in the Status of Women in the Age of Jackson," *American Studies Journal* 10 (Spring 1968): 5–15.

10. See Ellen Carol DuBois, "The Radicalism of the Woman Suffrage Movement: Notes Toward the Reconstruction of Nineteenth-Century Feminism," *Feminist Studies* 3 (Fall 1975): 63–71. On opposition to women's rights from a "traditional" woman, see Kathryn Kish Sklar, *Catherine Beecher: A Study in American Domesticity* (New Haven: Yale University Press), 266–67.

11. *History of Woman Suffrage,* reprinted in *The Feminist Papers: From Adams to de Beauvoir,* ed. Alice Rossi (New York: Bantam Books, 1973), 457–58. On the history of the women's rights movement, see Ellen Carol DuBois, *Feminism and Suffrage: The Emergence of an Independent Women's Movement in America, 1848–1860* (Ithaca: Cornell University Press, 1978); and Eleanor Flexner, *Century of Struggle: The Woman's Rights Movement in the United States* (New York: Atheneum, 1970).

12. William O'Neill, ed., *The Woman Movement: Feminism in the United States and England* (Chicago: Quadrangle Books, 1969), 47–54; and Gerda Lerner, ed., *Black Women in White America* (New York: Vintage, 1972), chap. 8.

13. DuBois, "Radicalism of the Woman Suffrage Movement," 69.

14. On personal networks and loving relationships in the women's colleges, see Judith Schwarz, "Yellow Clover: Katharine Lee Bates and Katharine Coman," *Frontiers* 4 (Spring 1979): 59–67; and Anna Mary Wells, *Miss Marks and Miss Woolley* (Boston: Houghton-Mifflin, 1978).

15. Barbara Welter, "The Cult of True Womanhood, 1820–1860," *American Quarterly* 18 (Summer 1966): 150–74.

16. Ryan, *Womanhood in America,* 229.

17. For biographical data on these and other reformers, see the entries in *Notable American Women, 1607–1950,* ed. Edward T. James, Janet Wilson James, and Paul S. Boyer (Cambridge: Harvard University Press, 1971).

18. On women in labor and radical movements, see Nancy Schrom Dye, "Feminism or Unionism? The New York Women's Trade Union League and the Labor Movement," and Robin Miller Jacoby, "The Women's Trade Union League and American Feminism," in *Feminist Studies* 3 (Fall 1975): 111–40; Allis Rosenberg Wolfe, "Women, Consumerism, and the National Consumers League in the Progressive Era, 1900–1923," *Labor History* 16 (Summer 1975): 378–92;

Mary Jo Buhle, "Women and the Socialist Party, 1901–1914," *Radical America* 4 (February 1970): 36–55; and Sherna Gluck, "The Changing Nature of Women's Participation in the American Labor Movement, 1900–1940s: Case Studies from Oral History (paper presented at the Southwest Labor History Conference, Tempe, Ariz., 5 Mar 1977).

19. Judith Paine, "The Women's Pavillion of 1876," *Feminist Art Journal* 4 (Winter 1975–76): 5–12, and *The Woman's Building, Chicago, 1893/The Woman's Building, Los Angeles, 1973* (Los Angeles, 1975).

20. Bertha Honoré Palmer, "The Growth of the Woman's Building," in *Art and Handicraft in the Woman's Building of the World's Columbian Exposition,* ed. Maud Howe Elliott (New York, 1893), 11–12.

21. See Ryan, *Womanhood in America,* for an exploration of these trends.

22. The New York World's Fair Bulletin 1 (December 1937): 20–21; the *New York City World's Fair Information Manual,* 1939, index. Amy Swerdlow kindly shared these references and quotations about the 1937 fair from her own research on women in the world's fairs.

23. Rosalind Rosenberg, "The Academic Prism: The New View of American Women," in *Women of America: A History,* ed. Carol Ruth Berkin and Mary Beth Norton (Boston: Houghton Mifflin, 1979), 318–38.

24. The following account of Blair is drawn from research for a biographical essay that appeared in *The Dictionary of American Biography,* supp., vol. 5 (New York: Charles Scribner, 1977), 61–63. For examples of her writings, see "What Women May Do with the Ballot" (Philadelphia, 1922); "Boring from Within," *Woman Citizen* 12 (July 1927): 49–50; "Why I Am Discouraged about Women in Politics," *Woman's Journal* 6 (January 1931): 20–22.

25. Radicalesbians, "The Woman-Identified Woman," *Notes from the Third Year: Women's Liberation* (reprinted in *Radical Feminism,* ed. Anne Koedt, Ellen Levine, and Anita Rapone [New York: Quadrangle, 1973] 240–45); Lucia Valeska, "The Future of Female Separatism," *Quest* 2 (Fall 1975): 2–16; Charlotte Bunch, "Learning from Lesbian Separatism," in *Lavender Culture,* eds Karla Jay and Allen Young (New York: Jove Books, 1978), 433–44.

26. A clear example of this contradiction is the contemporary gay subculture, which is both a product of the historical labeling of homosexuality as deviance and a source of personal affirmation and political consciousness. I am grateful to the San Francisco Gay History Project study group for drawing this parallel between the conflicts in women's and gay politics.

27. Rapp, 513.

Women in the 1920s'
Ku Klux Klan Movement

☐ In 1920, women won the right to vote, culminating a seventy-two-year struggle for greater access to the political sphere. Yet, women's politics changed in another way in the 1920s. When women gained the franchise, the issue that had united women with different backgrounds and politics disappeared. Women's political goals and ideologies had grown more diverse even before the ratification of the Nineteenth Amendment as the separate gender spheres of the nineteenth century dissolved. The extent of this diversity became even more clear without the unifying cause of suffrage. Cleavages of class, race, ethnicity, and region, constant features of women's politics in the United States, now increasingly eroded gender unity in political goals.[1]

The ways in which women became involved in postsuffrage politics were etched in the struggle for the franchise. Ideas born in the battle for the Nineteenth Amendment affected not only the activists but also their descendants and women who had refrained from politics. One outcome—the one most familiar in the popular imagery of the postsuffrage period—was the participation of women in progressive reform movements. Women whose belief in equality was nourished in the drive for the franchise found a logical extension of their suffrage politics in movements for social and urban reform. Women's votes supported candidates who favored maternity and infancy protection and opposed lynching and child labor. Female reformers of the 1920s led the fight for better schools, cleaner cities, more equitable labor relations, and honest politics.[2] Another outcome of the franchise, however, was the involvement of postsuffrage women in reactionary and right-wing political movements. If most women worked for, or were influenced by, the fight for women's suffrage because of its emphasis on political equity, a

Reprinted, with changes, from *Feminist Studies* 17, no. 1 (Spring 1991): 57–77. © 1991 by Feminist Studies, Inc.

significant minority found in the quest for votes for women an opportunity to solidify the political power of whites and native-born citizens. These women envisioned political equity between women and men as an issue relevant only within dominant racial and ethnic groups, as seen, for example, in campaigns to extend the franchise to white women.[3] Such racist and anti-immigrant tendencies within the movement for women's suffrage shared aspects of the political vision of nationalistic, militaristic, and racial supremacist movements in the 1910s and 1920s. Women who interpreted the struggle for women's votes through the prism of racial, ethnic, and class privilege thus experienced an apparently easy transition from women's suffrage to the plethora of white supremacist, nativist, and racist political movements of the early twentieth century.[4]

One of the largest and most influential right-wing women's organizations of the immediate postsuffrage period was the Women of the Ku Klux Klan (WKKK). From 1923 to 1930, women poured into the Klan movement to oppose immigration, racial equality, Jewish-owned businesses, parochial schools, and "moral decay." The mobilization of women into the 1920s' Klan was the product of a racist, nationalistic zeal, which also motivated men to join the Ku Klux Klan, combined with a specific, gendered notion of the preservation of family life and women's rights. The women's Klan copied the regalia, militarism, hierarchy, and political stances of the male Ku Klux Klan but insisted that they were no mere appendage of the KKK, claiming autonomy and a special mission for Klanswomen. They used the KKK's call for supremacy of white, native-born Protestants and interpreted it in a gender-specific way, as a vehicle to protect women and children, to preserve home and family life, and to demonstrate newly won women's rights. A 1923 advertisement recruited women for the WKKK, using "American" rights and "pure womanhood" as code words for racial and national privilege:

To the American Women of Washington: Are you interested in the welfare of our Nation? As an enfranchised woman are you interested in Better Government? Do you not wish for the protection of Pure Womanhood? Shall we uphold the sanctity of the American Home? Should we not interest ourselves in Better Education for our children? Do we not want American teachers in our American schools? IT IS POSSIBLE FOR ORGANIZED PATRIOTIC WOMEN TO AID IN STAMPING OUT THE CRIME AND VICE THAT ARE UNDERMINING THE MORALS OF OUR YOUTH. The duty of the American Mother is greater than ever before.[5]

The appeal of the Klan to large numbers of women in the 1920s raises more general questions about how and why women become involved in movements of political protest. A particularly intriguing aspect of the 1920s' WKKK was its complex political ideology. Klanswomen carried into their struggle against Blacks, Jews, Catholics, labor radicals, socialists, Mormons, and immigrants a belief in gender equality among white Protestants in politics, work, and wages. Such an ideology cannot be understood within theoretical frameworks that assume a bifurcation between progressive and proequality movements, on the one hand, and conservative, antifeminist, and "profamily" movements, on the other. The study of 1920s' Klanswomen is intended to contribute to an understanding of the varying, often contradictory, ideologies that underlie women's commitment to political movements, especially those of the political Right.[6]

Feminist scholarship on women in contemporary and historical right-wing movements suggests two additional issues that can be explored through an analysis of the 1920s' women's Klan movement. One issue is that of motivation. Did women enter the Klan for the same economic, ideological, and political reasons that brought men into the Klan? Or did women and men differ in the motivations, or the political agendas, that led to Klan membership? Research on other movements suggests different possibilities for women's mobilization into the Klan. Scholars of U.S. antifeminist movements, for example, argue that women's participation in politics, ranging from Victorian-era social purity to modern anti-abortion and anti-ERA movements, has been motivated by a complex mixture of defending and resenting male privilege and female vulnerability in the economic and social spheres. Men's participation in these movements, however, reflects a simpler assessment of collective male self-interest. However, the little research that exists on women in right-wing movements other than those with antifeminist agendas suggests that these women may not differ significantly in ideology or political motivation from their male counterparts on the Right.[7] The 1920s' WKKK, which supported both traditional right-wing politics and a certain degree of gender equality, provides an opportunity to examine gender differences in political motivation in a large and significant movement of the Right.

A second issue concerns political activity. What was the nature of women's involvement in the 1920s' Klan movement? Did women participate, as did men, in terroristic and violent activities, or were women's activities more peaceful, reformist, or "legitimate" than men's Klan activities? There is virtually no research on violent right-wing women's political activity in the United States with which to compare the WKKK. Is this, as traditional accounts imply, because women associated with the major reactionary and terroristic movements of the

Right in U.S. history have played insignificant roles in these movements? Historians of the various Klan movements, for example, typically dismiss women's Klan activities as incidental, auxiliary, or merely cultural screens behind which men carried out the real politics of the Klan. Or, as feminist theory suggests, are women's political activities on the far Right undocumented precisely because, as women's activities, they have been invisible or seen as trivial by most historians?[8] Traditional accounts of the Klan movement draw vivid images of episodic, deadly violence perpetrated by gangs of masked and hooded men. By defining the Klan movement through this image of male marauders, women disappear, becoming little more than peripheral onlookers to the crimes and violence of Klansmen. Such a picture distorts both women's role in the Klan and the reality of the Klan itself. If we take women's politics seriously, we find that in the 1920s, the activities of Klanswomen, commonly dismissed as inconsequential and apolitical, were responsible for some of the Klan's most destructive, vicious effects.

I explore these issues through analysis of the 1920s' Klan movement, using primary archival documents from the WKKK; the KKK; and from participants, observers, and critics of the Klan movement. I use documents from the national organizations of the WKKK and KKK to analyze the appeal of the Klan to women and the motivations that drew women into the Klan movement. The extensive propaganda machine of the 1920s' Klan left a considerable body of public documentation in the form of newspapers, pamphlets, and books, while surviving internal Klan letters, speeches, and memorandums preserve a sense of the ideology and goals of the organization.

To understand the specific processes of recruitment and activities of the WKKK, I also examine the large and powerful WKKK chapter in Indiana. With a membership estimated at 250,000 (half of Indiana's Klan membership of half a million), the Indiana WKKK was probably the largest state organization of Klanswomen. The Indiana WKKK was large but not unique; WKKK chapters existed in every state, with particularly strong chapters in Ohio, Pennsylvania, and Arkansas, in addition to Indiana. To assess why women joined the Klan in Indiana it is important to understand what kinds of women became Klanswomen. Unfortunately, as a secret organization, the Klan closely guarded, and later destroyed, its membership roster. No comprehensive or even partial listing of Indiana Klanswomen survives. My analysis of the composition of the women's Klan, therefore, is based on more indirect methods. Women are considered Klan members if they used their names publicly as leaders or spokeswomen for the Indiana WKKK, if their Klan membership was reported in the influential anti-Klan papers, *Tolerance* (Chicago) or the *Post-Democrat* (Muncie, Indiana), or if their membership was publicized at their deaths by public funeral ceremonies performed by fellow Klanswomen. I then traced the personal histories of these Klanswomen through local newspapers, genealogies, obituaries, county histories, and other biographical sources. In addition, I examined propaganda materials written and distributed by the Indiana WKKK; archival data from the women's and men's Klan in Indiana; non-Klan and anti-Klan accounts of Klan activity; and personal recollections of participants, observers, and opponents of the Klan in Indiana.

Background to the 1920s' Klan

☐ The Klan movement of the 1920s was the second historical occurrence of the Ku Klux Klan. The first Klan was organized in the rural South after the Civil War to assert claims of white, Southern supremacy during Reconstruction; it collapsed in the 1870s. The Klan lay dormant until the early twentieth century when it was reborn as a movement of white "100 percent American" Protestants, drawing strength from small towns and rural areas in the North, Midwest, and West as well as in the South.[9] This second wave of the Klan grew dramatically in the early 1920s, only to collapse precipitously in the late 1920s. In over a little more than a decade, the Klan managed to enroll an estimated three to six million persons in a crusade for a white, native-born Protestant America. A number of factors influenced the dramatic reemergence of the Klan movement in the 1920s. These included a public explosion of anti-Black racism and white supremacist sentiments that followed upon the postwar migration of Blacks from the South to the North, the nationalist hatred of immigrants and political "radicals" fueled by World War I propaganda, and the increase in bigotry and intolerance that accompanied the rise of religious and political fundamentalism.

Unlike its predecessor, the 1920s' Klan kept its organization in full public view, even as individual identities were safeguarded. The Klan movement built upon the network of lodges, Protestant churches, and clubs that structured daily life for many small-town and urban Protestant families. It recruited members in schools, clubs, and churches and used ministers and prominent local leaders as recruitment agents. In turn, the Klan built its own network of social ties. Numerous Klan newspapers and magazines were distributed across the United States. Klan lectures, rallies, and gatherings provided a focus for Protestant social life, and the Klan held out the promise of a Klan college to teach the children of loyal Klan parents. In a period of rapid change and great geographical mobility, the Klan positioned itself as the guarantor of the old virtues and the entrée into a cohesive social and cultural network.[10]

Some of the Klan's rapid growth can be attributed to the local specificity of its campaigns. Klan chapters had substantial autonomy to address community issues and fashion appropriate scapegoats—from Mormons in Utah to Catholics in the Midwest, Jews in the Northeast and Blacks in the South. Although a national ideology of anti-Catholicism, anti-Semitism, and anti-Black racism and conservative moralism always underlay Klan actions, recruits varied widely in their commitments to these. Local chapters, too, varied in their activities, which ranged from electoral politics, lobbying, and cultural activities, to terrorism, vigilantism, and violence.[11]

Women in the Klan Movement

□ Women's participation in the Klan movement began in the early 1920s, when male membership in the KKK was increasing rapidly. Various male Klan leaders throughout the country organized female auxiliaries, competing for membership and official chartering. The most successful of these affiliates was the WKKK, under the sponsorship of the powerful Klan leader, Hiram Evans.[12] The WKKK was open to white, native-born, Protestant women over sixteen years old. Although there were personal and organizational ties between the women's and men's Klan, the WKKK worked to maintain some degree of autonomy from the male KKK.

Women entered the Klan in various ways and for different reasons. Initially, the women's Klan built upon, then absorbed, many of the women's patriotic societies and Protestant women's clubs that began after World War I. Other women joined the Klan as the sisters, daughters, and wives of Klansmen, to assist the Klan cause and promote family togetherness. The WKKK also recruited women directly into a women's crusade for a white, Protestant America. The WKKK hired lecturers, organizers, and recruiters to establish new local chapters, usually in states where recruiters for the KKK had been successful. In this endeavor, the WKKK played upon notions of women's new status, as shaped in movements of female suffrage and gender equality. A recruitment ad for the Women's Klan in Indiana proclaimed: "Men no longer aspire to exclusive domination in any field of endeavor that is his authorship, and whether she wears the cool, sequestered veil of life in the home, or whether she is in the busy walks of business or fashion, woman is now called to put her splendid efforts and abilities behind a movement for 100 per cent American women."[13]

The devotion of the WKKK to an elaborate hierarchy and ritual proved attractive to women, as it had to men in the KKK. An Imperial Commander governed the WKKK on a national level. Under her, a complex series of state, regional, and local officers, with titles of Klaliff (vice-president), Klokard (lecturer), Kligraff (secretary), Klabee (treasurer), and Klarogo/Klexter (inner/outer guard), enforced the code of Klan conduct, collected membership dues, initiated new members, and organized events. Like their male counterpart, the WKKK had an array of social, cultural, and economic units, including drill teams, bands, choirs, a social service agency, kindergartens, and a robe-making factory.[14]

Recruitment of Women

☐ What sort of women joined the women's Klan? The common dismissal of the WKKK as a dependent auxiliary of the male KKK does not accurately capture the process through which women became involved in the Klan. Many—but certainly not all—women in the WKKK were related to male Klan members. Of the sixty-two nonleadership Indiana Klanswomen who are named in the *Tolerance* and *Post-Democrat* or in the Indianapolis Klan paper, *Fiery Cross,* twelve were widows or unmarried women and, we can assume, made their own decisions to participate in the Klan. Furthermore, married women in the Klan were not necessarily led into the movement by Klan husbands; in fact, it was their wives who sometimes convinced men to join the Klan.[15]

Further, most Indiana Klanswomen brought with them a history of extrafamilial involvement. Typically, they belonged to at least one voluntary organization, in addition to a Protestant church and the Klan; and a significant minority worked for wages, in occupations that ranged from positions such as physician, postmistress, real estate agent, and owner of a boardinghouse to skilled and semiskilled occupations that included dressmaker, office worker, courthouse employee, and nursing student.

Indiana Klanswomen in leadership positions, for whom more biographical information is available, clarify a pattern of Klan membership as an aspect of broad civic and social involvement. Daisy Douglas Barr, the fiery leader of the WKKK for Indiana and seven other states, was married to a bank examiner and raised a son but pursued an independent course. An ordained Quaker preacher, renowned for her oratory skills, Barr began preaching at sixteen; was ordained at eighteen; and served as pastor of churches in Muncie, Fairmount, and New Castle, Indiana. She was an active, powerful member of the Women's Christian Temperance Union (WCTU) and a famous crusader for the cause of the "drys" in Muncie.[16] Barr also was a leader in the Indiana Republican party, serving as the first woman vice-chair of the Republican state committee and as a member of the Indiana Women's Republican Club.[17] She was an active member of the American War Mothers (from which she was forced to resign when her Klan activities became known) and a member of the Women's Department Club. Daisy Douglas Barr, like many leaders of the women's Klan, was also an advocate of women's rights and public participation. In 1916, she wrote:

> One can hardly imagine, under our present day progress, that most of the religious denominations in our own country still refuse the rite of ordination to women applicants. Women have entered the professions of law, medicine, teaching, art, music and even are wrestling with the sciences.... And yet the relic of our barbarism and heathenism dogmas, when the belief was still current that women had no souls, is still evident in the fact that other doors are open while the holy ministry still bars her free entrance.[18]

Mary Benadum, prominent leader of the WKKK in Muncie, Indiana, and a rival of Daisy Barr, had a similar background prior to joining the Klan. Married to a prosecuting attorney, she worked for twelve years as a schoolteacher in Muncie and was involved in a variety of state and local civic associations. She was president of the Delaware County (Muncie) Republican Woman's Club and was active in the Business and Professional Women of Indiana and the Methodist church. She also was a vocal and open leader of the women's Klan in Indiana. Benadum embroiled the WKKK in several lawsuits, charging Daisy Barr first with stealing WKKK funds and later with slander, when Barr claimed that Benadum was the true culprit.[19] Her social prominence notwithstanding, Benadum did not fit the traditional conception of high-society womanhood. In 1924, she was arrested in Alliance, Ohio, in a battle with a rival faction of the WKKK in which one woman was injured seriously, and she and Daisy Barr competed intensively and viciously for leadership of the Muncie WKKK.[20]

Lillian Sedwick, named as president of the Marion County, Indiana (Indianapolis), WKKK, was a highly influential and active leader in Indianapolis. Married and the mother of three children, she served on the Indianapolis school board, through which she attempted to bring a Klan philosophy to questions of school policy and racial integration of the schools.[21] She also was active in Eastern Star, the Rebekah Lodge, the WCTU (in which she served as state superintendent), the Methodist Episcopal church, and the International Order of Odd Fellows.

Klanswomen in Indiana not only were likely to be women with a personal history of social and political involvement, but many also violated accepted notions of gender and wifely duty to participate in the Klan. Stories of women who joined the WKKK against the wishes of their husbands and families are common. The 16 May 1924 Muncie *Post-Democrat* noted that "in many Protestant homes the klan has done it's [*sic*] work breaking the ties that would never have been severed.... Some husbands have parted from their wives who joined the Kamelias [Women's Klan] and wives have deserted husbands who enlisted in the army of Satan."[22]

The Lynds' famous study of Muncie, Indiana, too, quotes a husband who attributed his divorce to his wife's participation in the Klan: "She and I split up over the G——d D—— Klan. I couldn't stand them around any longer." Divorce proceedings, given prominent play in the anti-Klan press, claimed that women neglected children and household in favor of Klan activities. The press emphasized the Klan's negative effect on marriage and family life in order to convince women to return to their "rightful" role as wife and mother. "Edna Walling ... led to believe that her sphere was politics and Klan activities, instead of the home life she deserved ... was arrested."[23]

Anti-Klan papers insisted that the Klan did not respect marriage and family life. Claims that the divorce rate was higher in the Klan stronghold of Muncie than in Nevada, that the Klan sponsored frivolous public weddings of fifty couples at a time, and that the Klan "placed Klangraft [Klan corruption] above the holy ordinance of marriage" were frequent. The existence of the WKKK was singled out as proof that the Klan was ignoring traditional morals and the rightful place of women and men. George Dale, the crusading anti-Klan editor of the Muncie *Post-Democrat* who was convicted of contempt of court by a local Klan judge, described Klanswomen spectators at his trial as "sister Amazons of Hate ... bob-haired Amazons [who] demanded my death." The WKKK itself was accused of being nothing more than a front for women's adulterous trysts and of fomenting the murderous tendencies of women unleashed from male direction.[24]

On the whole, this evidence offers a profile of Klanswomen that is remarkably congruent with decades of female activism in voluntary religious and reform associations. But why did they join the Klan? Recruitment literature from the WKKK played on the same racist and nativist themes as the male KKK, promising to safeguard the American family from "corrupting" influences; to guard against isolation and loneliness; to provide excitement; to preserve nationalistic pride; and to maintain racial, religious, and ethnic superiority. Other sources, however, indicate that women also joined the Klan to assert and increase their newfound political legitimacy. In a rare surviving document, an early women's Klan, the "Ladies of the Invisible Empire," of Shreveport, Louisiana, sought to simultaneously redirect American society and to assimilate women into the public, political life of the country. The group presented its objectives as

> the bringing together of the Protestant women of America . . . to cleanse and purify the civil, political and ecclesiastical atmosphere of our country; to provide a common meeting ground for American Protestant women who are willing to co-operate in bringing about better conditions in the home, church and social circles; to assist all Protestant women in the study of practical politics; to encourage a study by Protestant wives, mothers and daughters of questions concerning the happiness of the home and the welfare of the state.[25]

Klanswomen bemoaned immorality, racial integration, and religious pluralism, as did Klansmen, but it was in terms of the effect of these on women, children, and the family. Men needed protection from the economic competition of foreigners, the WKKK insisted, for the sake of those who were dependent upon men's livelihoods: "Foreigners can live and make money where a white man would starve because they treat their women like cattle and their swarms of children like vermin, living without fear of God or regard for man. . . . You should by voice and vote encourage for your husband's sake the restriction of immigration. Let us have fewer citizens and better ones. Women of America, wake up."[26]

The mobilization of women into the 1920s' Klan linked the racist, nationalistic zeal, which also motivated men to join the KKK, to a specific gendered notion of the preservation of family life and women's rights. Both Klansmen and Klanswomen promoted the idea of a white, Protestant America, but women, more so than men, were likely to fuse this political agenda with a vision of a perfected private family life. Advocates of a women's Klan organization, for example, linked antiforeign sentiments to a defense of the home and female morality. They charged that foreign influences were undermining morality by "public presentation of sex where the wife is always shown as inferior and the mistress as a heroine."

Similarly, the sermons of Quaker preacher and WKKK leader Daisy Douglas Barr adapted the rhetoric of the nineteenth-century temperance movement. Barr stressed the need for a "revival in our home [as] many of our family altars have been broken down," arguing that men's indulgence in the "serpent of alcohol . . . stings his family, degrades his wife, marks his children." She did not, however, consign women to the private sphere. Rather, she defended women's place in professional and civic life as necessary to the purification of the home.[27]

Indeed, through active involvement in the Klan, white, Protestant women claimed to find a new weapon against male immorality. The Klan promoted its ability to protect women from sexual harassment on the job and from abuse by husbands. Both the KKK and the WKKK issued warnings to men who cheated on their wives, owed child support, or neglected their families.[28]

As the WKKK recruited women on the basis of a conservative, racist ideology that stressed the interconnection between the public sphere of politics and the private sphere of the home, it expressed a political ideology that had been shaped in earlier women's political movements for temperance and moral reform. Like the WCTU, an organization to which many Klanswomen belonged and most Klanswomen probably were sympathetic, the WKKK expressed elements of a women's rights politics in which the interests of women were primary. The ideology of the women's Klan, however, was not identical to that of the temperance movement of the nineteenth century. Changes in women's roles in the early twentieth century were reflected in the politics of the 1920s' women's Klan. The restrictions of domesticity that gave rise to anger, antagonism, and resentment toward men's privileges and that motivated the women's rights politics of the WCTU[29] no longer completely defined and circumscribed the lives of many white, Protestant, native-born women by the 1920s. Rather, the entrance of women into the world of politics and business made divisions of race, social class, and religion more salient for, and among, women. Klanswomen still used a rhetoric of women's subordinate status and collective interests similar to that which brought women into the temperance movement; but it was now mixed with appeals for racial, ethnic, and national unity, appeals which depended upon the unity and commonality of purpose of white, native-born, Protestant women *and* men. With this political ideology, the WKKK was able to mobilize women from a great variety of employment and family backgrounds.

Activities of Klanswomen

☐ For the most part, the activities of Indiana Klanswomen did not differ significantly from those of Klansmen, except that Klanswomen were rarely involved in violence or vigilantism. Klansmen tended to be involved in either fraternal/social or terroristic activities. Klanswomen worked to solidify the Klan movement itself, led political assaults on non-Klan businesses, and organized to strengthen the Klan's political base, actions essential to the Klan's political and social impact.

On a national and state level, a central aspect of Klanswomen's work was organization building, antivice activities, and anti-Catholic propaganda and actions. The WKKK orchestrated rallies, festivals, and recreational events, some closed to all nonmembers, some for Klanswomen only, and others involving entire Klan families. The WKKK, like the KKK, specialized in ritual and spectacle, with day-long carnivals of sport and song followed by a twilight parade through town, a cross burning, and an evening series of lectures and speeches in a field outside town. Klanswomen organized entertainment meant to build internal solidarity and heighten recruitment, including orchestras, quartets, and parades. A typical event, held in Sullivan, Indiana, involved 3,000 Klanswomen who paraded through downtown, then marched to a park. There,

by the light of a burning cross, the speaking and demonstration were held. Floats, decorated autos, lady horseback riders, marching hosts, all the persons wearing the white robe and marks of the Ku Klux Klan with the exception of one young lady riding upon a specially decorated float. Mothers with sleeping babies in their arms marched with the others and the American flag was given a prominent place. At the park a speaker explained the aim and purpose of the women's organization and a male quartet sang.[30]

Klanswomen were also prominent in the creation of a political culture of "klannishness"—the use of family, leisure, social ties, and ritual to solidify the Klan movement internally and to mark the boundaries between insiders (Klan members) and outsiders ("aliens"). Although often regarded as politically insignificant, the political culture shaped by Klanswomen in the 1920s was critical to the Klan's success in convincing white, native-born, Protestants to enlist in the Klan's crusade and in shaping the solidarity of Klansmembers. Especially important in this culture were Klan rites of passage, including Klan wedding services, christening ceremonies, and funeral services to herald departed Klan sisters. These served both to create a sense of the totality of the Klan world and to present a politically palatable alternative to the culture, practices, and rituals of Catholicism, Judaism, Mormonism, and socialism that Klansmembers swore to oppose. Further, the WKKK had a public relations–oriented charity dimension. With great fanfare, they distributed food baskets to needy families and milk to public school children and raised money to build Protestant hospitals. They were also active in the effort to recruit churches into the Klan movement by descending on a church service in full regalia, striding to the front of the church and presenting an envelope of cash to the minister—sometimes a surprised potential recruit, but often a covert Klan propagandist. They crusaded against "immorality," drove liquor agents out of town, and worked to establish a "clean" motion picture company (the Cavalier Motion Picture Company).[31]

A second activity of Klanswomen was the attempt to "reform" the public schools. Klanswomen frequently visited public schools to distribute Bibles or copies of the Ten Commandments, attempted to have Catholic teachers fired from public school positions, pushed for racial segregation of schools, worked against school closings and the teaching of German in public schools, sought to remove Catholic encyclopedias from the public schools, and raised money in their communities to support public schools to undermine parochial education. Klanswomen also ran for school board seats in order to implement the Klan's program to "Americanize" and make Protestant the public school system.[32]

Third, Klanswomen worked to influence electoral politics, especially in Indiana. They were active in the drive to bring out the Klan vote by lobbying voters, distributing scandal sheets on non-Klan candidates, and caring for the children of women who pledged to vote the Klan ticket. More insidiously, Klanswomen were involved as "poison squads," organizing whispering campaigns to destroy the reputation of anti-Klan candidates by insinuating that they were Catholic or Jewish. Vivian Wheatcraft, a reputed Klanswoman and highly controversial vice-chair of the Indiana Republican State Committee, was accused of running an "organization of which she is pleased to call a 'poison squad of whispering women' "—five Klanswomen in each county in Indiana who could be counted upon to spread gossip and rumors for the Klan.[33]

Similar tactics were used by Klanswomen who organized boycotts of Jewish-owned and Catholic-owned businesses and newspapers opposed to the Klan. These boycotts often were very effective, especially in smaller cities. They were a part of the overall Klan boycott program, in which women's role as household consumer was essential. Boycotts were implemented via a series of codes that encouraged trade only with fellow Klan members. Ads proclaimed "100 percent" dry cleaners, grocers, or photo studios or contained the code "TWK" (Trade with a Klansman).[34]

Klanswomen took the message and vision of the Klan and acted upon it in a variety of ways, some of which were quite different from the actions of Klansmen. Although Klansmen tended toward more open displays of physical violence and intimidation, Klanswomen were the legitimators of the Klan, the covert manipulators of electoral plots, the cultural organizers of a Klan world, and the force behind the attempt to "Protestantize" the public schools of the 1920s. Certainly, Klanswomen demonstrated no more inclination toward progressive or peaceable politics than did men. On the contrary, the behind-the-scenes actions of Klanswomen had the same goals, and perhaps a greater effect, than the openly violent actions of Klansmen. To a great extent, the destructive fury of the 1920s' Klan lay in its use of rumors, boycotts, and electoral strength—tactics that ruined countless lives across the nation. In these tactics, Klanswomen were key actors.

Conclusion

□ In many respects, the involvement of women in the 1920s' WKKK was motivated by factors similar to those that brought millions of men into the Klan. Both women and men, reacting to a fear of social, cultural, racial, and religious difference, joined a movement to preserve and elevate traditional white Protestant dominance. Women, no less than men, perceived heterogeneity as threatening; it was Indiana, one of the most homogeneous of states, that produced the nation's largest chapters of female and male Klans in the 1920s. From the limited data available, it also appears that female and male Klan members had similar backgrounds. Both women and men spanned a wide range of ages and occupational/class positions, with those in leadership positions more likely to be older and wealthier.

Women and men in the Klan movement, however, differed in one significant way. The political agenda of the women's Klan wove together appeals to racism, nationalism, traditional morality, and religious intolerance with other appeals to white women's vulnerability and to the possibility for increased equity between white women and men. Klanswomen described their reasons for participating in the Klan as related to the precarious or subordinate positions that they—as women—held in the family and in society. Women argued that the Klan was the best vehicle for protecting women and children, asserting the rights of women relative to men, and incorporating women's political savvy into the political arena.

It is clear that women's participation in the 1920s' Klan movement was not trivial or insignificant in its consequences. Although Klanswomen were not involved in the violent terroristic and vigilante actions of Klansmen, women did participate in a full range of racist, antipacifist, and right-wing activities. Klanswomen organized racially targeted boycotts, electoral strategies, and character assassinations, in addition to the cultural and social forums that bound the Klan movement together. Their actions contributed significantly to the persecution of racial and religious minorities and to the poisoning of American public life that was the legacy of the 1920s' Klan.

The history of women's participation in the 1920s' Klan movement should caution against a simplistic equation of progressive and proequality politics. Klanswomen, as fully as Klansmen, promoted a right-wing agenda of racism and bigotry. But they linked the preservation of their families to the rights of women (white, native-born, Protestant women) in the public sphere. They promoted white women's entrance into professions, white women's right to vote, and the need of white women to shape the nation's political agenda. Just as progressive political movements have not always promoted gender equality, so, too, reactionary political movements have at times included women's rights agendas.

The Klan of the 1920s collapsed rapidly at the end of the decade, a victim of economic depression, internal battles, and financial scandals. In the Klan's next significant appearance in the 1950s, women and men no longer belonged to separate organizations. In the violent, extremist right-wing politics of today's Klan, women have become background figures, integrated with men in Klan organizations that no longer advocate gender equality. The fusion of women's rights with a reactionary and racist politics, at least in the Klan movement, did not stand the test of time.

What was it that permitted the inclusion of women's rights sentiments into the racist, reactionary political agenda of Klanswomen in the 1920s, but not thereafter? The answer rests on the specific historical conditions under which women joined the second Klan movement. The male Klan movement, desperate for female members to bolster the claims of competing Klan factions, recruited women who supported nativist and racist viewpoints but also supported women's rights politics. Further, anti-immigrant and racist sentiments within the women's suffrage, moral reform, and temperance movements created the historical possibility for a postsuffrage women's Klan that espoused women's rights while denying the rights of nonwhites, non-Protestants, and the foreign-born.

Feminist scholarship has uncovered a rich legacy of women's involvement in progressive and proequality political movements. It is now possible to turn more attention to the disturbing, but important, question of women's involvement in racist, reactionary, and fascist movements. The study of women in extremist right-wing movements may provide us with a richer understanding of the complexities of women's activities in political movements, as well as better strategies by which to challenge racist, reactionary movements in contemporary society.

Notes

A version of this paper was presented at the Seventh Berkshire Conference on the History of Women, held 17–21 June 1987 at Wellesley College, Wellesley, Massachusetts. This research has been made possible by a National Endowment for the Humanities summer stipend, a research grant from the Kentucky Foundation for Women, and travel grants from the National Endowment for the Humanities and the Southern Regional Education Board. The author thanks Paula Baker, Pam Goldman, Dwight Hoover, and archivists and librarians at the Indiana State Library, the Indiana Historical Society, the New York Public Library, the Special Collections of Ball State University Library, and other local public libraries and historical societies in Indiana.

1. See Nancy Cott, *The Grounding of Modern Feminism* (New Haven: Yale University Press, 1987); Paula Baker, "The Domestication of Politics: Women and American Political Society, 1780–1920," *American Historical Review* 84 (June 1984): 620–47; and Anne Firor Scott, "After Suffrage: Southern Women in the Twenties," *Journal of Southern History* 30 (August 1964): 298–318.

2. Dorothy M. Brown, *Setting a Course: American Women in the 1920s* (Boston: Twayne, 1987).

3. The complicated relationship between white supremacist and anti-immigrant ideologies and the women's equality movement of the nineteenth and early twentieth centuries is well documented in a number of historical accounts. In particular, see Bettina Aptheker, *Woman's Legacy: Essays on Race, Sex, and Class* (Amherst: University of Massachusetts Press, 1982), 9–52; Paula Giddings, *When and Where I Enter: The Impact of Black Women on Race and Sex in America* (New York: William Morrow, 1984), 159–70; and Rosalyn Terborg-Penn, "Discrimination against Afro-American Women in the Women's Movement, 1830–1920," in *The Afro-American Woman: Struggles and Images,* ed. Sharon Harley and Rosalyn Terborg-Penn (Port Washington, N.Y.: National University Publications, 1978), 17–27.

4. Joan Jensen, "All Pink Sisters: The War Department and the Feminist Movement in the 1920s," in *Decades of Discontent: The Women's Movement, 1920–1940,* ed. Lois Scharf and Joan Jensen (Westport, Conn.: Greenwood Press, 1983), 199–222; Rayna Rapp and Ellen Ross, "The Twenties' Backlash: Compulsory Heterosexuality, the Consumer Family, and the Waning of Feminism," in *Class, Race, and Sex: The Dynamics of Control,* ed. Amy Swerdlow and Hanna Lessinger (Boston: G.K. Hall, 1983), 93–107.

5. See *Watcher on the Tower,* 15 Sept. 1923, 12. This was published by the Seattle Klan.

6. An exception to this is the new historical scholarship on women in Nazi Germany which explores the contradictory nature of Nazi feminism in the early years of Nazism in Germany. See Renate Bridenthal, Atina Grossman, and

Marion Kaplan, *When Biology Became Destiny: Women in Weimar and Nazi Germany* (New York: Monthly Review Press, 1984).

7. Pamela Conover and Virginia Gray, *Feminism and the New Right: Conflict over the American Family* (New York: Praeger, 1983); Barbara Ehrenreich, *The Hearts of Men: American Dreams and the Flight from Commitment* (Garden City, N.Y.: Anchor/Doubleday, 1983), 144–68; Kristin Luker, *Abortion and the Politics of Motherhood* (Berkeley: University of California Press, 1984); Jane Mansbridge, *Why We Lost the ERA* (Chicago: University of Chicago Press, 1986); Susan E. Marshall, "In Defense of Separate Spheres: Class and Status Politics in the Antisuffrage Movement," *Social Forces* 65 (December 1986): 327–51; Carroll Smith-Rosenberg, *Disorderly Conduct: Visions of Gender in Victorian America* (New York: Oxford University Press, 1986), 109–28; Janet Saltzman Chafetz and Anthony Gary Dworkin, "In the Face of Threat: Organized Antifeminism in Comparative Perspective," *Gender and Society* 1 (March 1987): 33–60; Jensen; Rebecca Klatch, "Coalition and Conflict among Women of the New Right," *Signs* 13 (Summer 1988): 671–94, and *Women of the New Right* (Philadelphia: Temple University Press, 1987).

8. Traditional histories of the Klan include David Chalmers, *Hooded Americanism: The History of the Ku Klux Klan* (Durham, N.C.: Duke University Press, 1987); and Arnold S. Rice, *The Ku Klux Klan in American Politics* (New York: Haskell, 1972). See Anne Firor Scott, "On Seeing and Not Seeing: A Case of Historical Invisibility," *Journal of American History* 71 (June 1984): 7–21.

9. Max Bentley, "The Ku Klux Klan in Indiana," *McClure's Magazine* 57 (May 1924): 23–33; John A. Davis, "The Ku Klux Klan in Indiana, 1920–1930: An Historical Study" (Ph.D. diss., Northwestern University, 1966); John Bartlow Martin, *Indiana: An Interpretation* (Freeport, N.Y.: Books for Libraries, 1972); Larry R. Gerlach, *Blazing Crosses in Zion: The Ku Klux Klan in Utah* (Logan, Utah: Utah State University Press, 1982); Roger K. Hux, "The Ku Klux Klan in Macon, 1919–1925," *Georgia Historical Quarterly* 62 (Summer 1978): 155–68; Kenneth Jackson, *The Ku Klux Klan in the City, 1915–1930* (New York: Oxford, 1967). But see John Moffatt Mecklin, *The Ku Klux Klan: A Study of the American Mind* (New York: Harcourt, Brace, 1924). On the first Klan, see Walker L. Fleming, "The Prescript of the Ku Klux Klan," *Southern Historical Association* 7 (September 1903): 327–48; J.C. Lester, *The Ku Klux Klan* (New York: AMS Press, 1905); Mrs. S.E.F. Rose, *The Ku Klux Klan or Invisible Empire* (New Orleans: L. Graham, 1914); U.S. Congress, "Affairs in the Late Insurrectionary States," Report 22, pts. 1–3, 42d Cong., 2d sess., 1872.

10. David Chalmers, "The Ku Klux Klan in Politics of the 1920s," *Mississippi Quarterly* 18 (Fall 1965): 234–47; George S. Clason, *Catholic, Jew, Ku Klux Klan: What They Believe, Where They Conflict* (Chicago: Nutshell Publishing, 1924); Emerson Hunsberger Loucks, *The Ku Klux Klan in Pennsylvania* (New York: Telegraph, 1936); Rice. Extensive records of the 1920s' Klan can be found in the

Ku Klux Klan Collection, Archives Division, Indiana State Library; Ku Klux Klan Collection-Wayne County, Indiana, Indiana Historical Society; Depositions of Klan leaders in "Indiana–Attorney General," Ku Klux Klan Manuscripts, Archives Division, Indiana State Library; and at the New York Public Library, Library of Congress, and Ball State University Library.

11. The best sources for this are Klan newspapers, such as *Dawn*, 1922–24, published in Chicago; *Fellowship Forum*, 1921–27, published in Washington, D.C.; and *Kourier*, 1924–36, published in Atlanta. Also see "State of Indiana in the Circuit Court of Marion County, Case No. 41769, State of Indiana, Plaintiff v. The Knights of the Ku Klux Klan, a Foreign Corporation," in Papers of the Ku Klux Klan, Archives Division, Indiana State Library and "D.C. Stephenson Collection," Archives Division, Indiana State Library. Morality crusades were popular in most Klan chapters. The Klan saw itself as the defender of traditional values and the rights of women and the family. It terrorized wifebeaters, wifeabusers, men who deserted their families, and adulterers. See "Field Letters," Ku Klux Klan Collection, Indiana State Archives, box L-208; Kathleen M. Blee, "Gender Ideology and the Role of Women in the 1920s' Klan Movement," *Sociological Spectrum* 1 (1987): 73–97; "Protecting Womanhood," *Tolerance*, 15 Apr. 1923, 11. For a history of Klan terrorism in South Bend, Indiana, see Jill Suzanne Nevel, "Fiery Crosses and Tempers: The Ku Klux Klan in South Bend, Indiana, 1923–1926" (Senior thesis, Princeton University, 1977).

12. Other major women's Klan organizations were Kamelia, sponsored by the competing Klan leader, William Simmons, and the Queens of the Golden Mask (QGM), sponsored by the Midwestern Klan leader, D.C. Stephenson. Kamelia and the QGM, along with local and regional branches of Klanswomen, such as the Ladies of the Invisible Empire, merged into the more successful Women of the Ku Klux Klan in the mid-1920s. See Norman F. Weaver, "The Knights of the Ku Klux Klan in Wisconsin, Indiana, Ohio, and Michigan" (Ph.D. diss., University of Wisconsin, 1954). See also "Women of the Ku Klux Klan: Certificates of Incorporation," in Office of the Indiana Secretary of State, Corporation Division.

13. "Something for the Ladies," *Fiery Cross*, 9 Mar. 1923, 8. This newspaper was published in Indianapolis by the Ku Klux Klan.

14. *Fiery Cross*, 1922–24; *Fellowship Forum*, 1924–31; WKKK Publications, including *Constitution and Laws* (Little Rock, Ark.: WKKK, 1927); *Women of America!* (Little Rock, Ark.: WKKK, 1923); *Kloran* (Little Rock, Ark.: WKKK, 1923); *Ideals of the Women of the Ku Klux Klan* (Little Rock, Ark.: WKKK, 1923); *Installation Ceremonies* (n.p.: WKKK, n.d.).

15. *Fiery Cross*, 30 Mar. 1923, 5.

16. Minutes of the Yearly Meetings of Friends, Held at Richmond, Indiana, 1938; *Indiana Authors and Their Books, 1967–1980* (Crawfordsville, Ind.: Wabash

College, 1981); Indiana Biography, "Mrs. Daisy Douglas Barr" (n.d.), vol. 17; "Klan Women Sue Daisy Barr," *Muncie Star,* 3 June 1924, 1.

17. The female and male Ku Klux Klans of Indiana were involved heavily with the state Republican party. The Indiana Klan engineered the election of numerous mayors, police chiefs, county commissioners, and school boards across the state and was significant in the election of a pro-Klan governor and state assembly in 1924. See Frank Mark Cates, "The Ku Klux Klan in Indiana Politics, 1920–1925" (Ph.D. diss., Indiana University, 1970); Carrolyle M. Frank, "Politics in Middletown: A Reconsideration of Municipal Government and Community Power in Muncie, Indiana, 1925–1935" (Ph.D. diss., Ball State University, 1974); and Martin.

18. "Activities in Ku Klux Klan Resented: Indiana War Mothers Accept Resignation of Reverend Daisy Barr," *Muncie Press,* 27 Mar. 1923, 1; Daisy Barr, "Women in the Ministry," *Indianapolis News,* 1 Nov. 1916, supp. 2. See also Alice French Moore Manuscript Collection, box 1: Indiana Chapter, American War Mothers, Indiana Historical Society Library.

19. *Who's Who and What's What in Indiana Politics* (Indianapolis: James Perry Publisher, 1944), 755; "Former Teacher Charges Slander," *Muncie Star,* 3 Jan. 1924, 1; "Klan Women Sue Daisy Barr," ibid., 3 June 1924, 1; Delaware County (Ind.) Civil Order Book, 1924; "Sues Daisy Barr and Others for $50,000," *Indianapolis News,* 3 Jan. 1924, 17; "Mrs. Barr Defendant in Klan Women's Suit," ibid., 3 June 1924, 12; "Klan Women Sue Agent for $45,000," *Indianapolis Star,* 3 June 1924, 10; and "Klan Women Shift Slander onto Wizard," *Muncie Evening Post,* 14 Nov. 1924, 1.

20. "Ku Klux Women Battle," *New York Times,* 8 Jan. 1924, 10. For example, when Daisy Barr spoke to a gathering of 2,000 women in Muncie, she had Mary Benadum physically barred from the audience.

21. "Mrs. Sedwick Is New Klan Head," *Indianapolis Times,* 4 June 1926, 1; "Blame Klan for Segregation," ibid., 14 Jan. 1957, 11. See also Weaver.

22. "Klan Loses Its Terbacker in Primary Election," Muncie *Post-Democrat,* 16 May 1924, 3.

23. Robert Lynd and Helen Lynd, *Middletown* (New York: Harcourt Brace, 1929), 122; "Lays Separation to Klan," *New York Times,* 27 Mar. 1927, 19; "Kluck Politicians Desert Edna Walling," Muncie *Post-Democrat,* 23 May 1924, 1.

24. See Muncie *Post-Democrat:* "Marriage a Joke to the Klan," 10 Aug. 1923, 1; "The Klan and Divorce," 1 Aug. 1924, 1; "Bloodthirsty Women," 2 Jan. 1925, 1; "Elwood Klan Couple Divorced," 29 Aug. 1923, 1; Robert A. Warrner, "George Dale versus Delaware Klan No. 4" (M.A. thesis, Ball State University, 1972). See also George R. Dale Papers, Special Collections, Ball State University Library.

25. "Join 'Invisible Empire,'" *New York Times,* 7 Jan. 1923, 20.

26. "Women of Indiana Should Wake Up," *Fiery Cross,* 9 Mar. 1923, 6.

27. Ibid., Letter to the Editor, 9 Feb. 1923, 7; Barbara Leslie Epstein, *The Politics of Domesticity: Women, Evangelism, and Temperance in Nineteenth-Century America* (Middletown, Conn.: Wesleyan University Press, 1981); Daisy Douglas Barr, *Springs That Run Dry and Other Addresses* (Noblesville, Ind.: Butler Printing, n.d.), 46, 105, 128.

28. "Our Business Girls," *Fiery Cross,* 29 Dec. 1922, 4; Ku Klux Klan Papers, box L-208, Ku Klux Klan Collection, Indiana State Library; also, Martin, 192.

29. Epstein, 115–46, 1–6.

30. "Women Parade in Klux Meet," *Carlisle News,* 31 Aug. 1923, 1; also, Robert Coughlan, "Konklave in Kokomo," in *The Aspirin Age, 1919–1941,* ed. Isabel Leighton (New York: Simon & Schuster, 1949), 105–29.

31. "Women's Auxiliary of Klan Announces $1,000 Gift to Howard County Institution," *Kokomo Daily Dispatch,* 15 July 1923, 1. Also, Blee. The WKKK and KKK were adept at transforming the lyrics of popular songs into Klan messages. Consider the popular "We Belong to the Ku Klux Klan":

We like the Holy Bible, and we like the U.S.A./ We'll go out and fight for the Stars & Stripes any night or day;/ We like good old America, and we'll help her all we can;/ For we, oh we belong, to the Ku Klux Klan;/

Chorus

Yes, we belong to the Ku Klux Klan, we belong to the Ku Klux Klan;/ We'll stop and help a sister [brother] anywhere in this great land;/ [We'll protect your wives and mothers anywhere in this great land;]/ For we belong to the Ku Klux Klan;

We don't like the old bootlegger; we don't like the gambling man./ We don't like the crook in politics; we'll knock him all we can./ We're out to make America a fit place for Americans,/ For we, oh we belong to the Ku Klux Klan.

We like the little old schoolhouse where we used to go to school;/ Where the teacher read the Bible, and she taught the golden rule;/ We're going to place a Bible in every schoolhouse in the land;/ For we, oh we belong to the Ku Klux Klan.

(George R. Dale Papers, Special Collections, Ball State University).

32. See *Fiery Cross,* 1922–24.

33. "Women in G.O.P. Ask Removal of Mrs. Wheatcraft," *Indianapolis Star,* 2 Sept. 1926, 1. The most bizarre result of the whispering campaigns in Indiana was the assault on a train in North Manchester, Indiana, when poison squads spread the rumor that the pope was on the train en route from Cincinnati to Chicago where he was to proclaim the United States as part of the papal empire. A large crowd of Klan members halted the train, pulled off a traveling salesman and held him until they were satisfied that he was not the pope

traveling in disguise. See Morton Harrison, "Gentlemen from Indiana," *Atlantic Monthly* 141 (May 1928): 676–86.

34. "Why the Lid Came Off Ku Kluxed Indianapolis," *Tolerance,* 8 Apr. 1923, 6. See Bradford W. Scharlott on the WKKK boycott of the *South Bend Tribune,* "The Hoosier Newsman and the Hooded Order: Indiana Press Reaction to the Ku Klux Klan in the 1920s" (Paper presented at the Association for Education in Journalism annual convention, Houston, 1979). See also *Fiery Cross,* 1922–24; and Depositions of Klan Leaders, in "Indiana–Attorney General," Ku Klux Klan Collection, Archives Division, Indiana State Library.

"Where Are the Organized Women Workers?"

☐ "The organization of women," wrote Fannia Cohn, an officer of the International Ladies' Garment Workers' Union, to William Green, newly elected president of the American Federation of Labor, "is not merely a moral question, but also an economic one. Men will never be certain with their conditions unless the conditions of the millions of women are improved."[1] Her letter touched a home truth and yet in 1925, the year in which Cohn's letter was written, the AFL, after nearly forty years of organizing, remained profoundly ambivalent about the fate of more than eight million wage-earning women.

During these four decades of industrial growth, the women who worked in the industrial labor force had not passively waited to be organized. Yet their best efforts had been tinged with failure. Figures for union members are notoriously unreliable, and estimates fluctuate widely. But something like 3.3 percent of the women who were engaged in industrial occupations in 1900 were organized into trade unions. As low as that figure was, it was to decline even further. Around 1902 and 1903 trade union membership among women began to decrease, reaching a low of 1.5 percent in 1910. Then, a surge of organization among garment workers lifted it upwards. A reasonable estimate might put 6.6 percent of wage-earning women into trade unions by 1920. In a decade that saw little change in the relative proportion of female and male workers, the proportion of women who were trade union members quadrupled, increasing at more than twice the rate for trade union members in general. Even so, the relative numbers of wage-earning women who were trade union members remained tiny. One in every five men in the industrial work force belonged to a union, compared with one in every fifteen women. Although more than 20 percent of the

Reprinted, with changes, from *Feminist Studies* 3, nos. 1/2 (Fall 1975): 92–110. © 1975 by Feminist Studies, Inc.

labor force was female, less than 8 percent of organized workers were women. And five years later, when Fannia Cohn was urging William Green to pay attention to female workers, these startling gains had already been eroded.[2]

Figures like these have led historians of the working class to join turn-of-the-century labor organizers in lamenting the difficulty of unionizing female workers. Typically, historians argue that the traditional place of women in families, as well as their position in the work force, inhibited trade unionism. Statistical overviews suggest that these arguments have much to be said for them. At the turn of the century, most wage-earning women were young, temporary workers who looked to marriage as a way to escape the shop or factory. Eighty-five percent of these women were unmarried and nearly half were under twenty-five years old. Most women worked at traditionally hard-to-organize unskilled jobs—one-third were domestic servants and almost one quarter worked in the garment and textile industries. The remainder were scattered in a variety of industrial and service jobs, including the tobacco and boot and shoe industries, department stores, and laundries. Wage-earning women often came from groups without a union tradition: about one-half of all working women were immigrants or their daughters who shared rural backgrounds. In the cities, that figure sometimes climbed to 90 percent.[3]

For all these reasons, women in the labor force unionized with difficulty. Yet the dramatic fluctuations in the proportions of organized working women testify to their potential for organization. The large numbers of unions in which the proportion of women enrolled exceeded their proportion in the industry urge us to seek further explanations for the small proportions of women who actually became union members.[4]

No apparent change either in the type of women who worked or in the structure of jobs explains the post-1902 decline in the proportion of unionized women. On the contrary, several trends would suggest the potential for a rise in their numbers. The decline began just at the point when union membership was increasing dramatically after the devastating depression of 1893–97. The proportion of first-generation immigrant women who were working dropped after the turn of the century only to be matched by an increase in the proportion of their Americanized daughters who worked. Married women entered the labor force in larger numbers suggesting at once a more permanent commitment to jobs and greater need for the security unions could provide. Large declines in the proportion of domestic workers reduced the numbers of women in these isolated, low-paying, and traditionally hard-to-organize jobs. At the same time, increases in office and clerical workers, department store clerks, and factory operatives, offered fertile areas for promoting unionization among women. Strenuous organizing campaigns by and among women in all these areas achieved few results.

Although cultural backgrounds, traditional roles, and social expectations hindered some unionizing efforts, they were clearly not insurmountable barriers. Given a chance, women were devoted and successful union members, convinced that unionism would serve them as it seemed to be serving their brothers. In the words of a seventeen-year-old textile worker, "We all work hard for a mean living. Our boys belong to the miners' union so their wages are better than ours. So I figured that girls must have a union. Women must act like men."[5] In the garment workers union where women were the majority of members, they often served as shop "chairladies" and reached positions of minor importance in the union structure. Faige Shapiro recalled how her union activity began at the insistence of a business agent but quickly became an absorbing interest. In these unions, women arrested on picket lines thought highly enough of the union to try to save it bail money by offering to spend the night in jail before they returned to the line in the morning.[6]

In mixed unions, women often led men in militant actions. Iowa cigar makers reported in 1899 that some striking men had resumed work, but the women were standing pat.[7] Boot and shoe workers in Massachusetts were reported in 1905 to be tough bargainers. "It is harder to induce women to compromise," said their president, "they are more likely to hold out to the bitter end . . . to obtain exactly what they want."[8] The great uprising of 1909 in which 20,000 women walked out of New York's garment shops occurred over the objections of the male leadership, striking terror into the hearts of Jewish men afraid "for the security of their jobs."[9] Polish "spool girls" protesting a rate cut in the textile mills of Chicopee, Massachusetts, refused their union's suggestion that they arbitrate and won a resounding victory. Swedish women enrolled in a Chicago Custom Clothing Makers local lost a battle against their bosses' attempts to subdivide and speed up the sewing process when the United Garment Workers union, largely male, agreed to the bosses' conditions. The bosses promptly locked out the women, forcing many to come to terms and others to seek new jobs.[10] At the turn of the century, female garment workers in San Francisco and tobacco strippers, overall and sheepskin workers, and telephone operators in Boston ran highly successful sex-segregated unions.[11]

If traditional explanations for women's failure to organize extensively in this period are not satisfying, they nevertheless offer clues to understanding the unionization process among women. They reveal the superficiality of the question frequently asked by male organizers and historians alike: "Why don't women organize?" And they encourage us to adopt economist Theresa Wolfson's more sensitive formulation: "Where are the organized women workers?"[12] For when we stop asking why women have not organized themselves, we are led to ask how women were, and are, kept out of unions.

The key to this question lies, I think, in looking at the function that wage-earning women have historically played in the capitalist mode of production. Most women entered the labor force out of economic necessity. They were encouraged by expanding technology and the continuing division of labor which in the last half of the nineteenth century reduced the need for skilled workers and increased the demand for cheap labor. Like immigrant men, and Blacks today, women formed a large reservoir of unskilled workers. But they offered employers additional advantages. They were often at the mercy of whatever jobs happened to be available in the towns where their husbands or fathers worked, and they willingly took jobs that offered no access to upward mobility. Their extraordinarily low pay and exploitative working conditions enabled employers to speed up the process of capital accumulation. Their labor was critical to industrial expansion, yet they were expected to have few job-related aspirations and to look forward instead to eventual marriage. Under these circumstances, employers had a special incentive to resist unionization among women. As John Andrews, writing in the 1911 Report on the Condition of Women and Child wage earners, put it: "The moment she organizes a union and seeks by organization to secure better wages she diminishes or destroys what is to the employer her chief value."[13]

If the rising numbers of working women are any gauge, women for the most part nicely filled the expectations of employers. Traditional social roles and the submissive behavior expected of women with primary attachments to home and family precisely complemented the needs of their bosses. To those women whose old world or American family norms encouraged more aggressive and worldly behavior—Russian Jews, for example—unionization came easier. Yet, for the most part, women fought on two fronts—against the weight of tradition and expectation and against employers. If that were not enough, there was yet a third battlefront.

Unionists, if they thought about it at all, were well aware of women's special economic role. Samuel Gompers, head of the AFL, editorialized in 1911 that some companies had "taken on women not so much to give them work as to make dividends fatter."[14] In a competitive labor market, unionists tended to be suspicious of women who worked for wages and to regard them as potentially threatening to men's jobs. "Every woman employed," wrote an editor in the AFL journal, *American Federationist,* "displaces a man and adds one more to the idle contingent that are fixing wages at the lowest limit."[15]

Because employers clearly had important economic incentives for hiring women, male trade unionists felt they had either to eliminate that incentive or to offer noneconomic reasons for restricting women's labor force participation. In the early 1900s they tried to do both. In order to reduce the economic threat, organized labor repeatedly affirmed a commitment to unionize women wage earners and to extract equal pay for them. Yet trade unionists simultaneously argued that women's contributions to the home and their duties as mothers were so valuable that women ought not to be in the labor force at all. Their use of the home and motherhood argument had two negative effects—it sustained the self-image on which the particular exploitation of women rested, and it provided employers with a weapon to turn against the working class as a whole.

Buttressed by the grim realities of exploitative working conditions and the difficulties of caring for children while working ten or more hours a day, and supported by well-intentioned social reformers, the argument to eliminate women from the work force, in the end, held sway. It was, of course, impossible to achieve, so the AFL continued to organize women and to demand equal pay for equal work. But genuine ambivalence tempered its efforts. The end result was to divide the working class firmly along gender lines and to confirm women's position as a permanently threatening underclass of workers who finally resorted to the protection of middle-class reformers and legislators to ameliorate intolerable working conditions. The pattern offers us some lessons about what happens to the work force when one part of it attacks another.

The published sources of the AFL reveal some of the attitudes underlying AFL actions. I have focused attention on these because I want to illustrate how open and prevalent the argument was and because the AFL's affiliated unions together constituted the largest body of collective working-class opinion. We have amassed enough evidence by now to know that the AFL was a conservative force whose relatively privileged members sacrificed the larger issues of working-class solidarity for a piece of the capitalist pie. In the interest of creating what labor economist Selig Perlman called "a joint partnership of organized labor and organized capital," the AFL cooperated extensively with corporation-dominated government agencies, sought to exclude immigrants, and supported an imperialist foreign policy.[16] Its mechanisms for dealing with the huge numbers of women entering the labor force are still unclear. Yet they are an integral part of the puzzle surrounding the interaction of ideological and economic forces in regulating labor market participation.

In the period from 1897 to 1920, the AFL underwent dramatic expansion. It consolidated and confirmed its leadership over a number of independent unions, including the dying Knights of Labor. Membership increased from about 265,000 members in 1897 to more than four million by 1920 and included four-fifths of all organized workers. In the same period, the proportion of women working in the industrial labor force climbed rapidly. Rapid and heady expansion offered a golden opportunity for organizers. That they didn't take advantage of it is one of the most important facts in the history of labor organizing in America.

☐ Union leaders were sure that women did not belong in the work force. Anxious about losing jobs to these low-paid workers, they tried instead to drive women out of the labor force. "It is the so-called competition of the unorganized defenseless woman worker, the girl and the wife, that often tends to reduce the wages of the father and husband," proclaimed Samuel Gompers.[17] And the *American Federationist* was filled with tales of men displaced by women and children. "One house in St. Louis now pays $4 per week to women where men got $16," reported the journal in 1896. "A local typewriter company has placed 200 women to take the place of unorganized men," announced an organizer in 1903.[18]

The AFL's fears had some basis. In the late nineteenth and early twentieth centuries, new technology and techniques of efficiency pioneered by Frederick Taylor eroded the control and the jobs of skilled workmen, replacing them with managerial experts and the unskilled and semiskilled. Skilled members of the AFL, who might appropriately have directed their anger at the way technology was being manipulated, lashed out instead at women who dared to work. Gompers offers a good example. In an article published in 1904, he declared, "The ingenuity of man to produce the world's wealth easier than ever before, is utilized as a means to pauperize the worker, to supplant the man by the woman and the woman by the child. . . . " Some of the least appropriate bitterness was expressed by Thomas O'Donnell, secretary of the National Spinners Union, whose constituency, once largely female, had been replaced by men after the Civil War. The advent of simple electric-powered machinery caused him to complain that "the manufacturers have been trying for years to discourage us by dispensing with the spinning mule and substituting female and child labor for that of the old time skilled spinners. . . . "[19]

Real anxieties about competition from women stimulated and supported rationalizations about woman's role as wife and mother. Working men had argued even before the Civil War that women belonged at home, and both the harsh conditions of labor and the demands of rearing a family supported their contention. But the women who worked for wages in the early 1900s were overwhelmingly single and often supported widowed mothers and younger siblings with their meager pay. An argument that could have been used to improve conditions for all workers was directed at eliminating women from the work force entirely. By the early 1900s it had become an irrepressible chorus. "The great principle for which we fight," said the AFL's treasurer in 1905, "is opposed to taking . . . the women from their homes to put them in the factory and the sweatshop."[20] "We stand for the principle," said another AFL member, that it is wrong to permit any of the female sex of our country to be forced to work, as we believe that the man should be provided with a fair wage in order to keep his female relatives from going to work. The man is the provider and should receive enough for his labor to give his family a respectable living."[21] And yet a third proclaimed, "Respect for women is apt to decrease when they are compelled to work in the factory or the store. . . . More respect for women brings less degeneration and more marriages . . . if women labor in factories and similar institutions they bring forth weak children who are not educated to become strong and good citizens."[22] No language was too forceful or too dramatic. "The demand for female labor," wrote an official of the Boston Central Labor Union in 1897, is "an insidious assault upon the home . . . it is the knife of the assassin, aimed at the family circle."[23] The *American Federationist* romanticized the role of women's jobs at home, extolling the virtues of refined and moral mothers, of good cooking and even of beautiful needlework and embroidery.[24]

These sentiments did not entirely prevent the AFL from attempting to unionize women. Gompers editorialized on the subject in 1906: "We . . . shall bend every energy for our fellow workmen to organize and unite in trade unions; to federate their effort without regard to . . . sex." Yet the limited commitment implied by the wish that women would get out of the work force altogether was tinged with the conviction and perhaps the hope that women would, in the end, fail. The AFL's first female organizer, Mary Kenny, had been appointed as early as 1892. But the AFL had supported her only half-heartedly and allowed her position to expire when she gave up the job to marry. It was 1908 before the organization appointed another woman, Annie Fitzgerald, as full-time organizer. Although Gompers and others conceded the "full and free opportunity for women to work whenever and wherever necessity requires," Gompers did not address himself to the problem of how to determine which women were admissible by these standards, and his actions revealed that he thought their numbers relatively few.[25] The AFL repeatedly called for an end to discriminatory pay for women and men: "Equal compensation for equal service performed."[26] The demand was a double-edged sword. Although it presumably protected all workers from cheap labor, in the context of the early 1900s' labor market it often functioned to deprive women of jobs. The Boston Typographical Union, noted one observer, saw "its only safety in maintaining the principle of equal pay for men and women. . . ."[27] Officials must have been aware that equal compensation for women often meant that employers would as soon replace them with men. It was no anomaly, then, to find an AFL organizer say of his daughters in 1919 that although he had "two girls at work [he] . . . wouldn't think of having them belong to a labor organization."[28]

When the AFL did organize women, its major incentive was often the need to protect the earning power of men. Women were admitted to unions after men recognized them as competitors better controlled from within than allowed to compete from without. "It has been the policy of my associates and myself," wrote Gompers in 1906, "to throw open wide the doors of our organization and invite the working girls and working women to membership for their and our common protection."[29] *American Federationist* articles that began with pleas that women stay out of the work force concluded with equally impassioned pleas to organize those who were already in it. Alice Woodbridge, writing in 1894, concluded an argument that women who worked for wages were neglecting their duties to their "fellow creatures" with the following statement: "It is to the interest of both sexes that women should organize . . . until we are well organized there is little hope of success among organizations of men."[30] The AFL officially acknowledged competition as a primary motivation for organizing women in 1923. "Unorganized they constitute a menace to standards established through collective action. Not only for their protection, but for the protection of men . . . there should be organization of all women. . . ."[31]

These were not of course the only circumstances under which men suspended their hostility toward women's unions. Occasionally in small towns, female and male unions in different industries supported each other against the hostile attacks of employers. Minersville, Pennsylvania miners, for example, physically ousted railroad detectives who tried to break up a meeting of female textile workers.[32] The women in this case were the daughters, sisters, and sweethearts of miners. Far from competing with men for jobs, women were helping to support the same families as the miners. Similarly, women and men in newly established industries could cooperate more effectively in unionizing together. The garment industry saw parallel but equally effective organization among its various branches. Although female organizers complained bitterly of the way they were treated, male leadership depended on the numerical majority of female workers to bargain successfully with employers and did not deny women admission. Yet, even here, union leadership successfully decimated "home work" without offering to the grossly underpaid and often needy female workers who did it a way of recouping their financial losses.

Occasional exceptions notwithstanding, the general consequence of union attitudes toward women was to isolate them from the male work force. Repeatedly, women who organized themselves into unions applied for entry to the appropriate parent body only to be turned down or simply ignored. Pauline Newman, who had organized and collected dues from a group of candy makers in Philadelphia, in 1910 offered to continue to work with them if the International Bakery and Confectionery Workers union would issue a charter. The International stalled and put them off until the employers began to discharge the leaders and the group disintegrated.[33] Waitresses in Norfolk, Virginia, suffered a similar fate. Mildred Rankin, who requested a charter for a group of fifteen, was assured by the local AFL organizer that she was wasting her time. "The girls were all getting too much money to be interested," was his comment on denying the request.[34] New York's International Typographical Union refused to issue female copyholders a charter on the grounds that they were insufficiently skilled. When the group applied to the parent AFL for recognition, they were refused on the grounds that they were within the ITU's jurisdiction. The Women's Trade Union League (WTUL) got little satisfaction when it raised this issue with the AFL's executive council the following year. Although the AFL had agreed to issue charters to Black workers excluded from all-white unions, it refused to accord the same privilege to women. The parent body agreed only to "take up the subject with the trade unions and to endeavor to reach an understanding" as far as women were concerned.[35]

A strong union could simply cut women out of the kinds of jobs held by unionized men. This form of segmenting the labor market ran parallel to and sometimes contradicted the interests of employers who would have preferred cheap labor. A Binghamton, New York, printing establishment, for example, could not hire women linotype operators because "the men's union would not allow it."[36] The technique was as useful for excluding racial minorities as it was for restricting women.[37] Like appeals to racist beliefs, arguments based on the natural weakness of women worked well as a rationale, as the following examples will indicate. Mary Dreier, then president of the New York Chapter of the WTUL, recalled a union of tobacco workers whose leaders refused to admit women because "they could only do poor sort of work . . . because women had no colour discrimination."[38] A Boston metal polishers union refused to admit women. "We don't want them," an official told a Women's Bureau interviewer. "Women can only do one kind of work while men can polish anything from iron to gold and frame the smallest part to the largest," and besides, he added, "metal polishing is bad for the health."[39]

Women were often excluded from unions in less direct but equally effective ways. The International Retail Clerks Union charged an initiation fee of three dollars and dues of fifty cents a month. Hilda Svenson, a local organizer in 1914, complained that she had been unable to negotiate a compromise with the International. "We want to be affiliated with them," she commented, "but on account of the dues and initiation fee we feel it is too high at the present time for the salaries that the girls in New York are getting."[40] Sometimes union pay scales were set so high that the employer would not pay the appropriate wage to women. Joining the union could mean that a female printer would lose her job, so women simply refused to join.

Although the AFL supported its few female organizers only half-heartedly, male organizers complained of the difficulty of organizing women. Social propriety hindered them from talking to women in private or about moral or sanitary issues. Women felt keenly the absence of aid. When the Pennsylvania State Federation of Labor offered to finance the Philadelphia WTUL's program for organizing women, its secretary pleaded with Rose Schneiderman to take the job. "We have never had a wise head to advise, or an experienced worker," she wrote.[41]

But even membership in a union led by men guaranteed little to women. Such well-known tactics as locating meetings in saloons, scheduling them at late hours, and ridiculing women who dared to speak deprived women of full participation. And unions often deliberately sabotaged their female members. Fifteen hundred female street railway conductors and ticket agents, dues-paying members of New York City's Amalgamated Street Workers Union, complained in 1919 that their brother union members had supported a reformers' bill to deprive them of their jobs. When the women discovered they had been betrayed, they resigned from the union and formed their own organization, sending women throughout the state to Albany "to show them that they . . . were able to take care of their own health and morals." To no avail. Eight hundred of the fifteen hundred women lost their jobs, and the remaining seven hundred continued to work only at reduced hours.[42] Supporting union men was not likely to benefit women either. Mary Anderson, newly appointed head of the Women's Bureau, got a frantic telegram from a WTUL organizer in Joliet, Illinois, early in 1919. The women in a Joliet steel plant who, in return for the promise of protection, had supported unionized men in a recent strike, were fighting desperately for jobs that the union now insisted they give up. The company wanted to retain the women, but union men argued the work was too heavy for them.[43]

☐ As the idea of home and motherhood was used to exclude women from unions, so it enabled unionized workers to join legislatures and middle-class reformers in restricting women's hours and regulating their working conditions through protective labor legislation. The issue for the AFL's skilled and elite corps of male workers was clearly competition. Their wives did not work for wages, and most could afford to keep their daughters outside the marketplace. In an effort to preserve limited opportunity, they attacked fellow workers who were women, attempting to deny them access to certain kinds of jobs. Abused by employers who valued women primarily for their "cheap labor," women were isolated by male workers who were afraid their wages and their jobs would fall victim to the competition. Arguments used by male workers may have undercut their own positions, confirming the existence of a permanent underclass of workers and locking men psychologically and economically into positions of sole economic responsibility for their families. Appeals to morality and to the duties of motherhood obscured the economic issues involved, encouraging women and men alike to see women as impermanent workers whose major commitment would be to families and not to wage earning. Women would, therefore, require the special protection of the state for their presumably limited wage-earning lives.

The argument reached back at least as far as the 1880s and it was firmly rooted in the idea that the well-being of the state depended on the health of future mothers. But the line between the interests of the state and those of working men was finely drawn, and occasionally a protagonist demonstrated confusion about the issue. A few examples will illustrate the point. The cigar maker Adolph Strasser, testifying before a congressional committee in 1882, concluded a diatribe against the number of women entering the trade with a plea to restrict them.

"Why?" asked his questioner. "Because," replied Strasser, "I claim that it is the duty of the government to protect the weak and the females are considered among the weak in society."[44] Nearly forty years later, a Women's Bureau investigator reported that the secretary of the Amalgamated Clothing Workers Union, fearful that women were taking jobs from men, had argued that women were "going into industry so fast that home life is very much in danger, not to mention the propagation of the race."[45] As the idea spread, it took on new forms, leading a Boston streetcar union secretary to acknowledge that "he would not care to see [women] employed as conductors. . . . It coarsened [them] to handle rough crowds on cars.[46] But in more sophisticated form, the argument for protective legislation appeared as a patriotic appeal to enlightened national self-interest. "Women may be adults," argued one AFL columnist in 1900, "and why should we class them as children? Because it is to the interest of all of us that female labor should be limited so as not to injure the motherhood and family life of a nation."[47] Sometimes pleas were more dramatic. In a piece entitled, "The Kingdom of God and Modern Industry," Ira Howerth, a sociologist writing for the *American Federationist,* asserted:

> The highest courts in some of our states declare that a law limiting the hours of labor for these women is unconstitutional. It may be so, but if it is so, so much the worse for the state. The state or nation that permits its women to stunt their bodies and dwarf their minds by over-exertion in insanitary [sic] stores and mills and factories is thereby signing its own death warrant. For the degeneracy of women is the degeneracy of the race. A people can never be any better than its mothers.[48]

Gompers, as well as other AFL officials, at first opposed the idea of legislation. But in the period following World War I, their attitudes changed, perhaps as a result of what seemed like an enormous increase in the number of women in the industrial labor force. The AFL encouraged the Department of Labor to set up a Women's Bureau to defend the interests of wage-earning women.[49] The bureau, on investigation, found that many union officials viewed unionization and protective legislation as alternate means to the same goal—better working conditions. Sara Conboy, United Textile Workers' official and a WTUL activist, told a Women's Bureau interviewer that she believed in "legislation to limit long hours of work for women where and when the union [was] not strong enough to limit hours."[50] Some unionized workers thought legislation surer and faster or remarked that it was more dependable than possibly untrustworthy union leaders. A. J. Muste, then secretary of the Amalgamated Textile Workers Union of America, preferred unionization but was said to have believed that legislation did not hinder organization and might be essential in industries with many women and minors.[51] But some women union leaders were not so sanguine. Fannia Cohn of the International Ladies Garment Workers' Union (ILGWU) only reluctantly acquiesced to the need for protective legislation. "I did not think the problem of working women could be solved in any other way than the problem of working men and that is through trade union organization," she wrote in 1927, "but considering that very few women are as yet organized into trade unions, it would be folly to agitate against protective legislation."[52] Cohn laid the problems of female workers on the absence of organization.

In any event, exclusion from unions merely confirmed the discomfort many women felt about participating in meetings. Italian and southern families disliked their daughters going out in the evenings. Married and self-supporting women and widows had household duties at which they spent afterwork hours. Women who attended meetings often participated reluctantly. They found the long discussions dull and were often intimidated by the preponderance of men. Men, for their part, resented the indifference of the women and further excluded them from leadership roles, thereby discouraging more women from attending. Even fines failed to spark attendance. Some women preferred to pay them rather than to go to the meetings.[53]

Self-images that derived from a paternalistic society joined ethnic ties in hindering unionization. Wage-earning women, anxious to marry, were sometimes reluctant to join unions for what they felt would be a temporary period. Occasionally, another role conflict was expressed: "No nice girl would belong to one," said one young woman.[54] An ILGWU organizer commented that most women who did not want to join a union claimed that "the boss is good to us and we have nothing to complain about and we don't want to join the union."[55] A woman who resisted unionization told an organizer that she knew "that $6 a week is not enough pay but the Lord helps me out. He always provides . . . I won't ever join a union. The Lord doesn't want me to."[56] A recent convert to unionism apologized for her former reticence. She had always scabbed because church people disapproved of unions. Moreover, she and her sister had only with difficulty, she told an organizer, overcome their fear of the Italian men who were organizing their factory.[57]

Exceptions to this pattern occurred most often among women whose ethnic backgrounds encouraged both wage labor and a high level of social consciousness, as in the American Jewish community. Young Jewish women constituted the bulk of the membership of the ILGWU in the period from 1910 to 1920. Their rapid organization and faithful tenure is responsible for at least one-quarter of the increased number of unionized women in the second decade of the twentieth century. And yet, they were unskilled and semiskilled workers, employed in small, scattered shops, and theoretically among the least organizable workers. These women, unionized at their own initiative, formed the backbone of the ILGWU, which had originally been directed toward organizing the skilled, male, cutters in the trade.

As it became clear to many laboring women that unionists would offer them little help, many women turned to such middle-class allies as the Women's Trade Union League. Established in 1905, the WTUL, an organization founded by female unionists and upper-middle-class reformers, offered needed financial and moral support for militant activity. Its paternalistic and benevolent style was not unfamiliar to women and those who came from immigrant families seemed particularly impressed with its Americanizing aspects. Young immigrant girls spoke with awe of the "fine ladies" of the WTUL and did not object to the folk-dancing classes that were part of the Chicago League's program.[58] But help from these non-wage-earning women came at a price. Working women who became involved in the WTUL moved quickly from working-class militance to the search for individual social mobility through vocational training, legislation, and the social refinements that provided access to better-paying and the rapidly increasing number of clerical and secretarial jobs. Rose Schneiderman illustrates this syndrome well. Beginning as a fiery organizer of the hat and cap makers, she moved through the WTUL to become secretary of the New York State Department of Labor. Like the WTUL, which had begun by organizing women into trade unions, she began in the 1920s to devote herself to attaining protective legislation, even borrowing some of the arguments used by men who did not wish women to compete with them.

By this time many working women were themselves moving in the direction of legislative solutions to exploitative working conditions. It seemed to be the most accessible solution to the problems of exploitation. Female workers interviewed by the Women's Bureau at first felt that both women and men should be included in any legislation. Later, they asked that office workers be exempted.[59] Other women acquiesced reluctantly. "I have always been afraid," wrote a supervisor in a Virginia silk mill, "that if laws were made discriminating for women, it would work a hardship upon them." By 1923 she had changed her mind. "It would in time raise the entire standard rather than make it hard for women."[60] As women came to accept the necessity for legislation, they, like men, saw it as an alternative to unionization and rationalized its function in terms of their female "roles." A Women's Bureau agent noted of the reactions to a forty-eight-hour law passed in Massachusetts that "the girls felt that legislation establishing a 48-hour week was more 'dignified' and permanent than one obtained through the union as it was not so likely to be taken away."[61] By the mid-1920s only business and professional women remained staunchly opposed to protective legislation.

□ Within this framework of trade union ambivalence and the real need of wage-earning women for some form of protection, employers who were particularly anxious that women not unionize pressed their advantage. Using crude techniques, rationalized by the home and motherhood argument, they contributed more than their share toward keeping women out of unions. In the small businesses in which women most often worked, employers used a variety of techniques to discourage organization, some of them familiar to men. Department store employees whose union membership became known were commonly fired. Many stores had spy systems so that employees could not trust their coworkers. Blacklists were common. A representative of the year-old retail clerks union testifying before a congressional committee in 1914 was afraid even to reveal the number of members in her union. Owners of New York's garment shops, fighting a losing battle by 1910, nevertheless frequently discharged employees who were thought to be active organizers or union members.[62]

Other tactics were no more subtle. Employers often played on ethnic and racial tensions in order to prevent women from unionizing. Rose Schneiderman, who formed the Hat and Cap Makers Union in 1903, fought against bosses who urged immigrant workers to stick to the "American shop"—a euphemism for an antiunion shop. Jewish owners sometimes hired only Italian workers who were thought to be less prone to unionization than Jews.[63] Others hired "landsmen" from the same old-country community, hoping that fraternal instincts might keep them from striking. Blacks were played off against whites. Waitresses picketing Knab's restaurant in Chicago were met with counterpickets paid by the employers. A representative of the waitresses union reported indignantly that the employer "placed colored pickets on the street, colored women who wore signs like this 'Gee, I ain't mad at nobody and nobody ain't mad at Knab.'" When the nonunion pickets attracted a crowd, police moved in and arrested the union members. The women were further discouraged by trials engineered by employers who had previously given "every policeman a turkey free."[64]

Police routinely broke up picket lines and outdoor union meetings. Women who were accused of obstructing traffic or were incited into slapping provocateurs were arrested. More importantly, women who might have been interested in unionization were intimidated by police who surrounded open-air meetings or by department store detectives who mingled obtrusively with potential recruits. Department store owners diverted workers from street meetings by locking all but one set of doors or sending trucks, horns honking full blast, to parade up and down the street in which a meeting was scheduled.[65]

Small employers formed mutual assistance associations to help them resist their employees' attempts to unionize. The Chicago Restaurant Keepers Association, for example, denied membership to any "person, firm or corporation . . . having signed agreements with any labor organization."[66] Garment manufacturers in both New York and Chicago created protective associations to combat what they called "the spreading evil of unionism."[67] In small towns, the power of town officials was called into play. Ann Washington Craton, organizing textile workers in Minersville, Pennsylvania, was warned by the town burgess: "You are to let our girls alone . . . Mr. Demsky will shut the factory down rather than have a union. . . . The town council brought this factory here to provide work for worthy widows and poor girls. We don't intend to have any trouble about it."[68]

Employers justified their continued refusal to promote women or to offer them access to good jobs on the grounds that women's major contribution was to home and family. When they were challenged with the argument that bad working conditions were detrimental to that end, they responded slowly with paternalistic amelioration of the worst conditions and finally by acquiescing to protective labor legislation. Often, concessions to workers were an effort to undercut mounting union strength, as, for example, when department store owners voluntarily closed their shops one evening a week. Some employers introduced welfare work in their factories, providing social workers or other women to help smooth relationships between them and their female employees. Mutual benefit associations, sometimes resembling company unions, were a more familiar tactic. Though they were presumably cooperative and designed to incorporate input from workers, membership in them was compulsory and dues of ten to twenty-five cents per month were deducted from wages. In return, employees got sickness and health benefits of varying amounts but only after several months of continuous employment. A 1925 investigation of one widely publicized cooperative association operated by Filene's department store in Boston revealed that in all its twelve years, only store executives had ever served on its board of directors.[69]

Manufacturers seemed to prefer legislation regulating the hours and conditions of women's work to seeing their workers join unions. One, for example, told the Women's Bureau of the Department of Labor that a uniform forty-eight-hour week for women would equalize competition and would, in any event, only confirm existing conditions in some shops. Some went even further hoping for federal legislation that would provide uniform standards nationwide.[70]

When occasionally employers found it in their interests to encourage unionism they did so in return for certain very specific advantages. One of these was the union label. In the garment industry the label on overalls in certain parts of the country assured higher sales. To acquire the right to use it, some employers rushed into contracts with the United Garment Workers and quite deliberately urged their workers into the union.[71] New York garment manufacturers negotiated a preferential union shop, higher wages, and shorter hours with the ILGWU in return for which the union agreed to discipline its members and to protect employers against strikes. The garment manufacturers' protective association urged employers to "make every effort to increase the membership in the union so that its officers may have complete control of the workers and be enabled to discipline them when necessary."[72] Southern textile mill owners, otherwise violently opposed to unions, were similarly interested in the disciplinary functions of unionism. They would, an observer reported, modify their opposition "if the purposes of the union were to improve the educational, moral and social conditions of the workers."[73]

In general, however, employers made valiant attempts to keep women out of unions. The paternalism, benevolence, and welfare they offered in compensation were supported by other sectors of their society, including the trade unions. Middle-class reformers and government investigators had long viewed the harsh conditions under which women worked as detrimental to the preservation of home and family, and government regulation or voluntary employer programs seemed to many an adequate alternative. Unions played into this competitive structure, adopting the home and motherhood argument to restrict women's labor force participation. In the process they encouraged women to see their interests apart from those of male workers.

☐ Limited labor force opportunities, protective labor legislation, and virtual exclusion from labor unions institutionalized women's isolation from the mainstream of labor. Not accidentally, these tendencies confirmed traditional women's roles, already nurtured by many ethnic groups and sustained by prevailing American norms. Together they translated into special behavior on the part of female workers that isolated them still further from male workers and added up to special treatment as members of the labor force.

In acquiescing, women perhaps bowed to the inevitable, seeking for themselves the goals of employers who preferred not to see them in unions, of male workers who hoped thereby both to limit competition and to share in the advantages gained, and of middle-class reformers who felt they were helping to preserve home and motherhood. Echoing labor union arguments of twenty years earlier, Women's Bureau head Mary Anderson defended protective legislation in 1925 on the grounds that such laws were necessary to conserve the health of the nation's women.[74]

A final consequence for women was to lead them to search for jobs in newly developing sectors of the labor market that were not yet sex-stereotyped. Employers' needs in the rapidly expanding white-collar sector led women increasingly to secretarial and clerical work. Vocational education to train women for office jobs, teaching, and social work expanded rapidly in the early twentieth century. Working women rationalized these jobs as steps up the occupational ladder; state and local governments and employers provided financial aid; and middle-class women launched a campaign to encourage women to accept vocational training.[75] It took an astute union woman like Fannia Cohn to see what was happening. She drew a sharp line between her own function as educational director of the ILGWU and the functions of the new schools. Her hope was to train women to be better union members, not to get them out of the working class.

The parallel development of protective legislation and vocational education confirmed for many working women their marginal positions in the labor force, positions they continued to rationalize with obeisance to marriage and the family. As Alice Henry said of an earlier group of female wage earners, "they did not realize that women were within the scope of the labor movement."[76] Fannia Cohn understood what that meant. That hard-headed and clear-sighted official of the ILGWU prefaced a call for a revolution in society's view of women with a plea for an end to competition between working women and men. Because it was destructive for all workers, she argued, "this competition must be abolished once and for all, not because it is immoral, yes inhuman, but because it is impractical, it does not pay."[77] But in the first two decades of the twentieth century, the moral arguments prevailed— releasing some women from some of the misery of toil but simultaneously confirming their place in those jobs most conducive to exploitation.

Notes

I wish to thank the Louis M. Rabinowitz Foundation and the American Philosophical Society for essential financial support and Jan Shinpoch for assistance in research.

1. Fannia Cohn to William Green, 6 Mar. 1925, box 4, Fannia Cohn Collection, New York Public Library.

2. Figures are derived from John Andrews and W. D. P. Bliss, *History of Women in Trade Unions: Report on the Condition of Women and Child Wage Earners in the U.S.* (Washington, D.C.: GPO, 1911), vol. 10, pp. 136–39; Leo Wolman, *Ebb and Flow in Trade Unionism* (New York: National Bureau of Economic Research, 1936), 74, 116; Leo Wolman, *The Growth of American Trade Unions, 1880–1923* (New York: National Bureau of Economic Research, 1923), chap. 5. Wolman estimates that about 40 percent of organized women were in the three garment industry unions: ILGWU, Amalgamated Clothing Workers, and United Garment Workers, unions that had been either literally or virtually nonexistent before 1910. See Wolman; and Alice Henry, *Women and the Labor Movement* (New York: George Doran, 1923), chap. 4, for discussions of the difficulty of collecting trade union figures. Henry illustrates the numbers of women in specific unions.

3. The proportion of foreign-born and native-born daughters of foreign-born women declined slightly in this period, and women continued to shift from manual sectors to low-level clerical sectors of the work force. See U.S. Bureau of the Census, *Fourteenth Census of Populations* (Washington, D.C.: GPO, 1920), 3:15. Such occupations as taking in boarders, home work, and working on husband's farms or in family businesses are not counted by census takers. Including these legitimate forms of labor would create drastic upward revisions in the proportion of working women, but we have no way of knowing by how much. The figures include Black women, more than 40 percent of whom worked for wages, compared with about 20 percent of white women. However, about 32 percent of married Black women worked, compared with fewer than 6 percent of married white women. Black wage-earning women are far more heavily concentrated in agricultural and domestic service jobs than their white counterparts. Figures are from Joseph Hill, *Women in Gainful Occupations: 1870–1920,* Census Monographs no. 9 (Washington, D.C.: GPO, 1929), chaps. 5 and 9; Janet Hooks, *Women's Occupations through Seven Decades,* Women's Bureau Bulletin no. 218 (Washington, D.C.: GPO, 1947), 37, 39.

4. Andrews and Bliss, 138–39. Even before the great uprising of 1909–10, women, who made up 63 percent of the workers in the garment trades, represented 70 percent of the trade union members. This is all the more remarkable because their skill levels did not, by and large, match those of men. Of hat and cap makers, 32.5 percent were women, and 54 percent of union

members were women. Women made up 50 percent of bookbinders and 40 percent of the trade union members in that industry.

5. Ann Blankenhorn, miscellaneous notes, chap. 2, p. 12, file no. 23, box no. 1, Ann Craton Blankenhorn Collection, Archives of Labor History, Wayne State University. For another example, see interview with Netti Chandler, Virginia Home visits, Bulletin no. 10, accession no. 51A101, Women's Bureau (hereafter cited as WB) Collection, Record Group 86, National Archives, Washington, D.C.

6. Faige Shapiro interview, 6 Aug. 1964, pp. 2, 7, Amerikaner Yiddishe Geschichte Bel-pe, YIVO Institute, New York.

7. *American Federationist* 6 (November 1899): 228.

8. Quoted in Andrews and Bliss, 173.

9. New York Women's Trade Union League, *Report of the Proceedings, Fourth Annual Conference of Trade Union Women* 9 and 10 Oct. 1926, 18.

10. Vera Shlakman, *Economic History of a Factory Town: A Study of Chicopee, Massachusetts*, Smith College Studies in History 20 (October 1934–July 1935): 216; Andrews and Bliss, 166.

11. Andrews and Bliss, 168; Massachusetts, Women's Trade Union League, *The History of Trade Unionism among Women in Boston* (Boston: WTUL, n.d. [but c. 1907]), 22, 23.

12. Theresa Wolfson, "Where Are the Organized Women Workers?" *American Federationist* 32 (June 1925): 455–57.

13. Andrews and Bliss, 151.

14. *American Federationist* 17 (November 1911): 896; James Kenneally, "Women and Trade Unions," *Labor History* 14 (Winter 1973), describes but does not explain the AFL's mixed feelings.

15. Eva McDonald Valesh, "Women and Labor," *American Federationist* 3 (February 1896): 222.

16. Selig Perlman, *A History of Trade Unionism in the U.S.* (New York: Macmillan, 1923), 166. For illustrations of AFL policies, see James Weinstein, *The Corporate Ideal in the Liberal State: 1900–1918* (Boston: Beacon Press, 1968), esp. chaps. 1 and 2; Ronald Radosh, *American Labor and United States Foreign Policy* (New York: Vintage, 1970); Stanley Aronowitz, *False Promises* (New York: McGraw-Hill, 1973).

17. Samuel Gompers, "Should the Wife Help Support the Family?" *American Federationist* 13 (January 1906): 36. See also Stuart Reid, "The Joy of Labor? Plutocracy's Hypocritical Sermonizing Exposed—A Satire," *American Federationist* 11 (November 1904): 977–78.

18. "Mainly Progressive," *American Federationist* 3 (March 1896): 16; "What Our Organizers Are Doing," *American Federationist* 10 (April 1903): 370.

19. Editorial, *American Federationist* 11 (July 1904): 584; "Trade Union History," *American Federationist* 9 (November 1902): 871.

20. John Safford, "The Good That Trade Unions Do," pt. 1, *American Federationist* 9 (July 1902): 353, 358; "Talks on Labor," 12 (November 1905): 846.

21. William Gilthorpe, "Advancement," *American Federationist* 17 (October 1910): 847.

22. John Safford, "The Good That Trade Unions Do," pt. 2, *American Federationist* 9 (August 1902): 423.

23. Edward O'Donnell, "Women as Breadwinners: The Error of the Age," *American Federationist* 4 (October 1897): 186. The article continued: "The wholesale employment of women in the various handicrafts must gradually unsex them as it most assuredly is demoralizing them, or stripping them of that modest demeanor that lends a charm to their kind, while it numerically strengthens the multitudinous army of loafers, paupers, tramps and policemen."

24. Safford, "The Good That Trade Unions Do," pt. 1, 357–58.

25. Gompers, 36. See also Louis Vigoreux, "Social Results of the Labor Movement in America," *American Federationist* 6 (April 1899): 25.

26. "Women's Labor Resolution," *American Federationist* 5 (January 1899): 22; "Talks on Labor," *American Federationist* 10 (June 1903): 477.

27. Massachusetts WTUL, *History of Trade Unionism among Women in Boston*, 13; Elizabeth Baker, *Technology and Women's Work* (New York: Columbia University Press, 1964), 33.

28. Mildred Rankin to Mrs. Raymond Robins, 30 Mar. 1919, Margaret Dreier Robins Collection, University of Florida, Gainesville, Florida. In 1918, two women members of the federation offered a resolution to the national convention urging the addition of two women to the all-male executive board. It was quietly suppressed.

29. Gompers, 36.

30. Alice Woodbridge, "Women's Labor," *American Federationist* 1 (April 1894): 66–67; Valesh, "Women and Labor," 222; and Massachusetts WTUL, *History of Trade Unionism among Women in Boston*, 32.

31. WTUL Action of Policies, 3, 8, box 4, accession no. 55A556, WB; Proceedings of the AFL convention, 1923. See also Massachusetts WTUL, *History of Trade Unionism among Women in Boston*, 32.

32. Blankenhorn manuscript notes, chap. 4, p. 17, box 1, file 24. Such examples of family unity are not unusual in the mine/mill towns of Western Pennsylvania and the Appalachian mountains. Women helped to picket during strikes, provided essential support services, and sometimes spearheaded attacks against mine management.

33. Pauline Newman interview, undated, p. 21, Amerikaner Yiddishe Geschichte Bel-pe. Gladys Boone, *The Women's Trade Union League in Great Britain and the U.S.A.* (New York: Columbia University Press, 1942), 166, recounts a similar incident as having taken place in 1918. I suspect that it might be the same one and that her date is incorrect. Andrews and Bliss, 149, note that

women practically disappeared from this union between 1905 and 1910—a period in which master bakers were rapidly being eliminated by machinery.

34. Mildred Rankin to Mrs. Raymond Robins, 30 Mar. 1919, Robins Collection.

35. Boone, 167; Henry, 102.

36. Vail Ballou Press interview, Effects of Legislation: Night Work Schedule, New York, WB.

37. See, for example, Rankin to Robins, 30 Mar. 1919; and M. E. Jackson, "The Colored Woman in Industry," *Crisis* 17 (November 1918): 14.

38. New York Women's Trade Union League, *Report of the Proceedings,* 14.

39. Undated interviews, unions, for Bulletin no. 65, WB.

40. Testimony of Hilda Svenson, *Final Report and Testimony of the Commission on Industrial Relations* (hereafter CIR), Senate Documents, Vol. 21, 64th Cong., 1st Sess., vol 3, 1914, p. 2307; the testimony was taken in June 1914.

41. Florence Sanville to Rose Schneiderman, 28 Nov. 1917, box A94. Rose Schneiderman Collection, Tamiment Institute Library. For examples of union discrimination, see Massachusetts WTUL, *History of Trade Unionism among Women in Boston,* 13; Andrews and Bliss, 156, 157; Alice Henry, *The Trade Union Woman* (New York: Burt Franklin, 1973), 150.

42. Testimonies, box 15, accession no. 51A101, WB. The women had been hired when the war broke out.

43. Emma Steghagen to Mary Anderson, 15 Jan. 1919, WTUL Action on Policies.

44. U.S. Education and Labor Committee, *Report upon the Relations between Capital and Labor* (Washington, D.C.: GPO, 1882), 1, 453. See Andrews and Bliss, 94, for Strasser's often-quoted "We cannot drive females out of the trade but we can restrict their daily quota of labor through factory laws," and 155 of the same volume for Samuel Gompers' fears of female competition as expressed in 1887.

45. Mr. Salerno interview, Amalgamated Clothing Workers, interviews, unions, accession no. 51A101, WB.

46. Mr. Hurley interview, July 1919, Women Street Car Conductors, accession no. 51A101, WB.

47. Sir Lyon Playfair, "Children and Female Labor," *American Federationist* 7 (April 1900): 103. See also Martha Moore Avery, "Boston Kitchen Help Organize," *American Federationist* 10 (April 1903): 259, 260.

48. Ira Howerth, "The Kingdom of God and Modern Industry," *American Federationist* 14 (August 1907): 544.

49. Mary Anderson, "The Federal Government Recognizes Problems of Women in Industry," *American Federationist* 32 (June 1925): 453.

50. Individual interviews, Massachusetts, 12 Apr. 1920, accession no. 51A101, WB. Conboy's preference rested on the union's ability to ask for wage raises to compensate for the reduction in hours.

51. Individual interviews, Massachusetts and New Jersey, accession no. 51A101, WB. See esp. interviews with A. J. Muste; Mr. Sims, secretary of the Weavers union; and Amalgamated meeting of workers at Princeton Worsted Mills. These are undated but must have occurred in early 1921.

52. Fannia Cohn to Dr. Marion Phillips, 13 Sept. 1927, box 4, Fannia Cohn Collection.

53. Tony Salerno, interview, Amalgamated Clothing Workers Union and Hat and Cap Makers Local 7, Boston, individual interviews, unions, accession no. 51A101, NA; Massachusetts WTUL, *History of Trade Unionism among Women in Boston,* 11.

54. Lizzie Swank Holmes, "Women Workers of Chicago," *American Federationist* 12 (August 1905): 507–10; Eva McDonald Valesh, "Women in Welfare Work," *American Federationist* 15 (April 1908): 282–84; "Mainly Progressive," *American Federationist* 3 (March 1896): 16.

55. Shapiro interview, 25.

56. *Justice,* 19 Apr. 1919, 2.

57. Blankenhorn manuscript notes, chap. 13, p. 4, box 1, file 25.

58. For example, see Mary Dreier, address to New York WTUL in *Report of the Proceedings,* 1926, p. 14. Dreier refers in this speech to the difficulty the WTUL had getting female workers to serve on the executive board at first. See Nancy Schrom Dye, "Creating a Feminist Alliance: Sisterhood and Class Conflict in the New York WTUL, 1903–1914," *Feminist Studies* 2, no. 2–3 (1975): 24–38. Keneally treats the WTUL's relations with the AFL at length.

59. Individual interviews, California, effects of legislation, accession no. 51A101, WB.

60. Quoted in a letter from Mary Van Kleeck to Mary Anderson, 2 Feb. 1923, Mary Van Kleeck Collection, Smith College, Northampton, Massachusetts, unsorted.

61. Breman and O'Brien, individual interviews, Massachusetts, accession no. 51A101, WB. Such sentiments must, however, be treated cautiously. We know, for example, that the National Consumers League in Philadelphia orchestrated an anti-ERA letter-writing campaign by wage-earning women in 1922. The league urged women to write letters arguing that the ERA would limit or eliminate protective labor legislation. See Barbara Klazcynska, "Working Women in Philadelphia: 1900–1930" (Ph.D. diss., Temple University, Philadelphia, 1975). Janice Hedges and Stephen Bemis point out that most "protective" legislation has now been invalidated by EEOC decisions. See "Sex Stereotyping: Its Decline in Skilled Trades," *Monthly Labor Review* 97 (May 1974): 18.

62. Sylvia Shulman testimony, CIR, 2285, 2292; Hilda Svenson testimony, CIR, 2311, 2317; Elizabeth Dutcher testimony, CIR, 2392. Exceptions sometimes occurred in small western towns where workers would not patronize nonunion stores. Dutcher testified that seventy-five employees of Macy's were

discharged in 1907 after they attended a union ball. Svenson testimony, CIR, 2307; Lillian Mallach to David Dubinsky, 18 Dec. 1964, YIVO Institute, New York. See also minutes of the Waistmakers Conference, 10 Jan. 1911, ILGWU, Ladies Waist and Dress Makers Union file, box A95, Rose Schneiderman Collection.

63. Rose Schneiderman with Lucy Goldthwaite, *All for One* (New York: Paul Erickson, 1967), 59; Shapiro interview, 9.

64. Elizabeth Maloney testimony, CIR, 3246–47. See Jackson, 12–17.

65. Agnes Nestor testimony, CIR 3389; Dutcher testimony, CIR, 2405.

66. Maloney testimony, CIR, 3245.

67. Leon Stein, *The Triangle Fire* (Philadelphia: J. B. Lippincott, 1952); Nestor testimony, CIR, 3382.

68. Blankenhorn, manuscript notes, chap. 4, p. 17, box 1, file 24.

69. Nestor testimony, CIR, 3382; and Svenson testimony, CIR, 3382, 2308 reveal the degree to which this was an attempt to undercut union strength. See also an unsigned typescript entitled "Personnel and Management in a Retail Store: A Study of the Personnel Policies and Practices of William Filene's Sons Co., Boston, Mass.," 14, in the Van Kleeck Collection; Marie Obenauer and Charles Verrill, *Wage-Earning Women in Stores and Factories: Report on the Condition of Women and Child Wage Earners* (Washington, D.C.: GPO, 1911), 5:48; and Svenson testimony, CIR, 2309.

70. See Cambridge Paper Box Company, Long Hour Day Schedule, accession no. 51A101, WB.

71. Andrews and Bliss, 169.

72. U.S. Department of Labor, Bureau of Labor Statistics, Bulletin no. 145, 1914, p. 37.

73. *The Cotton Textile Industry: Report on the Condition of Women and Child Wage Earners* (Washington, D.C.: GPO, 1910), 1:608.

74. Mary Anderson, "Industrial Standards for Women," *American Federationist* 32 (July 1925): 21.

75. See Massachusetts WTUL, *History of Trade Unionism among Women in Boston*, 7, 32; New York WTUL, *Report of the Proceedings*, 21.

76. Henry, 108.

77. Typescript of "Complete Equality between Men and Women," from the December 1917 issue of the *Ladies Garment Worker*, box 7, Fannia Cohn Collection.

Race, Sex, and Class: Black Female Tobacco Workers in Durham, North Carolina, 1920–1940, and the Development of Female Consciousness

☐ This chapter examines how race, sex, and class affected the lives and consciousness of Black female tobacco workers in Durham, North Carolina, and how they conceptualized work and its meaning in their lives. The research was based on fifteen interviews. The interviewees fall into three broad age categories: five were born before 1908, seven between 1908 and 1916, and three between 1916 and 1930. All were born in the rural South. The majority migrated to Durham in the 1920s, subsequently entering the labor force.

Historically, Black labor of both females and males has been critical to the tobacco manufacturing industry. As cigarette manufacture became mechanized, Blacks were hired as stemmers, sorters, hangers, and pullers. These "dirty" jobs were seen as an extension of field labor and therefore as "Negro work" for which whites would not compete.[1] The rapidly expanding number of tobacco factories employed the thousands of Black females and males migrating from the rural South. The pull of better-paying jobs and the push of falling farm prices, perennial pests, and hazardous weather induced a substantial number of Black share-croppers, renters, and landowners to seek refuge in Durham.

Charlie Necoda Mack, the father of three future female tobacco workers, remembered the difficulties of making an adequate living out of farming in Manning, South Carolina. "I was a big cotton farmer; I made nine bales of cotton one year. Next year I made, I think, one or

Reprinted, with changes, from *Feminist Studies* 10, no. 3 (Fall 1984): 441–51. © 1984 by Feminist Studies, Inc.

two, and the next year I didn't make none. I left in July; I had to leave. I borrowed money to get up here—Durham. I had six children and I know no jobs available. Well, then I came up here in July in 1922 and got a job at the factory. And by Christmas I had all my children with clothes and everything." Unlike the Mack family who were pushed out of South Carolina, others were pulled into the city. Dora Miller, after marrying in 1925, left Apex, North Carolina, because she heard of the "better-paying jobs in Durham." Mary Dove, at age ten and accompanied by her family, left Roxboro, North Carolina, because a "Duke agent told us that a job in the factory at Liggett Myers was waiting for my daddy." Rosetta Branch, age eighteen and single, left Wilmington, North Carolina, because her mother had died, and "there were no other kinfolks."[2]

Thus, Durham's gainfully employed Black population swelled from 6,869 in 1910 to 12,402 in 1930. (The city's total Black population in 1930 was 23,481.) According to the census, the number of Black female tobacco workers in 1930 was 1,979 out of a total Black female population of 12,388. (See table 1.)

Table 1. Tobacco Industry Employment by Race and Gender

Durham County: 1930			
White		Negro	
Male	Female	Male	Female
2,511	2,932	1,336	1,979
North Carolina: 1940			
White		Negro	
Male	Female	Male	Female
6,517	3,175	5,899	5,898

Source: U.S. Bureau of the Census, *Population: 1930* (Washington, D.C.: GPO, 1930), vol. 3, pt. 2, pp. 355, 378; *Labor Force: 1940* (Washington, D.C.: GPO, 1940), vol. 3, pt. 4, p. 566.

Durham and Winston-Salem tobacco factories employed more Black females than other cities: one-half of the number of women employed in tobacco factories in 1930 in these cities were Black compared with the 19.7 in Petersburg and Richmond in Virginia.[3]

Upon disembarking at the central train station, the newly arrived southern migrants were immediately faced with race restrictions. Rigidly segregated communities were the dominant feature of Durham's Black life. Many of the migrants settled in the dilapidated housing in the larger communities of East End and Hayti, a bustling commercial district of Black businesses, and in the smaller areas of Buggy Bottom and Hickstown. Almost all Black workers rented either from the company and white landlords or from Black real estate agents. The comments of Annie Barbee, the daughter of Charlie Necoda Mack, reflect her first impressions of Durham.

> We were renting in the Southern part of Durham—the Negro section—on Popular Street, second house from the corner, across the railroad tracks. The house was small, two rooms, but somehow we managed. The street was not paved and when it rained it got muddy and in the fall, the wind blew all the dust into your eyes and face. There were no private family bathrooms. But it was an exciting life. See, in the country things were so dull—no movie houses. . . . Up here people were always fighting and going on all the time.[4]

Despite the exploitive living conditions described by Barbee, urban employment did have some liberating consequences for rural daughters.

Race restricted the Black population to segregated neighborhoods and also determined the kinds of jobs Black females could get. Black female tobacco workers also faced discrimination as poor people and as females. Although class and sex restraints punctuated the lives of white female tobacco workers, their impact was reinforced by management policies. Although white females' wages were a fraction of white males' and inadequate to support a family, Black females' wages were even lower. According to some Black female tobacco workers, the wage inequity led many white women to consider Black women inferior. This in turn led to an atmosphere of mistrust between Black and white females. Management strengthened racial and class inequities in hiring practices, working conditions, and spatial organization of the factory and therefore impeded the formation of gender bonds among working-class women.

Black females were usually hired as if they were on an auction block. "Foremen lined us up against the walls," one worker stated, "and chose the sturdy robust ones." Mary Dove recalled that she had "to hold up one leg at a time and then bend each backwards and forwards."[5] Once hired, Black and white women were separated on different floors at the American Tobacco Company and in entirely different buildings at the Liggett Myers Tobacco Company. In the 1920s and 1930s, according to a report by the Women's Bureau (the federal agency created in 1920), and confirmed by my interviews, 98 percent of these Black females were confined to the prefabrication department where they performed the "dirty" jobs—sorting, cleaning, and stemming tobacco.[6] White females had the "cleaner" jobs in the manufacturing and packing department as they caught, inspected, and packed the tobacco. However, both jobs were defined by the sex division of labor—jobs to be performed by women. Black men moved between the areas pushing 500-pound hogsheads of tobacco while white men worked as inspectors, safeguarding the sanctity of class and sex segregation.[7]

Reflecting on these blatant differences in the working conditions, some fifty years later, many Black women expressed anger at their injustice. Annie Barbee recalled: "You're over here doing all the nasty dirty work. And over there on the cigarette side white women over there wore white uniforms.... You're over here handling all the old sweaty tobacco. There is a large difference. It ain't right!" Rosetta Branch spoke of her experience with anger. "They did not treat us Black folks right. They worked us like dogs. Put us in separate buildings . . . thinking maybe we were going to hurt those white women. Dirty work, dirty work we had to do. Them white women think they something working doing the lighter jobs."[8] These comments reflect both the effectiveness of management policies to aggravate racial and sexual differences in order to preclude any possible bonds of gender but also illustrate the unhealthy working conditions to which Black women were exposed.

In fact, the interviews indicate that the health of some Black women suffered in the factories. Pansy Cheatham, another daughter of Charlie Necoda Mack, maintained that the Georgia leaf-tobacco "was so dusty that I had to go to the tub every night after work. There was only one window and it got so hot that some women just fainted. The heat and smell was quite potent." Mary Dove recounted one of her fainting spells. "You know on the floor there was a salt dispenser, because it would get so hot. I did not feel so well when I came to work but I had to work. After about two hours standing on my feet, I got so dizzy—I fell out. My clothes was soaking wet from my head to my feet. When I woke up I was in the dispensary."[9]

Blanche Scott and another worker were forced to quit for health reasons. Scott, who began working for Liggett Myers in 1919, quit four years later. "When I left the factory, it became difficult for me to breathe. The dust and fumes of the burly tobacco made me cough. The burly tobacco from Georgia had chicken feathers and even manure in it. Sometimes I would put an orange in my mouth to keep from throwing up. I knew some women who died of TB." The other worker had miscarried twice. Pregnant again, she decided not to return to the American Tobacco Company. "I felt that all that standing while I stemmed tobacco," she stated, "was the reason I lost my two children." Some women found momentary relief from the dust by retreating outside the confines of the factory complex to breathe the fresh air while sitting under trees or on the sidewalk during lunch.[10]

These comments on the poor, unhealthy working conditions were verified by research on Durham's death records between 1911 and 1930. In many instances, the records were imprecise and failed to provide information about race and occupation. Of the 105 certificates that identified Black women as tobacco workers, who died between 1911 and 1920, 48 (about 46 percent) died of tuberculosis, sometimes listed as phthisis and consumption. Of the 134 recorded deaths of Black female tobacco workers between 1920 and 1930, 86 (64.5 percent) died of tuberculosis. Because tuberculosis is a bacteria that can be transmitted by a tubercular person through the cough, it is likely that poorly ventilated rooms and incessant coughing by workers, possibly by a carrier, made some workers susceptible to the disease, although deplorable living conditions of workers cannot be dismissed as a contributing factor.[11]

As studies have found in other cities, Black females in Durham were more likely to work than white females.[12] Black females also earned lower wages than white females. In the early 1900s, wages for Black tobacco workers, both female and male, ranked the lowest in the nation. In 1930, 45.5 percent of native-born white women in Durham were gainfully employed—27.7 percent in tobacco. While 44 percent of Black women were working, 36.2 percent were employed in tobacco. From 1920 to 1930, Durham's white female tobacco workers averaged about 29 cents per hour, while Black female hand stemmers earned about 11.9 cents an hour. However, Black men, as well as Black women, who stemmed tobacco by machine, averaged about 27 cents an hour, still less than white women.[13]

Wage differential continued and worsened throughout the 1930s. By the eve of the New Deal, a Women's Bureau survey reported figures for North Carolina which revealed an even higher wage discrepancy. White women working in the making and packing departments reported a median weekly wage of $15.35. Wages ranged from $14.10 earned as catchers to $20.50 on older packing machines. On the newest packing machines, the median wage was $18.15. Black women, working in the leaf department, reported a median weekly wage of $7.95. Hand stemmers earned a median wage of $6.50.[14]

The low wage was itself demeaning to Black female workers. But the inadequate wages also forced many into the labor force at an early age. Black women thus worked for a longer part of their lives and henceforth were more vulnerable to diseases and other health problems. Blanche Scott, for example, began working at the age of twelve. "Since my mother stayed so sick, I had to go to work. I worked at Liggett Myers after school got out. I attended West End School. I'd normally get out at 1:30 and worked from 2 o'clock to 6 p.m. I was just twelve years old. In the summer, they're let children come and work all day until 4 o'clock." Pansy Cheatham began working at age thirteen. "My father talked to the foreman," she stated. "I worked because my sisters Mae and Annie worked; I stemmed tobacco by hand. But Papa did collect the money and use it for food and clothing." Cheatham's statement would indicate that the gender hierarchy of the Black family resided in the father who controlled the daughter's wages.[15]

Many women saw their employment as a means of "helping out the family." Better stated in the words of Margaret Turner, "that's what a family is all about, when we—the children—can help out our parents."[16] Out of the fifteen interviewees, the ten women who entered the work force at an early age all conceptualized the central meaning of their work in relation to their families.

By the late 1920s and early 1930s, the enforcement of the Child Labor Law of 1917 arrested the practice of employing children under the age of sixteen. "They began to ask for your birth certificate," one worker stated. A study done by Hugh Penn Brinton, substantiated the decrease of child labor employment in Durham's factories. Brinton found that from 1919 to 1930 the percentage of Black laboring-class households sending children into the labor force had decreased from 35 to 14 percent.[17]

However, the legislation against child labor did not force the wages up for Black tobacco workers, and the constant low earning power of both female and male breadwinners continued to affect the lives of Black female workers psychologically. Many women submitted to the demands of the foreman and other company officials. Viewed as short-term cheap labor, some females submitted to physical and verbal harassment, because in many instances defiance would have certainly resulted in the loss of jobs. Dora Miller asserted that "since the foreman knew you needed the job, you obeyed all of his demands without question. He called you dirty names and used foul language but you took it." Mary Dove recalled what it was like to work under one "of the toughest bosses." "Our foreman was a one-eyed fella named George Hill. He was tight! He was out of South Carolina, and he was tight. I mean tight! He'd get on top of them machines—they had a machine that altered the tobacco—he'd get on top of that machine and watch you, see if you was working all right and holler down and curse. Holler down and say, "GD ... get to work! GD ... go to work there; you ain't doin' nothin." Janie Mae Lyons remembered one who walked in on her while she "was in the sitting position on the stool" and told her "that if you ain't finished then you can pack up and leave. I was so embarrassed and that's what I did."[18]

Lyons's departure from the factory represented a form of militancy—a definitive stance against further harassment. Other women resisted verbally. Annie Barbee publicly castigated "women who allowed the foreman to fumble their behind" and further stated that if "one did that to me he would be six feet under." She indicated no one ever did. One worker resisted "by playing the fool." "The foreman thought I was crazy and left me alone."[19]

Constantly resisting physical and verbal abuse and trying to maintain their jobs, the workers were further threatened by increased mechanization. "I don't think it is right," one woman stated, "to put them machines to take away from us poor people." "Because of the strain we work under," another maintained, "they don't care nothing for us." One woman recalled crying at the machines because she could not quit in the face of high unemployment. "With them machines you have to thread the tobacco in. Them machines run so fast that after you put in one leaf you got to be ready to thread the other. If you can't keep pace the foreman will fire you right on the spot. Sometimes I get so nervous but I keep on goin'."[20]

The increased mechanization of the tobacco factories resulting in physical hardships of female workers can to some degree be attributed to Franklin D. Roosevelt's National Industrial Recovery acts of 1933 and 1934. On the one hand, President Roosevelt's New Deal measure fostered economic stability for many Black families by establishing standard minimum wages and maximum hours. On the other hand, this standardization exacerbated the job insecurity of Black workers by indirectly catalyzing many companies to maximize profits by replacing hand labor with technology. During the latter part of the 1930s, Liggett Myers closed its green leaf department that had employed the majority of Black women.[21]

The long-term insecurities of their jobs led Black female stemmers to organize Local 194. The limited success of the union was reflected in the decline of its membership of two thousand in January 1935 to less than two hundred by May 1935. Black female union members found little support from either Local 208, Black-controlled, or Local 176, white-controlled. In the eyes of the male unionists, the temporary nature of women's jobs excluded them from any serious consideration by the locals.[22] Conscious of their auxiliary position and the lack of support from male-led unions, Black females chose not to support the April 16, 1939, strike at Liggett Myers. Reporting for work on that day, they were turned away as management had no other recourse but to close the factory. Dora Miller recalled that the Black stemmery workers "were never involved in the strike because demands for wage increases did not include us."[23] On April 26, 1939, the company capitulated. The contract indeed reaffirmed Miller's assessment because the stemmery workers were not mentioned.[24]

The factory policies of hiring, wages, working conditions, and spatial segregation, inherently reinforced by racism, the "cult of true white womanhood," and the inadvertent effect of New Deal governmental measures, all came together to touch the lives of Black women tobacco workers, with sex, race, and class exploitation. These practices further dissipated any possible gender bonds between Black women and white women workers. As a race, Black female tobacco workers were confined to unhealthy segregated areas either in separate buildings or on separate floors. As a working class, they were paid inadequate wages. As a sex, they were relegated to the worst, lowest paid, Black women's jobs.

Black females conceptualized work as a means of "helping out the family." Denied self-respect and dignity in the factory, Black female tobacco workers felt a need to validate themselves in other spheres. Victimized by their working conditions, female tobacco workers looked to the home as a preferred if not powerful arena. The home became the inner world that countered the factory control over their physical well-being. The duality of their lives—workers of production and nurturers of the family—could be assessed as a form of double jeopardy. But it was their role as nurturers, despite the hardship of work, that provided them with a sense of purpose and "joy." As Pansy Cheatham described her daily routine, "I get up at 5:30 a.m. I feed, clothe, and kiss my children. They stay with my sister while I work. At 7 a.m. I am on the job. A half-hour for lunch at about 12 noon. At 4 p.m. I quit work. At home about 4:30 then I cook, sometimes mend and wash clothes before I retire. About 11:30 I go to bed with joy in my heart for my children are safe and I love them so."[25]

Black females who worked together in the tobacco factories also had the positive experience of creating networks of solidarity. Viewing their plight as one, Black females referred to one another as "sisters." This sisterhood was displayed in the collection of money during sickness and death and celebration of birthdays. The networks established in the factory overlapped into the community and church. Many of these workers belonged to the same churches—Mount Vernon, Mt. Gilead, and White Rock Baptist Church—and functioned as leaders of the usher boards, missionary circles, and Sunday School programs. These bonds were enhanced in the community by the development of clubs. These church groups and female's clubs overlapped the factory support networks and functioned in similar ways.

Finally, the resistance to the physical and verbal abuse that was a constant in the work lives of Black women fostered among some a sense of autonomy, strength, and self-respect. Annie Barbee was one of those women. The assertiveness, dignity, and strength she developed through work became an intricate part of her private life. At age forty and pregnant, she decided to obtain private medical assistance despite her husband's resistance. "When you know things ain't right God gave you a head and some sense. That's my body. I knew I wasn't going to Duke Clinic. And I was working and making my own money, I went where I wanted to go. You see, being married don't mean that your husband controls your life. That was my life and I was carrying his child, it's true, but I was going to look after myself."[26]

Although the work experience of Black women tobacco workers was one of racial, sex, and class oppression, the early advent into the labor force, the resistance to exploitation, and the longevity of work created a consciousness that fostered a sense of strength and dignity among some women in this working class. Management tactics of wage inequity, hiring practices, and racial-sexual division of labor pitted Black women against white women economically as workers and made the formation of gender bonds across race lines all but impossible. Yet among Black women, the linkages of sisterhood engendered a consciousness of female strength, if not feminism.

Notes

I am deeply grateful to North Carolina Central University for a Faculty Research Grant and for the excellent editorial comments of the *Feminist Studies* editors.

1. For discussion of the historical involvement of Black labor in tobacco manufacturing, see Joseph C. Robert, *The Tobacco Kingdom* (Durham, N.C.: Duke University Press, 1938).

2. Charlie Necoda Mack, interview with author, 22 May 1979, on file in the Southern Oral History Program, University of North Carolina, Chapel Hill, hereafter cited as SOHP/UNC. Dora Miller, interview with author, 6 June 1979, SOHP/UNC; Mary Dove, interview with author, 7 July 1979, SOHP/UNC; Rosetta Branch, interview with author, 15 Aug. 1981.

3. The 1940 labor force figures do not include information for Durham County. U.S. Bureau of the Census, *Population: 1930* (Washington, D.C.: GPO, 1930), 3:341. In 1900, the major tobacco industries in the South were the American Tobacco Company and Liggett Myers in Durham, R.J. Reynolds in Winston-Salem, and P. Lorillard in Richmond, Virginia.

4. Annie Barbee, interview, 28 May 1979, SOHP/UNC.

5. Interview, 30 May 1981; Mary Dove interview.

6. Women's Bureau, *The Effects of Changing Conditions in the Cigar and Cigarette Industries,* Bulletin no. 110 (Washington, D.C.: GPO, 1932), 774–75. The Women's Bureau was established by Congress in 1920 under the aegis of the U.S. Department of Labor. Its purpose was to gather information and to provide advice to working women.

7. Mary Dove interview; interviews, 15 and 28 Aug. 1981.

8. Annie Barbee and Rosetta Branch interviews.

9. Pansy Cheatham, interview with author, 9 July 1979, SOHP/UNC; Mary Dove interview.

10. Blanche Scott, interview with author, 11 July 1979, SOHP/UNC; interviews, 8, 15 June, 1981; Mary Dove and Annie Barbee interviews.

11. Death Certificates, 1911–1930, Durham County Health Department, Vital Records, Durham, North Carolina. I was also interested in the correlation of working conditions and female-related maladies such as stillbirths, miscarriages, and uterine disorders. Further perusal of death certificates of stillbirths were less valuable for there were no indications of mothers' occupations. Even hospital statistics lacked occupational data. This area of inquiry as it relates to the health of Black female workers and working conditions needs further research. Further questions that will have to be explored include: Was there a higher percentage of female tobacco workers dying of tuberculosis than non-female tobacco workers? How long were stricken female workers employed in the factory? How much weight must be given to the working environment over that of home environs? Despite the lack of solid data on these questions, the interviews and death records clearly indicate that racial division of labor had a negative impact upon the health of many Black female tobacco workers.

12. Elizabeth H. Pleck, "A Mother's Wage: Income Earning among Married Italian and Black Women, 1896–1911," in *The American Family in Social-Historical Perspective,* 2d ed., edited by Michael Gordon (New York: St. Martin's Press, 1978), 490–510; "Culture, Class, and Family Life among Low-Income Urban Negroes," in *Employment, Race, and Poverty,* ed. Arthur M. Ross and Herbert Hill (New York: Harcourt, Brace and World, 1967), 149–72; "The Kindred of Veola Jackson: Residence and Family Organization of an Urban Black American Family," in *Afro-American Anthropology: Contemporary Perspective,* ed. Norman E. Whitten, Jr., and John F. Szwed (New York: Free Press, 1970), chap. 16.

13. U.S. Bureau of the Census, *Population: 1930,* vols. 3 and 4; U.S. Department of Labor, Women's Bureau, *Hours and Earning in Tobacco Stemmeries,* Bulletin no. 127 (Washington, D.C.: GPO, 1934).

14. Women's Bureau, *Effects of Changing Conditions,* 172–75.

15. Blanche Scott and Pansy Cheatham interviews.

16. Margaret Turner, interview with author, 25 Sept. 1979, SOHP/UNC.

17. Interview, 8 June 1981; Hugh Penn Brinton, "The Negro in Durham: A

Study in Adjustment to Town Life" (Ph.D. diss., University of North Carolina, Chapel Hill, 1930).

18. Dora Miller and Mary Dove interviews; Janie Mae Lyons, interview with author, 4 Aug. 1981.

19. Annie Barbee interviews, 28 May 1979, 10 July 1981.

20. Interviews, 4 and 15 June 1981.

21. For the best discussions of the National Industrial Recovery Act's impact on Blacks, see Raymond Wolters, *Negroes and the Great Depression: The Problem of Economic Recovery*, ed. Stanley E. Kutler (Westport, Conn.: Greenwood Publishing Co., 1970); and Bernard Sternsher, ed., *The Negro in the Depression and War: Prelude to Revolution, 1930–45* (Chicago: Quadrangle Books, 1969). Also see Dolores Janiewski, "From Field to Factory: Race, Class, and Sex and the Woman Worker in Durham, 1880–1940" (Ph.D. diss., Duke University, Durham, North Carolina, 1979).

22. *Durham Morning Herald*, 17, 18 Apr. 1939, p. 1; Janiewski.

23. Dora Miller interview.

24. For terms of contract, see *Durham Morning Herald* and *Durham Sun*, 27 Apr. 1939, pp. 1, 2; Janiewski.

25. Pansy Cheatham interview.

26. Annie Barbee interview, 28 May 1979.

9 Sharon Hartman Strom

Challenging "Woman's Place": Feminism, the Left, and Industrial Unionism in the 1930s

☐ An important work which helped us see the history of women's work in a new way is Alice Kessler-Harris's 1975 article, " 'Where Are the Organized Women Workers?' " Attacking the traditional question asked by organizers and historians, "Why don't women organize?" Kessler-Harris argued that the sexual segregation of women's jobs, their life cycles of work and marriage, and the overwhelming sexism of male unionists made the organization of any women workers remarkable. She suggested that a focus on women workers who had organized would be a more positive and instructive category in the new women's history.[1]

Historians have begun to look for more organized women workers and, not surprisingly, have found them, particularly in the industrial sector. The fact remains, however, that women have organized less frequently than men; by the mid-1970s, 12 percent of working women were unionized while 29 percent of working men were. Despite increases in unionization among women, some observers of women's work still see the relatively low level of organized female workers as evidence that women are inherently less organizable than men. Although acknowledging that women have had more difficulties to overcome in organizing, these observers still believe there is a psychological component in women's attitudes toward union organization that makes them less assertive, less willing to take risks, more willing to be victims of employer exploitation. Illustrating that women have organized—such as the clerical organizing in the 1930s I described in this essay—is not enough. We need to go beyond the question, "Where are the organized women

Reprinted, with changes, from *Feminist Studies* 9, no. 2 (Summer 1983): 359–86. © 1983 by Feminist Studies, Inc.

workers?" and explain why women workers haven't been able to organize as effectively as men. In other words, what historical conditions needed to be present for women to perceive that protests against employers and sexist unions were worth risking their jobs? Why haven't such protests generally led to the forming of viable trade unions? What will make it possible for women to organize *en masse* in the primarily female occupations? When can women organize?

In this article I will explore Depression-era organizing with these questions in mind. In so doing I will avoid attributing psychological motives to women workers. Instead, I will try to show that economic, ideological, and political variables can explain why some women workers succeeded in organizing but did not organize in as large numbers as men. The most important of these variables were women's occupational positions in the U.S. economy, the discriminatory policies of the New Deal, prevailing cultural and ideological views of women's roles in the work force, the failure of industrial unionism to reach most women workers, the lack of community and family support networks for striking women workers, and the absence of a feminist critique within the progressive labor movement, especially the Communist party. I will argue that although women did engage in job actions and spontaneous labor protests in the 1930s they were at an intrinsic disadvantage in getting the kind of wholehearted support men received. That support could not have been provided without a feminist ideology to justify changing the status of working women. As Ruth Milkman has argued, "minimally any successful struggle to organize women had first to challenge the ideology of 'women's place'—a problem that did not arise in organizing men."2

Unemployment, underemployment, and drastically reduced wages became a national experience during the 1930s. Under the banner of Franklin D. Roosevelt's New Deal, the federal government responded on a number of levels to ease the suffering of working people. Women did not receive equal assistance. The 1933 National Industrial Recovery Act (NIRA) minimum wage codes sanctioned lower pay rates for women workers than for men in the same occupations, and they excluded domestic and agricultural jobs—both major occupations for women, especially poor and minority women. Salaried workers and clerical workers in the insurance industry were also excluded. There was widespread evasion of maximum hour codes for clerical workers as employers changed titles, assigned salaries, increased duties, and then forced secretaries to work overtime with no extra pay. The domestic work, agricultural, and government sectors were not covered by Social Security; all three were employers of large numbers of women. The NIRA work relief section ignored women altogether, and the Civilian Conservation Corps camps were originally for men only. When camps for females were set up, women received one-half of what men were paid. The Works Projects Administration (WPA) provided more jobs, but only one member of a family could earn relief, and that member had to be the main wage earner. Aid to Dependent Children (ADC) was widely seen in local communities as a way to get women off the WPA rolls and therefore out of the work force, although ADC payments were lower than WPA work rates. When the NIRA was found to be unconstitutional and was replaced by the Fair Labor Standards Act of 1938, clerks, seasonal employees, and domestic workers found themselves with no protection against substandard wages.[3]

National legislation lashed out at married women workers. Section 213 of the Economy Act of 1932 allowed the firing of one spouse if both husband and wife worked for the government, and of the fifteen hundred married persons fired within the next year, nearly all were women. A crop of proposed state laws tried to follow suit. Frances Perkins, secretary of labor and the first woman to hold a cabinet position, had, as state industrial commissioner of New York, called on women who did not need jobs to stay at home and deplored women who worked for "pin-money."[4]

Federal and state governments were in some ways merely expressing sentiments held by the public at large. Many people believed that working married women were partly responsible for unemployment, and there was widespread sentiment for the firing of married teachers and government workers. The president of the California Institute of Technology proposed that 75 percent of all jobs be reserved for men, and George Gallup, who repeatedly polled Americans on their attitudes toward working wives, claimed that he had never seen poll respondents "so solidly united in opposition" to an economic issue.[5]

Section 213 and other discriminatory policies against married women played a direct role in forcing women out of better jobs in the 1930s. Local and state employees had increased by 400 percent between 1900 and 1930, civilian employees of the federal government had tripled, and school workers had grown by two and one-half times. Women received many of these new jobs, and one-fifth of the women were married. The Women's Bureau found that Section 213 was usually applied to married typists and stenographers and rarely to married charwomen or elevator operators. These policies were repeated in private industry. In 1931, New England Telephone and Telegraph fired all its married women workers. Most large companies, and almost all banks and insurance firms, simply refused to hire married women as clericals. Numerous commentators observed that many workers lied about their married status in order to get or keep jobs. When Social Security cards were issued for the first time in 1937, regional offices were besieged by calls from women who feared their marriages would be revealed to their employers.[6]

Married women were not excluded from the labor force during the Depression. In fact, the number of married women at work increased because families were forced to earn a living in any way they could. Overall, women's status in the job market declined in the thirties; men made gains in proportion to women in teaching, library work, social work, and nursing. Meanwhile, many women had to enter the lower-paid female occupations like domestic service, part-time work, canning, and farm labor. These were also job categories either not covered or only partially covered by Social Security, collective-bargaining legislation, NIRA, and the Fair Labor Standards Act. They were also the only job categories available to most Black and minority women.[7]

The ramifications of attacks on married women workers were of grave import for all women workers, married or not. Because most women eventually married, the working woman was by default considered to be a young adult, or "working girl." She was not a permanent member of the work world and therefore should not have the same say in government and union policy as the "working man." Every married working woman was an anomaly, present in the work force either through temporary financial necessity or personal selfishness. The implication for women was that work outside the home was a stage, not a right, and that the mature woman belonged at home.

Movies hammered home the same message. As Molly Haskell has observed, although many movies of the thirties portrayed an adventurous young working woman who could hold her own in a man's world, she usually capitulated to marriage and home by the film's end.[8] In any event, she worked because she had to.

Thus, the makers of popular culture, government legislators, the general public, and private industry, although somewhat sympathetic to the plight of the working man, were ambivalent about the working woman. She was evidently a necessary evil but should remain confined to the lower-paying feminized occupations, which did not, for the most part, deserve the same benefits as male jobs. She faced a complicated range of problems in the work force, only one of which was union organization.

Women workers responded to Section 7 (a) of the NIRA in 1933, which gave workers the legal right to bargain collectively for wages and working conditions. They were often helped by Communist activists, many of them women, in the Trade Union Unity League (TUUL) and the Unemployed Councils. In Detroit, 6,000 workers, 2,000 of them women, went on strike at the Briggs Mack Avenue plant and won substantial wage gains for women. In Philadelphia, female and male workers at the Philadelphia Storage Battery Company (Philco) won an agreement which gave a 10 percent wage increase to men and a 15 percent increase to women aimed at narrowing the disparity between female and male wages. In May of 1933, 4,500 workers, mostly women, struck nonunion Philadelphia dress plants. A revitalized International Ladies' Garment Workers' Union (ILGWU) was able to launch a general strike of dressmakers, mostly female, in New York, New Jersey, and Connecticut and won an agreement in four days. Similar strikes were conducted by the Amalgamated Clothing Workers in Pennsylvania, New York, and Connecticut. In St. Louis 1,400 women, mostly Black, went on strike to protest a piece-rate reduction in the city's pecan-shelling factories. The strikers, who had gone out in 1927 as well, had the support of the TUUL and the Unemployed Councils. Husbands and children of the strikers joined them on the picket line, and sympathetic unionists and businesses in the Black community provided food for meals. After the employers brought in scabs and strikebreakers, the local Jewish community and the American Civil Liberties Union provoked sympathy for the strikers in the press, and the mayor of the city helped to mediate negotiations.[9]

In 1934, textile workers went out on strike from Maine to Mississippi, and women, who made up 40 percent of all textile workers, were instrumental in the protracted and bloody strike which ensued. They fought state militias, participated in huge demonstrations, sat down on railroad tracks, and led "flying squadrons" from plant to plant to recruit new strikers and intimidate scabs. Thirty thousand women and men hotel workers struck fifty hotels in New York early in 1934 to gain union recognition. In December 1936, 4,000 female and male workers struck five of Philadelphia's six leading department stores. Warehouse workers, truckers, sales clerks, packers, porters, and waitresses were joined on the third day of the strike by seventy-five bookkeepers and office workers. Although the strike was hushed up in the newspapers and numerous arrests were made, workers achieved union recognition and a forty-eight-hour week.[10]

The entire labor movement entered a dynamic new phase in 1936 and 1937 when workers in basic production waged sit-down strikes. In both Akron, Ohio, and Flint, Michigan, despite the fact that they made up substantial numbers of workers in both the rubber and automobile industries, women workers—many of them young and single—were sɛnt home by strike leaders and not allowed to sit-down. Women were discouraged from sitting in with men in factory strikes, for mixed groups of women and men might give employers a chance to charge sexual promiscuity or to provoke "unfit mother" cases in the courts.[11] Both men and married women, given the traditional allocation of childcare responsibilities in the thirties, probably feared that children would be neglected if mothers were not at home to care for them.

Sit-downs were perceived as men's affairs in the Congress of Industrial Organizations (CIO). One union official defined a sit-down in 1937 as "a cessation of work with the men remaining at work." But women workers throughout the country were quick to perceive that sit-downs might be of use to them. Jeremy Brecher found that both Chicago and Detroit experienced waves of sit-down strikes in stores and smaller factories following the great General Motors strike in the spring of 1937. There were eighty-seven sit-downs involving 3,000 workers in Detroit alone, many of them in the auto parts and manufacturing firms which employed large numbers of women. Two hundred women, not allowed to participate in the Flint sit-down strike which led to a United Automobile Workers (UAW) contract with General Motors, sat down in a sewing room in the Fischer Body Plant No. 1 and were joined in sympathy an hour later by 280 additional women sewers. When sixty men in the shipping department also sat down, the entire plant was forced to close.[12] Clerks sat down in Detroit, Chicago, and New York department stores and five-and-tens, and women workers barricaded themselves in three tobacco plants in Detroit for several weeks. When 150 police attacked sit-downers at one of them, "hysterical cries echoed through the building as, by ones, and twos, the eighty-six women strikers, ranging from defiant girls to bewildered workers with gray hair, were herded into patrol wagons and sped away, while shattering glass and the yells of the street throng added to the din."[13] The UAW protested against such forced evictions, threatened to call 180,000 auto workers out on strike, and even raised the specter of a citywide general strike. The police stopped their raids. In Chicago there were sixty sit-downs in a two-week period in March of 1937, including 9,000 female and male Loop workers, ranging from peanut baggers to stenographers. Brecher reports that "1,800 workers, including 300 office workers, sat down at the Chicago Mail Order Company and won a ten percent pay increase; 450 employees at three deMet's tea rooms sat down as 'the girls laughed and talked at the tables they had served' until they went home that night with a twenty-five percent pay increase. . . ."[14]

We should also remember that women participated in strikes and job actions not only as workers but also as wives or relatives of workers, mainly in women's auxiliaries. Male unionists at the time were more likely to respond to women who participated in women's auxiliaries than to women workers. The image of the woman standing behind her man and his job became a sentimental theme in union rhetoric, while the working woman was conspicuously absent. Women's auxiliaries often picketed and even fought the police, and they also provided meals for the duration of strikes, clearly an important key to their success.[15] There were obviously no "men's auxiliaries" to provide meals and childcare for striking women, although we need to know more about the ad hoc arrangements created by the friends, relatives, and communities of striking women. Working women and wives and relatives of working men all belonged to the auxiliaries; women workers who were sent out of plants in the Akron and Flint sit-downs of 1934 and 1937 participated by joining the UAW and United Rubber Workers (URW) auxiliaries.[16]

The auxiliaries did not lead to permanent union organizations which might have begun to articulate women workers' grievances. Although most male sit-downers were happy to have the support of women's emergency brigades during strikes, they expected that women would return to traditional roles once the emergencies were over. Some women resented this idea and saw the auxiliaries as a forum for discussion of women's concerns. Sometimes they were encouraged by Communist party (CP) organizers to address such issues as birth control, childcare, and who should do the housework, but the mere fact of organizing together as women was evidently a problematic idea for all concerned.

> In some cases the women through their activities won the respect of their striking husbands, and were given representation on strike committees. In other situations, the militancy of the CP-led auxiliaries enraged the male union leadership, who wanted women to stay home. Women in auxiliaries, as in the CP's women's units, developed some cooperative methods of child care, and occasionally forced their husbands to assume some of these responsibilities. These organizations did not equal liberation, of course, as tasks such as preparing food for the strikers still remained for the women. The CP often failed to push the auxiliaries and unions to go beyond sex-stereotyped roles.[17]

Yet some working-class women clearly articulated the larger issues their organizing as women had raised; one participant in the Flint Emergency Brigade said, "Just being a woman isn't enough anymore. I want to be a human being with the right to think for myself."[18] Beatrice Marcus reported in a December 1934 issue of the CP's *Working Woman*

that women from coal miner families in Hillsboro, Illinois, had organized to demand adequate relief. They "held meetings, travelled through
the countryside, raised money, and, in defiance of the male leadership
of the Progressive Miners' Association, led demonstrations. As one
march began on City Hall, the male demonstrators 'made vain efforts to
keep their wives from the front ranks.' "[19] One of the most salient
features of the thirties is the failure of any organized groups to develop
this working-class women's new consciousness and militance into a
feminist position.

Feminist organizations, for the most part made up of middle-class
women, were on the defensive in the thirties. In fact, because they had
not recruited many younger women to join their ranks, older feminists
found themselves increasingly talking to each other. Many of the goals
they had been working toward since 1920 seemed to be under attack,
particularly the right to combine marriage and work. In an attempt to
gain some protection for the jobs of married women, feminists tended
to emphasize that women workers did not usually compete with men
and that most of them needed their wages to support families. Although
useful in the short run, these arguments tended to reinforce popular
notions of the thirties that women should work only when they had to
and only when they did not take men's jobs.[20] Feminists in the thirties
were also unable to establish any sustained point of view in the industrial union movement; they either ended up criticizing the role of
Communists and other leftists, or they joined popular front alliances in
which leftist women—most of whom were suspicious of traditional
feminism—dominated. Although they had never been very successful
in attracting working-class women to their groups, the failure of feminists
to remain visible in the thirties meant that working-class women had no
public sanction for articulating feminist ideas.

Communist party dogma officially viewed feminism as a bourgeois
reform movement; women's problems would automatically be corrected
with the arrival of true communism. Yet this view, as Robert Schaffer
has recently argued, barely kept the lid on a smoldering debate within
the party and in its publications on the "woman question." Party writers
did discuss birth control, unequal pay, maternity insurance, and the
role of men in housework. It was always clear, however, that industries
dominated by male workers would be the target of vanguard organizing.
Official writings also did not "admit to any conceivable antagonism
between working-class men and women," and any struggle against male
supremacy within the party had to be balanced against the party's desire
to have its members live like ordinary workers and therefore accept
ordinary workers' behavior—including the subordination of women to

men.[21] These party lines, however, must be counterpointed by the actual experience of Communist women in the 1930s. There is no doubt that the experience of party membership, of organizing women's auxiliaries, consumer boycotts, and picket lines gave many a female Communist the organizing experience and self-respect she needed to become an independent woman. We must remember, however, that sometimes standing up for women, working with women, or becoming independent of men was not the same as possessing a feminist consciousness.

The labor struggles of the Great Depression took on a new dimension after 1937 as the CIO rapidly expanded. The effects of increasing bureaucratization in the union movement on women's organizing efforts were somewhat contradictory. Certainly the financial resources, institutional support, and power to impose a unionized shop of the CIO made it possible to bring unionism to women who would otherwise have missed it. Any unionized shop was likely to raise women's wages significantly.[22] But there is also evidence to suggest that the early militancy of strikes and the wide-ranging scope of issues they raised in the early thirties began to disappear by 1937, as collective bargaining replaced confrontation and focused on the narrow range of issues laid out by contract negotiations.[23]

In a primer on how to organize an industrial union, Clinton S. Golden and Harold J. Ruttenberg argued that "the written collective-bargaining contract is the means through which workers secure . . . a voice. . . . Once wage earners successfully establish organization and collective bargaining at their point of actual employment, their relationship with management undergoes a transition from one of conflict in varying degrees to that of cooperation in some degree."[24] Unions called for grievances to be handled by shop stewards and union committees. In many unions women were denied access to this hierarchy, although they were a significant influence in some.[25] These new developments probably prevented women from capitalizing on effective use of job actions to rectify their grievances.

Although the CIO was more receptive to women workers than the American Federation of Labor (AFL) had been, women usually joined when they were present in industries with large numbers of men, as in, for example, the garment and electrical industries or when they organized themselves. Self-organization occurred particularly among minority women. When 400 Black women stemmers in Richmond, Virginia, tobacco factories walked out in a spontaneous strike in 1937, they were told by the AFL that Black workers couldn't be organized. The Southern Negro Youth Congress and the National Negro Congress, not the

CIO, helped them form the Tobacco Stemmers and Laborers' Union. The ILGWU, which had a better record on helping southern workers than some other CIO unions, sent 500 women pickets to a Richmond tobacco strike in 1938, and the newly formed locals were passed on to the CIO in 1939. A similar strike by Mexican-American pecan shellers in San Antonio, Texas, in 1938 helped to establish the United Cannery, Agricultural, Packing and Allied Workers of America, a leftist union which was expelled from the CIO in 1950.

Yet only a "negligible proportion" of the 519 delegates to the first CIO convention were women (most of them from office worker unions); and by 1946 only 20 of the 600 delegates to the national convention were female. Only one woman, Eleanor Nelson of the United Federal Workers (UFW), was ever a president of any of the unions chartered by the CIO in the thirties. None of the 1938 constitutional convention's resolutions mentioned working women. The only specific reference to women thanked members of the women's auxiliaries, "the mothers, wives, sisters and daughters of industrial workers," thus ignoring entirely the contribution made by women workers to the auxiliaries. The *CIO News* either buried articles on women's strikes or failed to report them at all, and pictures of women workers in cheesecake poses were far more common than pictures of women on picket lines. Wisconsin CIO members in 1938 thought "a good union girl" should only work to support herself or her family, be intelligent, a good housekeeper, and shorter than her boyfriend. She should use makeup moderately and keep her stocking seams straight. She should go out on the picket line "with her man," because having "girls come on the line . . . puts more pep in the gas."[26] Male unionists clearly had trouble maintaining the contradiction of the ornamental "union girl" that their ideology upheld with the militant union woman whom they frequently encountered. One UFW member told a meeting of unionists that he wanted "to say a word in praise of this little girl of ours, Eleanor Nelson, who . . . has the tenacity of a bulldog and has been out there facing the guns for our union!"[27]

The narrow application of industrial unionism by the CIO to workers in basic production and manufacturing hurt women workers as well. Fewer than 22 percent of all working women worked in manufacturing by 1940, so the failure to reach out to service, domestic, sales, and clerical workers by the CIO played a crucial role in excluding women. Whether this failure was based on disinterest in nonindustrial occupations or on disinterest in women is not very important because it amounted to the same thing.[28]

Although it was not so obvious in the thirties, it is very clear now that the decision to ignore clerical workers was especially portentous. The census of 1940 indicated that more than 21 percent of all women workers were in clerical work, and the size of the occupation increased by nearly 85 percent from 1940 to 1944.[29] To ignore clerical workers was, then, to ignore a significant portion of women workers. Inevitably, however, clericals also caught the union spirit. Leftist clericals and office workers, both female and male, had begun by the mid-thirties to agitate within long-dormant AFL locals for industrial unionism. In 1937 the CIO agreed to charter three office worker unions: the UFW, the State, County and Municipal Workers of America, and the United Office and Professional Workers of America (UOPWA). These unions grew substantially during the 1930s and 1940s but were all purged by the CIO in 1950 and rapidly disappeared. Only the UOPWA could really follow the male industrial union model, because national state and local government employees were usually prohibited by law from going on strike.

The CIO never poured any effort into organizing assistance for the UOPWA and in fact repeatedly restricted its influence. Conceding to the protests of male industrial unions like the UAW and the URW, the CIO prohibited the UOPWA from organizing clerical workers in industries already represented by CIO nationals. Office workers in the steel, mining, auto, rubber, and electrical industries, therefore, were left to the whims of industry or of male unionists, none of whom made any significant attempt to organize clericals. In fact, many manufacturing unions tried to exclude office workers from their locals, a significant action because office workers made up 14.2 percent of all workers in manufacturing by 1938. The 1941 UAW contract with Ford Motors, for instance, specifically excluded most white-collar workers. Sometimes industrial unions made gains explicitly at the expense of white-collar workers. A United Electrical Workers contract with General Electric in 1937 cut salaries for office workers. In the late thirties, rubber workers in Jeanette, Pennsylvania, and Akron, Ohio, agreed to contracts which raised factory wages significantly but cut or froze those of office workers.[30]

Not all office workers or blue-collar workers wanted to be grouped with each other, and the National Labor Relations Board (NLRB) usually ruled that office workers should not be members of the same locals. One of the consequences of this bifurcation of the work force was that blue-collar wages increased at a faster pace than white-collar wages, with clerical workers increasingly earning lower wages than organized workers in manufacturing. Some office employees formed independent unions, but we don't know whether women clerical workers were in favor of this arrangement or not or if they were even involved in the decisions to organize these. Certainly these independent unions were dominated by men, who had the better-paying and more responsible office jobs. The Federation of Westinghouse Independent Salaried Unions even tried to exclude married women from the Westinghouse offices.[31]

The indifference of the CIO at best and its hostility at worst to the organizing of clericals was one problem, which helped prevent the widespread organizing of clericals. Confusion within clerical worker unions over issues of class and gender was another. Young Communist women were particularly likely to be in a position to organize in the offices. The social character of the Communist party had changed dramatically since World War I, with many of the second-generation children of working-class parents receiving high school and even college educations by the 1930s. Many young leftist women with degrees in teaching could not find jobs and were forced to work as secretaries. By 1938 the CP estimated that 22 percent of its new recruits were technically "middle class." Young Communist women were working in business offices, social agencies, publishing houses, government offices, and trade union offices. As Communists they were expected to participate directly in the building of militant unions. They had received speaking, organizing, and protest experience in the CP, a vitally important ingredient for women workers, who often had trouble getting this experience elsewhere. They became the main leaders and organizers of the fledgling office worker unions which emerged in 1936 and 1937, an activity encouraged by the CP during the popular front.[32] Leftists helped break new ground in the organization of clericals in the thirties, but their antifeminist position and their class analysis of clericals hindered their effectiveness.

What class did clerical workers belong to in the thirties? Certainly many secretaries, especially older ones, came from the middle class, and some were college-educated women who had been pushed into lower-status jobs by the effects of the Depression. However, the new compulsory school laws and fewer industrial jobs for teenagers during the Depression meant that countless young working-class women were taking a "business curriculum" in high school and becoming clericals. Business had partly responded to hard times by reducing wages for office workers, instituting speedup, and increasing mechanization. This process involved a more clear-cut sexual division of labor with male office workers doing the managing and earning the best salaries and women performing the more tedious "assembly line" functions and earning the lowest wages. Most hard data on office workers indicated that female stenographers, typists, filing clerks, and other clericals were rapidly descending into the working class at least in terms of wages.[33]

Nonetheless, most leftists continued to lump all female and male office workers together as though their interests and values were the same. They believed that the "social prestige" of office workers usually made them identify with the middle class and that female and male office workers' interests were necessarily inseparable. No one in the Left in the thirties was able to fully articulate the sexual division of office work or to grasp that women might prefer to be or even should be organized *as women* in an industrial clerical workers' movement. Organizers were also unable to discard the notion that because they were theoretically—if not actually—"middle class," office workers were a kind of parentheses to the main thrust of the industrial labor movement.[34]

In fact, the motives for organizing office workers sometimes bordered on the cynical. Communists routinely asserted in the thirties that fascism in Germany and Italy had relied on the support of the *petite bourgeoisie*, including white-collar workers, for its political success. Fearful of the same social phenomenon in the United States, leftist theorists and organizers argued that the American middle class—especially the white-collar sector—should be organized primarily to prevent it from supporting right-wing political causes and to facilitate the spread of unions in the industrial sector. According to Len DeCaux, editor of the *CIO News*, "if democracy and liberalism are to prevail over the menacing forces of fascism, unionization of white collar, office and professional workers is one of the most effective means of spreading labor sympathy and understanding among the middle classes."[35] This line of reasoning often obscured the actual grievances of working-class clericals and made them mere supporters of the struggle to help industrial workers. Such attitudes on the part of the CP leadership probably helped prevent widespread organizing.

Despite all these obstacles, thousands of female clerical workers joined the UOPWA in the thirties, and hundreds went out on strike.[36] Some of these strikes were successful; others were not. A few examples should illustrate that female office workers could be militant, determined, and effective unionists and should also indicate the problems they might encounter.

In early 1936 machinists at the Margon Corporation, a small manufacturing firm in New York City, went on strike. The entire office staff of seven workers, all of them women and members of the leftist Bookkeepers, Stenographers, and Accountants Union (BSAU), precursor of the UOPWA, refused to cross the machinists' picket line. The strike was quickly won, and the factory workers went back to work with "increased wages, union recognition, and improved working conditions." On January 18, Sunny Grill, who had worked for Margon for six years, was fired and given her severance check. Three days later union shop steward Claire Mitchell "interviewed the employers and told them that Miss Grill's discharge made them all feel insecure and if it were actually necessary to have any layoff, it be done on the basis of seniority." Mitchell was fired, and the remaining women were asked to sign pledges that "under no circumstances, especially in the case of a strike of the factory workers, would they go on strike or refuse to walk through the inside workers' picket lines." When they refused to sign, the women were fired, and the BSAU called a strike. Fifty-eight arrests were made in front of the Margon office in the next eight days, and eighteen members of BSAU were arrested in front of the house of one of the owners in Brooklyn. One picketer was beaten by a hired thug. Approximately 200 factory workers did not honor the office workers' picket line until March 2, and by then the position of the owners was frozen. The strike continued into April, when the Margon owners moved their factory to Bayonne, New Jersey, where they had received "assurances that they would not be annoyed with labor disputes."37

Margon was the kind of small firm UOPWA often organized, and the 1936 strike typified some of the special dilemmas of organizing clericals. First, the clerical staff was far outnumbered by the industrial workers. That industrial workers, usually male, would honor clerical picket lines was not a foregone conclusion. One also senses here that employers were more threatened by the betrayal of their office staffs than they were by the militancy of factory workers; they were willing to move the factory rather than "tolerate the idea of their office girls belonging to a union and being as loyal to their fellow workers as they had been" to their bosses.38 As for the factory workers, the message was crystal clear; saving jobs and union membership might necessitate throwing clerical workers overboard.

The advantages of unionizing a "clerical worker factory" were obvious in the wave of credit clearinghouse strikes in the Northeast in 1937–38. The 225 employees of the New York Credit Clearing House, the largest credit information bureau in the country, won union recognition and negotiated a contract under the leadership of office chair Lena de Pasquale. Salaries were as low as $11.88 a week, and employees were expected to work as many as two extra days a week without pay. An arbitrator set new minimum pay rates at $14 a week, but a strike ensued in 1940 over continued union recognition and new wage scales. Workers devised a new strike tactic—telephone picketing. New York Credit Clearing House had seventy-seven trunk lines, and unionists and their friends and relatives kept two thousand calls an hour coming in to jam the phones and stop business.[39]

Taking on a huge corporation, however, was far more difficult. At the New York office of L. Sonneborn Sons, Inc., an oil and paint company with widespread operations throughout the Northeast, Beatrice Limpson and six of her officemates organized and won a NLRB election for Local No. 16 in 1941. A strike in February ensued when contract negotiations broke down, and sympathetic picket lines were thrown up by UOPWA locals around Sonneborn operations all over the country. Longshoremen, seamen, teamsters, and painters all refused to cross picket lines, and names of scabs were advertised daily on picket signs.[40]

UOPWA organizers realized early on they would have to reach Sonneborn's customers to make the strike effective. Accounts had to be visited, and if persuasion failed they were to be picketed or boycotted. The company's executives were hit with a barrage of telephone calls from strikers and their families; the "swanky Savoy Plaza," residence of the company president, was the target of a demonstration. Although Sonneborn eventually agreed to some of the union's demands, it refused to reinstate strikers, and rumor had it that new defense orders were making the company stronger than ever. Office workers at Sonneborn went back to work without a contract.[41]

The UOPWA had a better record than most CIO unions in organizing women workers, but it also incorporated prevailing gender attitudes of the period, despite its leftist leadership. The president of the national was always a man, and national organizers of the UOPWA frequently aired patronizing views of clerical workers in articles like the condescending weekly column signed by "Susie the Secretary." Susie said in 1937 that she didn't know if there were "any other girls in my department who have sense enough to stick together. They seem to be just out for themselves and not to care about how anyone else gets along. I used to be pretty dumb too, thinking that unions were just for common laborers and mechanics, so perhaps I can show them that organization is the thing."[42]

The UOPWA consistently allowed professional and higher-paid office workers, most of whom were men, to write contracts which excluded clerical workers or bargained away their contract rights. And in 1939 the union decided to launch a major campaign to organize insurance agents, almost all of whom were men. Although the insurance agents had suffered reduced salaries and worsened working conditions as a result of the Depression, they were not really devoted to industrial unionism and routinely excluded clericals from their contracts and their locals. Clericals had to join separate locals of the UOPWA. The national accepted this sexism as the price it had to pay for attracting insurance agents to the union, but it meant that dues collected from clerical workers were sent to male locals with no intention of ever serving them.

The UOPWA had successfully organized insurance agents at most of the major insurance corporations by the middle of World War II. In its desire to make these inroads, however, it essentially abandoned any attempt to include clerical workers in the insurance industry. Eventually, the insurance workers bolted from the CIO and created independent craft unions or joined the AFL.

Not surprisingly, these unions specifically excluded clericals. In 1952 striking AFL insurance agents set up a picket line outside a Prudential office building in Newark, New Jersey, hoping to convince clericals not to go to work; the clericals crossed the line. This episode was recorded as another example of how women workers, especially clerical workers, will not honor picket lines, but the story, as we have seen, was far more complicated.[43]

The arrival of the CIO in the 1930s must be viewed as a mixed blessing for women workers. Although many made gains in wages and working conditions, countless others were never offered industrial unions. The CIO acquiesced in the sexual division of labor and even actively sought to maintain it. And, whenever women were organized into unions without some sense of themselves as women, they tended to abrogate their rights. They usually became an adjunct to male unionism, paying in dues and receiving little else but a union card in return.

Women workers needed to challenge women's place to organize effectively in the thirties. They were not only establishing unions but also the right to work, to have feminized occupations accorded equal treatment under federal statute, to earn comparable pay, and to win the support and cooperation of working-class men. In other words, women faced a complicated mesh of ideological, social, and economic obstacles in organizing that were peculiar to them. Where was this challenge to come from? To argue that working-class women could somehow have mounted a viable feminist movement on their own is to engage in the worst sort of wishful thinking. To perceive as an individual woman that one's exploitation as a wife, a mother, a daughter, an employee, and a unionist were all connected was one thing; to struggle collectively on occasion against one or more of these conditions was another; to band together in the face of women's economic dependence on men and attack them all at once was impossible. There were no existent forms of protest or organization along these lines, no popular symbols to evoke, no terms with which to identify the process of liberation, no audiences who would have taken such rhetoric seriously. Unions should have been the forum where the connections between women's problems as workers and as women were made, where the beginnings of a feminist consciousness should have emerged.

Leftist activists from both the working and middle classes were most likely to perceive these connections and to be able to act on them at the same time. Already in an antiestablishment posture, they might be able to see similarities between forms of patriarchy and forms of capitalism. As members of political groups or parties they would have alternative means of personal support other than traditional patriarchal families. Socialist feminists had developed such connections earlier in the century. Women in the Socialist party articulated a far-reaching platform of goals for working women, including suffrage, birth control, and pay for housework. Anarchist Emma Goldman and socialist theorist Charlotte Perkins Gilman had attacked marriage as a capitalist institution ensuring male property rights. Their point of view was missing from leftist ideology in the thirties. The Communist party viewed women's issues as important but inferior to the issues of race and industrial unionism. When all three of these issues combined, as in the pecan sheller's strike in St. Louis in 1933, the Communists did some of their best work. But in organizing women they were prone to use them for the greater good of the party not for engaging in an ongoing struggle to eliminate sexism. Yet Communist women were probably more engaged with women workers than were any other groups in American politics during the Depression. They helped women to articulate their own issues in a movement which would otherwise probably have ignored women as much as possible.

Whatever the failings of both feminists and leftists in the thirties, they did try to organize women workers and pioneered in the organization of clerical workers. Hundreds of clerical workers responded by joining CIO office workers' unions, and their numbers grew larger during World War II. The contributions of leftist and feminist women during the thirties and during the war stand out in high relief when we look at women in unions in the fifties, a time when feminism was at its lowest point since the early nineteenth century. The Left was driven from the industrial union movement, and all three industrial unions for office workers were expelled from the CIO.

When can women organize? Women workers—whether they are domestics, nurses, clericals, hairdressers, or seamstresses—must be given the impression by someone—male unionists, middle-class feminists, or leftist activists—that unions are appropriate for women, that unions are receptive to the elimination of sexism, and that taking the risks of losing jobs by striking will be worth the effort. The recent public attention paid to such sobering examples as Crystal Lee Jordan, on whom the film character Norma Rae was based, and the Willmar Eight may provoke more fear than courage, and it is easy to see why—women fighting for unions seem to get themselves fired.

Women workers as a group remain ambivalent about their feminism and its role in union organizing. Although they want to draw on some of the issues related to equal pay and equal representation raised by the feminist movement they are also reluctant to identify themselves as "women's libbers."[44] Recent strikes have shown that union women can use some aspects of feminist ideology to bolster their own self-esteem and create a rationale for the redressing of their grievances. "Feminist baiting," however, is also a tactic available to the opposition, and it will probably be increasingly used in the future.[45] Feminists who are also socialists will probably be particular targets of the corporations, hospitals, banks, and insurance companies, just as communist women and men were particular targets in the McCarthy era. A unionist movement for women in this country will be successful to the extent that it acknowledges its past in radical industrial unionism and its future in militant feminism.

Notes

I would like to thank Susan Porter Benson, Kate Dunnigan, and Bruce Laurie for reading an earlier draft of this paper and providing helpful suggestions.

1. Alice Kessler-Harris, " 'Where Are the Organized Women Workers?' " *Feminist Studies* 3 (Fall 1975): 92–110.

2. Ruth Milkman, "Organizing the Sexual Division of Labor: Historical Perspectives on 'Women's Work' and the American Labor Movement," *Socialist Review* 10 (January–February 1980): 119.

3. Philip S. Foner, *Women and the American Labor Movement,* 2 vols. (New York and London: Free Press, 1979–80), 2:279–81; and Lois Scharf, *To Work and To Wed: Female Employment, Feminism, and the Great Depression* (Westport, Conn., and London: Greenwood Press, 1980), 110–33.

4. Scharf, 45–50; Foner, 2:278.

5. Foner, 2:257; Scharf, 50.

6. Scharf, 45, 104, 106–7; Grace Coyle, "Women in the Clerical Occupations," *Annals of the American Academy of Political and Social Science* 143 (May 1929): 183–84; U.S. Department of Labor, Women's Bureau, *The Employment of Women in Offices,* by Ethel Erickson, Bulletin no. 120 (Washington, D.C.: GPO, 1934), 12–13.

7. For an overall analysis of the impact of the Depression on women's

work, see Ruth Milkman, "Women's Work and the Economic Crisis: Some Lessons from the Great Depression," *Review of Radical Political Economics* 8 (Spring 1976): 73–97; Scharf, 86–109.

8. Molly Haskell, *From Reverence to Rape: The Treatment of Women in the Movies* (New York: Holt, Rinehart & Winston, 1974), 141–52.

9. James J. Keneally, *Women and American Trade Unions* (St. Albans, Vt., and Montreal: Eden Press, 1978), 155; Foner, 2:270, 272–73, 281–82, 285, 314–18.

10. Foner, 2:286–88; Keneally, 155–56; Irving Bernstein, *The Turbulent Years: A History of the American Labor Movement, 1933–1941* (Boston: Houghton Mifflin, 1970), 122–23; "Store Clerks Win Philadelphia Strike," *Ledger* 2 (December 1936): 1.

11. Sidney Fine, *Sit-down: The General Motors Strike of 1936–1937* (Ann Arbor: University of Michigan Press, 1969), 156; Robert Schaffer, "Women and the Communist Party, USA, 1930–1940," *Socialist Review,* no. 45 (May–June 1979): 99.

12. Jeremy Brecher, *Strike!* (San Francisco: World Publishing, 1972), 203, 207–9; Foner, 2:311–12.

13. Foner, 2:312–13.

14. Brecher, 208–9.

15. For discussions of women's auxiliaries see Rosalyn Baxandoll, Linda Gordon, and Susan Reverby, eds., *America's Working Women: A Documentary History—1600 to the Present* (New York: Random House, 1976), 264–65; Fine, 200–201, 279–80; Foner, 2:290–92, 302–12. One of the most important sources on the auxiliaries is the 1977 film *With Babies and Banners: The Story of the Women's Emergency Brigade,* directed by Lorraine Gray, produced by Anne Bohlen, Lyn Goldfarb, and Lorraine Gray and distributed by New Day Films.

16. *With Babies and Banners;* Foner, 2:303–4. Ruth Meyerowitz found that working women were instrumental participants in the brigade ("Organizing the UAW: Women Workers at the Ternstedt General Motors Plant," in *Women, Work, and Protest: A Century of U.S. Women's Labor History,* ed. Ruth Milkman (Boston: Routledge & Kegan Paul, 1985), 235–58.

17. Schaffer, 99–100.

18. Fine, 201.

19. Beatrice Marcus, quoted by Shaffer, 89.

20. Scharf, 43–65.

21. Shaffer, 86–87.

22. Ruth Milkman, "Redefining 'Women's Work': The Sexual Division of Labor in the Auto Industry during World War II," *Feminist Studies* 8 (Summer 1982): 357.

23. David A. Brody, *Workers in Industrial America: Essays on the Twentieth-Century Struggle* (New York: Oxford University Press, 1980), 127–35.

24. Clinton S. Golden and Harold J. Ruttenberg, *The Dynamics of Industrial Democracy* (New York and London: Harper & Brothers, 1942), 82, 310.

25. Ruth Milkman, "The Reproduction of Job Segregation by Sex: A Study of the Changing Sexual Position of Labor in the Auto and Electrical Manufacturing Industries in the 1940s" (Ph.D. diss., University of California, Berkeley, 1981). Milkman argues persuasively that the greater numbers of women working in industry during World War II allowed them to exert more influence in the CIO and to raise women's issues more frequently.

26. U.S. Department of Labor, Women's Bureau, *The Woman Wage Earner: Her Situation Today*, by Elizabeth D. Benham, Bulletin no. 172 (Washington, D.C.: GPO, 1939), 44; *Office and Professional News* 13 (December 1946): 4; Foner, 2:327, 329; and "Sweetheart of the CIO," *CIO News* 1 (6 Aug. 1938): 7.

27. Anne Prosten, interview; "Regions Give 'All-Out' Aid to Organizing Drives," *Federal Record* 4 (3 Apr. 1941): 1.

28. Valerie Kincade Oppenheimer, *The Female Labor Force in the United States: Demographic and Economic Factors Governing Its Growth and Changing Composition* (Westport, Conn.: Greenwood Press, 1976), 149.

29. Milkman, "Women's Work and the Economic Crisis," 530.

30. Jurgen Kocka, *White-Collar Workers in America, 1890–1940: A Sociopolitical History in International Perspective* (London and Beverly Hills, Calif.: Sage, 1980), 20, 218–19, 226; Carl Dean Snyder, *White-Collar Workers and the UAW* (Urbana: University of Illinois Press, 1973); "Wage Cuts in Steel Offices Hit by Union," *Ledger* 4 (February 1938): 1, 8; "Union Grows in Rubber Company," *Office and Professional News* 6 (March–April 1940): 1, "Organizing the Unorganized White-Collar Workers," *Career* 2 (15 Oct. 1949): 4.

31. Kocka, 224–25, 227, 230–31.

32. Nathan Glazer, *The Social Basis of American Communism* (New York: Harcourt, Brace & World, 1961), 116–17, 130. Len DeCaux, editor of the *CIO News*, said that the "new-type" leaders of white-collar unions "differed little from the blue collars. Some college was common for all . . . many . . . were trained in the Communist movement as I knew it—a movement, that is, of militant unemployed; of Union pioneers before New Deal permitted or CIO paid salaries; of rebels against corrupt inaction or reaction in AFL unions." See his *Labor Radical: From the Wobblies to CIO: A Personal History* (Boston: Beacon Press, 1970), 288–89.

33. Coyle, "Women in the Clerical Occupations"; *The Employment of Women in Offices*; C. Wright Mills, *White Collar: The American Middle Classes* (New York: Galaxy Paperback, 1956), 189–212; Orlie Pell, *The Office Worker—Labor's Side of the Ledger*, pamphlet published by the League for Industrial Democracy (New York, January 1937); Lewis Corey, *The Crisis of the Middle Class* (New York: Covici, Freide, 1935), 259; and Hans Speir, "The Salaried Employee in Modern Society," *Social Research* 1 (February 1934): 116–18.

34. See Joseph Starobin, *American Communism in Crisis, 1943–1957* (New York: Harvard University Press, 1972), 96–97.

35. Len DeCaux, "Unionizing the White Collared," *CIO News* 1 (21 May 1938): 4.

36. The UOPWA claimed 22,000 members and 40 locals in 1937 out of an estimated white-collar work force of four or five million. See "Merrill Article Shows White-Collar Progress," *Ledger* 3 (November 1937): 5. By 1943 the UOPWA had 43,000 members and 118 locals. See Florence Peterson, *Handbook of Labor Unions* (Washington, D.C.: American Council on Public Affairs, 1934), 259.

37. Murray Nathan, "The Margon Strike," *Ledger* 2 (March 1936): 5–6; "Unity Pledged at Joint Rally," *Ledger* 2 (March 1936): 9; "The Margon Strike Continues," *Ledger* 3 (April 1936): 9.

38. Nathan, "Margon Strike."

39. "Union Recognized in Credit Firm . . . ," *Ledger* 3 (September 1937): 1; "Local 16 Pickets CCH by Telephone," *Office and Professional News* 6 (February 1940): 1, 3.

40. "Local 16 Wins NLRB Poll in Oil Office by Two to One," *Office and Professional News* 7 (January 1941): 1; "Sonneborn Strikers Win Coast to Coast Support," and "Strikers Burned Up—Put Heat on Oil Company" 7 (February 1941): 1, 2, both in *Office and Professional News*.

41. "Strike Spirit Rises As Sonneborn Accounts Fall" (March 1941): 8; "Sonneborn Begins Talk in Strike's 9th Week" (April 1941): 12; and "Local 16 Maps Changes in Sonneborn Strike" (May 1941): 8, all in *Office and Professional News*.

42. "Susie Steno Discovers the Union," *Ledger* 3 (June 1937): 6.

43. Harvey J. Clerment, *Organizing the Insurance Worker: A History of Labor Unions of Insurance Employees* (Washington, D.C.: Catholic University Press, 1966), 176; and Strom.

44. "Women's Group Set to Organize Office Workers," *New York Times*, 4 Mar. 1981, A12; "Women Clerical Workers and Trade Unionism," Interview with Karen Nussbaum, *Socialist Review* 10 (January–February 1980): 151–59.

45. See, for instance, Gail Gregory Sansbury, " 'Now, What's the Matter with You Girls?' Clerical Workers Organize," *Radical America* 14 (November–December 1980): 67–75; and the 1980 film *Willmar 8*, directed by Lee Grant, produced by Mary Beth Yarrow and Julie Thompson, and distributed by California Newsreel.

Rethinking Troubled Relations between Women and Unions: Craft Unionism and Female Activism

☐ The underrepresentation of women in the activities and leadership of the U.S. labor movement has been a long-standing problem shared by virtually all unions. In the early decades of the twentieth century, men even officered organizations that boasted a majority of female members, such as the International Ladies' Garment Workers' Union (ILGWU). The patterns of male dominance survived the rise of the industrial union movement in the 1930s and 1940s and the influx of women into unions during World War II. In 1986, researchers could still report that despite the growing ranks of women in unions, the number in higher levels of leadership (both elective and appointive) had increased only slightly.[1]

Because of this poor aggregate record, feminist scholars initially dismissed unions as vehicles for female activism, arguing that unions historically operated as patriarchal institutions, steeped in masculine culture and tradition. Many deemed the structure and philosophy of the U.S. labor movement inhospitable to female empowerment and held male union officials responsible for women's low rate of unionization and participation. The harshest criticism was directed at the American Federation of Labor (AFL) and its affiliates. The conventional notion has been that their elitist "craft" ideology and organizational practices acted as almost insurmountable barriers to the mobilization of women.[2] This skeptical perspective also predominated among practitioners of the new labor history, many of whom located worker militance outside the bureaucratic structures of trade union institutions. Trade unions were viewed as "confining

Reprinted, with changes, from *Feminist Studies* 16, no. 3 (Fall 1990): 519–98. © 1990 by Feminist Studies, Inc.

institutions, designed to hold workers in check rather than to liberate them."[3]

Despite their anti-institutional sentiment, these writings have been important in countering earlier analyses which posited women as inherently less militant than men and less concerned with economic justice and workplace representation. Clearly, the gender gap in labor activism resulted from situational factors as much as psychological attributes purportedly shared by women as a sex. The new scholarship documented numerous instances where male workers enhanced their own status by excluding and subordinating women; similarly, it uncovered situations where unions reflected male cultural values and habits—by holding their meetings at night or in a local saloon, for example—and hence thwarted female participation. Yet, as Ruth Milkman and Carole Turbin have emphasized in their most recent works, the "wide range of historical variation in union behavior toward women" and the specific conditions under which unions have been effective vehicles for female collective action and empowerment have received less attention.[4] Moreover, the most systematic treatments of female union activism have focused on situations in which mobilization has been sporadic or short-lived; we know even less about the circumstances necessary for sustained activism among women workers.[5]

The impressive record of participation among union waitresses in the AFL-affiliated Hotel Employees and Restaurant Employees (HERE) International Union offers the researcher an opportunity not only to specify the conditions that facilitated long-term activism but also to reevaluate craft unionism as an arena for female mobilization. Among those unions in which female leadership has been documented, HERE ranks at the top in the proportion of women among its leaders, even though women were a minority of its membership. HERE waitresses also evidenced a high degree of participation in union activities and, in marked contrast to the traditional portrait of intense but short-lived mobilization among women workers, they maintained their heightened level of activity from the early decades of the twentieth century into the post–World War II period.[6] Yet the achievements of HERE women have gone unrecognized. Manufacturing unions, such as the ILGWU or the United Auto Workers, have received the preponderance of attention. The few reports that include service workers have focused solely on the national level—thus bypassing the activism of HERE women on the local level—or on unions with a majority of female members. Relying on previously untapped records from food service locals across the country, this essay will rectify that neglect by first detailing the impressive degree of activity among AFL waitresses.[7]

But once the extensive record of waitress activism is established, how is it to be explained? Previous researchers have credited separate female locals and other structures, such as women's departments and women's committees, with a key role in augmenting the activity of women in the labor movement. Separatism has not been viewed uncritically, however. These same writers acknowledge that separatism has been a problematic long-range strategy for women, capable of sustaining women's leadership in some situations yet undermining female equality and authority in others.[8]

Separate female structures, I will argue, played a critical role in stimulating leadership among waitresses. Beginning in 1900 with the founding of the Seattle waitresses' union, female waiters established their own all-female locals in Chicago, San Francisco, St. Louis, Los Angeles, and other communities across the country; they also joined mixed culinary locals of waiters, cooks, and bartenders. By the early 1950s, the apex of HERE strength numerically, union waitresses had expanded their ranks to one-fourth of their trade. The participation of waitresses within their international union, however, reached its peak in the 1920s when the greatest number of waitresses belonged to separate-sex locals; similarly, the decrease in waitress activity from the 1930s onward closely paralleled the decline of female locals.

Yet separatism alone can not fully explain the remarkable extent of waitress activism. After all, women garment workers, launderers, and bookbinders, among others, set up separate female structures, and waitress leaders rose from thoroughly integrated culinary organizations as well as from the separate locals and women's divisions. An adequate explanation must move beyond separatism per se to recognize the particular *character* of sex separatism in the food service industry.

Unlike women's locals in other industries which included women from many different trades, waitress locals had an "occupational homogeneity" and a legitimacy as a craft-based organization.[9] Because the sexual divisions were also perceived as "craft" divisions, waitress locals received the same treatment and were accorded the same benefits as any other craft-based local. They had equal voting rights with waiter or bartender locals on the Local Joint Executive Boards (LJEBs), and, like every other local, they elected delegates to HERE conventions based on the size of membership. Their institutional legitimacy as craft organizations also helped waitress locals survive the vagaries of male opinion regarding separate gender-based structures.

Thus, in contrast to the situation of "Ladies' Branches" or "Women's Committees," waitress locals enjoyed an autonomy and a separate institutional status that augmented their political power. Yet because the locals were all female, they could function to increase gender consciousness, build leadership skills among women, and voice the special concerns of women workers. In other words, the autonomy and craft legitimacy of the waitress locals ensured that the "ghettoizing" impact that can accompany separatism was minimized and the positive aspects of female institution building were maximized.

But to fully understand the proclivity for activism among waitresses, one must also examine the particularities of their work situation and their household arrangements. Recent research shows that many groups of women workers developed work cultures that were expressed through informal organization at the workplace.[10] Waitresses, however, were one of the few female-dominated work groups to institutionalize their informal work-place practices and build permanent labor organizations. They created a work culture that nourished union building and participation.[11] I will argue that this activist-oriented culture derived from particular values waitresses brought to the workplace from their families as well as those engendered by the nature of food service work itself.

The Extent of Waitress Activism

□ Waitresses first joined with other culinary workers in forming local labor organizations in the 1880s. Many of these early locals affiliated briefly with the Knights of Labor, but by the 1890s most either disbanded or cast their lot with the newly charted AFL union, HERE. HERE membership hovered around 40,000—with the exception of the World War I period—until the unprecedented growth of the 1930s and 1940s. By the early 1950s, HERE represented more than 400,000 food service workers, and in labor strongholds such as San Francisco, New York, and Detroit, unionization approached 80 percent.[12]

Women were never a majority of HERE membership in this period, but their numbers jumped from approximately 2,000 (5 percent of the total) in 1908 to about 181,000 (45 percent) in 1950. The rise of HERE female membership paralleled the expansion and feminization of the hotel and restaurant industry. In 1900, barely a hundred thousand workers worked in commercial table service and the majority were male; by the 1950s, food service was one of the leading retail industries in the United States, and 80 percent of all waiting work was done by women.[13]

Despite their persistent minority status, female food servers sat on the General Executive Board (GEB) of their International from 1909 on and participated vigorously in its international conventions, state bodies, LJEBs, and local unions. Waitress activists also took on paid work as full-time labor officials, and many became lifetime "career" labor leaders. Although their dynamism did not always secure favorable policy decisions, they played a decisive role in shaping the character of their union. After the first female delegate broke the ice at the HERE convention of 1901, women attended every succeeding convention. Significantly, female participation in convention life was greatest from World War I to the early thirties, coincident with the flowering of the movement for separate female locals. In 1919, when women were approximately one-tenth of the total membership, one-tenth, or 231, of the delegates to the HERE convention were women. And in the late twenties and early thirties, when women represented one-fifth of the membership, they occupied between 21 and 26 percent of the delegate slots.[14] Female representation at HERE conventions dipped in the 1930s and 1940s as more women joined mixed organizations, but even in this later period, waitress activity was disproportionately high when compared with women in other unions.[15]

HERE women were also elected to convention committees in disproportionately high numbers, and beginning with the 1911 convention, they secured representation on the GEB and maintained it throughout the twentieth century. At various periods in the history of the union, women occupied two and sometimes three seats on the GEB, a board whose total membership averaged fifteen. Of the women serving on the GEB, only one, Detroit's Myra Wolfgang, was from a mixed local. The other women—Elizabeth Maloney, Kitty Donnelly, Kitty Amsler, Bea Tumber, Olivia Moore, Gertrude Sweet, Fay Rothring—were all from separate locals.[16] Indeed, most waitresses who rose to national prominence came from separate locals. In a 1940 tribute to significant women culinary leaders of the past and present, the editor of the *Catering Industry Employee,* the national journal of HERE, listed twenty-six outstanding women; twenty were from separate locals.

Waitress leadership in male-dominated mixed locals and LJEBs was impressive, however. Cooks and Waiters' Local 550 in Bakersfield, California, survived the Depression because of the "inestimable fortitude and perseverance" of its secretary-treasurer, Josephine Perry Rankin. Originally a member of Waitresses' Local 639, Rankin "loaned her guiding influence" to Bartenders Local 378 and was "so effective" that Bakersfield bartenders achieved 100 percent organization. Rankin was not an isolated case. Teresa Wolfson, writing in 1926, estimated that nationally at least forty-three culinary locals had female "secretaries." Although she thought that more women should have been elected president instead of secretary—a position she considered stereotypic for women—in reality, labor organizations often deemed the secretary their chief officer. Beulah Johnson, secretary and principal officer of Local 324 in Glendale, California, proudly told of her research on California female leaders in the March 1944 *Catering Industry Employee*. Out of seventy-five culinary locals in California, twenty-one had women secretaries. Only three of these were composed exclusively of women, Johnson added; the rest were mixed locals. Gertrude Sweet, a carpenter's daughter who became International vice-president for the Northwest region, recalled that "in Oregon, Washington, and Montana, we had more women officers in the union than we had men [officers]. I find that the women did work and talk and did as good a job as did the men."[17]

Waitresses held their own in the state culinary alliances as well. At the sixth annual convention of the California State Council of Culinary Workers, Bartenders, and Hotel Service Employees, held in 1949, about 30 percent of the 185 delegates, 37 percent of the committee members, and 25 percent of the executive board were female. The president of the council, Frankie Behan, was a San Francisco waitress from Local 48. In the 1930s, the council had also been led by a woman, Bee Tumber, a veteran waitress organizer from Southern California. The picture in Oregon, Washington, and other states with strong separate-sex locals was no different.

Local Strategies for Representation

☐ These accomplishments in part grew out of waitresses' own keen sense of the importance of equitable female representation. The means by which to achieve this equality were not so self-evident, however, and waitresses debated amongst themselves over the proper strategies for enhancing female participation and power. On a local level, the majority of waitresses favored sex separatism, at least until the 1930s.[18] After that, most newly organized waitresses adjusted to the new industrial structures of the union. Even in mixed locals, however, waitresses sought a sphere of autonomy by creating women's committees and councils. Both strategies proved problematic, each in its own way, but the separate-sex route granted a degree of organizational power that the women's committees could not duplicate.

Waitresses who preferred separate locals gave many reasons, but one recurring rationale involved the effect such organizations had in developing women's leadership. Separate locals ensured that women would hold responsible positions within the union and that the knowledge required to run a local—from grievance-handling and negotiating contracts, to public relations and parliamentary procedure—would be learned by women. Female participation was neither expected nor encouraged in mixed organizations, but in separate locals, women had no choice but to participate, even if the activities struck them as unappealing and unfeminine. Alice Lord, twenty-five-year officer of the Seattle waitresses' union, understood this principle. "In a mixed local," she wrote to the editor of the January 1906 *Mixer and Server,* "the girls do not take the interest that they should; they always leave the work to the boys, . . . but if the girls know that the success of the local depends on their efforts, they will put their shoulders to the wheel, and most invariably they will come out ahead, as the few waitresses' locals which are in existence prove that such is the case."

Waitresses also recognized the role of separate locals in creating the proud history of waitress representation. "A great deal has been said about having one local union for waiters and waitresses," Carrie Alexander of Chicago's Local 484 began, when the issue of merging the waiter and waitress locals at the 1927 HERE convention was raised, but "if the waiters and waitresses were in a local union, we would not have 51 delegates at this convention." After the applause died down, she underscored her point: "What is the matter with the local union . . . [in New York]? They have waitresses . . . , but there are no women here." She closed her speech with a final appeal for separate locals. "Let me tell you that the women will have to get up and fight for their own and stay in their own local. I hope no delegation here will consider amalgamating with the men because I believe it would be the elimination of the waitresses."

Waitresses took pride in the accomplishments of their all-female organizations and in their ability to take on jobs that the culture deemed inappropriate or too difficult for women. In 1906, Lord encouraged the press secretaries of female locals across the country to write letters for the opinion column of the national journal by pointing out the similarity between writing for the public audience—an unfamiliar task—and talking with each other in private, a common, everyday activity. "Now, girls, I would like to see an article every month in the Forum from one of our number. Do not be afraid, or imagine you cannot do so. Write just as you would talk to one another, even if it is not just correct. I am sure our broad-minded editor will find space for it."

Local 48 of San Francisco bragged of being "completely officered by women and [of constituting] an outstanding example of women's ability both as executives and administrators." In the 1950s, the Los Angeles waitress local printed the following slogan on the back cover of their bylaws: "Who Says 'Women are the Weaker Sex?' We are the largest culinary craft union in the World."

Women's Committees and Female Participation

☐ By the 1930s, the majority of new waitresses were entering mixed-gender locals. For these women, new strategies were required. The story of the women's committees they created—their brief organizational life and frustratingly piecemeal accomplishments—contrast markedly with the longevity and achievements of the separate locals. The comparison demonstrates that separatism in and of itself could not always guarantee increased power and participation for women—the form in which separate organizing occurred was critical.

Of the culinary locals in New York City, at least four—Locals 1, 42, 302, and 6—had large functioning women's committees at various times between the 1930s and the 1950s. Women were never the majority in any of these locals, but they comprised between 30 and 40 percent of the membership in Locals 302 and 6. The failure of these committees is noteworthy in light of their numerical potential, persistence, and creativity.

Although the committees defined their first task as promoting female leadership, they made little headway. The executive board of Hotel and Club Workers' Local 6 generally had two women out of approximately fifteen to twenty members; the staff ratio of women to men was similar.[19] Ironically, Local 6 prided itself on its progressive democratic character, but, because one-third of the union throughout the 1940s and 1950s was female, clearly a major portion of their rank and file was not represented. The records of other New York City locals were worse. Cafeteria Workers' Local 302 did not have a female business agent representing its 3,000 women members until 1942. Fifteen years later, the picture was remarkably stable: only one of the fifty executive board members was female. The New York LJEB reflected the dearth of female leadership in its affiliate locals: Gertrude Lane, general organizer and later secretary-treasurer for Local 6, was frequently the sole woman in a delegate body of thirty to fifty members.[20]

Women's committees also aimed to increase female participation in the life of the union. The barriers were numerous and ultimately impossible to surmount. Ida Brown, a Local 1 waitress, explained the source of the problem: "Many of us who can talk the legs off an iron pot when in our shops are smitten with stage fright at general membership meetings—and to tell the truth, we do not receive any particular encouragement from our brothers." A Local 302 cafeteria server admitted that "too many of us have qualms about going before a General Membership meeting and stating our opinions, but we wouldn't have any stage fright if we were part of a Council for women. Men just don't understand these things."[21]

Women's committees initiated various programs to foster women's participation. In conjunction with the New York Women's Trade Union League (WTUL), Local 6 held leadership training classes for "women only" in organizing techniques and public speaking. Local 1 organized a parliamentary procedure class. Other committees organized social and sporting events to draw the "women members closer to the union." Bingo parties, swim and bicycling clubs, dancing events, and softball teams were commonplace. A women's dramatics class held through Local 302 helped create a musical, "Sunny Side Up," about the lives of cafeteria workers.

Women's columns in the union newspaper were begun. Even the women's committee of Local 6, which carefully pointed out that they "were not segregating" themselves "from the men ... far from it ... [because] men and women are dependent on cooperation with each other for the success of the trade unions," started a "women's corner" in the *Hotel and Club Voice*. "Yes, this is something new, a little corner all to ourselves" where we can get "by ourselves and let our hair down." The *Voice of Local 1* encouraged women to write letters for the "Woman's View" column and to attend their union meetings. Local 302's *Cafeteria Call* had a "Hello Sister" column for a number of years and later an "Our Sisters Talk It Over" column.[22]

Early on, the columns emphasized the needs of women on the job, but as the committees lost steam, the columns shifted, appealing to women as housewives and mothers. Local 302's column changed tone in 1943, concomitant with a change in the Local's administration. After five years of broadsides directed toward workplace issues, a new columnist appeared who urged women to "join union activities to make this a better world for [their] children." In 1954, the "Woman's View" column in the Local 1 newspaper became the "Ladies' Corner" with articles on preserves, fashions, and household hints.[23]

Significantly, women's home responsibilities were rarely mentioned as a potential source of conflict for women activists, nor were home responsibilities perceived as a duty from which women should be relieved. The chair of the women's committee in Local 6 reminded women that they had a duty to participate in their union even though they had household responsibilities and had to "go home, clean house and prepare meals." Remember the pioneer women, she exhorted. When the Indians attacked, they "didn't say 'excuse me, I have to bake a cake' ... they came to the front and helped their men." Instead of attempting to rectify the problem of women's dual responsibilities in the workplace and in the home, women were expected to do both.[24]

Determined to gain representation, women's committees pressured male-dominated locals for quotas regarding women and minorities. Local 6 passed a bylaw provision in the 1940s requiring that one Black officer and one female officer be appointed "in the event that no Negro . . . or no woman has been elected to serve either as a General Officer of the union or the Board of Vice-Presidents." Local 1 women pushed through a resolution early in 1936 that at least two women would be elected to the Executive Board of the union. In the late 1940s, they amended the local bylaws to "provide that both the delegates to the WTUL must be women in addition to the mandatory two executive board members."

The most ambitious activities devised by women's committees involved organizing semi-independent all-female councils that functioned almost as separate branches within the main local. The women of Local 302 started a Women's Council composed of representatives from each shop where women were employed. The Women's Council formulated bylaws and collective-bargaining demands, and "other matters effecting [*sic*] women more than men. Similarly, under the auspices of the New York LJEB, Gertrude Lane set up a Women's Advisory Committee consisting of five women from each local with female membership. This all-woman group paralleled the male joint committee structurally but differed ideologically. As opposed to the collective-bargaining thrust of the virtually all-male LJEB, the female group was committed primarily to legislative and organizing activity in regard to minimum wages and maximum hours.

Ironically, success could create problems for committees. Women's committees were in something of a double bind. The male leadership saw the principal function of women's committees as attracting women to the work of building the general union organization, yet the most effective way of involving women was by appealing to their special interests. Because the gender concerns of women were often at odds with the priorities of a male-dominated union, the committees were stifled at precisely the point at which they developed a strong following among the women members of the local.

The demise of Local 302's committee is a case in point. From its inception in 1938, the committee defined broad and bold concerns. Besides the traditional entreaties for women's involvement in ongoing union activities, they wanted equal pay, a portion of the best jobs, and "important positions" in the union. They were tired of taking a "backseat" to the men. When the committee ran a letter-writing contest on "What do you want the Union to do for you as a woman member?" the winning essayist wanted a forty-hour week with no reduction in pay—clearly a useful demand for women with family responsibilities—and the runner-up opted for the union "to create equal opportunity for women to earn equal money for equal work with men." During the 1941 negotiations, the women's committee distributed "7-hour day for women" buttons and made other suggestions to the negotiating team "such as having cots in the dressing room for emergencies . . . and having sanitary dressing rooms." The committee members elaborated further objectives, including a veiled reference to the problem of sexual harassment: "We felt that not enough girls in the union . . . [knew] their rights and that sometimes they are laid off, or bothered, or something else like that."

During the early years of World War II, the committee toned down its feminist orientation in the actual activities they pursued, but their sassy rhetoric continued. One 1942 column grabbed attention with this opening: "What do you say to the wise guy who tells you that women belong at home in the kitchen? Or the bright boy who tells you women are taking men's jobs? Or the know-it-all who says girls are not as capable as men? Do you feel a slow burn creeping all over you while you want to tell him off—but good! Well, we have all the answers to those very short-sighted males who strut around this earth feeling that all things begin and end with them."

Nevertheless, although the committee elicited enthusiastic response from women members, the male-dominated executive board withdrew its support after a few years, effectively crippling the committee. Few lasting changes had occurred. The number of women in leadership remained small, and glaring inequalities in wages between women and men persisted.

On the other hand, those committees advancing only goals which complemented the interests of male coworkers found they lost the support of the very constituency they were trying to reach. The committees within Locals 6 and 1, for example, steered clear of "divisive issues" and in the end died from lack of female support. While agitating for more female staff for Local 6 and exhorting women to get more involved in the life of their union, the calls for women "to pitch in" and "shoulder the load" were directed at involving women in activities that did not challenge the ongoing traditional priorities of the union.

In the end, without the autonomy, power, and institutional legitimacy enjoyed by the separate female locals, the impact of women's committees was episodic and ephemeral. Without a majority vote within the local or a separate institutional base of power, women could neither change the priorities of the male leadership, nor could they act independently. Moreover, the basic legitimacy of women's committees was always in question. The separate waitress locals had to overcome male (and female) skepticism toward their sex-segregated structure before they gained separate charters, but once their local was established, their basic right to exist was not challenged. The committee form, however, was not an organizational structure recognized by the international union constitution. Waitress locals also garnered credibility because they represented not just the women of the union but also the waitress craft; in contrast, women's committees justified their existence through establishing the special needs and interests of women. Waitress locals forged unity through combining craft and organizational loyalty with gender concerns; in the case of women's committees, organizational and craft loyalties often were at odds with gender.

Strategic Dilemmas on the National Level

☐ Waitresses also experimented with various schemes for enhancing female power on the national level, alternating between arguments for equal treatment and special protection. Before the 1930s, for instance, female delegates to union conventions agitated against HERE's policy, instituted in 1909, "that one member of the Board shall be a woman to represent the women workers of our craft." In 1921, women delegates, all from separate-sex locals, submitted a resolution to abolish the special seat reserved for women. During the floor fight that ensued, women objected to the quota as a "protective" measure that set a maximum for female representation rather than a minimum. Others saw it as demeaning and encouraging the view of women as the weaker sex in need of special treatment. "You must get away from the idea that women are less able than men," one delegate said. "We don't want to be patronized and that is what the present law produces." Male delegates opposed the motion and prevailed.[25]

Unable to do away with the quota or elect more women to the board, female delegates switched tactics. In 1938, they embraced a recommendation that backed special protection for both women and dining car workers and increased the female quota from one to two. In these debates, waitresses now argued that women needed protection from the prejudices of their male colleagues and that, although the quota system at times seemed to limit the number of women board members, at least it ensured some female participation. Women delegates also expressed less optimism about their chances in open elections and appeared less sensitive to being categorized as a distinct constituency. In part, this shift may have been due to the increasing number of women entering mixed locals, the corresponding decline in female delegate proportions, and the general perception that the chances for increasing female representation by abolishing the quota system were slim.[26] The resolution requiring two seats for women passed, and in the election following, waitresses secured three of the fifteen elected seats on the board.[27]

Dissatisfied with the new policy, the general officers of HERE backed a resolution at the next convention eliminating one of the female vice-presidential slots. In contrast to previous conventions, male delegates now argued against paternalistic treatment of women, using the rhetoric of impartiality and equal treatment of the sexes. How can you support equal wages, GEB member and noted progressive Hugo Ernst asked the women delegates, yet desire differential treatment when it comes to elections? In reality, of course, because women were at least one-third of the membership, two board seats were hardly overrepresentation.

Despite pressure from male colleagues, not one of the 150 women delegates spoke in favor of the amendment. They stressed their numbers and their entitlement to proportionate representation. As delegate Anna Farkas succinctly put it: "We have probably one-half females in this Hotel and Restaurant International Alliance, and I think we are entitled to female representatives." Taking a different tack, Gertrude Lane of New York City admitted that "women had very little chance to be elected on a district basis and that was one of the reasons it would be a fatal error for the organization to take away any of the women's representation."[28] Despite "sharp debate from many different quarters," the quota requiring two female vice-presidents met defeat, and, as a result, HERE women lost one of the three women on the board. Nevertheless, waitresses retained two vice-presidential seats on the GEB throughout the 1950s and 1960s even though they competed against men for those positions.[29]

Thus, many waitresses supported sex-segregated policies on a local level, but they rejected the full implications of the "separate-sphere ideology" at the national level. They argued against quotas for female representation on the highest body of the international until the late 1930s. Nevertheless, with the decline of female delegate strength, and increasingly frustrated with the lack of progress, waitresses shifted their tactics and argued for special seats reserved for female delegates. Although they never devised a system to ensure proportionate representation for women, waitress activists did manage to maintain and even increase their presence on the board—despite the declining female delegate pool.

Work and Family

☐ To fully explain the achievements of women within HERE, one must look beyond the strategies devised by waitresses, even those as effective as separate locals. One must look to the nature and structure of the food service workplace itself and to the special family characteristics of waitresses. Waitresses created a work culture and community that promoted and sustained their collective activity. This activist consciousness was rooted primarily in the particularities of their work experience and family backgrounds.

The organization of the culinary workplace fostered women's leadership in subtle but powerful ways. The craft and sex segregation of work, for instance, solidified the occupational ties between waitresses while mitigating their identity with male workers in their craft. The strict categorizing of waiting jobs by sex meant that waitresses and waiters rarely worked together in the same house—women served at breakfast and lunch and in the lower-priced, informal restaurants; men worked dinner jobs in the fancier, more formal houses. This internal segregation of waiting work physically separated women and men food servers and created the basis for a collective identity among waitresses.

Yet unlike women in many other sex-segregated workplaces, waitresses continuously interacted with male cooks, bartenders, and busboys, as well as male customers. These exchanges were often fraught with conflict that derived in large part from the structure and demands of the workplace itself. Waitresses needed food and liquor immediately if their customers were to be satisfied; the cooks and bartenders, removed from the watchful and hungry eye of the patron, responded more to their own inclinations for a steady, unpressured work pace. In order to fulfill their work duties, waitresses developed ways of manipulating these interactions and asserting their own ends. The daily adversarial maneuverings with men prepared waitresses for the conflicts that emerged in their own union. Indeed, the spats between waitresses and their male coworkers on the shopfloor affected their readiness to engage in conflict with these same union brothers in the union hall. How could they accept paternalism in the union when they so firmly rejected it in the workplace?[30]

The kinds of skills acquired by waitresses in their daily interactions with customers were also directly transferable to union leadership. At work, waitresses learned to take charge verbally with customers, to deflect criticism and sarcasm by developing their own quick-witted retorts, and to be persuasive in their communication. Practice in "thinking on your feet" and in sharpening sparring skills came in handy during union debates, grievance meetings, and negotiation sessions. As William Whyte discovered in his classic study of the restaurant workplace, the women who survived as waitresses learned to control situations by initiating action rather than letting the customer define the interaction.[31] This boldness became a habit with some waitresses and aided them in their union activities. They were not intimidated by men nor were they accustomed to following the male lead. Unlike the office environment, for example, waiting work discouraged traditional female behavior.

Expert waitresses were keen judges of human character. They could assess an individual quickly, reading her or his nonverbal cues, and adjust their behavior to the mood of the other person. This grasp of character allowed the waitress to interpret the best approach with the particular customer—the one which would not only enhance the tip but would also protect the waitress from potentially abusive behavior.[32] A customer perceived as a bully or a pest could be put in his place before he got a chance to launch into his routine. This ability to size up individual customers and predict their behavior became a resource upon which waitresses could draw in their labor activities. The very qualities women needed in order to survive in the fast-talking, person-oriented, conflictual world of labor relations were fostered daily at the workplace.

Other aspects of the food service industry encouraged solidarity and group identity. Irregular hours and the custom of "split shifts" (which left workers stranded at the worksite between their stints of duty) fostered intergroup interaction and bonding. The employer practice of providing room and board also facilitated personal ties among workers. Those who "lived-in" formed the closest relationships, but even waitresses who resided off the employer premises could develop "passionate loyalties" based on the considerable amount of time they spent socializing and eating meals together. Some women in fact "chose" waitressing because of the opportunities for friendships and a substitute family it offered. As one young recruit explained: "It's very unpleasant thinking about being a girl in a big city who . . . must sit down alone and eat. The waitress however, doesn't do this. When her work is done she sits down with the other girls at a table and eats a good meal."[33] The occupational community of rank-and-file waitresses which formed at so many workplaces underlay and nourished the waitress representatives who braved the masculine world of union conventions and high-level executive boards.

Waitressing may have also attracted a more unconventional type than other occupations, such as clerical or sales or even factory labor. Certainly, before Prohibition, waitressing was looked upon as a disreputable trade. Waitresses interacted with male strangers in public places and even served them liquor. The intimacy of food service, the tip exchange required, and the association—perhaps unconscious—between eating and sex, led many observers to link waitressing and prostitution. Even later in the century, after more native-born women entered waitressing[34] and attitudes toward sexual mixing loosened, waitressing still retained a somewhat unsavory cast. The "intemperate" personal qualities exhibited by waitresses on the job were also noticed by the public and frowned upon. The stereotype of the bold, free-talking, aggressive waitress was partially based in reality. For these women then, already working in an "unladylike" job, becoming a labor activist—clearly nontraditional behavior for women—did not seem like much of a change of pace.

Lastly, the distinctive family backgrounds of waitresses may have predisposed them to workplace activism. Waitresses more than women in many other occupations tended to be either divorced, separated, or widowed, or if single, living apart from their family of origin.[35] As recent scholarship has demonstrated, the particular household arrangements of women workers can be tied systematically with their propensity for collective action. In his study of the union pioneers in the electrical industry, for instance, Ronald Schatz found that the distinguishing factor shared by the women leaders was their nontraditional family homelife—many were living alone, with sisters or peers, or divorced. These women rose to leadership, Schatz maintained, because they had either broken the patriarchal ties of their past family or challenged the authority structures in their current family.[36] Waitress activists conform to Schatz's schema because they, like the women organizers in the electrical industry, also diverged from other women in their tendency to shun conventional married life.

Equally important, the nontraditional family status of waitresses meant that a disproportionate number were the primary support of themselves and their family and, at least until the 1950s, were attached to the workplace in a permanent fashion as full-time, long-tenure workers. The implications of these particular attributes for female mobilization are profound, as Louise Tilly and Carole Turbin have recently pointed out. Women who were primary wage earners were more likely to take the lead in labor struggles; they had a greater stake in improving their wages and enjoyed more independence from male authority. Older women with more years in the labor force also appeared more committed to workplace struggles. They perceived their work as continuous and permanent, had developed more extensive workplace networks of support, and hence were more willing to invest in long-term union building.[37] Moreover, as I have noted elsewhere, older waitresses may have been more likely to take on union responsibilities because their energies were less absorbed in childrearing.[38]

Conclusion

☐ On the most obvious level, many of the factors which scholars have identified as linked to women's propensity for collective activity are also central to any understanding of women's ability to sustain such action. The particular family position of women and the characteristics of their "production unit" or workplace are critical in explaining women's ongoing union participation as well as their initial mobilization. Yet of the instances of female mobilization detailed by Louise Tilly, only the cigar makers played a significant leadership role in their union and turned their activism into "an ongoing affair." Tilly attributes their unusual leadership flair in part to their "opportunities for solidarity and association not unlike male craftsmen" and their organization into predominantly female union groupings.[39] The case of the waitresses suggests further generalizations about why activism among certain groups of women endured.

For HERE waitresses, like many other groups of women wage earners, the barriers to women's leadership—male hostility, the labor movement's masculine culture, the socialization of women for supportive roles, the often temporary attachment of women to the workplace, and the patriarchal institution of the family—could be mitigated in certain circumstances and ultimately overcome.[40] But the particular character of the craft and gender separatism that operated within the hotel and restaurant union proved key to preserving that participation. In other words, to understand the survival of collective action, we must analyze not only the family and work experiences of women but also the nature of the institutions within which they operated and the strategies they employed in negotiating their institutional arrangements.

It is not surprising that working-class women, like their middle-class sisters, found sustenance in the sex-segregated structures of their union organizations. What is startling, however, is that the craft form of unionism also proved nourishing. The few writers who have explored the relation between union organizational structure and women's subordinate status have emphasized the superiority of industrial unionism. And indeed, the "logic of industrial unionism" ensured that thousands of semiskilled and unskilled workers, including women, were organized.[41] The history of waitress activism suggests, however, that although industrial union structures were more conducive to the entrance of women into unions, craft structures may have been superior in sustaining female participation and leadership.

Indeed, HERE waitresses benefited from a propitious mix of craft and industrial unionism. Food service workers—like many other AFL unionists in fact—never really adopted the exclusionary membership policies so often associated with craft unionism. HERE organized "semiskilled" workers, such as waitresses and dishwashers, as well as "skilled" workers, such as cooks and bartenders. What made them craft unionists was their adherence to *other* organizational practices and philosophies. It was these aspects of craft unionism that promoted ongoing collective activity among women. The separation of workers by trade provided women with a space apart from male hostility and allowed the development of female perspectives and leadership skills. The tradition of local control and decentralization—so characteristic of craft unionism—also allowed for female autonomy.[42] Lastly, the craft union emphasis on pride in the trade and loyalty to others who belonged to the same occupation encouraged women's identity with work and with their sisters in the craft. The success of the waitress locals thus demonstrates how an organizational structure based on the logic of craft, rather than being incompatible with female mobilization, proved instrumental in its creation and maintenance.

Unions, then, are not static unchanging entities into which women must be integrated. Union responsiveness to women has varied widely over time and place. Even within the same international, let alone the same federation, labor organizations have exhibited a remarkable range of reactions. For those of us concerned with explaining that variation, the history of waitress activism redirects our attention beyond the stated ideological orientation of these institutions to the peculiarities of their organizational structures. The surprising impact of craft unionism discloses an important caveat. Although the gender ideology of organizations may imply one outcome for women, their organizational structures, seemingly gender-neutral, may produce a totally different result. As Roslyn Feldberg has recently noted, those concerned about the future of women within the contemporary labor movement would do well to demand not merely a change in attitude but also the creation of structures that would allow women the space to define and implement their own priorities.[43]

Notes

I am grateful for the encouragement and insights offered by Barbara Bergmann and the *Feminist Studies* reviewers who read earlier drafts of this essay.

1. Naomi Baden, "Developing an Agenda: Expanding the Role of Women in Unions," *Labor Studies Journal* 10 (Winter 1986): 229–30, 236–37.

2. Alice Kessler-Harris's early article, " 'Where Are the Organized Women Workers?' " *Feminist Studies* 3 (Fall 1975): 92–110, details the practices of male craft unionists which discouraged female participation. Ruth Milkman has also analyzed the barriers to female organization inherent in the craft form of unionism. See her "Organizing the Sexual Division of Labor," *Socialist Review* 10 (January–February 1980): 95–150.

3. David Brody, "Elements of Paradox in U.S. Labor History," *Monthly Labor Review* 110 (August 1987): 50.

4. Ruth Milkman, "Gender Trouble and Trade Unionism in Historical Perspective," in *Women, Politics, and Change,* ed. Louise A. Tilly and Patricia Gurin (New York: Russell Sage Foundation, 1990), 88, 90. Carole Turbin, "Beyond Conventional Wisdom: Women's Wage Work, Household Economic Contribution, and Labor Activism in a Mid-Nineteenth-Century Working-Class Community," in *"To Toil the Livelong Day": America's Women at Work, 1780–1980,* ed. Carol Groneman and Mary Beth Norton (Ithaca: Cornell University Press, 1987).

5. See Louise Tilly's paradigm in "Paths of Proletarianization: Organization of Production, Sexual Division of Labor, and Women's Collective Action," *Signs* 7 (Winter 1981): 400–17.

6. For comparison with other unions, consult Roger Waldinger, "Another Look at the ILGWU: Women, Industry Structure, and Collective Action"; and Alice Kessler-Harris, "Problems of Coalition-Building: Women and Trade Unions in the 1920s," both in *Women, Work, and Protest: A Century of U.S. Women's Labor History,* ed. Ruth Milkman (London: Routledge & Kegan Paul, 1985), 86–138; Susan A. Glenn, *Daughters of the Shtetl: Life and Labor in the Immigrant Generation, 1880–1920* (Ithaca: Cornell University Press, 1990), chap. 6; Michael Harrington, *The Retail Clerks* (New York: John Wiley & Sons, 1962); Barbara Wertheimer and Anne H. Nelson, *Trade Union Women: A Study of Their Participation in New York City* (New York: Praeger, 1975); Mary Margaret Fonow, "Women in Steel: A Case Study of the Participation of Women in a Trade Union" (Ph.D. diss., Ohio State University, 1977).

7. In addition to the files of the HERE International Union, which contained work rules, contracts, meeting minutes, correspondence, and newsletters from hundreds of local food service unions, I used the archives of individual HERE locals and the union serials available at the Robert F. Wagner Archives, Tamiment Library, New York City, and the U.S. Department of Labor.

8. For an analysis emphasizing the role of separate female locals, consult Nancy MacLean, *The Culture of Resistance: Female Institution Building in the ILGWU, 1905–1925,* Michigan Occasional Paper no. 21 (Ann Arbor: Winter 1982). Sherna Gluck and Susan Glenn discuss the variety of attitudes toward

separate locals held by working-class women activists. Consult Gluck, "The Changing Nature of Women's Participation in the American Labor Movement, 1900–1940: Case Studies from Oral History" (Paper presented at the Southwest Labor History Conference, 5 Mar. 1977, Arizona State University, Tempe, Arizona), 1; and Glenn, chap. 6. The controversy over the impact of separate female institutions is by no means limited to the trade union activities of women. One of the more illuminating essays is by Estelle B. Freedman, "Separation as Strategy: Female Institution Building and American Feminism, 1870–1930," *Feminist Studies* 5 (Fall 1979): 512–29.

9. The women's locals in the garment industry, for example, cut across occupational and ethnic lines, taking in all women within a given geographical location.

10. Susan Porter Benson, *Counter Cultures: Saleswomen, Managers, and Customers in American Department Stores, 1890–1940* (Urbana: University of Illinois Press, 1987); and Temma Kaplan, "Female Consciousness and Collective Action: The Case of Barcelona, 1910–1918," *Signs* 7 (Spring 1982): 545–66.

11. The debate over the relation between women's work culture and labor activism is addressed by Micaela di Leonardo's Introduction, "Women's Work, Work Culture, and Consciousness" (491–95); and Cynthia B. Costello, " 'WEA'RE Worth It!': Work Culture and Conflict at the Wisconsin Education Association Insurance Trust" (497–518), both in *Feminist Studies* 11 (Fall 1985).

12. See Dorothy Sue Cobble, "Sisters in the Craft: Waitresses and Their Unions in the Twentieth Century" (Ph.D. diss., Stanford University, 1986), chaps. 3 and 4.

13. For an account of the expansion and feminization of waiting work, see Cobble, chap. 1.

14. Although the numbers are not available for every convention year, in many cases separate locals also sent a higher proportion of the female delegates than their local numbers warranted. This line of argument concerning the importance of separate locals is at odds with those made by Matthew Josephson in *Union House, Union Bar: History of the Hotel and Restaurant Employees and Bartenders International Union* (New York: Random House, 1956). Josephson states that during the 1930s, the character of the unions was transformed, with many female officers coming to the fore for the first time. However, the women he names (Gertrude Sweet, Bea Tumer, Mae Stoneman, and others) were all from separate locals and had been officers prior to the 1930s. See Josephson, 225.

15. See note 6.

16. From 1909 to 1938, women held one seat on a board numbering between ten and twelve. In 1938, women captured three seats on an eighteen-member board. During the 1940s and 1950s, women continued to hold two and sometimes three seats. The composition of the GEB is listed year by

year in the HERE national journals, *Mixer and Server* and *Catering Industry Employee*.

17. Interview with Gertrude Sweet by Shirley Tanzer, conducted for the University of Michigan/Wayne State Oral History Project, "Twentieth-Century Trade Union Women: Vehicle for Social Change," on 2 Aug. 1976, 28. In general, the record of the East Coast waitresses fell behind that of the Midwest and West—in part because of the larger proportion of male workers in the industry and the smaller number of separate-sex locals. See Cobble, 480–81.

18. For a fuller discussion of the founding of the major separate-sex locals and the initiatives taken by women, consult Cobble, 116–77.

19. For example, see the listing of the 1942 officers and staff of Local 6 in *Catering Industry Employee*, February 1942, 25; or consult *Hotel and Club Voice*, 7 Feb. 1942, 1.

20. In 1939, the New York LJEB appeared to have one female member on a council of roughly fifty. In 1943 two of its thirty members were female.

21. Ida Brown, *Voice of Local 1*, January 1950, 2; *Cafeteria Call*, November 1940, 7.

22. *Hotel and Club Voice*, 15 Feb. 1941, 7; *Voice of Local 1*, November 1948, 5; *Cafeteria Call*, 1938–1945.

23. *Cafeteria Call*, June 1943, 2; *Voice of Local 1*, August 1954, 7. See the *Dining Room Employee*, 1954–55, the successor to the *Voice of Local 1*.

24. Women were continually being called upon to "do their share" and "to shoulder the load." See *Hotel and Club Voice*, 24 Aug. 1940, 1–8; "Listen Sister" columns written by Charlotte Ferris throughout 1940 and 1941; *Voice of Local 1*, November 1948, 5.

25. *Proceedings*, HERE convention, 1909, 145, and 1921, 171. Ibid., 1921, 116, 171.

26. Women may also have felt less singled out and demeaned by these policies of special board seats because quotas were now being applied not only to women but to dining car workers and to hotel service workers as well.

27. Bea Tumber of Waitresses' Local 639 in Los Angeles and Olivia Moore from Local 567 in Olympia, Washington, filled the vice-presidential positions reserved for women. Gertrude Sweet became the first woman to win a board seat in open competition with men; she secured a regular vice-presidential slot as the representative of the Pacific Northwest district. See *Catering Industry Employee*, October 1938, 33; Hotel and Restaurant Employees International Alliance and the Bartenders International League of America, *Fifty Years of Progress: A Brief History of Our Union, 1891–1941* (Cincinnati: HERE, 1941), 14.

28. *Proceedings*, HERE Convention, 1941, 130–33.

29. Myra Wolfgang and Gertrude Sweet represented their districts throughout this period. Consult the GEB minutes as reprinted in *Catering Industry Employee*, March 1953, 26; and *Cafeteria Call*, June 1941, 5.

30. The more passive and conservative culture of women wage earners described by Tentler, for example, was based almost exclusively on factory women where sex-segregated assembly work often limited their interaction with men to male supervisory personnel. See Leslie Tentler, *Wage-Earning Women: Industrial Work and Family Life in the United States, 1900–1930* (New York: Oxford University Press, 1979). Other service workers, such as department store clerks, worked more independently of men than did waitresses and hence fractious encounters between women and men were less frequent. Consult Benson for the work life of department store clerks.

31. William Whyte, *Human Relations in the Restaurant Industry* (New York: McGraw-Hill Book Co., 1948), 65–81, 92–128, 228–87, and "The Social Structure of the Restaurant," *American Journal of Sociology* 54 (January 1949): 305–11. Also consult Frances Donovan, *The Woman Who Waits* (Boston: Gorham Press, 1920); James Spradley and Brenda Mann, *The Cocktail Waitress: Women's Work in a Man's World* (New York: John Wiley & Sons, 1975); and Cobble, chap. 2.

32. Gerald Mars and Michael Nicod, *The World of Waiters* (London: George Allen & Unwin, 1984); and Leon Elder and Lin Rolens, *Waitress: America's Unsung Heroine* (Santa Barbara, Calif.: Capra Press, 1985).

33. William Whyte et al., *Action Resource for Management* (Homewood, Ill.: Richard D. Irwin, 1964), 44; Whyte, *Human Relations in the Restaurant Industry,* 153–56; Donovan, 94; Dagny Hansen, "Don't Kid the Waitress," *Collier's,* 4 May 1929, 14; Everett Hughes, "Personality Types and the Division of Labor," in *Personality and the Social Group,* ed. Ernest W. Burgess (Chicago: University of Chicago Press, 1929), 78–94; "Being a Waitress in a Broadway Hotel," *Scribner's Magazine,* September 1921, 317.

34. The majority of waitresses in the twentieth century were native-born and of Northern European background. Consult chapter 1 of "Sisters in the Craft" for documentation. Ethnic homogeneity affected the ability of waitresses to organize, and ethnic traditions probably encouraged separate-sex locals. Susan Glenn argues, for example, that separatism did not appeal to Jewish garment workers as much as it did to native-born women. See *Daughters of the Shtetl,* chap. 6.

35. Cobble, chap. 1, and concluding tables.

36. Ronald Schatz, "Union Pioneers: The Founders of Local Unions at GE and Westinghouse, 1933–37," *Journal of American History* 66 (December 1979): 586–602, and *The Electrical Workers: A History of Labor at General Electric and Westinghouse, 1923–60* (Urbana: University of Illinois Press, 1983), 80–101.

37. Tilly, 411–17. Turbin, 59–63, has an excellent summary of the recent literature which supports these suppositions.

38. Chapter 8 of "Sisters in the Craft" compiles biographical data on forty waitress leaders and finds that one-third were divorced, separated, or widowed and that most did not begin their careers until their thirties or later. These

findings are consistent with studies of contemporary women union leaders which note the disproportionate number of older, divorced activists.

39. Tilly, 414–17.

40. These barriers are detailed in Karen S. Koziara and David A. Pierson, "The Lack of Female Union Leaders: A Look at Some Reasons," *Monthly Labor Review* 104 (May 1981): 30–32; and Wertheimer and Nelson.

41. Milkman, "Organizing the Sexual Division of Labor," 114–44.

42. The initial structure of many industrial unions enhanced the participation of women. As they matured, however, becoming more bureaucratic and top-down, the activism of women declined. See Richard Lester, *As Unions Mature: An Analysis of the Evolution of American Unionism* (Princeton: Princeton University Press, 1958). Recently, Elizabeth Faue has traced the loss of local autonomy and community-based practice among the unions in Minneapolis and the dampening effect this transformation had on female activism. See her *Community of Suffering and Struggle: Women, Men, and the Labor Movement in Minneapolis* (Chapel Hill: University of North Carolina Press, 1991).

43. Roslyn Feldberg, "Women and Trade Unions: Are We Asking the Right Questions?" in *Hidden Aspects of Women's Work,* ed. Christine Bose et al. (New York: Praeger, 1987), 299–322.

"We Are That Mythical Thing Called the Public": Militant Housewives during the Great Depression

"We are that mythical thing called the public
and so we shall demand a hearing."
—Jean Stovel, organizer of a housewives'
flour boycott, Seattle, 1936

☐ The last fifteen years have seen a growing literature on women in the 1930s. These new histories have examined organizing among working women of various ethnicities, illuminated women's political networks in the New Deal, and assessed the relationship of women to New Deal social welfare programs. But we still know next to nothing about how poor and working-class housewives fared during the Great Depression. To a large extent our view is shaped by popular imagery of the time, which glorified the self-sacrificing wife and mother. Black-and-white documentary photographs like Dorothea Lange's portrait of a gaunt migrant woman sheltering her frightened children, novels like Sholem Asch's *The Mother,* and films like *The Grapes of Wrath* reinforced the popular view of poor mothers as the last traditionalists, guardians of the beleaguered home. In many ways, this idealization of motherhood placed on poor women's shoulders the responsibility for easing the hardships of hunger and joblessness.[1]

In her 1933 book, *It's Up to the Women,* Eleanor Roosevelt argued that mothers, through self-sacrifice and creativity, would save their families from the worst ravages of the Depression. There is abundant evidence

Reprinted, with changes, from *Feminist Studies* 19, no. 1 (Spring 1993): 147–72. ©1993 by Feminist Studies, Inc.

to show that poor wives and mothers did approach their traditional responsibilities with heightened urgency during the Depression. They did not, however, suffer alone their inability to provide food or shelter for their families; nor did they sacrifice silently for the sake of their husbands and children. Quite the contrary. From the late 1920s through the 1940s, there was a remarkable surge of activism by working-class American housewives.[2]

From New York City to Seattle; from Richmond, Virginia, to Los Angeles; and in hundreds of small towns and farm villages in between, poor wives and mothers staged food boycotts and anti-eviction demonstrations, created large-scale barter networks, and lobbied for food and rent price controls. Militant and angry, they demanded a better quality of life for themselves and their children. Echoing the language of trade unionism, they asserted that housing and food, like wages and hours, could be regulated by organizing and applying economic pressure.

This was not the first time Americans were treated to the spectacle of housewives demanding food for their families. Since the early nineteenth century, hard times in New York, Philadelphia, and other major cities had moved housewives in immigrant neighborhoods to demonstrate for lower food prices. But never before had Americans seen anything this widespread or persistent. The crisis conditions created by the Depression of the 1930s moved working-class wives and mothers across the United States to organize on a scale unprecedented in U.S. history. By organizing themselves as class-conscious mothers and consumers, they stretched the limits both of working-class and women's organizing in the United States.

Housewives' activism, like that of every other group of Americans during the Depression era, was profoundly influenced by Franklin Roosevelt's New Deal. During the early years of the Depression, prior to the 1932 presidential election, housewives organized to stave off imminent disaster. Their focus was on self-help—setting up barter networks, gardening cooperatives, and neighborhood councils. After 1933, the tactics and arguments used by militant housewives reflected their acceptance of Roosevelt's corporatist vision. By the mid-1930s, poor and working-class housewives, like farmers and factory workers, had begun to see themselves as a group that could, by organizing and lobbying, force the New Deal state to respond to their needs.

Press coverage reflected the ambivalence with which many Americans greeted the idea of politically organized housewives. Both mainstream and radical editors took their movement seriously. Housewives' strikes and demonstrations were featured in major newspapers and national magazines. Still these publications could not resist poking fun at the very idea of a housewives' movement. Writers never tired of suggesting that, by its very existence, the housewives' movement emasculated male adversaries. A typical headline ran in the *New York Times* in summer 1935 at the height of housewives' activism nationwide. "Women Picket Butcher Shops in Detroit Suburb," it blared. "Slap. Scratch. Pull Hair. Men Are Chief Victims." A more pointed headline, about Secretary of Agriculture Henry Wallace, ran a few weeks later in the *Chicago Daily Tribune:* "Secretary Wallace Beats Retreat from Five Housewives." Underlying this tone of ridicule was a growing tension over the fact that housewife activists were politicizing the traditional roles of wives and mothers.[3]

In New York City neighborhoods, organized bands of Jewish housewives fiercely resisted eviction, arguing that they were merely doing their jobs by defending their homes and those of their neighbors. Barricading themselves in apartments, they made speeches from tenement windows, wielded kettles of boiling water, and threatened to scald anyone who attempted to move furniture out on to the street. Black mothers in Cleveland, unable to convince a local power company to delay shutting off electricity in the homes of families who had not paid their bills, won restoration of power after they hung wet laundry over every utility line in the neighborhood. They also left crying babies on the desks of caseworkers at the Cleveland Emergency Relief Association, refusing to retrieve them until free milk had been provided for each child. These actions reflected a sense of humor but sometimes housewife rage exploded. In Chicago, angry Polish housewives doused thousands of pounds of meat with kerosene and set it on fire at the warehouses of the Armour Company to dramatize their belief that high prices were not the result of shortages.[4]

This activity was not simply a reaction to the economic crisis gripping the nation. It was a conscious attempt on the part of many housewives to change the system that they blamed for the Depression. In Seattle in 1931, urban and farm wives orchestrated a massive exchange of timber and fish from western Washington for grain, fruits, and vegetables from eastern Washington. As a result, tens of thousands of families had enough food and fuel to survive the difficult winter of 1931–32. Similar barter networks were established in California, Colorado, Ohio, and Virginia in which housewives gathered and distributed food, clothing, fuel, and building materials.[5]

Understanding their power as a voting bloc, housewives lobbied in state capitals and in Washington, D.C. They also ran for electoral office in numerous locales across the country. In Washington State and in Michigan, housewife activists were elected in 1934 and 1936 on platforms that called for government regulation of food prices, housing, and utility costs. And in Minnesota, in 1936, farm wives were key players in the creation of a national Farmer-Labor Party.[6]

These actions were not motivated by desire on the part of poor wives and mothers to be relieved of their responsibilities in the home—although certainly many were attracted by the excitement and camaraderie of activism. These were the actions of women who accepted the traditional sexual division of labor but who found that the Depression had made it impossible for them to fulfill their responsibilities to the home without leaving it.

Housewife activists argued that the homes in which they worked were intimately linked to the fields and shops where their husbands, sons, and daughters labored; to the national economy; and to the fast-growing state and federal bureaucracies. Mrs. Charles Lundquist, a farmer's wife and president of the Farmer-Labor Women's Federation of Minnesota, summed up this view in a 1936 speech before a gathering of farmers and labor activists.

> Woman's place may be in the home but the home is no longer the isolated, complete unit it was. To serve her home best, the woman of today must understand the political and economic foundation on which that home rests—and then do something about it.[7]

The extent and variety of housewives' activism during the Depression suggests that this view of the home was widely accepted by Black as well as white women, farm as well as urban women. The housewives' rebellions that swept the country during the 1930s cannot be seen as only spontaneous outcries for a "just price." Like so many others during the Depression, working-class housewives were offering their own solutions to the failure of the U.S. economic system.[8]

Roots of a Housewives' Uprising

☐ This essay focuses primarily on urban housewives' organizing, but farm women also played an essential role in Depression-era housewives' activism. Apart from organizing on their own behalf—establishing farmer-labor women's committees and food-goods exchanges with urban women—farm women provided urban women with information about the gap between what farmers were paid and what wholesalers charged. This profit taking formed the basis for activists' critique of what they called "food trusts." Farm wives' activism during the 1920s and 1930s must be studied before a full assessment of this phenomenon is possible. However, because of space limitations, this essay focuses on three of the most active and successful urban housewives' groups: the New York-based United Council of Working-Class Women, the Seattle-based Women's Committee of the Washington Commonwealth Federation, and the Detroit-based Women's Committee against the High Cost of Living.

Greater availability of sources on New York housewives' activism has made possible a deeper analysis of New York than of Detroit or Seattle, both of which merit further study. Still, there is sufficient evidence on the latter two cities to make for a fruitful comparison and to discern some key patterns in working-class housewives' organizing during the Depression.

An examination of these three groups illustrates that although there were some important regional differences in housewives' political style and focus, there were also commonalities. Most significantly, each had a strong labor movement affiliation. Housewives' activism developed in union strongholds, flourishing in the Bronx and Brooklyn, among the wives and mothers of unionized garment workers; in Detroit, among the wives and mothers of United Auto Workers' (UAW) members; and in Seattle, among the wives of unionized workers who had begun to argue the importance of consumer organizing during the 1920s.[9]

This union link is important for several reasons. Union husbands' fights for higher wages during the 1910s had resulted in a fairly comfortable standard of living for many families by World War I. But spiraling inflation and the near-destruction of many trade unions during the 1920s eroded the working-class quality of life. By 1929 it had become increasingly difficult, even for families of employed union workers, to make ends meet.[10]

The militance of the Depression-era housewives' movement was an outgrowth of this sudden and rapid decline in working-class families' standard of living. But it was also rooted in women organizers' own experiences in trade unions. There are no statistics detailing exactly how many housewife activists were formerly union members. However, in all the areas where housewives' organizations took hold, it was common for women to work for wages before marriage. And given the age of most leading activists in New York, Seattle, and Detroit, their working years would have coincided with the years of women's labor militance between 1909 and 1920.[11]

Certainly the key organizers of the housewives' movement were all labor leaders before the Depression. In Seattle, Jean Stovel and Mary Farquharson were active in the American Federation of Labor (AFL) before they became leaders of the Women's Committee of the Washington Commonwealth Federation. Detroit's Mary Zuk was the daughter of a United Mine Workers' member and was raised on the violent mine strikes of the 1920s. As a young woman she migrated to Detroit to work on an automobile assembly line and was fired for UAW organizing before founding the Detroit Women's Committee against the High Cost of Living. In New York, Rose Nelson was an organizer for the International Ladies' Garment Workers' Union (ILGWU) before she became co-director of the United Council of Working-Class Women (UCWCW). And the career of the best-known housewife organizer of the 1930s, Clara Lemlich Shavelson, illustrates the importance of both labor movement and Communist party links. (Only the New York organizers had explicit CP ties, although charges of CP involvement were leveled against nearly all the housewife leaders.)[12]

Shavelson's career also roots the housewives' rebellions of the 1930s in a long tradition of Jewish immigrant women's agitation around subsistence issues. Because few immigrant or working-class families in the early twentieth century could afford to live on the salary of a single wage earner, wives, daughters, and sons contributed to the family economy. Clara Lemlich Shavelson's mother ran a small grocery store. Other immigrant women took in boarders, ran restaurants, peddled piece goods, and took in washing or sewing. Their experience with small-scale entrepreneurship gave them a basic understanding of the marketplace that carried over to their management of the home. This economic understanding was deepened by their exposure to unionist principles through their husbands, daughters and sons, and sometimes through their own experience as wage workers.[13]

These experiences nourished a belief among working-class women that the home was inextricably bound in a web of social and economic relationships to labor unions, the marketplace, and government. That view of the home was expressed in a series of food boycotts and rent strikes that erupted in New York; Philadelphia; Paterson, New Jersey; and other East Coast cities between the turn of the century and World War I. Clara Lemlich came of age on Manhattan's Lower East Side where married women led frequent food boycotts and rent strikes during the first decade of the twentieth century. Long before she made the famous speech that set off the massive 1909 shirtwaist makers' strike—"I am tired of the talking; I move that we go on a general strike!"—Lemlich was aware that the principles of unionism could be applied to community activism.[14]

Blacklisted by garment manufacturers after the 1909 strike, fired from her new career as a paid woman's suffrage advocate after conflicts with upper-class suffragists, Lemlich married printer Arthur Shavelson in 1913 and immediately began looking for ways to channel spontaneous outbursts of housewives' anger into an organizational structure. During World War I, the U.S. government made her task easier by mobilizing housewives in many city neighborhoods into Community Councils for National Defense. Now, when housewives decided to protest rapidly increasing food prices, they had an organizational structure to build on and halls in which to meet. In 1917 and 1919 Shavelson and other community organizers were able to spread meat boycotts and rent strikes throughout New York City by winning support from the community councils, as well as synagogue groups and women's trade union auxiliaries.[15]

By 1926, when Shavelson established the United Council of Working-Class Housewives (UCWCH), she was working under the auspices of the Communist party. However, Shavelson's insistence on organizing women made her a maverick within the CP, as she had been in the labor and suffrage movements. The male leadership of the CP expressed little interest in efforts to win working-class wives to the party. And the women who ran the UCWCH put no pressure on women who joined the housewives' councils to also join the CP.[16]

Around the same time that the united councils were founded, non-Communist organizers like Rose Schneiderman of the Women's Trade Union League (WTUL) and Pauline Newman and Fania Cohn of the ILGWU were also trying to bring housewives into the working-class movement. In the twenty years since the 1909 shirtwaist strike—the largest strike by U.S. women workers to that time—these labor organizers had run up against the incontrovertible fact that working-class women lacked the economic power to achieve their social and political aims unless they allied themselves with more powerful groups such as middle-class women or working-class men.[17]

Seeking a way to maximize working-class women's economic power, they decided to organize women both as consumers and as workers. As workers, women were segregated into the lowest-paid, least-skilled sectors of the labor force. Economic deprivation and discrimination in male-dominated labor unions limited their power, even when they organized. But as consumers, U.S. working-class women spent billions of dollars annually. Organized as consumers, even poor women could wield real economic power. By the late 1920s, women organizers were ready to try to link the home to labor unions and government in a dynamic partnership—with wage-earning women and housewives as full partners.[18]

That goal brought women organizers into direct conflict with male leaders in the trade union movement and in the CP, who were unwilling to accept the home as a center of production or the housewife as a productive laborer. Nor did they see a relationship between production and consumption. Poor housewives, whatever their political stripe, understood that relationship implicitly. They responded to the neighborhood organizing strategy because they saw in it a chance to improve day-to-day living conditions for themselves and their families.[19] Jean Stovel explained the surge of militance among Seattle housewives this way: "Women," she said, "have sold the idea of organization—their own vast power—to themselves, the result of bitter experience. We are that mythical thing called the public and so we shall demand a hearing."[20]

It is important to distinguish the aims of veteran women's organizers from the aims of the majority of women who participated in housewives' protests. For the most part, these housewives had no intention of challenging the traditional sexual division of labor. Nor were they interested in alternative political philosophies such as socialism or communism. But, desperate to feed, clothe, and shelter their families, poor women challenged traditional limits on acceptable behavior for mothers and wives. In so doing, they became political actors.[21]

From Self-help to Lobbying the Government

☐ Between 1926 and 1933 housewives' self-help groups sprang up across the United States. In cities surrounded by accessible growing areas (such as Dayton, Ohio; Richmond, Virginia; and Seattle, Washington), housewives and their husbands created highly developed barter networks. Unemployed workers, mostly male, exchanged skills such as carpentry, plumbing, barbering, and electrical wiring. Women—some workers' wives, others unemployed workers themselves—organized exchanges of clothing and food. These organizations grew out of small-scale gardening collectives created by housewives during the late 1920s to feed their communities.[22]

In Seattle, unemployed families organized quickly in the aftermath of the 1929 stock market crash; but then this was an unusually organized city, described by a local paper in 1937 as "the most unionized city in the country." In 1919, Seattle had been the first city in the United States to hold a general strike. During the 1920s, Seattle's labor unions again broke new ground by calling on working-class women and men to organize as consumers. When the Depression hit, Seattle's vast subsistence network was described in the national press as a model of self-sufficiency, "a republic of the penniless," in the words of the *Atlantic*. By 1931–32, 40,000 Seattle women and men had joined an exchange in which the men farmed, fished, and cut leftover timber from cleared land, and the women gathered food, fuel, and clothing. The women also ran commissaries where members could shop with scrip for household essentials. By 1934, an estimated 80,000 people statewide belonged to exchanges that allowed them to acquire food, clothing, and shelter without any money changing hands.[23]

In larger cities like New York, Chicago, Philadelphia, and Detroit, self-help groups also sprang up during the early years of the Depression, but housewives there had little chance of making direct contact with farmers. Rather than establishing food exchanges, they created neighborhood councils that used boycotts and demonstrations to combat rising food prices. And, rather than rehabilitating abandoned buildings for occupation by the homeless, as the unemployed did in Seattle, housewives in larger cities battled with police to prevent evictions of families unable to pay their rents.[24]

Tenant and consumer councils in those cities took hold in neighborhoods where housewives had orchestrated rent strikes and meat boycotts in 1902, 1904, 1907, 1908, and 1917.[25] They organized in the same way as earlier housewife activists had done—primarily through door-to-door canvassing. Boycotts were sustained in the latter period, as in the earlier one, with picket lines and streetcorner meetings. Even their angry outbursts echoed the earlier housewives' uprisings: meat was destroyed with kerosene or taken off trucks and thrown to the ground. Flour was spilled in the streets, and milk ran in the gutters.[26]

But although its links to earlier housewives' and labor union struggles are important, the 1930s' housewives' revolt was far more widespread and sustained, encompassing a far wider range of ethnic and racial groups than any tenant or consumer uprising before it. The earlier outbursts were limited to East Coast Jewish immigrant communities, but the housewives' uprising of the 1930s was nationwide and involved rural as well as urban women. It drew Polish and native-born housewives in Detroit, Finnish and Scandinavian women in Washington State, and Scandinavian farm wives in Minnesota. Jewish and Black housewives were particularly militant in New York, Cleveland, Chicago, Los Angeles, and San Francisco.[27]

The 1930s' housewives' movement can also be distinguished from earlier housewives' actions by the sophistication and longevity of the organizations it generated. Depression-era housewives moved quickly from self-help to lobbying in state capitals and Washington, D.C. Leaders like the "diminutive but fiery" Mary Zuk of Detroit displayed considerable skill in their use of radio and print media. Their demands of government—regulation of staple food prices; establishment of publicly owned farmer-consumer cooperatives—reflected a complex understanding of the marketplace and the potential uses of the growing government bureaucracy.

Leaders of these groups also demonstrated considerable sophistication about forming alliances. Shortly after Roosevelt was elected president, hostilities between Communist and non-Communist women in the labor movement were temporarily set aside. AFL-affiliated women's auxiliaries and CP-affiliated women's neighborhood councils worked together to organize consumer protests and lobby for regulation of food and housing costs. This happened in 1933, well before the CP initiated its Popular Front policy urging members to join with "progressive" non-Communist groups and well before the Congress of Industrial Organizations extended its hand to Communists to rejoin the labor movement.[28]

This rapprochement highlighted the desperation that gripped so many working-class communities during the Depression. Although anti-Communist charges were leveled against housewife organizers throughout the Depression, such accusations did not dampen the enthusiasm of rank-and-file council members. To many non-Communists in the movement, the question of who was Communist and who wasn't did not seem terribly relevant at a time when millions faced hunger and homelessness. Detroit housewife leader Catherine Mudra responded this way to charges of Communist involvement in the Detroit meat strike of 1935: "There may be some Communists among us. There are a lot of Republicans and Democrats too. We do not ask the politics of those who join. . . . All we want is to get prices down to where we can feed our families."[29]

Despite this tolerance of Communist leadership, housewife organizers affiliated with the CP were careful not to push too hard. Party regulars like Clara Lemlich Shavelson were open about their political beliefs, but they did not push members of the housewives' councils to toe the party line. And they organized as mothers, not as Communists. Shavelson did not use the name Lemlich, which still reverberated among New York City garment workers who remembered her fiery speech in 1909. Instead, she organized under her married name and made sure to point out her children whenever they passed by a streetcorner where she was speaking.[30]

Seasoned organizers like Shavelson sought to build bonds between women in the name of motherhood. They understood that when appealed to as mothers, apolitical women lost their fears about being associated with radicalism in general and the CP in particular. Meeting women organizers day after day, in the local parks with their babies, in food markets, and on streetcorners, shy housewives gained the confidence to express their anger. The deepening Depression hastened such personal transformations. Once all sense of economic security had dissolved, temperamentally conservative women became more open to radical solutions. Sophia Ocher, who was a member of a Mother and Child Unit of Communist organizers in the Bronx, wrote that "work among these women was not difficult for there was the baby, the greatest of all issues, and there were the women, all working-class mothers who would fight for their very lives to obtain a better life for their babies."31

In New York, ethnic bonding among women facilitated the growth of housewives' councils. Although many community organizers like Shavelson, Rose Nelson Raynes, Sonya Sanders, and Sophia Ocher were CP members, they were also genuine members of the communities they sought to organize, familiar with local customs, needs, and fears. They addressed crowds of housewives in Yiddish as well as English. And steering clear of Marxist doctrine, they emphasized ethnic and community ties in their speeches, likening housewives' councils to the women's charitable associations traditional in East European Jewish culture.32

Conscious of the hardship of poor women's lives, the organizers never hesitated to roll up their sleeves and help out. In one Bronx neighborhood, Sonya Sanders created an entire neighborhood council by winning over one resistant housebound woman. After Sanders came into the woman's house when she was sick, cleaned it, bathed the children, and prepared a kosher dinner for the family, the woman gave up her suspicion of Sanders and became an enthusiastic supporter. She invited all her friends to come to her home and listen to Sanders discuss ways to fight evictions and high prices. Before long a new neighborhood council was born. Of course, successes like these were predicated on the shared ethnicity of organizer and organized. The ploy would not have worked as well if Sanders did not understand the laws of *kashrut* or know how to cook Jewish-style food.33

This strength was also a weakness. As a result of New York's ethnic balkanization, the city's neighborhood councils were not ethnically diverse. Organizers tended to have most success organizing women of their own ethnic group. The United Council of Working-Class Women (UCWCW), founded and run by Jewish immigrant women, was primarily composed of Jewish immigrant housewives; owing to the CP's strength in Harlem, Black women were the second largest group; small numbers of Irish and Italian housewives also joined.

"We never intended to be exclusively a Jewish organization," Rose Nelson Raynes recalls.

But we built in areas where we had strength. Maybe it was because of the background of so many Jewish women in the needle trades, maybe it was because of the concentration of immigrants from the other side, I don't know. But there was a feeling in the Jewish working class that we had to express ourselves in protest of the rising prices.[34]

As in New York, the Detroit and Seattle housewives' actions were initiated by immigrant women of a particular ethnic group—Polish Catholics in Detroit and Scandinavian Protestants in Seattle. Because those cities were less ghettoized than New York, organizers were more successful in creating coalitions that involved Black as well as white women; Protestants, Jews, and Catholics; immigrants and native born. However, ethnic differences were not unimportant, even outside New York. For example, American-born Protestants in the Detroit housewives' councils were far less confrontational in their tactics than their Polish, Jewish, or Black counterparts. They signed no-meat pledges rather than picketing butcher shops and handed in petitions rather than marching on city hall.[35]

Women had different reasons for joining housewives' councils in the 1930s, but those who stayed did so because they enjoyed the camaraderie, the enhanced self-esteem, and the shared sense of fighting for a larger cause. During an interview in her Brighton Beach apartment, eighty-eight-year-old Rose Nelson Raynes offered this analysis of why the councils inspired such loyalty:

> Women were discriminated against in all organizations in those years and the progressive organizations were no exception. When women joined progressive organizations with men they were relegated to the kitchen. There was a need on the part of the mother, the woman in the house. She wanted to get out. There were so many things taking place that she wanted to learn more about. So women came to our organization where they got culture, lectures. Some developed to a point where they could really get up and make a speech that would meet any politician's speech today. It came from the need, from the heart. We felt we wanted to express ourselves, to learn to speak and act and the only way was through a women's council.[36]

The Meatless Summer of 1935

☐ Depression-era organizing against high food prices reached its peak during the summer of 1935. Working-class women activists from Communist and non-Communist organizations convened two regional conferences the previous winter, one for the East Coast, another for the Midwest, to coordinate protests against the sales tax and high cost of living. Representatives from AFL women's union auxiliaries, parents' associations, church groups, farm women's and Black women's groups attended. By that summer, they had laid plans for the most ambitious women's consumer protest to that time.[37]

It began when the Chicago Committee against the High Cost of Living, headed by Dina Ginsberg, organized massive street meetings near the stockyards to let the meat packers know how unhappy they were with rising meat prices. New York housewives in the UCWCW quickly raised the ante by organizing a citywide strike against butcher shops.[38]

On May 22 women in Jewish and Black neighborhoods around New York City formed picket lines. In Harlem, according to historian Mark Naison, the meat strike "produced an unprecedented display of coordinated protest by black working-class women."[39] The strike lasted four weeks. More than 4,500 butcher shops were closed down by housewives' picket lines. Scores of women and men around the city were arrested. The New York State Retail Meat Dealers Association threatened to hold Mayor Fiorello LaGuardia responsible for damage to their businesses as a result of the strike. The mayor, in an attempt to resolve the strike, asked federal officials to study the possibilities for reducing retail meat prices.[40]

Raynes, citywide coordinator of the meat strike, describes what happened next.

> It was successful to a point where we were warned that the gangsters were going to get us. . . . We decided to call the whole thing off but first we organized a mass picket line in front of the wholesale meat distributors. . . . About three, four hundred women came out on the picket line. It was supposed to be a final action. But . . . instead of being the windup it became a beginning.[41]

Housewives across the United States promptly joined in. Ten thousand Los Angeles housewives, members of the Joint Council of Women's Auxiliaries, declared a meat strike on June 8th that so completely shut down retail meat sales in the city that butchers cut prices by the next day. In Philadelphia, Chicago, Boston, Paterson, St. Louis, and Kansas City, newly formed housewives' councils echoed the cry of the New York strike: "Stop Buying Meat Until Prices Come Down!"[42]

On June 15, a delegation of housewives from across the country descended on Washington, D.C., demanding that the Department of Agriculture enforce lower meat prices. Clara Lemlich Shavelson described the delegation's meeting with Secretary of Agriculture Henry Wallace. "The meat packers and the Department of Agriculture in Washington tried to make the strikers' delegation . . . believe that the farmer and the drought are to blame for the high price of food. But the delegation would not fall for this. They knew the truth."[43]

The Polish housewives of Hamtramck, Michigan, a suburb of Detroit, did not believe Wallace's explanation either. A month after the end of the New York strike, thirty-two-year-old Mary Zuk addressed a mass demonstration of housewives gathered on the streets of Hamtramck to demand an immediate reduction in meat prices. When the reduction did not come by that evening, Zuk announced a meat boycott to begin the following day.[44]

On July 27, 1935, Polish and Black housewives began to picket Hamtramck butcher shops, carrying signs demanding a 20 percent price cut throughout the city and an end to price gouging in Black neighborhoods. When men, taunted by onlookers who accused them of being "scared of a few women," attempted to cross the lines, they were "seized by the pickets . . . their faces slapped, their hair pulled and their packages confiscated. . . . A few were knocked down and trampled." That night Hamtramck butchers reported unhappily that the boycott had been 95 percent effective.[45]

Within a matter of days the meat boycott spread to other parts of Detroit, as housewives in several different ethnic communities hailed the onset of "a general strike against the high cost of living." Jewish women picketed kosher butcher shops in downtown Detroit neighborhoods. Protestant women in outlying regions such as Lincoln Park and River Rouge declined to picket or march but instead set up card tables on streetcorners to solicit no-meat pledges from passing housewives.[46]

Housewives also sought government intervention. Detroit housewives stormed the city council, demanding that it set a ceiling on meat prices in the metropolitan area. "What we can afford to buy isn't fit for a human to eat," Joanna Dinkfeld told the council. "And we can't afford very much of that." Warning the council and the state government that they had better act, Myrtle Hoaglund announced that she was forming a statewide housewives' organization. "We feel that we should have united action," she said. "We think the movement of protest against present meat prices can be spread throughout the state and . . . the nation." As evidence, she showed the city council bags of letters she had received from housewives around the country, asking her how to go about organizing consumer boycotts.[47]

Throughout August the meat strikers made front-page news in Detroit and received close attention in major New York and Chicago dailies. The women staged mass marches through the streets of Detroit, stormed meat-packing plants, overturned and emptied meat trucks, and poured kerosene on thousands of pounds of meat stored in warehouses. When these actions resulted in the arrest of several Detroit women, hundreds of boycotters marched on the city jails, demanding the release of their friends. Two hours after her arrest, Hattie Krewik, forty-five years old and a mother of five, emerged from her cell unrepentant. A roar went up from the crowd as she immediately began to tell, in Polish, her tale of mistreatment at the hands of police. By the end of the first week in August, retail butchers in Detroit were pleading with the governor to send in state troops to protect their meat.[48]

Although without a doubt the butchers suffered as a result of this boycott, the strikers in Detroit, like the strikers in New York, frequently reiterated that the strike was not aimed at retail butchers or at farmers. It was aimed, in Clara Shavelson's words, at the "meat packer millionaires." To prove that, in the second week of August, a delegation of Detroit housewives traveled to Chicago where they hooked up with their Chicago counterparts for a march on the Union stockyards.

Meeting them at the gates, Armour & Company president R.H. Cabell attempted to mollify the women. "Meat packers," he told them, "are not the arbiters of prices, merely the agencies through which economic laws operate." The sudden rise in prices, he explained, was the fault of the Agricultural Adjustment Administration which had recently imposed a processing tax on pork.[49]

"Fine," Mary Zuk responded. The housewives would return to Washington for another meeting with agriculture secretary Wallace. On August 19, 1935, Zuk and her committee of five housewives marched into Wallace's office and demanded that he end the processing tax, impose a 20 percent cut on meat prices, and order prompt prosecution of profiteering meat packers.[50] Wallace, perhaps sensing how this would be played in the press, tried to evict reporters from the room, warning that he would not speak to the women if they remained. Zuk did not blink. She replied: "Our people want to know what we say and they want to know what *you* say so the press people are going to stay." The reporters stayed and had a grand time the next day reporting on Wallace's unexplained departure from the room in the middle of the meeting.[51] "Secretary Wallace Beats Retreat from Five Housewives," the *Chicago Daily Tribune* blared. *Newsweek* reported it this way:

> The lanky Iowan looked down into Mrs. Zuk's deep-sunken brown eyes and gulped his Adam's apple.
> Mrs. Zuk: Doesn't the government want us to live? Everything in Detroit has gone up except wages.
> Wallace fled.[52]

In the aftermath of Zuk's visit to Washington, *Newsweek* reported housewives' demonstrations against the high price of meat in Indianapolis, Denver, and Miami. The *New York Times* reported violent housewives' attacks on meat warehouses in Chicago and in Shenandoah and Frackville, Pennsylvania. And Mary Zuk, the "strong-jawed 100 lb. mother of the meat strike," became a national figure. The Detroit post office announced that it was receiving letters from all over the country addressed only to "Mrs. Zuk—Detroit."[53]

Although boycotts and strikes continued to be used as a tool in the housewives' struggle for lower prices, the movement became more focused on electoral politics as the decade wore on. Both Shavelson and Zuk used the prominence they'd gained through housewife activism to run for elected office. Shavelson ran for New York State Assembly in 1933 and 1938 as a "real . . . mother fighting to maintain an American standard of living for her own family as well as for other families. . . ." She did not win but she fared far better than the rest of the CP ticket.[54]

Zuk ran a successful campaign for the Hamtramck City Council in April of 1936. Although the local Hearst-owned paper warned that her election would be a victory for those who advocate "the break-up of the family," Zuk was swept into office by her fellow housewives. She won on a platform calling for the city council to reduce rents, food prices, and utility costs in Hamtramck. After her election she told reporters that she was proof that "a mother can organize and still take care of her family."[55]

In some ways what the Hearst papers sensed was really happening. Zuk's campaign represented an express politicization of motherhood and the family. On Mother's Day, 1936, seven hundred Zuk supporters rallied outside the city council to demand public funding for a women's healthcare clinic, childcare centers, playgrounds, and teen centers in Hamtramck. They also called for an end to evictions and construction of more public housing in their city. The government owed this to mothers, the demonstrators told reporters.[56]

Two years earlier, in Washington State, the Women's Committee of the Washington Commonwealth Federation (WCF) had successfully elected three of its members to the state senate—Mary Farquharson, a professor's wife; and Marie Keene and Katherine Malström, the wives of loggers. Their campaign had been built around a Production-for-Use initiative to prohibit the destruction of food as a way of propping up prices. Such waste, they said, was an outrage to poor mothers in the state, who had been fighting the practice since the beginning of the Depression. The ballot measure also proposed a state distribution system for produce so that farmers could get a fair price and workers' families could buy food directly from farmers. Led by Katherine Smith and Elizabeth Harper, committee members collected 70,000 signatures to put the measure on the 1936 ballot.[57]

The Production-for-Use initiative failed by a narrow margin, but it made national news as columnists across the country speculated on the impact it might have had on the U.S. economic system. Other WCF campaigns were more successful, however. The most important of these was the campaign to create publicly owned utilities in Washington State. Washington voters were the only ones to approve state ownership of utilities, but voters in localities across the country endorsed the creation of city and county utility companies during the 1930s.[58]

Housewife activists also kept their sights on the federal government during this period. From 1935 to 1941, housewives' delegations from major cities made annual trips to Washington, D.C., to lobby for lower food prices. These trips stopped during World War II but resumed afterward with a concerted campaign to save the Office of Price Administration and to win federal funds for construction of public housing in poor neighborhoods.[59]

The alliance of housewives' councils and women's union auxiliaries continued to grow through the late 1930s, laying the groundwork for two more nationwide meat strikes in 1948 and 1951. These strikes affected even more women than the 1935 action because housewives now had an organizing tool that enabled them to mobilize across thousands of miles: the telephone. "We have assigned fifty-eight women ten pages each of the telephone directory," said one strike leader in Cincinnati. In August of 1948, housewives in Texas, Ohio, Colorado, Florida, Michigan, and New York boycotted meat. And during the winter of 1951, a housewives' meat boycott across the country forced wholesalers dealing in the New York, Philadelphia, and Chicago markets to lower their prices. In New York City alone, newspapers estimated, one million pounds of meat a week went begging. Fearing for their own jobs, unionized butchers, then retailers, and finally even local wholesalers, called on the federal government to institute price controls on meat.[60]

But even as these actions made front-page news across the country, the housewives' alliance was breaking apart over the issue of Communist involvement. As early as 1933, the Washington State legislature had passed a bill requiring that Seattle take over the commissaries created by the unemployed two years earlier. Conservative politicians claimed that Communists had taken control of the relief machinery in the city and were seeking to indoctrinate the hungry. In 1939, Hearst newspapers charged that the housewives' movement nationwide was little more than a Communist plot to sow seeds of discord in the American home. The Dies Committee of the U.S. Congress took these charges seriously and began an investigation. U.S. entry into World War II temporarily ended the investigation but also quelled consumer protest, because the government instituted rationing and price controls.[61]

Investigations of the consumer movement began again soon after the war ended. During the 1948 boycott, housewife leaders were charged by some with being too friendly to Progressive party presidential candidate Henry Wallace. In 1949, the House Committee on Un-American Activities began investigating the organizers of a 1947 housewives' march on Washington, and in 1950 they were ordered to register with the Justice Department as foreign agents. By the early 1950s national and local Communist-hunting committees had torn apart the movement, creating dissension and mistrust among the activists.[62]

The unique alliance that created a nationwide housewives' uprising during the 1930s and 1940s would not reemerge, but it laid the groundwork for later consumer and tenant organizing. Housewives' militance politicized consumer issues nationwide. "Never has there been such a wave of enthusiasm to do something for the consumer," *The Nation* wrote in 1937. Americans have gained "a consumer consciousness," the magazine concluded, as a direct result of the housewives' strikes in New York, Detroit, and other cities. The uprising of working-class housewives also broadened the terms of the class struggle, forcing male union leaders to admit that "the roles of producer and consumer are intimately related."[63]

Housewives' groups alleviated the worst effects of the Depression in many working-class communities by bringing down food prices; rent and utility costs; preventing evictions; and spurring the construction of more public housing, schools, and parks. By the end of World War II, housewives' activism had forced the government to play a regulatory role in food and housing costs. Militant direct action and sustained lobbying put pressure on local and federal politicians to investigate profiteering on staple goods. The meat strikes of 1935 and of 1948 through 1951 resulted in congressional hearings on the structure of the meat industry and in nationwide reductions in prices. The intense anti-eviction struggles led by urban housewives and their years of lobbying for public housing helped to convince New York City and other localities to pass rent-control laws. They also increased support in Congress for federally funded public housing.[64]

Perhaps an equally important legacy of housewives' activism was its impact on the consciousness of the women who participated. "It was an education for the women," Brooklyn activist Dorothy Moser recalls, "that they could not have gotten any other way." Immigrant women, poor native white women, and Black women learned to write and speak effectively, to lobby in state capitals and in Washington, D.C., to challenge men in positions of power, and sometimes to question the power relations in their own homes.[65]

By organizing as consumers, working-class housewives not only demonstrated a keen understanding of their place in local and national economic structures, but they also shattered the notion that because homemakers consume rather than produce, they are inherently more passive than their wage-earning husbands. The very act of organizing defied traditional notions of proper behavior for wives and mothers—and organizers were often called upon to explain their actions.

Union husbands supported and sometimes, as Dana Frank argues in her study of Seattle, even instigated their wives' community organizing. However, that organizing created logistical problems—namely who was going to watch the children and who was going to cook dinner? Some women managed to do it all. Others could not. Complaining of anarchy in the home, some union husbands ordered their wives to stop marching and return to the kitchen. In November 1934, *Working Woman* magazine offered a hamper of canned goods to any woman who could answer the plaint of a housewife whose husband had ordered her to quit her women's council.

First prize went to a Bronx housewife who called on husbands and wives to share childcare as "they share their bread. Perhaps two evenings a week father should go, and two evenings, mother." The same woman noted that struggle keeps a woman "young physically and mentally" and that she shouldn't give it up for anything. Second prize went to a Pennsylvania miner's wife who agreed with that sentiment. "There can't be a revolution without women. . . . No one could convince me to drop out. Rather than leave the Party I would leave him." And an honorable mention went to a Texas farm woman who warned, "If we allow men to tell us what we can and cannot do we will never get our freedom."[66] The prize-winning essays suggest that, like many women reformers before them, Depression-era housewife activists became interested in knocking down the walls that defined behavioral norms for women only after they had personally run up against them.[67]

In defending their right to participate in a struggle that did not ideologically challenge the traditional sexual division of labor, many working-class housewives developed a new sense of pride in their abilities and a taste for political involvement. These women never came to think of themselves as feminists. They did, however, begin to see themselves as legitimate political and economic actors. During this period, poor wives and mothers left their homes in order to preserve them. In so doing, whether they intended to or not, they politicized the home, the family, and motherhood in important and unprecedented ways.

Notes

1. For an analysis of the impact of one school of documentary photography on our impressions of poor mothers during the Depression, see Wendy Kozol, "Madonnas of the Field: Photography, Gender, and Thirties' Farm Relief," *Genders*, no. 2 (Summer 1988): 1–23.

2. Eleanor Roosevelt, *It's Up to the Women* (New York: Frederick A. Stokes, 1933). A less friendly version of this argument can be found in Norman Cousins's 1939 article skewering those who suggested that women who left the home to work were somehow responsible for the ongoing unemployment crisis. See Norman Cousins, "Will Women Lose Their Jobs?" *Current History and Forum* (September 1939): 14–18; 62–63.

3. The *New York Times, Newsweek, The Nation, New Republic*, the *Saturday Evening Post, Harper's*, the *Christian Century, Business Week*, and *American Mercury* all covered and commented on housewife organizing. The *Chicago Daily Tribune* and the *Detroit Free Press* also provided detailed coverage of housewives' activism in their cities. *Working Woman*, the monthly publication of the Women's Commission of the Communist party, was invaluable. Although extremely dogmatic in its early years, the magazine is one of the most complete sources available on working-class women during the Depression. The two main archives consulted for this paper were the Tamiment Library in New York City and the Robert Burke Collection in the Manuscripts Division of the University of Washington Library, Seattle. See *New York Times*, "Buyers Trampled by Meat Strikers," 28 July 1935, "Secretary Wallace Beats Retreat from Five Housewives," *Chicago Daily Tribune*, 20 Aug. 1935.

4. See *Working Woman*, April 1931, June 1931, April 1933, June 1935; *New York Times*, 30 Jan.–28 Feb. 1932; *Detroit Free Press*, 6–9 Aug. 1935; *Chicago Daily Tribune*, 18 Aug. 1935.

5. See *Atlantic*, October 1932; *Collier's*, 31 Dec. 1932; *Literary Digest*, 11 Feb. 1933; *The Nation*, 1 Mar. 1933, and 19 Apr. 1933; *Survey*, 15 Dec. 1932, and July 1933; *Saturday Evening Post*, 25 Feb. 1933; *Commonweal*, 8 Mar. 1933; *Good Housekeeping*, March 1933.

6. *Working Woman*, June 1935; *Woman Today*, April 1936; *New York Times*, 10 Apr. 1936; *Party Organizer*, September 1935. Meridel Le Sueur describes the radicalization of one of those farm women, Mary Cotter, in her 1940 short story, "Salute to Spring," in Meridel Le Sueur, *Salute to Spring* (New York: International Publishers, 1940).

7. *Woman Today*, April 1936.

8. Selected sources on housewife activism early in the Depression include

Working Woman, 1931–35. See *New York Times,* 23, 30 Jan.; February; 22 Mar.; 22 May; 7 June; 7, 11 July; 13–26 Sept.; 9 Oct.; 7, 21 Dec. 1932; January–February; 23, 30 Mar.; 13, 24 May; 1, 2, 8 June; 2, 31 Aug.; 7, 9, 26 Sept.; 9 Dec. 1933. See *Atlantic,* October 1932; *The Nation,* 1 Mar. 1933; 19 Apr. 1933; 14, 18 Mar. 1934; *New Republic,* 15 Nov. 1933; *Ladies' Home Journal,* October 1934.

9. For information on the links between union activity and community organizing in New York City neighborhoods between 1902 and 1945, see Annelise Orleck, "Common Sense and a Little Fire: Working-Class Women's Activism in the Twentieth-Century United States" (Ph.D. diss., New York University, 1989); on Seattle politics in the post–World War I period, see Albert Acena, "The Washington Commonwealth Federation: Reform Politics and the Popular Front" (Ph.D. diss., University of Washington, 1975); and Dana Frank, "At the Point of Consumption: Seattle Labor and the Politics of Consumption, 1919–1927" (Ph.D. diss., Yale University, 1988).

10. A leaflet distributed by the UCWCW in 1929 noted that "the prices of most essential foodstuffs are still very high, while . . . the wages of those workers still employed, and part time workers, have been cut more and more." See "Working-Class Women, Let Us Organize and Fight," leaflet, n.d., Tamiment Library.

A *Working Woman* study in the winter of 1931 reported that even among those workers still employed in the big cities of the United States, income had declined 33 percent, but food prices had decreased only 7 percent. See *Working Woman* 3 (March 1931).

11. Rose Nelson Raynes, one of the chief organizers of the UCWCW, recalls that in 1931, when she first became involved with the organization, most of the women were older than thirty-five. Interview with Rose Nelson Raynes, New York City, 8 Oct. 1987. *New York Times* reports of arrests in anti-eviction actions and consumer boycotts between 1931 and 1935 show that all the women were married and the vast majority were between the ages of thirty and forty-two. *Detroit Free Press* accounts of arrests in the 1935 meat strike list the majority as having been between the ages of twenty-eight and forty-eight. In 1932, T.J. Parry (*Atlantic,* October 1932), writing about members of the food exchanges in Seattle, commented that most of them were "near life's half-way mark or beyond."

12. See *Woman Today,* July 1936; Mary Farquharson Papers, Burke Collection, boxes 12–14, and folders 30 and 94; and Frank, "At the Point of Consumption."

13. In *The Jewish Woman in America* (New York: New American Library, 1976), pp. 99–114, Charlotte Baum, Paula Hyman, and Sonya Michel review some of the voluminous immigrant literature highlighting the entrepreneurship of Jewish immigrant mothers. See Orleck, chap. 1, for a fuller analysis of the literature on working-class women's entrepreneurship, their conception of home, and their involvement in activism around tenant and consumer issues in the first decade of the twentieth century.

14. Paula Hyman makes this point in her essay on "Immigrant Women and Consumer Protest: The New York City Kosher Meat Boycott of 1902," *American Jewish History*, no. 70 (September 1980): 91–105. See also *New York Times* for May–June 1902; 13 July–2 Sept. 1904; 30 Nov.–9 Dec. 1906; 26 Dec. 1907–27 Jan. 1908. These sources indicate that many of the women involved were the wives and mothers of garment workers.

15. See *New York Times*, 3, 4, 7–10, 12–15 May; 17 June; 4–6 Sept. 1919. Also see "Women's Councils in the 1930s," a paper presented by Meredith Tax at the June 1984 Berkshire Conference on the History of Women, Smith College, Northampton, Mass. *Daily Worker*, 23 May 1927.

16. CP women complained consistently in the *Party Organizer* during the 1930s that CP men were hindering or ignoring their efforts at organizing women in urban neighborhoods. See particularly the August 1937 issue in which Anna Damon, head of the CP Women's Commission, lashes out at CP leaders for undercutting her efforts with Black women in St. Louis.

17. See New York Women's Trade Union League, *Annual Reports*, 1922, 1926, 1928; and Summary of Speeches, Women's Auxiliary Conference, Unity House, Forest Park, Penn., 30 June–1 July 1928, New York Women's Trade Union League Papers, Tamiment Library. Mary Van Kleeck Papers, Sophia Smith Collection, Smith College, Northampton, Mass. See also correspondence between Fania M. Cohn and women's auxiliary leaders, Grace Klueg and Mary Peake. Cohn to Klueg, 27 Aug. 1926; 15 Jan. 1927; 3 Mar. 1927; Cohn to Peake, 20 Apr. 1927; Klueg to Cohn, 7 Apr. 1927, in Fania Cohn Papers, New York Public Library.

18. A study by the American Federation of Women's Auxiliaries of Labor estimated in 1937 that U.S. women in union households spent $6 billion annually. See *Working Woman*, March 1937.

19. Robert Shaffer notes that the national CP leadership condemned CP feminist theorist Mary Inman particularly for her assertion that the home was a center of production and that housewives did productive labor. See his "Women and the Communist Party, USA, 1930–1940," *Socialist Review*, no. 45 (May–June 1979): 73–118. See also Mary Inman, "Thirteen Years of CPUSA Misleadership on the Woman Question" (Published by the Author, Los Angeles, 1949).

20. *Woman Today*, July 1936.

21. See Temma Kaplan, "Female Consciousness and Collective Action: The Case of Barcelona, 1910–1918," *Signs* 7 (Spring 1982): 545–66.

22. See *Atlantic*, October 1932; *Collier's*, 31 Dec. 1932; *Literary Digest*, 11 Feb. 1933; *The Nation*, 1 Mar. 1933; 19 Apr. 1933; *Survey*, 15 Dec. 1932; July 1933; *Saturday Evening Post*, 25 Feb. 1933; *Commonweal*, 8 Mar. 1933; *Good Housekeeping*, March 1933.

23. See Parry; *New York Times*, 7 June, 3 Sept. 1936; *Woman Today*, July 1936;

Ladies' Home Journal, October 1934; *Seattle Post-Intelligencer,* 11 Jan. 1937; *American Mercury,* February 1937.

24. *Working Woman,* June–September 1931. For anti-eviction activity, see *New York Times* almost daily in February, as well as 1, 2, 13 Mar.; 28 May; 7 June; 7 July; 13, 15–18, 20, 26 Sept.; 7, 21 Dec. 1932; 6, 12, 17, 28 Jan.; 1, 22 Feb.; 8, 23, 30 Mar.; 13, 24 May; 1, 2, 8 June; 2, 3 Aug.; 7, 9, 26 Sept.; 9 Dec. 1933.

25. Identifiable links to these earlier events, in addition to Clara Lemlich Shavelson, include Dorothy Moser, another New York activist of the 1930s, who remembers her mother's involvement in the 1917 boycotts. See Moser, interview with the author, New York City, 8 Oct. 1987. Judging from the age of the women arrested in New York and Detroit actions (see *New York Times* and *Detroit Free Press,* 1931–1935), mostly in their forties, most of the 1930s' activists were old enough to remember earlier actions.

26. See Hyman, 91–105; and Dana Frank, "Housewives, Socialists, and the Politics of Food: The 1917 New York Cost-of-Living Protests," *Feminist Studies* 11 (Summer 1985): 255–85. See also Kaplan.

27. Rose Nelson Raynes, interviews with author, 8 Oct. 1987, and 17 Feb. 1989. *Working Woman,* June, July, and August 1935; *Woman Today,* July 1936; *New York Times, Chicago Daily Tribune, Detroit Free Press, Newsweek,* and the *Saturday Evening Post* also provided coverage of housewife actions. See particularly, *New York Times,* 28 July; 4, 6, 11, 18, 24, 25 Aug. 1935; *Saturday Evening Post,* 2 Nov. 1935; *Chicago Daily Tribune,* 18, 20, 21 Aug. 1935; *Newsweek,* 17, 31 Aug. 1935.

28. In 1933, pleased with the success of their neighborhood organizing strategy, the UCWCW, the umbrella organization for New York housewives' councils, began working to build a coalition with other New York women's organizations, many of which had previously been quite hostile to anyone with CP affiliations. This was an important turning point in the housewives' movement. (See *Working Woman,* October 1933; December 1933.)

29. *New York Times,* 6 Aug. 1935.

30. "Who Is Clara Shavelson?" A leaflet from her 1933 campaign for New York State Assembly in the 2d Assembly District (courtesy of her daughter, Rita Margulies); interview with daughter Martha Shaffer, 11 Mar. 1989.

31. *Party Organizer,* 10 (July 1937): 36.

32. Brighton Beach, Brooklyn, where Clara Shavelson organized, is a perfect example of this strategy. Shavelson built on a highly developed network of Jewish women's religious and cultural associations to create the effective Emma Lazarus Tenant's Council during the 1930s. See Orleck, chap. 8.

33. *Party Organizer* 11 (March 1938): 39–40.

34. Raynes interview, 8 Oct. 1987.

35. Information on the New York UCWCW comes from interviews with

Raynes, 8 Oct. 1987, and 17 Feb. 1989. Also, both *New York Times* and *Working Woman* coverage of New York City housewives' actions from 1932 to 1937 show that the most consistently militant sections of the city were Jewish immigrant communities. Information on the composition of the Seattle housewives' groups was drawn from membership lists of the Renter's Protection, Cost of Living, and Public Ownership committees of the Women's League of the Washington Commonwealth Federation, Burke Collection, folders 30, 94, 182, 183, 188. Information on the composition of the Detroit housewives' movement comes from the *Detroit Free Press,* 26 July–25 Aug. 1935 when housewife activists made the paper, quite often the front page, almost every day.

36. Raynes interview, 8 Oct. 1987.

37. *Working Woman,* March 1935.

38. *Chicago Daily Tribune,* 18 Aug. 1935; *Working Woman,* August 1935.

39. Mark Naison, *Communists in Harlem during the Depression* (New York: Grove Press, 1983), 149.

40. See *New York Times,* 27–31 May; 1, 2, 6, 10–12, 14–16 June 1935.

41. Raynes interview, 8 Oct. 1987.

42. *Working Woman,* June 1935; *New York Times,* 15, 16 June 1935.

43. *Working Woman,* August 1935.

44. *Detroit Free Press,* 27 July 1935; *New York Times,* 28 July 1935.

45. *Detroit Free Press,* and *New York Times,* both for 28 July 1935.

46. *Detroit Free Press,* 29–31 July 1935; *New York Times,* 30 July 1935.

47. *Detroit Free Press,* 1 Aug. 1935; *New York Times,* 4 Aug. 1935.

48. *Detroit Free Press,* 3–5 Aug. 1935.

49. *Chicago Daily Tribune,* 18 Aug. 1935; *Newsweek,* 17 Aug. 1935; *Saturday Evening Post,* 2 Nov. 1935.

50. *New York Times,* 20 Aug. 1935.

51. Ibid.

52. *Newsweek,* 31 Aug. 1935.

53. *Detroit Free Press,* 6–7, 9 Aug. 1935; *Newsweek,* 31 Aug. 1935; *New York Times,* 19 Aug.; 1, 5 Sept. 1935.

54. "Who Is Clara Shavelson?" Martha Shaffer, interview with the author, 11 Mar. 1989; and Sophie Melvin Gerson, interview with the author, 17 Feb. 1989.

55. *Detroit Free Press,* and *New York Times,* both for 10 Apr. 1936; *Woman Today,* July 1936.

56. *Woman Today,* July 1936.

57. Ibid.; *New York Times,* 7, 13 June; 5, 26 July; 3, 9, 10, 13 Sept.; 1, 9 Nov. 1936; "A Few Honest Questions and Answers about Initiative 119" (Handbill, n.d., Burke Collection).

58. "A Few Honest Questions and Answers" (Leaflet of the Washington Commonwealth Federation, n.d., Burke Collection). See *The Nation,* 28 Nov. 1934; 19 Aug. 1939.

59. *Woman Today,* March 1937; *New York Times,* 4 Dec. 1947; 20 May; 20 July; 3–31 Aug. 1948; 24, 26–28 Feb.; 25, 26 May; 14 June; 18 Aug. 1951.

60. Raynes interview, 17 Feb. 1989; *New York Times,* 3, 5, 8–11, 19, 28, 31 Aug. 1948; 24, 26–28 Feb.; 14 June 1951.

61. *New York Times,* 26 Feb. 1933; *Woman Today,* March 1937; *The Nation,* 5, 12 June 1937; 18 Feb. 1939; *Business Week,* 11 Nov. 1939; *Forum,* October 1939; *New Republic,* 1 Jan. 1940.

62. *New York Times,* 23 Oct. 1949; 7 Jan. 1950.

63. *The Nation,* 5, 12 June 1937; *New Republic,* 8 Apr. 1936.

64. *New York Times,* 20, 24, 25 Aug. 1935; 20 May; 20 July; 3–31 Aug. 1948; 24, 26–28 Feb.; 25, 26 May; 14 June; 18 Aug. 1951.

65. Moser interview.

66. *Working Woman,* March 1935.

67. Frank argues that, during the 1920s, working-class women in Seattle resisted their husbands' and brothers' calls to consumer action, because they resented their exclusion from meaningful participation in governance and policy making of the labor unions. See Frank, "At the Point of Consumption." Shaffer interview.

Ladies' Day at the Capitol: Women Strike for Peace versus HUAC

☐ In mid-December of 1962 in the Old House Office Building of the U.S. Congress, a confrontation occurred between a recently formed women's peace group called Women Strike for Peace (WSP) and the House Committee on Un-American Activities (HUAC). The confrontation, which took place at a hearing to determine the extent of Communist party infiltration into "the so-called 'peace movement' in a manner and to a degree affecting the national security,"[1] resulted in a rhetorical victory for the women of WSP and a deadly blow to the committee.[2] It is a moment in the history of peace movements in the United States in which women led the way by taking a more courageous and principled stand in opposition to cold war ideology and political repression than that of their male counterparts.[3]

This study seeks to reconstruct the WSP-HUAC confrontation and the reasons it took the form it did.[4] By analyzing the ideology, consciousness, political style, and public demeanor of the WSP women as they defended their right as mothers "to influence the course of government," we can learn a great deal about the strengths and weaknesses of women's movements for social change that build on traditional sex role ideology and on female culture.[5]

WSP burst upon the American political scene on November 1, 1961, when an estimated fifty thousand women in more than sixty cities across the United States walked out of their kitchens and off their jobs in a one-day women's strike for peace. As a radioactive cloud from a Russian nuclear test hung over the American landscape, these women strikers staged the largest female peace action in the nation's history.[6] In small towns and large cities from New York to California, the women visited government officials, demanding that they take immediate steps

Reprinted, with changes, from *Feminist Studies* 8, no. 3 (Fall 1982): 453–520. ©1982 by Feminist Studies, Inc.

to "End the Arms Race—Not the Human Race."[7] Coming on the heels of a decade noted for cold war consensus, political conformity, and the celebration of female domesticity, this spontaneous women's initiative baffled both the press and the politicians. The women seemed to have emerged from nowhere. They belonged to no unifying organizations, and their leaders were totally unknown as public figures.

The women strikers were actually responding to a call from a handful of Washington, D.C., women who had become alarmed by the acceleration of the nuclear arms race. So disheartened were they by the passivity of traditional peace groups that they had sent a call to women friends and contacts all over the country urging them to suspend their regular routine of home, family, and job to join with friends and neighbors in a one-day strike to end the nuclear arms race.[8]

The call to strike spread rapidly from Washington through typical female networks: word of mouth and chain letter fashion from woman to woman, from coast to coast, through personal telephone calls, and Christmas card lists. Contacts in Parent Teacher Associations (PTAs), the League of Women Voters, church and temple groups, as well as the established peace organizations, such as the Women's International League for Peace and Freedom (WILPF) and the Committee for a Sane Nuclear Policy (SANE), also spread the word.

The nature of the strike in each community depended entirely on what the local women were willing and able to do. Some marched, others lobbied local officials, a few groups took ads in local newspapers. Thousands sent telegrams to the White House and to the Soviet embassy, calling upon the two first ladies of the nuclear superpowers, Jacqueline Kennedy and Nina Khrushchev, to urge their husbands on behalf of all the world's children to "stop all nuclear tests—east and west." Amazed by the numbers and composition of the turnout on November 1, *Newsweek* commented:

> They were perfectly ordinary looking women, with their share of good looks; they looked like the women you would see driving ranch wagons, or shopping at the village market, or attending PTA meetings. It was these women by the thousands, who staged demonstrations in a score of cities across the nation last week, protesting atomic testing. A "strike for peace," they called it and—carrying placards, many wheeling baby buggies or strollers—they marched on city halls and Federal buildings to show their concern about nuclear fallout.[9]

The strikers' concern about the nuclear arms race did not end with the November 1 actions. Within only one year, the one-day strike for peace was transformed by its founders and participants into a national women's movement with local groups in sixty communities and offices in ten cities. With no paid staff and no designated leaders, thousands of women in different parts of the country, most of them previously unknown to each other, managed to establish a loosely structured communications network capable of swift and effective direct action on both a national and international scale.

From its inception, the WSP was a nonhierarchical participatory network of activists opposed both to rigid ideologies and formal organizational structure. The WSP women called their format simply "our un-organization." It is interesting to note that the young men of Students for a Democratic Society (SDS), a movement founded in the same year as WSP, more aware of their place in the radical political tradition, more aware of the power of naming, and more confident of their power to do so, named their loose structure "participatory democracy." Eleanor Garst, one of the Washington founders, explained the attractions of the un-organizational format:

> No one must wait for orders from headquarters—there aren't any headquarters. No one's idea must wait for clearance through the national board. No one waits for the president or the director to tell her what to do—there is no president or director. Any woman who has an idea can propose it through an informal memo system; if enough women think it's good, it's done. Those who don't like a particular action don't have to drop out of the movement; they just sit out that action and wait for one they like. Sound "crazy"?—it is, but it also brings forth and utilizes the creativity of thousands of women who could never be heard from through ordinary channels.[10]

The choice of a loose structure and local autonomy was a reaction to hierarchical and bureaucratic structures of traditional peace groups like WILPF and SANE to which some of the early leaders belonged. These women perceived the WILPF structure, which required that all programmatic and action proposals be cleared with state and national offices, as a roadblock to spontaneous and direct responses to the urgent international crisis.[11] The willingness of the Washington founders to allow each group to act in the way that suited its particular constituency was WSP's greatest strength and the source of the confidence and admiration that women across the country bestowed on the Washington founders. Washington came to be considered the WSP national office not only because it was located in the nation's capital but also because the Washington group was trusted by all.

There was also another factor militating against a traditional membership organization. Only the year before the WSP strike, Linus Pauling, the Nobel Laureate in physics and opponent of nuclear testing, had been directed by the Senate Internal Security Subcommittee to turn over the names of those who had helped him gather signatures on a scientists' antinuclear petition. The commandeering of membership lists was not an uncommon tactic of political intimidation in the 1950s. Membership lists of radical organizations could therefore be a burden and responsibility. As they served no purpose in the WSP format, it was a sensible strategy to eliminate them. Another benefit was that WSP never had to assess accurately its numerical strength, thus allowing its legend to grow even when its numbers did not.

From its first day onward, WSP tapped a vast reservoir of moral outrage, energy, organizational talent, and sisterhood—female capacities that had been submerged and silenced for more than a decade by McCarthyism and the "feminine mystique." Using standard pressure-group tactics, such as lobbying and petitioning, coupled with direct demonstrative action and civil disobedience, executed with imagination and "feminine flair," the WSP women succeeded in putting women's political demands on the front pages of the nation's newspapers, from which they had largely disappeared since the days of the suffrage campaign. WSP also managed to influence public officials and public policy. At a time when peace marchers were ignored, or viewed as "commies" or "kooks," President John F. Kennedy gave public recognition to the women strikers. Commenting on WSP's first antinuclear march at the White House, on January 15, 1962, the president told the nation that he thought the WSP women were "extremely earnest."

> I saw the ladies myself. I recognized why they were here. There were a great number of them, it was in the rain. I understand what they were attempting to say, therefore, I consider their message was received.[12]

In 1970, *Science* reported that "Wiesner [Jerome Wiesner, President Kennedy's science advisor] gave the major credit for moving President Kennedy toward the limited Test Ban Treaty of 1963, not to arms controllers inside the government but to the Women Strike for Peace and to SANE and Linus Pauling."[13]

Although WSP, in its first year, was well received by liberal politicians and journalists, the surveillance establishment and the right-wing press were wary. They recognized early what the Rand Corporation described obliquely as the WSP potential "to impact on military policies."[14] Jack Lotto, a Hearst columnist, charged that although the women described themselves as a "group of unsophisticated wives and mothers who are loosely organized in a spontaneous movement for peace, there is nothing spontaneous about the way the pro-Reds have moved in on our mothers and are using them for their own purposes."[15] On the West Coast, the *San Francisco Examiner* claimed to have proof that "scores of well-intentioned, dedicated women . . . were being made dupes of by known Communists . . . operating openly in the much publicized Women Strike for Peace demonstrations."[16]

That WSP was under Federal Bureau of Investigation (FBI) surveillance, from its first public planning meeting in Washington in October 1961, is abundantly evidenced in the forty-three volumes of FBI records on WSP which have been made available to the movement's attorneys under the provisions of the Freedom of Information Act. The records show that FBI offices in major cities, North, East, South, and West—and even in such places as Mobile, Alabama, Phoenix, Arizona, and San Antonio, Texas, not known for WSP activities—were sending and receiving reports on the women, often prepared in cooperation with local "red squads."[17]

Having just lived through the Cuban Missile Crisis of October 1962, WSP celebrated its first anniversary in November with a deep sense of urgency and of heightened political efficacy. But as the women were making plans to escalate their commitment and their protests, they were stopped in their tracks in the first week of December by HUAC subpoenas to thirteen women peace activists from the New York metropolitan area, as well as Dagmar Wilson of Washington, D.C., the WSP national spokesperson.[18]

It is difficult today to comprehend the emotions and fears such a summons could invoke in individuals and organizations. Lillian Hellman's *Scoundrel Time* gives a picture of the tension, isolation, and near-hysteria felt by an articulate and prominent public figure, as she prepared her defense against the committee in 1953.[19] By 1962, cold war hysteria had abated somewhat, as the United States and the USSR were engaged in test ban negotiations, but HUAC represented those forces and those voices in American politics that opposed such negotiations. As a congressional committee, it still possessed the awesome power of an agency of the state to command headlines, cast suspicion, and by labeling individuals as subversives, destroy careers, lives, and organizations.

The HUAC subpoenas gave no indication of the subject of the hearings, or of their scope. So there was, at first, some confusion about whether it was the WSP connection or other aspects of the subpoenaed women's political lives that were suspect. To add to the confusion, it was soon discovered that three of the women called were not even active in WSP. They were members of the Conference of Greater New York Peace Groups, an organization founded by New Yorkers who had either been expelled from, or who had willingly left, SANE because of its internal red hunt. Of these three women, two had already been named by the committee informers as communists in previous HUAC hearings. One of these women, Elizabeth Moos, had achieved considerable notoriety when she was identified by accused Russian spy William Remington as his mother-in-law and a card-carrying communist. Given these circumstances it was clear that the WSP leadership had some important decisions to make regarding their response to the HUAC hearings. There were two important questions to be faced. First, as WSP had no official membership list, would the group embrace any woman working for peace even if she were not directly involved in WSP activity? Second, would WSP disavow its members who had past or present communist affiliations, and if WSP did not disavow them, would the movement lose its following and its effectiveness?

The key to WSP unity in the face of the "communist issue," which had divided and disrupted peace, labor, and even civil liberties organizations in the previous decade, was the fact that WSP had previously decided to handle forthrightly, and in advance of any attack, the issue of communist inclusion. WSP had, even before the HUAC hearings, decided to reject political screening of its members, deeming it a manifestation of outdated cold war thinking. This decision, the women claimed, was based not on fear or expediency but on principle. The issue of accepting communists in the movement was brought to the floor of the first national WSP conference in June 1962 by the Los Angeles coordinating council. A prepared statement by the Los Angeles group declared: "Unlike SANE and Turn Toward Peace, WSP must not make the error of initiating its own purges." Treating the issue of communist membership as a question of personal conscience, the Los Angeles group asked, "If there are communists or former communists working in WSP, what difference does that make? We do not question one another about our religious beliefs or other matters of personal conscience. How can we justify political interrogation?" The Los Angeles statement continued, "If fear, mistrust and hatred are ever to be lessened, it will be by courageous individuals who do not hate and fear and can get together to work out tolerable compromises."[20] The argument that "this is a role women would be particularly equipped to play" won over the conference and resulted in the inclusion of a section in the WSP national policy statement which affirmed: "We are women of all races, creeds and political persuasions who are dedicated to the achievement of general and complete disarmament under effective international control."[21]

An emergency meeting of about fifty New York area "key women," along with Dagmar Wilson and other representatives from Washington, was called a few days after the HUAC summonses began to arrive.[22] The first decision made at this meeting was that WSP would live up to the national policy statement that had been arrived at six months earlier and make a reality of the phrase, "We are women of all ... political persuasions." Following from this decision it was clear that WSP would support and embrace every woman summoned before HUAC, regardless of her past or present affiliations, as long as she supported the movement's campaign against both Russian and American nuclear policies. This meant that in addition to supporting its own women, the three women not active in WSP would also come under the movement's protection if they so desired. They would be given access to the same lawyers as the WSP activists. They would not be isolated or attacked either for their affiliations or for the way they chose to conduct themselves at the hearing. This decision was in sharp contrast to the action taken by SANE in 1960 when it expelled a leading member of its New York chapter after he invoked the Fifth Amendment at a Senate Internal Security Subcommittee hearing and then refused to tell Norman Cousins, a cochair of SANE, whether he had ever been a communist.[23]

The decision made by the New York and Washington women not "to cower" before the committee, to conduct no internal purges, to acknowledge each woman's right to act for peace and to conduct herself according to the dictates of her conscience was bold for its day. It was arrived at within the movement, by the women themselves, without consultation with the male leaders of traditional peace and civil liberties groups, many of whom disagreed with this WSP policy.[24] It was based not only on the decision to resist the demonology of the cold war but also on a sense of sisterhood, on feelings of identification with and empathy for the women singled out for attack. Even the subpoenaed women themselves turned for counsel and support more to each other and the WSP leadership than to their families and lawyers. Working together at a feverish pace, night and day for three weeks, writing, phoning, speaking at rallies, the key women seemed to be acting as if they were a family under attack, for which all personal resources, passions, and energies had to be marshaled. But the family, this time, was "the movement" and it was the sisters, not the fathers, who were in charge.

In response to the subpoenas, a massive campaign was organized for the cancellation of the hearings and for support of WSP from national organizations and public figures. An anti-HUAC statement was composed in New York and Washington which spoke so well to the concerns and the consciousness of "the women" that it succeeded in unifying a movement in shock. The WSP statement on the HUAC inquisition was quoted widely by the press, used by local groups in ads and flyers, in letters to editors, and in speeches. "With the fate of humanity resting on a push button," the statement declared, "the quest for peace has become the highest form of patriotism."[25] In this first sentence, the women set the ground rules for their confrontation with the committee: it was going to be a contest over which group was more patriotic. But the test of "Americanism" according to the WSP rules was the extent of one's dedication to saving America's children from nuclear extinction. Addressing the issue of communism in the movement, WSP declared: "Differences of politics, economics or social belief disappear when we recognize man's common peril . . . we do not ask an oath of loyalty to any set of beliefs. Instead we ask loyalty to the race of man. The time is long past when a small group of censors can silence the voice of peace." These words would be the WSP *leitmotif* in the Washington hearings. The women were saying, once again, as they had throughout their first year, that for them, the arms race, cold war ideology, and cold war politics were obsolete in the nuclear age, as was the committee itself. This is the spirit Eric Bentley caught and referred to when he wrote: "In the 1960s a new generation came to life. As far as HUAC is concerned, it began with Women Strike for Peace."[26]

The WSP strategy against HUAC was innovative. An organizing memorandum from the Washington office declared: "the usual response of protest and public statements is too traditional and ineffectual. . . . Let's Turn the Tables! Let's meet the HUAC challenge in the Good New WSP way!"[27] The "new way" suggested by women all over the country was to insist that WSP had nothing to hide. Instead of refusing to testify, as radicals and civil libertarians had done in the 1950s, large numbers of WSP participants volunteered to "talk." Approximately one hundred women sent wires to Representative Francis Walter, chair of HUAC, offering to come to Washington to tell all about their movement. The offers were refused by HUAC. But, this new WSP tactic pointed up the fact that the committee was less interested in securing information than in exposing and smearing those it chose to investigate. Some WSP groups objected to the free testimony strategy on the grounds that there was a contradiction between denying the right of the committee to exist and at the same time offering to cooperate with it. But these groups were in a minority. Carol Urner of Portland, Oregon, spoke for all those who volunteered to testify, making it clear that she would not be a "friendly witness." "I could not, of course, divulge the names of others in the movement," she wrote to Representative Walter. "I suppose such a refusal could lead one to 'contempt' and prison and things like that . . . and no mother can accept lightly even the remote possibility of separation from the family which needs her. But mankind needs us too. . . . "[28]

Only three weeks' time elapsed between the arrival of the first subpoenas from HUAC and the date of the Washington hearings. In this short period, the WSP key women managed to develop a legal defense, a national support system for those subpoenaed, and a broad national campaign of public protest against the committee. The women's performance at the hearings was so original, so winning, and so "feminine" in the traditional sense that it succeeded in capturing the sympathy and the support of large sections of the national media and in strengthening the movement instead of destroying it.

The hearings opened on December 11, 1962, at 10:00 A.M. in the caucus room of the Old House Office Building of the U.S. Congress in Washington, D.C. Fear, excitement, and exhilaration were in the air as each WSP woman in the audience looked around to see every seat in the room occupied by sisters who had come from eleven states, some from as far as California, in response to a call for their presence from the national leadership. Clyde Doyle, chair of the subcommittee of HUAC conducting the WSP hearings, opened with a statement of their purpose. Quoting from Lenin, Stalin, Khrushchev, and Gus Hall, he explained:

> Communists believe that there can be no real peace until they have conquered the world. . . . The initiated Communist, understanding his Marxist-Leninist doctrine, knows that a Moscow call to intensify the "fight for peace" means that he should intensify his fight to destroy capitalism and its major bastion, the United States of America.[29]

The WSP women in the audience rose as one as the committee called its first witness, Blanche Posner, a retired schoolteacher who was the volunteer office manager for New York WSP. The decision to rise with the first witness, to stand *with* her, was spontaneous. It was proposed only a few minutes before Posner was called, as a note from an unknown source was circulated around the room. Posner refused to answer any questions about the structure or personnel of WSP. She resorted to the Fifth Amendment forty-four times, as the press pointed out in dozens of news stories covering the first day of the hearings. They also reported the way in which Posner took matters into her own hands, lecturing the committee members as though they were recalcitrant boys at DeWitt Clinton High School in the Bronx, where she had taught. Talking right through the interruptions and objections raised by the chair and by committee counsel Alfred Nittle, Posner declared:

I don't know, sir, why I am here, but I do know why you are here, I think . . . because you don't quite understand the nature of this movement. This movement was inspired and motivated by mothers' love for children. . . . When they were putting their breakfast on the table, they saw not only the wheaties and milk, but they also saw strontium 90 and iodine 131. . . . They feared for the health and life of their children. That is the only motivation.

Each time Posner resorted to the Fifth Amendment, she did it with a pointed criticism of the committee or a quip that endeared her to the women in the hearing room who needed to keep their spirits up in the face of charges that Posner had been identified by an FBI informer as a Communist party member while working in New York City as a schoolteacher. One prize exchange between Nittle and Posner led to particularly enthusiastic applause and laughter from WSP women. Nittle asked, "Did you wear a colored paper daisy to identify yourself as a member of the Women Strike for Peace?" Posner answered, "It sounds like such a far cry from communism it is impossible not to be amused. I still invoke the Fifth Amendment."[30]

Most of the witnesses were called because the committee believed it had evidence to link them with the Communist party through identification by FBI informers or the signing of party nominating petitions. But the strategy backfired with Ruth Meyers, of Roslyn, Long Island. She stepped forward, according to Mary McGrory's report in the *Washington Evening Star,* "swathed in red and brown jersey, topped by a steeple crowned red velvet hat," and "she was just as much of a headache to the committee as Posner had been."[31] There was much sparring between Meyers and the committee about the nature and structure of WSP. "Are you presently a member of a group known as Women Strike for Peace?" Nittle asked. "No, sir, Women Strike for Peace has no membership," Meyers answered. Nittle then asked, "You are familiar, I understand, with the structural organization of Women Strike for Peace as evidenced by this plan?" Meyers replied, "I am familiar to the extent of the role that I play in it. I must say that I was not particularly interested in the structure of Women Strike for Peace. I was more involved in my own community activities. . . . I felt that structure, other than the old telephone, has not much of what I was interested in." Nittle then proceeded to deliver what he believed would be the coup de grace for Meyers. "Mrs. Meyers," he barked, "it appears from the public records that a Ruth Meyers, residing at 1751 East 10th Street, Brooklyn, New York, on July 27, 1948, signed a Communist Party nominating petition. . . . Are you the Ruth Meyers who executed that petition?" Meyers shot back, "No, sir." She then examined the petition carefully and announced, "I never lived in Brooklyn, and this is not my signature."[32] Although the official transcript does not contain this statement, many, including the author, remember that she added, "My husband could never get me to move there." This female remark brought an explosion of laughter and applause. Meyers also invoked the Fifth Amendment. As she left the witness stand, Meyers received a one-minute ovation for humor, grace, and mistaken identity. In the corridor outside the caucus room in front of the TV cameras, she told reporters that she had never been a communist. "But I'll never acknowledge the Committee's right to ask me that question."[33]

Another witness, Lyla Hoffman, chose to tell the committee of her past communist affiliation, asserting that she had left the Communist party but would not cooperate in naming names or in citing the cause of her resignation. In a statement written after the hearings Hoffman explained, "I felt that it was high time to say, 'What difference does it make what anyone did or believed many years ago? That's not the problem facing humanity today.' But I had to say this in legal terms." She found it very difficult to do so, as the committee was interested only in whether she was a genuine anticommunist or a secret fellow-traveler.[34] Hoffman invoked the First Amendment.

The witnesses who followed Posner, Meyers, and Hoffman, each in her own style, invoked whatever legal and rhetorical strategy her conscience and her situation dictated. They lectured the committee eloquently and courageously on the danger of nuclear holocaust, on women's rights and responsibility to work for peace. In attempting to explain the nonstructured format of WSP, several witnesses suggested that the movement was too fluid and too unpredictable to be comprehended by the masculine mind.

In their most optimistic projections, the WSP women could not have predicted the overwhelmingly favorable press and public response they would receive and the support and growth for the movement that would result from the HUAC episode. From the outset, the WSP leadership understood that HUAC needed the press to make its tactics of intimidation and punishment work. So, WSP played for the press—as it had done from its founding—and won! The Washington and New York leadership knew that it had two stories; both were developed to the hilt. The first was "motherhood under attack" and the second was the age-old "battle of the sexes." The contest between the sexes, according to the WSP version, involved female common sense, openness, humor, hope, and naiveté versus male rigidity, solemnity, suspicion, and dark theories of conspiracy and subversion. The WSP women, in their middle-class, feminine, political style, turned the hearings into an episode of the familiar and funny "I Love Lucy," rather than the tragic and scary inquisition of Alger Hiss.

For the first time, HUAC was belittled with humor and treated to a dose of its own moral superiority. Headlines critical of the committee and supportive of WSP were featured on the front pages of prominent newspapers from coast to coast. The *Chicago Daily News* declared: "It's Ladies Day at Capitol: Hoots, Howls—and Charm; Congressmen Meet Match." *New York Times* syndicated columnist Russell Baker's column was headed "Peace March Gals Make Red Hunters Look Silly," and a *Detroit Free Press* story was entitled, "Headhunters Decapitated." A cartoon by Herblock in the *Washington Post* of December 13 showed three aging and baffled committee members: One is seated at the hearing table. One is holding a gavel. Another turns to him and says, "I Came in Late, Which Was It That Was Un-American—Women or Peace?"[35] A story in the *Vancouver Sun* of December 14 was typical of many other reports:

> The dreaded House Un-American Activities Committee met its Waterloo this week. It tangled with 500 irate women. They laughed at it. Kleig lights glared, television cameras whirred, and 50 reporters scribbled notes while babies cried and cooed during the fantastic inquisition.

Bill Galt, author of the *Vancouver Sun* story, gave a blow-by-blow description of WSP civil disobedience in the Old House Office Building:

> When the first woman headed to the witness table, the crowd rose silently to its feet. The irritated Chairman Clyde Doyle of California outlawed standing. They applauded the next witness and Doyle outlawed clapping. Then they took to running out to kiss the witness. . . . Finally, each woman as she was called was met and handed a huge bouquet. By then Doyle was a beaten man. By the third day the crowd was giving standing ovations to the heroines with impunity.[36]

The hearings were a perfect foil for the humor of Russell Baker:

> If the House Un-American Activities Committee knew its Greek as well as it knows its Lenin, it would have left the women peace strikers alone. . . . Instead with typical male arrogance it has subpoenaed 15 of the ladies, . . . spent several days trying to show them that women's place is not on the peace march route, and has come out of it covered with foolishness.

Baker, a liberal columnist, understood the committee's purpose and also the "drama of the absurd" that WSP had staged to defeat that purpose. "The Committee's aim was simple enough," Baker pointed out:

Their sleuths studying an organization known as Women Strike for Peace had learned that some of the strikers seemed to have past associations with the Communist Party or its front groups. Presumably if these were exposed, right thinking housewives would give up peace agitation and go back to the kitchen.

The committee had reckoned without female logic, according to Baker:

How could WSP be infiltrated, witness after witness demanded, when it was not an organization at all? . . . Try as he might, Alfred Nittle, the committee counsel, never managed to break through against this defense.[37]

The *Detroit Free Press* commented: "The House Committee can get away with attacking college students in California, government flunkies who are forced to shrive their souls to save their jobs, and assorted misguided do-gooders. But when it decides to smear an estimated half-million angry women, it's in deep trouble. We wish them nothing but the worst."[38]

Mary McGrory in the *Washington Evening Star* played up the difference between the male HUAC perceptions and those of the female WSP:

"Why can't a woman be like a man?" sings Henry Higgins in *My Fair Lady*. That is precisely the question the House Committee on Un-American Activities is asking itself today. . . . The committee is trying to find out if the ladies' group is subversive. All it found out was that their conduct in the caucus room certainly was.

"The leader of the group kept protesting that she was not really the leader at all," McGrory observed. Pointing out that few men would deny being leaders or admit they didn't know what was going on, Mary McGrory reported that

Dagmar Wilson of Washington, when asked if she exercised control over the New York chapter merely giggled and said, "Nobody controls anybody in the Women Strike for Peace. We're all leaders."

Characterizing Wilson's appearance as the "coup de grace in the battle of the sexes," McGrory noted that the ladies had been using the Congress as a babysitter, while their young crawled in the aisles and noisily sucked their bottles during the whole proceedings. With a mixture of awe and wonder McGrory described how the ladies themselves, as wayward as their babies, hissed, gasped, clapped entirely at will. When several of their number took the Fifth Amendment, to McGrory's surprise, the women applauded, and

when Mrs. Wilson, trim and beguiling in red wool, stepped up to take the stand, a mother with a baby on one hip worked her way through the crowd and handed her a bouquet of purple and white flowers, exactly as if she were the principal speaker at a ladies' luncheon.

McGrory caught the flavor of Wilson's testimony, which was directed not only at the committee but also at her sisters in the audience. She reported that when Mr. Nittle asked whether the New York chapter had played a dominant role in the group, Wilson replied, "Other cities would be mortified if you said that."

> "Was it," Mr. Nittle wanted to know, "Mrs. Wilson's idea to send delegates to a Moscow peace conference?" "No," said Mrs. Wilson regretfully, "I wish I'd thought of that." When Mr. Nittle pursued the question of whose idea it was to send observers to Moscow, Dagmar Wilson replied, "This is something I find very difficult to explain to the masculine mind."

And, in a sense, it was. "Mr. Nittle pressed forward to the clutch question," one, according to McGrory, "that would bring a man to his knees with patriotic protest: 'I would like to ask you whether you would knowingly permit or encourage a Communist Party member to occupy a leadership position in Women Strike for Peace.' " Wilson replied:

> Well, my dear sir, I have absolutely no way of controlling, do not desire to control, who wishes to join in the demonstrations and the efforts that women strikers have made for peace. In fact, I would also like to go even further. I would like to say that unless everybody in the whole world joins us in this fight, then God help us.

"Would you knowingly permit or welcome Nazis or Fascists?" asked Mr. Nittle. Mrs. Wilson replied, "if we could only get them on our side."[39] Mr. Doyle then thanked Wilson for appearing and being so helpful. "I want to emphasize," he said,

> that the Committee recognizes that there are many, many, many women, in fact a great, great majority of women, in this peace movement who are absolutely patriotic and absolutely adverse to everything the Communist Party stands for. We recognize that you are one of them. We compliment you on your leadership and on your helpfulness to us this morning.

Dagmar Wilson tried to get the last word: "I do hope you live to thank us when we have achieved our goal." But Doyle replied, "Well, we will."[40]

The way in which WSP, a movement of middle-class, middle-aged, white women mobilized to meet the attack by a feared congressional committee was energetic and bold, politically nontraditional, pragmatic rather than ideological, moralistic, and maternal. It was entirely consistent with the already established program, tactics, rhetoric, and image of this one-year-old group, labeled by the University of Wisconsin's student newspaper as "the bourgeois mother's underground."[41]

Were these courageous women who bowed to traditional notions of female behavior merely using the politics of motherhood for political advantage? Or had they internalized the feminine mystique? It is useful to examine the backgrounds of the WSP women in seeking to understand their use of their own female culture to legitimate a radical critique of national, foreign, and military policies. The WSP key women were mostly in their late thirties to mid-forties at the inception of the movement in 1961. Most of them, then, had come into adulthood in the late 1930s and early 1940s. They were students or workers in the years of political ferment preceding World War II. Many had married just before, during, or right after the war. The majority of these women participated in the postwar baby boom, the rise of middle-class affluence, and the privatism and consumerism connected with suburban life. It was during the 1950s that they made their adjustment to family, parenting, community, and consensus politics.

As a movement born out of, and responding to, the consciousness of the 1950s, WSP projected a middle-class and politically moderate image. In an article celebrating WSP's first anniversary, Eleanor Garst, one of WSP's early image makers, proclaimed:

> Breaking all the rules and behaving with incredible disorder and naivete, "the women" continue to attract recruits until the movement now numbers hundreds of thousands. . . . Furthermore, many of the women behaving in these unaccustomed ways are no odd-ball types, but pillars of the community long courted by civic organizations. Others—perhaps the most numerous—are apolitical housewives who have never before lifted a finger to work for peace or any other social concern.[42]

Although the movement projected an image of political innocence and inexperience, WSP was actually initiated by five women who were already active members of SANE. The women—Dagmar Wilson, Jeanne Bagby, Folly Fodor, Eleanor Garst, and Margaret Russell—had gravitated toward each other because of their mutual distaste for SANE's internal red hunt, which they felt contributed to an escalation rather than an end to cold war hysteria. Perhaps, more important, they shared a frustration over the slow pace with which the highly structured SANE reacted to international crises. They also resented the reluctance of SANE's male leadership to deal with "mother's issues" such as the contamination of milk by radioactive fallout from nuclear tests.

Dagmar Wilson was forty-five years old and a political novice when she was moved to call a few friends to her home in the late summer of

1961 to discuss what could be done about the nuclear crisis. At this meeting WSP was born. Wilson was at that time a successful free-lance children's book illustrator, the mother of three daughters, and wife of Christopher Wilson, a commercial attache at the British embassy. Wilson had been born in New York City, had moved to Germany as a very young child, and had spent most of her adult years in England where her father, Cesar Searchinger, was a well-known broadcast correspondent for CBS and NBC.

Wilson came to the United States prior to World War II, held a variety of professional jobs as an artist and teacher, and finally became a free-lance illustrator. She worked in a studio at home, so as to be available to her children and to insure a smooth-running household. Despite the fact that Wilson was so successful an artist that one of her children's books had become a best-seller, she nevertheless identified herself as a housewife.

> My idea in emphasizing the housewife rather than the professional was that I thought the housewife was a downgraded person, and that we, as housewives, had as much right to an opinion and that we deserved as much consideration as anyone else, and I wanted to emphasize ... this was an important role and that it was time we were heard.[43]

A gifted artist, an intelligent person of good sense, good grace, and charm, Wilson possessed the charisma of those who accurately represent the feelings and the perceptions of their constituency, but excel them in passion and the capacity for creative articulation. Having been most of her life a "nonjoiner," Wilson was, as the *New York Times Magazine* reported in a feature story in May 1962, a "political neophyte."[44] Because Wilson had not been involved in U.S. radical politics of the 1940s, she was free from the self-conscious timidity that plagued those who had been involved in leftist organizations and who feared either exposure or a repetition of the persecution and the political isolation they had experienced in the 1950s.

Among the women who met at Wilson's house to plan the emergency peace action was Eleanor Garst, whose direct, friendly, practical, yet passionate political prose played a powerful role in energizing and unifying the WSP women in their first year. It was she who drafted the call for November 1 and later helped create most of the anti-HUAC rhetoric.

Garst came from a conservative Baptist background. She recalls that everything in her upbringing told her that the only thing a woman should do was marry, have babies, care for her husband and babies, and "never mind your own needs." Despite this, Garst was the only one of the inner circle of Washington founders, who in 1961 was a completely self-supporting professional woman, living on her own. She was the mother of two grown children. At the time of the founding of WSP, Garst was employed as a community organizer for the Adams Morgan Demonstration project, administered by American University, working to maintain integrated neighborhoods in Washington, D.C. She had become a pacifist in her early childhood after reading about war in novels and poems. Her husband, a merchant seaman, refused to be drafted prior to World War II, a decision that he and Eleanor made together without consulting any other pacifists because they knew none. They spent their honeymoon composing an eighty-page brief against peacetime conscription.

After the war, Garst became a professional political worker, writer, and peace activist on the West Coast before coming to Washington. She had been a founder of the Los Angeles SANE and editor of its newsletter. A forceful and easy writer, Garst had already been published in the *Saturday Evening Post, Reporter, Ladies' Home Journal,* and other national publications when she was asked to draft the letter that initiated the successful November 1 strike.

Folly Fodor, a leading figure in the founding group, had come to Washington in 1960 to follow her husband's job with the U.S. Labor Department. She joined SANE on her arrival in Washington and had been elected to the board. Thirty-seven years old at the time of the founding of WSP, Fodor was the mother of two. She was the daughter of parents who had been involved in liberal-to-communist political causes and had herself been a leader in political organizations since her youth. As an undergraduate at Antioch College, in Yellow Springs, Ohio, Fodor had become active in the Young People's Socialist League, eventually becoming "head of it," as she put it. In retrospect she believes she spent too much time fighting the communists on campus and "never did a goddamn thing." Fodor had been chair of the Young Democrats of California and as a Democrat she had clandestinely supported Henry Wallace in 1948. During the mid-1950s, after the birth of her second child, Fodor organized a mother's group to oppose nuclear testing. So Fodor, like Garst, was not new to radical causes, to peace activity, or to women's groups. She was ready and eager for a separate women's peace action in the fall of 1961.

Two other women who founded WSP, Jeanne Bagby and Margaret Russell, were also already active in the peace cause at the time of the founding of WSP. Bagby was a frequent contributor to *Liberation* magazine. Together, the founders possessed research, writing, organizing, and speaking talents that were not unusual for women active in a variety of community, civic, and church groups in the 1950s. All the founders shared a conviction that the men in the peace movement and the government had failed them and that women had to take things into their own hands.

But what of the thousands of women who joined the founders? What was their social and political background and their motivation to take to the streets in peace protest? Elise Boulding, a sociologist and long-time pacifist activist, who became involved in the WSP communications network right after November 1, decided to try to find out. During the six months in which Boulding edited the *Women's Peace Movement Bulletin*, an information exchange for WSP groups, she kept asking herself whether the WSP women were really political neophytes as they claimed, or "old pros with a well defined idea of some kind of world social order?" Using the resources of the Institute for Conflict Resolution in Ann Arbor, Michigan, where she was working, and with the help of WSP colleagues in Ann Arbor, she composed a questionnaire that was sent to every eighth name on the mailing lists of forty-five local groups. By the fall of 1962, shortly before the summonses from HUAC, 279 questionnaires had been returned from thirty-seven localities in twenty-two states. According to Boulding, the respondents represented a cross section of the movement—not only leaders.[45]

Boulding found that the overwhelming majority of the WSP women were well-educated mothers and that 61 percent were not employed outside the home. But she concluded that the women who went out on strike for peace on November 1, 1961, and stayed on in the movement in the following months, appeared to be a more complex and sophisticated group than the "buggy-pushing housewife" image the movement conveyed. She characterized the early WSP participants as "largely intellectual and civic-minded people, mostly of the middle class"—very much like the Washington founders themselves.[46]

Most of the women strikers had been liberals, radicals, or pacifists in the 1940s. Although few had been political leaders of any kind, they shared the 1940s' belief that society could be restructured on humanistic lines through the direct political action of ordinary people. Dorothy Dinnerstein described the psychological process of depoliticization and privatization that many politically active people experienced in the 1950s. Many radicals, according to Dinnerstein, spent the 1950s in a state of moral shock, induced by the twin catastrophes of Stalinism and McCarthyism. They lost their capacity for social connectedness, and "in this condition they withdrew from history—more or less totally, more or less gradually, more or less blindly—into intensely personalistic, inward-turning, magically thing-and-place-oriented life." According to

Dinnerstein they withdrew their passion from the larger human scene and sought to invest in something less nightmarish, more coherent, and mentally manageable.[47] What the WSP women withdrew into, with society's blessing and encouragement, was the domestic sphere, the management of family, children, home, and local community. Many, when their school-age children no longer required full-time care, were propelled into the PTAs, League of Women Voters, Democratic party politics, church, synagogue, or cultural activities by their earlier social, political, and humanitarian concerns.

It took the acceleration of nuclear testing by both the capitalist United States and the socialist USSR to convince the WSP women of something they already suspected—that there was no political force in the world acting morally and humanely in the interest of the preservation of life. It took a series of international crises, the example of the civil rights sit-ins, and the Aldermarston antibomb marches in Britain to give the WSP women both the sense of urgency and of possibility that are the necessary ingredients for a political movement. Once out in the political arena, the women found that their moral outrage, their real fear for their children's future, and their determination never to be pushed back into the nonpolitical domestic sphere made them unafraid of a mere congressional committee before which others had quaked.

The women who were drawn to WSP certainly took the job of motherhood seriously. They had willingly chosen to sacrifice careers and personal projects to raise society's children, because they had been convinced by the post-Freudians that the making of human beings is a far more important vocation than anything else and that the making of human beings was a sex-specific vocation requiring the full-time duties of a resident mother.[48] But where the WSP women differed from the majority of their middle-class cohorts was that they saw motherhood not only as a private function but also as a contribution to society in general and to the future. When they built on their rights and responsibilities to act politically in defense of the world's children, they were invoking not only their maternal consciousness but their social conscience as well. They were women of heart, emotion, ingenuity, wit, and guile, but they were also serious political thinkers and activists. They chose to rely on their femininity, as most women did in the fifties and early sixties, to create whatever space and power they could carve out for themselves.

The Birmingham (England) Feminist History Group in an article, "Feminism as Femininity in the Nineteen Fifties?" suggests that feminism of the fifties seemed to be more concerned with integrating and foregrounding femininity than in transforming it in a fundamental way.[49] The conduct of WSP before the House Committee on Un-American Activities follows this pattern. The WSP women were not concerned with transforming the ideology of femininity but rather with using it to enhance women's political power. But in so doing they were transforming that ideology and foreshadowing the feminism that emerged later in the decade.

Very much in the way that the concept of Republican motherhood was used in the late eighteenth century to justify the demand for women's education, and the cult of true womanhood was built upon to project women into the antebellum reform movements, WSP used the feminine mystique of the 1950s to legitimize women's right to radical dissent from foreign and military policies. In the repressive political climate of the early 1960s, WSP relied heavily upon sex role stereotypes to legitimize its opposition to cold war policies. But by emphasizing the fact that the men in power could no longer be counted on for protection in the nuclear age, WSP implied that the traditional sex-gender contract no longer worked. And by stressing global issues and international sisterhood, rather than domestic responsibilities, WSP challenged the privatization and isolation of women which was a key element of the feminine mystique. Most importantly, by performing in relation to HUAC with more courage, candor, and wit than most men had done in a decade of inquisitions, WSP raised women's sense of political power and self-esteem. One of the negative effects for WSP of relying so heavily on the politics of motherhood to project its political message was that it alienated a new generation of younger women who admired the movement's stand for peace but saw its acquiescence to sex role stereotypes as regressive. In the late 1960s these younger women insisted upon working for peace not as wives, mothers, and sisters but as autonomous persons.

Sara Evans in *Personal Politics: The Roots of Women's Liberation in the Civil Rights Movement and the New Left* points out that those few young women in the civil rights movement who first raised feminist issues within the movement had to step *outside* the sex role assumptions on which they were raised in order to articulate a radical critique of women's position.[50] For WSP it was obviously different. The founders and leaders of WSP certainly did not step outside the traditional sex role assumptions; rather, they stood squarely upon them, with all their contradictions. By using these contradictions to present a radical critique of man's world, WSP began the transformation of woman's consciousness and woman's role.

Notes

I wish to thank my sisters in WSP, particularly Barbara Bick, Eleanor Garst, Ruth Meyers, Ethel Taylor, and Dagmar Wilson, for their helpful comments regarding an earlier version of this paper delivered at the Fifth Berkshire Conference on the History of Women, Vassar College, 16 June 1981. I am indebted also to Alice Kessler-Harris, Joan Kelly, Gerda Lerner, Melanie Gustafson, and Warren Susman for their valuable insights, advice, and criticism. Research for this article was funded in part by a Woodrow Wilson Women's Studies Dissertation Fellowship, 1980.

1. U.S. Congress, House, Committee on Un-American Activities, *Communist Activities in the Peace Movement (Women Strike for Peace and Certain Other Groups), Hearings before the Committee on Un-American Activities on H.R. 9944,* 87th Cong., 2d. sess., 1962, p. 2057.

2. Historians and political opponents of HUAC agree that the WSP hearings marked the beginning of the end of the committee's power. Eric Bentley called the WSP-HUAC confrontation "the fall of HUAC's Bastille." See Eric Bentley, *Thirty Years of Treason* (New York: Viking Press, 1971), 951. Frank Wilkerson of the National Committee to abolish HUAC wrote to the Washington office after the hearing: "Magnificent women. . . . You have dealt HUAC its greatest setback." Frank Wilkerson to Eleanor Garst et al., 14 Dec. 1962, WSP Document Collection in custody of the author. (This collection went to the Swarthmore College Peace Collection in 1983.) Peace historian Charles De Benedetti said of the HUAC investigation of WSP, "WSP activists challenged for the first time the House Un-American Activities Committee's practice of identifying citizen peace seeking with Communist subversion. . . . The open disdain of the WSP for HUAC did not end the Congress's preference for treating private peace actions as subversive. But it did help break the petrified anti-Communism of Cold War American politics and gave heart to those reformers who conceived peace as more than military preparedness." See Charles De Benedetti, *Peace Reform in American History* (Bloomington: Indiana University Press, 1980), 167–78.

3. In May 1960, Senator Thomas Dodd, vice-chair of the Senate International Security Subcommittee, threatened SANE with congressional investigation if it did not take steps to rid itself of communist infiltrators. SANE responded by voting to exclude all those with communist sympathies. Whole chapters that did not go along with internal red hunts were expelled, as was Henry Abrams, a leading New York activist who refused to tell the Senate committee whether he was a communist. Turn Toward Peace also rejected communists or former communists. See Milton S. Katz, "Peace, Politics, and Protest: SANE and the American Peace Movement, 1957–1972" (Ph.D. diss., Saint Louis University, 1973), 109–30. Homer Jack, executive director of national

SANE, criticized WSP's "welcome everybody" stand. He claimed that it would call into question the political sagacity of groups like his own. See Homer A. Jack, "The Will of the WISP Versus the Humiliation of HUAC" (transcript of a talk on Radio Station WBAI, New York, 28 Dec. 1962), WSP Document Collection. After 15 Jan. 1962, many WSP groups and the Washington office referred to themselves as Women's International Strike for Peace (WISP).

4. The way in which WSP's militant role in the peace movement has been either ignored or trivialized by journalists, peace movement leaders, and historians is illustrated by the following examples. Mary McGrory in her syndicated column described a WSP visit to the White House in the following manner: "This week's Cinderella story has to do with Women Strike for Peace, which after 15 years of drudgery in the skullery of anti-war activity has been invited to the White House" (*New York Post*, 8 Mar. 1977, 24). Dave Dellinger, one of the most prominent of the male leaders of the 1960s' peace movement, devoted about 10 lines to WSP in a 317-page book on the history of the civil rights and peace movements from 1965 to 1973. He described WSP as a group fearful of engaging in civil disobedience in the 1967 "Mobilization March on the Pentagon." Nowhere in the book did Dellinger mention that nine months earlier 2,500 WSP women broke through police barricades to bang their shoes on the Pentagon doors which had been shut in their faces. See Dave Dellinger, *More Power Than We Know* (Garden City, N.Y.: Anchor Press, 1975). Lawrence Wittner, in a critical survey of American politics from 1945 to 1974 that focuses on movements of dissent, devoted only four words to WSP. He included the movement in a list of early critics of radioactive fallout. See his *Cold War America from Hiroshima to Watergate* (New York: Praeger, 1974), 232.

5. For a symposium on the relationship of feminism, women's culture, and women's politics, see Ellen DuBois, Mari Jo Buhle, Temma Kaplan, Gerda Lerner, and Carroll Smith-Rosenberg, "Politics and Culture in Women's History: A Symposium," *Feminist Studies* 6 (Spring 1980): 26–64. Also see Temma Kaplan, "Female Consciousness and Collective Action: The Case of Barcelona, 1910–1918," *Signs* 7 (Spring 1982): 545–66. Kaplan points out that women's defense of traditional rights, while fundamentally conservative, can have revolutionary consequences.

6. The figure of fifty thousand claimed by the Washington founders after November 1 was accepted in most press accounts and became part of the WSP legend. It was based on reports from women in sixty cities and from newspapers across the country. Often the women's reports and that of the newspapers differed, but even in using the highest figures available I can substantiate only a count of approximately twelve thousand women who struck on November 1. Nevertheless, this was still the largest women's peace demonstration on record.

7. "End the Arms Race—Not the Human Race" was the central slogan of the November 1 "strike": "Help Wanted" flyer, 25 Oct. 1961, Washington, D.C. See WSP Document Collection (mimeographed).

8. "Dear ———, Last night I sat with a few friends in a comfortable living room talking of atomic war." Draft of call to strike by Eleanor Garst, Washington, D.C., 22 Sept. 1961. WSP Document Collection.

9. *Newsweek,* 13 Nov. 1961, 21.

10. Eleanor Garst, "Women: Middle-Class Masses," *Fellowship* 28 (1 Nov. 1962): 10–12.

11. Minutes of the WILPF National Executive Committee stated: "Each branch taking direct action should clear with the National Action Projects Committee. The committee should have, and send out to branches, a list of approved action and a list of the organizations with which we formally cooperate." Women's International League for Peace and Freedom, Minutes of the National Executive Committee, meeting of 28–29 Sept. 1961. Swarthmore College Peace Collection, DG 43, Series A-2, box 18, 5.

12. "Transcript of the President's News Conference on World and Domestic Affairs," *New York Times,* 16 Jan. 1962, 18.

13. *Science* 167 (13 Mar. 1970): 1476.

14. A.E. Wessel, *The American Peace Movement: A Study of Its Themes and Political Potential* (Santa Monica: Rand Corporation, 1962), 3.

15. *New York Journal American,* 4 Apr. 1962, 10.

16. *San Francisco Examiner,* 21 May 1962, 10.

17. The FBI files on WSP are located in the offices of the Washington, D.C., law firm of Gaffney, Anspach, Shember, Klimasi, and Marx. These contain hundreds of documents from security officers in major cities to the director of the FBI and from the directors to the security officers. For instance, as early as 23 Oct. 1961, one week before the November 1 strike, the Cleveland office of the FBI already identified one of the WSP planning groups as communist (FBI Document 100-39566-8). When WSP sent a delegation to lobby the Geneva Disarmament Conference, 2–7 Apr. 1962, the FBI involved Swiss federal police and covert Central Intelligence Agency agents in the American embassy to spy on the women (Legat Bern to Director, FBI, 4 Apr. 1962, FBI Document 100-39574-187). An internal security memorandum on 24 July 1962 stated that an informant, who had furnished reliable information in the past, made available a list of women "who will be guests of the Soviet Women's Committee in the USSR, 12–26 July 1962." The list which had been circulated to the press by WSP included the names of twelve women from various parts of the country (FBI Document 100-39566-222).

18. Those subpoenaed were (in order of appearance) Blanche Posner, Ruth Meyers, Lyla Hoffman, Elsie Neidenberg, Sylvia Contente, Rose Clinton, Iris Freed, Anna Mackenzie, Elizabeth Moos, Ceil Gross, Jean Brancato, Miriam Chesman, Norma Spector, and Dagmar Wilson. Spector never testified; she was excused due to illness. *Hearings before Committee on Un-American Activities,* 3.

19. Lillian Hellman, *Scoundrel Time* (Boston: Little, Brown & Co., 1976), 99.

20. Los Angeles WISP, Statement 1, Ann Arbor Conference, 9–10 June 1962, WSP Document Collection; *Women Strike for Peace Newsletter,* New York, New Jersey, Connecticut, Summer 1962, 1–2.

21. "WSP National Policy Statement," *Women Strike for Peace Newsletter,* New York, New Jersey, Connecticut, Summer 1962, 1–2.

22. "Key women" was the name used by WSP for those women who were part of the national and local communications network. They were the ones who were called upon to initiate actions or who called upon others to do so.

23. Katz, 122–26.

24. Jack.

25. The anti-HUAC statement by WSP was composed by the New York and Washington leadership in their usual collaborative fashion, with no pride or claim of authorship, so it is difficult to know which group wrote what part. It was distributed through official WSP channels via the national office in Washington.

26. Bentley, 951.

27. Women Strike for Peace, Washington, D.C., to "Dear WISP's," 6 Dec. 1962, WSP Document Collection.

28. Carol Urner to Representative Francis Walter, reprinted in *Women's Peace Movement Bulletin* 1 (20 Dec. 1962): 5.

29. *Hearings before Committee on Un-American Activities,* 2064–65.

30. Ibid., 2074, 2085.

31. Mary McGrory, "Prober Finds 'Peacemakers' More Than a Match," *Washington Evening Star,* 12 Dec. 1962, A-1.

32. *Hearings before Committee on Un-American Activities,* 2095, 2101.

33. McGrory, A-1.

34. Lyla Hoffman, undated typewritten statement, WSP Document Collection.

35. Thirty-seven favorable news stories, columns, and editorials were reprinted in a hastily prepared WSP booklet, published less than two weeks after the hearings. Facsimile copies of Russell Baker's column, "Peace March Gals Make Red Hunters Look Silly," appeared on p. 2; The *Detroit Free Press* story declaring "Headhunters Decapitated," appeared on p. 4; "It's Ladies' Day at Capitol" from the *Chicago Daily News* appeared on p. 9; and the Herblock cartoon appeared on p. 5. *So Many Great Things Have Been Said* (Washington, D.C.: Women Strike for Peace, 1963).

36. *Vancouver Sun,* 14 Dec. 1962, 2.

37. "The Ladies Turn Peace Quiz into Greek Comedy," *Detroit Free Press,* 16 Dec. 1962, 1.

38. *Detroit Free Press,* 13 Dec. 1962, 8-A.

39. "Nobody Controls Anybody," *Washington Evening Star,* 14 Dec. 1962, A-1, A-9.

40. *Hearings before Committee on Un-American Activities,* 2201.

41. *Madison Daily Cardinal,* 14 Dec. 1962, 2.

42. Garst, 10–11.

43. Interview with Dagmar Wilson, Leesburg, Virginia, September 1977.

44. *New York Times Magazine,* 6 May 1962, 32.

45. On a WSP activity measure, 38 percent rated themselves as "very active," 10 percent as "active," and 42 percent rated themselves as "not active," or only "slightly active." The profile of the majority of the WSP participants that emerged was indeed that of middle-class, well-educated housewives. Sixty-five percent of the women had either a B.A. or a higher degree, at a time when only 6 percent of the female population over age twenty-five had a B.A. or more. Seventy-one percent of the WSP women were suburb or city dwellers, with the highest concentrations in the East Central states, the West Coast, and the Midwest, and with low participation in the Mountain states and the South. The WSPers were concentrated in the twenty-five-to-forty-four age bracket. Only 5 percent of the group were "never married." Of the married women 43 percent had from one to four children under six; 49 percent had from one to four or more children over eighteen. Sixty-one percent of the women involved in WSP were not, at the time of the questionnaire, employed outside the home. Nearly 70 percent of the husbands of the WSP women who responded to the survey were professionals.

Thirty-eight percent of the women who responded claimed to belong to no other organizations or at least did not record the names of any organizations in response to questions concerning other community activities. Forty percent of the women were active in a combination of civic, race relations, civil liberties, peace, and electoral political activities. Only 11 percent were members of professional organizations. Boulding concluded that many of the WSP women were nonjoiners. As for their goals in joining WSP activities, the Boulding questionnaire revealed that 55 percent gave abolition of war or multilateral disarmament as their primary goals, and 22 percent gave nonviolent solution of all conflict, political and social. The remainder chose as their goals a variety of proposals for world government or limited international controls such as a test ban treaty. As to their reasons for participating in WSP activities: 28 percent of the women said they had joined the movement over concern about fallout, testing, and civil defense, another 4 percent because of the Berlin Wall crisis; but 41 percent listed no specific event, just an increasing sense of urgency about the total world situation and a feeling of the need to make a declaration of personal responsibility. See Elise Boulding, *Who Are These Women?* (Ann Arbor, Mich.: Institute for Conflict Resolution, 1962).

46. Ibid., 15.

47. Dorothy Dinnerstein, *The Mermaid and the Minotaur: Sexual Arrangements and Human Malaise* (New York: Harper Colophon Books, 1977), 259–62.

48. Ashley Montagu, "The Triumph and Tragedy of the American Woman,"

Saturday Review, 27 Sept. 1958, 14; Dr. Benjamin Spock, *The Common Sense Book of Baby and Child Care* (New York: Duell, Sloan & Pearce, 1945), 484.

49. "Feminism as Femininity in the Nineteen Fifties?" Birmingham History Group, *Feminist Review,* no. 3 (1979), 48–65.

50. Sara Evans, *Personal Politics: The Roots of Women's Liberation in the Civil Rights Movement and the New Left* (New York: Alfred A. Knopf, 1979), 23.

13   Madeline Davis and Elizabeth Lapovsky Kennedy

Oral History and the Study of Sexuality in the Lesbian Community: Buffalo, New York, 1940–1960

□ We began a study of the history of the Buffalo lesbian community, 1930–1960, to determine that community's contribution to the emergence of the gay liberation movement of the 1960s.[1] Because this community centered around bars and was highly role defined, its members often have been stereotyped as low-life societal discards and pathetic imitators of heterosexuality. We suspected instead that these women were heroines who had shaped the development of gay pride in the twentieth century by forging a culture for survival and resistance under prejudicial conditions and by passing this sense of community on to newcomers; in our minds, these are indications of a movement in its prepolitical stages.[2] Our original research plan assumed the conceptual division between the public (social life and politics) and the private (intimate life and sex), which is deeply rooted in modern consciousness and which feminism has only begun to question. Thus we began our study by looking at gay and lesbian bars—the public manifestations of gay life at the time—and relegated sex to a position of less importance, viewing it as only incidentally relevant. As our research progressed we came to question the accuracy of this division. This article records the transformation in our thinking and explores the role of sexuality in the cultural and political development of the Buffalo lesbian community.
　At first, our use of the traditional framework that separates the public and private spheres was fruitful.[3] Because the women who patronized the lesbian and gay bars of the past were predominantly working class and left no written records, we chose oral history as our method of study. Through the life stories of over forty narrators, we found that

Reprinted, with changes, from *Feminist Studies* 12, no. 1 (Spring 1986): 7–26. ©1986 by Feminist Studies, Inc.

there were more bars in Buffalo during the forties and fifties than there are in that city today. Lesbians living all over the city came to socialize in these bars, which were located primarily in the downtown area. Some of these women were born and raised in Buffalo; others had migrated there in search of their kind. In addition, women from nearby cities, Rochester and Toronto, came to Buffalo bars on weekends. Most of the women who frequented these bars had full-time jobs. Many were factory workers, taxi drivers, bartenders, clerical workers, hospital technicians; a few were teachers or women who owned their own businesses.[4]

Our narrators documented, beyond our greatest expectations, the truth of our original hypothesis that this public bar community was a formative predecessor to the modern gay liberation movement. These bars not only were essential meeting places with distinctive cultures and mores, but they were also the central arena for the lesbian confrontation with a hostile world. Participants in bar life were engaged in constant, often violent, struggle for public space. Their dress code announced them as lesbians to their neighbors, to strangers on the streets, and of course to all who entered the bars. Although confrontation with the straight world was a constant during this period, its nature changed over time. In the forties, women braved ridicule and verbal abuse but rarely physical conflict. One narrator of the forties conveys the tone: "There was a great difference in looks between a lesbian and her girl. You had to take a streetcar—very few people had cars. And people would stare and such."[5] In the fifties, with the increased visibility of the established gay community, the concomitant postwar rigidification of sex roles, and the political repression of the McCarthy era, the street dyke emerged. She was a full-time "queer," who frequented the bars even on week nights and was ready at any time to fight for her space and dignity. Many of our fifties' narrators were both aware and proud that their fighting contributed to a safer, more comfortable environment for lesbians today.

> Things back then were horrible, and I think that because I fought like a man to survive I made it somehow easier for the kids coming out today. I did all their fighting for them. I'm not a rich person; I don't even have a lot of money. I don't even have a little money. I would have nothing to leave anybody in this world, but I have that that I can leave to the kids who are coming out now, who will come out into the future, that I left them a better place to come out into. And that's all I have to offer, to leave them. But I wouldn't deny it; even though I was getting my brains beaten up I would never stand up and say, "No, don't hit me, I'm not gay, I'm not gay." I wouldn't do that.

When we initially gathered this material on the growth and development of community life, we placed little emphasis on sexuality. In part we were swept away by the excitement of the material on bars, dress, and the creation of public space for lesbians. In addition, we were part of a lesbian feminist movement that opposed a definition of lesbianism based primarily on sex. Moreover, we were influenced by the popular assumption that sexuality is natural and unchanging and the related sexist assumption of women's sexual passivity—both of which imply that sexuality is not a valid subject for historical study. Only recently have historians turned their attention to sexuality, a topic that used to be of interest mainly to psychologists and the medical profession. Feminists have added impetus to this study by suggesting that women can desire and shape sexual experience. Finally, we were inhibited by the widespread social reluctance to converse frankly about sexual matters. Thus for various reasons, all stemming, at least indirectly, from modern society's powerful ideological division between the public and the private, we were indisposed to consider how important sexuality might have been to the women we were studying.

The strength of the oral history method is that it enables narrators to shape their history, even when their views contradict the assumptions of historians. As our work progressed, narrators volunteered information about their sexual and emotional lives, and often a shyly asked question would inspire lengthy, absorbing discourse. By proceeding in the direction in which these women steered us, we came to realize that sexuality and sexual identity were not incidental but were central to their lives and their community. Our narrators taught us that although securing public space was indeed important, it was strongly motivated by the need to provide a setting for the formation of intimate relationships. It is the nature of this community that it created public space for lesbians and gay men, while at the same time it organized sexuality and emotional relationships. Appreciation of this dynamic interconnection requires new ways of thinking about lesbian history.

What is an appropriate framework for studying the sexual component of a lesbian community's history and for revealing the role of sexuality in the evolution of twentieth-century lesbian and gay politics? So little research has been done in this area, that our work is still exploratory and tentative. At present, we seek primarily to understand forms of lesbian sexual expression and to identify changes in sexual norms, experiences, and ideas during the 1940s and 1950s. We also look for the forces behind these changes in the evolving culture and politics of the lesbian community. Our goal has been to ascertain what part, if any, sexuality played in the developing politics of gay liberation. As an introduction to this discussion, we shall present our method of research because it has been crucial in our move to study sexuality, and so little has been written on the use of oral history for research on this topic.

Using Oral History to Construct the History of the Buffalo Lesbian Community

☐ The memories of our narrators are colorful, illuminating, and very moving. Our purpose, however, was not only to collect individual life stories but also to use these as a basis for constructing the history of the community. To create from individual memories a historically valid analysis of this community presented a difficult challenge. The method we developed was slow and painstaking.[6] We treated each oral history as a historical document, taking into account the particular social position of each narrator and how that might affect her memories. We also considered how our own point of view influenced the kind of information we received and the way in which we interpreted a narrator's story. We juxtaposed all interviews with one another to identify patterns and contradictions and checked our developing understanding with other sources, such as newspaper accounts, legal cases, and labor statistics.

As mentioned earlier, we first focused on understanding and documenting lesbian bar life. From the many vibrant and humorous stories about adventures in bars and from the mountains of seemingly unrelated detail about how people spent their time, we began to identify a chronology of bars and to recognize distinctive social mores and forms of lesbian consciousness that were associated with different time periods and even with different bars. We checked and supplemented our analysis by research into newspaper accounts of bar raids and closings and actions of the State Liquor Authority. Contradictions frequently emerged in our material on bars, but, as we pursued them, we found they were rarely due to idiosyncratic or faulty memory on the part of our narrators but to the complexity of bar life. Often the differences could be resolved by taking into account the different social positions of our narrators or the kinds of questions we had asked to elicit the information we received. If conflicting views persisted we tried to return to our narrators for clarification. Usually, we found that we had misunderstood our narrators or that contradictions indeed existed in the community at the time. For instance, narrators consistently told us about the wonderful times in bars as well as how terrible they were. We came to understand that both of these conditions were part of the real experience of bar life.

When we turned our attention to sexuality and romance in this community, we were at first concerned that our method would not be adequate. Using memories to trace the evolution of sexual norms and expression is, at least superficially, more problematic than using them to document social life in bars. There are no concrete public events or institutions to which the memories can be linked. Thus, when a narrator talks about butch-fem sexuality in the forties, we must bear in mind the likelihood that she has modified her view and her practice of butch-fem sexuality in the fifties, sixties, seventies, and eighties. In contrast, when a narrator tells about bars in the forties, even though social life in bars might have changed over the last forty years, she can tie her memories to a concrete place like Ralph Martin's bar, which existed during a specific time period. Although not enough is known about historical memory to fully evaluate data derived from either type of narrative, our guess is, that at least for lesbian communities, they are equally valid.[7] The vividness of our narrators' stories suggests that the potential of oral history to generate full and rich documents about women's sexuality might be especially rich in the lesbian community. Perhaps lesbian memories about sexual ideals and experiences are not separated from the rest of life because the building of public communities is closely connected with the pursuit of intimate relationships. In addition, during this period, when gay oppression marked most lesbians' lives with fear of punishment and lack of acceptance, sexuality was one of the few areas in which many lesbians found satisfaction and pleasure. This was reinforced by the fact that, for lesbians, sexuality was not directly linked with the pain and/or danger of women's responsibility for childbearing and women's economic dependence on men. Therefore, memories of sexual experience might be more positive and more easily shared. But these ideas are tentative. An understanding of the nature of memory about sexuality must await further research.

The difficulty of tying memories about sexual or emotional life to public events does present special problems. We cannot identify specific dates for changes in sexual and emotional life, such as when sex became a public topic of conversation or when role-appropriate sex became a community concern. We can talk only of trends within the framework of decades. In addition, we are unable to find supplementary material to verify and spark our narrators' memories. There are no government documents or newspaper reports on lesbian sexuality. The best one can find are memoirs or fiction written about or by residents in other cities, and even these don't exist for participants in working-class communities of the forties.[8] In general, we have not found these problems to require significant revision of our method.

Our experience indicates that the number of people interviewed is critical to the success of our method, whether we are concerned with analyzing the history of bar life or of emotional and sexual life. We feel that between five and ten narrators' stories need to be juxtaposed in order to develop an analysis that is not changed dramatically by each new story. At the present time, our analysis of the white lesbian community of the fifties is based on oral histories from over fifteen narrators. In contrast, we have only five narrators who participated in the white community of the forties, four for the Black community of the fifties, and one from the Black community of the forties. Therefore, we emphasize the fifties in this article and have the greatest confidence in our analysis of that decade. Our discussion of the forties must be viewed as only tentative. Our material on the Black community is not yet sufficient for separate treatment; so Black and white narrators' memories are interspersed throughout the article. Ultimately, we hope to be able to write a history of each community.

Sexuality as Part of the Cultural-Political Development of the Buffalo Lesbian Community

☐ Three features of lesbian sexuality during the forties and fifties suggest its integral connection with the lesbian community's cultural-political development. First, butch-fem roles created an authentic lesbian sexuality appropriate to the flourishing of an independent lesbian culture. Second, lesbians actively pursued rich and fulfilling sexual lives at a time when sexual subjectivity was not the norm for women. This behavior was not only consistent with the creation of a separate lesbian culture, but it also represented the roots of a personal and political feminism that characterized the gay liberation movement of the sixties. Third, although butch-fem roles and the pursuit of sexual autonomy remained constant throughout this period, sexual mores changed in relation to the evolving forms of resistance to oppression.

Most commentators on lesbian bar life in the forties and fifties have noted the prominence of butch-fem roles.[9] Our research corroborates this; we found that roles constituted a powerful code of behavior that shaped the way individuals handled themselves in daily life, including sexual expression. In addition, roles were the primary organizer for the lesbian stance toward the straight world as well as for building love relationships and for making friends.[10] To understand butch-fem roles in their full complexity is a fundamental issue for students of lesbian history; the particular concern of this article is the intricate connection between roles and sexuality. Members of the community, when explaining how one recognized a person's role, regularly referred to two underlying determinants—image, including dress and mannerism, and sexuality.[11] Some people went so far as to say that one never really knew a woman's role identity until one went to bed with her. "You can't tell butch-fem by people's dress. You couldn't even really tell in the fifties. I knew women with long hair, fem clothes, and found out they were butches. Actually I even knew one who wore men's clothes, haircuts and ties, who was a fem."

Today, butch-fem roles elicit deep emotional reactions from many heterosexuals and lesbians. The former are affronted by women assuming male prerogatives; the latter by lesbians adopting male-defined role models. The hostility is exemplified by the prevalent ugly stereotype of the butch-fem sexual dyad: the butch with her dildo or penis substitute, trying to imitate a man, and the simpering, passive fem who is kept in her place by ignorance. This representation evokes pity for lesbians because women who so interact must certainly be sexually unfulfilled; one partner cannot achieve satisfaction because she lacks the "true" organ of pleasure, and the other is cheated because she is denied the complete experience of the "real thing." Our research counters the view that butch-fem roles are solely an imitation of sexist heterosexual society.

Inherent to butch-fem relationships was the presumption that the butch is the physically active partner and the leader in lovemaking. As one butch narrator explains, "I treat a woman as a woman, down to the basic fact it'd have to be my side doin' most of the doin'." Insofar as the butch was the doer and the fem was the desired one, butch-fem roles did indeed parallel the male/female roles in heterosexuality. Yet unlike the dynamics of many heterosexual relationships, the butch's foremost objective was to give sexual pleasure to a fem; it was in satisfying her fem that the butch received fulfillment. "If I could give her satisfaction to the highest, that's what gave me satisfaction." As for the fem, she not only knew what would give her physical pleasure, but she also knew that she was neither object of nor receptacle for someone else's gratification. The essence of this emotional/sexual dynamic is captured by the ideal of the "stone butch," or untouchable butch, that prevailed during this period. A "stone butch" does all the "doin'" and does not ever allow her lover to reciprocate in kind. To be untouchable meant to gain pleasure from giving pleasure. Thus, although these women did draw on models in heterosexual society, they transformed those models into an authentically lesbian interaction. Through role playing they developed distinctive and fulfilling expressions of women's sexual love for women.

The archetypal lesbian couple of the 1940s and 1950s, the "stone butch" and the fem, poses one of the most tantalizing puzzles of lesbian history and possibly of the history of sexuality in general.[12] In a culture that viewed women as sexually passive, butches developed a position as sexual aggressor, a major component of which was untouchability. However, the active or "masculine" partner was associated with the giving of sexual pleasure, a service usually assumed to be "feminine." Conversely, the fem, although the more passive partner, demanded and received sexual pleasure and in this sense might be considered the more self-concerned or even more "selfish" partner. These attributes of butch-fem sexual identity remove sexuality from the realm of the "natural," challenging the notion that sexual performance is a function of biology and affirming the view that sexual gratification is socially constructed.

Within this framework of butch-fem roles, individual lesbians actively pursued sexual pleasure. On the one hand, butch-fem roles limited sexual expression by imposing a definite structure. On the other hand, this structure ordered and gave a determinant shape to lesbian desire, which allowed individuals to know and find what they wanted. The restrictions of butch-fem sexuality, as well as the pathways it provided for satisfaction, are best captured and explored by examining what it meant for both butch and fem that the butch was the doer; how much leeway was there before the butch became fem, or the fem became butch?

Although there was complete agreement in the community that the butch was the leader in lovemaking, there was a great deal of controversy over the feasibility or necessity of being a "stone butch." In the forties, most butches lived up to the *ideal* of "the untouchable." One fem, who was in a relationship with an untouchable butch at that time, had tried to challenge her partner's behavior but met only with resistance. Her butch's whole group—those who hung out at Ralph Martin's—were the same. "Because I asked her one time, I said, 'Do you think that you might be just the only one?' 'Oh no,' she said. 'I know I'm not, you know, that I've discussed with . . . different people.' [There were] no exceptions, which I thought was ODD, but, I thought, well, you know. This is how it is."

In the fifties, the "stone butch" became a publicly discussed model for appropriate sexual behavior, and it was a standard that young butches felt they had to achieve to be a "real" or "true" butch. In contrast to the forties, a fifties' fem, who was out in the community, would not have had to ask her butch friend why she was untouchable, and if there were others like her. She would have known it was the expected behavior for butches. Today our narrators disagree over whether it was, in fact, possible to maintain the ideal and they are unclear about the degree of latitude allowed in the forties or fifties before a butch harmed her reputation. Some butches claim that they were absolutely untouchable; that was how they were, and that's how they enjoyed sex. When we confronted one of our narrators, who referred to herself as an "untouchable," with the opinion of another narrator, who maintained that "stone butches" had never really existed, she replied, "No, that's not true. I'm an 'untouchable.' I've tried to have my lover make love to me, but I just couldn't stand it. . . . I really think there's something physical about that." Like many of our butch narrators, this woman has always been spontaneously orgasmic; that is, her excitement level peaks to orgasm while making love to another woman. Another "stone butch" explains: "I wanted to satisfy them [women], and I wanted to make love—I love to make love. I still think that's the greatest thing in life. But I don't want them to touch me. I feel like that spoils the whole thing—I am the way I am. And I figure if a girl is attracted to me, she's attracted to me because of what I am."

Other butches who consider themselves, and had the reputation of being, untouchable claim that it is, as a general matter, impossible to be completely untouchable. One, when asked if she were really untouchable replied, "Of course not. How would any woman stay with me if I was? It doesn't make any sense. . . . I don't believe there was ever such a class—other than what they told each other." This woman preferred not to be touched, but she did allow mutual lovemaking from time to time during her long-term relationships. A first time in bed, however:

> there's no way in hell that you would touch me . . . if you mean untouchable like that. But if I'm living with a woman, I'd have to be a liar if I said that she hadn't touched me. But I can say that I don't care for it to happen. And the only reason it does happen is because she wants it. It's not like something I desire or want. But there's no such thing as an untouchable butch—and I'm the finest in Buffalo and I'm telling you straight—and don't let them jive you around it—no way.

This narrator's distinction between her behavior on a first night and her behavior in long-term relationships appeared to be accepted practice. The fact that some—albeit little—mutuality was allowed over the period of a long relationship did not affect one's reputation as an untouchable butch, nor did it counter the presumption of the butch as the doer.

This standard of untouchability was so powerful in shaping the behavior of fifties' butches that many never experienced their fems making love to them. By the seventies, however, when we began our interviewing, norms had changed enough so that our butch narrators had had opportunities to experience various forms of sexual expression. Still, many of them—in fact all of those quoted above on "stone butches"—remained untouchable. It was their personal style long after community standards changed. Today these women offer explanations for their preference that provide valuable clues about both the personal importance and the social "rightness" of untouchability as a community norm in the forties and fifties. Some women, as indicated in one of the above quotations, continue to view their discomfort with being touched as physical or biological. Others feel that if a fem were allowed the physical liberties usually associated with the butch role, distinctions would blur and the relationship would become confusing. "I feel that if we're in bed and she does the same thing to me that I do to her, we're the same thing." Another narrator, reflecting on the fact that she always went to bed with her clothes on, suggests that "what it came to was being uncomfortable with the female body. You didn't want people you were with to realize the likeness between the two." Still other butches are hesitant about the vulnerability implicit in mutual lovemaking. "When the first girl wanted to make a mutual exchange sexually, . . . I didn't want to be in the position of being at somebody's disposal, or at their command that much—maybe that's still inside me. Maybe I never let loose enough."

But many untouchables of the fifties did try mutual lovemaking later on, and it came as a pleasant surprise when they found they enjoyed being touched. "For some reason . . . I used to get enough mental satisfaction by satisfying a woman . . . then it got to the point where this one woman said, 'Well, I'm just not gonna accept that,' and she started venturing, and at first I said, 'No, no,' and then I said, 'Well, why not?' and I got to enjoy it." This change was not easy for a woman who had spent many years as an "untouchable." At first she was very nervous and uncomfortable about mutual sex, but "after I started reaching physical climaxes instead of just mental, it went, that little restlessness about it. It just mellowed me right out, y'know." The social pressure of the times prevented some women from experiencing expanded forms of sexual expression they might have enjoyed, and it also put constraints upon some women who had learned mutual sex outside of a structured community. One of our narrators had begun her sex life with mutual relations and enjoyed it immensely, but in order to conform to the community standard for butches, adopted untouchability as her sexual posture. She acceded to this behavioral change willingly and saw it as a logical component of her role during this period.

How was a community able to monitor the sexual activities of its members, and how might people come to know if a butch "rolled over"—the community lingo for a butch who allowed fems to make love to her? The answer was simple; fems talked! A butch's reputation was based on her performance with fems.

Despite the fact that sexual performance could build or destroy a butch's reputation, some butches of the fifties completely ignored the standard of untouchability. Our narrators give two reasons for this. One reason is the opinion that a long-term relationship requires some degree of mutuality to survive. One butch, a respected leader of the community because of her principles, her affability, and her organizational skills, was not only "touchable" but also suspects that most of the butches she knew in the fifties were not "stone butches." "Once you get in bed or in your bedroom and the lights go out, when you get in between those sheets, I don't think there's any male or there's any female or butch or fem, and it's a fifty-fifty thing. And I think that any relationship . . . any true relationship that's gonna survive has got to be that way. You can't be a giver and can't be a taker. You've gotta both be givers and both gotta be takers." The second reason is the pleasure of being touched. Some women experienced this in the fifties and continued to follow the practice.

> When it came to sex [in the fifties] butches were untouchable, so to speak. They did all the lovemaking, but love was not made back to them. And after I found out how different it was, and how great it was, I said, "What was I missing?" I remember a friend of mine, that I had, who dressed like a man all her life . . . and I remember talking to [her] and saying to her, you know you've got to stop being an untouchable butch, and she just couldn't agree. And I remember one time reaching over and pinching her and I said, "Did you feel that?" and she said, "Yes," and I said, "It hurt, didn't it? Well, why aren't you willing to feel something that's good?"

We do not know if in the forties, as in the fifties, butches who preferred a degree of mutuality in lovemaking existed side by side with the ideal of untouchability because we have considerably less information on that decade. Therefore, we cannot judge whether there was in fact a development toward mutual sexuality, the dominant form of lesbian lovemaking of the sixties and seventies, or whether the "stone butch" prescribed ideal and mutual lovemaking couples existed side by side consistently throughout the forties and fifties.

Our information on fem sexuality is not as extensive as that on butch sexuality because we have been able to contact fewer fem narrators. Nevertheless, from the fems we have interviewed and from comments by butches who sought them out and loved them, we do have an indication that fems were not passive receivers of pleasure but, for the most part, knew what they wanted and pursued it.[13] Many butches attributed their knowledge of sex to fems, who educated them by their sexual responsiveness as well as by their explicit directions in lovemaking.

As implied by our discussion of butch sexuality, many fems had difficulty accepting "untouchability." One fem narrator of the forties had a ten-year relationship with an untouchable butch, and the sexual restrictions were a source of discomfort for her. "It was very one-sided, you know, and . . . you never really got a chance to express your love. And I think this kind of suppressed . . . your feelings, your emotions. And I don't know whether that's healthy. I don't think so." But at the same time the majority of these fems appreciated being the center of attention; they derived a strong sense of self-fulfillment from seeking their own satisfaction and giving pleasure—by responding to their butches. "I've had some that I couldn't touch no parts of their bodies. It was all about me. Course I didn't mind! But every once in a while I felt like, well, hey, let me do something to you. I could NEVER understand that. 'Cause I lived with a girl. I couldn't touch any part of her, no part. But boy, did she make me feel good, so I said . . . All right with me . . . I don't mind laying down."

What emerges from our narrator's words is in fact a range of sexual desires that were built into the framework of role-defined sexuality. For butches of the period, we found those who preferred untouchability; those who learned it and liked it; those who learned it and adjusted to it for a time; those who preferred it, but sensed the need for some mutuality; and those who practiced mutuality regularly. For fems, we found those who accepted pleasure, thereby giving pleasure to their lovers; usually such women would aggressively seek what they wanted and instruct their lovers with both verbal and nonverbal cues. Some fems actively sought to make love to their butches and were successful. And finally, we found some women who were not consistent in their roles, changing according to their partners. In the varied sex lives of these role-identified women of the past, we can find the roots of "personal-political" feminism. Women's concern with the ultimate satisfaction of other women is part of a strong sense of female and potentially feminist agency and may be the wellspring for the confidence, the goals, and the needs that shaped the later gay and lesbian feminist movement. Thus, when we develop our understanding of this community as a predecessor to the gay liberation movement, our analysis must include sexuality. For these lesbians actively sought, expanded, and shaped their sexual experience, a radical undertaking for women in the 1940s and 1950s.

Although butch-fem roles were the consistent framework for sexual expression, sexual mores changed and developed throughout this period; two contradictory trends emerged. First, the community became more open to the acceptance of new sexual practices, the discussion of sexual matters, and the learning about sex from friends as well as lovers. Second, the rules of butch-fem sexuality became more rigid, in that community concern for role-appropriate behavior increased.

In the forties there were at least two social groups, focused in two prominent bars, Ralph Martin's and Winters. According to our narrators, the sexual mores of these two groups differed: the former group was somewhat conservative; the latter group was more experimental, presaging what were to become the accepted norms of the fifties. The lesbian patrons of Ralph Martin's did not discuss sex openly, and oral sex was disdained. "People didn't talk about sex. There was no intimate conversation. It was kind of hush, hush . . . I didn't know there were different ways." By way of contrast, this narrator recalls a visit to Winters, where other women were laughing about "sixty-nine." "I didn't get it. I went to [my partner] and said, 'Somebody says "sixty-nine" and everybody gets hysterical.'" Finally her partner learned what the laughter was all about. At that time our narrator would have mentioned such intimacies only with a lover. It wasn't until later that she got into bull sessions about such topics. Not surprisingly, this narrator does not recall having been taught about sex. She remembers being scared during her first lesbian experience, then found that she knew what to do "naturally." She had no early affairs with partners older than herself.

The Winters' patrons had a more open, experimental attitude toward sex; they discussed it unreservedly and accepted the practice of oral sex. These women threw parties in which women tried threesomes and daisy chains. "People would try it and see how it worked out. But nothing really happened. One person would always get angry and leave, and they would end up with two." Even if their sexual adventures did not always turn out as planned, these women were unquestionably innovative for their time. Our narrator from the Winters' crowd reminisced that it was always a contrast to go home to the serene life of her religious family. She also raved about two fems who were her instructors in sexual matters, adding, "I was an apt pupil."

During the fifties the picture changed, and the mores of the Ralph Martin's group virtually disappeared. Sex came to be a conversation topic among all social groups. Oral sex became an accepted form of lovemaking, so that an individual who did not practice it was acting on personal preference rather than on ignorance or social proscription. In addition, most of our fifties' butch narrators recall having been teachers or students of sex. As in the Winters' group in the forties, an important teacher for the butch was the fem. "I had one girl who had been around who told me. I guess I really frustrated the hell out of her. And she took a piece of paper and drew me a picture and she said, 'Now you get this spot right here.' I felt like a jerk. I was embarrassed that she had to tell me this." According to our narrator, the lesson helped, and she explains: "I went on to greater and better things."

The fifties also saw the advent of a completely new practice— experienced butches teaching novice butches about sex. One narrator remembers that younger women frequently approached her with questions about sex: "There must be an X on my back. They just pick me out. . . . " She recalls one young butch who "had to know every single detail. She drove me crazy. Jesus Christ, y'know, just get down there and do it—y'get so aggravated." The woman who aggravated her gives the following account of learning about sex:

> And I finally talked to a butch buddy of mine. . . . She was a real tough one. I asked her "What do you do when you make love to a woman?" And we sat up for hours and hours at a time. . . . "I feel sexually aroused by this woman, but if I take her to bed, what am I gonna do?" And she says, "Well, what do you feel like doing?" and I says, "Well, the only thing I can think of doing is . . . all I want to do is touch her, but what is the full thing of it . . . you know." So when [she] told me I says, "Really," well there was this one thing in there, uh . . . I don't know if you want me to state it. Maybe I can . . . well, I won't . . . I'll put in terms that you can understand. Amongst other things, the oral gratification. Well, that kind of floored me because I never expected something like that and I thought, well, who knows, I might like it.

She later describes her first sexual experience in which she was so scared that her friend had to shove her into the bedroom where the girl was waiting.

At the same time that attitudes toward discussions of and teachings about sexuality relaxed, the fifties' lesbian community became stricter in enforcing role-appropriate sexuality. Those who deviated from the pattern in the forties might have identified themselves as "lavender butch" and might have been labeled by others as "comme ci, comme ça." Although their divergence from the social norm would have been noticed and discussed, such women were not stigmatized. But the community of the fifties left little room to deviate. Those who did not consistently follow one role in bed were considered "ki-ki" (neither-nor), or more infrequently "AC/DC," both pejorative terms imposed by the community. Such women were viewed as disruptive of the social order and not to be trusted. They not only elicited negative comments, but they also were often ostracized from social groups. From the perspective of the 1980s, in which mutuality in lovemaking is emphasized as a positive quality, it is important to clarify that "ki-ki" did not refer to an abandonment of role-defined sex but rather to a shifting of sexual posture depending upon one's bed partner. Therefore, it was grounded absolutely in role playing. One of our narrators in fact defined "ki-ki" as "double role playing."[14]

These contradictory trends in attitudes and norms of lesbian sexuality parallel changes in the heterosexual world. Movement toward open discussion of sex, the acceptance of oral sex, and the teaching about sex took place in the society at large, as exemplified by the publication of and the material contained in the Kinsey reports.[15] Similarly, the lesbian community's stringent enforcement of role-defined behavior in the fifties occurred in the context of straight society's postwar move toward a stricter sexual division of labor and the ideology that accompanied it.[16] These parallels indicate a close connection between the evolution of heterosexual and homosexual cultures, a topic that requires further research.[17] At this point, we wish to stress that drawing parallels with heterosexuality can only partially illuminate changes in lesbian sexual mores. As an integral part of lesbian life, lesbian sexuality undergoes transformations that correspond with changing forms of the community's resistance to oppression.

Two developments occurred in this prepolitical period that are fundamental for the later emergence of the lesbian and gay liberation movement of the sixties. The first development was the flourishing of a lesbian culture; the second was the evolving stance of public defiance. The community of the forties was just beginning to support places for public gatherings and socializing, and during this period lesbians were to be found in bars only on weekends. Narrators of the forties do not remember having role models or anyone willing to instruct them in the ways of gay life. The prevalent feeling was that gay life was hard, and if people wanted it, they had to find it for themselves. In the fifties, the number of lesbian bars increased, and lesbians could be found socializing there every night of the week. As bar culture became more elaborate and open, lesbians more freely exchanged information about all aspects of their social lives, including sexuality. Discussion of sex was one of many dimensions of an increasingly complex culture. The strengthening of lesbian culture and the concomitant repression of gays in the fifties led the community to take a more public stance. This shift toward public confrontation subsequently generated enough sense of pride to counter the acknowledged detriments of gay life so that members of the community were willing to instruct newcomers both socially and sexually. Almost all our narrators who came out in the fifties remember a butch who served as a role model or remember acting as a role model themselves. Instruction about sexuality was part of a general education to community life that developed in the context of expanding community pride.

However, the community's growing public defiance was also related to its increased concern for enforcing role-appropriate behavior in the fifties. Butches were key in this process of fighting back. The butches alone, or the butch-fem couple, were always publicly visible as they walked down the street, announcing themselves to the world. To deal effectively with the hostility of the straight world, and to support one another in physical confrontations, the community developed, for butches in particular, rules of appropriate behavior and forms of organization and exerted pressure on butches to live up to these standards. Because roles organized intimate life, as well as the community's resistance to oppression, sexual performance was a vital part of these fifties' standards.

From the vantage point of the 1980s and twenty more years of lesbian and gay history, we know that just as evolving community politics created this tension between open discussion and teaching about sex and strict enforcement of role-appropriate sexual behavior, it also effected the resolution. Our research suggests that in the late sixties in Buffalo, with the development of the political activities of gay liberation, explicitly political organizations and tactics replaced butch-fem roles in leading the resistance to gay oppression. Because butch-fem roles were no longer the primary means for organizing the community's stance toward the straight world, the community no longer needed to enforce role-appropriate behavior.[18] This did not mean that butch-fem roles disappeared. As part of a long tradition of creating an authentic lesbian culture in an oppressive society, butch-fem roles remain, for many lesbians, an important code of personal behavior in matters of either appearance, sexuality, or both.

Notes

This article is a revision of a paper originally presented at the "International Conference on Women's History and Oral History," Columbia University, New York, 18 November 1983. We want to thank Michael Frisch, Ellen DuBois, and Bobbi Prebis for reading the original version and offering us helpful comments. We also want to thank Rayna Rapp and Ronald Grele for their patience throughout the revision process.

1. This research is part of the work of the Buffalo Women's Oral History Project, which was founded in 1978 with three goals: (1) to produce a comprehensive, written history of the lesbian community in Buffalo, New York, using as the major source, oral histories of lesbians who came out prior to 1970; (2) to create and index an archive of oral history tapes, written interviews, and relevant supplementary materials; (3) to give this history back to the community from which it derives. Madeline Davis and Elizabeth (Liz) Kennedy are the directors of the project. Avra Michelson was an active member from 1978 to 1981 and had a very important influence on the development of the project. Wanda Edwards has been an active member of the project since 1981, particularly in regard to research on the Black lesbian community and on racism in the white lesbian community. For our expanded discussion of lesbian sexuality, see *Boots of Leather, Slippers of Gold: The History of a Lesbian Community* (New York: Routledge, 1993), chap. 6, " 'Now You Get This Spot Right Here': Butch-Fem Sexuality during the 1940s and 1950s," 191–230.

2. This hypothesis was shaped by our personal contact with Buffalo lesbians who came out in the 1940s and 1950s, and by discussion with grassroots gay and lesbian history projects around the country, in particular, the San Francisco Lesbian and Gay History Project, the Boston Area Gay and Lesbian History Project, and the Lesbian Herstory Archives. Our approach is close to and has been influenced by the social constructionist tendency of lesbian and gay history. See, in particular, Jonathan Katz, *Gay American History: Lesbians and Gay Men in the U.S.A.* (New York: Thomas Y. Crowell Co., 1976); Gayle Rubin, Introduction to *A Woman Appeared to Me* by Renée Vivien (Nevada: Naiad Press, 1976), iii–xxxvii; Jeffrey Weeks, *Coming Out: Homosexual Politics in Britain from the Nineteenth Century to the Present* (London: Quartet Books, 1977). We want to thank all these sources which have been inspirational to our work.

3. The Buffalo Women's Oral History Project has written two papers on bar life, both by Madeline Davis, Elizabeth (Liz) Kennedy, and Avra Michelson: "Buffalo Lesbian Bars in the Fifties," presented at the National Women's Studies Association, Bloomington, Indiana, May 1980, and "Buffalo Lesbian Bars: 1930–1960," presented at the Fifth Berkshire Conference on the History of Women, Vassar College, Poughkeepsie, N.Y., June 1981. Both papers are on file at the Lesbian Herstory Archives, P.O. Box 1258, New York, NY 10116.

4. We think that this community could accurately be designated as a working-class lesbian community, but this is not a concept many members of this community would use; therefore, we have decided to call it a public bar community.

5. All quotations are taken from the interviews conducted for this project between 1978 and 1984. The use of the phrase "lesbian and her girl" in this quote reflects some of our butch narrators' belief that the butch member of a couple was the lesbian and the fem member's identity was less clear.

6. A variety of sources were helpful for learning about issues and problems of oral history research. They include the Special Issue on Women's Oral History, *Frontiers* 2 (Summer 1977); Willa K. Baum, *Oral History for the Local Historical Society* (Nashville, Tenn.: American Association for State and Local History, 1974); Michael Frisch, "Oral History and *Hard Times:* A Review Essay," *Oral History Review* (1979): 70–80; Ronald Grele, ed., *Envelopes of Sound: Six Practitioners Discuss the Method, Theory, and Practice of Oral History and Oral Tradition* (Chicago: Precedent Publishing, 1975); Ronald Grele, "Can Anyone over Thirty Be Trusted? A Friendly Critique of Oral History," *Oral History Review* (1978): 36–44; "Generations: Women in the South," *Southern Exposure* 4 (Winter 1977); "No More Moanin'," *Southern Exposure* 1 (Winter 1974); Peter Friedlander, *The Emergence of a UAW Local, 1936–1939* (Pittsburgh: University of Pittsburgh Press, 1975); William Lynwood Montell, *The Saga of Coe Ridge: A Study in Oral History* (Knoxville: University of Tennessee Press, 1970); Studs Terkel, *Hard Times: An Oral History of the Great Depression* (New York: Pantheon Books, 1970); Martin B. Duberman, *Black Mountain: An Exploration in Community* (Garden City, N.J.: Doubleday, 1972); Sherna Gluck, ed., *From Parlor to Prison: Five American Suffragists Talk about Their Lives* (New York: Vintage, 1976); and Kathy Kahn, *Hillbilly Women* (New York: Doubleday, 1972).

7. For a helpful discussion of memory, see John A. Neuenschwander, "Rememberance of Things Past: Oral Historians and Long-Term Memory," *Oral History Review* (1978): 46–53; many sources cited in the previous note also have relevant discussions of memory; in particular, see Frisch; Grele, *Envelopes of Sound;* Friedlander; and Montell.

8. See, for instance, Joan Nestle, "Esther's Story: 1960," *Common Lives/Lesbian Lives* 1 (Fall 1981): 5–9; Joan Nestle, "Butch-Fem Relationships, Sexual Courage in the 1950s," *Heresies* 12 (1981): 21–24; Audre Lorde, "Tar Beach," *Conditions,* no. 5 (Autumn 1979): 34–47; and Audre Lorde, "The Beginning," in *Lesbian Fiction,* ed. Elly Bulkin (Watertown, Mass.: Persephone Press, 1981), 255–74. Lesbian pulp fiction can also provide insight into the emotional and sexual life of this period; see, for instance, Ann Bannon's *I Am a Woman* (Greenwich, Conn.: Fawcett Publications, 1959), and *Beebo Brinker* (Greenwich, Conn.: Fawcett Publications, 1962).

9. See, for instance, Nestle, "Butch-Fem Relationships"; Lorde; Del Martin and Phyllis Lyon, *Lesbian/Woman* (New York: Bantam Books, 1972); John D'Emilio, *Sexual Politics, Sexual Communities: The Making of a Homosexual Minority in the United States, 1940–1970* (Chicago: University of Chicago Press, 1983).

10. For a full discussion of our research on butch-fem roles, see Madeline Davis and Elizabeth (Liz) Kennedy, "Butch-Fem Roles in the Buffalo Lesbian Community, 1940–1960" (Paper presented at the Gay Academic Union Conference, Chicago, October 1982). This paper is on file at the Lesbian Herstory Archives.

11. These two main determinants of roles are quite different from what would usually be considered as indicators of sex roles in straight society; they do not include the sexual division of labor.

12. The origins of the "stone butch" and fem couple are beyond the scope of this paper. For an article that begins to approach these issues, see Esther Newton, "The Mythic Mannish Lesbian: Radclyffe Hall and the New Woman," *Signs* 9 (Summer 1984): 557–75.

13. Our understanding of the fem role has been enhanced by the following: Nestle's "Butch-Fem Relationships" and "Esther's Story"; Amber Hollibaugh and Cherrie Moraga, "What We're Rolling Around in Bed With: Sexual Silences in Feminism: A Conversation toward Ending Them," *Heresies* 12 (1981): 58–62.

14. For indications that "ki-ki" was used nationally in the lesbian subculture, see Jonathan Katz, *Gay/Lesbian Almanac, A New Documentary* (New York: Harper & Row, 1983), 15, 626.

15. Alfred C. Kinsey, Wardell B. Pomeroy, and Clyde E. Martin, *Sexual Behavior in the Human Male* (Philadelphia: W.B. Saunders Co., 1948); and Alfred Kinsey et al., *Sexual Behavior in the Human Female* (Philadelphia: W.B. Saunders Co., 1953). Numerous sources document this trend; see, for instance, Ann Snitow, Christine Stansell, and Sharon Thompson, eds, *Powers of Desire: The Politics of Sexuality* (New York: Monthly Review Press, 1983), in particular, Introduction, sec. 2, "Sexual Revolutions," and sec. 3, "The Institution of Heterosexuality," 9–47, 115–71, 173–275; and Katz, *Gay/Lesbian Almanac.*

16. See Mary P. Ryan, *Womanhood in America: From Colonial Times to the Present* (New York: Franklin Watts, 1975).

17. A logical result of the social constructionist school of gay history is to consider that heterosexuality is also a social construction. Katz, in *Gay/Lesbian Almanac,* begins to explore this idea.

18. Although national homophile organizations began in the fifties, no such organizations developed in Buffalo until the formation of the Mattachine Society of the Niagara Frontier in 1969. But we do not think that the lack of early homophile organizations in this city made the bar community's use of roles as an organizer of its stance toward the straight world different from that of cities where homophile organizations existed. In general, these organizations, whether mixed or all women, did not draw from or affect bar communities. Martin and Lyon in chap. 8, "Lesbians United," *Lesbian/Woman* (238–79), present Daughters of Bilitis (DOB) as an alternative for those dissatisfied with bar life, not as an organization to coalesce the forces and strengths of the bar community. Gay liberation combined the political organization of DOB and the defiance and pride of bar life and therefore affected and involved both communities.

The Rise and Fall of Feminist Organizations in the 1970s: Dayton as a Case Study

☐ In 1972 the U.S. Congress passed the Equal Rights Amendment (ERA), *Ms.* magazine published its first issue, and women ran in the Boston marathon for the first time. A decade of federal congressional and executive decision making had created a new legal structure that seemed to nourish feminism. Who could doubt that the movement would continue to make gains when in less than a decade it had achieved the Equal Pay Act, affirmative action programs, Title VII and Title IX, the Equal Employment Opportunity Commission, and other programs? Who could doubt, given the overwhelming majority favoring the amendment in the Washington vote, that state ratification for the ERA would take place quickly and easily? Who could doubt, given the continued flood of women into the work force, that wage disparities would soon begin to disappear? Who could doubt that by the 1980s the prospects for feminism would not seem even brighter?

What feminist would have thought that instead, in 1981, even such a staunch supporter of the women's movement as Barbara Ehrenreich would write that feminism had "peaked" and that forces of antifeminism were becoming ever more powerful?[1] What feminist in 1972 would have predicted a decade's bitter battle and final defeat for the ERA? What feminist would have predicted the overwhelming re-election in 1984 of a president who headed an administration that openly derided the need for affirmative action programs and lobbied for a constitutional amendment banning abortion?

Feminists, then, do not enjoy the luxury to wax proud over victories or to be nostalgic over past battles lost or won. Instead, we need the kind of clear insight into the history of the movement that derives from careful analysis and documented research. Yet such research is not

Reprinted, with changes, from *Feminist Studies* 12, no. 2 (Summer 1986): 321–410. © 1986 by Judith Sealander and Dorothy Smith.

readily available. In 1968 feminist protest at the annual Miss America Contest got front page coverage as American newspapers filled with stories of man-hating bra burners. Almost twenty years later, much of the analysis of contemporary feminism has remained on that condescending and inaccurate level. Although a few scholars have attempted to study gains and failures of contemporary feminism, their articles remain tentative and speculative, more concerned with the origins than the nature of the movement, and in need of the concrete detail a case study can provide.[2]

Why choose Dayton, Ohio, for such a case study? First, a wealth of evidence exists. Due to the aggressive collecting policies of a Wright State University archivist, the complete organizational files of three important feminist groups have been saved and inventoried. Membership lists in the files of each organization provided the names of many people to contact for interviews. The extensive nature of written and oral evidence about the history of feminist organizations in Dayton may, in fact, be unparalleled. To our knowledge, the records of contemporary feminist organizations in many other cities are still held in private hands or have been lost or destroyed.

Second, the fact that the records of Dayton Women's Liberation, the Dayton Women's Center, and Dayton Women Working sit in cardboard boxes at a university archive rather than in cabinets in organizational offices suggests another reason to choose Dayton, Ohio, for historical case study. The decade, 1970 to 1980, exists as a meaningful and completed period in the history of contemporary Dayton feminism, for three major organizations began and ended within that period. A look at their rise and fall raises questions and suggests answers about the nature of contemporary feminism that would be more difficult to derive from an examination of existing organizations.

Third, since the early twentieth century, Dayton has shared with Muncie, Indiana, a reputation as a typical small American city. Pollsters in the 1970s continued to choose the city of roughly 200,000 citizens for random sampling with decidedly unrandom regularity. It was a frequent test market, and its population was given sneak previews of new movies, soaps, and underarm deodorants.[3] Pollster Richard Scammon claimed that the average American voter was "a forty-seven-year-old housewife from the outskirts of Dayton, Ohio, whose husband is a machinist."[4]

Moreover, Dayton typified the problems of many American towns and communities trying to make the often painful shift from an industrial to a service economy. Although manufacturing in Dayton declined by over 20 percent during the 1970s, and one company alone laid off more than 14,000 workers, Dayton achieved a net gain for the decade of 17,000 new jobs. Most of the jobs, however, were "women's jobs"—jobs in the lower-paying service sectors. In 1950, Dayton, per capita, possessed the highest number of color televisions in the country. It was a city filled with people whose healthy paychecks, earned in the area's auto, tire, and printing factories, made the purchase of such luxuries possible. By 1970, Dayton no longer enjoyed that enviable image of a city of highly paid, skilled, union workers. Service sector work had filled the gaps caused by the closing of plants but had not fattened wallets. The new "typical" Dayton worker was a female bank teller, not a unionized auto worker. Therefore, a history of feminism in Dayton can provide an examination of organizational success and failure in a city widely viewed as far more typical than New York, Chicago, San Francisco, or Boston—the four "movement" cities which, to date, remain the focus of most journalistic comment about feminism. Such a history can also provide an examination of feminist organizations in a city which typified, sometimes even prophesied, changes in the national economy that had the most direct and important implications for female roles and status.

☐ The women's movement arrived in Dayton in September 1969, via Ann Arbor, Michigan, not, as might have been expected, via nearby Antioch College in Yellow Springs, Ohio. Cheryl Radican, a University of Cincinnati student, had herself newly arrived in Dayton, accompanying her divinity school student husband. While commuting back and forth to Cincinnati to finish her degree, Radican also began to write for Dayton's recently established "underground" newspaper, the *Minority Report*, a Left-liberal newsletter staffed by volunteers who wrote the stories and then sold the issues on street corners and area college campuses. At a national underground newspaper conference in Ann Arbor in the summer of 1969, Radican met other women angry about their subordinate roles on their publications. As had happened at earlier meetings of student radicals, the women at the newspaper conference formed a separate caucus and told the men to stay away.[5]

Radican, "filled with the power of sisterhood," enthusiastically returned home and formed Dayton's first consciousness-raising (CR) group.[6] This first group grew rapidly by word of mouth. By January 1970 a new CR group formed every month, first in Dayton neighborhoods and then on nearby college campuses like Antioch and Wright State University in Dayton. The typical woman in these groups was not a radical even though Radican and many of her friends saw themselves as social activists, committed especially to protesting the war in Vietnam. A member of a CR group was likely to be white, "liberal Democrat," college-educated, married, and middle class. In 1969, she was far more likely to be in school or at home than she was to be at work full-time, although she was not necessarily at home with small children.[7] At least one-quarter of the women in the first CR groups were middle-aged, self-described "*Better Homes and Gardens* housewives . . . casualties of the 1950s."[8] Radican first organized her friends, and not surprisingly, these friends were often students, wives of ministers or divinity students, wives of teachers or college professors, or women active in the League of Women Voters and church children's education groups.[9]

The experience of joining CR groups, however, often proved radicalizing to these nonradical women. In the mid-sixties, hundreds of similarly earnest middle-class white women had gone south demanding civil rights for Blacks. They expected opposition. They did not expect to be treated as inferiors and maids by their own coworkers and as "loose" women by the press. Similarly, in 1970, members of three CR groups in Dayton traveled to Columbus, Ohio, to take part in a large proabortion rally. They returned to find themselves described by the local media as "fourteen braless, make-up-less women." In fact, as one participant exclaimed, "We were all carefully dressed. One of us was in a mink coat and open-toed shoes. . . . They [reporters] just kept asking if the women were wearing bras."[10]

By mid-1970, these kinds of patronizing experiences convinced women in several CR groups that they had to unite, take their case to the public, and work with more than the ten to twelve women in their own groups. Dayton Women's Liberation emerged from these discussions. It quickly established a phone bank, staffed by members who answered questions about feminism. It set up a speakers' bureau; members traveled to high schools, police stations, and—on a regular basis—the television studio where Phil Donahue, still a local Dayton talk show host, filmed his programs. Although the organization issued a pamphlet denouncing the Vietnam War, Dayton Women's Liberation generally continued to emphasize small CR groups, rather than political activism. And most of these CR groups continued to explore personal issues, such as relationships with mothers, children, and husbands. By 1975, however, two other feminist organizations that were more concerned with programs to change politics and society—the Women's Center and Dayton Women Working—had joined Dayton Women's Liberation.

In 1973, the Dayton City Commission granted Dayton Women's Liberation funds to establish a "neighborhood Women's Center, focusing on the needs of women in the surrounding area . . . establishing a place for women to explore common concerns, to share and expand their knowledge." The proposal outlined several programs: self-help classes, a walk-in center and meeting place for women, an advocacy and referral service for women in need, political and personal counseling, a lending library, childcare for women using the center, and educational programs.[11]

Dayton Women Working initially was a product of one Dayton Women's Center member's efforts to engage in "political counseling and action."[12] In 1975, frustrated that her male colleagues in the Dayton chapter of the socialist New American Movement (NAM) did not take women's employment issues seriously, Sherrie Holmes organized the first Dayton chapter of the National Organization for Women (NOW) and drew up plans for a Women in the Work Force Task Force. Within months the NOW task force decided to establish itself as a separate organization, choosing in April 1975 the name, Dayton Women Working.

Dayton Women Working, begun in protest of her male colleagues' inattention by a woman who saw herself as a socialist and radical, linked the women's movement in Dayton to the New Left and linked Dayton to a national network of feminist groups interested in workplace problems. In fact, Dayton Women Working helped to create that network. In 1977, Dayton Women Working was a founding member of the National Women's Employment Project (NWEP), a consortium of six working women's organizations. The NWEP, launched with a $25,000 grant from the Rockefeller Family Fund, chose to emphasize the problems of office workers and to focus first on an employer "notorious" for discrimination against women clerical workers: the banking industry.[13] Dayton Women Working joined with the older and better-established consortium members, especially Boston's 9 to 5, and adopted this emphasis.

What did these three groups accomplish? How did they fail? In what ways did their troubles illustrate problems faced by other feminist groups in other cities? What is their legacy? Examination of programs, finances, and membership can provide partial answers to these questions. Organized feminism in Dayton in the 1970s achieved communitywide visibility with well-planned campaigns and successful projects. Because it did not succeed, however, in anchoring itself to a stable base of committed dues-paying members, it suffered continual money and membership problems.

The Women's Center rented a two-story frame house on North Main Street near downtown Dayton in October 1973. Cleaning, painting, and floor-waxing parties generated enthusiasm and prepared the building for occupancy. More than 100 women attended a grand opening party in January 1974.[14] Within months the center had a full program of activities, including classes in self-defense, women's legal rights, careers, health, sexuality, auto mechanics, pottery, and yoga. Two therapy groups met weekly. There were regular community forums on topics of interest to women, such as daycare options and married women's property rights. Building on the Dayton Women's Liberation tradition, the staff compiled information for a referral service for women in need of community services.

Several women's groups met at the center, including a parent support group, a socialist/feminist discussion group, the Women on Rape Task Force, and a large lesbian organization called Sappho's Army. The center's four paid staff members, as well as members of its collective, accepted invitations to speak at local universities, church groups, Parent Teacher Association groups, social workers' associations, and women's clubs. The Women's Center began to issue a newsletter, and stories about the center appeared in eight local newspapers, and on two radio and two television stations. After the center had been open for two months, the collective reported that more than 300 women had used the center's facilities.[15]

By 1975, the Women's Center programs had expanded significantly. Hundreds of women used its facilities for classes, counseling and feminist therapy, and activities and discussion groups. The center's referral service thrived, passing along the names of feminist doctors, lawyers, and welfare workers. It also provided advice to women about employment and legal rights and maintained regularly updated files on educational opportunities, as well as files of job listings and financial aid.[16] In 1975, the center opened an extremely popular Daycare Parents' Cooperative.[17] The Women's Center's many programs thus made feminism quite visible in Dayton. It "was a smorgasbord of services," and during its seven-year history approximately two thousand Dayton women a year helped themselves.[18]

Dayton Women Working also spread the feminist message in Dayton with initially successful, attention-getting projects. Member organizations of the National Women's Employment Project—Women Employed in Chicago, 9 to 5 in Boston, Dayton Women Working, Cleveland Women Working, Women Organized for Employment in San Francisco, and Women Office Workers in New York—agreed to monitor and investigate the effectiveness of post-1964 federal antidiscrimination laws and executive orders.[19] NWEP's own effectiveness suffered from serious internal disputes about equitable distribution of grant monies which led to the departure, by October 1977, of Women Employed in Chicago. Nevertheless, the five remaining organizations set to work on a national investigation of conditions for female clerical workers in banks.[20]

Dayton Women Working plunged enthusiastically into the project, which was designed to provide both a case study of employment discrimination against women and a study of the degree of employer compliance with antidiscrimination laws. The group's analysis of the banking industry of Dayton was to be its most important project and most significant success. It soon learned that three-quarters of the employees of the three major banks in Dayton were women, and more than 89 percent of these women worked in poorly paid office and clerical jobs. Using bank affirmative action reports, surveys and interviews with female bank employees, annual reports, banking directories, and other documents in the public record, Dayton Women Working printed a pamphlet that charged, among other things, that major Dayton banks were not seriously committed to equal employment opportunity. As one letter to a bank stated, banks limited affirmative action efforts to the creation of affirmative action plans that were "inadequate" and out of date.[21] Banks, as holders of federal deposits, had the status of federal contractors and as such had to fulfill federal guidelines regarding affirmative action in employment. The Labor Department, as the agency charged with enforcement of contract compliance, agreed in 1978 to investigate Dayton Women Working's charges that Third National, First National, and Winters National banks of Dayton practiced employment discrimination against women.[22]

The "banking study" generated much local publicity, and open meetings attracted large crowds.[23] Women employed in banks began to mail in anonymous testimonials. Citing fear of job reprisal, one woman (who, like most bank employees, asked that her name not be used in Dayton Women Working publicity) wrote: "I used to be a person who was hurt that I was paid so little. I thought there was something wrong with me, that I was being singled out. However, I recently learned that this is not the case, that many of the women in my department that have been with the bank a long time, make even less than I do."[24]

Barred from distributing materials within banking offices, members of Dayton Women Working stood on downtown street corners handing out more than two thousand questionnaires to women office workers headed toward banks. Women who filled out the twenty-six-item questionnaires were to use a point system to rate their jobs: a "yes" equaled two points, a "not sure" was one point, and a "no" was zero points. Questions included: "Are you permitted to discuss salaries with coworkers?" "Are there training programs available within your bank?" "Are women promoted at the same rate as men?" "Is there an effective grievance procedure to deal with discrimination?" Banks rating fewer than twenty points were "not good places to work. Watch out or call D.W.W."[25] In May of 1980, U.S. Department of Labor investigators charged Third National Bank with a "pattern of discrimination against its minority and women employees" and in initial review documents assessed nearly one million dollars in back pay for 110 employees who had "suffered the effects of past discrimination."[26]

However, by 1980 Dayton Women Working, on the verge of disbanding, was unable to capitalize on this victory. Despite its many programs and its contact with thousands of Dayton women who used its services, the Dayton Women's Center was equally unable to use the visibility and success of many of its projects to enter the next decade as a strong and growing feminist organization. As early as 1975 most Dayton Women's Liberation CR groups had ceased to meet. Personal and ideological conflicts, declining activism, and small membership, as well as recurrent financial crises, were all problems that plagued organized feminism in Dayton.

A staff of four paid workers ran the Women's Center and oversaw its programs. A Women's Center collective, with a rotating leadership, provided that staff with program and policy direction. Almost from the beginning, conflicts marred relationships between collective and staff. Even more importantly, the collective itself often divided into two warring camps. One group identified itself as socialist and saw women as an oppressed class to be organized as part of a larger movement to transform society. The other group defined itself as feminist, wanted an independent women's movement, saw women's issues as most important, and feared a close association with male-led politics. The conflict became bitter and open early in 1977, when some NAM members, including men, used the printing facilities at the Women's Center. Angry memos flew between the two factions, and collective meetings became battlegrounds.[27]

In retrospect, Kathy Ellison, who judged herself to be a neutral collective member, felt that the fights were more personal than political. "From time to time these great political struggles would happen. I never thought the conflict was real, I felt it was more personality and power struggles. For whatever reasons, these strong-minded women didn't get along, and they had to imbue their interpersonal fights with issue overtones."[28] But Robin Suits, a longtime member of both the collective and the staff, perceived that in the women's movement the personal *was* political. "As your consciousness got raised, and you began to see things in more political ways, you got a sense that there was only one right way. Everybody had a slightly different way, and the groups became smaller and more splintered over the most ridiculous things."[29]

Both the Women's Center and Dayton Women's Liberation, each with at least some connections to student activism or the New Left, adopted the antihierarchical, antileader stances of these other movements.

Members of Students for a Democratic Society (SDS), for instance, proclaimed: "Let the people decide." A rhetoric of shared decision making, however, did not prevent many New Left groups from following a strong leader. An emphasis on democracy, in fact, contributed to split many groups into competing factions. And Dayton feminist groups were not unique. With so many problems facing women demanding attention, disagreement readily surfaced about which problems were most important. By 1970, across the country, feminists debated priority lists for problems and challenged each other's analyses of the causes of sexism. Radical feminists, such as the New York Radical Feminists, the Feminists, and the Redstockings, emphasized the universality of male oppression. Socialist feminist groups like Bread and Roses considered class structure important too. Male domination could not be explained or countered in universalist terms. More moderate groups like NOW called for neither drastic changes in traditional marriage and childrearing patterns nor for an economic revolution. Instead, they urged legal, educational, and employment opportunity reforms; changes in states' property rights laws; the passage of the ERA; and equal access for women to schools and jobs.[30]

The emphasis on equality and democracy itself caused tension. In Dayton Women's Liberation, for instance, women selected CR groups by lot. The random choice procedure obviously emphasized common sisterhood and equality, but also it meant that groups were formed of women who sometimes had little in common. An early member of one such group, Carrie LaBriola recalled: "I actively disliked some of the people [in my group]." It meant, for some, that discussions of controversial topics, like abortion, were "too painful" and ceased. Here too the Dayton experiences echoed those in other cities. In New York one disgruntled member called the Feminists' emphasis on egalitarianism "an anti-individual mania." By 1970, the Feminists' lot system for division of tasks had become more elaborate; new rules sought to prevent the formation of cliques or the emergence of "stars." But the system, instead of bringing egalitarian harmony, contributed to conflicts that caused many members to resign.[31]

Painful discussions and memberships splintered into factions were not problems for Dayton Women Working, but apathy was. Noreen Willhelm and Sherrie Holmes, the two driving forces behind Dayton Women Working, were white political activists in their twenties. The average member of Dayton Women Working was also a young white woman.[32] Nevertheless, neither Willhelm nor Holmes led lives similar to those of their members. Neither had ever married; both had borne babies out of wedlock. Both lived in communal houses, had come of age in the late sixties as anti-Vietnam War protestors, and had ties with leftist politics. In fact, to blur the differences between themselves and the more traditional members Willhelm and Holmes once discussed wearing phoney wedding rings to meetings.[33] Kathy Ellison, a friend of Holmes and a member of Dayton Women Working while a law student, remembered that Holmes and Willhelm made decisions to avoid certain feminist issues that might "alienate your average secretary or clerk." She recalled that abortion, socialism, and lesbianism, for instance, were not to be debated.

The leaders of Dayton Women Working staged many imaginative events that grabbed newspaper headlines. For instance, the group's Pettiest Boss awards earned the organization plenty of free local publicity. Contenders for one Petty Boss contest included the head of a jewelry firm who used clear nail polish on his fingernails and had his secretary paint the right hand nails, a boss who required an employee to go to his home to feed his dog, a physician who sent his bookkeeper downtown to buy a plunger to fix a clogged toilet, and a businessman who required his secretary to check him over carefully each day to see that he was properly dressed and that his socks matched. Charles Moody, the physician, received his award when several Dayton Women Working members showed up at his offices unannounced to deliver a toilet plunger, with a rose attached.[34]

Still, despite the efforts of Holmes and other "spokespersons"[35] who generated publicity and avoided controversial topics such as lesbianism, Dayton Women Working leaders failed to recruit an active membership. A memo Holmes sent to the national NAM program coordinating board illustrated a major problem. Rather than viewing her members as friends and compatriots, she seemed to see them as "the clerical sector." Unsuccessfully urging the national NAM leadership to support her efforts, she argued that "this (Dayton) project is important because (1) it is an important part of a nation-wide test of the organizing potential of clericals, (2) it is important for N.A.M. to build ties with this sector, (3) it is important to build ties with other clerical organizers."[36]

Of course, historical examples of successful movements in which leaders were not friends with their followers abound. Holmes did not have to be "your average secretary or clerk"; she did not have to marry and share her members' personal lives or moral values. But she did have to build ties. She did have to convince members that Dayton Women Working deserved their loyalty, support, and dedication, that the organization could be a vehicle for change in their lives.

In fact, Dayton Women Working leaders did build some ties with other clerical organizers, government officials, and private philanthropists.

But ties with their own members, who became accustomed to having programs delivered to them ready-made, were the crucial and neglected ones. Phrases in Holmes's letter echoed those used to justify projects such as the 1965 Economic Research and Action Projects (ERAP) of SDS, meant to build ties with the "urban poverty sector." The northern college student radicals who decamped to urban poverty in 1965 and 1966 were often genuinely committed to helping. They worked hard, received no salary, and lived on peanut butter. Some ERAP projects, such as those in Boston and Cleveland, succeeded in organizing welfare mothers, sowing the seeds for a national welfare rights movement. But many ERAP projects failed at least partially because their leaders were unable to communicate a sense of shared interest and mission with the often confused, sometimes hostile, residents of urban ghettoes.[37]

Holmes's rhetoric also echoed that of some early-twentieth-century American feminists. Alice Paul, for instance, had tried during the 1920s to make the National Woman's Party a "vanguard" party, promoting absolute equality for women, including "industrial equality" for women workers. But few workers joined the National Woman's Party; it remained a small organization of well-educated women, run in an authoritarian fashion by Paul and her coterie.[38] Sherrie Holmes was not another feminist generation's version of Alice Paul, however. She was no blue blood, sporting graduate degrees. She defined herself as a leftist but had no master plan for Dayton Women Working to emerge as a vanguard party—still her attempts to forge links between leftist activists and women workers echoed Paul's. And like Paul, she seemed to possess greater skill in constructing phrases strategically calculated to appeal to leftists than to politically moderate women workers.

Of course, Dayton Women Working was part of a larger network and linked its work to that of the NWEP. In each of the NWEP chapters, Noreen Willhelm argued, one woman "*was*" the organization. If Sherrie Holmes "was" Dayton Women Working, Helen Williams "was" Cleveland Women Working, and Karen Nussbaum "was" Boston 9 to 5. In that respect, at least, the entire NWEP resembled the National Woman's Party, in which "[Alice Paul] is the party."[39] These strong, intelligent women took on big challenges. But in many cases, not just that of Dayton Women Working, the romance of battles against American banking czars or federal power brokers wooed them away from the tedium of membership drives and they, with feminist leaders from past decades, reproduced organizations without sufficient grass-roots strength. And women office workers, socialized already by job and family to be deferential and quiet, were often silent when they confronted their own organizations' authority figures. Unlike meetings at the Dayton Women's

Center, which often boiled with charges, countercharges, and both good and bad feelings, Dayton Women Working held its meetings punctually at the end of workdays and followed Robert's Rules. Thousands of women utilized the services of the Women's Center; only a small percentage joined the collective and worked hard to keep the center a vital force in the community. Over two hundred women filled out membership cards and joined Dayton Women Working, but far fewer came regularly to meetings. Many did not even pay the nominal $3.00 yearly dues. If these groups had focused on grass-roots organization, would they have enjoyed greater success? A great influx of new members would not automatically have assured strength and stability. New Left organizing provides a cautionary example. In 1965, spurred by the escalation of the war in Vietnam, thousands of new members flooded into SDS, but such quick growth, Todd Gitlin has argued, did not really help the organization. All the new members and concomitant attention changed SDS into a mass movement too quickly, with leaders who increasingly became media stars, whose speeches were shaped by television and not constituency demands.[40]

Hundreds, even thousands, of active, committed members would not have ensured the longevity of Dayton Women Working, the Women's Center, or Dayton Women's Liberation. But such a membership could have provided a potential for strength. Through dues and donations it certainly could have provided funds. And lack of money became, along with membership recruitment and involvement, a serious problem for Dayton feminist groups, as well as their national umbrellas. On both a national and local level, leaders depended heavily on monies granted by the federal government or private philanthropies. When those funding sources disappeared, so too did the organizations they fostered. In that sense, feminist organizations in Dayton were not just outgrowths of 1960s' activism or products of the women's movement. They were also legacies of the national programs that had made federal monies available for local community action projects.

During the mid- and late-1960s, Dayton received large amounts of federal money under one of Lyndon Johnson's Great Society programs, Model Cities. Healthy Model Cities grants continued under the Nixon administration. In Dayton, locally elected Priority Boards made recommendations to the City Commission about projects in their neighborhoods to be funded by Model Cities.[41] In November 1973, the Dayton City Commission, using federal Model City monies, awarded the Women's Center $15,000.[42] Comprehensive Employment and Training Act (CETA) and Volunteers in Service to America (VISTA) money provided part-time staff positions and interns. At all times, between 1976 and 1980, the great bulk of monies available to Dayton Women Working were federal funds. CETA paid the salaries of its full-time director-organizer, its full-time program-organizer, and its part-time office manager.[43]

Between 1978 and 1979, the VISTA program provided funds for a VISTA worker, who was, ironically, installed at Dayton Women Working offices with federal money in order to "allow constituents to develop their leadership skills and make decisions" affecting Dayton Women Working. The paid VISTA worker was to "encourage members to volunteer their time."[44]

Dayton churches, like the Miami/Presbytery and the United Church of Christ, provided a few thousand dollars to Dayton Women Working and the Women's Center. By 1980, however, both organizations found that they "had worn out their welcome" at these private charities, which were inclined to give only one or two years of seed money.[45] In both organizations, membership dues provided only token support.

By 1980, Dayton Women's Liberation, Dayton Women Working, and the Dayton Women's Center had died. A preliminary autopsy would suggest that causes of death included excessive dependence on federal funding and ambitious programs that eclipsed grass-roots organizing. Such an autopsy would also note changes in political and economic climates. By 1980, Dayton organizations were certainly not the only feminist groups in the country to find funding sources less sympathetic and to experience a backlash against feminism. Finally, an autopsy would indicate that these three organizations died when subjected to the great stresses inherent in any social movement as it ages and moves from initial dreams and optimism to long-range realistic assessment. As Noreen Willhelm realized in retrospect, Dayton Women Working leaders "did get caught up in our myth before we had even created it."[46] Sherrie Holmes had "this initial fantasy about the Women's Center, that all we had to do was provide this place and women who wanted to change society would all come there and continue to build the movement."[47] Clearly, the slow building of a movement proved to be a harder task.

The task was complicated by the fact that organized feminism in Dayton, in common with organized feminism in other cities, failed to embrace working-class or minority women in any significant numbers, even though the Women's Center house was located in one of Dayton's few truly mixed-race neighborhoods. The leaders of the groups were white and overwhelmingly middle-class, women who sometimes seemed oblivious to a patronizing attitude when they tried to organize even white working-class women. Not surprisingly, meaningful contacts with the Black community proved difficult. Moreover, as Cheryl Radican explained, "We [in feminist organizations] felt a lot of hesitation" about recruiting Blacks. Radican and others who sympathized with the civil rights movement "did not want to drive a wedge into their Black unity."[48] These white women, who had little direct contact with the Black community and few friendships with Blacks, seemed to feel that, for Black women, issues of race superseded those of sex. The fact that many Black women might have agreed with such an assessment did not negate the fact that few were consulted.

Also complicating the task of building a movement was the fact that neither Dayton Women Working nor the Women's Center achieved a clear focus and sense of purpose. Dayton Women Working did not see itself as a union for clerical workers; in fact, its leaders made little attempt to contact leaders of Dayton unions. The union leadership in Dayton, a town where traditional heavy-industry unions like the Steel Workers and the United Auto Workers still dominated, returned the disdain. But Dayton Women Working did not really see itself as functioning as a women's center for women clerical workers, providing a place for women office workers to come to be together to talk about home lives, social relationships, and struggles at work.

Interestingly, the NWEP, which Dayton Women Working had helped create, did solve the dilemma of focus by forming a firm alliance with the union movement. NWEP, which ceased to exist formally in 1979, did not cease to exist in the same way that Dayton Women Working did. It became, under the new name "Working Women," a project of the National Association of Office Workers. In 1981, Working Women and the Service Employees International Union formed District 925, specifically to organize office workers.[49]

The Women's Center, by 1977 torn by dissension, had its own problems setting an agenda. Frequent and bitter controversies erupted. Some collective members thought the center should be more openly socialist; others sought to downplay leftist politics. Some wanted a more visible role for lesbians; some did not. Even the wildly successful daycare co-op caused conflict as babies and children crowded into space formerly devoted to other programs. This disunity led to a Women's Center where angry resignations and statements of "exhaustion" were commonplace.[50] Many of the young, middle-class women who had given their energies to Dayton Women Working and the Women's Center began to direct their energies elsewhere. Many took full-time jobs; some went to graduate or law school; others started families.

This analysis chronicles the rise and fall of feminist organizations in Dayton. It does not, however, chronicle the rise and fall of feminism itself. Although none of the three organizations here examined survived, not all their ideas and programs disappeared. In that sense, their deaths were not a failure for feminism. Dayton Women Working played a central role in stirring interest among national unions in organizing office workers, and District 925 exists partly as Dayton Women Working's legacy. The feminist organizations here studied fell, but feminism itself survived. Although disillusioned with infighting or specific projects, no members of these Dayton feminist groups contacted for interviews were disillusioned with feminism itself. In fact, they continued to live independent, self-confident lives centered by feminism. Some entered traditional male-only occupations—one, for instance, became a forester, another an engineer. Others continued to work long hours for feminist causes, staffing rape hot lines and battered women shelters. Moreover, in important ways, feminism in Dayton itself became, as one Dayton Women's Center member put it, "mainstreamed" by the late-1970s.[51] Other groups, with fewer radical connections, began to offer some of the services first provided by Dayton Women's Liberation, Dayton Women Working, and the Women's Center. For instance, the Dayton YWCA opened a Career Development Center, offering seminars and workshops for women workers. A city-funded Victim-Witness Project offered advocacy and counseling for rape victims.[52]

But mainstreaming always imposes a price. Today, many of the objectives of organized feminism in Dayton during the 1970s remain goals and dreams. Most Dayton women clerical workers remain unorganized and poorly paid. Women still have problems with childcare, healthcare, and the host of other issues that concerned the Women's Center. And many federally funded programs meant to help women cope with those problems have disappeared. An organization called the Dayton Women's Center remains listed in the Dayton phonebook, but those calling its number hear the voices of members of a local chapter of a "Right to Life" group. In 1980, the Dayton Women's Center collective sent a letter to the women on its mailing list, announcing its "difficult decision" to close. "We need new strategies, new weapons, and new blood," the letter writers concluded.[53] In the 1980s, many Dayton feminists were still seeking those visions, tools, and energies.

Notes

1. Barbara Ehrenreich, "The Women's Movements: Feminist and Anti-feminist," *Radical America* 15 (Spring 1981): 101.

2. See, for example, William Chafe, "Feminism of the 1970s," *Dissent* 21 (Fall 1974): 508–17.

3. For a popularized summary of Dayton's history, see Bruce Ronald, *Dayton, the Gem City* (Tulsa: Continental Heritage Press, 1981). See also Judith

Ezekiel, "Contribution à l'histoire du mouvement féministe américaine: L'Étude de cas de Dayton, Ohio, 1969–1980" (in English; Ph.D. diss., University of Paris VIII, 1986), which was unfortunately not completed in time to be available for our story.

4. Richard Scammon, quoted in *Dayton Daily News,* 20 July 1980.

5. Cheryl Radican, telephone interview from Richland, Washington, with Judith Sealander, 4 Jan. 1985. For discussion of women in Students for a Democratic Society, see Sara Evans, *Personal Politics: The Roots of Women's Liberation in the Civil Rights Movement and the New Left* (New York: Vintage, 1979), esp. chaps. 6, 7.

6. Ibid.

7. Carrie LaBriola, interview with Judith Sealander, Dayton, Ohio, 17 Oct. 1984.

8. Tape-recorded group discussion with Jan Griesinger, Joan Ruth Rose, Mary Morgan, Katie Egart, Yellow Springs, Ohio, 17 Oct. 1983.

9. *Dayton Women's Liberation Newsletter,* September 1970, Records of Dayton Women's Liberation (hereafter cited as DWL), Department of Archives and Special Collections, Wright State University Library, Dayton, Ohio.

10. LaBriola interview.

11. Model Cities grant proposal submitted by Dayton Women's Liberation, 15 Oct. 1973, box 1, no. 1, records of the Dayton Women's Center (hereafter cited as DWC), Department of Archives and Special Collections, Wright State University Library, Dayton, Ohio.

12. Sherrie Holmes, interview with Dorothy Smith, San Rafael, California, 30 June 1983.

13. Minutes of National Women's Employment Project meeting, 8 Oct. 1977, Chicago, "N.W.E.P. Memos and Correspondence," box 4, no. 1, Records of Dayton Women Working (hereafter cited as DWW), Department of Archives and Special Collections, Wright State University Library, Dayton, Ohio.

14. Susan Zurcher, interview with Dorothy Smith, Dayton, Ohio, 17 Feb. 1984; Robin Suits, interview with Dorothy Smith, Yellow Springs, Ohio, 25 Feb. 1984; Minutes, Women's Center collective, 23 Jan. 1974, box 1, no. 4, DWC.

15. Letter from Women's Center collective to Fair River Oaks Council Priority Board, 12 Mar. 1974, box 1, no. 2, DWC.

16. Suits interview. See also "What's Happening at the Women's Center," printed newsletter, box 4, no. 3, DWC.

17. Holmes and Suits interviews.

18. Holmes interview.

19. Memo to National Women's Employment Project Board from Heleny Cook, 13 Apr. 1977, "N.W.E.P. Memos and Correspondence," box 4, no. 2, DWW. Also Noreen Willhelm, interview with Judith Sealander, Dayton, Ohio, 18 July 1983.

20. Memo to National Women's Employment Project Board from Heleny Cook, 31 Oct. 1977, "N.W.E.P. Memos and Correspondence," box 4, no. 2, DWW. See also Willhelm interview.

21. Noreen Willhelm to Marvin Michel, Vice-President, Personnel, First National Bank, Dayton, 13 Feb. 1978, "Correspondence, Banking Study," box 3, no. 14, DWW.

22. Introduction, "Banks: Discrimination in Employment, a Dayton Working Women Study: Employment Discrimination in Dayton's Three Largest Commercial Banks," 10 July 1978, DWW.

23. Ibid.

24. Notes on Banking Industry Research, evidence compiled by Dayton Women Working and Cleveland Women Working, 1979, 15, box 3, no. 15, DWW.

25. Dayton Women Working, "Progress Report," January–July 1978, box 1, no. 8, DWW.

26. Banking Industry Research, 3.

27. Minutes of Women's Center collective, 26 Jan. and 2, 9, and 23 Feb. 1977, box 1, no. 4, DWC. See also letter from Roberta Fischer to Women's Caucus of New American Movement, 17 Jan. 1977; letter from Women's Caucus of New American Movement to Women's Center collective, 27 Jan. 1977, both in box 1, no. 3, DWC.

28. Kathy Ellison, interview with Judith Sealander, Dayton, Ohio, 10 Aug. 1983.

29. Suits interview.

30. See, for example, Evans, chap. 9; Chafe; Wini Breines, *Community and Organization in the New Left, 1962–1968: The Great Refusal* (South Hadley, Mass.: Bergin & Garvey, 1982); Todd Gitlin, "The Dynamics of the New Left," *Motive* (November 1970): 45; Kirkpatrick Sale, *S.D.S.* (New York: Vintage Books, 1973); and Judith Hole and Ellen Levine, *Rebirth of Feminism* (New York: Quadrangle, 1971).

31. Hole and Levine, 145–49.

32. Dayton Women Working was made up primarily of white women. Membership cards do not list race, and although recollections about percentages of Black members differ, all agreed that there were few Black members. A rise in Black members occurred after Deborah Walker, a Black hospital worker, joined in 1979 and began actively to recruit members.

33. Holmes and Willhelm interviews.

34. See *Dayton Daily News* and *Dayton Journal Herald,* both for 5 May 1978.

35. Holmes interview.

36. Sherrie Holmes, Typewritten memo, [early 1977?], DWW.

37. See Evans, chap. 6; Sale, chaps. 2–4; and Mitchell Goodman, ed., *The Movement toward a New America* (Philadelphia: Pilgrim Press, Knopf, 1970).

38. Nancy Cott, "Feminist Politics in the 1920s: The National Woman's Party," *Journal of American History* 71 (June 1984): 43–61.

39. Inez Haynes Irwin, quoted in Cott, 45.

40. Todd Gitlin, *The Whole World Is Watching: Mass Media in the Making and Unmaking of the New Left* (Berkeley: University of California Press, 1980).

41. The Dayton City Manager's Office Special Projects Files: Model Cities Program, Department of Archives and Special Collections, Wright State University Library.

42. *Dayton Women's Liberation Newsletter,* November 1973, DWL.

43. See Financial Statements of Dayton Women Working, "Financial Records," box 1, no. 3, DWW.

44. Volunteers in Service to America Study, "Project Report," HQ02-390-3 (interviewer, Charles Hefner), 8 Sept. 1978; Fundraising—V.I.S.T.A.," both in box 1, no. 19, DWW.

45. Financial Statements of Dayton Women Working. See also letter to women on Women's Center mailing list, June 1974; October 1975; 8 Nov. 1976; 25 July 1977, box 4, no. 3, DWC; Minutes, Women's Center collective, 9 Mar. 1977, box 1, no. 4, DWC.

46. Willhelm interview.

47. Holmes interview.

48. Radican interview.

49. Memo, Ellen Cassedy to National Women's Employment Project Board, "Future of N.W.E.P.," 10 May 1979, box 4, no. 2, DWW; Steve Askin, "Female Rights Spell Trouble for Bosses," *In These Times* 27 July–9 Aug. 1983, 11.

50. Morgan interview

51. Ellison interview.

52. Letter to women on Women's Center mailing list, 31 Dec. 1980, box 4, no. 3, DWC.

53. Ibid.

Race, Class, and Gender: Prospects for an All-inclusive Sisterhood

☐ The concept of sisterhood has been an important unifying force in the contemporary women's movement. By stressing the similarities of women's secondary social and economic positions in all societies and in the family, this concept has been a binding force in the struggle against male chauvinism and patriarchy. However, as we review the recent past, it becomes apparent that the cry "Sisterhood is powerful!" has engaged only a few segments of the female population in the United States. Black, Hispanic, Native American, and Asian American women of all classes, as well as many working-class women, have not readily identified themselves as sisters of the white middle-class women who have been in the forefront of the movement.

This essay examines the applications of the concept of sisterhood and some of the reasons for the limited participation of racially and ethnically distinct women in the women's movement, with particular reference to the experience and consciousness of African-American women. The first section presents a critique of sisterhood as a binding force for all women and examines the limitations of the concept for both theory and practice when applied to women who are neither white nor middle class. In the second section, the importance of women's perception of themselves and their place in society is explored as a way of understanding the differences and similarities between Black and white women. Data from two studies, one of college-educated Black women and the other of Black female household workers, are presented to illuminate both the ways in which the structures of race, gender, and class intersect in the lives of Black women and the women's perceptions of the impact of these structures on their lives. This essay concludes with a discussion of the prospects for sisterhood and suggests

Reprinted, with changes, from *Feminist Studies* 9, no. 1 (Spring 1983): 131–50. © 1983 by Feminist Studies, Inc.

political strategies that may provide a first step toward a more inclusive women's movement.

The Limitations of Sisterhood

☐ In a political critique of the concept of sisterhood, historian Elizabeth Fox-Genovese identifies some of the current limitations of this concept as a rallying point for women across the boundaries of race and class.[1] Sisterhood is generally understood as a nurturant, supportive feeling of attachment and loyalty to other women which grows out of a shared experience of oppression. A term reminiscent of familial relationships, it tends to focus upon the particular nurturant and reproductive roles of women and, more recently, upon commonalities of personal experience. Fox-Genovese suggests that sisterhood has taken two different political directions. In one, women have been treated as unique, and sisterhood was used as a basis for seeking to maintain a separation between the competitive values of the world of men (the public-political sphere) and the nurturant values of the world of women (the private-domestic sphere). A second, more recent and progressive expression of the concept views sisterhood as an element of the feminist movement which serves as a means for political and economic action based upon the shared needs and experiences of women. Both conceptualizations of sisterhood have limitations in encompassing the racial and class differences among women. These limitations have important implications for the prospects of an all-inclusive sisterhood.

Fox-Genovese argues that the former conceptualization, which she labels "bourgeois individualism," resulted in "the passage of a few middle class women into the public sphere" but sharpened the class and racial divisions between them and lower-class minority women. In the latter conceptualization, called the "politics of personal experience," sisterhood is restricted by the experiential differences that result from the racial and class divisions of society.

> Sisterhood has helped us, as it helped so many of our predecessors, to forge ourselves as political beings. Sisterhood has mobilized our loyalty to each other and hence to ourselves. It has given form to a dream of genuine equality for women. But without a broader politics directed toward the kind of social transformation that will provide social justice for all human beings, it will, in a poignant irony, result in our dropping each other by the wayside as we compete with rising desperation for crumbs.[2]

These two notions of sisterhood, as expressed in the current women's movement, offer some insights into the alienation many Black women have expressed about the movement itself.

The bourgeois individualistic theme present in the contemporary women's movement led many Black women to express the belief that the movement existed merely to satisfy needs for personal self-fulfillment on the part of white middle-class women.[3] The emphasis on participation in the paid labor force and escape from the confines of the home seemed foreign to many Black women. After all, as a group they had had higher rates of paid labor force participation than their white counterparts for centuries, and many would have readily accepted what they saw as the "luxury" of being a housewife. At the same time, they expressed concern that white women's gains would be made at the expense of Blacks and/or that having achieved their personal goals, these so-called sisters would ignore or abandon the cause of racial discrimination. Finally, and perhaps most importantly, the experiences of racial oppression made Black women strongly aware of their group identity and consequently more suspicious of women who, initially at least, defined much of their feminism in personal and individualistic terms.

Angela Davis, in "Reflections on the Black Woman's Role in the Community of Slaves," stresses the importance of group identity for Black women. "Under the impact of racism the black woman has been continually constrained to inject herself into the desperate struggle for existence. . . . As a result, black women have made significant contributions to struggles against racism and the dehumanizing exploitation of a wrongly organized society. In fact, it would appear that the intense levels of resistance historically maintained by black people and thus the historical function of the Black liberation struggle as harbinger of change throughout the society are due in part to the greater objective equality between the black man and the black woman."[4] The sense of being part of a collective movement toward liberation has been a continuing theme in the autobiographies of contemporary Black women.

> Ideas and experiences vary, but Shirley Chisholm, Gwendolyn Brooks, Angela Davis and other Black women who wrote autobiographies during the seventies offer similar . . . visions of the black woman's role in the struggle for Black liberation. The idea of collective liberation . . . says that society is not a protective arena in which an individual black can work out her own destiny and gain a share of America's benefits by her own efforts. . . . Accordingly, survival, not to mention freedom, is dependent on the values and actions of the groups as a whole, and if indeed one succeeds or triumphs it is due less to individual talent than to the group's

belief in and adherence to the idea that freedom from oppression must be acted out and shared by all.[5]

Sisterhood is not new to Black women. It has been institutionalized in churches. In many Black churches, for example, membership in the church entitles one to address the women as "sisters" and the men as "brothers." Becoming a sister is an important rite of passage which permits young women full participation in certain church rituals and women's clubs where these nurturant relationships among women are reinforced.[6] Sisterhood was also a basis for organization in the club movements that began in the late 1800s.[7] Finally, it is clearly exemplified in Black extended family groupings that frequently place great importance on female kinship ties. Research on kinship patterns among urban Blacks identifies the nurturant and supportive feelings existing among female kin as a key element in family stability and survival.[8]

Although Black women have fostered and encouraged sisterhood, we have not used it as the anvil to forge our political identities. This contrasts sharply with the experiences of many middle-class white women who have participated in the current women's movement. The political identities of African-American women have largely been formed around issues of race. National organizations of Black women, many of which were first organized on the heels of the nineteenth-century movement for women's rights, "were (and still are) decidedly feminist in the values expressed in their literature and in many of the concerns which they addressed, yet they also always focused upon issues which resulted from the racial oppression affecting *all* black people."[9] This commitment to the improvement of the race has often led Black women to see feminist issues quite differently from their white sisters. And racial animosity and mistrust have too often undermined the potential for coalition between Black and white women since the women's suffrage campaigns.

Many contemporary white feminists would like to believe that relations between Black and white women in the early stages of the women's movement were characterized by the beliefs and actions of Susan B. Anthony, Angelina Grimké, and some others. The historical record suggests, however, that these women were more exceptional than normative. Rosalyn Terborg-Penn argues that "discrimination against Afro-American women reformers was the rule rather than the exception within the woman's rights movement from the 1830's to 1920."[10] Although it is beyond the scope of this article to provide a detailed discussion of the incidents that created mistrust and ill-feeling between

Black and white women, the historical record provides an important legacy that still haunts us.

The movement's early emphasis upon the oppression of women within the institution of marriage and the family, and upon educational and professional discrimination, reflected the concerns of middle-class white women. During that period, Black women were engaged in a struggle for survival and a fight for freedom. Among their immediate concerns were lynching and economic viability. Working-class white women were concerned about labor conditions, the length of the working day, wages, and so forth. The statements of early women's rights groups do not reflect these concerns, and, "as a rigorous consummation of the consciousness of white middle-class women's dilemma, the (Seneca Falls) Declaration all but ignored the predicament of white working-class women, as it ignored the condition of Black women in the South and North alike."[11]

Political expediency drove white feminists to accept principles that were directly opposed to the survival and well-being of Blacks in order to seek to achieve more limited advances for women. "Besides the color bar which existed in many white women's organizations, black women were infuriated by white women's accommodation to the principle of lynch law in order to gain support in the South . . . and the attacks of well-known feminists against anti-lynching crusader, Ida Wells Barnett."[12]

The failure of the suffrage movement to sustain its commitment to the democratic ideal of enfranchisement for all citizens is one of the most frequently cited instances of white women's fragile commitment to racial equality. "After the Civil War, the suffrage movement was deeply impaired by the split over the issue of whether black males should receive the vote before white and black women . . . in the heated pressures over whether black men or white and black women should be enfranchised first, a classist, racist, and even xenophobic rhetoric crept in."[13] The historical and continued abandonment of universalistic principles in order to benefit a privileged few, on the part of white women, is, I think, one of the reasons why Black women today have been reluctant to see themselves as part of a sisterhood that does not extend beyond racial boundaries. Even for those Black women who are unaware of the specific history, there is the recognition that under pressure from the white men with whom they live and upon whom they are economically dependent, many white women will abandon their "sisters of color" in favor of self-preservation. The feeling that the movement would benefit white women and abandon Blacks or benefit whites at the expense of Blacks is a recurrent theme. Terborg-Penn concludes: "The black feminist movement in the United States during the mid

1970's is a continuation of a trend that began over 150 years ago. Institutionalized discrimination against black women by white women has traditionally led to the development of racially separate groups that address themselves to race determined problems as well as the common plight of women in America."[14]

Historically, as well as currently, Black women have felt called upon to choose between their commitments to feminism and to the struggle against racial injustice. Clearly, they are victims of both forms of oppression and are most in need of encouragement and support in waging battles on both fronts. However, insistence on such a choice continues largely as a result of the tendency of groups of Blacks and groups of women to battle over the dubious distinction of being the "most" oppressed. The insistence of radical feminists upon the historical priority, universality, and overriding importance of patriarchy in effect necessitates acceptance of a concept of sisterhood that places one's womanhood over and above one's race. At the same time, Blacks are accustomed to labeling discriminatory treatment as racism and therefore may tend to view sexism only within the bounds of the Black community rather than see it as a systemic pattern.[15] On the one hand, the choice between identifying as Black or female is a product of the "patriarchal strategy of divide-and-conquer"[16] and, therefore, a false choice. Yet the historical success of this strategy and the continued importance of class, patriarchal, and racial divisions perpetuate such choices both within our consciousness and within the concrete realities of our daily lives.

Race, of course, is only one of the factors that differentiate women. It is the most salient in discussions of Black and white women, but it is perhaps no more important, even in discussions of race and gender, than is the factor of class. Inclusion of the concept of class permits a broader perspective on the similarities and differences between Black and white women than does a purely racial analysis. Marxist feminism has focused primarily upon the relationship between class exploitation and patriarchy. Although this literature has yielded several useful frameworks for beginning to examine the dialectics of gender and class, the role of race, though acknowledged, is not explicated.

Just as the gender-class literature tends to omit race, the race-class literature gives little attention to women. Recently, this area of inquiry has been dominated by a debate over the relative importance of race or class in explaining the historical and contemporary status of Blacks in this country. A number of scholars writing on this issue have argued that the racial division of labor in the United States began as a form of class exploitation which was shrouded in an ideology of racial inferiority. Through the course of U.S. history, racial structures began to take on a life of their own and cannot now be considered merely reflections of class structure.[17] A theoretical understanding of the current conditions of Blacks in this country must therefore take account of both race and class factors. It is not my intention to enter into this debate but instead to point out that any serious study of Black women must be informed by this growing theoretical discussion. Analyses of the interaction of race, gender, and class fall squarely between these two developing bodies of theoretical literature.

Black women experience class, race, and sex exploitation simultaneously, yet these structures must be separated analytically so that we may better understand the ways in which they shape and differentiate women's lives. Davis, in her previously cited article, provides one of the best analyses to date of the intersection of gender, race, and class under a plantation economy.[18] One of the reasons this analysis is so important is because she presents a model that can be expanded to other historical periods. However, we must be careful not to take the particular historical reality which she illuminated and read it into the present as if the experiences of Black women followed some sort of linear progression out of slavery. Instead, we must look carefully at the lives of Black women throughout history in order to define the peculiar interactions of race, class, and gender at particular historical moments.

In answer to the question: Where do Black women fit into the current analytical frameworks for race and class and gender and class? I would ask: How might these frameworks be revised if they took full account of Black women's position in the home, family, and marketplace at various historical moments? In other words, the analysis of the interaction of race, gender, and class must not be stretched to fit the proscrustean bed of any other burgeoning set of theories. It is my contention that it must begin with an analysis of the ways in which Black people have been used in the process of capital accumulation in the United States. Within the contexts of class exploitation and racial oppression, women's lives and work are most clearly illuminated. Davis's article illustrates this. Increasingly, new research is being presented which grapples with the complex interconnectedness of these three issues in the lives of Black women and other women of color.[19]

Perceptions of Self in Society

□ For Black women and other women of color an examination of the ways in which racial oppression, class exploitation, and patriarchy intersect in their lives must be studied in relation to their perceptions of the impact these structures have upon them. Through studying the lives of particular women and searching for patterns in the ways in which they describe themselves and their relationship to society, we will gain important insights into the differences and similarities between Black and white women.

The structures of race and class generate important economic, ideological, and experiential cleavages among women. These lead to differences in perception of self and their place in society. At the same time, commonalities of class or gender may cut across racial lines, providing the conditions for shared understanding. Studying these interactions through an examination of women's self-perceptions is complicated by the fact that most people view their lives as a whole and do not explain their daily experiences or worldview in terms of the differential effects of their racial group, class position, or gender. Thus, we must examine on an analytical level the ways in which the structures of class, race, and gender intersect in any woman's or group of women's lives in order to grasp the concrete set of social relations that influence their behavior. At the same time, we must study individual and group perceptions, descriptions, and conceptualizations of their lives so that we may understand the ways in which different women perceive the same and different sets of social structural constraints.

Concretely, and from a research perspective, this suggests the importance of looking at both the structures which shape women's lives and their self-presentations. This would provide us not only with a means of gaining insight into the ways in which racial, class, and gender oppression are viewed but also with a means of generating conceptual categories that will aid us in extending our knowledge of their situation. At the same time, this new knowledge will broaden and even reform our conceptualization of women's situations.

For example, how would our notions of mothering, and particularly mother-daughter relationships, be revised if we considered the particular experiences and perceptions of Black women on this topic? Gloria I. Joseph argues for and presents a distinctive approach to the study of Black mother-daughter relationships, asserting that

> to engage in a discussion of Black mothers and daughters which focused on specific psychological mechanisms operating between the two, the dynamics of the crucial bond, and explanations for the explicit role of patriarchy, without also including the important relevancy of racial oppression ... would necessitate forcing Black mother/daughter relationships into pigeonholes designed for understanding white models.

In discussing Black mothers and daughters, it is more realistic, useful, and intellectually astute to speak in terms of their roles, positions, and functions within the Black society and that society's relationship to the broader (White) society in America.[20]

Unfortunately, there have been very few attempts in the social sciences to systematically investigate the relationship between social structure and self-perceptions of Black women. The profiles of Black women that have been appearing in magazines like *Essence*, the historical studies of Black women, fiction and poetry by and about Black women, and some recent sociological and anthropological studies provide important data for beginning such an analysis. However, the question of how Black women perceive themselves with regard to the structures of race, gender, and class is still open for systematic investigation.

Elizabeth Higginbotham, in a study of Black women who graduated from college between 1968 and 1970, explored the impact of class origins upon strategies for educational attainment. She found that class differences within the Black community led not only to different sets of educational experiences but also to different personal priorities and views of the Black experience.[21] According to Higginbotham, the Black women from middle-class backgrounds who participated in her study had access to better schools and more positive schooling experiences than did their working-class sisters. Because their parents did not have the economic resources to purchase the better educational opportunities offered in an integrated suburb or a private school, the working-class women credited their parents' willingness to struggle within the public school system as a key component in their own educational achievement. Social class also affected college selections and experience. Working-class women were primarily concerned with finances in selecting a college and spent most of their time adjusting to the work load and the new middle-class environment once they had arrived. Middle-class women, on the other hand, were freer to select a college that would meet their personal, as well as their academic, needs and abilities. Once there, they were better able to balance their work and social lives and to think about integrating future careers and family lives.

Among her sample, Higginbotham found that a larger proportion of women from working-class backgrounds were single. She explained this finding in terms of class differences in socialization and mobility strategies. She found that the parents of women from working-class backgrounds stressed educational achievement over and above other personal goals.[22] These women never viewed marriage as a means of mobility and focused primarily upon education, postponing interest in, and decisions about, marriage. In contrast, women from middle-class backgrounds were expected to marry and were encouraged to integrate family and educational goals throughout their schooling.

My own research on household workers demonstrates the ways in which class origins, racial discrimination, and social conceptions of women and women's work came together during the first half of the twentieth century to limit work options and affect family roles and the self-perceptions of one group of African-American women born between 1896 and 1915.[23] Most of them were born in the South and migrated North between 1922 and 1955. Like the majority of Black working women of this period, they worked as household workers in private homes. (During the first half of the twentieth century, labor force participation rates of Black women ranged from about 37 percent to 50 percent. Approximately 60 percent of Black women workers were employed in private household work up until 1960.)[24]

The women who participated in this study came from working-class families. Their fathers were laborers and farmers; their mothers were housewives or did paid domestic work of some kind (cooking, cleaning, taking in washing, and so forth). As a result, the women not only had limited opportunities for education but also often began working when they were quite young to help support their families. Jewell Prieleau (names are pseudonyms used to protect the identity of the subjects), one of eight children, described her entrance into work as follows:

> When I was eight years old, I decided I wanted a job and I just got up early in the morning and I would go from house to house and ring doorbells and ask for jobs and I would get it. I think I really wanted to work because in a big family like that, they was able to feed you, but you had to earn your shoes. They couldn't buy shoes although shoes was very cheap at that time. I would rather my mother give it to the younger children and I would earn my way.

Queenie Watkins lived with her mother, aunt, and five cousins and began working in grammar school. She described her childhood jobs in detail.

> When I went to grammar school, the white ladies used to come down and say "Do you have a girl who can wash dishes?" That was how I got the job with the doctor and his wife. I would go up there at six o'clock in the morning and wash the breakfast dishes and bring in scuttles of coal to burn on the fireplace. I would go back in the afternoon and take the little girl down on the sidewalk and if there were any leaves to be raked on the yard, I'd rake the leaves up and burn them and sweep the sidewalk. I swept off the front porch and washed it off with the hose and washed dishes again—for one dollar a week.

Although class position limited the economic resources and educational opportunities of most of these women, racial discrimination constricted work options for Black women in such a way as to seriously undercut the benefits of education. The comments of the following women are reflective of the feelings expressed by many of those in this sample:

> When I came out of school, the black man naturally had very few chances of doing certain things and even persons that I know myself who had finished four years of college were doing the same type of work because they couldn't get any other kind of work in New York.

> In my home in Virginia, education, I don't think was stressed. The best you could do was be a schoolteacher. It wasn't something people impressed upon you you could get. I had an aunt and cousin who were trained nurses and the best they could do was nursing somebody at home or something. They couldn't get a job in a hospital. I didn't pay education any mind really until I came to New York. I'd gotten to a certain stage in domestic work in the country and I didn't see the need for it.

> Years ago there was no such thing as a black typist. I remember girls who were taking typing when I was going to school. They were never able to get a job at it. In my day and time you could have been the greatest typist in the world but you would never have gotten a job. There was no such thing as getting a job as a bank teller. The blacks weren't even sweeping the banks.

For Black women in the United States, their high concentration in household work was a result of racial discrimination and a direct carryover from slavery. Black women were in essence "a permanent service caste in nineteenth and twentieth century America."[25] Arnold Anderson and Mary Jean Bowman argue that the distinguishing feature of domestic service in the United States is that "the frequency of servants is correlated with the availability of Negroes in local populations." By the time most of the women in this sample entered the occupation, a racial caste pattern was firmly established. The occupation was dominated by foreign-born white women in the North and Black freedwomen in the South, a pattern which was modified somewhat as southern Blacks migrated north. Nevertheless, most research indicates that Black women fared far worse than their white immigrant sisters, even in the North. "It is commonly asserted that the immigrant woman has been the northern substitute for the Negro servant. In 1930, when one can separate white servants by nativity, about twice as large a percentage of foreign as of native women were domestics. . . . As against this 2:1 ratio between immigrants and natives, the ratio of Negro to white servants ranged upward from 10:1 to 50:1. The immigrant was not the northerner's Negro."[26]

Two major differences distinguished the experiences of Black domestics from that of their immigrant sisters. First, Black women had few other employment options. Second, Black household workers were older and more likely to be married. Thus, although private household work cross-culturally, and for white women in the United States, was often used as a stepping-stone to other working-class occupations, or as a way station before marriage, for Black American women it was neither. This pattern did not begin to change substantially until World War II.

Table 1. Percentage of Females of Each Nativity in U.S. Labor Force Who Were Servants, by Decades, 1900–1940

	1900	1910	1920	1930	1940
Native white	22.3	15.0	9.6	10.4 ⎫	11.0
Foreign-born white	42.5	34.0	23.8	26.8 ⎬	
Negro	41.9	39.5	44.4	54.9	54.4
Other	24.8	22.9	22.9	19.4	16.0
Total	30.5	24.0	17.9	19.8	17.2
(N, in thousands)	(1,439)	(1,761)	(1,386)	(1,906)	(1,931)
(Percent of all domestic servants)	(95.4)	(94.4)	(93.3)	(94.1)	(92.0)

Source: George J. Stigler, *Domestic Servants in the United States: 1900–1940,* Occasional Paper no. 24 (New York: National Bureau of Economic Research, 1946), 7.

Table 1 indicates that between 1900 and 1940 the percentage of Black women in domestic service actually increased, relative to the percentage of immigrant women which decreased. The data support the contention that Black women were even more confined to the occupation than their immigrant sisters. At the turn of the century, large numbers of immigrants entered domestic service. Their children, however, were much less likely to become household workers. Similarly, many Black women entered domestic service at that time, but their children tended to remain in the occupation. It was the daughters and granddaughters of the women who participated in this study that were among the first generation of Black women to benefit from the relaxation of racial restrictions which began to occur after World War II.

Finally, Black women were household workers because they were women. Private household work is women's work. It is a working-class occupation, has low social status, low pay, and few guaranteed fringe benefits. Like the housewife who employs her, the private household worker's low social status and pay is tied to the work itself, to her class, gender, and the complex interaction of the three within the family. In other words, housework, both paid and unpaid, is structured around the particular place of women in the family. It is considered unskilled labor because it requires no training, degrees, or licenses, and because it has traditionally been assumed that any woman could or should be able to do housework.

The women themselves had a very clear sense that the social inequities which relegated them and many of their peers to household service labor were based upon their race, class, and gender. Yet different women, depending upon their jobs, family situations, and overall outlooks on life, handled this knowledge in different ways. One woman described the relationship between her family and her employer's as follows:

> Well for *their* children, I imagine they wanted them to become like they were, educators or something that-like [*sic*]. But what they had in for my children, they saw in me that I wasn't able to make all of that mark but raised my children in the best method I could. Because I wouldn't have the means to put *my* children through like they could for their children.

When asked what she liked most about her work, she answered, "Well, what I like most about it, the things that I weren't able to go to school to do for my children. I could kinda pattern from the families that I worked for, so that I could give my children the best of my abilities."

A second woman expressed much more anger and bitterness about the social differences which distinguished her life from that of her female employer.

> They don't know nothing about a hard life. The only hard life will come if they getting a divorce or going through a problem with their children. But their husband has to provide for them because they're not soft. And if they leave and they separate for any reason or [are] divorced, they have to put the money down. But we have no luck like that. We have to leave our children; sometime leave the children alone. There's times when I have asked winos to look after my children. It was just a terrible life and I really thank God that the children grow up to be nice.

Yet while she acknowledged her position as an oppressed person, she used her knowledge of the anomalies in her employers' lives—particularly the woman and her female friends—to aid her in maintaining her sense of self-respect and determination and to overcome feelings of despair and immobilization.

When asked if she would like to switch places with her employers, she replied,

> I don't think I would want to change, but I would like to live differently. I would like to have my own nice little apartment with my husband and

have my grandchildren for dinner and my daughter and just live comfortable. But I would always want to work. . . . But, if I was to change life with them, I would like to have just a little bit of they money, that's all.

Although the women who participated in this study adopted different personal styles of coping with these inequities, they were all clearly aware that being Black, poor, and female placed them at the bottom of the social structure, and they used the resources at their disposal to make the best of what they recognized as a bad situation.

Contemporary scholarship on women of color suggests that the barriers to an all-inclusive sisterhood are deeply rooted in the histories of oppression and exploitation that Blacks and other groups encountered upon incorporation into the American political economy.[27] These histories affect the social positions of these groups today, and racial ethnic women[28] in every social class express anger and distress about the forms of discrimination and insensitivity which they encounter in their interactions with white feminists. Audre Lorde has argued that the inability of women to confront anger is one of the important forces dividing women of color from white women in the feminist movement. She cites several examples from her own experience which resonate loudly with the experiences of most women of color who have been engaged in the women's movement.

> After fifteen years of a women's movement which professes to address the life concerns and possible futures of all women, I still hear, on campus after campus, "How can we address the issues of racism? No women of color attended." Or, the other side of that statement, "We have no one in our department equipped to teach their work." In other words, racism is a Black women's problem, a problem of women of color, and only we can discuss it.

> White women are beginning to examine their relationships to Black women, yet often I hear you wanting only to deal with the little colored children across the roads of childhood, the beloved nursemaid, the occasional second-grade classmate. . . . You avoid the childhood assumptions formed by the raucous laughter at Rastus and Oatmeal . . . the indelible and dehumanizing portraits of Amos and Andy and your daddy's humorous bedtime stories.[29]

Bell hooks points to both the racial and class myopia of white feminists as a major barrier to sisterhood.

> When white women's liberationists emphasized work as a path to liberation, they did not concentrate their attention on those women who are most exploited in the American labor force. Had they emphasized the plight of working class women, attention would have shifted away from the college-educated suburban housewife who wanted entrance into the

middle and upper class work force. Had attention been focused on women who were already working and who were exploited as cheap surplus labor in American society, it would have de-romanticized the middle class white woman's quest for "meaningful" employment. While it does not in any way diminish the importance of women resisting sexist oppression by entering the labor force, work has not been a liberating force for masses of American women.[30]

As a beginning point for understanding the potential linkages and barriers to an all-inclusive sisterhood, Lorde concludes that "the strength of women lies in recognizing differences between us as creative, and in standing to those distortions which we inherited without blame but which are now ours to alter. The angers of women can transform differences through insight into power. For anger between peers births change, not destruction, and the discomfort and sense of loss it often causes is not fatal, but a sign of growth."[31]

Prospects for an All-inclusive Sisterhood

☐ Given the differences in experiences among Black women, the differences between Black and white women, between working-class and middle-class women, between all of us, what then are the prospects for sisterhood? Although this essay has sought to emphasize the need to study and explicate these differences, it is based upon the assumption that the knowledge we gain in this process will also help enlighten us as to our similarities. Thus, I would argue for the abandonment of the concept of sisterhood as a global construct based on unexamined assumptions about our similarities, and I would substitute a more pluralistic approach that recognizes and accepts the objective differences between women. Such an approach requires that we concentrate our political energies on building coalitions around particular issues of shared interest. Through joint work on specific issues, we may come to a better understanding of one another's needs and perceptions and begin to overcome some of the suspicions and mistrust that continue to haunt us. The limitations of a sisterhood based on bourgeois individualism or on the politics of personal experience presently pose a very real threat to combined political action.

For example, in the field of household employment, interest in the needs of a growing number of middle-class women to participate in the work force and thus find adequate assistance with their domestic duties (a form of bourgeois individualism) could all too easily become support for a proposal such as the one made by writer Anne Colamosca in a 1980 article in the *New Republic*.[32] She proposed solving the problems of a limited supply of household help with a government training program for unemployed immigrant women to help them become "good household workers." Although this may help middle-class women pursue their careers, it will do so while continuing to maintain and exploit a poorly paid, unprotected, lower class and will leave the problem of domestic responsibility virtually unaddressed for the majority of mothers in the work force who cannot afford to hire personal household help. A socialist feminist perspective requires an examination of the exploitation inherent in household labor as it is currently organized for both the paid and unpaid worker. The question is, what can we do to upgrade the status of domestic labor for ALL women, to facilitate the adjustment and productivity of immigrant women, and to insure that those who choose to engage in paid private household work do so because it represents a potentially interesting, viable, and economically rewarding option for them?

At the same time, the women's movement may need to move beyond a limited focus on "women's issues" to ally with groups of women and men who are addressing other aspects of race and class oppression. One example is school desegregation, an issue which is engaging the time and energies of many urban Black women today. The struggles over school desegregation are rapidly moving beyond the issues of busing and racial balance. In many large cities, where school districts are between 60 and 85 percent Black, Hispanic, or Third World, racial balance is becoming less of a concern. Instead, questions are being raised about the overall quality of the educational experiences low-income children of all racial and ethnic groups are receiving in the public schools. This is an issue of vital concern to many racially and ethnically distinct women, because they see their children's future ability to survive in this society as largely dependent upon the current direction of public education. In what ways should feminists involve themselves in this issue? First, by recognizing that feminist questions are only one group of questions among many others that are being raised about public education. To the extent that Blacks, Hispanics, Native Americans, and Asian Americans are miseducated, so are women. Feminist activists must work to expand their conceptualization of the problem beyond the narrow confines of sexism. For example, efforts to develop and include nonsexist literature in the school curriculum are important. Yet this work cannot exist in a vacuum, ignoring the fact that schoolchildren *observe* a gender-based division of labor in which authority and responsibility are held primarily by men while women are concentrated in nurturant roles or that schools with middle-class students have more funds, better facilities, and better teachers than schools serving working-class populations. The problems of education must be addressed as structural ones. We must examine not only the kinds of discrimination that occur within institutions but also the ways in which discrimination becomes a fundamental part of the institution's organization and implementation of its overall purpose. Such an analysis would make the linkages between different forms of structural inequality, like sexism and racism, more readily apparent.

While analytically we must carefully examine the structures that differentiate us, politically we must fight the segmentation of oppression into categories such as "racial issues," "feminist issues," and "class issues." This is, of course, a task of almost overwhelming magnitude, and yet it seems to me the only viable way to avoid the errors of the past and to move forward to make sisterhood a meaningful feminist concept for all women, across the boundaries of race and class. For it is through first seeking to understand struggles that are not particularly shaped by one's own immediate personal priorities that we will begin to experience and understand the needs and priorities of our sisters—be they Black, brown, white, poor, or rich. When we have reached a point where the differences between us ENRICH our political and social action, rather than divide it, we will have gone beyond the personal and will, in fact, be "political enough."

Notes

The author wishes to acknowledge the comments of Lynn Weber Cannon and Elizabeth Higginbotham on an earlier version of this essay.

1. Elizabeth Fox-Genovese, "The Personal Is Not Political Enough," *Marxist Perspectives* (Winter 1979–80): 94–113.

2. Ibid., 97–98, 112.

3. For discussions of Black women's attitudes toward the women's movement, see Linda LaRue, "The Black Movement and Women's Liberation," *Black Scholar* 1 (May 1970): 36–42; Renee Ferguson "Women's Liberation Has a Different Meaning for Blacks," in *Black Women in White America: A Documentary History*, ed. Gerda Lerner (New York: Pantheon, 1972); Inez Smith Reid, *"Together" Black Women* (New York: Emerson-Hall, 1972); Cheryl Townsend Gilkes, "Black Women's Work As Deviance: Social Sources of Racial Antagonism within Contemporary Feminism" (Paper presented at the Seventy-fourth Annual Meeting of the American Sociological Association, Boston, August 1979).

4. Angela Davis, "Reflections on the Black Woman's Role in the Community of Slaves," *Black Scholar* 2 (December 1971): 15.

5. Mary Burgher, "Images of Self and Race," in *Sturdy Black Bridges*, ed. Roseann P. Bell, Bettye J. Parker, and Beverly Guy-Sheftall (Garden City, N.Y.: Anchor Books, 1979), 118.

6. For a related discussion of Black women's roles in the church, see Cheryl Townsend Gilkes's paper "Institutional Motherhood in Black Churches and Communities: Ambivalent Sexism or Fragmented Familyhood."

7. For a discussion of the club movement among black women, see, in addition to Lerner's book, Alfreda Duster, ed., *Ida Barnett, Crusade for Justice: The Autobiography of Ida B. Wells* (Chicago: University of Chicago Press, 1970); Rackham Holt, *Mary McLeod Bethune: A Biography* (Garden City, N.Y.: Doubleday & Co., 1964); Jeanne L. Noble, *Beautiful, Also, Are the Souls of My Black Sisters: A History of the Black Woman in America* (Englewood Cliffs, N.J.: Prentice-Hall, 1978); Mary Church Terrell, *A Colored Woman in a White World* (Washington, D.C.: Ransdell Publishing Co., 1940).

8. Carol Stack, *All Our Kin* (New York: Harper & Row, 1970); and Elmer P. Martin and Joan Martin, *The Black Extended Family* (Chicago: University of Chicago Press, 1977).

9. Gilkes, "Black Women's Work as Deviance," 21.

10. Rosalyn Terborg-Penn, "Discrimination against Afro-American Women in the Woman's Movement, 1830–1920," in *The Afro-American Woman: Struggles and Images,* ed. Sharon Harley and Rosalyn Terborg-Penn (Port Washington, N.Y.: Kennikat Press, 1978), 17.

11. Angela Davis, *Women, Race, and Class* (New York: Random House, 1981), 54.

12. Gilkes, "Black Women's Work As Deviance," 19. In this quotation Gilkes cites Jay S. Walker, "Frederick Douglass and Woman Suffrage," *Black Scholar* 4 (7 June 1973).

13. Adrienne Rich, "'Disloyal to Civilization': Feminism, Racism, and Gynephobia," *Chrysalis,* no. 7 (1978): 14.

14. Terborg-Penn, 27.

15. Elizabeth Higginbotham, "Issues in Contemporary Sociological Work on Black Women," *Humanity and Society* 4 (November 1980): 226–42.

16. Rich, 15.

17. This argument has been suggested by Robert Blauner in *Racial Oppression in America* (New York: Harper & Row, 1972); and William J. Wilson in *The Declining Significance of Race: Blacks and Changing American Institutions* (Chicago: University of Chicago Press, 1978).

18. Davis, "Reflections on the Black Woman's Role."

19. See Cheryl Townsend Gilkes, "Living and Working in a World of Trouble: The Emergent Career of the Black Woman Community Worker" (Ph.D. diss., Northeastern University, 1979); and Elizabeth Higginbotham,

"Educated Black Women: An Exploration in Life Chances and Choices" (Ph.D. diss., Brandeis University, 1980).

20. Gloria I. Joseph and Jill Lewis, *Common Differences: Conflicts in Black and White Feminist Perspectives* (Garden City, N.Y.: Anchor Books, 1981), 75–76.

21. Higginbotham, "Educated Black Women."

22. Elizabeth Higginbotham, "Is Marriage a Priority? Class Differences in Marital Options of Educated Black Women," in *Single Life*, ed. Peter Stein (New York: St. Martin's Press, 1981), 262.

23. Bonnie Thornton Dill, "Across the Boundaries of Race and Class: An Exploration of the Relationship between Work and Family among Black Female Domestic Servants" (Ph.D. diss., New York University, 1979).

24. For detailed data on the occupational distribution of Black women during the twentieth century, see U.S. Bureau of the Census, *Historical Statistics of the United States: Colonial Times to 1970*, H. Doc. 83-78 (Washington, D.C.: GPO, 1973).

25. David Katzman, *Seven Days a Week: Women and Domestic Service in Industrializing America* (New York: Oxford University Press, 1978), 85.

26. Arnold Anderson and Mary Jean Bowman, "The Vanishing Servant and the Contemporary Status System of the American South," *American Journal of Sociology* 59 (November 1953): 216, 220.

27. Elizabeth Higginbotham, "Laid Bare by the System: Work and Survival for Black and Hispanic Women," in Amy Swerdlow and Hannah Lessinger, *Race, Class, and Gender: The Dynamics of Control* (Boston: G.K. Hall, 1983); and Bonnie Thornton Dill, "Survival as a Form of Resistance: Minority Women and the Maintenance of Families" (Working Paper no. 7, Inter University Group on Gender and Race, Memphis State University, 1982).

28. The term "racial ethnic women" is meant as an alternative to either "minority," which is disparaging; "Third World," which has an international connotation; or "women of color," which lacks any sense of cultural identity. In contrast to "ethnic," which usually refers to groups that are culturally distinct but members of the dominant white society, "racial ethnic" refers to groups that are both culturally and racially distinct and in the United States have historically shared certain common conditions as oppressed and internally colonized peoples.

29. Audre Lorde, "The Uses of Anger," *Women's Studies Quarterly* 9 (Fall 1981): 7.

30. Bell hooks, *Ain't I a Woman? Black Women and Feminism* (Boston: South End Press, 1981), 146.

31. Lorde, 9.

32. Ann Colamosca, "Capitalism and Housework," *New Republic*, 29 Mar. 1980, 18–20.

My Black Mothers and Sisters; or, On Beginning a Cultural Autobiography

☐ In most societies, it is from women that you get the most consistent concept of nationhood of any people. Women usually are very nationalistic in the way we determine what we are supposed to be doing with our lives. With Black people in the United States, we understand that one of our responsibilities is to live and struggle so that there will be another generation of people. This makes us, Black women, as a group within the Black community, nationalistic. We have to take on the task of understanding what or who Black people are as a people and how we, Black women, must move so that there will be our people today and tomorrow. Historically, we have confronted with our very beings the premise that Black people were not brought here to be here always. If we look at early years of Black existence in this society, we find that in the brutality of the slave system, we died in greater numbers than we were born. The problem of our people then was to turn around this dying recipe of slavery so that there would be a Black people. To take on that job is to be a nationalist, to be about the formation and continuance and survival of a nation. Black women as mothers have been the heart of that battle.

We are, at the base of our identities, nationalists. We are people builders, carriers of cultural traditions, key to the formation and continuance of culture. We are the ones who touch the children first and most consistently. Social researchers tell us that by the time we are two or three years old, much of our cultural identity has been set. The experiences and data that go into making up that identity come to the child carried by the personnel charged with the maintenance of the environment in which life begins and grows. In the Black community, this environment has historically been our responsibility. Whether it is

Reprinted, with changes, from *Feminist Studies* 8, no. 1 (Spring 1982): 81–96. © 1981 by Bernice Johnson Reagon.

from the mother or the grandmother or the aunt or the babysitter or the nursery, the first words that the child begins to speak, the first smells, the songs, the body stances, the tastes, come from the women part of the society. Black women are nationalists in our efforts to form a nation that will survive in this society, and we are also the major cultural carriers and passers-on of the traditions of our people.

The roles that Black women have played in making a Black space in the United States of America in which Black life can grow have been nationalistic, cultural, and also revolutionary. Revolution, as I understand it, is the stopping of something, the turning around of something, the radical change of direction. It involves a lot of violence, and it has to be a cleansing process. I go back to my earlier statement that we were brought here to do certain kinds of work, to carry out a certain kind of function. That function and responsibility did not have with it a concern with our continuance or existence as a people through time. Sometimes I think by the time they made the cotton-picking machines, we were just not supposed to be here anymore. The continuing process of stopping that, the act of turning that around, this kind of nationalism is revolutionary; and Black women have played a major role in that particular struggle.

For the development of my thinking in this area, I owe much to Dr. Vincent Harding. Vincent talks about Black American existence in this country as the longest revolutionary struggle we know to date. As a people, we began to fight when they took us from Africa and we have not yet stopped. When you look at Black American history, you see skirmishes and battles in the war. In between, are mending periods, even some slipping-back periods. We call it backsliding. However, it is good to keep in mind that natural flow of things. *Waves go out. When they come in there is always a rock-back. It is not the same wave in the same place and the sands have shifted to never again be the same.*

I am in fact doing the same thing that my mother did and that my sisters did. The sands have shifted, but the motion I carry is from them. If we understand that we are talking about a struggle that is hundreds of years old, then we must acknowledge a continuance: that to be Black women is to move forward the struggle for the kind of space in this society that will make sense for our people. It is different today. Things have changed. The search for high levels of humanity and space to be who we know we are is the same. And if we can make sense of our people in this society, we will go a long way in making sense for the rest of the peoples who also live and suffer here. From that perspective, nationalism goes outside of what I call cocoon nationalism or isolationist nationalism. It has to have in its view the knowledge that what we do affects a larger scene. We cannot wrap ourselves in a wall and survive. In some ways, a wall threatens survival, making a clearer target. Being a nationalist may mean a centering in purpose inside oneself and then being sure of being everywhere so that as my nation goes, so will you, my enemy.

My mothers.
My mother was born in Worth County
Her mother was a seamstress
Words from my mother about her mother were like
"I never knew when she went to bed"
She was a farmer
When she got home from working the farm
my grandmother would do her work as a seamstress
To my mother she was always a seamstress
Even while she picked cotton or pulled corn or cooked peas and rice
My mother's mother's mother was very heavy
When my mother talks about her,
(who she did not know) she says
"They said that because of her—"
(Her husband was a scholar—he read books—and he would sit down
    and talk to you about books)
"Because of her—"
My mother's mother's mother took on the practical existence of her
    family
"Because of her—
they owned a plantation"
When she died the plantation fell apart
To talk about this lady's strength and talent is to talk of tenaciousness
I don't say nothing negative about Jordan Hill (her husband)
because if you do—
you have to fight everybody in the family.
"Because of her—"
Because of Hannah Hill
all of the children went to school
At least up until she died
We're talking about the 1890s, 1900, Worth County, Georgia
There were no Black schools in Worth County, Georgia
She had to earn money to send them off to school

My grandmother
who is my mother's mother
had her clothes packed to go off to school when Hannah Hill died.

Hannah Hill died in August
Grandmother was to leave for school in September
But when Hannah Hill died
Grandmother never caught the ride
so she didn't go off to school.
She sewed and sharecropped her way through.
Now what Hannah Hill did is what I saw my mother do
And what she saw her mama do

If you live as a Black person in this country
you see these people
who show you how to be
Men are supposed to be like *this*
and women are supposed to be like *this*
The powers that be
told Black men they could not be men unless—
Unless they had a job
Unless they supported their family
Unless they protected their women
Then the powers that be
froze the jobs
starved the babies
raped us
And then said
See you are not a man
'cause you are not responsible
'cause you don't have a job
'cause you don't support your family
'cause you don't protect your women
And do you know that
there are some of us—
buy that.

Women
Black women
looking at white women
Never had illusions about being that
There was never any possibility
It was just not in the offering
Too far away from keeping Black folks alive
So when you look at what Black women do
You are looking at people who have to fashion a something else
A way out of no way

When we look across time at Black women
We're looking at women who come to this country in bondage, with a
  tradition
And we had to do whatever we could to continue that tradition.

We have to do whatever we have to do in order for there to be a new
day. That means dealing with practical reality in a way that keeps you
very close to the ground, always knowing what you have to deal with in
the everyday sense. I think there must be dreams someplace in this
picture. The reality, the practical reality, hits you so hard that—
Maybe you propel your dreams two or three generations down the line.
Lay it on your daughters or your sons or their children. You understand that what you have to do is make up the difference, whatever that
is

My father would work from sunup to sundown
and would come home exhausted
eat, and go to bed
My mother would work from sunup to sundown
would come home
and work from sundown to sunup
to work from sunup to sundown again
The bottom line
Nobody else to turn to
If my father came home from work
and dinner was not done
hell broke loose
because he had worked from sunup to sundown
The only person who did that dinner
until we could do it
was mama
My father had a turning place
mama
We had a turning place
mama
white folks had a turning place
all of us
There was nobody for mama to turn to
She was it
When a dress had to be made for a play
if my father did not have the money to buy the material that was
  it
For mama that was just the beginning

She then had to figure out a way to get the cloth for the dress
and stay up all night making it
for this child to be in this play

It's called
making a way out of no way
I'm not talking about magicians.
I'm talking about people who have to handle the things that they find in
    the society
I'm talking about people who have to scrub walls
and do whatever they have to do—so
that they can deliver the goods
when there is no way laid out to deliver the goods.

I had a teacher named Mamie Daniel
I thought Mamie Daniel was old.
I thought she must have been teaching for hundreds of years.
Not hundreds
but at least she was 50 when I went to school
and I started school when I was three because Mamie Daniel told
    everybody to send their three year olds to school so by the time they
    were six they would be ready for the first grade
I went to school when I was three
and I thought I was supposed to learn to read
so I did and I passed into the second grade
When I was four.
Mamie Daniel would let you do that
By the time I was in fourth grade
I was teaching
At least I thought I was teaching
I think I was teaching first grade—
reading and math.
Mamie Daniel would let you do that
Well, she couldn't really do anything more because she had seven
    grades in one room in a little red schoolhouse

I thought Mamie Daniel was really old
I went back to talk to her as part of this research project
and it turns out that at Blue Springs School, she had her first teaching
    job
In fact, she was very young
How did she go to college?
Mamie Daniel got married

Her husband went into the service and sent back $50.00 a month
On $50.00 a month
she put herself through school
and the first job she had was at Blue Springs
which was this little school I went to at three years old.

Mamie Daniel was an extraordinary teacher
but I'm talking about her as a prototype of extraordinary teachers
I don't want to give you the impression that she was rare
She is rare today
If you tried to find her today
you'd be up the creek
But she was not a rarity in 1940
Black teachers understood that if they managed to get a degree
that degree put them in another class
The only thing that did was make them more responsible for handling
    more material things to complete the delivery of goods to their
    community
Mamie Daniel had a vision of how to open up our world and point us
    outward
My father was a carpenter
He built a stage in our one-room schoolhouse so that we didn't have
    programs that were on the floor
We had a real stage
That meant that Mamie Daniel could put the first grade on the stage
and turn them so that they could get their lessons out when I was
    helping them
And the third grade would be turned another way, looking out *that*
    window.
She could make space where there was none
And she could organize the space she had
My mama
My grandmama
My great grandmama
Mrs. Daniel . . .
dreamers who believed in being materialists—
revolutionaries
who were also nationalists
who were also cultural carriers.

My children games I learned from Mamie Daniel.
Sometimes she'd yell that we were not clapping right.
Every day at lunch time you would finish your lunch and go outside

and Mamie Daniel would lead all of the games, to make sure you got
them right.
It did not matter that you were three and the seventh graders were—
they looked to be six feet tall.
When I would see one coming
I would run because they were so big.
Today in school you don't go up against those kinds of giants
They're way down the hall someplace and you're in your little room if
you're in kindergarten
But if you were a third grader at Blue Springs
and you had to go to the outdoor toilet and you were coming back
through the garden
that Mamie Daniel made your PTA plant
so that you would cook greens so you'd learn to cook
and then here come R. C. Norman
you would just run.
You would also cry, because he was just so huge
But at recess all of you would be in this game
and you would be shaking it to the east
and shaking it to the west with R. C. Norman
And Mrs. Daniel would be running it all.
Then R. C. Norman would look very good because in a group you
could fantasize about him being your boyfriend.

My mama
My grandmama
My great grandmama
Mrs. Daniel . . .
were dreamers who believed in being materialists—
revolutionaries
who were also nationalists
who were also cultural carriers.

Mamie Daniel found out we had never been on a train trip.
She took us on a trip from Albany to Americus, Georgia.
She found out we were not drinking milk and made the milkman
who stopped at a store a few miles away
swing by our school
so that we could have milk.
She found out we weren't brushing our teeth
and taught us to make toothbrushes out of pine needles.
If somebody came in and hadn't brushed
they had to go make a brush and brush their teeth

She made the PTA build a playhouse
I know you've seen playhouses made out of cardboard
That is not what I'm talking about
I'm talking about a playhouse one-fourth the size of our one-room
  schoolhouse
a playhouse that my father and other fathers designed and put together
and built including all of the things in it
a playhouse that we could walk into and sit down in
Nobody at our house could buy a playhouse
Nobody could get one
But we had a playhouse you could walk in
and if you did everything right, you got to clean it up
While you cleaned it up
you could sing your little songs and do all the things you saw your
  mama doing

There was a Miss Nana in every church
My father pastored a church every Sunday
Miss Nana was in two or three of his churches
Miss Nana was like thunder
I called her Miss Nana
My mama called her Nana
and Nana was a great singer
She couldn't sing all kind of songs
but certain songs she could really get a grip on
This was the way my mama would talk about it
"Nana could get a grip on a song and rock a church with it"
She used to sing—
"Time, oh, time, time is a-winding up"
and if you don't hear Nana singing it, you don't know the song.
I mean you could hear *me* singing,
"Time, oh, time, time is a-winding up"
that would be sort of a weak reference point for what
Miss Nana did when she sang
"Time, oh, time, time is a-winding up"

Everybody in church talked about
Miss Nana's relationship with God
People thought she had a sort of audacity
Everybody else would say
"Now, Lord, here comes me your meek and undone servant and you
  know me and you know my condition"
This was a way of saying

"Now, Lord, I don't even need to go over my situation
Let us start now with where I am and what I need today"
Black people have a familiarity with God
But Miss Nana would take it to an extreme
She would get ahold of God in a special way especially during a revival
    meeting.
Miss Nana was big
I don't know now how old she was
She just looked real old to me
I was a teenager at the time
My Daddy would open the doors of the church and somebody would
    come to join
and everybody would have to watch Miss Nana
Miss Nana would either grab the child who had just come in
or she would grab my father
The ushers would race to get Miss Nana so she wouldn't get ahold of the
    little converts
Miss Nana would be making a streak for a convert—
or the preacher
and all the while she would be talking in a very everyday, familiar way
    with God
She would be saying things like—
"All right, thank you, Jesus.
Thank you Lord—
Thank you
I really appreciate that, Jesus
And tomorrow night you can just send us some more now
You just send us some more."
Miss Nana was grateful for what she got but she didn't let up on God for
    what she wanted
God had already given her a soul, right?
But then she'd say,
"That ain't all I need, Lord.
You are not off the hook.
I expect you to be here on time tomorrow night."
People thought Miss Nana was amazing
    and didn't know what to do with her
You just sort of protected yourself from her so
    she didn't get too close.
It was like when you put an extension cord into a socket and the
power ain't right
You could blow the socket

or the extension cord.
Miss Nana could blow a lot of sockets in our church.

Trois J. Latimer was my history teacher at Albany State College.
I don't remember a lot of history she taught me.
I know I learned about World War II and I remember Hitler.
I made A's out of both classes.
I did not become a historian until later.
She did not give me my love for history.
But Trois J. Latimer was an educated—degreed Miss Nana.
Church people talked about Miss Nana the same way we students
    talked about Miss Latimer.
We called her Ma Lat.
The thing I remember about Miss Latimer was that the first day we
    organized a Movement demonstration,
Ma Lat said,
as we went by trying to get people out of their classes,
"Get out. Go do something for your freedom. You ain't doing nothing
    here."
She ran the class out of the room into our demonstration line.
That was Trois J. Latimer.

Miss Rogers taught me history in high school
and I remember two things
One, she thought I could go to Talladega College which from Albany,
    Georgia, was a really fancy-select school that was very difficult to get
    into
    She thought I should go to Talladega.
The other thing was
I was reading my history book and it said
"Black people were better off in slavery than they were in Africa
    because in Africa they ate themselves."
Miss Rogers popped her girdle and said
"Well, I don't know about that."
And that's what I know about Miss Rogers.

Miss Patricia Webb taught me sociology
and she was the person who when we were talking in class would say
"Integration is coming and you all had better be ready." She said this to
    us consistently in preparation for this day when we'd be sitting next
    to white people
Then we were talking one day—

somebody started talking about the bomb. Patricia Webb said she
didn't think the bombs were supposed to be dropped
This was in the 1950s in Albany, Georgia, and she thought it was a
bad idea to drop those bombs on Japan.
That was very different from anything anybody else had ever told me
about the bomb
And Patricia Webb told me that

Autherine Lucy was my first Black woman fantasy partner
Me and Autherine Lucy went to the University of Alabama
We went there together
I was with her there every day
I would dream about her
She said something wrong one day
I know it was because they were pushing her up against the wall
And they suspended her
So I just went home and helped her get together
because the NAACP was going to get her back in
which they did
And she went back
me and Autherine Lucy—
I'm in junior high school—
went back to the University of Alabama
Then she got suspended again
which was no problem
since she had gotten suspended one time before
I'd just go home and eat me some more grits
Me and Autherine Lucy were going back as soon as the NAACP forced
the University of Alabama to let us back in
But she didn't go back
She got married to this preacher who took her to Texas
I still have not forgiven him
because I never got to go back to the University of Alabama with
Autherine Lucy
She was my fantasy partner.
One day I know I'll meet her and I'll be able to tell her that.

The Civil Rights Movement was simply a continuance
or *more complexly* a continuance
The list reads the same way
I'm talking about Black people in different times
on different levels
but the list reads the same way

The mother of my church
I heard her pray every Sunday
But I didn't really hear the prayer
   until she was in a Civil Rights
   Movement mass meeting
She said, "Lord, here come me your meek and undone servant knee
   bent and body bowed to the mother dust of the earth asking you to
   have mercy and come by here
   You know me
   You know my condition"
And a new
feeling came over me.
It was the first time I had really heard it
I don't mean that the mother of the church had not prayed that prayer
   before
But it took a march
a Civil Rights Movement march
for me to hear it
to understand what this woman had been saying all of her life
I knew for the first time what it took for me to be able to hear those prayers
In order to stand in the shoes of this old woman
who I had never seen march before or do sit-ins
or any of the fantastic things
we were doing for the first time
   in our lives
that Black people hadn't done before us
or so we thought
In order to even be able to understand what she had been telling me in
   her prayers for the 17 years I had lived till then,
It took my being in the struggle
marching
fighting in the
   Civil Rights Movement
to be able to finally hear
and feel the meaning of her words.
Till my marching and going to jail
   my ears had not lived enough to hear her prayers.

What Black women did in the Civil Rights Movement was to continue
   looking at what else we had to do in order for there to be another
   day for our people.

The Civil Rights Movement, in that respect, is not necessarily this
gigantic, unbelievable leap.
It is, in this light, a continuance.

We used to look at Fannie Lou Hamer
who weighed cotton for 17 years on a plantation
as if one day she suddenly went down to register and vote.
It was not one day suddenly going to register and vote.
It was changing jobs to go on carrying out her real work.
If you exist to—
If it is your job to—
If your role is to somehow manipulate this society so you can deliver
the goods for the survival of your people,
If somebody says there are more Black people in this country than
white people—and if you all will register to vote, you may be able to
deliver more goods
then you don't go on weighing cotton on
somebody else's plantation
If you could believe that
then you could go down and try to register to vote.
What is revolutionary about registering to vote in Mississippi in the
sixties is you know you're going to get killed
When you decide in Mississippi you're going to register to vote you
have already passed the point that revolutionaries pass when they
know that what they have to give
is their life.

Black women are a part of a Black nation, trained, defined, shaped in a
way that says
"We must give our lives"
We settle our peace with that very early
Very early we know that one of the things we have to do in order to
deliver the goods is give our lives
So it is not surprising that the Civil Rights Movement had more women
than men
A majority of the people who were in jail were women
We were the majority of the people who were in the marches
We were the majority of people who were in the mass meetings
When you look at an intensive campaign that lasts without let-up for a
year
When you look and see who comes to the mass meetings
It is Black women who are there every night

Somehow understanding that in *this* movement we might be able to
    increase the space that we had to work in
    in order to deliver the goods
    so that there will be another day for our folks.

When we look at people like Fannie Lou Hamer
and Victoria Gray
When we look at that woman out of Little Rock
When we look at Dorothy Cotton
When we look at Septima Clark
When we look at Ella Baker
Betty Mae Fikes
Cleo Kennedy
We are looking at my sisters
regardless of age or generation
Black women who jumped at the opportunity to enlarge the space we
    had to work in in order to do what we have to do.

Today I perceive Black women as being given another opportunity
to enlarge the working and living space
That space is us
we—ourselves
We must apply energy to the development of our potential
as parents
as creative producers
as the new way-makers.

There must not be a woman's place for us
We must be everywhere our people are
or might be—
in order to continue to do
what my mother did
and her grandmother did
and what my sisters of the Civil Rights Movement did
Fighting each generation
Each decade
to seize and hold more space
to continue to deliver the goods of survival
in a society that does not know how big we are
and how much room we need
to stand to our full height.

17 Kristin Booth Glen

Abortion in the Courts: A Laywoman's Historical Guide

☐ On June 20, 1977, the Supreme Court of the United States drasti-cally reduced the availability of abortion for poor women by its rulings in three cases. In these cases, *Beal v. Doe, Maher v. Doe,* and *Poelker v. Doe,* the Court ruled that (1) The Equal Protection Clause of the United States Constitution does not require a state to reimburse for "elective" abortions under Medicaid, even though the state *does* reimburse for childbirth and birth related expenses; (2) A state may require the written consent of the Department of Social Services prior to an abortion, even though no such consent is required for any other medical proce-dure because a "potential human life" is at stake; (3) Title XIX of the Social Security Act (Medicaid) does not require states to fund nonthera-peutic abortions, because states may refuse to fund "unnecessary," although desirable, medical services; and (4) Publicly funded municipal hospitals may legally refuse to provide elective abortions. These deci-sions represented a significant retreat from the legal protection of the right to abortion feminists thought they had gained in 1973 with *Roe v. Wade*—a critical right for which they had struggled so hard and which they appeared to have won. As Justice Thurgood Marshall argued in his dissenting opinion in *Beal v. Doe:*

> The governmental actions in these [new abortion cases], ostensibly taken to "encourage" women to carry pregnancies to term, are in reality intended to impose a moral viewpoint that no State may constitutionally enforce. Since efforts to overturn [earlier abortion decisions] have been unsuccessful, the opponents of abortion have attempted every imaginable means to circumvent the commands of the Constitution and impose their moral choices upon the rest of society. As the Court well knows, these regula-tions will inevitably have the practical effect of preventing nearly all poor

Reprinted, with changes, from *Feminist Studies* 4, no. 1 (February 1978): 1–29. © 1978 by Feminist Studies, Inc.

women from obtaining safe and legal abortions. . . . I am appalled at the ethical bankruptcy of those who preach a "right to life" that means, under present social policies, a bare existence in utter misery for so many poor women and their children.

In 1977 these decisions and their painful implications came as a complete surprise to most women and their proabortion allies, but the warning signs of potential backlash and the vulnerability of the legal "right to abortion" had been apparent for some time. The problem is that this struggle, unlike many other struggles against the oppression of women, took place almost entirely in the courts. Women organized and lawyers went into court to argue their cases, emerging with what frequently appeared to be victories. After the applause died down, women went off to fight other battles, like those for daycare, welfare rights, and the Equal Rights Amendment. Women without legal training generally did not suspect how fragile their "abortion victories" really were.

This is not to say that the legal strategy was not a wise or correct one or that other strategies were not simultaneously pursued.[1] Nor is it to say that the struggle for freely available abortion would not continue in the courts. It does suggest that when a political struggle takes place primarily in a legal arena, everyone concerned with the outcome has a responsibility to inform herself about the concepts and strategies employed and their ultimate political ramifications.

Understanding what happened to abortion in the courts in the 1970s first requires some knowledge of certain basic concepts of constitutional law, such as equal protection, substantive and procedural due process, and the "right to privacy." These concepts, which have been employed in attempts to strike down restrictive abortion legislation, are complex, but they are not incomprehensible. In this article, I will first explain the key legal issues by reviewing the history of abortion litigation through the 1970s.

Understanding the history also requires review of the social and political context in which the abortion decisions have been rendered. The Supreme Court's apparent repudiation of the "right to abortion" occurred in the context of a gradual but alarming shift in the content of governmental population policy. In the second section of the article, I will attempt to explain the legal backlash by suggesting a class analysis of population policy that links the declining fortunes of feminist abortion rights to the rising specter of state-encouraged sterilization procedures for poor and predominately nonwhite women.

Finally, because the shift in governmental and judicial policy took place simultaneously with a decline in mass mobilized feminist protest,

I will discuss the political and practical implications of that recent history. It is clearly necessary that feminists and all proponents of reproductive freedom regroup, consolidate the few gains they have won, and reformulate the abortion "problem" in a way that links it to other struggles against women's race and class oppression.

☐ A close look at the history of abortion litigation reveals the weaknesses and warning signals that have led us to this present disaster. When the abortion movement began in the mid- to late 1960s, it took the form of a legal attack on statutes which defined the performance of abortion as a crime. Generally speaking, there were three major types of criminal abortion statutes. One involved an outright ban on all abortions; it made performance of, procuring of, or participating in an abortion illegal, regardless of the circumstances. The second, more "liberal" type of law permitted abortions performed under certain clearly specified circumstances, such as the termination of a pregnancy resulting from rape or incest.[2] The third type was a statute which did not prohibit abortions performed to save the pregnant woman's "life or health." It was such a statute that was first challenged in the Supreme Court in 1967.

In that case a licensed physician, Milan Vuitch, was indicted for performing an abortion in the District of Columbia. The District's abortion law proscribed abortions done by a person, "unless the same were done as necessary for the *preservation of the mother's life or health* and under the direction of a competent licensed practitioner of medicine."[3] Prior to his trial, Vuitch moved for a determination as to whether the statute was unconstitutionally vague. His arguments were similar to those used by many other foes of restrictive abortion laws at the time and stemmed from the legal concept of unconstitutional "vagueness."

The concept of "void for vagueness" emerged from the Fourteenth Amendment's general proscription that no person shall be deprived of life, liberty, or property "without due process of law."[4] This enormously broad and elastic provision has been interpreted by the courts to include two separate kinds of "due process," substantive and procedural. It is the latter with which we are concerned here.

"Procedural due process" means, most simply, that people should not be convicted of crimes[5] without certain procedural protections such as the right to jury trial or to confrontation of witnesses. These protections have been historically required in Anglo-American law and are deemed "fundamental" to a fair trial.

One of the most "fundamental" protections is that of adequate advance notice that the behavior for which one is to be tried and possibly punished is actually proscribed. Thus, a statute that criminalizes certain behavior must describe the behavior with sufficient clarity not only to warn the potential wrongdoer but also to provide standards (for arrest or conviction) for the police charged with enforcing the law and for judges and juries who must determine guilt under it. When a criminal statute lacks such specificity, adequate "notice" has not been given, and we say that the law is unconstitutionally vague.

Using this kind of analysis, Vuitch argued that the statutory term "health" was so broad in meaning—stretching from the prevention of fatality to emotional well-being—that neither he nor anyone else could be certain what it meant. Consequently, it was impossible to tell in advance whether *any* abortion performed by a physician was or was not criminal.

The first court to which this argument was addressed—the District Court for the District of Columbia—agreed and struck down the statute as unconstitutional.[6] By the time the Supreme Court heard the case, other District of Columbia courts had construed the statute to permit abortions for "mental health" reasons; the Court found this interpretation of the statute "in accord with the general usage and modern understanding of the word 'health' which includes psychological as well as physical well-being."[7] Given such a construction, the Supreme Court held that the statute was *not* "unconstitutionally vague."

Thus, although the Court refused to strike down the abortion statute, its decision provided a short-term victory for women seeking abortions under similar "life and health" statutes. The problem was, as one of the dissenting judges pointed out, that the decision was still an entirely subjective one which would vary from physician to physician. Clearly, in order to obtain abortions, each woman was going to have to find a physician who agreed that her "mental health" might be injured by an unwanted pregnancy and birth.

The *Vuitch* decision was hardly a victory for women's rights. Its practical result was to insure inequality of access to abortion based on economic and geographic lines. The existence of such inequality bolstered the need for legal arguments being made elsewhere that the criminal abortion statutes denied equal protection of the laws.

The next round of litigation involved the constitutional requirement of "equal protection of the laws" derived from the Fifth and Fourteenth amendments. Next to "due process," "equal protection" is the favorite choice of litigators who seek to strike down unfair or unreasonable legislation. The basic premise of the equal protection clause is that the state may not treat similarly situated individuals differently unless it has good reason to do so. Almost all laws single out certain persons or groups for special treatment, whether for benefits or punishment. The initial inquiry is always whether the state has good reason for the differing treatment, or, as the courts say, whether there is a "legitimate state purpose" to the discriminatory law.

Once a legitimate purpose has been found, as it almost invariably is, the inquiry turns to whether the means chosen by the statute for discriminating among various persons (wrongdoers/nonwrongdoers; recipients of benefits/nonrecipients) bears a "rational relationship" to that purpose. The "rational relationship" test places the legal burden of proving *irrational* relationship between statutory means and ends on the party seeking to overturn the legislation. As a practical matter, this is a difficult burden to overcome. The courts are required to sustain constitutionality wherever possible and will frequently stretch to find a reasonable—if not always readily apparent—ground.

There are two major exceptions to this "reasonable relationship test," and each shifts the burden of proof to the party (usually the state) who seeks to uphold the challenged legislation. In each of these two exceptions, the courts are required to impose "strict scrutiny" on the discriminatory classification and to uphold it only on the showing of a compelling state interest. The two areas where this special "strict scrutiny" test is required are where a "suspect class" is involved or where a "fundamental right" is at stake.

"Suspect classes" include classes defined by race, national origin, or "illegitimacy." When legislation is considered by the Court to discriminate against all members of a suspect class, whether directly or indirectly, it will almost inevitably be struck down.[8] "Suspect classes" appear to be based on immutable, readily identifiable characteristics; the special scrutiny they are accorded is based on the liberal view that individuals should not be penalized for inherited characteristics—for something that is "not their fault." Despite the fact that a person's gender clearly meets all those criteria, sex has not been held to be a "suspect" classification.[9]

"Fundamental rights" recognized by the courts prior to the abortion litigation included the right to vote, to travel across state lines, to prosecute a criminal appeal, and to procreate. Such rights could not be abridged or burdened under the "strict scrutiny" test without the requisite showing of overwhelming or "compelling" state interest.[10]

Obviously, abortion statutes of all kinds were excellent targets for attack under the equal protection clause, both under the "rational relation" test and the more favorable, but less clearly available, "strict scrutiny" test. The arguments took various forms, depending on the statutes involved. Statutes of the type permitting abortion where pregnancy was the result of rape or incest were attacked because the classification chosen to be protected against abortion (i.e., fetuses conceived in one set of circumstances versus those conceived in another) bore no reasonable relationship to the purpose of the statute—the preservation of human life.[11] Statutes of the type permitting abortions only to save the woman's "life or health" were attacked because they indirectly discriminated against poor women. A woman who could not afford or who did not have access to psychiatrists who would attest to the need for abortion to protect her "mental" health could not obtain an abortion under these statutes.[12] The challengers argued that if the purpose of the statutes was to balance protection of a woman's health against the preservation of the fetus's life, this could not be "rationally" accomplished by making the operative discriminatory criteria the wealth or connections of the pregnant woman.[13]

This argument was accepted by several lower courts in setting aside abortion statutes; it eventually formed much of the rationale for the Medicaid cases when they were decided in the lower courts. It, like the first argument, was frequently joined with a more basic challenge, the claim that abortion involved a "fundamental right" and, as such, required strict scrutiny such as to invalidate virtually all legislative restriction on abortion. The fundamental right alleged in equal protection challenges—whether for poor women or those otherwise excluded from legal abortion—was the right of reproductive choice deriving from the "right of privacy."

The real issue at stake in all these legal wranglings was a woman's right to control her own body and her reproductive functions in particular. The Constitution does not specifically identify such a right nor is it surprising that the founding *fathers* were not concerned with it. Feminists and abortion rights litigators were thus forced to look for some more general constitutional right from which this specific one might be derived.

The most promising area originated with the lengthy, complex, and ultimately successful litigation to legalize the availability of contraception. The contraception decisions had developed a "right of privacy" which proabortion forces argued should include an individual's right to all forms of reproductive control, not just to conventional birth control devices.

The first contraception case which the Supreme Court decided on the merits was *Griswold v. Connecticut*,[14] in which an absolute ban on the use of contraceptive devices by married persons was struck down as violative of the "right of privacy." Although Justice Douglas, who wrote the opinion, admitted that no such right could be specifically located in the Constitution, he found a "zone of marital privacy" which was protected by a "penumbra of rights" emanating from other constitutional guarantees. These included the First Amendment's right to freedom of association and the Fourth Amendment's protection against "unreasonable searches and seizures."

The Court's specific reliance on "marital" privacy was seen as a possibly devastating limitation on the right of privacy. Accordingly, some litigators began to argue that the concept was derived directly from the Ninth Amendment, which provides that "the enumeration in the Constitution of certain rights shall not be construed to deny or disparage others retained by the people" and that all rights "possessed" by the people at the time the Constitution was enacted were retained by the people, unless they were explicitly given up in the Constitution itself. Therefore, any common-law rights enjoyed under Anglo-American law in 1776 were themselves preserved and guaranteed by the Ninth Amendment, just as other enumerated rights were guaranteed by earlier amendments. This theory of the Ninth Amendment as "repository" of, *inter alia,* the right of privacy was important for abortion litigation. Extensive historical research clearly demonstrated that abortion, at least in the first trimester (pre-"quickening"), was not criminal at the time the Constitution was adopted.

The possible locus of the right of privacy in the Ninth Amendment was first set forth in 1965 in Justice Goldberg's concurring opinion in *Griswold.* [15] The right of privacy itself received its fullest expression in the next contraceptive case, *Eisenstadt v. Baird,* [16] in which a ban on distribution of certain nonhazardous contraceptive devices to unmarried persons was struck down as violative of equal protection. In the opinion of the Court, although not the majority opinion, Justice Brennan spoke ringingly of the right of privacy as "the right of the individual, married or single, to be free from unwarranted governmental intrusion into matters so fundamentally affecting a person as the decision whether to bear or beget a child."[17]

Buoyed by this broad construction of the right of privacy, a number of lower courts, following what they saw as the Supreme Court's lead, struck down various kinds of antiabortion statutes as violative of the right of privacy or as denying equal protection by overly burdening so "fundamental" a right. On this basis the forces of abortion reform marched into the Supreme Court confident of victory. Unfortunately, they had not grasped the significance of the changes in the Supreme Court's composition which had occurred after *Eisenstadt.* [18]

By 1973, when the germinal cases of *Roe v. Wade* and *Doe v. Bolton* [19] were finally decided, Nixon's Supreme Court appointments had already caused a marked turn to the Right. Accordingly, the decisions in those cases were not the vindication to reproductive freedom they were seen to be but something entirely different. In fact, they contained the seeds of a long-term retreat from libertarian visions held out by Justice Brennan in *Eisenstadt*, even though they appeared initially to be victories. The *Roe* case involved a Texas statute prohibiting abortion except to save the life of the mother. *Doe* involved a Georgia law permitting abortion where the life or health of the pregnant woman was endangered, where the fetus was likely to be born deformed,[20] or where the pregnancy resulted from forceable or statutory rape.

The Court's decisions in these cases began in a promising fashion, with a lengthy discussion of the historical bases of abortion, seemingly supporting the Ninth Amendment repository theory. In addition, the Court completely disposed of the argument of antiabortionists that the right to life of a fetus is protected by the Constitution. The Court's opinion specifically found that there was a "right of privacy" which precluded all state interference with abortions during the first twelve weeks of pregnancy and limited state interference in the second twelve weeks to restrictions necessary for the mother's health. Only in the final period of pregnancy could a state's interest in continuing the life of a now-viable fetus possibly outweigh an abortion decision based on the right of privacy.[21]

But what was this "right to privacy" and where did it come from? Not from the Ninth Amendment but from the Fourteenth Amendment's guarantee of "substantive" due process. Because the Court used the Fourteenth rather than the Ninth Amendment in its ruling, this seemingly progressive decision in fact had a reactionary basis.[22] Unlike procedural due process, which is concerned with the way in which legal decisions are made, substantive due process decrees that there are areas in which legislative bodies have no power to make laws.

Although at first glance the idea of substantive due process might seem a "liberal" proscription against undue governmental involvement in people's lives, it has been used by U.S. courts almost entirely in the service of vested property interests and not in support of meaningful individual rights. Significantly, the idea of substantive due process was last used by a reactionary Supreme Court to strike down progressive labor legislation in the early part of the century.

The 1973 decisions were also shaky victories in another respect, for the Supreme Court was not upholding a *woman's* right to determine whether to bear a child, as abortion proponents and feminists had argued. Instead, it was upholding a *physician's* right to make a medical decision. The most startling portion of the abortion opinions, frequently ignored in the flush of apparent victory, was the statement that "the abortion decision in all its aspects is inherently, and primarily, a medical decision, and basic responsibility for it must rest with the physician."[23] The Supreme Court, speaking through Justice Harry Blackmun (who was, not coincidentally, the former counsel to the Mayo Clinic) described its decision in striking down the Texas and Georgia statutes as "vindicat[ing] the right of the physician to administer medical treatment according to *his* professional judgment . . . [italics added]." In this "victory," the seeds of *Beal, Maher,* and *Poelker* were clearly sown.

The threat of those future decisions was, however, temporarily overshadowed by an apparently ominous aside in the *Roe* case. In footnote 67, the Court specifically excluded from its decision any suggestion as to whether spousal or parental consent could be constitutionally required before an abortion could be performed. The immediate dangers suggested by footnote 67, and the speedy attempts by right-to-lifers to capitalize on this possible loophole,[24] led to the next, misleadingly optimistic round of Supreme Court abortion cases.

The next two abortion cases, heard by the Supreme Court in 1976, were *Danforth v. Planned Parenthood of Central Missouri* and *Belotti v. Baird.*[25] The former involved a Missouri statute with, *inter alia,* a spousal consent provision and an outright prohibition on saline abortions after the first trimester. The latter concerned a Massachusetts statute which required parental consent before an abortion could be performed on an unmarried woman under eighteen.

In *Danforth,* the Court struck down the spousal consent requirement, arguing that the "State does not have the constitutional authority to give a third party an absolute and possibly arbitrary veto over the *decision of the physician* and his patient to terminate the patient's pregnancy [italics added]."[26] The prohibition on post-first-trimester saline abortions was similarly struck down as not being a "reasonable regulation for the protection of maternal health,"[27] because, as the record showed, it was the method "most commonly used nationally by physicians after the first trimester."

On the other hand, record-keeping procedures which were argued to impose an unnecessary and unconstitutional burden on the abortion decision were upheld as not "unreasonable" and placing no prohibited "restrictions" on the "medical" decision or the "physician-patient relationship."[28] Again, although the case looked like a victory, it was surely a qualified one, not only in result but also in its reiteration of just what—and whose—rights were really being protected.

The *Belotti* decision was more ambiguous. Rather than deciding that a parental consent requirement, like that of spousal consent, simply imposed impermissible restrictions on the "abortion decision," the Court sent the case back to the Massachusetts courts for their interpretation of the procedure required by the statute. Although the *Belotti* opinion was in some respects consistent with general, neutral principles of "abstention,"[29] it nevertheless signified some retreat from the apparently absolute position of *Doe* and *Roe*. The warning signs in *Belotti* and *Danforth* were overlooked by most women, who were diverted by the Supreme Court's more dramatic, although indirect, repudiation of women's reproductive freedom in the contemporaneous pregnancy disability decisions.

In *Gedulig v. Aiello* and *Gilbert v. General Electric,*[30] the Supreme Court was confronted with two challenges to insurance plans containing disability benefits which excluded pregnancy and pregnancy-related disabilities. The challenge in the first case, *Gedulig v. Aiello,* was premised entirely upon the Fourteenth Amendment's equal protection clause. The Court held that discrimination against pregnancy is *not* discrimination against women, because not all women get pregnant.[31] The fact that *only* women get pregnant and that a denial of benefits may affect *all* women's decisions as to whether to become pregnant, or whether to enter or remain in the work force if they wish to become pregnant, was conveniently, albeit sophistically, ignored.

Recovering from their dismay at the *Gedulig* decision, feminists pinned their hopes on lower court decisions that *Gedulig* did not control litigations under Title VII of the Civil Rights Act of 1964,[32] which was seen as taking a broader view of sex-based discrimination. Such hope proved short-lived. In the second case, *Gilbert v. General Electric,* the Court considered a lower court determination striking down a disability plan that excluded pregnancy as violative of Title VII and of the accompanying guidelines issued by the Equal Employment Opportunity Commission (EEOC). Although regulations of enforcing agencies are generally given great weight and deference because of the agency's supposed expertise, and although the EEOC's regulations were clear on the subject of discrimination by virtue of pregnancy being considered discrimination on the basis of sex, the Court cavalierly ignored the regulations and the EEOC's decisional law. Instead, as in *Gedulig,* it flatly stated that because not all women are or become pregnant, blatant discrimination based on pregnancy is not considered to be statutorily prohibited discrimination by sex.[33] This unconvincing, artificial, but politically expedient separation of reproduction and gender advanced in *Gilbert* presaged the Supreme Court's turnabout on the fundamental "right" to abortion in *Beal, Maher,* and *Poelker.*

As was noted earlier, an especially strict standard is imposed in equal protection cases where a "fundamental right" is burdened or abridged. In reading *Roe* and *Doe* as establishing just such a right, lower courts almost uniformly struck down statutory or regulatory schemes which deprived poor women of their "fundamental" right to abortion (or, perhaps more accurately, their right to have a *physician* decide that they should have an abortion) by denying Medicaid or state-funded payment of the costs of such an abortion.

Thus, a federal court invalidated the directive of the New York State Commissioner of Social Services, who distinguished between "medically necessary" and "elective" abortions for purposes of Medicaid reimbursement. It reasoned that because women who could afford "elective" abortions could exercise their right, but poor women could not, the directive involved an unconstitutional discrimination. The lower court also noted that such discrimination against poor women did not rationally relate to the state's avowed purpose of saving money, because the costs of childbirth, covered by Medicaid, were higher than those of abortion.[34] When the Supreme Court agreed to take a Medicaid reimbursement case, it was generally felt that the Court would merely affirm what the lower courts had almost unanimously been doing all along—invalidating regulations which discriminated against poor women in the exercise of their "right" to abortion. Unfortunately, it was forgotten that this right did not belong to the woman at all, and, according to the Supreme Court, never had.

The first of three test Medicaid cases, *Beal v. Doe,* involved the provisions of Title XIX of the Social Security Act (Medicaid), which permits participating states to establish "reasonable standards" for determining the extent of medical assistance to be provided. Pennsylvania's Medicaid regulations restricted reimbursement to abortions certified as "medically necessary." The plaintiffs in *Beal* challenged the regulation as violating their right to equal protection and as contravening the policy of Medicaid. The U.S. Court of Appeals for the Third Circuit found that Title XIX prohibits participating states from requiring a medical necessity as a funding condition during the first two trimesters of pregnancy. The Supreme Court reversed, finding that although Medicaid would not allow a state to refuse to fund *necessary* medical treatment, nontherapeutic abortions are not necessary. If the state chooses to "encourage normal childbirth" by withholding funds for abortion it may legally do so by refusing to fund nontherapeutic abortions.

The Court did not confront the constitutional issue in *Beal,* but it did so in *Maher v. Roe,* where the plaintiffs had challenged similar regulations issued by the Connecticut Welfare Department. Because the Connecticut program was entirely state-funded, there was no Medicaid participation and therefore no question of the applicability of the Medicaid statute. Only the constitutional question remained. The lower court had held that the Equal Protection Clause forbids the exclusion of nontherapeutic abortions from a state welfare program that generally subsidizes the medical expenses incident to childbirth. It relied on language in the Supreme Court's earlier decisions in *Roe* and *Doe* that "abortion and childbirth—are simply two alternative medical methods of dealing with pregnancy." In judging the state's decision to fund one and not the other, the lower court applied the "strict scrutiny" test required when fundamental rights are involved. Because a woman has a fundamental right to an elective abortion, the court ruled that

> The state may not justify its refusal to pay for one type of expense arising from pregnancy on the basis that it morally opposes such an expenditure of money. To sanction such a justification would be to permit discrimination against those seeking to exercise a constitutional right on the basis that the state simply does not approve of the exercise of that right.[35]

The Supreme Court reversed by employing the "rational relationship" test of equal protection in conjunction with its acceptance of the argument that the state has an interest in encouraging normal childbirth. It refused to apply the "strict scrutiny" standard which would have placed the burden on the state for two reasons. The Court found that "indigent pregnant women" do not constitute a "suspect class" and, more important, it found that "the District court misconceived the nature and scope of the fundamental right recognized in *Roe.*" According to this logic, Connecticut's refusal to fund elective abortions did not deny a woman's fundamental right to an abortion, because there was no such right! The Court "reasoned":

> *Roe* did not declare an unqualified "constitutional right to an abortion," as the District Court seemed to think. Rather, the right protects the woman from unduly burdensome interference with her freedom to decide whether to terminate her pregnancy. It implies no limitation on the authority of a State to make a value judgment favoring childbirth over abortion, and to implement that judgment by the allocation of public funds.
>   The Connecticut regulation before us is different in kind from the laws invalidated in our previous abortion decisions. The Connecticut regulation places no obstacles—absolute or otherwise—in the pregnant woman's path to an abortion. An indigent woman who desires an abortion suffers no disadvantage as a consequence of Connecticut's decision to fund childbirth; she continues as before to be dependent on private sources for the service she desires. The State may have made childbirth a more attractive alternative, thereby influencing the

woman's decision, but it has imposed no restriction on access to abortions that was not already there. The indigency that may make it difficult—and in some cases, perhaps impossible—for some women to have abortions is neither created nor in any way affected by the Connecticut regulation.[36]

Because no "fundamental right" was involved, the Court found that "the state's strong interest in protecting the potential life of the fetus" was "rationally related" to its choice not to fund elective abortions and that the statute was thus constitutional under the applicable equal protection standard.

Finally, in the third case, *Poelker v. Doe,* the Supreme Court used similar reasoning to validate an antiabortion policy of St. Louis's municipal hospitals.[37] The lower court had applied a "strict scrutiny" test to the city's practice of not funding abortions while funding childbirth. In enjoining St. Louis from refusing to perform elective abortions, the lower court had emphasized "the contrast between women who can afford abortions in private hospitals and indigent women who cannot." The Supreme Court found the constitutional question presented by a municipal hospital's refusal to provide abortions identical to a state's refusal to provide Medicaid reimbursements, and for the reasons set forth in *Maher,* it found "no constitutional violation by the city of St. Louis electing, as a policy choice, to provide publicly financed hospital services for childbirth without providing corresponding services for nontherapeutic abortions."[38]

Thus, in a single day the Court struck down all guarantees of state or local assistance for the medical costs of an abortion. As a result, all women, whether medically indigent or not, who could afford private care or the transportation costs necessary to find such care, lost their hard-won "right to abortion."

☐ These new abortion decisions and what occurred after they were handed down had both immediate and long-term implications, including legislative implementation of the newly determined governmental right to "encourage normal childbirth" and the political response to such legislation; actual and potential political pressure on elected officials, particularly municipal officers; and the actual effects on poor women or women who were dependent on abortion facilities and services that were no longer available to them. But the results of the Court's decisions were probably *not* what the dissenting justices expected. Rather than a drastic increase in illegal, "back-alley" abortions or unwanted pregnancies carried to term, what appears to have occurred was an increase in the "choice" of sterilization as a birth control measure. This "option" was made readily available and almost unavoidable by government agencies anxious to slow or halt the birth rate among poor women and women of color. The legally sanctioned cutback in abortion services appears to have been directly connected to an increasingly powerful movement for the compulsory sterilization of women of specific race and class groups. Thus, the struggle for freely available abortion was inextricably linked to, and must still be seen as part of, the struggle against sterilization abuse. An appropriate feminist response to this development must proceed on several fronts. We must oppose antiabortion legislation on the national level, local electoral campaigns of antiabortion candidates, and forced sterilization measures wherever they appear. Massive organizing, on the national and ultimately district-by-district levels, is a necessity in order to roll back this vicious and far-reaching federal legislation. The "right-to-life" forces (or, as one writer accurately calls them, the "mandatory motherhood" crowd)[39] are tremendously well-financed and organized and have displayed extraordinary influence over legislators. In contrast, the women's movement has not shown itself capable of such long-term, concerted effort in the recent past, but as the halcyon days of reliance on the courts have passed, such effort can no longer be avoided. Organization on the state level is especially critical, for the fact that Medicaid funds are no longer available to the states for elective abortions does not mean that individual states may not choose to fund abortions out of their own coffers.

Antiabortion, or "mandatory motherhood," proponents are frequently best organized and most vociferous and powerful on the local level. The *Poelker* case demonstrated graphically how this strength could be transformed into an immediate, almost totally effective ban on abortion. When local mayoral candidates like St. Louis's Henry Poelker, or other municipal officials, were elected on platforms of ending abortion services in public hospitals, the effect on abortion rights for women was immediate and drastic.[40] As Justice Marshall warned: "I fear that the Court's decisions will be an invitation to public officials, already under extraordinary pressure from well financed and carefully orchestrated lobbying campaigns, to approve more such restrictions."[41] It is clear that this "fear" was well founded, and this underscores the need for educational campaigns and organization. To be ultimately effective, however, this work must be infused with an understanding of the racism and classism inherent in many "pragmatic" proabortion arguments and of the connection between abortion and sterilization.

In states where welfare costs make up a large proportion of the state budget, legislators may be persuaded that it is ultimately cheaper to pay the full costs of abortion than to support an ever-increasing welfare population. This is the argument most likely to prove persuasive,[42] but it is clearly unacceptable to feminists not only because of its overt race and class hostility but also because its way of posing the "problem" suggests a cheaper, easier, and more efficient "answer" than freely available abortion—namely, forced sterilization.

Even before the 1973 Supreme Court decisions favoring abortion rights, the experience of some states suggested that liberalizing abortion policy might have "benefits" in the area of population control. In New York, for example, the so-called illegitimacy rate had declined for the first time in years, and the rate of new additions to Aid to Families with Dependent Children rolls slowed.[43]

The national increase in the welfare population, as well as the significantly higher birth rate and rate of children born outside marriage among women of color, made legalized abortion seem the best, if not the only, solution to these perceived "problems." This analysis was grounded not in feminism but in racism and classism; nevertheless, it seemed to assure that the "right to abortion" was secure, albeit for ugly and unacceptable reasons.

The proabortion movement's tacit acceptance of these arguments and its lack of understanding of how its gains in "reproductive freedom" could and would be used against minority women caused some Black and Hispanic women to see the legalization of abortion and/or the provision of free abortion services as a policy of genocide against people of color.[44] This in turn led to the deepening of race and class splits within the women's movement. Many middle-class white women continued to see the legalization of abortion as a key "right" to be fought for, but many minority and poor women understood abortion in the broader context of reproductive and population *control.* Although most minority women did not actively oppose abortion reform, that struggle was often of far less importance to them than daycare, welfare, and other economic issues.

At the same time that minority women made these analyses of abortion, they were confronted with a more overt threat, that of forced sterilization. Increased sterilization abuse, facilitated by the development of new and inexpensive technology, completely changed the political climate in which the early abortion battles were won.[45] Although the "right" to abortion was being won in the courts, we began to learn of apparently massive sterilization abuse of young Black women in the South, Puerto Rican women on the island, and Native American women on reservations.[46] Sterilizations were being performed on women as young as twelve years of age, without informed consent, and frequently as a condition of continuing to receive government benefits.

According to federal statistics, an estimated 100,000 to 150,000 low-income persons were sterilized annually during the 1970s under federally funded programs.[47] In Puerto Rico, where sterilization had been made the most readily accessible method of birth control, an estimated 35 percent of women of childbearing age were sterilized.[48]

It became apparent that sterilizing people, with or without their consent, was a decidedly more efficient and less costly means of controlling poor and minority population increases than providing abortion services or other less drastic means of birth control. At the same time, the "illegitimacy" rates that had started to decline with the availability of free abortion began to shoot up again.[49] Obviously, free abortion was not working to solve the "illegitimacy" and welfare "mess," although it was resulting in a further decline in the birth rate for married women.[50]

The political implications of these facts suggest that some of the Supreme Court's previous reasons for insuring the availability of abortion no longer operated—especially with the appearance of a more "reliable" solution to the "illegitimacy" and welfare "problems." The decisions in *Beal, Maher,* and *Poelker,* otherwise difficult to explain, seem to support this analysis and suggest certain conclusions and strategies for the days to come.

First, the availability of sterilization as a means of poor and minority population control drastically decreases the political necessity or desirability of freely available abortion. Accordingly, we can no longer afford to separate the issues of free abortion and sterilization abuse.[51] Effective struggles for the first must be intimately linked to effective struggles *against* the latter. Second, in organizing to restore the availability of free abortion, alliances must be built across class and race lines; reliance on a white middle-class movement is simply not going to work.[52]

One result of the unavailability of free abortions may well be that poor women, otherwise unable to control their reproductive lives, will increasingly "choose" sterilization—especially where it is free or inexpensively available. This suggests certain strategies for feminists to pursue.

First, with a decrease in the number of publicly funded facilities doing abortions, the cost of abortions in private facilities will almost surely increase, putting them well beyond the capability of those poor women who the Supreme Court said should look to "private" sources of service. Early in the struggle to legalize abortion, feminists organized and developed referral services which kept the prices of abortion down and the quality up. Where possible, feminist efforts to channel women needing abortions to conscientious physicians and health facilities providing good service at low cost must be renewed and given high priority as an immediate goal.

Similarly, the efforts to democratize the technology of birth control, menstrual extraction, and/or abortion begun by various women's self-help groups in the late 1960s and early 1970s must be revived.[53] If women are no longer dependent on male physicians and a male health establishment to perform the abortions they may need, they will be equally independent of the necessity to have the state provide such services. Achieving real control over the technology of reproduction is a utopian goal but not an impossible one. It should not be abandoned.

Whichever strategy or strategies are chosen, it is indisputable that feminists will have to engage in a vigorous and long-term struggle to reverse the vicious backlash against abortion rights. It is equally clear that only struggles which are rooted in a broader understanding of the nature of abortion rights and their place in state population control policy can replace pyrrhic victories with real ones.

Notes

The author thanks Diane Polan, Sandra Harding, and Michael Ratner for reading and commenting on the original draft.

1. I am thinking here of the women's self-help movement, which began to develop and take control of the technology of reproductive freedom in such a way that the male-dominated medical establishment could never regain a complete monopoly of control.

2. This type of law was based on a model proposed by the American Law Institute, a prestigious body of lawyers and law professors who draft "model" legislation in many areas of the law. Its model statutes are considered more progressive than those generally in effect and are usually enacted by more "liberal" legislatures. The ALI abortion provision was found in its Model Penal Code, sec. 230.3(2) (Proposed Official Draft 1962).

3. D.C. Code Anno. sec. 22-201 (1967).

4. The Fourteenth Amendment technically applies only to the states, but the law growing up around "due process" is equally applicable to the federal government or its subdivisions (e.g., the District of Columbia) through the Fifth Amendment.

5. Procedural due process also applies to certain noncriminal proceedings where valuable property or liberty rights are at issue, such as termination of welfare assistance, removal from public housing, and school suspensions.

6. The effect of finding a statute unconstitutional is not to automatically remove it from the statute books. Rather, the person involved in the actual

proceeding where it is challenged is freed from its effects. Once a statute has been found unconstitutional, further prosecutions under it are unlikely, although not impossible, unless and until the U.S. Supreme Court affirms the finding of unconstitutionality.

7. U.S. v. Vuitch, 401 U.S. 62, 72 (1971).

8. An example of direct, blanket prohibition would be a statute or ordinance requiring all Black people to use a separate entrance to public buildings. An indirect but similarly blanket discrimination might arise from a seemingly neutral statute, such as Reconstruction Era "grandfather clauses" for voting, which effectively disenfranchised all Blacks whose grandfathers couldn't vote because they were slaves.

9. Had the Supreme Court held sex a suspect classification, all courts would have been required to impose a strict scrutiny under ordinary equal protection law similar to that which an equal rights amendment would impose. A number of cases specifically raised the issue, but the Court declined to so hold.

10. The only Supreme Court decision to uphold a blatantly racially (suspect class) discriminatory classification abridging a fundamental right (to travel freely) involved the incarceration of Japanese-Americans during World War II and was premised on the "compelling" governmental need for security in wartime. See Korematsu v. U.S., 319 U.S. 432 (1943).

11. The legal issue of whether a fetus had a "right to life" under the Fourteenth Amendment had generally been decided by holding that a fetus was not a "person" within the meaning of that amendment. See, for example, People v. Belous, 71 Cal. 2d 954, 458 P. 2d 194 (1969), *cert. den.* 397 U.S. 915 (1970).

12. States with the Vuitch-type statute generally required a certification by two psychiatrists, or by a hospital committee, that the abortion was medically "necessary." Accordingly, poor women had a far smaller chance of obtaining psychiatric justification for abortion. See Hall, "Therapeutic Abortion, Sterilization, and Contraception," *American Journal of Obstetrics and Gynecology* 91 (1965): 518–22. Statistics from states or municipalities with such requirements predictably showed that a far higher proportion of medically necessary abortions were being performed in voluntary (in other words, private) hospitals used by the well-to-do than in municipal hospitals used by the poor. See Hall, "Abortion in American Hospitals," *American Journal of Public Health* 57 (1967): 1933–34.

13. See Charles and Alexander, "Abortions for Poor and Nonwhite Women: A Denial of Equal Protection?" *Hastings Law Journal* 23 (1971): 147.

14. 381 U.S. 479 (1965).

15. Ibid., 486.

16. Eisenstadt v. Baird, 405 U.S. 438 (1972).

17. Ibid., 453.

18. Between *Griswold* and *Roe* and *Doe*, Justice Goldberg resigned from the

Court to go to the United Nations; Justice Fortas was forced into retirement; and Chief Justice Warren and Justice Black retired. All were replaced by far more reactionary Nixon appointees.

19. Roe v. Wade, 410 U.S. 113 (1973), Doe v. Bolton, 410 U.S. 179 (1973).

20. This provision was generally added to the "liberal" ALI-type statutes after the birth of the Thalidomide babies in the late 1960s.

21. Although the state could not "interfere" with first-trimester abortions, the Court found it virtually beyond question that the state could require early abortions to be performed only by physicians.

22. The danger of the transitory and clearly politically determined reliance on "substantive due process" was recognized and pointed out by some commentators. See Ely, "The Wages of Crying Wolf: A Comment on *Roe v. Wade,*" *Yale Law Journal* 81 (1973): 920.

23. Roe v. Wade, 166. [In the 1991 Rust v. Sullivan decision the Court specifically restricted the free-speech rights of physicians and other medical personnel working at federally funded facilities, forbidding them from informing their patients of their legal right to abortion.—Eds.]

24. Right-to-lifers, in addition to proposing constitutional amendments which would prohibit abortion, have also sought enactment of restrictive state provisions requiring the consent of husbands, where the pregnant woman was married, and of parents, where she was a minor.

25. Danforth v. Planned Parenthood of Central Missouri, 428 U.S. 52 (1976); Belotti v. Baird, 428 U.S. 132 (1976).

26. Danforth, 74.

27. Although, according to *Roe* and *Doe,* the state cannot entirely prohibit second-trimester abortions, it can impose greater regulation because of the increased "danger" to maternal health from abortion during this period.

28. Danforth, 80–81.

29. Abstention is a general doctrine which requires federal courts to "abstain" from determining the constitutionality of an apparently ambiguous statute until the state courts are given an opportunity to definitively interpret the statute. The hope is that they will do so in a way which precludes the constitutional question.

30. Gedulig v. Aiello, 417 U.S. 484 (1974); Gilbert v. General Electric, 429 U.S. 125 (1976).

31. As the Court wrote: "The lack of identity between the excluded disability and gender as such under this insurance program becomes clear upon the most cursory analysis. The program divides potential recipients into two groups—pregnant women and non-pregnant persons. While the first group is exclusively female, the second includes members of both sexes. The fiscal and actuarial benefits of the program thus accrue to members of both sexes." Gedulig v. Aiello, 497, n. 20.

32. Title VII prohibits discrimination on the basis of sex, in hiring, firing, or the "terms and conditions" of employment, of which insurance coverage was deemed to be one.

33. [The effect of *Gilbert* was overturned by passage of the Pregnancy Discrimination Act by Congress in 1978—Eds.]

34. Klein v. Nassau County Medical Center, 347 F. Supp. 496 (E.D.N.Y. 1972).

35. Roe v. Norton, 408 F. Supp. 660, 669 (D. Conn. 1975).

36. 45 U.S.L.W., 4790.

37. The defendant in the case, Henry Poelker, ran for mayor of St. Louis on a vicious antiabortion platform, and this policy was the result. A seemingly irrelevant local win for the right-to-lifers was transformed by the Court's decision into a virtually total national victory.

38. 45 U.S.L.W., 4795.

39. Garrett Hardin, *Mandatory Motherhood* (Boston: Beacon Press, 1974).

40. Justice Brennan described some of the more far-reaching results of the *Poelker* decision as follows: "The importance of today's decision is greatly magnified by the fact that during 1975 and the first quarter of 1976 only about 18% of all public hospitals in the country provided abortion services, and in 10 States there were no public hospitals providing such services. . . . Public hospitals that do not permit the performance of elective abortions will frequently have physicians on their staffs who would willingly perform them. This may operate in some communities significantly to reduce the number of physicians who are both willing and able to perform abortions in a hospital setting. . . . The Court's holding will also pose difficulties in small communities where the public hospital is the only nearby health care facility. If such a public hospital is closed to abortions, any woman—rich or poor—will be seriously inconvenienced; and for some women—particularly poor women—the unavailability of abortions in the public hospital will be an insuperable obstacle. Indeed, a recent survey suggests that the decision in this case will be felt most strongly in rural areas, where the public hospital will in all likelihood be closed to elective abortions, and where there will not be sufficient demand to support a separate abortion clinic. 97 S. Ct. at p. 2393 (Brennan, J. dissenting).

41. Poelker v. Doe, 97 S. Ct., 2392–94 (Brennan, J. dissenting); Beal v. Doe, 97 S. Ct. 2394, 2398 (Marshall, J. dissenting).

42. The overwhelming rhetoric will, no doubt, be that of the right of individual choice; abstract rights seldom sway legislators, but dollars, racism, and class interest do.

43. See, for example, Tietze, "Two Years' Experience with a Liberal Abortion Law: Its Impact on Fertility Trends in New York City," *Family Planning Perspective* 5 (1973): 36. The New York experience had also demonstrated that enormous profits could be reaped by those connected with legalized abortion,

from physicians doing abortions to entrepreneurs running clinics or referral services.

44. There is at least a partial justification in seeing the provision of free reproductive control services as "genocidal" when it is contrasted with the almost total lack of other essential medical and health services available to poor people and people of color, especially women and children.

45. Female sterilization, which had previously been accomplished only through tubal ligation—considered "major surgery"—was revolutionized by the onset of laparoscopies, or "band-aid" sterilizations which could be performed on an outpatient basis. Similarly, new techniques made male sterilization by vasectomy a "simple" and inexpensive procedure.

46. National attention was drawn to this situation by a lawsuit which focused on the plight of two sisters, aged twelve and fourteen, who had been sterilized in Alabama without their informed consent or that of their parents. The court in that case, Relf v. Weinberger, 327 F. Supp. 1196 (D. Ala. 1974), noted that there was "uncontroverted evidence" that "an indefinite number of poor people have been improperly coerced into accepting a sterilization operation under the threat that various federally supported welfare benefits would be withdrawn unless they submitted to irreversible sterilization."

47. Relf v. Weinberger, 1199.

48. Family Planning Digest 1 (May 1972).

49. For example, in 1971 when abortion was legalized in California, the nonmarital birth rate dropped by a dramatic 16 percent. By 1972, however, the decline had significantly slowed to 2.7 percent, causing the researchers who compiled the statistics to note that "despite the availability of legal abortion, many women are deliberately choosing unwed motherhood." See Sklar and Berkov, "The Effects of Legal Abortion on Legitimate and Illegitimate Birth Rates: The California Experience," Studies in Family Planning 4 (November 1973): 281. Nonmarital rates increased more rapidly for young white women, but the nonmarital rates for nonwhites continue to be substantially higher than those for whites.

50. For example, the Sklar and Berkov study (note 49) showed a decline in marital birth rates of 10.3 percent and 10.1 percent in 1971–72. This decline was seen as directly related to the legalization of abortion.

51. It is also important to understand the difference between a libertarian view of the right to sterilization, where freely chosen, and forced, uninformed, or otherwise nonconsensual sterilization abuse. Allies in the abortion struggle have sometimes been painfully pitted against each other over what is really a false but dangerously persuasive dichotomy. A case in point was the American Civil Liberties Union suit to set aside the progressive Guidelines for Elective Female Sterilization issued by the New York City Health and Hospitals Corporation.

52. This was, unfortunately, the experience of the ERA movement as well. In both instances, of course, middle-class white women were and are mobilized to take the opposing position, often with devastating effect.

53. See, for example, the discussion of the development of "period" or menstrual extraction developed by the Los Angeles Women's Self-Help Clinic in Ellen Frankfort, *Vaginal Politics* (New York: Quadrangle Books, 1972), 226.

Debating Difference: Feminism, Pregnancy, and the Workplace

☐ In January 1987, the U.S. Supreme Court ruled on a case that posed the question of whether it is possible to reconcile equality norms with policies treating pregnant workers differently from other workers. The case involved a bank receptionist, Lillian Garland, who sought to return to her job under a California statute requiring employers to provide unpaid job-protected disability leaves to their pregnant employees. When the Supreme Court upheld the legitimacy of the California law, its decision was widely welcomed as a victory for working women.

The meaning of the Lillian Garland case was, however, complex. Feminist attorneys were divided on the case and on the merits and dangers of providing special benefits to pregnant workers.[1] Although the debate at times appeared technical and obscure to nonlawyers, it raised questions analogous to those already emerging in other policy arenas about the limits of equality, the meaning of difference, and the direction of feminist strategy.[2]

Underlying the debate over pregnancy policy was the theoretical question of how to construe sexual difference. For the lawyers, the question initially turned on the nature of pregnancy. Is pregnancy a temporary disability? Is it a unique condition which for the practical purpose of enhancing equal employment opportunity can be analogized to other conditions? Or is pregnancy so special that such analogies demean women and actually impede equal employment opportunity? Implicitly or explicitly, the lawyers found themselves confronting basic problems of feminist theory and long-term goals. As feminists, is our objective simply the dismantling of barriers to equal participation in social life? Do we want to push beyond assimilation, which effectively leaves male norms in place, toward a balanced androgyny in a social

Reprinted, with changes, from *Feminist Studies* 16, no. 1 (Spring 1990): 9–32. © 1990 by Lise Vogel.

structure transformed to symmetrically meet women's and men's needs? Or should we frankly recognize woman's special and different nature through the development of woman-centered analysis and a rich women's culture? Is it reasonable to focus just on sexual specificity in a world torn apart by class, race, national, and other differences? What if a person's identity is not fixed but, rather, fluctuates—drawing variously on multiple sources, only one of which is gender? Perhaps we should view feminist goals as more transcendent—pointing beyond equality and difference, and past all dichotomies, to a future community of marvelously diverse persons, simultaneously united and autonomous.

The concerns of the participants in the debate over special treatment of pregnancy in the workplace thus converge with those of recent feminist theory, for pregnancy poses the dilemma of difference in an especially sharp and poignant form. In this essay I outline the controversy over special treatment of pregnancy, briefly explore how feminist legal scholarship conceptualized it, and suggest some broader implications. My purpose is to move beyond the polarization that characterized the debate without losing sight of the larger political context.

Pregnancy and Equality

☐ Lillian Garland had been employed as a receptionist in a Los Angeles branch of the California Federal Savings and Loan Association (Cal Fed). Her difficult first pregnancy and delivery necessitated several months' disability leave in early 1982, and she expected her position to be protected by a California law mandating that employers grant workers temporarily disabled by pregnancy up to four months of unpaid leave with job security. When she attempted to return to work at the end of the leave, however, Cal Fed claimed no receptionist or similar positions were available. Garland then sought her rights under the state statute. In response, Cal Fed, joined by the California Chamber of Commerce and the Merchants and Manufacturers Association, initiated a suit to invalidate the state law, arguing that it was preempted by the federal Pregnancy Discrimination Act (PDA). At issue was the conflict between the state law's requirement that pregnant employees be treated in a special manner and the federal law's mandate that they be treated the same as other workers. Cal Fed did not provide job-protected leaves to employees temporarily disabled by conditions other than pregnancy, and it wished to treat its pregnant employees in the same niggardly way. The Supreme Court determined, however, that California's disability leave statute was not in conflict with the federal PDA. That is, the Court ruled that special treatment of pregnancy in the workplace does not necessarily contradict the imperatives of equality.

The Supreme Court ruling meant that Garland did indeed have the right to reclaim her job. In this sense, the decision was an unambiguous victory. The question feminist lawyers had been debating was not whether Garland should have her job back but how best to achieve this outcome. To understand the controversy sparked in the feminist legal community by the California case, the litigation must be examined in the context of U.S. maternity and parenting policy.

It is always a shock to find out just how little substantive support for pregnancy and parenting is available in the United States. Despite an entrenched public ideology venerating motherhood and family, the level of tangible benefits and rights supporting parenting in the United States is sharply below world standards. Most industrialized countries, as well as many developing nations, provide comprehensive benefits to eligible workers for childbirth and childrearing. Medical costs are covered, and paid job- and benefit-protected leaves for maternity and parenting are the norm. In Europe, for example, maternity leave ranges from twelve weeks to twelve months and is paid at 80 to 100 percent of the maximum insured wage. Leaves can be extended should pregnancy or delivery prove difficult. Some countries provide additional leave to single mothers, for second and subsequent children, or for multiple births. Many permit mothers (or parents) to take more time, with the additional leave paid at a lower rate or simply job protected. Benefits in Canada, although less generous than those in Europe, are light years ahead of those available on this side of the border—approximately seventeen weeks' leave at 60 percent pay, usually with job, pension, and seniority preserved. The United States is thus unique in the stinginess of its support for maternity and parenting.[3]

Current maternity policies in the United States have evolved out of a history quite different from that shaping developments elsewhere. In the early twentieth century, when European countries were developing extensive social insurance programs coupled with comprehensive labor legislation, the United States trailed far behind. Its relatively weak set of substantive maternity supports were mainly instituted through state legislation affecting the employment of women and children but not men. Protective laws limited women's hours of work, regulated their working conditions, and prohibited female labor in certain "dangerous" occupations. Many women workers benefited from such laws, but others were not covered at all, and some found themselves excluded from jobs they wanted.[4]

Over time, special treatment for women through protective legislation not only reinforced sex segregation in the labor market, but it also increasingly became the basis for policies and practices that harmed women workers. In the name of protection, special—but often unfavorable —treatment of pregnant workers thus became a norm that was still in place in the early 1970s. Employers could and did fire workers because of pregnancy; they could also refuse to hire a female applicant on the basis of her pregnancy. Maternity leaves could be required regardless of the employee's desire to work; many employers forced pregnant workers to stop working three to six months after conception. Health insurance policies often excluded from coverage normal and cesarean deliveries, or even childbirth altogether. When covered, pregnancy-related expenses were usually reimbursed at a much lower rate than other medical costs. Employers (or states) could not only force a woman onto maternity leave, they could also determine the point at which she was permitted to return; a new mother ready to go back to work might have to wait. While waiting, she had little chance for any income replacement because most states explicitly excluded pregnant women and those recovering from childbirth from eligibility for disability or unemployment benefits. Maternity leaves generally had to be taken without income replacement, extension of benefits, retention of seniority, or rights to reinstatement. Where employees enjoyed relatively good maternity benefits—the minority of cases—these were usually the product of either collective bargaining or employer goodwill, the latter not necessarily extended to all female employees. For example, some employers provided benefits only if the employee was married.[5]

Feminist legal strategies in the 1960s and 1970s focused on eliminating discrimination against women. Given the ambiguous legacy of protectionist policy in the United States and the burgeoning activity on the civil rights front, it made sense to address the needs of women as a question of rights and equality rather than as protective legislation. Feminist equality strategy sought to make sex-based generalizations generally impermissible and to delegitimate the use of sex as a proxy for specific traits, functions, or behaviors. In the area of employment, the approach was to replace sex-based classifications with distinctions based on function. Instead of designating a job as male, for example, an employer would have to develop job-related criteria, such as strength or height. Characteristics specific to one sex—for example, pregnancy —could, for certain purposes, be viewed as comparable to other characteristics; by establishing comparability in the workplace, unfavorable treatment based on sex-specific characteristics could be identified as discriminatory, hence impermissible.[6]

The campaign to bring pregnancy within the scope of equality norms was thus part of a larger effort, and by the late 1970s it had produced substantial results. Employers and courts began to establish a record of treating pregnant workers as comparable to other workers whose ability to work was similarly affected. Practices that had seemed normal only a decade earlier were redefined as discriminatory and unacceptable. Job security and benefits for pregnant workers, especially in the areas of health, disability, and unemployment insurance, improved.[7] In effect, an implicit national maternity policy was being shaped. Modest and, indeed, peculiar by European standards, it did not center on specific substantive benefits for pregnant workers, nor did it define its goals in terms of social welfare. Instead, its touchstone was an antidiscrimination principle: pregnancy could not be the basis for unequal treatment of a woman worker.

Consistent with this legal framework, Congress enacted the Pregnancy Discrimination Act in 1978. The PDA was designed to nullify several Supreme Court decisions that used pregnancy as a basis to deny women benefits and seemed to be trying to turn back the clock on equality. In these rulings, the Court had insisted that pregnancy is not comparable to other conditions. Rather, said the justices, pregnancy is a unique "*additional* risk"—an extra burden that can properly be treated in a special and unfavorable manner.[8] The Court found that General Electric, for example, was not discriminating against women when it excluded pregnancy from its disability coverage. Outraged, a coalition of feminist, labor, civil rights, church, and even antiabortion groups mobilized to support the passage of the PDA.[9]

The PDA extends the 1964 Civil Rights Act to cover discrimination on the basis of pregnancy and specifically mandates that employers treat pregnant workers the same as other workers who are comparably able or unable to work.[10] To comply with the PDA, employers must generally make decisions about pregnant workers based on their capacity to work, just as such decisions would be made about other employees. If able to work, a pregnant worker cannot be fired or forced to take a leave of absence. If not able to work, she must be treated no differently than other workers similar in their inability to work. An employer who ordinarily permits workers temporarily disabled by illness to return to their old jobs, for instance, must provide the same option to workers temporarily disabled by pregnancy.

The PDA does not shape the substantive content of the pregnant worker's rights and benefits. Rather, the treatment a pregnant worker might receive under the PDA largely depends on her employer's particular policies. Unexpectedly, the federal act seemed to conflict with a handful of recently enacted state laws designed to provide benefits to pregnant women.[11] By attempting to address the substantive needs of pregnant workers directly, these state laws departed from the strategic approach embodied in the PDA. Rather than follow an antidiscrimination principle requiring that pregnant workers be treated in a manner comparable to other workers, pregnancy disability laws provide special benefits for one group of persons with special needs. The contradiction between the two strategies led inevitably to the litigation which culminated in the Supreme Court's Cal Fed decision.

The outcome of the litigation was of great importance to women workers. Employers were attempting to use the PDA to void state laws mandating the provision of benefits on the basis of pregnancy. If successful, their efforts threatened women with the loss of significant benefits. The equality framework that had seemed to be unequivocally on the side of women was revealing hidden ambiguities. At one level, the Cal Fed case pitted mean-spirited employers against pregnant workers needing job-protected disability leave. At another, it posed extremely difficult questions for feminist strategy and theory.

Feminist Legal Scholarship: Special versus Equal Treatment

☐ Feminist lawyers across the country discussed the implications of the litigation with more than a little consternation. For over a decade, their attention had been focused on equality. Only a few years earlier, they had mobilized to circumvent backward-looking Supreme Court decisions through the passage of the PDA. The feminist legal community was ill-prepared for an assault on women in the very name of equality.

The issues were intensively debated at numerous meetings and conferences and split the feminist legal community.[12] Participants conceptualized the problem as a choice between two approaches to pregnancy in the workplace: "special treatment" and "equal treatment."[13] Advocates of both positions supported Lillian Garland's right to her leave. Unlike her employer, they agreed that California's disability leave provision is not preempted by the federal PDA and that Cal Fed could and should comply with both statutes. Within this shared framework, they followed differing reasoning and suggested different remedies. Proponents of special treatment argued that the real sexual difference constituted by pregnancy made special treatment necessary to achieve real equality; if Cal Fed complied with California's statute it would automatically meet the requirements of the PDA, because both laws were intended to promote equal employment opportunity. Advocates of equal treatment also argued that Cal Fed could comply with both statutes but only by making unpaid, job-protected leave available on a nondiscriminatory basis to all its temporarily disabled employees. From the special-treatment perspective, then, narrowly drawn laws providing benefits to pregnant workers to accommodate the specific physical burdens of pregnancy were consistent with the equality mandate of the PDA. From the equal-treatment perspective, however, consistency with the PDA required that the benefits provided by such laws be extended equally to all workers.

Distinct strategic, ideological, and theoretical views informed the contending positions. The debate focused on the state statute and the PDA, but it implicated deeper concerns about the meaning of difference and the nature of equality. As the California case proceeded through the courts, divisions hardened, and the controversy flowed beyond the boundaries of the feminist legal community. Feminists and progressives mobilized to represent plaintiffs, file *amicus* briefs, and participate in support coalitions. Most of the major organizations litigating women's rights and developing policy for women—for example, the National Organization for Women, the American Civil Liberties Union, and the National Women's Political Caucus—backed the equal-treatment position. Activists as well as organizations in the labor, health, gay, and women's movements frequently sided with the special-treatment position. In California, strong support developed for the state's defense of its pregnancy disability leave statute. Indeed, members of the Southern California ACLU endorsed an *amicus* brief in opposition to that written and submitted by the national organization.[14]

Feminist legal scholarship articulated the competing positions. Two articles, one by Wendy Williams and the other by Linda J. Krieger and Patricia N. Cooney, were especially critical to the debate.[15] In "The Equality Crisis: Some Reflections on Culture, Courts, and Feminism," published in 1982, Williams pointed to increasing feminist concern about the meaning of equality. Having dealt with the "easy" cases, feminists now confront the "hard" ones, such as rape, military service, pregnancy, and maternity. These cases "touch the hidden nerves of our most profoundly embedded cultural values," causing feminists to question their traditional equality strategy.[16] Williams defended the equality framework as providing, even for the hard cases, both a practical approach and an adequate feminist vision of sexual difference.

In the hard case of pregnancy, for example, Williams maintained that women's special needs can be addressed without creating a classification based on sexual difference, thus removing the pretext for disadvantageous special treatment. The very real physiological uniqueness of pregnancy creates burdens for women workers that can be acknowledged by analogy to other burdensome physiological conditions. Williams cautioned against advocacy of a pregnancy-based classification. New pregnancy laws cannot, she argued, be narrowly drawn to reflect only "real" biological differences; the history of protective legislation shows that an emphasis on the special nature of maternity, however well-intentioned, can provide a basis for unfavorable as well as favorable treatment. Already she observed, there was an ominous convergence between feminist support for special treatment of special needs and the Supreme Court's damaging opinion that pregnancy is an extra burden. Feminists who seek special recognition for pregnancy through maternity legislation cannot guarantee that their interpretation of the special nature of motherhood will be adopted by the state.[17] Only ten years had passed since the Supreme Court first acknowledged sex discrimination could be unconstitutional, she noted, and gains under the emerging norms of gender neutrality were still fragile.[18] In sum, to endorse the doctrine of difference would put women at risk.

The equality approach, Williams argued, establishes a norm of gender-neutral treatment which employers must respect; such disadvantageous treatment as forced maternity leave or unequal medical benefits is prohibited. To the extent that pregnancy creates special physiological needs, women have access to the same provisions for medical coverage, sick leave, and temporary disability insurance their employers provide for other workers. Should women find themselves disadvantaged by an employer's policy that appears to be neutral but disproportionately harms pregnant women, they can use adverse impact analysis to seek relief from the courts. A woman whose employer provides the same inadequate sick leave to all workers, for example, could argue that the policy differentially affects women and therefore constitutes discrimination under the PDA. In the long run, Williams wrote,

> the solution is not state statutes specially aimed at pregnancy but statutes that require pregnancy-related disabilities to be treated like other disabilities, reasonable employer disability rules, and the provision, at the employee's option, of some amount of leave time for rearing of the infant. The child-rearing leave would be available to either parent on a gender-neutral basis.[19]

Williams also commented on the deeper implications of the special-treatment/equal-treatment dilemma. The special-treatment perspective, she suggested, projects a view of women that is essentially identical to the separate spheres ideology of the past, which assumed women and men to be by nature different and thus provided a basis for discrimination against women. By contrast, the equality approach exemplified by the PDA helps to dismantle the ideology of separate spheres. Feminists need to make a choice, she concluded: "Do we want equality of the sexes—or do we want justice for two kinds of human beings who are fundamentally different?"[20] In a later article, Williams specified that "the equal treatment approach [seeks] to overcome the definition of the prototypical worker as male and to promote an integrated—and androgynous—prototype."[21] In Williams's view, the special-treatment position collapses into endorsement of retrograde separate spheres ideology, but the equal-treatment perspective offers the more feminist vision of androgyny.

In 1983, Krieger and Cooney argued the opposing position, in defense of laws providing special benefits to pregnant workers. They maintained that women's special role as childbearers creates obstacles to equal employment opportunity that men do not face. In the presence of real physiological sex differences, equal treatment can yield unequal results. In particular, an inadequate disability leave policy can amount to a policy of terminating pregnant workers. Given the extra burden of maternity, Krieger and Cooney suggested, women require extra benefits on a permanent basis if they are to achieve real equality. In making special provision for pregnancy, special-treatment legislation "places women on an *equal* footing with men and permits males and females to compete *equally* in the labor market."[22] That is, it enhances equal employment opportunity and is not in conflict with the PDA.

Krieger and Cooney claimed to have a broader and more feminist vision of sexual difference than equal-treatment proponents. They castigated the equal-treatment framework as thoroughly liberal and abstract—focused on form rather than results, denying the reality of difference, and implicitly adopting men as the norm. The relentless individualism of equal treatment may work relatively well for upper-middle-class women, they asserted, but it fails to meet the immediate needs of working-class and single mothers. The masses of women have not made significant progress on the sex-specific issues of pregnancy and abortion, they argued, yet feminist litigators persist in offering the courts only this narrow liberal view of equality. "It is incumbent upon feminists," they concluded, "to provide a new, more humanistic vision for society, a new ideology of equality."[23]

Within the feminist legal community, the articles by Williams and by Krieger and Cooney set the terms of the increasingly bitter debate over special treatment versus equal treatment of pregnancy in the workplace. Subsequent exchanges refined and amplified the arguments, producing several versions of each position, but the parameters of discussion remained the same. Participants in the debate distinguished the immediate physical needs of childbearing from the demands of childrearing, and they all agreed that the needs of workers as childrearers can best be met through gender-neutral parenting programs and legislation. The dispute centered on childbearing. Although each side recognized that equal employment opportunity requires woman's experience as childbearer to be acknowledged in the workplace, they differed on the means to be used. Those in favor of special treatment supported narrowly drawn pregnancy laws as a way to provide the extra help pregnant women need to achieve equal employment opportunity. Advocates of equal treatment opposed female-specific legislation, cautioning that special treatment in the law has traditionally translated into inferior treatment of the targeted group. They argued that a continued emphasis on equality analysis, which includes sensitivity to adverse impacts of seemingly neutral rules, is consistent with past gains and is the best way to meet the special needs created by pregnancy. Fundamental to the policy dispute, although only partially acknowledged in the debates, were divergent feminist views of sexual difference and women's liberation.

Different but Not Unequal

☐ When the Supreme Court ruled on the Cal Fed case in January 1987, its opinion did not settle the special-treatment/equal-treatment controversy. The decision established the legal viability of statutes providing benefits on the basis of pregnancy, but gender-neutral legal norms continue to govern in most other areas affecting women. Efforts to meet women's needs as childbearers can therefore follow either the special-treatment or the equal-treatment strategy. Indeed, the flurry of confused legislative activity following the Cal Fed decision shows that state lawmakers seeking to enact pregnancy or parenting legislation are befuddled; they do not know which approach to adopt.[24] One effect of the Supreme Court decision has been, then, to return the debate to the legislatures. Uncertainty about the relative merits of special and equal treatment of pregnant workers persists.

The debate over pregnancy policy must be recast in order to be resolved or, better, transcended. Polarized by the need to take a stand on the litigation, participants in the debate often stereotyped the two available positions. Only recently have some feminist scholars, within and without the legal profession, begun to question the terms of the debate itself. "Are we," they ask, "doomed forever to oscillate between dualities—group vs. individual equality, assimilation vs. accommodation, 'formal' equality vs. 'real' equality? Or is there a way to move legal doctrine beyond these dualities to some richer synthesis?" More generally, can we develop a pregnancy policy within the framework of a politics that both cherishes difference and respects equality?[25]

In order to go beyond the debate over special treatment of pregnancy, several issues must be disentangled. First, the actual impact of the PDA on women workers has been an object of dispute and needs to be evaluated. Second, the underpinnings and ideological implications of the various positions in the debate have to be examined more closely. And, third, the debate should be placed in the context of the general problem of developing and evaluating feminist strategy. I consider these questions in the following sections. What emerges is a case in favor of a version of the gender-neutral approach to pregnancy policy.[26]

The PDA and Women Workers

☐ Participants in the debate over special treatment disagreed about the actual effect of the PDA on women workers. Those favoring special-treatment legislation argued that gender-neutral treatment disproportionately fails to meet the needs of working-class and poor women. Focusing mainly on benefit plans, they implied that the PDA has harmed rather than helped women. Its immediate practical effect has been, they suggested, at best, mixed—benefiting some women but harming many others, especially poor and working-class women, in the name of a purely formal equality.[27] The attempt to deny pregnancy benefits to Lillian Garland, a Black single mother caught in the low-wage ghetto of routine clerical work, seemed to epitomize this interpretation.

Evidence for the critique of the PDA has been largely anecdotal and impressionistic. An adequate evaluation of the statute's practical impact requires more extensive data, weighing costs and benefits on several dimensions, over time and on a national scale. Although comprehensive studies have not yet been carried out, some data exist. Evidence from the insurance industry, for example, which provides employers with policies to cover employee benefits, can shed light on the PDA's impact on disability and medical coverage.[28] The insurance industry had vigorously opposed the passage of the PDA, arguing that costs would be high and that women malingerers would abuse the benefits the statute would provide.[29] Its fears with respect to costs were confirmed by several studies based on insurance company data that find generally higher short-term disability costs due to payment of benefits mandated by the PDA.[30] A similar increase in costs has been documented in states with temporary disability laws that provide income replacement.[31] A 1984 study of the health plans of twenty-one companies in Iowa, Missouri, and Indiana furnishes additional evidence. Before the PDA's passage, medical benefits for pregnancy in all twenty-one firms were inferior to benefits for other conditions; four of the firms offered no coverage whatsoever for either normal or cesarean delivery. After implementation of the PDA, all the firms covered pregnancy and pregnancy-related conditions on the same basis as other conditions.[32] Improved medical coverage and increased aggregate cash benefits suggest that on average the PDA has aided women monetarily, although no one knows just how many women have benefited nor who they are. The fact that monetary benefits have risen could suggest that the PDA especially benefits working-class women, generally more in need of cash and less able to sustain the unpaid leaves that "middle-class" women can sometimes afford.[33]

Many women work for firms employing fewer than fifteen persons and are therefore not covered by the PDA. With jobs at the bottom of the employment scale and with minimal or no benefits, these are the low-income women for whom special pregnancy legislation at the state level should be especially helpful, according to special-treatment proponents. The actual experience of California is instructive. The guarantee of up to four months of job-protected pregnancy disability leave was one of nine provisions in a package passed by the California legislature in 1978. The statute was originally proposed as a gender-neutral prohibition on pregnancy-based discrimination, along the lines of the PDA, but it emerged from the legislative process in female-specific form. Of the nine provisions mandating special treatment of pregnant workers, two provide benefits but seven are more ambiguous, permitting employers to treat pregnancy unfavorably. For example, employers are required to provide pregnant workers with the unpaid, job-protected pregnancy disability leave that was at the center of the Cal Fed litigation, but unlike larger employers, they are allowed to exclude pregnancy from medical benefit plans.[34] This mixed bag of benefits and exclusions is in effect for California firms with six to fourteen employees. If Lillian Garland had not worked for a big bank, she might have found herself with an unpaid disability leave but without medical coverage for her difficult and expensive pregnancy. All women need both medical coverage and adequate leave provisions, but again, I would argue that for working-class women the medical benefits are especially important. In California, then, the special-treatment approach resulted in statutes that treated pregnancy in contradictory and sometimes unfavorable ways.

More studies are necessary, but available evidence on the PDA's immediate impact suggests that on balance it has resulted in improved pregnancy benefits for large numbers of working women. Any overall evaluation of the PDA's impact must include, furthermore, its protection of all women's access to work. Without the PDA, pregnant women's rights to be hired, to enter training programs, and to continue working while pregnant would be threatened. In an economy in which women increasingly participate in the labor force, the issue of access to work is at least as important to poor and working-class women as it is to "middle-class" women. In terms of practical results, then, the gender-neutral approach to pregnancy cannot be evaluated as negatively as the special-treatment critics would claim.

The Meanings of Pregnancy

☐ In addition to practical impact, the choice of a particular strategy carries with it ideological implications. For many of the participants in the special-treatment/equal-treatment debate, these implications have been at the core of the controversy over pregnancy legislation. Special-treatment proponents are repelled by what they see as the equal-treatment approach's representation of pregnancy as a disability and its imposition of male norms on women. At issue in their critique are the meanings attributed to pregnancy and sexual difference. The PDA, in this view, is irreparably tainted by the identification it supposedly makes of pregnancy with disability.[35] By treating pregnancy as a temporary disability, the PDA is said to stigmatize childbearing as a pathological departure from an implicitly male norm. As physician Wendy Chavkin puts it, "pregnancy . . . is not an illness. Rather, it is a unique condition, that may be accompanied by special needs, and sometimes by illness."[36] In sum, according to the critics, the gender-neutral approach to pregnancy devalues its special biological and social nature, attempts inappropriately to standardize women's experience within male-defined medical and work norms, and represents pregnancy as, literally, an abnormal and unhealthy condition.

The image of pregnancy that special-treatment advocates seem to prefer focuses on woman's uniqueness. We should not shrink, they argue, from endorsing difference.

> In observing that [pregnancy and breastfeeding] are the capabilities which *really* differentiate women from men, it is crucial that we overcome any aversion to describing these functions as "unique." Uniqueness is a "trap" only in terms of an analysis . . . which assumes that maleness is the norm. "Unique" does not mean uniquely handicapped.[37]

There is, in this view, a profound and definitional character to the phenomenon of childbearing. It marks all women, constituting a strength and source of unity but also creating specific needs. Policies that positively acknowledge the uniqueness of childbearing, such as those in many European countries, need not be judged by an equality standard. Instead, they show that women's special needs can be accommodated within a framework that emphasizes caring and responsibility.

The special-treatment representation of pregnancy and sexual difference is in many ways compelling. It emphasizes the inadequacy of traditional liberal views that deny sexual difference and seek individualistic assimilation to a single standard. It offers a vision of women and their special needs as not only unique but also profoundly important. It claims to be the best defense of the most needy women, as well as the foundation for the far more adequate maternity policies found in other countries. And it resonates with feminist aspirations to go beyond conventional formulations toward more radical solutions. For many feminists, these characteristics have proven irresistible.[38]

Chief among the ideological accusations made against the gender-neutral framework are that its proponents endorse male norms and that they commit the sin of liberalism. Although the charges can validly be directed at some backers of equal treatment, others seek to transcend the liberalism of which they are accused. Nadine Taub and Wendy Williams, for example, are well aware that the traditional liberal framework tends to override difference and set up a male model as the norm. They point out that "the model is, of course, not only male but also white, able-bodied, English-speaking, and a member of a mainstream religion."[39] And they depict pregnancy as only one of many unique conditions that human beings have or develop—conditions that invariably involve special needs society ought to accommodate. Where special-treatment advocates insist on woman's categorical difference and propose special policies to represent globally special female needs, Taub and Williams move toward an understanding of all persons as differentiated individuals, each with her or his own special needs. To meet these needs, the workplace must be transformed. "The vision is not . . . a workplace based on a male definition of employee, with special accommodation to women's differences from men, but rather a redefinition of what a typical employee is that encompasses both sexes."[40]

Implicit in Taub and Williams's comments is a significantly revised version of the gender-neutral approach to the pregnancy dilemma. Rather than categorize workers into two groups, female and male, this approach acknowledges that all employees have special needs—as expectant mothers; as parents; as aging, handicapped, or temporarily infirm workers; and so forth. It replaces, in other words, the fixed dichotomy of male versus female with attention to individual needs that is simultaneously sensitive to group-based hierarchy. This approach, then, rejects both the formal equality model of traditional liberalism and the special-treatment model proposed by some contemporary feminists. Neither individual assimilation to male norms nor group-based accommodation to categorically defined female needs provides an adequate framework.

In sum, gender neutrality has, like liberalism itself, a radical edge. Disentangled from the abstract individualism of its liberal origins, gender neutrality can support a view of difference that goes beyond the simplistic oppositions haunting the special-treatment/equal-treatment debate. Within such an expanded gender-neutral perspective, pregnancy and breastfeeding are no longer seen as abnormal conditions; neither are they viewed as immutably defining characteristics of sexual difference. Rather, childbearing is represented as one among many important categorical specificities that must be accommodated in a society transformed to equally meet the special needs of all.[41]

Equality and Difference as Strategy

□ The debate over special treatment of pregnancy took place in a charged strategic context. Benefits of immediate usefulness to women were at risk, as was the categorization of women as a class within the U.S. legal framework. Questions of immediate impact and short-term strategy thus converged with problems of long-term feminist vision. Within the feminist legal community, one either supported the California statute as an adequate implementation of the special-treatment perspective or opposed it on the basis of some version of the equality approach. In the heated atmosphere of the developing litigation, too little attention was paid to evaluating the competing positions as strategies proposed for a particular time and place and equally fraught with dangers and contradictions. At most, feminist legal scholars sought to transcend the dichotomized opposition of difference to equality in abstract terms.[42]

Some commentators have recently begun to conceptualize dilemmas concerning rights and equality as problems in the use of reforms to effect social change. Lawyer Elizabeth M. Schneider proposes, for example, that struggles using the discourse of rights and equality should be evaluated in terms of multiple criteria. "The assertion or 'experience' of rights can express political vision, affirm a group's humanity, contribute to an individual's development as a whole person, and assist in the collective political development of a social or political movement." Instead of dismissing rights claims as irredeemably shaped by their liberal origins, litigators can both acknowledge the limits of equality discourse and use it to move the struggle forward. Schneider offers the feminist demands for equality and reproductive rights as examples of the transformative potential of reform struggles centered on rights claims. "By concretizing an abstract idea and situating it within women's experience, these rights claims did not simply 'occupy' an existing right, but rather modified and transformed the nature of the right." Legal scholar Patricia J. Williams similarly underscores the consciousness-raising and empowering aspects of rights discourse. Focusing on African-Americans, she argues compellingly that subordinate groups experience the assertion of rights differently from dominant groups. For Blacks, she shows, rights discourse can be "deliciously empowering," and the struggle for equal rights is not a "dry process of reification . . . [but] the resurrection of life from 400-year-old ashes."[43]

Viewed as alternative reform strategies, variants of both the special-treatment and equal-treatment approaches to pregnancy ought to be carefully evaluated at several levels. As with any reform, feminists cannot, unfortunately, retain full control over the use and implementation of their conceptualizations—in this case, by legislators, judges, policymakers, and the media. Nor can we fully anticipate the ramifications of the positions we adopt. A number of questions therefore arise. To what extent, for example, will a particular policy approach to pregnancy in the workplace respond to women's immediate needs? In what ways might it be vulnerable to antiwoman revision in the courts and legislatures? How does a given approach to pregnancy in the workplace contribute to individual empowerment, to political education and organizing, and to the building of the movement? What are the implications of the approach for the future, and are they adequate to the feminist vision? Which feminist vision?

I can only sketch answers to these questions. With respect to short-term impact and vulnerability to atavistic revision, I find the practical arguments in favor of the so-called equal-treatment approach hard to counter. Classifications based on difference have always, in the U.S. context, had a sinister capacity to be used against groups so categorized. Nothing occurred during the Reagan years that might suggest a reduced vulnerability to such disadvantageous interpretations, nor is there much basis to predict a major shift in the near future. Although equality strategies are all flawed or incomplete to some extent, they have in fact served U.S. women of diverse class and race origins relatively well.[44] It is true that equality is a diffuse and limited notion, but those who on this basis reject the quest for equal rights spin a risky discourse and practice. From the perspective of subordinate groups, denial of equality is a burden too heavy to bear, while the assertion of rights can be practically useful and politically empowering.

Still, arguments stressing expediency are not enough to justify a position in favor of equal treatment of pregnancy in the workplace. The theoretical foundations for a radical version of this position must be more completely developed and the linkages to feminist aspirations for the future strengthened. The expanded gender-neutral perspective described here is, in my view, a start. In terms of immediate results and resistance to retrograde misinterpretation, gender neutrality provides minimum standards of equal treatment in the liberal sense. But it need not remain imprisoned in traditional liberal notions of the desirable sameness of abstract individuals. An expanded concept of gender neutrality can move beyond the imperatives of universal conformity to a single standard.

In short, gender neutrality can underpin policies that treat difference and diversity as entirely normal rather than as phenomena to be ignored or suppressed. The goal, in philosopher Iris M. Young's words, is "to de-normalize the way institutions formulate their rules by revealing the plural circumstances that exist, or ought to exist, within them." Rights could thus be extended to all persons in their human variety— rather than measured out in contradictorily equal portions to some on the basis of a presumed uniformity. Inclusion rather than exclusion would become the standard. Along the way, the meaning of difference could be transformed. As poet Audre Lorde appreciates, diversity is a boundless resource: "Difference must be not merely tolerated, but seen as a fund of necessary polarities between which our creativity can spark like a dialectic. . . . Difference is [a] raw and powerful connection."[45]

Notes

I would like to thank the many friends and colleagues whose thoughtful comments and suggestions—provided in myriad and diverse ways, and sometimes in sharp disagreement—have helped me develop the ideas presented here. I am particularly grateful to Eleanor Bader, Ava Baron, Joan Bertin, Kathleen Daly, Alice Kessler-Harris, Donna Lenhoff, Susan Reverby, Ronnie Steinberg, and Nadine Taub. Grants from Rider College and the American Council of Learned Societies partially supported the research. This article is dedicated to James S. Ackerman on his seventieth birthday.

1. The California suit and controversy had been foreshadowed by litigation over a similar pregnancy disability statute in Montana. For a brief summary of the litigation in both cases, see Herma Hill Kay, "Equality and Difference: The Case of Pregnancy," *Berkeley Women's Law Journal* 1 (Fall 1985): 1–38, esp. 10–15.

2. For example, feminists concerned with policy in the areas of divorce

and sexual harassment have questioned the ability of traditional equality strategies to confront sexual difference. See Lenore J. Weitzman, *The Divorce Revolution: The Unexpected Social and Economic Consequences for Women and Children in America* (New York: Free Press, 1985); Catharine A. MacKinnon, *Sexual Harassment of Working Women: A Case of Sex Discrimination* (New Haven: Yale University Press, 1979). Feminist understandings of difference and equality were also at issue in the controversial Sears case. See "Women's History Goes to Trial: EEOC v. Sears, Roebuck and Company," *Signs* 11 (Summer 1986): 751–79; Ruth Milkman, "Women's History and the Sears Case," *Feminist Studies* 12 (Summer 1986): 375–400.

3. For this overview, see Sheila B. Kamerman, *Maternity and Parental Benefits and Leaves: An International Review* (New York: Columbia University Press, 1980). Alena Heitlinger includes in-depth discussions of maternity and parental benefits in Eastern Europe in *Reproduction, Medicine, and the Socialist State* (New York: St. Martin's Press, 1987).

4. For the evaluation of protective legislation in this and the following paragraph, see Alice Kessler-Harris, *Out to Work: A History of Wage-Earning Women in the United States* (New York: Oxford University Press, 1982), chap. 7, and "The Debate over Equality for Women in the Work Place: Recognizing Differences," *Women and Work: An Annual Review* 1 (1985): 141–61. The feminist legal community often emphasizes the exclusionary aspects of protection in a presentist manner; see Ann Corinne Hill, "Protection of Women Workers and the Courts: A Legal Case History," *Feminist Studies* 5 (Summer 1979): 247–73; or Barbara Allen Babcock et al., *Sex Discrimination and the Law: Causes and Remedies* (Boston: Little, Brown & Co., 1975), 261–78.

5. For a useful summary of the situation as of the early 1970s, see Women's Bureau, U.S. Department of Labor, *1975 Handbook on Women Workers*, Bulletin no. 297 (Washington, D.C.: GPO, 1975), chap. 8, "Maternity Standards." On medical coverage as of 1976, see Dorothy R. Kittner, "Maternity Benefits Available to Most Health Plan Participants," *Monthly Labor Review* 101 (May 1978): 53–56. See also Elizabeth Duncan Koontz, "Childbirth and Childrearing Leave: Job-Related Benefits," *New York Law Forum* 17 (1971): 480–502. For a sampling of typical pregnancy rules deemed unacceptable by the courts in the past fifteen years, see Wendy W. Williams, "Equality's Riddle: Pregnancy and the Equal Treatment/Special Treatment Debate," *New York University Review of Law and Social Change* 13, no. 2 (1984–85): 325–80, esp. nn. 125, 127.

6. For discussion of the feminist legal framework developed and implemented in the 1960s and 1970s, see Williams, "Equality's Riddle," 329–32. Readers who are neither lawyers nor philosophers may wish to remind themselves that the term "equality" does not mean sameness or identity. On this issue I have found the following helpful: Hugo Adam Bedau, "Egalitarianism and the Idea of Equality," in *Equality: Nomos IX,* ed. J. Roland Pennock and

John W. Chapman (New York: Atherton Press, 1967), 3–27; Steven Lukes, *Individualism* (Oxford: Blackwell, 1973); and Bernard Williams, "The Idea of Equality," in *Philosophy, Politics, and Society,* 2d series, ed. Peter Laslett and W.G. Runciman (Oxford: Blackwell, 1962), 110–31. See also Deborah L. Rhode, "Feminist Perspectives on Legal Ideology," in *What Is Feminism?* ed. Juliet Mitchell and Ann Oakley (New York: Pantheon, 1986), 151–60; and Juliet Mitchell, "Women and Equality," in *The Rights and Wrongs of Women,* ed. Juliet Mitchell and Ann Oakley (Harmondsworth: Penguin Books, 1976), 379–99.

7. Sheila B. Kamerman, Alfred J. Kahn, and Paul Kingston, *Maternity Policies and Working Women* (New York: Columbia University Press, 1983); Williams, "Equality's Riddle."

8. General Electric Company v. Gilbert (1976), cited in Williams, "Equality's Riddle," 345.

9. Joyce Gelb and Marian Lief Palley, *Women and Public Policies* (Princeton: Princeton University Press, 1982), chap. 7.

10. The Pregnancy Discrimination Act amends Title VII of the Civil Rights Act specifying that "the terms 'because of sex' or 'on the basis of sex' include, but are not limited to, because of or on the basis of pregnancy, childbirth, or related medical conditions; and women affected by pregnancy, childbirth, or related medical conditions shall be treated the same for all employment-related purposes, including receipt of benefits under fringe benefit programs, as other persons not so affected but similar in their ability or inability to work."

11. In the 1970s, five states—California, Connecticut, Massachusetts, Montana, Wisconsin—enacted maternity leave legislation, generally mandating that an employer provide unpaid leave and a measure of employment security and benefit protection to eligible women workers. All but the Massachusetts law explicitly specify that the leave is to be based on pregnancy-related disability; Massachusetts defines the leave as childbirth-related. For an overview of the new maternity legislation, see Nancy E. Dowd, "Maternity Leave: Taking Sex Differences into Account," *Fordham Law Review* 54 (April 1986): 699–765, esp. 720–35.

12. The early stages of the debate are briefly described in Linda J. Krieger and Patricia N. Cooney, "The Miller-Wohl Controversy: Equal Treatment, Positive Action, and the Meaning of Women's Equality," *Golden Gate University Law Review* 13 (Summer 1983): 513–72, esp. 515–16.

13. Although the debate is generally characterized as opposing "special treatment" to "equal treatment," participants note the diversity of views within their camp, and some reject the terminology. Equal-treatment advocates are generally more comfortable with their label; for consideration of an alternative formulation, see the discussion in Nadine Taub and Wendy W. Williams, "Will Equality Require More Than Assimilation, Accommodation, or Separation from the Existing Social Structure?" *Rutgers Law Review* 37 (1985): 825–44.

Some proponents of so-called special treatment view the term as a derisive caricature. See, for example, Ruth Colker, "The Anti-Subordination Principle: Applications," *Wisconsin Women's Law Journal* 3 (1987): 62.

I generally retain the special-treatment/equal-treatment terminology in the following discussion, even though neither position is fully captured by its respective label. "Special" can convey, it seems to me, the sense of difference, affirmatively understood, that feminists want to endorse. "Equal" may too often be heard to mean "same" (see n. 6), however, and the equal-treatment perspective might more appropriately be called "gender-neutral," although that term also carries connotations of liberal individualism and the denial of difference. For lack of a better alternative, I adopt the term "gender-neutral" rather than "equal" in the latter sections of this essay.

14. Brief of the American Civil Liberties Union et al., amici curiae, in California Federal Savings and Loan Association v. Guerra, 85-494 U.S. Supreme Court, pp. A2–3; see also Tamar Lewin, "Pregnancy-Leave Suit Has Divided Feminists," *New York Times,* 28 June 1986, 52.

15. Wendy Williams, "The Equality Crisis: Some Reflections on Culture, Courts, and Feminism," *Women's Rights Law Reporter* 7 (Spring 1982): 175–200; Krieger and Cooney.

16. Williams, "Equality Crisis," 176.

17. Ibid., 195–96.

18. Reed v. Reed, 404 U.S. 71 (1971).

19. Williams, "Equality Crisis," 197 n. 122. See also 196 n. 113, for adverse impact analysis. Title VII of the 1964 Civil Rights Act has long been interpreted as prohibiting formally neutral rules where they have substantively negative consequences for a group. The solution in such a situation is a new rule that affects all employees in a truly neutral manner, not one that applies only to adversely impacted employees.

20. Ibid., 200.

21. Williams, "Equality's Riddle," 363, 367; and Taub and Williams, 838.

22. Krieger and Cooney, 533.

23. Ibid., 551. See also Krieger and Cooney, 545–46.

24. Of twenty-six states that introduced new pregnancy disability and/or parenting legislation following the Supreme Court decision in early 1987, about one-half adopted the special-treatment model and the rest took the gender-neutral approach. See "Parental Leave and Maternity Benefits Legislation Introduced 1987 Legislative Sessions," unpublished list, Women's Legal Defense Fund, April 1987.

25. Taub and Williams, 835–36. In this article, the authors extend their earlier discussions of the gender-neutral approach, addressing in particular critiques made by special-treatment proponents. Lucinda Finley uses Carol Gilligan's work in "Transcending Equality Theory: A Way Out of the Maternity

and the Workplace Debate," *Columbia Law Review* 86 (October 1986): 1118–82; the results still seem to fall squarely within a special-treatment perspective. Ava Baron emphasizes contradictions inherent in both positions in the debate and conceptualizes the issues in terms of the opposition between freedom or privacy and protection in "Feminist Legal Strategies: The Powers of Difference," in *Analyzing Gender: Perspectives from the Social Sciences,* ed. Myra Marx Ferree and Beth Hess (Beverly Hills, Calif.: Sage, 1987), 474–503. Joan W. Scott touches on issues relevant to the debate in "Deconstructing Equality-Versus-Difference: Or, the Uses of Poststructuralist Theory for Feminism," *Feminist Studies* 14 (Spring 1988): 33–50. Although deconstructionist theory seems to have a profoundly heuristic value for many, feminists (and others) have long been sensitive to the dangers to which it points: fixed oppositions, dualism, seemingly unitary categories, and language as a powerful and ambiguous mode of representation. We have, after all, been deconstructing "woman," "the family," and the socialism/feminism couplet since the late 1960s. Iris M. Young seeks to develop the foundations for a politics of difference; see, for example, "The Ideal of Community and the Politics of Difference," *Social Theory and Practice* 12 (Spring 1986): 1–26, and "Difference and Policy: Some Reflections in the Context of New Social Movements," *University of Cincinnati Law Review* 56 (1987): 535–50. For the politics of difference in history; see, among others, Kessler-Harris, "The Debate over Equality," and Nancy F. Cott, "Feminist Theory and Feminist Movements: The Past before Us," in *What Is Feminism?* 49–62.

26. For the full discussion, see my book, *Mothers on the Job: Maternity Policy in the U.S. Workplace* (New Brunswick, N.J.: Rutgers University Press, 1993). For the term "gender-neutral," see n. 13.

27. For the claim that the PDA harms poor and working-class women, see, for example, Krieger and Cooney, 545–46; Ann C. Scales, "Towards a Feminist Jurisprudence," *Indiana Law Journal* 56 (1980–81): 375–444, esp. 427; Reva B. Siegel, "Employment Equality under the Pregnancy Discrimination Act of 1978," *Yale Law Journal* 94 (March 1985): 929–56, esp. 932–33; and Wendy Chavkin, "Walking a Tightrope: Pregnancy, Parenting, and Work," in *Double Exposure: Women's Health Hazards on the Job and at Home,* ed. Wendy Chavkin (New York: Monthly Review Press, 1984), 196–213. For similar charges against the gender-neutral approach in the area of divorce and family law, see Martha Fineman, "Illusive Equality: On Weitzman's *Divorce Revolution,*" *American Bar Foundation Research Journal* (Fall 1986): 781–90.

28. I thank Nadine Taub for directing my attention to the insurance industry as a source of data and for discussing the data with me.

29. Laura Messina, "Maternity Benefits in Group Health and Disability Policies," *CPCU Annals* 29 (December 1976): 282–88; Mitchell Meyer, *Women and Employee Benefits* (New York: Conference Board, 1978), 7.

30. Carol C. McDonough and Linda H. Kistler, "An Evaluation of the Costs

of Pregnancy Disability," *Employee Benefits Journal* 6 (December 1981): 7–11. See also Kathryn McIntyre, "Pregnancy Law Hikes Short-Term Disability Costs," *Business Insurance,* 8 Feb. 1982, 1, reporting a survey of sixty-eight companies.

31. Daniel N. Price, "Cash Benefits for Short-Term Sickness, 1948–81," *Social Security Bulletin* 47 (August 1984): 23–38; esp. 37–38. Some of the rise in maternity costs could be due to a relative increase in the numbers of women of childbearing age in the labor force.

32. Janet Witte Burgstahler, "The Impact of the Pregnancy Discrimination Act of 1978 on Employee Health Insurance Benefit Levels" (Ph.D. diss., University of Iowa, 1984). See also Price, 37–38; and, for the pre-PDA norms, Kittner.

33. Williams, "Equality's Riddle," 350 n. 102; Koontz, 502.

34. For the text of the California statute, see Kay, 12 n. 16. For its history, see Brief of the National Organization for Women et al., amici curiae, in California Federal Savings and Loan Association v. Guerra, 85–494 U.S. Supreme Court, pp. 14–17; Susan M. Damplo, *"California Savings and Loan Ass'n. v. Guerra* and the Feminist Debate: Sameness/Difference Assumptions about Pregnancy in the Workplace," Georgetown University Law Center, 1987.

35. Special-treatment advocates are confused, I believe, in their analysis of how the notion of disability is used in both the PDA they critique and the special-treatment laws they support. The PDA nowhere mentions disability (see n. 10), although it did arise out of an attempt to counter the Supreme Court's denial of disability benefits to pregnant women. An early feminist identification of pregnancy with disability was in fact abandoned in the PDA (see my *Mothers on the Job*). Somewhat more startling is the fact that the pregnancy legislation favored by special-treatment advocates is in most cases legislation that explicitly designates its benefits as disability dependent; see n. 11.

36. Chavkin, 202.

37. Scales, 435.

38. Three other factors perhaps contribute to the spontaneous support many feel for the special-treatment approach. The first involves personal experience. Numerous women have told me how deeply drawn they are to the special-treatment position, often punctuating their comments with examples drawn from their own pregnancies. The second has to do with the legacy of protectionism. Most people interpret any benefits associated with childbearing as special treatment, even when in fact they may derive from gender-neutral provisions or policies. The third involves a philosophical confusion about the concept of equality. Equality does not mean identity or sameness and in fact can only be envisioned in the presence of difference (see the literature cited in n. 6). These three factors together seem to identify the gender-neutral approach in the minds of many with a position advocating no benefits for pregnancy—a policy view most feminists rightly abhor.

39. Taub and Williams, 839–40.

40. Williams, "Equality's Riddle," 367–68.

41. My approach to the transcendence of liberalism is indebted to Lukes. See also Young, "The Ideal of Community and the Politics of Difference" and "Difference and Policy."

42. For example, Finley; Kathleen Lahey, "...Until Women Themselves Have Told All That They Have to Tell...," *Osgoode Hall Law Journal* 23 (1985): 519–41; Ann Scales, "The Emergence of Feminist Jurisprudence: An Essay," *Yale Law Journal* 95 (1986): 1373–1403.

43. Elizabeth M. Schneider, "The Dialectic of Rights and Politics: Perspectives from the Women's Movement," *New York University Law Review* 61 (October 1986): 589–652, esp. 590, 642. Patricia J. Williams, "Alchemical Notes: Reconstructing Ideals from Deconstructed Rights," *Harvard Civil Rights–Civil Liberties Law Review* 22 (Spring 1987): 401–33, esp. 431, 430. See also Charlotte Bunch's discussion of reforms in *Passionate Politics: Feminist Theory in Action* (New York: St. Martin's Press, 1987), 103–17.

44. The skepticism voiced by many feminists concerning the results of the equality legislation seems to me too negative. Kessler-Harris suggests, for example, that the various federal laws designed to remove barriers to equality "have had little discernible impact for women as a whole" ("The Debate over Equality," 153). Schneider comments that "even with concrete legal gains, it is not clear how the lives of most women, particularly poor women and women of color, have changed. Certainly, women's economic realities have not improved" (633). As with any reform, equality legislation can only be evaluated through a complex multileveled analysis which includes the perspective of subordinate groups. The particular question of women's economic situation needs to be analyzed in the context of the general economic deterioration of the past decade and a half; my guess is that without the equality legislation, women today would be even worse off than they are.

45. Young, "Difference and Policy," 550. Audre Lorde, *Sister Outsider: Essays and Speeches* (Trumansburg, N.Y.: Crossing Press, 1984), 111–12.

Something Old, Something New: Auxiliary Work in the 1983-1986 Copper Strike

☐ The Arizona copper miners' strike against the Phelps Dodge Corporation gained national attention soon after it began in the summer of 1983. This bitter conflict was one of many dramatic defeats that organized labor suffered in the 1980s. The decade began with the destruction of the Professional Air Traffic Controllers Union (PATCO) in 1981, when Ronald Reagan dismissed thousands of striking controllers. Since then, once-mighty unions like the auto and steel workers have made concessions on a scale unheard of since the 1930s. And in Minnesota, Hormel meatpacking workers battled the National Guard as well as the company, the courts, and national officials of their own union, only to suffer defeat.[1]

The Phelps Dodge strike, like these other episodes in the labor history of the 1980s, received substantial coverage in the national media. Yet one central feature of the strike remains virtually unknown outside the local community—the political activity and struggle of the Morenci Miners Women's Auxiliary (MMWA), an organization composed primarily of miners' wives. This account of the MMWA strike participation shows that women can be central actors in labor struggles even when the workers involved are almost all male. However, the women's contribution to the Phelps Dodge strike was ignored or underestimated by the media, by the local community, and even by some of the women themselves. We write this account of their struggle in the hope that it will not remain hidden from history.

The MMWA efforts recall those of earlier women's labor auxiliaries. Feminist historians have recently reconstructed the history of several such organizations: the Ladies' Auxiliary in the 1934 Teamsters' strike in Minneapolis, the "Red Berets" in the Flint auto workers' strike of 1937,

Reprinted, with changes, from *Feminist Studies* 14, no. 2 (Summer 1988): 251–68. © 1988 by Feminist Studies, Inc.

and the auxiliary in the 1950–52 zinc miners' strike made famous by the film, *Salt of the Earth,* among others.[2] All these women's auxiliaries received much more public and media attention from contemporaries than the MMWA today—an ironic contrast in light of the much greater visibility of women in public life in the late twentieth century. Yet it is useful to place the MMWA in the historical perspective provided by these earlier examples of women's labor auxiliaries.

Background: The Strike and the Community

☐ On 1 July 1983, more than 2,300 workers from thirteen unions went out on strike against the copper mines owned by Phelps Dodge Corporation in Morenci, Arizona, rather than accept a two-tiered wage scale, elimination of cost-of-living allowances (COLA), and cuts in vacation and medical benefits. Phelps Dodge quickly moved to replace the striking workers. Governor Babbitt ordered more than 400 state troopers and 300 National Guards to "control" the strikers when Phelps Dodge began bringing in scabs in August 1983.[3]

The unions and Phelps Dodge negotiated sporadically during the strike. Almost a year after the strike began, the unions offered major concessions—a two-year freeze on COLA, a two-dollar-an-hour wage cut, and some shifting of medical costs to the workers if Phelps Dodge would take back the strikers and fire the replacement workers. Rejecting the unions' demands and apparently intent on busting the unions, Phelps Dodge refused to accept the concessions. Shortly after that, on the first anniversary of the walkout, the strike gained new notoriety when the police marched into town in full riot gear and used tear gas to break up a rally that most observers described as peaceful until the entrance of the National Guard.[4]

In October 1984, an election was held to decertify the unions. By that time, the union members had been out on strike for fifteen months, so only the 1,055 replacement workers and the 1,345 union members who had chosen to scab were eligible to vote.[5] Thus, the vote in favor of decertification surprised no one. A series of appeals by the unions delayed the official decertification by the National Labor Relations Board (NLRB) until 19 February 1986.

The strike brought profound changes to the mining communities of Morenci and Clifton, two adjacent towns totally dependent on Phelps Dodge for survival. Morenci is a company town where almost all the land and buildings, including all the housing, are owned by Phelps Dodge. Residents do not elect a town council. Clifton is not a company town, but it has no other industry and is economically dependent on

Phelps Dodge. Both towns are geographically isolated, high up in the eastern Arizona mountains. Because of the centrality of Phelps Dodge to the local economy, everyone in these two communities was affected by the strike and most had a strong opinion about it. Clifton and Morenci together had a total population of approximately 7,400[6] and are typical small towns where "everybody knows everybody." Thus, a person's position on the strike became a principal identifying characteristic, and the conflict pitted longtime neighbors, relatives, and friends against each other. It was common for people to fight, yell at each other, give each other "the finger," or simply refuse to say "hello" because of disagreements about the strike. Because there are few places to shop or to seek entertainment in this area, it was difficult, if not impossible, to avoid unpleasant encounters. In addition to open displays of hostility toward those on opposing sides, both strikers and scabs tried to control those who agreed with them. Scabs would chastise friends who were too cordial to strikers. Strikers would criticize those who shopped at the grocery store owned by Phelps Dodge. (To boycott the Phelps Dodge store, the only large, fully stocked store in the area, much cheaper than the smaller markets, was a serious sacrifice.)

The community split by the strike was also marked by ethnic divisions. Since the late 1800s, Hispanics had been relegated to the least skilled jobs in the copper industry. Older Hispanic women and men in Clifton and Morenci tell of being barred from the Morenci Club (this was changed in 1955), of segregated bathroom facilities and company housing, and of official restrictions on the use of Spanish.[7] Although the legal restrictions have changed, the stratification continues.

The strike both reflected that stratification and exacerbated ethnic hostilities. As one graffiti writer, responding to the word "SCAB" painted on a building, put it: "I'd rather be rich than an ignorant fucking Mexican union-loving son of a bitch." Although the majority of loyal union members were Hispanic, the majority of replacement workers (as well as Phelps Dodge management) were Anglo. Most union/nonunion conflicts were conflicts between Hispanics and Anglos. Furthermore, the company used ethnicity during the strike to divide the strikers. The police and the company treated the Hispanic strikers more harshly, for example, by dropping charges against Anglo strikers.

Most of the women we observed and interviewed were Hispanic, although some of the central actors were Anglo. Members tended to downplay the importance of ethnicity, in part because their organization was class-based and ethnically mixed, with friendships crossing ethnic lines. During moments of tension, however, ethnic identities would surface. Thus, the story of the strike involves the complex interaction of ethnicity, class, and gender.

The Work of the Morenci Miners Women's Auxiliary

☐ The MMWA was formed over forty years ago as part of the community support network for copper miners and their unions.[8] The copper miners were regularly drawn into strikes when their contracts came up for renegotiation, and the auxiliary was reactivated for each of those strikes.[9] In 1983, the auxiliary was once again reactivated to support the strike against Phelps Dodge.

The majority of MMWA members were the wives of miners, but the auxiliary was open to any woman even if she was not "directly" connected through family or work to the strike. The women in the auxiliary reported that they had more than 100 active members in 1984 at the height of the strike. By 1985, however, the number of active members had dropped to about 20, and after decertification became official, the auxiliary slowly disbanded.

Auxiliary members in the 1983–86 strike contrasted "their" work with that of the auxiliary in previous strikes. Fina Roman, the first president of the 1983 auxiliary, stated in a women's newspaper in Tucson that "historically the Women's Auxiliary was reinforcement for the family, finding ways to keep the children occupied, taking food to the picket line."[10] Although still committed to this aspect of the auxiliary in the 1983–86 strike, members prided themselves on being an important political organization. In contrasting the "new" auxiliary with the old, Roman told us that "the membership is different now. We don't just do what the auxiliary used to do. . . . When Governor Babbitt sent in the National Guard and the police to suppress the people who were fighting for an equitable contract, then it became political."[11]

The auxiliary engaged in a variety of activities during the strike. Some of the auxiliary work we observed was traditional, an extension of its members' domestic responsibilities. The members helped provide food, fuel, money, rides to the physician, and school supplies for strikers and their families. This work was maintained by the auxiliary's fund-raising events and joint work with the unions and the local food bank. The auxiliary also served as reinforcement for family when the members planned activities for the strikers, such as a Christmas party, Easter picnic, Labor Day cookout, Cinco De Mayo festival, and Fourth of July fiesta.

These activities not only provided nurturance and support for striking families, but they also served to build feelings of solidarity, commitment, and self-sufficiency among the strikers. In addition, the weekly meetings established by the auxiliary to discuss the subsistence needs of the strikers provided a forum for the exchange of political information and linked strikers to other organizations within the community like the union and the food bank.

MMWA members also participated in work not associated with the "traditional female role," and they were especially animated when they spoke about this. The maintenance of a picket line in Clifton was the most important example of what the women saw as the new political work of the auxiliary. The unions maintained an official picket line in Morenci at the gate of the mine. The impact of this line was limited because Phelps Dodge obtained legal restrictions on the pickets and made it physically difficult to picket by removing a picket shack and moving in piles of dirt to make it impossible to gather many people in this area.

The auxiliary's unofficial picket line was at the town line between Morenci and Clifton on a road that could not be avoided by miners going to work. The unofficial line created an opportunity for larger numbers of people and for nonminers (such as wives and retirees) to support the strike every day. Furthermore, the unofficial picket line was near some buildings owned by strike sympathizers who became involved by providing parking for picketers as well as places to store signs and other strike materials, like leaflets, balloons, and helium. In this way, the unofficial line allowed the strike to spill over into the community.

Auxiliary members also worked to bring the strike to the attention of people outside of Arizona. The Clifton-Morenci area is geographically isolated so that events there could be easily overlooked. The "informal" picket line organized by the MMWA was most effective at attracting the press, because it was larger and more colorful than the tightly restricted official line. On 5 May 1984, the auxiliary organized one of the largest rallies of the strike, attracting thousands of people. Importantly, this particular rally was not only not organized by the unions, but local union officials publicly denounced the plans for the rally and left town the day it took place in order to emphasize their decision not to participate.

The auxiliary also took the strike to others through national outreach. In 1984, four members went on a speaking tour of the West to raise funds and to publicize the strike. Two other members went to speak at the National Coalition of Labor Union Women (CLUW) meeting in Chicago. CLUW organization rules were suspended in order to pass the hat because the audience was so moved by their presentation. Jorge O'Leary, a company physician who was fired by Phelps Dodge for supporting the strike, together with members of the auxiliary, met with Bruce Springsteen to accept $10,000 to help provide healthcare services for the strikers. In 1985, MMWA members went to a national meeting of women miners in Utah. Anna O'Leary, the last president of the auxiliary, went to Nairobi on a scholarship to represent minority and poor women at the concluding session of the "Decade of Women."

Although the work of the MMWA supported the efforts of the striking miners in their fight against Phelps Dodge, auxiliary members also had their own particular concerns as wives. The "traditional" concerns of the auxiliary were not just reflections of their position in subordination to their husbands; the women were not "simply" helping or supporting their husbands. The goals of the strike and the strike itself became the women's as well.

The women organized to help each other put food on the table and provide clothing and school supplies for their children. As one member explained:

> And like I tell them [auxiliary members] we're all going to eat from the same plate. So, today I don't have a loaf of bread, I can always say I'll call this person or that person, "Do you have any bread? Do you have any salt?" And like I tell them, you're welcome to call me—if I have it, it's yours. Because we are going to have to help each other.[12]

Furthermore, their activities did not stop at helping each other to survive the strike. The auxiliary also actively fought Phelps Dodge and even the police in defense of the strike. As one member put it:

> Women are more aggressive when they see something harming their kids. . . . When the strikebreaker or scab, he's taking her husband's jobs away, taking the food away from your kids, taking the shoes off their feet, I think women are the first to respond to that. . . . They're seeing the destruction of the family, and they are going to come out with tooth and claw.[13]

The particular situation of women in their families and in their community gave them, at times, a vision of appropriate strategies that differed from that of the unions. We noted earlier that the auxiliary was central to the 1984 Cinco De Mayo rally that brought out thousands of strike supporters, although it was unsanctioned by the unions. The unions were not always happy with the auxiliary and attempted to contain it. Some members of the Steelworkers Union, the largest union involved in the strike, suggested at one point that the leaders of "their" auxiliary should be wives of Steelworkers. Because some of the more vocal leaders, including Anna O'Leary, the wife of the outspoken physician, Jorge O'Leary, were not wives of Steelworkers, this suggestion was interpreted by auxiliary members as an attempt to control them. MMWA members were happy when they "discovered" that the auxiliary historically had not been associated with any particular union.[14]

The planning of the second anniversary of the walkout illustrates not only the auxiliary's role in challenging the unions during the strike but also the way in which the unions were able to sometimes contain their challenge.[15] The unions and the MMWA did not agree on the best way to recognize the second anniversary. The unions wanted it to be commemorated in Tucson, 170 miles away from Clifton-Morenci, but the auxiliary wanted the event to be held in the striking community. Auxiliary members did not shy away from risking another violent encounter with the police, because they believed they needed to keep national attention focused on their plight.[16] The unions wanted to avoid violence, and the union position prevailed, in part because the unions made it clear that they would not provide legal assistance to anyone who was arrested during a rally in Clifton on that day.[17] So, the anniversary was celebrated by a $100-a-plate fund-raiser in Tucson followed by a musical program in a large hotel to which miners were bussed from Clifton.

The auxiliary also challenged gender within the families of several members. Although the women in the auxiliary never became card-carrying feminists (they frequently declared that they were not "libbers"), they did start talking about their rights and encouraging each other to make demands of their husbands. For example, the MMWA women began violating a community norm by going to a local bar with other women instead of their husbands. They justified this by saying they had worked hard and deserved it. Simply setting aside one night a week to attend a meeting often meant a challenge to the husband's authority (such challenges were significant to the auxiliary members). The women were trying to be good wives and mothers by supporting the strike. Ironically, by doing so they put themselves in a situation that offered a potential challenge to domesticity.

Auxiliary Work: Historical Continuities

☐ The activities of the MMWA seemed new to most participants and observers. However, they were strikingly similar to those of previous women's auxiliaries in the 1934 Teamsters' strike, the 1937 Flint auto workers strike, the Colorado Coal Strike of 1913, the Harlan County strikes in the 1970s in Kentucky, and the zinc miners' strike of 1950–52, portrayed in *Salt of the Earth*.[18] Some of the common themes we found include the distinction participants made between "domestic" work and political work; the transition made between these two types of work as the strike wore on; the political effect of apparently domestic activities; the separate challenge posed by the auxiliary to the company on the basis of a set of interests that were related but not identical to their husbands' interests; and the spillover of the women's strike work into another area of politics—gender relations within their families.

The MMWA distinguished between the "old" work of family reinforcement and "new" work that was more conventionally political. Marjorie Penn Lasky observed the same kind of distinction in the 1934 Teamsters' strike auxiliary.

> Auxiliaries performed highly stereotypical "women's work" with the labor movement—preparing food, administering first aid, and performing union office work during the strikes, for example. . . . Sometimes, however, auxiliary activities spilled beyond the boundaries of conventional female roles, especially during strikes, when women often assumed quasi-military responsibilities.[19]

In both the MMWA and the 1934 auxiliary, a distinction was made between these two types of work, and the strike seemed to bring out the second kind of activity. That is, the auxiliary in both cases assumed the familial support work, but as the strike progressed, its activities more clearly began to encompass other political work. In the MMWA case, the president of the auxiliary, Fina Roman, as quoted earlier, actually dated this transition as being a result of police violence against the strikers.

In the MMWA, the women distinguished between the two kinds of work and tried to get others to acknowledge their "nontraditional" work. Lasky notes this distinction but it is not clear that the Teamsters' auxiliary women did. Furthermore, Lasky suggests that the distinction may have been blurred because all the work of the auxiliary was understood to have the same motivation. That is, no matter what the activities were—making sandwiches or fighting the scabs—the motivation was explicitly defined as an extension of the women's domestic roles and responsibilities.[20]

Lasky observed, as we did, that the work of the auxiliary, even when it appeared to be the old traditional work, actually accomplished a political task of unifying the strikers. She noted that "tactically, the workers' kitchen was an inspiration. It not only fed its army well, but, just as importantly, it encouraged community solidarity—providing the only arena where strikers from many businesses, and their families, could stay in touch with each other and strike events."[21] Priscilla Long also noted that women in the Colorado coal miners' strike "played an indispensable role in helping form a cohesive unified striker's community —a community of resistance."[22] Patricia Yeghissian writes that the kitchens were so politically important in the 1937 Flint strike that General Motors attempted to destroy them.[23]

These examples present an interesting contrast to the zinc miners' strike documented in *Salt of the Earth*. In that case, the men took over the domestic tasks and the women took over the strike. The political contribution of the "women's" activities was not acknowledged as important and the women themselves did not gain the limelight until they took up "men's" work. Even the writers of *Salt of the Earth* assumed that effective, important, political work does not include making sandwiches or other "domestic" activities.

Our observation, that strike support work (even when it was "simply" domestic work) affected gender relations between auxiliary members and their husbands, was shared by Long and Lasky. Another important similarity in our observations, and in those of other miners' strikes, is that the women—despite the fact that they were not directly employed by the mine owners—had their own conflicts with the company that they expressed by their strike support work. One of the most famous examples of the conflict between the wives of the miners and the owners of the mine was depicted in *Salt of the Earth*, when the women demanded that the company provide a better water supply system. At first, this demand was not recognized as important by the men because they did not have to haul water for cooking and washing as the women in the community did. The MMWA demands on Phelps Dodge were mainly for better pay, job security, and safety for the miners. However, the women's own interests were also served by these demands, because their ability to do their work as housewives (not to mention their ability to survive) was affected by the money coming into their households.

Auxiliary Work in the 1980s: New Tensions

☐ Despite all the similarities between the MMWA and these other auxiliaries, there was one important difference. In the 1983–86 copper strike, the relationship between the union and the auxiliary was not entirely happy; there were tensions as well as agreement about goals and strategies. In contrast, most contemporaries and historians record harmony between auxiliaries and unions. For example, Roy Reuther said of the women in the 1937 Flint strike: "They are crusaders in the new American Labor Movement and their fighting spirit is an inspiration to all workers."[24] Of the Colorado strike, Long said that "the union viewed the participation of the women as an essential strategy. The women were at least as effective as the men in a demonstration or a picket line and they were less likely to be physically attacked."[25] In the zinc strike, the local went so far as to initiate the involvement of the wives in the strike by delivering the union newspapers to miners' homes so that they would be seen by wives.[26] In contrast, we recorded incidents of conflict between MMWA and the unions. What accounts for the conflict which was apparently missing from earlier strikes? We offer three possibilities.

First, the conflict—or more precisely the lack of conflict—may be a methodological artifact. Auxiliaries and unions agree in general on the goal, and both define themselves in opposition to management or capital. In studies relying on retrospective interviews, it is this general level of agreement (and whether the strike was won or lost) that is perhaps most salient. Furthermore, it makes sense for union sympathizers to avoid public displays of disagreement. In our study, most of the conflict was observed behind the scenes—in auxiliary meetings. It is quite likely that if these women were interviewed today, their antagonisms toward Phelps Dodge would overshadow any conflict they had with the unions.

This methodological problem may be especially apparent in *Salt of the Earth*, which was created in retrospect, but more importantly was a historically based but partly fictitious creation by filmmakers who had definite ideas about the message they wished to convey. Deborah Rosenfelt said that "the film carefully shapes, selects, and synthesizes characters and episodes. Not every incident in the film happened in this particular strike; obviously not every incident in the strike went into the film. . . . The film's use of the various resources of the medium underlines its themes instead of complicating them." Furthermore, she suggests that one of those themes is the "coalescence of the different struggles."[27] The goal of the filmmakers was to present a focused and simplified picture of the strike instead of one that showed all the diversity and conflicts that may have characterized the real strike.

Assuming that the higher level of conflict in the copper strike is real, there are two possible explanations. First the organization of gender is currently in flux, so any threat to the status quo may be taken more seriously by men. The women of the MMWA could invoke feminist rhetoric, whereas women in earlier studies did not have this rhetoric available. As mentioned earlier, the women protested that they were not "libbers," but their organization nevertheless frequently resembled a consciousness-raising group. In the MMWA meetings, the women talked about rights and fairness when dealing with their personal problems and encouraged each other to make demands on their husbands. They began to question norms of behavior which they had once tolerated, such as being allowed to go to a bar alone. At times, women also acted together as a group in opposition to men. For example, at the beginning of the strike, the husbands of some of the women sat outside the auxiliary meetings, ostensibly to protect the women from possible assaults. After some time, only one man continued to come. He was tolerated for some time; but then the group began to see his behavior as inappropriate (he was perceived as overly possessive of his wife), and they demanded that he no longer attend. This story does not have a happy ending, with the wife gaining a feminist consciousness. Instead, she quit coming to the meetings. But the group did redefine acceptable behavior with a more feminist ideology. And the redefinition was public and potentially threatening to the men.

Some of the women began using gender politics to explain other politics. One member, in discussing a conflict with the union, explained that the relationship between the union and the auxiliary "is like a marriage. We are underfoot. If we agreed to everything they did, we'd just be at home letting them do it. That's probably what they want."[28]

Lasky argues that a lack of this kind of feminist understanding and rhetoric was at least part of the explanation (albeit not the most important one) for why the Ladies' Auxiliary in the 1934 strike did not challenge union orders.

> Women's internalization of conventional gender ideology and the lack of an alternative ideology only partially explain their inability to challenge union order. Also crucial were men's actions to discourage female autonomy ... the Trotskyists actively curbed women's behavior and defused women's militancy. So, too, did the union rank and file. Most men only grudgingly accepted women's presence at the headquarters. Occasionally a picket demanded to know why a woman wasn't home where she belonged, or who was caring for her children while she was working. Although women responded with cutting retorts, these exchanges rarely moved beyond traditional ideas of female subservience.[29]

In 1934, the potential for conflict between the auxiliary and the union was clear, but apparently its expression was suppressed.

The union movement in the 1980s was different in two important ways from prior decades; these differences may also have contributed to the "new tensions" we observed. At this time, the union movement was declining and was more clearly on the defensive. The gains made by the union movement in the past fifty years appear to be rapidly deteriorating through concessions, decertifications, and changes in the interpretation of labor laws. In addition, the proportion of workers in organized unions has declined steadily in the past decade, and employers have grown bolder in breaking the law to stop organizing campaigns.[30] Although there were certainly union defeats in the first half of the century and organizers and participants were undoubtedly discouraged at times, the union movement as a whole was on the rise. The 1983–86 Arizona copper strike appears to be part of a trend in the opposite direction toward the demise of unions. This may make unions less tolerant of criticisms and disagreements.

Another difference in unions today is that they are more bureaucratized and entrenched at the national level.[31] Conflicts between the unions and the MMWA may have been rooted not only in gender but also in other political differences. The auxiliary was deeply embedded in a community; the local union officials were tied to the internationals. Therefore, the conflict expressed was between local rank-and-file strikers, along with strike supporters in the community, and representatives of national unions based in faraway Washington and New York. Indeed, early in the strike, Jorge O'Leary became a popular "unofficial" leader—much to the chagrin of local union officials. The internationals' approach to the strike was legalistic, in sharp contrast to the innovative and militant approach advocated by the MMWA and some rank-and-file strikers. The internationals' entire strategy was to win the strike in the NLRB hearings. Many rank-and-file strikers, the MMWA, and leaders like O'Leary instead attempted to call for more widespread national support. At one point, O'Leary went so far as to call for a general strike.[32]

Community organizations often develop a perspective on labor struggles that differs from that of the unions. In her account of the 1973–74 Brookside Miners Strike in Harlan County, Linda Ewen suggests that local women had a broader view of their struggle than did the union officials and were more likely to support other local strikes.[33] Similarly, writing about the coal miners' strike in Britain, Jeremy Harding argues that those most embedded in the community were more militant in their support of the strike.

> The most committed support for the miners came not from the national centralized political and labor institutions but from the political cultural margins, from beleaguered left-wing councils running inner city areas, from certain isolated sectors of the church, from women, from gays, from blacks who perceived a direct relation between police handling of the pickets and the nature of the police in their own areas—in other words, from "crisis ridden communities."[34]

Conclusions: Auxiliary Work as Invisible

☐ Despite all their activity, the work of the MMWA was generally ignored. One of the most astonishing examples of this was continued in a 1985 article about the strike in *Newsweek*.[35] The update consisted of a written report and a picture. The report described the strike and discussed the effects of the strike on the community. The picture showed a group of people at a rally holding signs and jeering scabs. The article stated that the main actors in the group were the miners, the unions, and Jorge O'Leary. The people in the picture were not miners or union officials; they were members of the auxiliary—an organization not mentioned in the article. Furthermore, the women pictured were not simply participants in the rally; they had organized it.[36]

When the MMWA was recognized, it was acknowledged in narrow ways. Strikers tended to focus on the auxiliary's domestic activities, such as providing "menudo" (a soup made with entrails) for those on the picket line. For example, when asked by an interviewer what he thought about the MMWA, one striker praised the auxiliary's tortilla sales and Christmas party. Listening to him, an auxiliary member tried to coach him by repeating "la línea, la línea" (referring to the picket line the auxiliary had organized).[37]

When the media recognized the auxiliary at all, it ignored its "political" work. Most of the coverage of the MMWA women was limited to "human interest" stories.[38] Even the leftist media ignored the activities of the auxiliary.[39] One of the few articles to focus on women's role in the strike examined the contribution of women miners (a distinct minority) instead of the auxiliary.[40]

This lack of attention is particularly ironic because earlier auxiliary work, especially that documented in *Salt of the Earth*, received more attention than the MMWA. Why? Perhaps women's broader participation in public life today makes any particular instance of political work less newsworthy. In the 1950s when the famous New Mexico strike occurred, the nontraditional work of the auxiliary was in stark contrast to gender ideology of the times. Thus, it made a good news story.

Although certainly women's participation in public life is more newsworthy during some historical periods than in others, we do not think this explains the lack of recognition of the work of the MMWA. After all, it does not require a dramatic story—only a sentence—for *Newsweek* to report that the rally it photographed was organized by the MMWA.

We think that the work of the women was ignored because it was not understood partly because the women stood outside the traditional arena of labor disputes—they were neither workers nor management. Perhaps more importantly, the work of the MMWA was not understood because most observers lacked a feminist perspective. What little coverage the MMWA received evidenced a superficial awareness of feminism. As noted earlier, pieces focused on either "exceptional" women (such as women miners) or, in a rather patronizing manner, on the gender socialization of Hispanic women. Feminism was, in essence, reduced to a perspective that acknowledges that women can "be like men" or one that tells women they must overcome inadequate socialization.

A feminist perspective calls for new ways of thinking about the world; yet the media clings to the old categories. The work of the MMWA was viewed by the media, the community, and even the women themselves through a lens that places domestic work in opposition to political work. People know of the "traditional" work of the MMWA but, mirroring societal judgments about domestic work, essentially dismiss it. (Domestic work may make life more pleasant but it is not "really" important.) The strong association of the auxiliary with domestic work, coupled with a view that political and domestic work are incompatible, blinded people to MMWA's "political" work. In contrast, the auxiliary in *Salt of the Earth* was remembered largely because it rejected "women's work" in favor of "men's work."

Michelle Rosaldo wrote of the domestic and public dichotomy:

> There is some cause to think our acceptance of these terms makes sense; but at the same time, it would now appear that understandings shaped by oppositional modes of thought have been—and will most likely prove themselves to be—inherently problematic for those of us who hope to understand the lives that women lead in human societies.[41]

This oppositional mode of thinking certainly helped obscure the contribution of the MMWA. Although some auxiliaries have received more publicity than this one, the work of working-class women in auxiliaries remains largely ignored and underestimated. Women may be praised when they do "men's work," but the total range of their work and the significance of their contribution remains invisible.

Notes

1. William Serrin, "Labor Movement: Era of Hard Times," *New York Times,* 7 June 1986, sec. I, 8; Ed Townsend, "For Fifth Year in a Row, Unions Accept Smaller Wage Increases to Protect Jobs," *Christian Science Monitor,* 23 Oct. 1985, 8; "Thousands Struck and Lost Jobs," *New York Times,* 7 June 1986.

2. Marjorie Penn Lasky, "Where I Was a Person: The Ladies' Auxiliary in

the 1934 Minneapolis Teamsters' Strikes," in *Women, Work, and Protest: A Century of U.S. Women's Labor History*, ed. Ruth Milkman (Boston: Routledge & Kegan Paul, 1985), 181–206; Patricia Yeghissian, "Emergence of the Red Berets," *Michigan Occasional Papers*, no. 10 (Winter 1980); Linda Ewen, *Which Side Are You On?* (Chicago: Vanguard Books, 1979); Priscilla Long, "The Women of the Colorado Fuel and Iron Strike, 1913–1914," in *Women, Work, and Protest*, 62–86; Michael Wilson and Deborah Rosenfelt, *Salt of the Earth* (Old Westbury, N.Y.: Feminist Press, 1978).

3. Leo Banks, "The Strike: One Year on the Line," *Arizona Daily Star*, 1 July 1984, 1. Of the 2,900 strikers who were out at this time, 2,300 had walked out and 600 had been laid off prior to the actual strike.

4. For summaries, see Ed Lopez, "Copper Strikers Cut Demands in New Talks," *Arizona Daily Star*, 9 June 1984, 1; and John DeWitt, "The Anatomy of a Riot," *Arizona Daily Star*, 9 July 1984.

5. William Serrin, "Fury Etches Strikers' Life in Crumbling Fight at Arizona Mines," *New York Times*, 30 July 1984, A8.

6. These figures are for 1984, from *Arizona Statistical Review*, Valley National Bank, 40th Annual Edition (September 1984).

7. For a review of ethnic stratification in the copper industry, see Terry Boswell, "Race, Class, and Markets: Ethnic Stratification and Labor Market Segmentation in the Metal Mining Industry, 1850–1880" (Ph.D. diss., University of Arizona, 1984); and Michael E. Parrish, *Mexican Workers, Progressives, and the Wilson Years* (La Jolla: Chicano Research, 1979). For some local history, see A. Blake Brophy, *Foundlings on the Frontier: Racial and Religious Conflicts in Arizona Territory, 1904–1905* (Tucson: University of Arizona Press, 1972).

8. Auxiliary brochure, no date.

9. Confidential interview, conducted March 1985, Clifton, Arizona.

10. Barbara Golseth, "Break in Tradition Shatters Their Lives," *Clarion*, September 1984.

11. Interview conducted with Fina Roman, Clifton, Arizona, 9 Jan. 1985. This quotation is a typical example of the political sophistication and organizational skills of members of the MMWA. Roman, who had been an organizer for the United Farm Workers for many years, was particularly experienced, but others did not have as much organizational experience. However, lifetimes spent in union families in a mining town constantly in conflict with the company had created an articulate and politically aware group of people.

12. Confidential interview, Morenci, Arizona, 18 Jan. 1985.

13. Confidential interview, 28 Jan. 1985.

14. Field notes, 30 July 1985. The women were overjoyed to "discover"—it was never clear how—that they were never officially affiliated with the Steelworkers. If they had discovered otherwise, they would have declared themselves a new, independent organization.

15. Here we are identifying the local union officials who were controlled by the internationals as "the unions." They were sometimes in agreement with the local rank and file and sometimes not.

16. In this study we often speak of the auxiliary as a homogeneous entity, but this was definitely not the case. Members disagreed on a variety of issues, such as the direction the auxiliary should take, the level of radicalism, and so forth. An analysis of the various "factions" and their interactions would be another study in itself.

17. Field notes, 26 June 1985.

18. See note 2.

19. Lasky, 181.

20. Ibid.

21. Ibid., 190.

22. Long, 72.

23. Yeghissian.

24. Roy Reuther, cited in ibid., 12.

25. Long, 75.

26. Wilson and Rosenfelt, 137.

27. Ibid., 146–47.

28. Telephone conversation with Anna O'Leary, 25 Sept. 1985.

29. Lasky, 197.

30. Jack Barbash, "Trade Unionism from Roosevelt to Reagan," *Annals of the American Academy of Political and Social Sciences* 437 (May 1984): 11, 22; Robert Ziegler, *American Workers, American Unions, 1920–1985* (Baltimore: Johns Hopkins University Press, 1986), 193; Paul Weiler, "Promises to Keep: Securing Workers' Rights to Organization under the NLRB," *Harvard Law Review* 96 (June 1983): 1769–1827; Alan Kistler, "Union Organizing: New Challenges and Prospects," *Annals of the American Academy of Political and Social Sciences* 437 (May 1984): 96–107; Thomas Edsall, *The Politics of Inequality* (New York: W.W. Norton, 1984).

31. Arthur Schwartz and Michele Hoyman, "Changing the Guard: The New American Labor Leader," *Annals of the American Academy of Political and Social Sciences* 437 (May 1984): 664–75; and Samuel Friedman, *Teamster Rank and File: Power, Bureaucracy, and Rebellion at Work* (New York: Columbia University Press, 1982). These two pieces present very different points of view on the issue of bureaucracy. Although they agree that an intense bureaucratization has occurred in unions in recent U.S. history, Schwartz and Hoyman argue that bureaucracy is useful, but Friedman maintains that bureaucracy is a political vehicle for the repression of labor activity that would serve the real interest of the workers. Although many people have written on this question, these two present an especially good contrast.

32. At one point during the strike, rank-and-file miners attempted to challenge the international by running a slate of officers who did not agree

with the direction of the strike being promoted by the international. The challengers lost the election.

33. Ewen, 54.

34. Jeremy Harding, "After Miners' Strike: What Next for Labor?" *In These Times*, 29 May–11 June 1985, 9.

35. David Gates, "Losing Battle in Arizona," *Newsweek*, 22 July 1985, 9.

36. We are not trying to argue here that the MMWA was the most important factor in the strike. However, its invisibility contrasts sharply with the important role it did play.

37. Conversation at a rally, 30 June 1985 in Tucson. This was first brought to our attention by Barbara Russell who videotaped the interview.

38. See, for example, Pam Izakowitz, "Anna O'Leary," *Arizona Daily Star*, 30 June 1985.

39. We looked at the *People's Tribune, World Magazine, Guardian, Militant, Bulletin, Progressive, Village Voice*, and *In These Times*. See, for example, David North, "Class Wars at Phelps Dodge," *Bulletin*, November 1984; "Copper Strikers Rally: Governor Calls Guard," *People's Tribune*, 4 June 1984, 5; "Unions Rally to Back Phelps Dodge Strikers," *World Magazine*, 15 Dec. 1984, M3; Scott Egan, "Copper Miners Barricade Town during Police Riot," *Guardian*, July 1984, 9; "Copper War," *Village Voice*, 19 Mar. 1985, 7.

40. Barbara Kingsolver and Jill Fein, "Women on the Line," *Progressive* (March 1984).

41. Michelle Rosaldo, "The Use and Abuse of Anthropology: Reflections on Feminism and Cross-Cultural Understanding," *Signs* 5 (Spring 1980): 389–417.

Women Workers and the Yale Strike

☐ In 1971 Lucille Dickess, the registrar of the Yale University Geology Department, served on an anti-union committee. Yet in the fall of 1984, after working at Yale for sixteen years, she became a spokeswoman for the striking clerical and technical employees, or C&Ts, at Yale. In 1985 she was president of her union, Local 34 of the Federation of University Employees. Like Dickess, most women workers at Yale had no experience with unions until they formed Local 34. Yet despite the antilabor climate of the 1980s, they organized an unusually democratic union which won nationwide support during its ten-week strike for pay equity.

One of the first major labor disputes to make economic discrimination against women and minorities a central issue, the Yale strike illuminates the issues and organizational forms likely to emerge as more pink-collar workers join unions. Perhaps because the women's movement has raised women's expectations and self-respect, and because they are spending more years in the paid labor force, growing numbers of women working in the expanding service sector are looking to unions to improve their working conditions. In the past decade, the number of unionized office workers (especially in the public sector) has increased dramatically. Clerical workers have also unionized at some universities, angered by the contrast between their inadequate salaries and working conditions and the prestige and humanitarian reputations of the institutions that employ them. Nevertheless, organizing office workers is difficult, both because management anti-union campaigns make union activism risky and because (in contrast to predominantly male unions) women's unions challenge their family role. By building women's confidence and sense of self-worth so that they no longer subordinate their own needs to those of their employer (and by taking time and energy away from their families), women's union activism challenges not only the power relations at work but also those at home

Reprinted, with changes, from *Feminist Studies* 11, no. 3 (Fall 1985): 465–89. © 1985 by Feminist Studies, Inc.

and in the community. For this reason, addressing "women's" issues alone may not lead women to become active in unions. Only their participation in the leadership as well as the rank and file of the organization ensures a union that truly addresses women's concerns.

Like its predominantly female leadership and democratic structure, Local 34's strategies distinguish it from traditional unions. Rather than depending on withdrawal of services to win the strike, Local 34 organized the entire community to bring public pressure to bear on the university. Because of its unique character, the Yale strike captured the imagination of the nation and received uncommonly strong support from students, faculty, and, especially, the labor movement. Although women workers have often organized despite the opposition of labor leaders, Local 34 received unqualified backing from unions. Its parent union, the Hotel Employees and Restaurant Employees International Union (HERE), provided Local 34 with an office, a staff of experienced organizers, and substantial financial support, while allowing it local autonomy. The members of Local 35, Yale's blue-collar union, raised their dues to help cover the C&Ts' organizing expenses and honored Local 34's picket lines for ten weeks. The solidarity between students and employees, female and male, Black and white, and blue- and white-collar workers that resulted from the strike has permanently altered the social and political dynamics of Yale University.

The Yale strike was the culmination of a four-year organizing drive. Local 34 won its election by just thirty-nine votes in May 1983, but its effective organizing program and the frustration felt by workers after six months of fruitless negotiations led more C&Ts to vote to strike than had voted for the union ten months earlier. In an unorthodox move, union members narrowly averted a strike in March 1984 when they voted at the last minute to accept a partial contract that resolved the noneconomic issues yet retained the right to strike over outstanding items. Still unsuccessful at resolving their dispute through negotiations, 1,800 Local 34 members walked off their jobs on September 26, 1984. In yet another controversial action, they returned to work on December 3 without having settled their contract. They set a strike deadline for January 19, the date the contract of Local 35 (the service and maintenance workers who had honored the picket line throughout the strike) expired. Both unions won excellent contracts that made major strides in eliminating economic discrimination against women at Yale without having to strike a second time. Local 34 ratified its contract January 22, and Local 35 did so several days later. The historic struggle of women workers at Yale, settled just as Ronald Reagan was being inaugurated to a second term, ended with a stunning victory.

Building the Organization

☐ Although clerical and technical work assured the smooth functioning of the university, C&Ts' contribution to the university was undervalued and unseen because they worked in traditionally women's jobs. "Over a period of many years," they reported, "many of us felt that we were the invisible part of the Yale community: there to do the work without which the University couldn't function, but overlooked, ignored, voiceless."[1]

The diversity of the work force and physical isolation of the C&Ts made it difficult for them to see that they had common concerns. The clerical and technical group was 82 percent women, 14 percent Black, and 3 percent other minorities.[2] They were young and old, with significant differences in skill and wage levels. The bargaining unit comprised 257 job titles, including secretaries, computer programmers, editorial assistants, athletic trainers, laboratory aides, and licensed practical nurses. They included single mothers, long-term employees who had been wage earners all their lives, women who had returned to the work force after their children entered school, the wives of faculty and graduate students, and Yale alumni working in laboratories before attending medical school. Because the 2,600 C&Ts worked in 220 buildings across campus, many of them were isolated from other women facing similar conditions. Although workers in large units such as the library and administrative offices worked closely together, many others worked more closely with students and faculty than with fellow C&Ts, and they tended to identify with the "university" more than with other workers. As women used to working alone and without recognition, they had little sense of the value of their work.

The lack of value accorded women's work at Yale was evident in low C&T salaries. A faculty report found that the $13,424 average salary of Yale C&Ts fell below that of Connecticut office workers and that the average salary for Yale administrative assistants (the most common job classification) was less than the *minimum* for the comparable position at Harvard.[3] Job segregation by sex was the greatest cause of the low wages of Yale's female employees. Although (mostly female) administrative assistants earned an average salary of $13,524, Yale's truck drivers (all male) received $18,470. According to economics professor Raymond Fair, when age, time at Yale, time in labor grade, and education were held constant, women workers earned $694 less than men, and Blacks earned $1,061 less than whites.[4] Even within the clerical and technical group, Blacks and women worked in the lowest paying jobs. Although the average salary of white male C&Ts was $14,324, white women earned only $13,408. The average wage of Black women was only $12,603, even though, on the average, they had worked at Yale longest.[5]

Despite substantial employee dissatisfaction due to low wages and management's lack of appreciation for their work, the majority of Yale C&Ts were initially mistrustful of unions. District 65 and the Office and Professional Employees International Union lost elections by wide margins in 1971 and 1977, and a United Auto Workers (UAW) campaign was foundering when Local 34 began its organizing drive in 1980. Although they were accustomed to a union presence at Yale (the service and maintenance workers had been unionized since the 1930s), many of the clerical workers identified unions with blue-collar men with whom they felt they had little in common, considered unions (like the blue-collar workers) to be outside of the academic community with which they identified, and thought unions had little to say to a mostly female work force. Like Lucille Dickess, some of the clerical and technical workers who later joined Local 34 scabbed during the bitter blue-collar strikes of the 1970s.

Under the leadership of business manager Vincent Sirabella (who went on to become organizing director for HERE), Local 35 had become a tough and militant union whose long strikes in 1971, 1974, and 1977 had divided the campus but made Local 35 members among the highest paid service workers in the country.[6] Even before Local 34 was organized, Local 35 recognized the importance of unionizing the white-collar employees and uniting all the workers at Yale. Aware that with only 1,300 Yale workers, Local 35 did not have the power to shut down the university during a strike, Sirabella supported the three unsuccessful organizing drives of the 1970s. Although he left New Haven before the Federation of University Employees began to organize the C&Ts in 1980, HERE funded the organizing drive. Since the early 1970s, the international union had provided HERE Local 217 of southern Connecticut (which was also led by Sirabella) with an annual subsidy in order to train union leaders. Using that subsidy, which continues to this day, Sirabella trained the staff (including Local 34's chief negotiator John Wilhelm) who later directed the Yale drive. In turn, they trained the current leaders of Local 34.[7]

In order to build confidence and a collective commitment to their enterprise, as well as develop union leaders, Local 34's strategy focused on building a strong organization with rank-and-file leadership. Often intimidated by the university's power and intellectual arguments against the union, Yale office workers needed time to build a union that was truly their own. With a union staff borrowed from Local 35 and Local 217, Local 34's paid organizers began in the fall of 1980 to make home visits and hold lunch meetings in order to build rank-and-file leaders into an organizing committee. During the first year and a half of the union drive, they used no leaflets, buttons, or membership cards, just talk. Not until December 1981, after 400 organizing committee members signed their first public statement, called "Standing Together," did the union distribute membership cards. Local 34's organization-building strategy, which differs from the issue orientation of most unions now organizing women workers, was designed to ensure that workers would have the collective strength to win their demands.

The structure of the union was based on the layout of Yale so that ideally every group of workers would be represented. The organizing committee consisted of more than 400 leaders drawn from most departments and work groups. About 150 organizing-committee members able to assume additional responsibility joined the steering committee, and leaders of that group joined the union staff, which eventually included more than fifty rank-and-file as well as paid organizers. The union's complicated structure and bottom-up organizing plan was intended to ensure that communication flowed up as well as down the organization. Before any decision was made, it was discussed in small groups throughout campus so that everyone had the chance to formulate her thoughts and make her views known.

Although not explicitly "feminist," Local 34's emphasis on organization building allowed it to develop women union leaders in a way that focusing on particular issues would not have. By building a grass-roots organization based in small work groups, Local 34 ensured that the union's issues came from the workers themselves, not from preconceived notions of what women's issues were. Coming together in their union, women began to see that their "personal" problems were shared by others and to feel that their work should—and could—be valued more highly. Women who had never before stood up for themselves learned to run lunch meetings, speak before large groups, talk back to their supervisors, and lead other workers to stand up to Yale. Local 34 created a sisterly community that gave women the support they needed to challenge traditional power relations on the job and at home.

The university's response to the union drive exposed the limits of Yale's paternalism and revealed its assumptions about women's work. Although the university was constrained by its liberal reputation and—at least on the surface—nonadversarial atmosphere, Yale conducted a traditional anti-union campaign. The administration claimed that the union, as an "outsider" to the Yale community, would destroy Yale's collegial atmosphere and assured employees that it would "protect" them from harassment by union organizers. The administration's claim that vacation, personal leave, and health coverage compensated for low clerical salaries demonstrated their belief that most women were secondary wage earners, for whom wages were less important than the time off to be with their families.

Local 34 combated Yale's anti-union campaign by using the university's own rhetoric to expose the differences between its liberal image and the reality of working for Yale. As employees and, in some cases, graduates of Yale, the C&Ts collectively knew how Yale worked better than most faculty did, and they were able to fashion a strategy that struck at Yale's most vulnerable point—its reputation. When the university called for a "civilized debate" and "full and open discussion" on the issues, Local 34 pointed out its insincerity by requesting an open debate between A. Bartlett Giamatti, president of Yale, and a union representative. The president refused.[8]

Local 34 further revealed the anti-union strategy hidden behind Yale's rhetoric by publicizing Yale's efforts to delay a union election and by stalling at the National Labor Relations Board (NLRB) hearings on the scope of the bargaining unit and other procedural questions. In contrast to common union practice, which leaves such hearings for attorneys to handle privately, Local 34 used them to organize workers and win public support. Nearly 200 C&Ts took a vacation or personal day off work to observe the hearings, at which the union was represented not by an attorney but by John Wilhelm, the chief negotiator for Local 34 and business manager of Local 35 (and a Yale graduate). The hearings thus became an organizing tool rather than a legalistic diversion from the union-building process. Those who attended were insulted, in one union member's words, by Yale's "lack of respect" for the C&Ts. "I thought Yale, being an academic community, would want to foster an environment that would lead to a free exchange of ideas," wrote a research assistant who attended the hearings. "I was wrong."[9] The administration was forced to abandon its stalling tactic, and the election was set for May 18.

Yale C&Ts, appalled by the university's actions and impressed with Local 34's bottom-up organizing, continued to join the union. Local 34's actions, which centered on workers' lives, reflected its emphasis on building an organization. For example, at union rallies dozens of women and men spoke out about how, through the union, they were gaining control of their lives. An issue of *Common Sense,* the union newsletter, distributed two weeks before the election, consisted of the photographs and personal statements of twenty pro-union employees.[10] Hundreds of workers wore buttons, signed their names to a petition entitled "We Believe in Ourselves," and attended pro-union rallies.

They showed fellow employees and the rest of the Yale community that the union was not, as the university had alleged, an outside party, but the workers themselves. On Wednesday May 18, 1983, Yale C&Ts voted 1,267 to 1,228 for the union. Local 34 had won with just 50.2 percent of the vote.

Organizing for a Contract

☐ After the election, Local 34 members formulated their contract proposals and elected a thirty-five-member negotiating committee to represent them at contract talks with the university. More than 400 members of the organizing committee distributed questionnaires to almost 2,000 union and nonunion employees. In hundreds of departmental and small group meetings, workers decided on their major concerns: a wage increase; revised salary structure; pensions; dental care; educational benefits; procedures for promotion, transfer, grievances, and reviewing job classifications; and union security. The twenty-four-page proposal also included items like free parking and free lunches that workers felt they deserved but realized they were not likely to win in their first contract.

The university's strategy was designed to stall negotiations and frustrate union members. Although Yale President Giamatti called on both sides to "put aside our differences and in good faith . . . work together," serious negotiations were impossible because the university's bargaining team did not include anyone with the authority to make decisions.[11] For three months Yale claimed that there was no suitable room on campus in which to meet (even though the C&Ts who booked the rooms found several). The university also refused to give Local 34's negotiators paid time off work, even though Local 35 members traditionally were paid during negotiations and no other university workers had their pay docked for engaging in university business during the day. The union fought Yale's stalling tactic and demonstrated its own strength by organizing 1,200 union members to contribute one day of personal or vacation time to a "daybank" so that the take-home pay of negotiating committee members would not be reduced. The university's initial rejection of their offer dismayed many faculty and students, and public pressure eventually forced the administration to pay them.

As it did during the NLRB hearings, Local 34 tried to make the negotiating process more accessible to its members, and, in so doing, to expose Yale's anti-union campaign to public scrutiny. Union members and, later, faculty, were allowed to observe negotiations as part of the union's team and make a statement to Yale's negotiators at the end of each session. Like the C&Ts who sat in on the talks, faculty found the administration's style "aloof, condescending and patronizing."[12] According to law professor Lucinda Finley, "I detected an audible expression of relief from some members of the university negotiating team that there were no faculty members in attendance. That day the observers' chairs were all occupied by women. The negotiators' faces looked startled when, at the day's end, I introduced myself as a law professor and two other young women identified themselves as faculty members."[13] Clerical and faculty members alike encountered Yale's disrespect for women workers.

As the prospect of a strike loomed near, workers brought public attention to their cause. Wearing red and white buttons saying: "I don't want to strike. But I will," hundreds of C&Ts met with faculty and supervisors to inform them of their dissatisfaction with the pace of negotiations. They held a silent candlelight vigil in front of Giamatti's home and celebrated International Women's Day with a community-labor rally attended by 4,000. On March 1, Local 34 members voted 1,309 to 165 to authorize a strike for March 26, 1984. In contrast to the university's expectations and most unions' experience, more workers voted to strike than had voted for the union ten months earlier. Students and faculty began to see clerical and technical workers in a new way.

The university's apparent willingness to sacrifice educational goals for financial concerns goaded students and faculty into action. Two hundred fifty professors and, later, more than two thousand students signed petitions supporting the union's call for binding arbitration, which provided for a third party to resolve contract issues without a strike. Fourteen prominent faculty members wrote Giamatti that a strike would "harm the collegial atmosphere of the University. [Yale's] national and local reputation will be impaired if relations between labor and management are soured."[14]

Although the administration assured students and faculty that "normal academic activities" would continue in the event of a strike, Local 34's message to the community sent shock waves through the campus. The union urged the university community to honor its picket lines by moving classes off campus; boycotting the library, the gym, and other campus facilities; and not holding any parties, conferences, or lectures on campus. "It is a harsh reality, should the administration force us to strike, that there are no neutrals," Local 34's statement read. "Your actions will either contribute to the achievement of a settlement, by preventing 'business as usual,' or will prolong the strike."[15] Never before had Yale's clerical workers made such demands of faculty and students.

Even sympathizers had difficulty taking leadership from their secretaries and resented the union's hard line. Local 34's call for a voluntary boycott of the campus forced individuals to seriously confront the picket line each day. By turning Yale into a ghost town, the union did not intend to disrupt classes but to attack the university's collegial image, thus impeding its ability to raise funds and attract students and faculty.

The extent of the disruption caused by the strike preparations took the administration by surprise, and, for the first time, Yale made concessions at the bargaining table. Progress in negotiations led to three postponements of the strike deadline in one week. The campus was on edge; students and faculty discussed the strike in departmental meetings, sent delegations to tell the administration their concerns, and prepared to move five hundred classes off campus. Posters and buttons saying: "Local 34 We're With You" dotted the campus. Pro-union students circulated petitions and demonstrated on the steps of the administration building, and more than 1,000 workers stood vigil outside negotiations. Workers went home each night not knowing whether they would be at work or on strike the next morning.

The strength and commitment of union members was tested at the membership meeting on Tuesday evening, April 3. After a tense week in which the strike had been put off three times, workers entered the meeting fully expecting to walk off their jobs the next day. Instead, at the recommendation of Wilhelm and the negotiating committee, they voted 906 to 353 to accept an interim agreement that guaranteed the existence of the union and reserved the right to strike over the outstanding issues. The unusual proposal for a partial settlement came as a complete shock to union members, some of whom feared they had been sold out and worried that the administration would think they did not strike out of weakness. The hasty decision-making process and emotional letdown of those who had been ready to strike led some workers and supporters to feel manipulated by union leaders. Although the wounds took months to heal, most union members came to feel that the struggle to overcome the differences among them had made the union stronger. In addition, the partial contract derailed the university's attempt to provoke a strike just before the end of the school year and made it impossible to seek a new election to decertify the union (a union cannot be decertified if it has signed a contract within a year after the NLRB election). Local 34's partial contract, which differed from a normal labor agreement in that the union retained the right to strike, afforded workers the basic protections of a union contract before they had completed negotiations—and even while they were on strike.

Although the Yale administration may have hoped that the partial contract would destroy the union's momentum and divide the rank and file from their leaders, it greatly underestimated the resolve and solidarity of union members. Their decision not to strike and to accept a partial contract defied customary trade union strategy as well as the traditional (male) definition of what being a tough and militant unionist was.

A more efficient grievance procedure, stronger protection against discrimination and sexual harassment, improved promotion and transfer procedures, and health and safety on the job were among the contract provisions. The agreement also established an employee participation program so that workers would have a say in decisions affecting their work lives. It strengthened workers' power on campus by guaranteeing Local 34's right to respect any picket line at Yale. Perhaps, most importantly, the contract also established an agency shop, which required every C&T to pay union dues or their equivalent to the union. Once the union's future was secure, workers could use the terms of the partial contract to increase their control of the workplace by filing grievances, appointing shop stewards, and enforcing the contract. Negotiations focused on the remaining economic issues, and Local 34 launched its campaign against economic discrimination at Yale.

An Unequal Opportunity Employer

☐ As New Haven's largest employer, Yale and its employment practices affected the entire city. Yale's low salaries depressed the average wage of the city; its inadequate pension plan contributed to the financial uncertainty of its older citizens and to the feminization of poverty, and its nonprofit status and ability to avoid paying taxes to the city drained New Haven's resources. Yale's wealth contrasted with the poverty of its employees and of the surrounding city, the seventh poorest in the nation. Although the university claimed it did not have the funds to pay higher wages without freezing faculty salaries, cutting financial aid, or increasing tuition, it refused the union's request to prove financial hardship by opening its books. Finally, even Yale Vice-President Michael Finnerty admitted that "it's not a question of whether Yale has the money. It's a question of priorities."[16]

Local 34's public campaign against economic discrimination at Yale contrasted the university's beneficent image with its low wages. The administration dismissed Local 34's charge of discrimination, refusing the Yale chaplain's request for a fact-finding committee on salary discrimination and claiming that it could not afford to pay clerical and technical workers higher salaries.[17] "I know that one can't live the way one would like to, or the way one would like one's family to live, on a Yale clerical and technical salary," Provost William Brainard told a group of C&Ts in a much-quoted statement. "That's a national problem, which Yale can't be expected to solve." However, the C&Ts who worked in the payroll department, processed alumni gifts, and solicited government research grants knew the extent of the financial surplus at Yale. They publicized the amount of money the university spent on liquor bills, parties, and projects like the $1 million golf clubhouse inaugurated during the strike, and other workers told the rest of the university community about the difficulties of living on a C&T salary. One woman who had an M.A. in English explained how she earned only $13,000 after two and a half years as an editorial assistant and had to share a one-room apartment with her fourteen-year-old daughter. Another single mother spent almost one-quarter of her $12,550 annual income on childcare alone.[18] Workers attended union rallies carrying signs that announced their low salaries: "$9,600 after 4 years" or "$14,800 after 8 years at Yale." By sharing this "private" information about themselves, they came to see their low wages as part of a systemic problem rather than a personal embarrassment. Women who had been conditioned not to ask for money for themselves felt entitled to demand an end to the discrimination and low wages that they shared with fellow employees.

The union viewed the university's lack of benefits, like its low salaries, as contributing to the feminization of poverty. Workers wanted a benefits package that would address the family needs of women employees, including maternity leave, affordable childcare, and a dental plan that covered children. Yale's pension system was also a problem. According to union figures, 151 retired C&Ts, averaging 18.2 years of service, received only $171 per month from Yale between 1979 and 1983. Because the pension formula was tied to women's low wages and did not increase with inflation, and because retirees had to pay most of their medical expenses, long-term Yale employees frequently retired in poverty.[19]

Because the partial settlement had assured union security and resolved the noneconomic terms of the contract, Local 34 was able to focus on the economic discrimination against women and minorities at Yale. However, the union never explicitly demanded "comparable worth" pay. That phrase was created by the media, which simplified Local 34's more complex demands for respect and the recognition of women workers' contribution to the university (which would include their participation in decisions affecting the workplace as well as fair wages and benefits) into the popular term "comparable worth." Union members were concerned that pay equity, as the issue has typically been pursued, was a legalistic approach to economic discrimination that did not build women's power and self-worth—or a strong organization— because it relied on professionals conducting job evaluation studies behind closed doors. Workers in a union that included typists and lab aides as well as medical technicians feared that comparable worth might reproduce society's notions of worth and therefore not eliminate the discrimination experienced by the poorest among them. They knew from their own experience and that of Local 35 that wages were not related to productivity or labor's intrinsic value. Although the service and maintenance work that Local 35 members did was essential to the functioning of the university, their relatively high wages were the results of years of labor struggles, not the university's acknowledgment of the "value" of their work. According to Local 34's calculations, the university could correct most wage inequalities at Yale by increasing all C&T salaries, by instituting a labor-management committee to review job classifications (won in April), and by revising the salary structure so that it did not discriminate against the mostly Black and female long-term employees.[20]

New Haven residents overwhelmingly supported Local 34's fight with Yale University. Even before the partial settlement, Black and white clergy, community organizations, women's groups, and unions in New Haven had protested Yale's discriminatory policies. Campus and community women, carrying banners that read: "In supporting Local 34, we support ourselves," held a "bread and roses" vigil outside the administrative offices of the university. Women identified with Local 34's struggle because they too worked for low wages (often in clerical jobs) and had suffered from the devaluation of women's work. Women students and faculty felt that Yale's arrogant attitude toward female clerical and technical employees showed the same attitudes toward women expressed in its unwillingness to take serious action against rape and sexual and racial harassment at Yale. A faculty Committee on the Education of Women found that only 5 percent of the tenured professors were female, a percentage that had not improved in six years.[21] Even anti-union Yale economist Jennifer Roback wrote that women are treated like servants at Yale, "the most sexist institution I've ever had anything to do with."[22]

New Haven's minority community, especially the Black clergy, also supported Local 34's fight against discrimination. Although one-third of the surrounding community was Black, just 14 percent of the C&T group was Black. Although Black C&Ts had the most seniority of any group working at Yale, they earned the least pay. These patterns of discrimination resulted in a relative absence of Blacks on the rank-and-file staff and in positions of leadership within the union. In order to give a stronger voice to minority issues in Local 34 and to encourage Black leaders to come forward, Black C&Ts organized a Black caucus within the union. Minority students, faculty, and community members also participated in the Black caucus. Especially during the strike, the visibility of its Black members strengthened everybody's commitment to Local 34's antidiscrimination program.

On Strike for Respect

☐ Local 34 began its strike against Yale on September 26, 1984. Angered by the lack of progress in negotiations and by the university's refusal to implement its wage offer at the time of the usual July 1 salary increase, 1,800 C&Ts—dozens of whom had not planned to strike six months earlier—walked off their jobs. Apparently expecting that the women would become demoralized, lose support among students and faculty, and return to work, the administration stated that it would never increase its "final offer." It failed to consider four important factors: (1) the effects on education of the strikers' withdrawal of services; (2) solidarity between Local 34 and Local 35; (3) student, faculty, and community support for the strikers; and (4) the nontraditional tactics of the union.

The university drastically underestimated the extent to which the strike would disrupt academic business. That women's work was not easily replaced became evident when managerial and professional employees, student workers, and 800 C&Ts (one-third of the bargaining unit) who continued to work could not keep the university running smoothly. Although some facilities, such as the medical school, ran almost normally, the library, computer center, and gym operated on shorter hours; the art gallery shut down; broken machinery in the language lab went unrepaired; and research and laboratory work suffered. Five hundred classes were moved off campus—held in movie theaters, pizza parlors, and restaurants, in student apartments, and on the picket line. Because Local 35 honored clerical and technical workers' picket lines, dining halls were closed, bathrooms and dorm rooms were left uncleaned, and the grounds were littered with leaves.

The extent of the disruption went beyond the visible effects and included the increasing tension and depression among students and faculty. Clerical and custodial services (housework)—work that was normally invisible because it was always done—had preserved students' and faculty members' time and mental energy so that they could concentrate on the "higher" business of education. When students had to do their own cooking and cleaning—services they had paid for—and faculty suddenly had to do their own typing and make their own appointments, they found themselves increasingly frustrated, distracted by details, and unable to focus on scholarship.[23] Because department secretaries and the administrative assistants in the dormitories, whose jobs included acting as mothers and confidants, were on strike, students and faculty lost an important source of emotional comfort and support.

The administration also underestimated the solidarity and strength of the strikers. Although the long strike was a financial and emotional strain, women who had been isolated in small departments, and whose time had been limited because of double household and wage-earning responsibilities, found the strike liberating. Workers who had been invisible in offices and labs were now visible and vocal on the picket line. Strikers used the picket lines to talk to people and persuade them of the rightness of their cause, rather than merely trying to keep them out of buildings. Picket shifts ended with meetings of picket captains and parades or minirallies so that strikers would end their four-hour shifts together. Many women who had felt isolated at work, or who had been harassed by anti-union supervisors or coworkers, found a support-ive community on the picket line. "Personal" family and financial problems normally dealt with on an individual level were acknowl-edged as problems of the entire group. The union's resource committee provided free lunches and funds for needy strikers; and area clergy convinced landlords and banks to delay loan, mortgage, and rent collections. However, strikers first tried to resolve financial difficulties on the picket line. Those who could, donated their picket pay to workers on their line in more desperate need. Some picket lines took advantage of closed dining halls by selling baked goods and sandwiches to faculty and students. As they learned to deal with personal issues collectively, without having to answer to a boss, strikers broke down the isolation that characterized women's work at home and in the office. The strike also reached into many women's homes, as they no longer had time or patience to cook, clean, do the (invisible and unrecognized) housework, or put their own needs aside for their families.[24]

Although the service and maintenance workers in Local 35 had financially supported the clerical union, not until the strike did the two locals really begin to function as one. Like the rest of the community, Local 35 members had to learn the importance of office work and respect for the courage and determination of women workers. Moreover, the blue-collar union decided to reorganize on the model of Local 34's democratic structure. In turn, Local 35 taught the newly unionized

C&Ts (only two-thirds of whom had gone out on strike) the meaning of labor solidarity. In the face of financial hardship, threats of dismissal, harassment, and a grievance filed by the university that might have forced them back to work, all but a handful of Local 35 members honored the strikers' picket lines for the entire ten weeks of the strike.

The administration also underestimated the extent of student and faculty support. Many students, having worked closely with C&Ts and having experienced the lack of respect accorded office workers, were unwilling to scab. Sympathetic students picketed with department and college secretaries; protested films, plays, and lectures held on campus; and organized teach-ins, discussions, and departmental meetings to educate fellow students about the union. The activism and anger unleashed by the strike went beyond a small nucleus of student radicals. Although the majority of student and faculty tried to remain neutral, hundreds of students attended pro-union rallies, filed a lawsuit against the university for breach of contract, staged sit-ins at the library to protest reduced hours, and withheld their second-semester tuition. Approximately one hundred faculty members picketed the administration building every Monday afternoon. Some professors used class time to talk about the strike issues and even held office hours on the picket line. During the strike, a significant "gender gap" emerged among student and faculty supporters: women were far more likely than men to talk to strikers and to sign pro-union petitions and letters.

As students and faculty organized in support of the union, they defied intimidation and threats by anti-union administrators. Despite the policy cited in the Yale handbook that guarantees the right to "think the unthinkable, discuss the unmentionable, and challenge the unchallengeable," the administration tried to curb pro-union protests by limiting free speech. The curtailment of civil liberties revealed the contradiction between Yale's liberal ideals and its actual policies. When six cheerleaders wore "SETTLE" pinned to their sweaters at the first Yale football game, they were told they would be thrown off the squad. Only after they organized, and the case garnered media attention did the university back down. Similarly, graduate students in the Computer Science Department, who refused to do C&T work and criticized the prohibition of strike-related messages from being posted on the department's electronic bulletin board, received a warning from the department chair. One student had his computer accounts turned off. Several teachers who made strike-related assignments were verbally reprimanded. Managerial and professional employees who talked to strikers on the picket lines were threatened with unfavorable performance evaluations, and police barred six strikers from entering the payroll and administration building to deliver a letter to their supervisors.[25] In a desperate attempt to regain control of the university and preserve its public image, the administration even tried to ban the media from campus.

Local 34 also received support from unions, civil rights groups, feminists, and Yale alumni throughout the United States who supported Local 34's fight against economic discrimination and were unhappy with Yale's labor policy. Black labor and civil rights activist Bayard Rustin (who had received an honorary degree from Yale in May) returned in October 1984 to lead 434 strikers and their supporters in civil disobedience outside a meeting of the Yale Corporation, the university's board of trustees and governing body. Ralph Abernathy, Cesar Chavez, AFL–CIO president Lane Kirkland, and Judy Goldsmith and Eleanor Smeal, of the National Organization for Women, also came to Yale to show their support for Local 34, as did representatives of organizations as diverse as the Council of Unions of South Africa and Black Women for Wages for Housework. Out-of-town supporters, including feminists, concerned clergy, members of other unions, and faculty from other colleges and universities, attended a series of rallies in New Haven that helped boost morale. Clerical workers from other campuses and their unions, particularly District 65 at Columbia University, also provided financial and moral support. Women's groups and unions picketed Yale football games, the offices and speeches of Yale Corporation members, and the New York Yale Club. To the surprise and dismay of the administration, a number of Yale parents publicly and privately pressured the administration to settle the strike, and supportive alumni nominated feminist economist Heidi Hartmann as a pro-union candidate for the Yale Corporation. Their support helped counter the pressure that Yale was receiving from businesses and universities concerned about the precedent on comparable worth which would be set by a settlement with Local 34.

Rather than depending only on the withdrawal of services to win the strike, Local 34 also brought public pressure to bear on the university. Such tactics are particularly effective for clerical and service workers who do not manufacture a tangible product and for employees of institutions whose wealth and power make it difficult to hurt them financially by withdrawal of services alone. Local 34's strategy of appealing to the public to support the justice of its cause grew out of and reflected the growing sense of self-worth of Yale women employees. Several weeks after the strike began, 190 workers were arrested for blocking the street in front of President Giamatti's house, while another 1,000 union members looked on in silence. The silent three-hour protest, in the tradition of Gandhi and Martin Luther King, Jr., was a dignified and powerful statement of strikers' commitment and connected their struggle for economic equality to the civil rights movement. Three weeks later, 434 workers, students, New Haven residents, and faculty participated in another nonviolent mass arrest.

The strikers' call for a three-day moratorium just before Thanksgiving vacation provoked strong opposition from the university, forcing liberal and conservative academics alike to wrestle with their consciences. Union members met with faculty, students, professionals, and even top administrators to urge them to cancel classes for three days to bring a quicker end to the strike. In response, the administration threatened those who participated in the moratorium with bad performance evaluations and even with the loss of their jobs. Faculty members were compelled to make a decision that tested the limits of their support for the union. How many would risk tenure to stand up to an administration that oppressed women workers (and themselves)? Although almost ninety faculty members (and especially women) supported the moratorium, it divided the campus. Like their more conservative colleagues, some socialist and feminist academics resented the C&Ts' demands, afraid that canceling classes for three days to support the strikers would hurt their careers. Like Yale Corporation members Eleanor Holmes Norton and Deborah Rhode (who write on sex discrimination and comparable worth), a few feminist faculty remained virtually silent throughout the strike, no more willing than their less progressive colleagues to take a public stand in support of the striking women workers when that stand required some sacrifice. At the same time, the backlash against the moratorium from the administration appalled both the faculty who did not actively support the union and those who were union supporters, isolating the administration from the rest of the community. The disruption to the university was immense.

In its boldest and most controversial move, the union decided to go "home for the holidays," back to work without a contract over Christmas break. They hoped to subvert the university's dual strategy of "starving" the employees into returning to work and of dividing Local 34 and Local 35. In order to force Local 35 to cross the picket lines and return to work, the administration had taken to arbitration a grievance charging the union with violating the nostrike clause of its contract. Local 34 leaders originally proposed their return to work as a contingency plan if Local 35 lost the arbitration award (which it eventually won) and would therefore be legally required to work; the C&Ts would return to work with Local 35 and both unions would strike again in January, when Local 35's contract expired. But because the withdrawal of services would not affect the university over Christmas holidays, when it was basically shut down, they decided to do it regardless of the results of the grievance. Returning to work over the holidays enabled strikers to earn a few weeks' pay (including, for most C&Ts, a week's paid Christmas vacation) and avoid the demoralization of picketing empty buildings when the university was closed and students were away. Because they were protected by their partial contract, Local 34 members could file grievances, talk to their supervisors and coworkers, and reassert the power in the workplace that they did not have while on strike outside. By timing the new strike deadline to coincide with Local 35's, the plan cemented the solidarity between the two locals and gave the blue-collar workers time to organize and educate the community about their contract issues.

When the rank-and-file staff presented the idea to the strikers two days before Thanksgiving, picket lines shut down while strikers discussed strategy in local restaurants and churches. Initially, it appeared that almost everyone was opposed to the idea. Some workers feared that the union was losing the strike. Others were afraid to go back to the isolation of their offices, where they would have to confront scabs and anti-union supervisors away from the support of their sisters and brothers on the picket line. Some angry strikers, who felt that the plan was asking women who had just begun to stand up for themselves to subordinate their struggle to the "Local 35 guys," opposed the majority determined to support the blue-collar men and women who had stood beside them. On November 29, union members voted 800 to 200 to reject the university's latest contract offer and call a temporary hiatus to their strike. The unusual tactic was possible only because the union's democratic organization allowed every member to be part of the decision. The university, stunned by the strikers' plan to return to work, increased the value of its contract offer for the first time since the strike began.

Settlement

☐ As the new strike deadline approached in January 1985, the Yale campus began once again to prepare for a strike. Although workers had used the month inside to file grievances and confront anti-union supervisors, little progress had been made in negotiations. For the third time in less than a year, workers and their supporters demonstrated outside negotiations, signed up for picket shifts, held departmental meetings, and prepared to move classes off campus. The character of the demonstrations differed from the past, both because of the presence of Local 35 and the anger and bitterness everyone felt at the prospect of another strike. In January, on the first day of spring semester classes, thirty-one students occupied President Giamatti's office, leaving only when threatened with expulsion, after extracting assurances that the university would compromise with the union and avert a strike.

In the wee hours of the morning of January 20, Local 34 won its four-year struggle for recognition of the value of women's work. The contract, which was ratified two days later, represented a significant step toward eliminating economic discrimination at Yale. It provided an average wage increase of 35 percent over three years for current employees and revised the salary structure to correct discrimination against long-term employees whose incomes had been concentrated at the bottom of their salary grade. The revised salary structure slotted workers into salary steps according to their years of service at Yale. The elimination of the lowest labor grade, which included many older Black women working as lab aides, increased the wages of some of the poorest workers by 80 to 90 percent and brought the salaries of undervalued workers more in line with their worth. At the same time, the contract language won earlier (in the partial contract), guaranteeing employees' health and safety and job security, and improved procedures for grievances, promotions, and transfers, helped workers increase their power in the office.

Many of the benefits Local 34 won were geared toward the particular needs of women workers. The contract improved the pension formula and instituted the payment of medical benefits to retirees and their spouses. Provisions for protection of flex-time, a family dental plan, improved leaves of absence, and a labor-management committee to study childcare were instituted to help women to combine work outside the home with their family responsibilities. A "bridge" in the years of service enables women who leave Yale employment for less than eighteen months, either because of childrearing or layoffs, to accrue seniority during their time away from Yale. Those who leave Yale for more than eighteen months receive seniority credit for half the time they previously worked there. Because C&Ts often have breaks in their employment at Yale, the "bridge" in the years of service helps minimize the penalty women workers receive for taking time away from the paid job to work at home. It is a step toward compensating women workers for both their jobs.

Despite their victory, Local 34 members did not rest; Local 35's strike deadline was less than a week away. By the middle of the week, stalled negotiations had brought the two unions and their supporters together in an unusual (for the 1980s) display of solidarity and respect for blue-collar workers. Local 35's concerns included wages, dental and pension plans, and, especially, job security. They sought the option of twelve-month employment for employees who only worked during the nine-month academic year, because new Reagan administration policies on unemployment insurance prohibited these workers from receiving benefits. Stricter enforcement of contract language limiting subcontracting and, when subcontracting was necessary, preference to firms with affirmative action policies were also major concerns.

Students wearing signs saying: "Truck drivers deserve more money too!" picketed the administration building and plastered the campus with green ribbons to call attention to service and maintenance work, which, like the work performed by C&Ts, was invisible to most of the campus. In confrontations with supervisors, noisy demonstrations outside negotiations, and petitions promising to honor the picket line, the C&Ts showed their solidarity with the blue-collar workers.

On the eve of the final strike deadline, a hundred demonstrators gathered in the hall outside the negotiating room, chanting "settle" whenever the university's bargaining team left the room. Forty people stood vigil until 3:30 A.M. when Local 35's contract was settled. Like Local 34, Local 35 gained from the increased strength of two strong unions on campus. Members won job security; higher wages; and the medical protection for retirees, pension, and dental plans that they had struck for unsuccessfully in the past.

Conclusion

☐ Using innovative tactics, Local 34 built an unusually militant and democratic organization that rallied the community around them and won recognition of the value of women's work at Yale. Although the chairs of the President's Council of Economic Advisers and the Reagan-controlled U.S. Civil Rights Commission ridiculed the concept of comparable worth as a "truly crazy proposal" and "the looniest idea since the Looney Tunes," Yale workers won a major step toward the economic equality of wage-earning women.[26] Local 34's bylaws also reflect its unique character and purpose, not only to uphold the dignity of Yale C&Ts but also "to promote justice at Yale and to encourage the University to be a good citizen of the community ... to advance the interests of workers generally and working women in particular, [and] to repay in full measure the solidarity of the labor movement and the community which helped give birth to Local 34."[27]

The success of the Local 34 strike had benefits for its supporters, both on and off the Yale campus. Just two weeks after the final settlement, Columbia University officially recognized District 65 (UAW) as the union representing Columbia clerical workers—reversing the position it had taken for two years of refusing to accept the results of an NLRB election which District 65 had won. The strike also altered the dynamics of student politics at Yale. When six students were arrested and threatened with suspension for disrupting a Central Intelligence Agency recruitment interview (severe punishment that many suspect was due as much to their pro-union activities as to their protest against the CIA), they used the phone trees of union supporters, the media contacts, and the organizing experience they had acquired during the strike to mobilize the support that eventually forced the administration to back down. Finally, in a move that many Yale students and faculty attributed to the strike, A. Bartlett Giamatti resigned as president of Yale.

Local 34 members continued to work to keep alive the enthusiasm and activism of the rank and file that characterized their organizing drive and strike. With newly elected officers, almost 300 active stewards (formerly the organizing committee), and a paid staff hired out of the rank and file, Local 34 continued to recruit new members. It has tried to resolve disputes with management through direct confrontations, rather than through bureaucratic procedures such as arbitration. When grievances could not be solved at the first step, or by groups of workers meeting with their supervisors, the entire organization would take action. For example, in the library, a factorylike unit with a low-paid, largely minority work force, the union filed numerous grievances against supervisors who refused to allow union leaders to make phone calls and threatened them with discharge. In 1985, Local 34 brought public attention to library workers' grievances by holding a lunchtime rally and march through the library. Initially told that they would not be allowed to enter the building, union members took their case to the media. The university relented, and 400 union members, "card-carrying" members of the university community, marched silently through the library holding their Yale identification cards over their heads.

The strike itself was only part of a continuing process of recognizing and compensating women clerical workers at Yale for all the work they do. The innovative tactics and democratic organization that were hallmarks of the strike are still being used and developed further as the union consolidates its strength and builds upon the gains the strike victory brought. Local 34's work before, during, and after the strike provides an inspiring model for organizing women workers.

Notes

I am grateful to the members of Local 34 for many of the insights contained in this article. Special thanks also to Ann Braude, George Chauncey, and Paul Clifford for all of their help and encouragement.

1. "A Report to the Community from the Members of Local 34, Federation of University Employees, AFL–CIO," September 1984, 6. Copies of this document and others cited below are in the author's possession, unless otherwise indicated.

2. Ibid., 6.

3. Robert Cover, Faye Crosby, Robert Dahl, Margaret Ferguson, Gerald Jaynes, Charles E. Lindbloom, John Simon, Samuel Thier, James Tobin, Kathryn Dominguez, John Pound, Sean Redding, Peter Siegelman, Chris Udry (Robert Adair dissenting), "Yale and Local 34: Facts on the Current Dispute," 29 Nov. 1984.

4. Raymond Fair, "A Note on Local 34's Charge of Salary Discrimination by Sex and Race at Yale," 29 Mar. 1984.

5. "Report to the Community," 12. Black men, who comprised a very small percentage of Yale C&Ts, had less seniority than the other groups. Their average salary was $12,813.

6. Tony Reese and Jim Lowe, "United They Stand," *New Journal* 17 (19 Oct. 1984): 22–26.

7. Despite its alleged ties to organized crime (accusations union leaders consider part of a corporate union-busting strategy), HERE has recently acquired a reputation as a militant and progressive union. Under President Edward Hanley and Organizing Director Sirabella, HERE ran militant and successful hotel strikes in Las Vegas and New York and won the white-collar strike at Yale.

8. "An Open Letter to Yale President Giamatti from the 120 Clerical and Technical Employees Who Are Members of the Local 34 Steering Committee," *Full and Open Discussion,* no. 5 (16 May 1983).

9. Ibid., no. 2 (7 Mar. 1983).

10. *Common Sense,* no. 2 (2 May 1983).

11. A. Bartlett Giamatti to the Yale Community, 19 May 1983.

12. Julius Getman, Terry Odendahl, and Harlon Dalton to Colleagues, 16 Mar. 1984.

13. Lucinda Finley, "Women's Work at Yale Wins Respect," *Hartford Courant,* 27 Jan. 1985.

14. Nancy Cott, Robert Cover, Robert Dahl, Thomas Emerson, and ten others to A. Bartlett Giamatti, 5 Dec. 1983.

15. "Business as Usual Will Prolong the Strike," flyer, March 1984.

16. Edward A. Gargan, "Yale, as Strikers Return, Weighs the Damage to an Intellectual Community," *New York Times,* 1 Dec. 1984, 25.

17. John Vannorsdall to John Wilhelm and A. Bartlett Giamatti, 19 Mar. 1984; reprinted in "In Good Faith," 21 May 1984.

18. "Report to the Community," cover; ibid., 4–5.

19. Ibid., 11.

20. Local 34 negotiators considered this committee a way to allow negotiations on this difficult issue to continue during the life of the contract. As with its other efforts, Local 34 members planned to use the committee not only to study job classifications but also to organize, publicize the issue, and upgrade jobs even before the contract expired.

21. Donald Crothers, chair, "Report of the Yale University Faculty of Arts and Sciences Advisory Committee on the Education of Women," April 1984.

22. Jennifer Roback, "What Really Happened at Yale?" *Business Times,* March 1985.

23. At the same time, some students benefited from this situation. Although strikers, many of whom were the sole support of their families, received only $50 a week in picket pay, students received a meal refund of $72.80 a week. Although some students turned over part of their allowance to the strikers, most saved any surplus money. A few young entrepreneurs made a profit by selling food, laundry services, and T-shirts during the strike.

24. Negotiating committee member Andrea Ross made this point in a speech, 14 Nov. 1984, and at a press conference, 20 Nov. 1984.

25. William Olds, Executive Director, Connecticut Civil Liberties Union, to A. Bartlett Giamatti and the Yale Corporation, 11 Dec. 1984; "Winning Lines," no. 8 (13 Nov. 1984).

26. William E. Niskanen and Clarence E. Pendleton, Jr., quoted in *Hartford Courant,* 17 Nov. 1984, 12.

27. Local 34, Federation of University Employees, "Proposed By-Laws (revised)," typescript (adopted 25 Apr. 1985).

21 Joan Tronto

Changing Goals and Changing Strategies: Varieties of Women's Political Activities

☐ The question of success is a key one for any movement for social change. Short of revolution what can we realistically expect a progressive movement to achieve? When is such a movement over? There is a perception, in the 1990s, that the women's movement has slowed.[1] As a result, some of the new research on political women seems to search for an assessment of whether, how, and why this loss of momentum has occurred. We might formulate the questions: To what extent are the political fortunes of the feminist movement within the control of politically active women? In light of the present conditions, what should we do?

Thinking about political strategy requires that we think about conflict.[2] This point is useful to remember because conflict always involves multiple parties who try to shift situations and outcomes to their favor; no single side can be entirely responsible or blameless in success or failure.

In this essay I shall draw upon some recent writings by feminists that examine American women's political experiences throughout this century. My goal is both to assess the political accomplishments of women and to put these accomplishments and failures into a broader strategic framework. We need as well to recognize certain biases in U.S. political life that will inevitably make the goals of feminists more difficult to achieve. The most prominent of these biases are that the U.S. political system responds most easily to issues raised by those in the middle or upper-middle class and that Americans perceive the world through individualistic glasses so that any analysis that grows out of a nonindividualistic framework will encounter special difficulties. The strategy that is easiest, then, may not be the one that is most inclusive. I shall

Reprinted, with changes, from *Feminist Studies* 17, no. 1 (Spring 1991): 85–104. © 1991 by Feminist Studies, Inc.

proceed by looking closely at a group of recent books about women in mainstream politics throughout this century. At the end of this essay I shall try to draw out some broader implications for future feminist political strategy.

Nancy Cott's *The Grounding of Modern Feminism* is a history of the women's movement in the 1910s and 1920s, when the term "feminism" first gained wide currency in the United States. Cott traces this type of "consciousness" as it intersected with the suffrage movement and as feminists took up a number of other political and cultural concerns in the 1910s and 1920s, including the split over the Equal Rights Amendment; the role of sexuality in the family; portrayals of women in the media; women as workers, as college-educated citizens, as professionals, as activists in clubs and other organizations, and as wives and mothers. Cott describes her work as "principally a study of consciousness—women's willingness or reluctance to say *we*—a study of feminist intentions and how they do or do not materialize." By "feminist," Cott refers to three ideas: (1) a belief in women's equality, that is, that there should be no sex hierarchy; (2) that women's social condition is socially constructed; and (3) that women have a common identity as women.[3]

Cott chronicles the rapid growth of feminism in the 1910s, partly in tandem with the growing and ultimately successful movement for suffrage, and its dissipation in the 1920s. Although part of the reason for this waning in the twenties was a growing conservatism of the times and the red baiting of feminists, Cott also stresses what she sees as the inherent contradiction within feminism's goals as a cause for the decline. It is not logically possible, Cott notes, to call successfully for equal opportunity for women, to have women succeed as the equals of men, *and* to retain somehow a strong sense of group identity. Once women have gained the recognition they need, they no longer need to identify as women. Solidarity among women can only remain important for a brief period of time; then it becomes too divisive between women and men. Among professional women this dilemma was obvious and pronounced. Although women professionals realized that they were discriminated against as women, they were reluctant to identify as feminists and optimistically predicted that discrimination would soon disappear. By the 1940s, "there was the Feminist legacy and the feminist paradox: how to be human beings and women too."[4]

Cott set a somewhat difficult task for herself in tracing "feminism"; a movement propelled by a common form of consciousness is, of course, a more difficult thing to pin down than a movement with a more tangible political goal. Nevertheless, she does an excellent job of identifying a range of relevant actors, writers, and others to sort out the meaning and place of feminism as a form of consciousness during this period. Although the suffrage movement drew in women of different races and classes, the developing feminist movement was much smaller, and it was primarily urban, white, upper class and middle class. Is this bias inherent in the nature of feminism? Or is it, as Cott implies, a problem in finding the sources that would trace a change in "consciousness" among other groups in the population? Although feminists in the 1910s and 1920s no longer believed in a single "Woman" who would be involved in what had been known in the nineteenth century as "the Woman Movement," how far can we stretch the diversity of the first feminist movement? Indeed, might the notion of feminism defined as "consciousness" itself be a middle-class construction? Nancy Cott's work in this regard raises many new questions. Who searched for a group identity? Surely, working-class, ethnic, and African-American women in the early twentieth century had a sense of who they were, not necessarily as women, but as members of outgroups in U.S. society. Cott's portrayal of a group searching for a form of group identity, but then rapidly outgrowing this sense of solidarity as they strove to reestablish themselves as *individuals,* would only be important for those groups for whom individualism was both desirable and possible.

It is in this way that the split over the Equal Rights Amendment in the 1920s can be viewed. In the 1920s, one gets the sense from both Cott's account and from others[5] that the debate was not simply about the best means to achieve the goal of improving the lives of women but of two groups speaking past one another.[6] If class differences are deeply embedded in the "forms of life" that people lead,[7] then it may be that Cott's version of the feminist dilemma, the search for autonomy out of group identity, is specific to the middle-class version of feminism.

Bell hooks, a scholar of African American women's lives, raises the objection that modern feminism has become united much more by questions of life-style than by a doctrinal commitment to ending sexist oppression.[8] Hooks's suggestion, that feminism cannot become more inclusive unless it eschews its "life-style," thus restates and resituates the dilemma that Cott observes. Is it an individualistic goal that makes for the types of dilemmas that Cott describes and the types of waxing and waning that she would describe as part of the logic of the nature of feminism? If so, what kind of force would be strong enough to escape the gravitational pull of individualism?

These are broad and ambitious questions, and they might seem at first to be so overly philosophical that they have no bearing on politics at all. But if feminism inevitably becomes the struggle for individual autonomy then the political terms for feminism change. When success is measured by individual accomplishment, political conflict has become privatized rather than socialized. In the end, then, Cott's book may be both exquisitely good history and misleading if read as political strategy. The basic premise of her book, concerning the inherent contradiction within feminism itself, may well explain the decline of feminism in the 1920s and the decline of feminism in the 1970s and 1980s. But if we accept on face value her contention that this contradiction is inherent in feminism, it may be because we have not thought through far enough how we might conceive of feminism.

Cynthia Harrison's *On Account of Sex: The Politics of Women's Issues, 1945–1968*[9] and Leila Rupp and Verta Taylor's *Survival in the Doldrums: The American Women's Rights Movement, 1945 to the 1960s*[10] both concern the post-World War II era (1945–65), a period of time within which, according to conventional wisdom, there was no women's movement. Yet as these two books demonstrate, women's rights made substantial progress as a federal policy and remained the focus for a small but active group of political activists who helped to shape the "second wave," which would emerge in the late 1960s.

Harrison uses the traditional tools of historians of "high politics" (that is, the political elites of Washington lobbies, high-ranking bureaucrats, Congress, the presidency) to recount the politics of women's rights during a period when the issue did not seem to be prominent on the national agenda. Harrison describes the politics of the Equal Rights Amendment during this period, the task of trying to achieve presidential appointments for women, and the passage of federal legislation favorable to women, such as the Equal Pay Act and the addition to the Civil Rights Act of 1964 that barred discrimination "on account of sex" (hence the book's title). As important as "the new history" has been for expanding our knowledge of women, Harrison's book stands as proof that new techniques of historical investigation should supplement, not supplant, older forms of historical research and writing.

Indirectly, Harrison's book is about an unsuccessful political issue of this period: the Equal Rights Amendment. Harrison describes the lines drawn before the 1940s between those women who advocated the passage of the amendment and those who advocated the continuation of forms of protective legislation for women, a group Harrison collectively calls "the Women's Bureau coalition" after their most important institutional stronghold. The ERA was the specter that impelled much of the prowomen's action during this period. As a reaction to a renewed interest in the ERA, beginning with its adoption by the Republican party in its 1940 platform and moved by the relentless lobbying of the National Woman's Party (NWP), the Democrats tried to think of other political concessions to make for women in this period that would forestall the ERA. Harrison meticulously accounts for presidential appointments during this period. She reconstructs the passage of the Equal Pay Act of 1963 and the addition of "sex" to the Civil Rights Act of 1964. It was not, as the story is often told, simply the result of a last-minute joke, but rather of a long-standing Southern Democrat view that white women deserved civil rights as much as Black men. She recounts as well the politics of President Kennedy's Commission on the Status of Women. All this activity, however, could not contain or stop the emergence of a broad-based movement for women's rights in the mid-1960s.

One of the most surprising aspects of Harrison's account is how much indirect influence the NWP wielded. By staking out what to everyone else was an extreme position, the NWP was able to shift the terms of debate about what political concessions should be made to women. As one of the few active voices on the issue during this period, the NWP made the opposite extreme position, do nothing, politically unacceptable. Partly because (to use E.E. Schattschneider's term) the scope of conflict was so narrow, because those who were concerned about women's issues were so few in number, the voice of the small NWP was clearly heard and required some response. In one sense, then, Harrison presents a classic study of the role of small and dedicated interest groups in U.S. politics.

Harrison's history is not meant to be, nor is it, an account of all of the antecedents of feminist political activity. There is no account here, for example, of the origins of the more radical branch of second-wave feminism in the civil rights movement.[11] But this piece of the story is related. Harrison notes that John F. Kennedy's election in 1960 signaled an opening to new political ideas, and his small steps for women, that may seem insignificant in retrospect, did mark a shift in the way women and men in government thought about this issue. It is difficult for historians and political scientists to measure broad shifts in public attitudes, but this opening seems to have served emerging women's activities well.

Leila Rupp and Verta Taylor look at the same time framework from another perspective. Their goal is to argue that even though this was a period of "doldrums" for the women's movement, there was nonetheless a social movement for women's rights in existence during this period. It was an "elite sustained movement," as they call it, but citing the sociological literature about social movements, they feel justified in describing these women, primarily from the NWP and other groups that grew up around it, as a social movement.

Rupp and Taylor recount the controversies within the NWP, the party formed by its charismatic leader Alice Paul after the accomplishment of suffrage in 1920. They paint a full picture of this group's postwar quest for an equal rights amendment, their strategies to magnify their political impact, and how their personal lives intersected with their political work. At the center of the NWP is Alice Paul, who appears here as politically astute and single-minded in her commitments.[12] Read along with Harrison's book, *Survival in the Doldrums* is especially illuminating in its demonstration of how a small group (in 1947 there were 627 active members, in 1952 there were 200 active members, with about 1,400 paper members in 1965) was able to have a large impact on politics.

Clearly part of Rupp and Taylor's goal is to argue for historical continuity—that is, that the women's movement never died out, it just continued on in an "elite sustained" form. Had it died out, they argue, this small group would not have exercised such influence over its resurgence. The account of social movements from which Rupp and Taylor begin emphasizes the role of goals and organizations as the distinguishing features of a social movement. There is, however, an alternative tradition for understanding social movements that deemphasizes such continuities and stresses their explosive quality. Frances Fox Piven and Richard Cloward,[13] for example, argue that social movements only arise when cracks and fissures appear in the social fabric. At that point, people are able to see that the disorder of their own lives is not their private problem but a function of the disorderly social system. (Hence, Piven and Cloward argue, the movements of the unemployed during the 1930s were fostered by an obvious systemic failure, not by good leadership or goals. The logic of this argument suggests that what caused the women's movement to reemerge when it did was a change in social policy and growing conflicts over women's roles.) Such an argument does not deny that the kind of activities Rupp and Taylor chronicled are important, but it does suggest that the proper identification for such activity is not to call it a social movement. To call it a social movement changes the meaning of social movements and makes it more difficult to provide an account of why the emerging broader movement "outstrips" the older leadership. (Rupp and Taylor note that the NWP did not understand why issues such as reproductive choice and racism got mixed in to the women's movement.) Of course, if we identify the "second wave" of feminism only with the more focused and conventional women's rights organizations such as the National Organization for Women (NOW), Rupp and Taylor's point is persuasive. They describe the infiltration of the newly created NOW by NWP activists, who urged NOW to set up the ERA as one of its highest priorities.

NOW followed their advice. But this argument assumes that NOW is the social movement.

As noted earlier, however, what is at stake in which definition of social movement we find more convincing may be the question of class. To describe the continuity between the well-heeled women of the NWP and the earlier and later movements for women's rights is to see, at least in part, the middle class as the center of these movements. That vision may be historically correct; it may also be a function of where, and at what, we are looking.

Another conceptual problem that may exist with the notion of an elite sustained movement is that we may only be able to recognize one after the fact. The members of the NWP surely thought of themselves as the keepers of the feminist flame during the doldrums, but had a broad-based movement that bore some familiarity to their concerns not sprung up in the 1960s, would we still have argued for continuity? Can we argue today that the coterie of women warriors who follow say, Mary Daly, brave and few though they be, constitute an elite sustained movement? And if not, or if the judgments about who served as the bridge from here to there can only be made later, then does it really make sense to call the activities of women's rights activists in the 1940s through 1960s an "elite sustained movement"? In arguing for this conception, Rupp and Taylor are trying to accomplish more than simply telling us about this history, which they do brilliantly. But is the lesson they are offering also meant as more than a history lesson? Are they trying to console us as we stand on the edge of another stretch of "doldrums"? If their argument is correct, then we need to look again at questions of goals, strategies, and their interaction. An "elite-sustained movement" will sustain the movement from the elite's perspective. Given the "mobilization of bias" that operates to keep many issues off the U.S. political agenda, this step is surely the easiest to imagine happening. Is it the most desirable?

In contrast, Ethel Klein's account of feminism, in *Gender Politics: From Consciousness to Mass Politics,* [14] seeks to understand its hold upon the population at large. Although much of the data that Klein presents has been superseded by more recent analyses,[15] this book remains interesting and worthwhile for its perspective on the relationship between consciousness and politics. Klein dates the beginning of the second wave of feminism precisely as August 26, 1970, the day of the Strike for Equality. Much of Klein's approach is revealed in this starting point. Before the strike, Klein observes, the participants in the women's movement had been either too radical or too small in number to be taken seriously. This formulation certainly underplays the importance not only of the NWP and women's rights wings of the movement, but it also underplays the role of the women who came to feminism from the civil rights, antiwar, and other New Left movements. Klein's interest, however, is in looking at the sudden appearance of feminist consciousness, which she defines as a recognition of women as a group and an understanding of problems as public rather than as personal. What was it about August 26, 1970, that made this time ripe for a flourishing of such a consciousness?

Because Klein is interested in mass opinion, she looks at aggregate opinion data that have been collected for other purposes, thus making her analysis somewhat indirect. What she discovers is that women's increased participation in the work force, smaller families, and reduced home responsibilities created "role conflict" as they worked a "double day" at home and in the broader society. This conflict led women to perceive their problems as women's problems. Women who developed this sense of consciousness (primarily well-educated, middle-class, white women from urban and suburban areas), like race-conscious Blacks, were much more likely to support collective action.[16]

In stressing that women's changed political consciousness arose out of their experiences as women, Klein also distinguishes between women and men who have feminist attitudes. Men are likely to be feminist because it seems to conform with other liberal values that they hold. Women, however, become feminists out of changed consciousness.

Klein traces the implications of her argument by looking at the differences between women and men in voting. She notes that the options presented by choices in elections determine whether some voting differences will appear, not whether the differences are there or not. Women and men may have held different attitudes in 1952 or 1936, but the election choices were not structured in such a way as to heighten this contrast. The elections in 1972, 1976, and 1980 did reflect gender differences, but in an interesting way. Klein notes that a "feminist vote," a vote about equality for women, is not distinguishable among women and men. A "woman's vote," however, does sometimes emerge, centering on issues that involve violence.

Klein is therefore quite successful in describing the transformation in women's political attitudes caused by changes in feminist group consciousness, but she is less successful in explaining how this change in consciousness comes about. The most important cause seems to be role conflict. But not all women who experience role conflict develop a feminist consciousness. Klein also implies that the women's movement she describes is basically different from the feminist activities of the small and elite groups of the postwar era. Nevertheless, it is easy to exaggerate the kinds of mass results Klein sees being achieved. Mass changes in attitudes, after all, follow perceptions of current events, as Klein's treatment of voting makes clear.

Another problem with Klein's theory about the emergence of a mass movement in 1970 is that it proves too much. The trends that she identifies do not point precisely to August 1970. Another alternative suggests itself. Although Klein views earlier forms of women's activism as too extreme to prove useful as the basis of a mass movement, isn't there a possibility that they set the stage to legitimate a less radical step? As with Harrison's account of the role of the "radical" NWP in the 1950s and 1960s, the existence of a more radical alternative may be an important strategic consideration in the acceptance of seemingly more mainstream alternatives. If this view is correct, then one important strategic lesson for feminists from these books is that a radical fringe is essential for more mainstream accomplishment, rather than it being a nuisance or embarrassment.

Women and the Politics of Empowerment is, in a way, about the questions of consciousness as well, but it is consciousness understood as "empowerment." Editors Ann Bookman and Sandra Morgen carefully distinguish in their introductory essay between "empowerment," on the one hand, and "politics," on the other. Empowerment for them is not simply the psychological process of feeling powerful. "For these women, empowerment begins when they recognize the systemic forces that oppress them, and then they act to change the conditions of their lives." Politics is "conventionally understood as the activities of elected officials and the workings of government, both out of the reach of ordinary people."[17] Through a series of twelve case studies located in offices, homes, schools, factories, and hospitals, the essays in this collection show how women (and men) viewed as traditionally apolitical act to change the circumstances of their lives.

The case studies are organized around a variety of related themes. The first theme raises questions of political boundaries. For example, Bonnie Thornton Dill's " 'Making Your Job Yourself': Domestic Service and the Construction of Personal Dignity" illustrates that even the most privatized forms of employment contain political dimensions. A second theme is the development of women's political consciousness. Cynthia B. Costello, in "Women Workers and Collective Action: A Case Study from the Insurance Industry," describes how a small number of striking women transformed their complaints into a new consciousness through their collective action. A third theme explores the relationship between gender, women's collective action, and other aspects of institutional and ideological life. The account of changing consciousness in Wendy Luttrell's "The Edison School Struggle: The Reshaping of Working-

Class Education and Women's Consciousness" considers questions of class, race, family, and neighborhood, as the group experienced both resistance and change. Other essays also put these working-class efforts into the broader context of the U.S. political economy, including essays by Patricia Zavella on Chicana cannery workers in Northern California, Andree Nicola-McLaughlin and Zala Chandler on the struggle of Black women to win support in New York City for Medgar Evers College, and Roberta M. Spalter-Roth on street vendors and their regulation in Washington, D.C. Not all of these actions are ultimately successful and sometimes their success (e.g., in organizing a union) is undone elsewhere (e.g., when the company closes the plant or the industry takes a downturn). Bookman and Morgen make an extremely important contribution, then, in documenting the fact that change in the society around issues of gender is not only occurring at the highly visible level discussed by the other authors in this essay but within the relatively unsung working class as well.

Many of the working-class women described in these case studies do not explicitly identify themselves as feminists, and they would probably not qualify as feminists to many of the other authors discussed in this essay. Their primary identification may be with their community rather than their gender. Yet as the editors argue in their conclusion, in another sense this book could not have been written about the political experiences of working-class men. The difference comes in what Bookman and Morgen see as a crucial aspect of women's sense of self-understanding: women identify themselves not so much in terms of political "interests" as in terms of senses of relationship and connection with others. This way of thinking through relationships with others provides a much better sense of what moves women to act.

One wonders, however, whether this relational view of women's activities adequately represents these actors. It is adopted from the work of Nancy Chodorow and Carol Gilligan and was originally developed to describe patterns of development among middle-class women. Martha Ackelsberg, in her essay on "Communities, Resistance, and Women's Activism: Some Implications for a Democratic Polity," evokes a richer sense of community as the basis for political action. The authors may have surrendered their working-class perspective too soon. A politics built upon relationships can suffer from the same kind of privatization that Cott described. But a community with a different sense of its priorities may be more difficult to dislodge from its commitment to change.

Jane J. Mansbridge's *Why We Lost the ERA*, [18] raises the themes of the nature of the second wave of feminism, the ERA, and how to assess the success of the movement. Mansbridge begins by retelling the history of the ERA and then describes in detail the activities of feminists (including herself) in trying to win passage of the amendment. The main theme of Mansbridge's argument is that the ERA, more important as a symbol than for the actual changes it would bring, was lost on the requirement of symbolic politics that the fight for equality remain "pure." Mansbridge provides a careful account of the nature of public opinion throughout the ERA controversy and suggests that it was never as solidly supportive as proponents argued. Mansbridge also distinguishes between the concerns of the public and those of state legislators, who were, after all, the ones to vote. Thus, ERA advocates (especially feminist lawyers) took a strict egalitarian line on the controversy about the draft, rather than being willing to compromise. Mansbridge maps out political strategies that might have been more effective. For example, she suggests allowing the courts to decide whether the ERA would have applied to the draft, because even the First Amendment needs to be modified in order to apply to the military. This tactic would have removed the most successful final argument from opponents of the ERA.

As good as this book is, however, there are still some questions to raise about its analysis. In the first place, Mansbridge's argument asserts that "we" lost the ERA. We were not defeated, as the earlier analyst Janet K. Boles[19] had argued, by Gresham's law, that is, by bad arguments in politics driving out the good and thus changing the debate. We were not defeated by the difficulties of supermajoritarian politics or by a change in the times that made any action by government look dubious. (Mansbridge's own account of the arguments most relevant to the state legislators includes a concern about states' rights. Recall that the ERA was proposed to the states during the war in Vietnam, during fading hope in the Great Society, and that much of the unsuccessful ratification effort was post-Watergate, when suspicion and cynicism about governmental action was high. It was defeated finally while Ronald Reagan was in the White House.)[20] Nor does Mansbridge grapple with the ERA's past for a clue about its meaning. The ERA had been avowedly middle class in the 1920s through 1940s. It was opposed by organized labor and the Democratic party until the early 1970s. Nevertheless, the failure of the ERA campaign was a resounding defeat for organized feminism in the early 1980s.

Some of the mistakes in strategy and tactics might be directly attributable to NOW (although Mansbridge has not done sufficient archival research to establish this point); yet the main problem, according to Mansbridge, is trying to accomplish political ends within a diffuse movement that relies upon volunteers. The implications of this finding are disturbing for feminist strategists. Mansbridge seems to be critical of the movement in the 1970s for not being more like the movement in the 1950s. If that is true, then was the second wave really nothing to be proud of or happy about? Can we expect better results once the messy masses and meddling lawyers get out of the way and leave the political strategizing to experts such as Mansbridge?

This concern brings us back to the problem of strategy. In one sense, the consoling finding of all six of these books is that women's political actions, as varied as they have been, can all be successful. In the end, Mansbridge avers that even the unsuccessful ERA campaign had good effects. But beyond this momentary uplift of knowing that we can do it, the lessons that we might draw from these books are considerably more complex than might at first appear. Let me suggest some simple but useful generalizations that we might draw about political strategy from this century's experiences; then I shall use these lessons to evaluate current strategic questions.

First, political strategies sometimes influence the types of political results that are possible. Nonetheless, factors other than strategies also influence outcomes, especially, for example, the reaction of any opposition. Small incremental steps will be the most likely to succeed, but they will be small steps.[21]

Examples of relatively small incremental strategies illustrate this point. For example, the compromised way in which "sex" became part of the Civil Rights Act of 1964 probably explains its initial, lackadaisical, enforcement; nonetheless, a narrow lobbying effort did achieve its end. The few but highly placed women who struggled for more women's appointments through the 1940s and 1950s were able to get more women in office, but their ability to create major changes once in place was circumscribed. Community-based political movements sometimes can achieve community political reforms, such as a change in one school.

Moving to the opposite extreme from local and discrete political change, this lesson—that the type of strategy may influence the outcome— is especially important to warn us about the allure of constitutional amendments. To amend the U.S. Constitution is a peculiar and difficult political strategy to adopt. It requires, as Jane Mansbridge and others have observed, a supermajoritarian support in the public, and the battleground includes state legislatures as well as Congress. Given the constraints of the process, the opposition to any proposed amendment has many more strategic options available to it—opposition can distort the debate, adopt a regional strategy, exploit inconsistencies among the amendment's proponents. Only a single-minded political force can

successfully amend the Constitution. One of the likely results of choosing this strategy, then, is that it will affect the way proponents are
organized, how widely they can conceive their mission, and so forth.
Working for a constitutional amendment, given its breadth, is always a
strategy with other costs.

Second, often there are only limited choices available concerning
political strategy. This lesson is especially hard to learn because it seems
to take flexibility away from political actors. Insofar as politics is about
conflict, however, strategic thinking requires that actors think of their
opponents' positions as well as what they want.

Thus, many of the successes in this century were the result of
narrowed political objectives. Rupp and Taylor convincingly demonstrate that, given its small base of resources, the NWP and women's
rights movement in the postwar era could not have broadened its
political agenda and been as effective as it was. Although Mansbridge
suggests that there may have been other strategic choices that would
have rescued the ERA, even she seems to present more convincing
evidence that this cause was somewhat hopeless by the mid-1970s.
Having chosen to pursue a constitutional amendment, ERA advocates
in the 1920s made the split over questions of protective legislation
inevitable, regardless of changes in consciousness.

Third, what follows from this point is that some political questions
are beyond the boundaries of normal political strategies. As a result,
political actors must keep some distance from their ongoing fights to
assess how their strategies further or betray their goals.

These lessons are most obviously learned by reflecting on the examples of non-middle-class political efforts discussed in these books. As
Bookman and Morgen note, if "politics" is conceived of as governmental
action, then few working-class women engage in politics. Extending the
notion of politics to include questions of power; domination; and
"respect" at work, at home, and in the community, challenges usual
assumptions about how to think about politics and acceptable political
strategies. Yet despite hundreds of such activities, they too often escape
our notice when we think of political change.

There is a danger that the "tail" of strategy will wag the "dog" of
political goals. I have suggested that the definition of feminism that has
informed much twentieth-century thought is a middle-class conception.
Political strategies that fit into mainstream American politics also will fit
best with middle-class political goals and are likely to leave out questions that are more fundamental.

Indeed, many of the political problems that confront women are a
result of the constraints on women's lives that arise from the organiza-

tion of work (for example, the forty-hour work week as normal),[22] households (for example, the privatized nuclear family), transportation systems, class and race structures, and other broad social institutions. It is difficult to raise these broader problems in political terms; they appear to be private problems within the U.S. framework. Thus, there is a vicious circle of only considering the problems that can be most easily solved but which are not necessarily the most important ones.

What implications might we draw from these lessons about current strategic choices? First, we need to realize that making strategic choices is not always so open as it might seem. The desire to return to strategies of social movements, for example, may be beyond the realm of current possibilities. There are many levels on which this claim may be true. Americans today seem somewhat cynical about possibilities for change, an attitude which is not favorable to initiating social movements. Problems faced by women appear to be individual, not social, and the efforts of the last several decades make it look as if any continuing problems are the fault of women, not a consequence of a still unequal society.[23] As feminists, we also need to be honest about the problem of "burnout." The economist Albert O. Hirschmann argued that involvement in public life tends to be cyclical, because our assessments of the benefits we receive from social involvement change over time.[24] Although at one point, one might say, "[the movement] changed my life," later the same person may seek more private fulfillment. If we follow Piven and Cloward's account of social movements, the perception of normalcy in the face of crises that now exist in the United States does not seem to betoken any obvious disrupting point.

As these authors suggest, the end of movement does not mean the end of political gain, but there is an important lesson here. I think the reason feminists are nostalgic about movement politics is that a vibrant movement signals a greater openness about political possibilities. Here, then, is the difficult task for the coming years. While pursuing more narrow strategies, which this history has admirably demonstrated can be quite successful, we need constantly to remember that the goals of feminism remain (or should be) broader than what interest group politics can achieve.

Here are some of the issues that we have to be honest about and to keep constantly before us. First, we need to define what the second wave of feminism *is*. One way is to identify it with the ERA, just as the first wave was identified with suffrage. But as Cott noted, the suffrage movement and the feminist movement were not the same. The consciousness that Klein attributes to the second wave—"Women who . . . believed that they deserved equal treatment but were denied opportunities because of sex discrimination, had a feminist consciousness—"[25] is much like the consciousness that Cott attributed to feminists of the 1910s and 1920s, that is, a demand for a release from inequality as a way to establish equality. But exactly what such equality might mean, and how to sustain it, remained (and remains) unclear. This was not a problem for the women of the NWP or the elite women who were making policy in the postwar era, who had a clear vision of their account of equality, or for the ERA volunteers Mansbridge identifies. At this point it becomes worthwhile to remember that the working-class and minority women in the case studies included in Bookman and Morgen did not identify themselves as feminists, and for them the question of equality could not be treated as an abstract notion. Working-class and "minority" women often have asked: "equal to whom?"[26] As the very revealing "NOW Bill of Rights" of 1966 reveals, much second-wave feminism was not seen as a challenge to the individualism that characterizes mainstream, middle-class, U.S. culture. But this goal does not of itself address questions of racial and ethnic inequality, economic injustice, or the institutional barriers that arise out of the role of women as housekeepers and childrearers that continue to frame women's life choices, no matter what their class or degree of privilege.

What this analysis suggests is that the failure of the current feminist movement to move any further may not be a consequence so much of bad strategy as it is a problem of trying to achieve goals that are in conflict with each other or that do not fit neatly into U.S. political values. The question that feminist analysts might ask most appropriately is: How, in dealing with present political issues, can we frame the questions so that we move towards our ultimate goals rather than away from them?[27]

One strategy that seems possible is the strategy of addressing the widest realm of political conflict in the United States—voting. The gender gap seems to have given some political mileage to women. The threat of a women's voting bloc in the 1920s also influenced political events then, winning a number of real concrete gains for women.[28] Nonetheless, there is no clear message that emerges from gender gap voting, and as Klein perceptively observed, elections are structured so that voting blocs may or may not be important to the outcome of elections. The best evidence is that gender gap attitudes are exhibited most by women who already have achieved autonomy.[29] Focusing on this strategy, then, will not bring about any increase in autonomy for more women but simply will take advantage of the already existing core of supporters. The gender gap focus will not necessarily widen the base of support for the movement. In this regard, the narrow political strategies pursued by the women's rights movement in the 1940s through the 1960s as described by Harrison and Rupp and Taylor seem politically more astute.

The main strategic task for feminists, then, is somehow to take political possibilities and to broaden them into a political strategy that, in a non-self-defeating way, is nonetheless capable of raising questions that challenge other forms of inequality and the isolating individualism that dominate U.S. culture. Reproductive choice, once it is removed from being a question of individual right and wrong, is an issue capable of a much broader framework.[30] Advocates of choice can expand the context of the discussion to include, for example, questions of adequate available health care; options for the mother and child; different life choices open to women in different class, racial, and ethnic groups; as well as the question of individuals' abilities to make decisions for themselves that vitally affect their ability to be moral agents. In short, given the cultural context within which this debate occurs, it affords a good opportunity to change creatively the terms of feminist debate.

Perhaps the main conclusion that we can draw from the century's richly varied set of political experiences is that there is no single political strategy to achieve ultimate success for women. Different historical circumstances present their own opportunities. Whether we can make the most out of any opportunities presented really will depend on whether we can resist the constraints of our goals and assumptions, recognize the limits of possibility, and do what we can.

Notes

1. See, among other works, Betty Friedan, "How to Get the Women's Movement Moving Again," *New York Times Magazine,* 3 Nov. 1985, 6–8+.

2. E. E. Schattschneider presented this simple way to understand political conflict in America. Schattschneider suggests that we think of politics as a fight. The nature and outcome of a fight is determined not only by the strength of the participants but also by how widely the fight spreads. A fistfight between two people changes when others join into the fray. Schattschneider calls this factor "the scope of conflict." Thus, in U.S. politics, political outcomes are often determined by who joins into the battle. Persuading outsiders to join in or to stay out requires that political actors try to use to their advantage "the mobilization of bias" that can be created around issues. See *The Semisovereign People: A Realist's View of Democracy in America* (New York: Holt, Rinehart, & Winston, 1960).

3. Nancy F. Cott, *The Grounding of Modern Feminism* (New Haven: Yale University Press, 1988), 9, 4–5.

4. Ibid., 231, 226, 278.

5. Among other accounts, see J. Stanley Lemons, *The Woman Citizen: Social Feminism in the 1920s* (Urbana: University of Illinois Press, 1973); and William H. Chafe, *The American Woman: Her Changing Social, Economic, and Political Roles, 1920–1970* (New York: Oxford University Press, 1972).

6. My point here may seem similar to Joan Hoff-Wilson's: "Until women begin to speak to each other in a common language, their impact on the domestic and foreign policies of the United States will remain marginal." See her Introduction, *Rights of Passage: The Past and Future of the ERA*, ed. Joan Hoff-Wilson (Bloomington: University of Indiana Press, 1986), 7. I would add, however, that as long as language rests upon lived experience, class differences will make such a hope for a common language at best unattainable and at worst extremely divisive.

7. On the notion of "forms of life," see, Norbert Elias, *The Civilizing Process: The History of Manners*, trans. Edmund Jephcott (New York: Pantheon, 1978); and Thomas L. Haskell, "Capitalism and the Origins of the Humanitarian Sensibility, pt. 2," *American Historical Review* 90 (June 1985): 547–66.

8. Bell hooks, *Feminist Theory: From Margin to Center* (Boston: South End Press, 1984).

9. Cynthia Harrison, *On Account of Sex: The Politics of Women's Issues, 1945–1968* (Berkeley: University of California Press, 1988).

10. Leila J. Rupp and Verta Taylor, *Survival in the Doldrums: The American Women's Rights Movement, 1945 to the 1960s* (New York: Oxford University Press, 1987).

11. See, among others, Sara Evans, *Personal Politics: The Roots of Women's Liberation in the Civil Rights Movement and the New Left* (New York: Vintage Books, 1979); Paula Giddings, *When and Where I Enter: The Impact of Black Women on Race and Sex in America* (New York: William Morrow, 1984); Dick Cluster, ed., *They Should Have Served That Cup of Coffee* (Boston: South End Press, 1979).

12. It is a bit misleading to portray Alice Paul as single-mindedly committed to the ERA, however. She was single-mindedly committed to her version of women's equality; nonetheless, her quest for women's equality took her in many directions. In 1938, for example, she founded the World Woman's Party (Rupp and Taylor, 6). See also Amelia R. Fry, "Alice Paul and the ERA," in *Rights of Passage, 8–24.*

13. Frances Fox Piven and Richard Cloward, *Poor People's Movements: Why They Succeed, How They Fail* (New York: Vintage Books, 1979).

14. Ethel Klein, *Gender Politics: From Consciousness to Mass Politics* (Cambridge: Harvard University Press, 1984).

15. See, among others, Carol Mueller, ed. *The Politics of the Gender Gap: The Social Construction of Political Influence* (Newbury Park, Calif: Sage Publications, 1988); Robert Darcy, Susan Welch, and Janet Clark, *Women, Elections, and*

Representation (New York: Longman, 1987); E. J. Dionne, Jr., "Struggle for Work and Family Fueling Women's Movement" *New York Times*, 22 Aug. 1989, Alff.

16. Klein, 134–35.

17. Ann Bookman and Sandra Morgen, *Women and the Politics of Empowerment* (Philadelphia: Temple University Press, 1988), 4.

18. Jane J. Mansbridge, *Why We Lost the ERA* (Chicago: University of Chicago Press, 1986).

19. Janet K. Boles, *The Politics of the Equal Rights Amendment: Conflict and the Decision Process* (New York: Longman, 1979).

20. There is a large and interesting literature on why the ERA failed. See, among others, Gilbert Y. Steiner, *Constitutional Inequality: The Political Fortunes of the Equal Rights Amendment* (Washington, D.C.: Brookings Institution, 1985), who argues that the ERA lost when it became entangled in the abortion controversy; Mary Frances Berry, *Why ERA Failed: Politics, Women's Rights, and the Amending Process of the Constitution* (Bloomington: University of Indiana Press, 1986), who places the ERA in the context of other unsuccessful amendments; and Janet K. Boles, "Building Support for the ERA: A Case of 'Too Much, Too Late' " *PS: Political Science and Politics* 15 (Fall 1982): 572–77, who faults inadequate organization in the states early in the ratification struggle. Both Berry and Boles stress that no amendments pass once they have languished in the state legislatures for more than four years.

21. An excellent study of the limits to incrementalism, see Jennifer L. Hochschild, *The New American Dilemma: Liberal Democracy and School Desegregation* (New Haven: Yale University Press, 1984).

22. See Emily Stoper, "Alternative Work Patterns and the Double Life," in *Women, Power, and Policy: Toward the Year 2000*, ed. Ellen Boneparth and Emily Stoper, 2d ed. (Elmsford, N.Y.: Pergamon Press, 1988), 93–112.

23. An important example of this point is the unintended consequence of no-fault divorce. Judges now often expect divorcing women to earn their own livelihoods even after a long married life in which they likely sacrificed any marketability. Any woman who has a problem obtaining employment is at fault, not the society that has changed the rules about marital obligations, not the labor market that discriminates against women. Lenore J. Weitzman's political conclusion is thus ignored: "To grant equal rights in the absence of equal opportunity is to strengthen the strong and weaken the weak." See *The Divorce Revolution: The Unexpected Social and Economic Consequences for Women and Children in America* (New York: Free Press, 1985), 213.

24. Albert O. Hirschmann, *Shifting Involvements: Private Interest and Public Action* (Princeton: Princeton University Press, 1982).

25. Klein, 3.

26. " 'When white women demand from men an equal part of the pie, we say, "Equal to what?" ' asked Frances Beal. 'What makes us think that white

women, given the positions of white men in the system, wouldn't turn around and use their white skin for the same white privileges?'" (See Giddings, 308.)

27. Joyce Gelb and Marion L. Palley, *Women and Public Policies,* 2d ed. (Princeton: Princeton University Press, 1988), argue that feminists are most likely to succeed when they frame issues as issues of role equity rather than role change (cf. Schattschneider's point about the mobilization of bias). Charlotte Bunch, in "The Reform Tool Kit," looks at the question from a radical's standpoint and argues that reforms are useful when they concretely help and empower women. See her *Passionate Politics: Feminist Theory in Action* (New York: St. Martin's Press, 1987), 103–17.

28. See Lemons, chap. 4.

29. Susan J. Carroll, "Women's Autonomy and the Gender Gap: 1980 and 1982," in *Politics of the Gender Gap,* 236–57.

30. An important account of the reproductive rights movement from this perspective is Rosalind P. Petchesky's, *Abortion and Woman's Choice: The State, Sexuality, and Reproductive Freedom* (New York: Longman, 1984).

Reproductive choice is an important locus to test how broadly feminists will make their appeal. When formulated as population control, this issue can also be seen as an attack on Third World Women, thus limiting its appeal to a broader base of women than the white, mainstream, middle-class groups. See Angela Davis, *Women, Race, and Class* (New York: Random House, 1981). Alas, at the NOW National Convention in 1989, Molly Yard urged women to think of reproductive choice in population control terms, "asserting that environmental catastrophe awaited the world if the population continued to grow at its present rate" ("NOW Members Are Told to Seek New Allies in Fight on Abortion," *New York Times,* 23 July 1989, 25).

Contributors

JUDY AULETTE is associate professor at the University of North Carolina at Charlotte, where she teaches sociology and women's studies. A political organizer for many years, she focuses on working-class women in both her scholarly and political work. She is currently interested in the participation of southern women in the labor force and just published the text *Changing Families* (1994).

KATHLEEN M. BLEE is professor of sociology at the University of Kentucky. The author of *Women of the Klan: Racism and Gender in the 1920s* (1991), she is currently completing a book with Dwight Billings on the origins and persistence of poverty and interpersonal violence in rural Appalachia.

DOROTHY SUE COBBLE is an associate professor at the Institute of Management and Labor Relations, Rutgers University, where she teaches history, women's studies, and labor studies. Her books include *Dishing It Out: Waitresses and Their Unions in the Twentieth Century* (1991), which won the 1992 Herbert A. Gutman Award, and an edited collection, *Women and Unions: Forging a Partnership* (1993).

MADELINE DAVIS is the chief conservator for the Buffalo and Erie County Public Library System and a cofounder of the Buffalo Women's Oral History Project. Since 1970 she has been active in the gay liberation and lesbian feminist movements. She is a singer/songwriter, actress, and a member of Black Triangle Drum Ensemble. She is co-author of *Boots of Leather, Slippers of Gold: The History of a Lesbian Community* (1993) with Elizabeth Lapovsky Kennedy.

BONNIE THORNTON DILL is professor of women's studies and affiliate professor of sociology at the University of Maryland, College Park. Before coming to UMCP, she was a professor of sociology at Memphis State University where, from 1982 to 1988, she also founded and directed the Center for Research on Women. Her published works include *Women of Color in U.S. Society*, co-edited with Maxine Baca Zinn (1994), and *Across the Boundaries of Race and Class: Work and Family among Black Female Domestic Servants* (1994). In 1993 she received both the Distinguished Contributions to Teaching Award and the Jessie Bernard Award from the American Sociological Association for her work with the Memphis State Center for Research on Women.

ELLEN CAROL DUBOIS is professor of history at UCLA. She is the author of *Feminism and Suffrage: The Emergence of an Independent Women's Movement in America, 1848–1869* (1978), the editor of *The Elizabeth Cady Stanton–Susan B. Anthony Reader* (1981), and the co-editor, with Vicki Ruiz, of *Unequal Sisters: A Multicultural Reader in U.S. Women's History* (1990). She is currently completing a biography of Harriot Stanton Blatch.

ESTELLE FREEDMAN teaches history and feminist studies at Stanford University. She is the author of *Their Sisters' Keepers: Women's Prison Reform in America, 1830–1930* (1981) and the co-author of *Intimate Matters: A History of Sexuality in America* with John D'Emilio (1988). Her biography of prison reformer Miriam Van Waters will appear in 1996. A reconsideration of her earlier essay "Separatism Revisited: Women's Institutions, Social Reform, and the Career of Miriam Van Waters" appears in *American History as Women's History* (ed. Linda Kerber, Kathryn Kish Sklar, and Alice Kessler-Harris, 1995).

KRISTIN BOOTH GLEN is presently an associate justice of the appellate term, Supreme Court of the State of New York. She is an adjunct professor of law at New York Law School, where she teaches feminist jurisprudence and remains active in the women's movement in New York City.

LINDA GORDON, the Florence Kelley Professor of History at the University of Wisconsin, was originally a Russian historian whose first book treated the early history of the cossacks. Turning her attention then to U.S. women's and family history, she has specialized in examining the historical roots of contemporary social policy debates. She wrote *Woman's Body, Woman's Right: The History of Birth Control in America* (1976; 2d ed., 1990), edited *America's Working Women* with Rosalyn Baxandall and Susan Reverby (1976; 2d ed., 1994), and wrote *Heroes of Their Own Lives: The Politics and History of Family Violence* (1988). Most recently she has turned her attention to the history of welfare. Her anthology *Women, the State, and Welfare* (1990) collected historical and analytical essays about the impact of welfare on women. Her latest book is *Pitied but Not Entitled: Single Mothers and the History of Welfare* (1994). With Rosalyn Baxandall she is currently working on a scholarly compilation of documents (leaflets, posters, articles) from the women's liberation movement.

NANCY A. HEWITT is professor of history at Duke University. She is the author of *Women's Activism and Social Change: Rochester, New York, 1822–1872* (1984), editor of *Women, Families, and Communities: Readings in American History* (1990), and co-editor of *Visible Women: New Essays on American History* with Suzanne Lebsock (1993). She is currently completing a study of Anglo, African American, and Latin women in Tampa, Florida, 1885–1945.

BEVERLY W. JONES is professor of history and director of the Institute for the Study of Minority Issues at North Carolina Central University, Durham. She is the author of *Quest for Equality: The Life and Writing of Mary Church Terrell, 1863–1954* (1990) and *In Their Own Words: Tobacco Workers in Durham, North Carolina, 1920–1940* (1988). She has published extensively on the impact of race, class, and gender on the lives of black working-class women.

ELIZABETH LAPOVSKY KENNEDY is a founding member of the women's studies program at the State University of New York at Buffalo and a professor in the department of american studies. She was trained as a social anthropologist at the University of Cambridge, Cambridge, England, and did two years of fieldwork with the Waunan in Columbia, South America. Over the past twenty years she has worked to build the field of women's studies and pioneered studies of lesbian history. She is co-author of *Feminist Scholarship: Kindling in the Groves of Academe* with Ellen Carol DuBois, Gail Paradise Kelly, Carolyn W. Korsmeyer, and Lillian S. Robinson (1985), and *Boots of Leather, Slippers of Gold: The History of a Lesbian Community* with Madeline Davis (1993).

ALICE KESSLER-HARRIS teaches history and women's studies at Rutgers University. She is the author of *Women Have Always Worked: A Historical Overview* (1980), *Out to Work: A History of Wage Earning Women in the United States* (1982), and *A Woman's Wage: Historical Meanings and Social Consequences* (1992). Her current work involves the development of gender differences in twentieth-century American social policy.

MOLLY LADD-TAYLOR, an assistant professor of history at York University in Toronto, was a graduate student at Yale University and an active supporter of Locals 34 and 35. As a liaison between the union and its student supporters, she had the opportunity to attend the meetings of Local 34's rank-and-file staff during the strike. Her publications include *Mother-Work: Women, Child Welfare, and the State, 1890–1930* (1994).

TRUDY MILLS received her Ph.D. in sociology from the University of North Carolina at Chapel Hill. She has taught sociology and women's studies at UNC at Greensboro and at the University of Arizona and is currently the owner of Antigone Books, a feminist bookstore in Tucson.

ANNELISE ORLECK teaches twentieth-century U.S. history at Dartmouth College. She is the author of *Common Sense and a Little Fire: Working Class Women's Politics in the Twentieth Century U.S.* (1995), and co-editor of *Redefining Motherhood: Mothers, Politics, and Social Change* (with Diana Taylor and Alexis Jetter, forthcoming). Her current research on mothers' movements ranges widely. Most recently she has written about the Las Vegas welfare rights movement and the right-wing Italian Housewives' Federation.

BERNICE JOHNSON REAGON is a historian, composer, singer, and author. She is founder and artistic director of Sweet Honey In The Rock, distinguished professor of history at American University, and curator emeritus at the Smithsonian Institution, National Museum of American History. Her recent works include *We'll Understand It Better By and By: Pioneering African American Gospel Composers* (1992) and *We Who Believe in Freedom: Sweet Honey in the Rock—Still on the Journey* (1993). She was conceptual producer of the landmark twenty-six-hour radio series "Wade in the Water: African American Sacred Music Traditions" produced by the Smithsonian Institution and National Public Radio.

MARY P. RYAN teaches in women's studies and history at the University of California at Berkeley. Her most recent book is *Women in Public: Between Ballots and Banners* (1990).

JUDITH SEALANDER is a professor of history at Bowling Green State University. She is currently completing a book manuscript entitled "Private Wealth and Public Life: Foundation Philanthropy and the Re-Shaping of American Social Policy, 1901–1932."

DOROTHY SMITH is an archivist and collection development librarian in the Paul Laurence Dunbar Library at Wright State University in Dayton,

Ohio. Her interest in contemporary feminism has led to acquisition of the papers and records of several local women's movement organizations.

SHARON HARTMAN STROM teaches American women's history and women's studies at the University of Rhode Island. She has published articles on the suffrage movement and working women and is the author of *Beyond the Typewriter: Gender, Class, and the Origins of Modern American Office Work, 1900–1930* (1992). She is currently writing a three-generation biography of Florence Luscomb, Hannah Knox Luscomb, and Samuel Knox.

AMY SWERDLOW is professor emerita of history and director emerita of the graduate program in women's history and the women's studies program at Sarah Lawrence College. She is the author of *Women Strike for Peace: Traditional Motherhood and Radical Politics in the 1960s* (1994) and numerous articles on women, peace, and radical politics. Most recent are "Abolition's Conservative Sisters," in *The Abolitionist Sisterhood: Women's Political Culture in Antebellum America* (ed. Jean Fagan Yellin and John C. Van Horne, 1994), and "The Congress of American Women, Left Feminist Politics in the Cold War," in *American History as Women's History* (ed. Linda Kerber, Kathryn Kish Sklar, and Alice Kessler-Harris, 1995).

JOAN TRONTO is the coordinator of the women's studies program and an associate professor at Hunter College, City University of New York. She is interested in using an ethic of care to effect political change in the United States. Her most recent book is *Moral Boundaries: A Political Argument for an Ethic of Care* (1993).

LISE VOGEL's most recent books are *Mothers on the Job: Maternity Policy in the U.S. Workplace* (1993), and *Woman Questions: Essays for a Materialist Feminism*, a collection of her essays (forthcoming). A professor of sociology and women's studies at Rider University, she is the 1994–95 Harris Distinguished Visiting Professor at Denison University.

Index

Books in the Series Women in American History